palgrave advances in peacebuilding

Palgrave Advances

Titles include:

Michele M. Betsill, Kathryn Hochstetler and Dimitris Stevis *(editors)*
INTERNATIONAL ENVIRONMENTAL POLITICS

Terrell Carver and James Martin *(editors)*
CONTINENTAL POLITICAL THOUGHT

Michelle Cini and Angela K. Bourne *(editors)*
EUROPEAN UNION STUDIES

Jeffrey Haynes *(editor)*
DEVELOPMENT STUDIES

Oliver P. Richmond *(editor)*
PALGRAVE ADVANCES IN PEACEBUILDING

Jim Whitman *(editor)*
GLOBAL GOVERNANCE

Palgrave Advances
Series Standing Order ISBN 978–1–4039–3512–0 **(Hardback)**
Series Standing Order ISBN 978–1–4039–3513–7 **(Paperback)**
(outside North America only)

You can receive future titles in this series as they are published by placing a standing order. Please contact your bookseller or, in case of difficulty, write to us at the address below with your name and address, the title of the series and the ISBNs quoted above.

Customer Services Department, Macmillan Distribution Ltd, Houndmills, Basingstoke, Hampshire RG21 6XS, England

palgrave advances in peacebuilding
critical developments and approaches

edited by
oliver p. richmond
director of the centre for peace and conflict
studies, university of st andrews, uk

First published 2010 by
PALGRAVE MACMILLAN

Palgrave Macmillan in the UK is an imprint of Macmillan Publishers Limited,
registered in England, company number 785998, of Houndmills, Basingstoke,
Hampshire RG21 6XS.

Palgrave Macmillan in the US is a division of St Martin's Press LLC,
175 Fifth Avenue, New York, NY 10010.

PALGRAVE MACMILLAN is the global academic imprint of the above companies
and has companies and representatives throughout the world.
Palgrave® and Macmillan® are registered trademarks in the United States,
the United Kingdom, Europe and other countries.

ISBN: 978–0–230–55522–8 hardback
ISBN: 978–0–230–55523–5 paperback

This book is printed on paper suitable for recycling and made from fully
managed and sustained forest sources. Logging, pulping and manufacturing
processes are expected to conform to the environmental regulations of the
country of origin.

A catalogue record for this book is available from the British Library.

A catalog record for this book is available from the Library of Congress.

10 9 8 7 6 5 4 3 2 1
19 18 17 16 15 14 13 12 11 10

Printed and bound in Great Britain by
CPI Antony Rowe, Chippenham and Eastbourne

Keith Webb
In Memoriam

contents

vii

list of abbreviations and acronyms

AFP	Armed Forces of the Philippines
ANC	African National Congress
APODETI	Timorese Popular Democratic Association
ASDT	Timorese Social Democratic Association
AU	African Union
CDF	Liberian Civil Defence Forces
CIA	Central Intelligence Agency
CSR	Corporate Social Responsibility
DDI	Development Diamond Initiative
DDR	Disarmament, Demobilisation and Reintegration
DFID	Department for International Development
DONGO	Donor-Created Non-Governmental Organisation
DPA	United Nations Department of Political Affairs
DPI	United Nations Department of Public Information
DPKO	United Nations Department for Peace Keeping Operations
DRC	Democratic Republic of Congo
DUP	Democratic Unionist Party
ECOSOC	Economic and Social Council
EGI	Basque Youth Force
EITI	Extractive Industries Transparency Initiative
ETA	Basque Homeland and Freedom
EU	European Union
FDTL	Timor-Leste Defense Forces
FLICT	Facilitating Local Initiatives for Conflict Transformation
FMLN	Farabundi Martí National Liberation Front
FRETILIN	Revolutionary Front for the Liberation of East Timor

GAL	Anti-Terrorist Liberation Groups
GDP	Gross Domestic Product
GEAR	Growth, Employment and Redistribution
GEMAP	Governance and Economic Management Assistance Programme
HB	Herri Batasuna (Unity of the People)
HDI	Human Development Index
HINGO	Humanitarian Non-Governmental Organisation
IAG	Index of African Governance
ICC	International Criminal Court
ICG	International Crisis Group
ICISS	International Commission on Intervention and State Sovereignty
ICRC	International Committee of the Red Cross
ICTY	International Criminal Tribunal for the former Yugoslavia
IFIs	International Financial Institutions
IFRC	International Finance and Reconstruction Corporation
IGOs	Inter-Governmental Organisations
IHL	International Humanitarian Law
ILO	International Labour Organisation
IMF	International Monetary Fund
IMTF	United Nations Integrated Mission Task Force
INGO	International Non-Governmental Organisation
IPCC	International Panel on Climate Change
IR	International Relations
IRA	Irish Republican Army
KKK	Ku Klux Klan
KPCS	Kimberley Process Certification Scheme
LDC	Low Development Country
LPU	Land and Property Unit
LRA	Lord's Resistance Army
LTTE	Liberation Tigers of Tamil Eelam
MIPO	Multidimensional and Integrated Peace Operations
MONUC	United Nations Mission in the Democratic Republic of Congo
MQM	Mohajir Qaami Movement
NATO	North Atlantic Treaty Organisation
NEPAD	New Partnership for Africa's Development
NGOs	Non-Governmental Organisations
NPA	New People's Army

OECD	Organisation for Economic Co-operation and Development
PBC	United Nations Peace Building Commission
PBSO	United Nations Peace Building Support Office
PHARE	Poland and Hungary: Assistance for Restructuring their Economies
PLO	Palestine Liberation Organisation
PNTL	Timorese Defense Force and Police Service
PNV	Basque Nationalist Party
PP	Spanish Popular Party
PWYP	Publish What You Pay
QUANGO	Quasi-Non-Governmental Organisation
R2P	Responsibility to Protect
TNC	Trans-National Corporations
UDT	Timorese Democratic Union
UN	United Nations
UNAMSIL	United Nations Mission in Sierra Leone
UNCTAD	United Nations Conference on Trade and Development
UNCRC	United Nations Convention of the Rights of the Child
UNCTC	United Nations Center on Transnational Corporations
UNDP	United Nations Development Programme
UNHCR	United Nations High Commissioner for Refugees
UNICEF	United Nations Children's Fund
UNIFEM	United Nations Development Fund for Women
UNRISD	United Nations Research Institute for Social Development
USAID	United States Agency for International Development
UNTAET	United Nations Transitional Administration in East Timor
WBGU	German Advisory Council on Global Change
WFP	World Food Programme
WTO	World Trade Organisation

notes on contributors

Alex J. Bellamy is Professor of International Relations at the University of Queensland, Australia. He has written, co-written or edited eight books, including *Responsibility to Protect* (Polity 2009), *Security and the War on Terror* (Routledge 2008), *Just Wars: From Cicero to Iraq* (Polity 2006) and (with Paul D. Williams and Stuart Griffin) *Understanding Peacekeeping* (Polity 2004).

Roland Bleiker is Professor of International Relations at the University of Queensland. His books include *Popular Dissent, Human Agency and Global Politics* (Cambridge University Press 2000), *Divided Korea: Toward a Culture of Reconciliation* (University of Minnesota Press 2005) and *Aesthetics and World Politics* (Palgrave 2009). He is conducting research that examines the emotional dimensions of security threats through a range of aesthetic sources. Essays related to this project have already appeared in *International Studies Quarterly, Millennium, European Journal of Social Theory, Alternatives and Review of International Studies.*

Volker Boege is Research Fellow at the Australian Centre for Peace and Conflict Studies, the University of Queensland. Current Research interests are hybrid political orders and peacebuilding, extractive industries and violent conflict and customary conflict resolution, with a regional focus on the South Pacific and Southeast Asia. He has published numerous articles, papers and books in the areas of peace research and contemporary German history.

Morgan Brigg is Lecturer in Peace and Conflict Studies at the University of Queensland, School of Political Science and International Studies. His research deals with questions of culture, selfhood and governance in conflict resolution and development practice. Morgan is the author of *The New Politics of Conflict Resolution: Responding to Difference* (Palgrave, 2008), and he has published in a range of international journals and has extensive experience as a mediation practitioner. With Professor Roland Bleiker he conducts research bringing under-recognised Oceanic and Asian traditions into exchange with mainstream Western approaches to conflict resolution.

M. Anne Brown is Senior Research Fellow at the Australian Centre for Peace and Conflict Studies, the University of Queensland, Brisbane, Australia, a centre for research and practice. Research and applied interests focus on building political community across division, social dialogue processes, conflict prevention and peacebuilding, state formation in hybrid states and changing forms of citizenship. Publications include *Security and Development in the Pacific Islands: Social Residence in Emerging States*, ed., Lynne Rienner and *Human Rights and the Borders of Suffering: The Promotion of Human Rights in International Politics*, University of Manchester Press.

Henry F. Chip Carey is Associate Professor of Political Science at Georgia State University in Atlanta, GA (USA). His forthcoming books include *Dilemmas of NGO Peacebuilding among Former Enemies* (Palgrave 2010) and *The Consequences of Torture and Cruelty for Local and Geopolitics: France, Argentina, Israel and the US in Comparative Perspective* (Westport, CT: Praeger 2010). He is co-editor of the ISA Compendium Project on International Law (Oxford: Blackwell 2009) and editor of two forthcoming edited volumes, one on *The Challenges of International Criminal Tribunals* and the *Effects of the European Union on Human Rights and Democratization in the New EU Candidate Countries*.

Kevin P. Clements is the Foundation Professor of Peace and Director of the National Centre for Peace and Conflict Studies at the University of Otago, Dunedin, New Zealand. He was formerly the Foundation Professor at the Australian Centre for Peace and Conflict Studies at the University of Queensland, Australia. He is the Secretary General of the International Peace Research Association, and the author of numerous books, papers and articles on peacebuilding and conflict resolution.

Neil Cooper is Senior Lecturer in International Relations and Security at the Department of Peace Studies, University of Bradford. His research interests include the political economy of civil conflicts and peacebuilding; the politics of resource regulation and the arms trade and arms control. His recent publications include the co-edited (with Michael Pugh and Mandy Turner) book *Whose Peace? Critical Perspectives on the Political Economy of Peace* (Palgrave 2008) the co-authored (with Michael Pugh and Jonathan Goodhand) work *War Economies in Their Regional Context: The Challenges of Transformation* (Lynne Rienner 2004) He is also co-editor with Michael Pugh of a special issue of *Conflict, Security and Development* on 'War Economies, Peace and Globalisation' (2006).

John Darby is Professor of Comparative Ethnic Studies at the Joan B. Kroc Institute for International Peace Studies, University of Notre Dame, and co-director (with Peter Wallensteen) of the Kroc-Uppsala Initiative at Notre Dame. In 1990, Darby was founding director of INCORE, a joint program of the Tokyo-based United Nations University and the University of Ulster in Northern Ireland. He has held visiting positions in Harvard and Duke Universities and has been a fellow of the Rockefeller Foundation in Bellagio, the Woodrow Wilson Center in Washington, the United States Institute of Peace and the Fulbright New Century Scholars' Program. His publications include *The Effects of Violence on Peace Processes* (USIP 2001); *Contemporary Peacemaking*, edited with Roger Mac Ginty (Palgrave 2003); *Violence and Reconstruction*, (Notre Dame Press 2006); and *Peacebuilding after Peace Accords* (Notre Dame Press 2006), with Tristan Anne Borer and Siobhan Mevoy-Levy. He is currently working to establish the Peace Accords Matrix (PAM), which will provide reliable data on about thirty peace accords, their origins and their implementation.

Vivienne Jabri is Professor of International Politics in the Department of War Studies, King's College London. Her research and writing focus on critical and post-structural thought, with a particular interest in the implications for politics and political subjectivity of war and practices of security. She is currently engaged in research on cosmopolitan modernity and the post-colonial critique. Jabri's most recent book is *War and the Transformation of Global Politics* (Palgrave 2007).

Dirk Kotzé is Professor in Political Science at the University of South Africa (UNISA) in Pretoria. His areas of specialisation are political conflict resolution and South African politics. The common element in both is the transition in South Africa in the 1990s and the conflict resolution practices it established for similar peace processes. South Africa's involvement in the Sudanese peace process is a case in point. He is actively involved in the capacity-building programme for the government of southern Sudan.

Roger Mac Ginty is Reader at the School of International Relations, University of St Andrews. He has published extensively on issues of conflict and peacemaking including *No War, No Peace: The Rejuvenation of Stalled Peace Accords and Peace Processes; Contemporary Peacemaking: Conflict, Peace Processes and Post-War Reconstruction* (edited with John Darby); and *Conflict and Development* (with Andrew Williams).

Anna Nolan is Research Officer at the Australian Centre for Peace and Conflict Studies at the University of Queensland, Brisbane, Australia. Her research interests include hybrid political orders and peacebuilding, Indigenous peoples' relationships to land; conflict resolution and dialogue processes in relation to land-based conflicts; and peacebuilding in the Asia-Pacific region.

Nilanjana Premaratna is currently completing her Master of International Studies: Peace and Conflict at the University of Queensland under an Australian Leadership Award. She works and lives in Sri Lanka, researching into different aspects of the Sri Lankan conflict. Her interests mainly concern the potential of using aesthetics for peacebuilding.

Michael Pugh is Professor of Peace and Conflict Studies, University of Bradford and editor of the journal *International Peacekeeping* and the Cass Peacekeeping book series. He edited *Regeneration of War-torn Societies* (2000) and co-authored with Neil Cooper and Jonathan Goodhand *War Economies in a Regional Context* (2004). He led the ESRC-funded Transformation of War Economies team and is co-editor of *Whose Peace? Critical Perspectives on the Political Economy of Peacebuilding* (2008).

Mikkel Vedby Rasmussen is Associate Professor at the Department of Political Science, University of Copenhagen and previously served as head of the Danish Institute for Military Studies. He teaches International Relations and Strategy at the University of Copenhagen as well as the Royal Danish Defence College. He is the author of *The Society at War (2006) and The West, Civil Society and the Construction of Peace* (2003).

Oliver P. Richmond is Professor of International Relations at the University of St Andrews and Director of the Centre for Peace and Conflict Studies. His publications include *Maintaining Order, Making Peace* (Palgrave 2002), *The Transformation of Peace* (Palgrave 2005), *Peace in IR* (Routledge 2008), (with Roger Mac Ginty) *The Liberal Peace and Post-War Reconstruction* (Routledge 2009).

Fiona Rotberg is Lecturer in the Department of Eurasian Studies in Uppsala University, Sweden. Her research focuses on natural resource scarcity and state failure. She specialises in the roles that rule of law, community members and cultural issues play in managing environmental conflicts.

Chandra Lekha Sriram is Professor of Human Rights at the University of East London, School of Law. She is author and co-editor of various books and journal articles on international relations, international law, human rights and conflict prevention and peacebuilding. She is most recently author of *Peace as governance: Power-Sharing, Armed Groups, and Contemporary Peace Negotiations* (2008), co-editor of *Surviving Field Research: Working in Violent and Difficult Situations* (2009) and *Peace vs justice? The Dilemma of Transitional Justice in Africa* (2009) and co-author of *War, Conflict, and Human Rights: Theory and Practice* (2009). She is director of the Centre on Human Rights in Conflict, a policy-oriented interdisciplinary research centre.

Shahrbanou Tadjbakhsh is the Director of Concentration on Human Security at the Master's of Public Affairs (MPA) at Sciences Po, Paris and was, until September 2008, the Director of the CERI Program for Peace and Human Security at Sciences Po in Paris. She is the co-author of *Human Security, Concepts and Implications* (with Anuradha M. Chenoy; Routledge UK, 2007); *Peacemaking in Tajikistan and Afghanistan: Lessons Learned and Unlearned*. Etudes du CERI No 143, April 2008, Paris: CERI Sciences Po; *Security with a Human Face: Challenges and Responsibilities* (UNDP and Govt. of Afghanistan, 2005); *Human Security: Concept, Implications and Application for Post-Intervention Afghanistan* (Etudes du Ceri, Paris No. 118, September 2005) and *Normative and Ethical Frameworks for Human Security in Eastern and Central Europe: A Status Report*, with Odette Tomasco-Hatto, UNESCO Paris, July 2007.

Ian Taylor is Professor in the School of International Relations, University of St. Andrews, Professor Extraordinary, University of Stellenbosch, South Africa and an Honorary Professor, Zhejiang Normal University, China. He is the author of over 100 academic articles and book chapters on Africa's political economy. His recent books include *China's New Role in Africa* (2009); *The United Nations Conference on Trade and Development* (2007); *China and Africa: Engagement and Compromise* (2006); and *NEPAD: Towards Africa's Development or another False Start?* (2005). He has visited and/or conducted research in 31 African countries.

Ioannis Tellidis is Teaching Fellow at the School of International Relations, University of St Andrews. His areas of interest are on Peace and Conflict, Terrorism and Political Violence and Nationalism. His current research focuses on the Internet as a tool of Conflict Resolution and 'de-marginalisation' of minority groups.

Tarja Väyrynen is Research Director at Tampere Peace Research Institute. Her areas of interest include conflict theory, conflict resolution and gender. She is the author of *Culture and International Conflict Resolution: A Critical Analysis of the Work of John Burton* (Manchester University Press, 2001).

Jevgenia Viktorova Milne is a PhD Candidate at the School of International Relations, University of St Andrews, and Lecturer in International Relations at the Institute of Political Science and Public Administration, Tallinn University. Her current research focuses on the role of culture in the analysis of violent conflict and peacebuilding. She has also researched, and published on, the problematic of identity, borders and international security.

Alison Watson is Professor of International Relations at the University of St Andrews. Her main area of research is on the role of children in the international system and she has published articles in a variety of journals including *Third World Quarterly, New Political Economy, International Feminist Journal of Politics* and *Studies in Conflict and Terrorism*.

Andrew J. Williams is Professor of International Relations at the University of St Andrews. His main research interests include international history and international conflict analysis. His most recent book (with Roger Mac Ginty), *Conflict and Development*, was published by Routledge in March 2009. Other recent works include *Liberalism and War: The Victors and the Vanquished* (Routledge 2006) and *Failed Imagination? New World Orders of the Twentieth Century* (Manchester University Press, 2nd edition, 2007); and (with Peter Mandaville) *Meaning and International Relations* (Routledge 2003). He is now working on a volume provisionally entitled *Ménage à Trois? France, Britain and the United States in the 20th Century* and a textbook for Routledge entitled *International History – International Relations*, to be published in 2010.

introduction

oliver p. richmond

In keeping with the crisis-ridden zeitgeist of the latter part of the first decade of the twenty-first century, practices and theory associated with conflict resolution and peacebuilding are now undergoing a major reflective and critical evaluation. This has touched upon the heart of political, economic, social, and cultural systems; institutions, ideologies, and norms that have been held to be the core of liberal political theory for hundreds of years; and, currently, of generally held assumptions about IR, peace and conflict. The post-Cold War construction and reconstruction of peace praxis has been unmasked as being – to some degree at least – a triumph of process, technocracy, bureaucracy, and ideology over substance, and, more directly, over the lives of millions of ordinary people for a generation or more in politically unstable parts of the world. Though scholars would accept that there has been an overall reduction in the number of wars in recent times, the quality of the peace that has emerged has been low and fraught. The liberal emperor has been shown to be semi-clothed at best.[1]

Critical thinking has prospered in this interdisciplinary area of study over the last decade or so, despite (and perhaps because of) the certainties and systems offered by the comfortable, liberal–realist mainstream praxis. As the liberal state system, and the assumptions of the 'international community' and its capacity to control and govern, appear now to have begun to unravel, so too the vibrancy of the debate in these areas has gathered pace. Articles and books pack publishers' lists; conference halls are busy; students pack lecture theatres; and debates have become more and more heated.

The argument is no longer between conflict managers, conflict resolutionists, and structuralists,[2] but increasingly between dogmatic liberal and statist positions towards peace (representing peace through military security, sovereignty, territory, democracy, a rule of law,

1

human rights, neoliberal development), and a critical and reflective position centred on social and public concerns in their everyday political, social, economic, and cultural contexts and related to the same list of prerequisites for peace. The former offers rights, formulas, institutions, and relative parsimony, not to mention cheapness (though not the often vaunted efficiency or coherence). The latter offers deep complexity of rights and needs, human security, humility, empathy, human security, and at one end of the scale a cosmopolitan certainty of basic human sameness and goodness, with at the other end a more pluralist interest in difference and hybridity.[3] Both ends of these scales offer a relative form of emancipation and agree on basic issues like the need for security, self-determination, democracy, law, human rights, prosperity, and cultural engagement. Where they differ is on how detailed, how sensitised, how 'local' such processes may be, on basic norms like international responsibility, on sovereignty, on the market versus welfare-oriented systems, and how institutions may be weighed up against the everyday conditions post-conflict societies and conditions face. Ultimately, the former reifies and validates the existing global and orthodox project of liberalism built into the liberal state and international system and its attendant community, while the latter seeks to develop that system and reduce its reliance on hard security, basic rights, dominant a priori institutions, markets, territoriality, and acultural normative systems.

This debate has developed the contours of an epic intellectual struggle, but we should not forget that, while the praxis of peacebuilding is debated by academics and policymakers, post-conflict individuals and societies continue to struggle in their distant everyday contexts. Peacebuilding has now become a very broad church, with all of the attendant advantages and disadvantages of its becoming an institution and a dogma – in this case the liberal peace framework and its close association with the recently emerged practice of 'statebuilding'. However, the original and sophisticated agenda of 'conflict resolution' survives, even if it may be in need of rescue and submerged by the dogmatic practices associated with institutions and supporters of liberal peacebuilding and statebuilding approaches. This volume's ambitious agenda is to offer some avenues through which peacebuilding might be developed and reconnect with the research agendas suggested by conflict resolution (in its more contextual, rather than idealistic or liberal, forms), theoretically and 'strategically' (to use the term employed by Lederach, Philpott, and Appleby, in their forthcoming volume on 'strategic peacebuilding').[4]

This collection of essays aims to critique the current orthodoxy, and to uncover an everyday agenda for peacebuilding by which to critique recent practice and to establish the conditions for an everyday peace. It hopes to offer, most importantly, a venue for a broad range of attempts to think beyond the conventional approaches to important issues in the evolving debates on conflict resolution and peacebuilding. Each author in this volume has been asked to discard the rigours of social science research where they limit a creative vision, and to develop an account of his or her area and a response to its problems that is both innovative and challenging. Thus, this volume intends to provide readers – senior-level and postgraduate students as well as academics – with a clear, succinct statement of the main strands and themes emerging from cutting edge research in the field of peace and conflict studies, oriented towards a particular focus on the evolution of peacebuilding in theory and practice.

I hope that this book offers a state-of-the-art set of essays which are both theoretically and empirically informed, and which also do not shy away from the major ontological and epistemological puzzles and paradoxes of this area of research, and indeed of this era and its many distant contexts. It does not seek to provide a comprehensive review of peace and conflict studies, but instead focuses on what its authors regard as its most pressing areas and issues, thus mapping the 'new agenda' for peace and conflict research. It is not a standard textbook offering a review of the literatures and issues alone: each essay is also a research contribution in its own right. Each author has been asked to address the issue of what he or she envisages might contribute to a 'self-sustaining peace' (as opposed to an externally sustained peace) and prevent what Kant would have seen as 'backsliding' in his or her area of concern in post-conflict settings. All of the essays respond to several key underlying questions underpinning the roots of the discipline: what are the roots of conflict? what components are required for a self-sustaining peace? what type of theoretical and methodological innovations are required? how can an ontology of peace and a related epistemology of peace emerge from the discipline and influence the policy world in the area, and without endorsing dogmatic approaches to peace?

brief outline of chapters

Part I of this volume examines the development of critical theories, concepts and methods in peace and conflict studies. In the introductory chapter, I outline what I see to be the current state of thinking in these and related areas, and mention some of its attendant challenges, in similar vein, I hope, to the instructions that, as an editor, I provided for my authors. Before I turn to the evolution of thinking about peacebuilding I first outline the development of peace and conflict theory. I then provide a critical discussion of peacebuilding theory in my own terms, and offer some thoughts on what challenges, opportunities, and frameworks lie ahead, and what this means for the broader intellectual project which lies behind peacebuilding.

In Chapter 2 Vivienne Jabri provides a critical and Foucaultian response to what she terms the 'hegemony of the liberal peace'. She describes this project of peacebuilding as 'interventionist, cosmopolitan, and largely in the hands of Europeans and North Americans'. Yet it is applied in a wide range of diverse contexts resembling the contexts of neither. This may no longer tally with the aims of conflict resolution, and certainly has lost sight of conflict resolution's assumptions of equity and justice – along with peace. Instead there is a renewed programme of social engineering through institution-building, which is also connected with humanitarian militarism. Effectively, what occurs through these process is a 'dispossession' in which agency is taken away from those who receive this peace. It represents a project of war, for both humanity and the management of populations. Thus, the emancipatory claims of the liberal peace instead reinforce 'a hierarchical conception of subjectivities premised on the primacy of the European liberal self'. For Jabri, this means that self-determination needs to be reclaimed in order to return agencies and political subjectivity. In her chapter she offers some avenues through which this return may be achieved.

In Chapter 3 Andrew J. Williams examines the development of debates about post-war reconstruction. He suggests reconstruction has become a 'form of (perhaps enlightened) liberal imperialism', one that is confused by a profusion of interests and objectives, as well as norms amongst the international community. These are aimed at dealing with so-called failed states. This linking of the statebuilding and peacebuilding processes has led to the practice of importing statehood at the expense of indigenous forms of political organisation. This attempt to develop the liberal state in other locales is doomed to disaster, he argues. Rather, new and evolving situations should be responded to by locally generated 'reconstruction' programmes. These may not meet liberal standards, but neither have those associated with the liberal peace.

This is followed by Jevgenia Viktorova Milne's discussion of the role of ethnography. Peace and conflict researchers need access to policymakers and officials, which is easily done using more traditional International Relations (IR) research methods, but, if access is to be gained to the equally important civil society level, peace and conflict studies needs to deploy alternative methodological approaches. This chapter outlines the use of, and issues arising from, ethnographic method in post-conflict and conflict zones. Viktorova argues that such methods are vital to avoid the reproduction of antagonistic identities, and the transcendence of exclusivity. Thus, an ethnographic encounter enables the necessary encounter with the other but is unable to condone the reconstruction of universal practices, as peacebuilding may currently be constituted.

Chapter 5 develops a theoretical framework for understanding political hybridity as it appears to be emerging in the South Pacific, but also in more general terms where the liberal peace paradigm makes contact with local, post-conflict polities. This, Boege, Brown, Nolan, and Clements observe, has been the overriding phenomenon that emerges in their own empirical work, and carries very broad implications for peacebuilding and the aim of a self-sustaining peace, transcending the problems outlined in literature on fragile states. They argue that 'hybrid political orders' represent the uneasy coexistence of different types of governance. In particular they identify dynamics associated with forms of governance often based on customary and community life, which carry significant social legitimacy, alongside the state. Such dynamics indicate that the unintended consequence of statebuilding has been to miss important dynamics supporting social resilience, but also to overlook the really existing dynamics of modern peacebuilding, in which the international value systems meet local value systems.

In Chapter 6, Shahrbanou Tadjbakhsh examines the contribution and direction of human security and the debates surrounding it. A limited, narrow and liberal interpretation of human security has been associated with the doctrine of Responsibility to Protect, an ethical responsibility to act on behalf of individuals where their host states cannot or will not. She argues however that a broader read would engage with a different type of ethic, grounded in local and not necessarily external responsibilities and local perceptions of dignity. She proposes revitalising the praxis of human security by adopting 'a postcolonial ethic of non-hegemonic engagement' in the light of both international peacebuilding norms and local social, customary, and political dynamics, seeing this move almost as an act of mediation between the two. From this emerges an emancipatory rather than a liberal-institutionalist approach to human security in hybrid and organic forms.

In the following chapter, Tarja Väyrynen examines the vexed issue of
the interaction of peacebuilding and gender. She critiques top-down models of mainstreaming gender into peacebuilding processes that rely on the
managerialist solutions of liberal peace. She shows how modernity has
constructed a form of peacebuilding devoid of sensitivity to gender in
particular. Even feminists have instrumentalised women's roles in peacebuilding or see them as subjects. As ever, liberal forms of peacebuilding
rest on othering, on the undoing of difference, and on rationalist sim-
plifications of complex issues, on the claims that they want to engage
with and hear the locals, while constructing them as colonial subjects.
Väyrynen offers a possible pathway out of such self-defeating projects, in
that the local should be engaged with by the international via translation,
not merely by integration, or, worse, by biopolitical governmentalities.

Ian Taylor examines the relationship between liberal peace and liberal
imperialism in his Gramscian critique of contemporary peacebuilding
in Africa. He examines the ways in which peacebuilding in Africa has
encountered neoliberal debates on poverty, development, and peacebuilding and operates within the broader international political economy of
the continent and beyond. In this context, he confirms a widely held view
that the neoliberal taint of the liberal peace project has had unintended
consequences at the local level, particularly in the post-conflict spaces
of Africa, that have rarely been examined or even acknowledged in the
general haste to confirm the international sanctity of the liberal peace
project. Indeed, he argues that this has led to a paradoxical state, built by
local elites and external actors, but also weakened by the actions of both.

Chapter 9 examines the ideology of peacebuilding in the context
of the war in Iraq. Mikkel Vedby Rasmussen argues there has been a
tendency to reduce peacebuilding to a technocratic question, which
ignores more serious issues. He suggests that peace has become an ideology based on Western and liberal capacities. In Iraq this has meant an
inability to engage with what are seen as politically marginal and alternative conceptions of peace. The war in Iraq illustrates how the ideology works in practice and the policy options the ideology offers with
respect to the use of military force to produce victory and with respect
to 'winning the peace' by building a new Iraqi society.

The next part of this collection of essays turns to 'Key Agendas'. In
Chapter 10 Alex J. Bellamy examines the role of international institutions towards peacebuilding for a sustainable peace. He argues that it
has become clear that stable peace is more likely when missions are well
resourced, clearly mandated and politically supported. This implies a

concerted process of rebuilding. He examines this issue in the context of the Peacebuilding Commission; he is pessimistic about its capacity. It is heavily politicised and lacks the resources to make a significant difference to the UN peace missions. Thus its role is more one of marshalling political support and providing a forum for discussions about peacebuilding. Another well-meant international institution designed for peacebuilding, it has rapidly been stonewalled by the usual range of issues, bureaucracy, resources, lack of consensus, and political agendas.

In Chapter 11 Dirk Kotzé discusses the difficult relationship between forms and processes of democratisation and development. He critiques the accepted wisdom (at least until recently) that democratisation, marketisation, and neoliberal development strategies are complementary and sequential, and may be driven by the private sector. In particular his chapter examines different approaches from the above, and the relative merits and problems of pursuing democratisation while also engaging in neoliberal development. It suggests that social welfare issues have become the great unknown other than in general rhetorical terms, clouded by ideology. His chapter draws extensively on empirical experience in sub-Saharan Africa, including South Africa, Mozambique, Rwanda and Burundi, reaching some conclusions that may startle some scholars and policymakers, but will be evident to many others.

The following chapter, by Henry F. Carey, investigates dilemmas in NGO peacebuilding. He discusses the development of various NGOs, states and IGOs and their role in decentralising 'world power'. He outlines the pros and cons of NGO peacebuilding in theory and practice, and the obstacles that the sector has faced. Indeed, he argues that, and illustrates how, NGOs have 'transformed, reformed and undermined' peacebuilding in various ways. He shows how, with patience, the NGO sector can respond to the range of paradoxes that have emerged and contribute positively to a range of issues, without depoliticising the very actors and communities they are supposed to assist. Indeed, he offers the interesting proposition that an NGO able to make NGO peacebuilding accountable may be necessary.

In Chapter 13, Michael Pugh discusses the significance of welfare in war-torn societies. He argues that peacebuilding has been used to undermine sovereignty and self-determination in war-torn societies without the sorts of redistribution practices often expected in democratic states outside the Anglo-American environment. Thus, the liberal state that results from peacebuilding benefits the capitalist classes rather than the state's citizenry as a whole. The importance of welfare

in stabilising society and polity has been ignored, with predictable
results – instability, continuing poverty, and an absent social contract.
The state is a hollow liberal–international brand, failing in its everyday interactions with its society to offer a locally recognisable form of
peace.

Chapter 14 turns to an examination of the resolution of conflicts,
accountability, and an attempt to navigate beyond the clichéd arguments that pit justice and peace against each other. Chandra Lekha
Sriram argues that the choice is never one of either peace or justice,
but instead sees a symbiotic relationship between the two, where neither can sustainably exist without the other. This dictates that traditional parsimony and pragmatism in the peacebuilding mindset,
particularly in mainstream officialdom and academia, have oversimplified such debates. Instead a more sophisticated understanding of complex, continuous balancing of both is required. There are far-reaching
implications of this insight, with which all the chapters of this volume
generally concur, namely that very serious and detailed reflection is
required on how peacebuilding is constructed, how it prioritises, and
what its unintended consequences are. Indeed, it entails reflection and
soul-searching amongst the very peacebuilders themselves about the
political, social, economic, and cultural systems they are part of and are
propagating. Peace and justice are at the core of this debate.

John Darby then turns to the unfortunately unfashionable debate
about reconciliation. He examines how reconciliation in post-conflict
situations is dealt with, and in particular why genuine reconciliation at
the political level is so significant if a self-sustaining peace is to emerge.
Though reconciliation is generally only dealt with in a cursory fashion, it is always part of the rhetoric of peace processes. He argues that
the reluctance to address reconciliation is a flawed approach, driven
by a futile 'pragmatism'. Thus, peace agreements are not products of
negotiations between political leaders, but require the approval of the
communities concerned. This is a complex and long-term project, not
reducible to sound-bites or high-level agreement, even if signed with a
flourish by political leaders.

The following chapter turns to a discussion about the transformation
of the political economies of conflict, via a range of strategies including
voluntarism, regulation and supervision. Neil Cooper argues that the
roles played by economic actors and economic agendas in civil conflicts
shape the prospects for post-conflict peacebuilding. Challenges arise
from the trading of specific conflict goods, greed, grievance and natural

for local communities, and provide mechanisms to mitigate environmental disagreements. If these are not adequately addressed the risk of future conflict will remain high. More positively, she also illustrates how such issues have increasingly become part of the peacebuilding agenda as part of a move towards a more localised understanding of peacebuilding processes.

This volume concludes with Ioannis Tellidis' examination of how civil society appears to have defeated terrorism in the Basque country, and what this means for peacebuilding theories which engage with grassroots debates. He argues that terrorism may be constituted as politics conducted by other means to represent or respond to nationalist discourses, and the failure of the state as a dictatorship or even a liberal democracy to safeguard human rights. In this, he argues, the most significant actor for the resolution of the conflict in the Basque country is the Basque civil society. Thus, peace of sorts came about in this case not only through security services, government, or international pressure, but via the undermining of the legitimacy of the use of violence by local society. Obliquely, his chapter offers significant implications for the current securitisation of peacebuilding and development, and more broadly for mainstream approaches to terrorism.

conclusion

For reasons that are generally unclear (unless one sees the discipline of IR as a status quo discipline aimed at maintaining power and the status quo),[5] debates in some quarters of cultural studies, political anthropology, development studies, and post-colonial studies are far in advance in offering insights into how self-sustaining peaces might be built via peacebuilding praxis. For this reason this volume attempts to draw as broad a map of peacebuilding as possible, illustrating its interdisciplinary requirements, and the horizontal and vertical range of engagements – from traditional security to everyday life. In order to highlight the integrity of the peacebuilding project as it is often perceived, and might be further developed, this collection of essays looks beyond the constraints of orthodox theory and methodology, in order to develop new insights into the key issues that present themselves to contemporary peacebuilding and so to suggest possible venues for peacebuilding's development devoid of ideological constraints and methodological limitations. We are clearly at a turning point in our understanding of what can be done about conflict, and a consideration of what should be done, especially in the context of achieving an everyday peace, brings together many of the positive aspects of peacebuilding and also serves as a warning about its more problematic aspects.

The breadth that the academy, with its interdisciplinary focus, can offer in understanding such dynamics has now made possible a more comprehensive consideration of how to create a self-sustaining peace. This volume is necessarily limited in its scope, and there are many areas which have not been covered either directly or indirectly, partly because peacebuilding has become such a broad and complex area. It is now necessary to pay due regard to the quality of peace in its everyday context. This peace should recognise and respect difference, and reproduce a *via media* between differences without resorting to assimilation – even if this is predominantly in liberal state form. I think most of the authors in this volume share with me the view that a hybridised form of liberalism is necessary for peacebuilding to become more relevant to the wide variety of post-conflict individuals and societies that it has touched. Fewer, perhaps, share my view that it should eventually be led by local views of hybridity rather than by liberal approaches, because of the complexities this introduces to peacebuilding praxis. This is the challenge I see, however, if peacebuilding and conflict resolution theories and practices are to remain relevant and legitimate in the future.

Any shortcomings in the subsequent chapters should be blamed on my own instructions and ambitions: but the intellectual and experiential capacity gathered together in this volume make a very powerful case for a new, possibly post-liberal, but definitely emancipatory, empathetic, everyday form of peace to represent the goal and process of any form of intervention that is legitimated under the rubric of 'peacebuilding'. In the spirit of the positive epistemology of peace suggested in the work of a wide range of thinkers, this volume makes a case for an evolved and responsive agenda for peacebuilding, able in itself to arrive at a peace its participants would recognise and accept.

notes

1. For more on this critical theme, see O.P. Richmond and J. Franks, *Liberal Peace Transitions: Between Statebuilding and Peacebuilding*, Edinburgh: Edinburgh University Press, 2009.
2. See A.J.R. Groom, 'Paradigms in Conflict: The Strategist, the Conflict Researcher and the Peace Researcher', in J. Burton and F. Dukes, *Conflict: Readings in Conflict Management and Resolution*, Houndmills: Basingstoke, Hampshire: Macmillan, 1990.

3. This sketch of differences within liberal and critical thinking mirrors and extends the graduations of the liberal peace I have outlined elsewhere. See O.P. Richmond, *Transformation of Peace*, Basingstoke: Palgrave, 2005
4. D. Philpott and G. Powers, *Strategies of Peace*, Oxford: Oxford University Press, 2010.
5. Or, as many post-colonial scholars see it, as the product of a long process of imperial practices and thought.

1

a genealogy of peace and conflict theory

oliver p. richmond

the concept of peace

The orthodoxy of IR has been that peace and conflict studies deals only with specific instances of mediation, conflict resolution, conflict transformation, or peacebuilding, and that the broader questions of order, norms, structures, power, and international organisation and governance were best left to 'international theorists'. This of course, is indicative of mainstream IR theory's tendency towards reductionism (though at the same time it has quietly adopted many of peace and conflict theory's approaches).[1] Despite this, what has emerged from peace and conflict studies was the gradual extension of the subdiscipline to include areas such as human rights, development, reconstruction, gender, humanitarian assistance, international organisations (IOs), agencies, international financial institutions (IFIs), non-governmental organisations (NGOs) and non-state actors. In addition broader approaches to peacebuilding emerged, as well as research methods such as ethnography, in order to understand violence, conflict, war, and peace from the perspective of grass roots directly affected and not just from the perspective of states and elites. In this sense, it might be said that peace and conflict studies has been in advance of the orthodoxy of IR and more in line with its critical wings.

As might be expected, such approaches have now led to a significantly different, and quietly influential, view of the way peace is understood vis-à-vis peacebuilding, though such views tend to be relatively marginalised in a discipline and policy domain dominated by mainstream realist, liberal, and neoliberal theories. Peace and conflict studies cannot just be seen as an attempt to investigate their subdisciplinary

14

areas in combination with such mainstream IR theories (though many scholars did take this approach). Instead, it has taken on a more significant role, which has been to question what many researchers see as self-fulfilling militaristic or institutionalist paradigms focused on power and violence, interest and status,[2] and to endeavour to redesign or replace them. Such moves normally occurred via interdisciplinary and detailed empirical research.

Many of the concepts utilised and developed as a result challenge the dominant frameworks of IR. Structural violence and the notions of negative and positive peace, developed by Galtung,[3] illustrate the deficiency of realism and liberalism in understanding the extent of violence and its indirect impacts. The notion that the transnational networks made up much of international relations, and that within this context security was based upon interdependence and on 'humans',[4] challenged key concepts such as the hierarchical balance of power, which reordered states as the key actors in IR. The Burtonian presentation of a set of basic sociobiological human needs[5] as navigation points for policy gave agency to individuals and implied that a general peace was not idealistic, and, as Azar added,[6] would rest upon the satisfaction of the needs of individuals in their social context. This provided an important avenue through which peace could be defined in terms of an absence of structural violence and a win–win situation for all concerned actors.[7]

In the context of peacebuilding, what this has meant is that it has been torn between two versions of liberalism. On the one hand, it is often now seen to be based upon a very conservative form of liberalism, in which the state is created as the vehicle of security and regulation, overlaid over territorial sovereignty (though this approach is now generally becoming known as statebuilding).[8] On the other hand, drawing on the work of a range of liberal and more radical theorists, peacebuilding is seen as an emancipatory activity, more concerned with a sophisticated order of justice and equity in a societal context than a basic security enforced through institutions as with the former.[9] In essence, this has meant that peacebuilding theory has become essentially contested and unstable, shifting from state security and sovereignty to human emancipation, while struggling to find a balance between the two. I shall now sketch how, in my view, this came about, and whether the choice that we are seemingly presented with (statebuilding vs. emancipation) in a search for peace, order, and justice is indeed a real choice or merely an attempt to prevent the consideration of peacebuilding as a transformative activity, not just for conflict zones, but for IR more generally.

In earlier work I have argued that there are four main generations of theory relating to peace and conflict studies, and I follow this usage here.[10] In brief outline, the first generation is derived from conflict management approaches that attempt to produce order without open violence by preserving the state and its relations, such as traditional forms of UN peacekeeping, high-level diplomacy, mediation, and negotiation, and other activities that take place in the elite, state-centric realm of IR. This reflects a realist view of peace and the management of conflict. The second generation focuses on dealing with human needs, removing violence, structural violence, and injustice mainly for individuals. This combines elements of idealism, structuralism, and liberalism, and presents a more ambitious version of a mutual peace and conflict resolution. The third generation focuses on large-scale, multidimensional approaches to creating peace. This latter version effectively reflects the liberal peace I have outlined elsewhere, along with many others.[11] The fourth generation seeks ways of dealing with conflict that would not result in its replication in various forms, leading to a consensual and legitimate, discursive and material form of emancipation.[12] In my view this raises the issue of how liberal peacebuilding and liberal notions of IR, such as self-determination, democracy, the economy, development, human rights, the rule of law, and related issues, are transformed by their engagement with non-liberal, non-development, non-Western locals which peacebuilding often brings about. This indicates, in various ways, the possibilities of various types of peace, and the interaction of different types of polities and their politics.

an outline of four generations of theory and practice

first generation: conflict management

All Members shall settle their international disputes by peaceful means in such a manner that international peace and security, and justice, are not endangered.[13]

1. The parties to any dispute, the continuance of which is likely to endanger the maintenance of international peace and security, shall, first of all, seek a solution by negotiation, enquiry, mediation, conciliation, arbitration, judicial settlement, resort to regional agencies or arrangements, or other peaceful means of their own choice.[14]

I have used the above quotation from the UN Charter several times in previous writings. This is because it is so central to any modern conception of peacebuilding and conflict resolution in realist and liberal forms, where international consensus, agency, and prescriptions are deemed to be necessary to maintain an international peace, deemed to be a key priority of international relations. Yet, it is easily seen as a cliché, as optimistic and implausible, and so it is easily ignored. This clear statement represents the apogee of hundreds of years of thinking about how to attain peace at the international level. It also, by omission, underlines the gaping holes in the contemporary international process whereby peace, both international and social, is aspired to, but rarely fully achieved. Take another step back from this argument, and it becomes evident that there is little in the seminal statement on peace by the UN and its framers as to what peace means, other than an implication that members of the Security Council and the Secretary General have an innate understanding of it.

The first generation approach to ending conflict, commonly equated with political realism, rests on the assumption that conflict is biological (the inherency argument), and a limited state-centric discourse that excludes non-state actors and ignores non-state-centric issues. Relationships between disputants are balanced, controlled, or modified by the insertion and presence of neutral third parties, or a third party operating on the basis of its interests, acting upon the basic interest of reducing violence. This modifies the classic friend–enemy distinction in favour of an externally managed balance between disputants. This provides third parties with a significant resource. It requires states, individuals, institutions, or organisations to calculate their own relative interests in relation to the broader liberal goals of reducing and managing conflict.[15]

Such conflict management approaches aim at the production of a basic minimum order without overt violence. This is argued to require neutrality and impartiality of the interveners, or a recognition of their interests in intervening, and is aimed at a negative form of peace, or at least a very conservative or victor's peace. The related literature is also concerned with issues like trust and the timing and form of intervention (whether it is diplomatic, in the form of mediation, or coercive, in the form of peacekeeping, military intervention). Indicative of conflict management approaches and the ontological, epistemological, and methodological frameworks they suggest is the literature on hurting stalemates and ripe moments.[16] This argues that there are certain windows of opportunity where conflicts can be settled through conflict management strategies which aim at producing a basic peace, and the most obvious opportunity is presented when a hurting stalemate has been arrived at. This allows mediators, diplomats, and peacekeeping operations to mobilise.[17] This then raises the question of the techniques, resources, 'power', and capacities of the actors, who then deploy these methods with these limited aims in mind. Peace is therefore understood to depend solely upon the outcome of the contest between the world's most powerful states, played out through the military and diplomatic tools they control to maintain order. This suggests that managing conflict is a problem-solving process, which invokes sovereign man, who can then construct a limited version of peace representing self-interest through the rational application of scientific knowledge.[18]

Consequently, much of this literature focuses on the different generations of peacekeeping, from very narrow operations that simply patrol ceasefires to much more complex, multidimensional operations that seek to impose a specific order (normally liberal) in the territory where they are located. It also focuses on mediation as a diplomatic or quasi-diplomatic activity, requiring interactions between states over territory, alliances, constitutional agreements or boundaries, within the world of sovereign representation. Traditional UN peacekeeping[19] was designed to provide the UN with a cautious role in constructing a limited peace in places such as Cyprus, the Middle East, and the Congo, as compared with the ambitious version of peace alluded to in its own Charter. As peacekeeping developed, the version of peace it was intended to create also became more ambitious. Early forms of peacekeeping were essentially observer missions or disengagement missions, but later forms of peacekeeping were intended to provide the conditions of stability in which diplomacy, mediation, and negotiation could then be used to avoid any reliance on quasi-military forces.

This dynamics spans most of the discussion and practice of conflict management, which failed to cope with the conceptual and practical problems derived from cases revolving around claims for representation, statehood related to disputed historical possession of territory, identity, and culture. Even where such issues may not be priorities, the agents of first generation approaches work on the basis that an ambitious version of peace cannot be achieved in such conflicts. This limited peace is consequently based upon the fragile equation of state interests, issues, and resources, and often depends upon external guarantors, though it also recognises that elements of the liberal agenda – the capacity of international alliances, institutions, and organisations – bring a semblance of order through international cooperation over coercion.

second generation: conflict resolution

A second generation of debates crystallised around the concept of conflict resolution (partly as a critique of conflict management's limitations).[20] This took a more ambitious stance on peace, leading to the notion of a 'win–win' peace. This approach perceived conflict to be psychological, sociobiological, or a product of political, economic and social structures that deny or impede human needs.[21] It was specifically focused on an understanding of the root causes of conflict from the perspective of individuals, groups, and societies, and on mutual accommodation at this level of analysis. From this perspective conflict arises out of a repression of human needs, and is a social[22] as well as a psychological phenomenon. Relative deprivation theory, for example, identifies a sense of injustice as a source of social unrest, and the frustration–aggression approach sees frustration as a necessary or sufficient condition for aggression.[23] Human needs theory offers a framework for understanding what caused conflict and how it might be resolved, derived from a civil society-oriented discourse and aimed at constructing a positive peace which directly addresses the societal roots of conflict. These are rooted in discriminatory, biased, or inequitable social, economic, and political structures. By implication these contributions highlighted human needs, rather than state security and structural violence, and the need to develop alternative forms of communication that would enable the full representation of all voices and issues in conflicts and prevent realist and state-centric approaches from imposing a self-fulfilling minimum level order in which the roots of future conflict might lie.

This approach to conflict has been crucial, not just in the contribution of new perspectives on peace that move beyond simplistic notions of state security and state interests, but also in providing a conceptual and methodological framework for non-state actors (NGOs, for example) and civil society to respond to the misallocation of universal human needs. Such needs, for example identity, political participation, and security, are viewed as non-negotiable because they are founded on a universal ontological drive.[24] From this assertion it was a short step to the realisation that the repression and deprivation of human needs is the root of protracted conflicts,[25] along with structural factors, such as underdevelopment. This equated development with peace, and offered

a conceptualisation of peace based upon values and transnational networks shared by states, civil societies, and international organisations,
though the focus was on the claim that peace could be built from the
'bottom-up' by civil society actors. From these claims, the debates about
conflict resolution evolved towards 'multi-track diplomacy', peacebuilding, and contingency approaches[26] and connected with liberal
arguments about human security and the 'democratic peace'.[27] These
contributions to second generation thinking also imply that conflict
requires social, political, and economic engineering on the part of third
party interveners to remove the conditions that create violence. From
here it was a short step to what is now known as liberal peacebuilding.

Even though civil society actors and security issues pertaining to
societies rather than states are foremost in this approach, it remains
the role of the state to distribute these human needs fairly, and it is the
role of the individual and civil society to provide indications of where
such needs are required. Effectively, the peace represented by the conflict resolution and peace research debates is normative in character –
though it adopted a positivist research methodology – because of its
focus on the needs of individuals and on the injustices caused by structural violence. Its underlying ontology is resistant to the notion that
individuals are merely passive actors in international politics. Indeed,
it is heavily predicated upon the understanding that individual agency
should and can be exerted to assuage human needs and lead to social
justice. This is clearly an improvement on first generation approaches
and is often represented as a methodology through which citizens are
able to deal with their own or others' conflicts in a non-zero-sum manner. Indeed, it is intended to be non-threatening towards traditional
high-level interactions. Of course, this fails to acknowledge the connection between civil society and constitutional or institutional versions
of peace. Indeed, in providing a forum for the agency of individuals,
and assuming that they will be in favour of a liberal form of peace, conflict resolution is also an inherently political approach, which threatens elites who monopolise resources for their own alternative interests.
Thus, second generation thinking provides a radical perspective of a
peace dependent upon the agency of the individual and civil society,
which is also in tension with the acceptance of liberal norms.

The understanding of peace that has emerged from these approaches
focuses on one specific dimension of the conflict environment, be it
the individual, group, or structure. Because it is assumed that human
needs are universal, and that, effectively, conflict resolution leads to

a peace that is not in need of cultural negotiation, second generation approaches fall short of examining some key issues related to the nature of peace. They assume that contact with the 'other' leads to a deconstruction, rather than reification, of conflict, and that donors and facilitators are not self-interested but are neutral and benevolent. They also assume they have some impact upon official dialogues rather than the reverse (which is probably more likely given the dominance of states), and that the kind of human security discourse which emerges from second generation approaches illustrates how the roots of conflict can be addressed through cooperative means, rather than making participants more aware of the structural violence or injustice they may be undergoing. Many of conflict resolution's claims are difficult to sustain: including the clear-cut distinction between a negative and a positive peace; the identification of human needs; the scientific rather than normative, cultural, or emotional aspects of conflict structures; their impact upon, but separation from, first generation approaches; their complementary possibilities for official mediation; and claims of neutral facilitation. Yet, this positive peace, which has been conceptualised as a 'cosmopolitan turn' in conflict resolution,[28] has also empowered non-state actors and NGOs to assist in the development of peace based on the identification and allocation of human needs according to the voices of non-state and unofficial actors.

Indeed, the challenge offered by second generation approaches carries such discursive and normative power that what soon became apparent was the requirement for more sophisticated methods than either first or second generation approaches provided in the construction of what came to be known as the 'civil peace'. As Burton argued, human needs are fulfilled through a transnational 'cobweb model' of transactions that form a world society.[29] Conflict resolution debates owe much to a conceptualisation of peace derived from the empowerment of civil society and the individual, and the imaginary of peace it presents is constructed from the bottom-up, is not limited in geospatial terms, and is not greatly corrupted by realist obsessions with interests, state or power, or liberal obsessions with institutional frameworks.

third generation: liberal peacebuilding and statebuilding

Peacebuilding was initially theorised in the peace research literature as a grass-roots, bottom-up process in which a local consensus led to a positive peace.[30] As the concept evolved it came to represent a convergence between the agendas of peace research, conflict resolution, and conflict management approaches. This convergence culminated in the contemporary liberal peacebuilding project, which in itself has been partially subsumed within a liberal statebuilding enterprise. This has rested upon an implicit agreement between international actors, the UN, IFIs, and NGOs, on a 'peacebuilding consensus' aimed at the construction of the liberal peace as a response to post-Cold War conflicts, many of which revolved around collapsed or fragile states in the terminology of the day (meaning any non-liberal state that was subject to conflict). After the end of the Cold War this was in part based upon the development of more ambitious forms of peacekeeping, which evolved rapidly from multidimensional peacekeeping to statebuilding, at first with the consent of local actors and in a multilateral form, and now, on occasion, without consent. As a result the demands on the role of the UN and its supporting actors multiplied and diversified enormously during this period.[31]

The peacekeeping operations in Namibia, Cambodia, Angola, Mozambique and El Salvador seemed to offer the hope that the peace engendered by UN intervention could go beyond patrolling ceasefires and would instead contribute to the democratisation of failing and failed states. In this way peacekeeping was linked to the liberal peace, meaning that interveners (peacekeepers, NGOs, donors, and officials) were now required to focus on democratisation, human rights, development, and economic reform. This became the blueprint from Cambodia, Bosnia, Kosovo, Sierra Leone, Liberia, DR Congo, and East Timor. Peacekeeping, and the complexity of tasks associated with it, became part of global governance, which now became the new imaginary of peace in the minds of policymakers and peace and conflict researchers alike. Despite the combination of conflict management and conflict resolution approaches, however, peacebuilding still mainly focused on top-down, elite-led, official processes. In this way, peacebuilding represented a multilevel approach, attempting to incorporate the local, state, and regional aspects of, and actors in, conflict. It also became multidimensional in nature in that it brought together a wide range of actors who were able to deal with the conflictual dimensions of a wide range of issues and dynamics.

These debates offered a more sophisticated methodology, through which peace could be rationally created through the scientific application of liberal knowledge systems. This widespread acceptance that the liberal peace could be created by the proper actions on the part of international agencies, actors, and NGOs following the requisite procedures required that liberal institutions should be created, and that human needs should be provided for civil society actors. An important aspect of the liberal peace is the argument that conflict cannot really be 'resolved' unless the concerns of civil society are met, and, furthermore, that there cannot be a liberal peace unless there is a vibrant civil society. It is generally accepted that peacebuilding approaches should be particularly sensitive to civil society actors' expectations and needs.[32] This means that peacebuilding is a multidimensional and multilevel process including a broad range of actors,[33] which must respond to political, social, economic, and developmental tasks if an ambitious version of the liberal peace is to be established. Implicit in this discourse on peace is the cosmopolitan belief that a universal version of peace is normatively possible through a scientific perfecting of the strategies to be deployed. Contemporary debates have appropriated these norms, approaches, and frameworks to produce a third generation approach, which has now been widely deployed in many of the post-Cold War environment's conflict settings to construct the shell of the liberal state.

This third generation approach is heavily driven by the requirements and perceptions of policymakers, officials, and actors involved in both a top-down and a bottom-up vision of peace, and processes based upon both. The multiple interventions at multiple levels inherent in peace-building approaches represent a peace which is technically plausible, which can be constructed by external actors in cooperation with local actors, and which thus, it is presumed, can eventually be free-standing.

Third generation approaches to peacebuilding emphasise governance and top-down thinking about peace, rather than bottom-up approaches. This accentuates reform processes associated with liberal–democratic free market frameworks, human rights and the rule of law, and development models. Guidance in, or control of, almost every aspect of state and society is provided by external actors, which construct liberal regimes through a mixture of consensual and punitive strategies. All of these approaches effectively combine an outside-in construction of peace, whereby outside actors import the specialised knowledge, procedures, and structures, with an inside-out approach, whereby disputants attempt to renegotiate this process according to their own interests, culture, and frameworks.

Third generation approaches gave rise to more comprehensive ambitions for peace, but also raise questions about the nature of the universal peace that they imply. The liberal peace requires multiple forms of intervention, which the theories of peacebuilding supply: UN peace operations, mediation and negotiation, development and humanitarian relief, and specialised reform aimed at meeting international standards in areas from the security sector, the economy, the environment, border controls, human rights, and the rule of law. This effectively means that the liberal concept of peace revolves around the reform of governance, is highly interventionary, has a rational and mechanical, problem-solving character, and can be constructed by those in possession of such specialised knowledge as deemed necessary to pass on for its creation. *Agenda for Peace*, published in 1992, was an early blueprint for such a broad and ambitious project,[34] though the nature of the peace it represented was still inherently constrained by the need to consider sovereign states as the main actors and the right of non-intervention by states in their affairs, as well as, on a more theoretical level at least, its implicit claim that peace could be built according to a universal formula.[35] As Chopra argued,[36] it engenders a mechanism whereby the UN, regional organisations, member states, and local actors take control or monitor the instruments of governance.[37] It allows the use of force as well as persuasion, and the hegemony of the discourse of conditionality between donor, coordinating actors and local actors. This reflects an amalgam of constitutional, institutional, and civil components of the liberal peace packaged within a blueprint framework which provides both its institutional components and the methods and actors by which it is installed. This replicates the Kantian-derived democratic peace argument and its focus on democratisation,[38] adding a focus on development and marketisation, and on the rule of law and human rights.

Yet, out of 18 UN attempts at democratisation since the end of the Cold War, 13 had suffered some form of authoritarian regime within 15 years.[39] underlining the wider implications of peacebuilding beyond any simplistic assumptions that the holding of free and fair elections means that peace is automatically self-sustaining.[40] In addition, the role of IFIs has effectively driven economic structural adjustment and development projects through neoliberal strategies which have failed to provide the sorts of economic opportunities and welfare that would be expected within a liberal state. The relationship between peacebuilding and justice and the problems of establishing post-conflict justice have also been controversial. This revolves around the argument either that justice needs to be incorporated into any self-sustaining peace, or that justice may have to be secondary in the short to medium term to the creation of peace. Justice has often remained subservient to stability and a limited notion of peace because so many individuals and organisations in conflict environments are implicated in violence, corruption, or crimes against humanity.[41] In effect, liberal peacebuilding has been turned into a system of governance rather than a process of reconciliation.

What this indicates, as has been explored by Pouligny to great effect, is a failure to come to terms with the lived experiences of individuals and their needs in everyday life, or vis-à-vis their welfare, culture, or traditions.[42] There has emerged a monumental gap between the expectations of peacebuilding and what it has actually delivered so far in practice, particularly from the perspective of local communities. There have been several common complaints: that there are not enough resources available for the vast scale of what is essentially a statebuilding project; that there is a lack of local capacity, skill, participation or consent; that there is a lack of coordination and too much duplication amongst the agents of intervention; that the peacebuilding process is mainly owned by international actors rather than by its recipients; that the issues that face society in cultural and welfare terms are ignored; and that peacebuilding is mainly driven by neoliberal marketisation and development agendas. Indeed, it is probably true to say that the co-option of peacebuilding by statebuilding approaches in the recent context of Afghanistan and Iraq has pushed its conceptualisation of peace from a liberal to a neoliberal basis.

Such problems undermine the universal claims inherent in the peacebuilding consensus and have forced them to become more and more interventionary. From *Agenda for Peace* to the *High Level Panel Report*, however, the assumption that liberal peacebuilding is plausible and will lead to a self-sustaining peace has become the fundamental assumption behind dealing with conflict, through a mixture of conditionality, deferment, dependency, and offering local freedom, rights and prosperity at some point in the future. What lies hidden in these assumptions is that elements of the victor's peace remain, that peacebuilders are not just engaged in constructing the liberal peace though institutional, constitutional and civil society formulations, but are also involved in minor or major ways in renegotiating the nature of this peace and the nature of the 'local' through the establishment of multiple and normally external layers of 'peace-as-governance', as inferred by a liberal conceptualisation of peace. This renegotiation occurs between major international actors, donors, and liberal states' interests, capacities, and objectives, as well as with local recipients of these activities in conflict zones. Indeed, third generation approaches offer a peace that is a product of multiple intervener objectives, with perhaps only a marginal renegotiation by its local recipients.

a fourth generation: liberal–local hybridity?

The third generation peacebuilding project – and indeed the liberal peace or even neoliberal peace it aims to construct – has become a major research agenda, but it has also been criticised by a range of scholars influenced by critical approaches to IR. These critiques have underlined the intellectual incoherence of the third generation project in terms of its emancipatory potential, its reification of state sovereignty, its difficulties in dealing with issues relating to justice, reconciliation, identity, gender, culture, or welfare, among others, as well as issues of coordination resources. They have pointed to issues with its universal claims, its cultural assumptions, its top-down institutional, neoliberal and neocolonial overtones, and its secular and rationalist nature.

These aspects of the liberal peacebuilding project have led a body of theorists to develop a critical fourth generation of thinking about peace and conflict theory, which aims to develop approaches which move beyond the replication of Westphalian forms of sovereignty as a response to conflict.[43] The Critical strand of a fourth generation – derived for the most part from the work of Habermas – implies an emancipatory form of peace that reflects the interests, identities, and needs of all actors, state and non-state, and aims at the creation of a discursive framework of mutual accommodation and social justice which recognises difference. An everyday, post-Westphalian peace is its aim. The post-structuralist strand of fourth generation approaches – derived in some degree from the work of Foucault – raises problems with the universal emancipatory project and its transmission into conflict zones, however, focusing instead on questions of representation and sovereignty in the context of debates about identity, boundaries, hybridity, and culture and the binaries these often rest upon. An everyday, post-sovereign peace represents the more extensive aim of post-structuralism-informed approaches. Local agency, autonomy and resistance represents its emerging dynamics. Such concerns connect both Critical and post-structural IR theory in that they focus on the question of how one can move beyond the installation of a hegemonic peace, and move towards an everyday notion of peace sensitised to the local as well as the state, regional, and global.

Further differences have emerged within this fourth generation approach, however. In terms of governance, which is both a key tool and key objective in the theoretical and policy concurrence on the liberal peace, fourth generation approaches argue that reform reflects the liberal mode for redistribution of power, prestige, and 'rules and rights embodied in the system' led by a hegemonic actor, whereby the balance of power, hegemony, and constitutionalism converge in the liberal peace.[44] For Critical theorists governance must be reconstituted to provide and enable emancipation, reflected as a discourse ethic. For post-structuralist-oriented thinkers, this represents '...an era of "governmentality"'[45] in which peace is produced by sovereign governments, states, and their institutions operating in a traditional top-down manner. Whereas Critical theorists point to the importance of non-state, non-official forms of governance at the civil society level in constructing an emancipatory peace, post-structuralist critiques regard this as a form of biopower[46] through which actors are empowered and enabled to intervene in the most private aspects of human life as their contribution to the development of the liberal peace. This governance is driven by dominant states and their institutions for its direction, represented as neutral, objective, and benevolent for the most part, and yet at the same time?, it is often also accused of effectively maintaining insidious practices of intervention upon host and recipient communities.[47] It results in a relationship of conditionality between its agents and recipients. As Beck has pointed out, what emerges from the practices of liberal peacebuilding to reconstruct states is a 'peace-war' in which cosmopolitan thinking, defence ministers, and liberal states sanction violence to build peace, and also sanction the neoliberal privatisation of many of the elements of statebuilding.[48]

Much criticism has also been aimed at the general adoption of neoliberalism as a key framework for the liberal peace. This means that its cornerstones have increasingly been perceived as predatory and subject to a global peacebuilding market rather than to a renegotiation of norms by some of those actors who either deploy or receive liberal peacebuilding. For example, the recent consultation paper for the UK's Department for International Development (DFID) conflict policy (2006) recognised the close relationship between conflict and development and the importance of 'culture' but omitted the equally significant issue of social welfare during a transitional peacebuilding period. Yet, this recognition can be found as far back as the Declaration of Human Rights (Articles 22, 23, and 25) and the International Covenant on Economic, Social and Cultural Rights (Articles 6, 9, 11, and 13). It is widely accepted that peacebuilding must both create and promote a vibrant civil society, and it also expects to receive much of its support and legitimacy on the ground from civil society. Yet, liberal peacebuilding often conflates welfare and cultural rights in similar, but secondary, rhetorical categories, thus undermining the very civil society it aspires to. This, in effect, means that the liberal peace is a virtual peace, which looks far more coherent from the outside than from the inside, and effectively builds the empty shell of a state, but neglects any notion of a social contract between that shell and its constituencies. These are in many ways shadow states, replicating a milieu in which ordinary people matter less than their mainly hypothetical rights and opportunities.

Even the debates on human security and on local participation do not escape censure by this fourth generation debate. Human security is mainly associated with the work of non-state actors, quasi-state agencies, and especially NGOs. Such actors are engaged in constructing a version of the liberal peace at the grass-roots level[49] and have been widely accepted in key policy circles, as well as 'global civil society'. This linkage between civil society, NGOs, international agencies and international organisations, donors, and IFIs[50] allows for the subjects of security to be redefined from the 'state' to the 'individual'. Since their emergence, human security-oriented approaches and actors offer a vision of the liberal peace in which social welfare and justice can be incorporated into parallel constitutional and institutional projects for peace. While this concept and these types of actors seem to provide a challenge to the traditional conceptions of the international system, most humanitarian actors, NGOs, and associated non-state actors must, for their very existence, work within the confines of the dominant institutions and regimes of the state system. This tempers somewhat the challenge that they enable, something missing? though most commentators agree that non-state actors and agencies are a vital and key part of peacebuilding, and also that global governance would not be possible without their cooperation.[51] For example, one of the side effects of the human security-oriented role of NGOs has been that the provision of basic needs of populations in conflict zones has been privatised, following the neoliberal model of franchise and branding of the liberal peace's components. By the end of the 1990s most countries dispersed 25% of their overseas aid through NGOs.[52] This dispersal has effectively created a market situation where NGOs have to compete for funds, and must respect the conditionalities imposed upon them by donors intent on constructing the liberal peace.

In terms of local participation in conflict zones this is seen as a way of ensuring that any peace created is not only sustainable, but is self-sustaining. The argument on local participation, put forward by Chopra and others, suggests that peace cannot be foisted on others, even if it is built by an international and multilateral set of actors, without their consent and their participation in the process.[53] This begs the question of whether the liberal peace allows for local participation, or instead leads to the co-option of local actors. Another possibility is that this peace is vulnerable to being co-opted by locals. A further dimension to this debate has been a discussion of indigenous peace practices and process, working from the bottom-up, and founded upon local culture and traditional practices.[54] This debate has revolved around a romanticisation of the indigenous contribution as necessarily peaceful, and pragmatism about its possible replication of negative practices and a rejection of the local as corrupt, deviant, traumatised, and schooled in cultures of violence.[55] Thus, the notion of a bottom-up and localised, even indigenously based, peace is also problematic from a fourth generation perspective, especially as it is far from clear whether the liberal peace framework can adjust itself sufficiently to incorporate such dynamics without necessarily losing whatever institutional integrity it may carry.

From the fourth generation perspective, the liberal peace project is ontologically incoherent. It offers several different states of being: a state-centric world dominated by sovereign constitutional democracies, a world dominated by institutions, and a world in which human rights and self-determination are valued. The only way in which this peace system can be coherent is if it is taken to be hierarchical and regulative, led by hegemons who set political and economic priorities, and this provides the framework in which human rights and self-determination can be observed. Democracy provides the political system in which this process is made representative. The trouble with this is that the individual is subservient to the structure and system, which may be enabling in some contexts, but in others it may not. Where the gaze of the guardians of the liberal panopticon cannot reach,[56] abuses may follow, often committed by those elites who control the various systems that make up the liberal peace. Effectively this means that the individual, who is relatively powerless, is required to perform liberal peace acts such as voting, paying taxes, engaging in the free market, and expecting rights to keep the international gaze satisfied, but not to expect that this performance carries any weight. Quite clearly, the assumptions which go with the liberal peace are contested across the world, in Islamic settings or those of other religions, in authoritarian states, in tribal and clan settings, and in societies where traditional and cultural practices do not fit with the Western conception of human rights and democracy. At a very basic level, muted by the preponderance of the liberal international system, the very ontology and related epistemology of the liberal peace

are being disputed by local communities, not necessarily on an ideological basis, but quite often because of its inefficiencies, its distant
directors and executors, its cultural biases, and its failures to provide
sufficient resources to support the everyday lives of such communities.
The liberal peace is strongly contested by actors who want to determine their own peace. In the context of liberal peacebuilding, the
omission of the landscape of everyday life, including its welfare aspects,
cultural activity and recognition, and increasingly significant environmental base, forms a core blind spot negated by neoliberalism but vital
to any sustainable peace. This agenda would require that individuals
and families have sufficient welfare and resources to enable them to
enter into stable relationships with their neighbours, as well as with
the institutions of government and state. Their cultural and identity
dynamics would be recognised rather than negated, and their environment would be preserved and improved such that it also contributed to stable relationships within the local and state. Security, shelter,
food, income, transport, and cultural and educational facilities provide
continuity on which an emancipatory peace, or indeed an ontology of
peace, might then be built.

From a fourth generation perspective, a preliminary assertion can be
made for a new agenda for peace based upon emancipation as upon
developing an understanding of its ontologies – approximating what
Patomaki equates with Bourdieu's *heterodoxa*, which indicates a pluralist, critical and self-reflective approach.[57] This might start from the
exercise of agency of individuals and groups, leading to a democratic
process of representation, but one not necessarily encapsulated by the
Westphalian state. Individuals and groups must be able also to represent
themselves. In this context the right of opportunity for a productive
life, not just with respect to labour, but with respect to emotions, culture, and learning, must be expressed. This may result in a universal
form of peace in the fashion proposed by Critical theory's approach
to emancipation, but it is more likely that it will open up the broader
range of issues associated with understanding an ontology of peace as a
discourse and praxis.

This said, the version of peacebuilding that remains in sight of conflict resolution and its rescue from the specificities of liberal and cultural hegemony has greater local and international legitimacy, and, in
this fast evolving field, it holds great potential if the lessons of the past
can be learned and the integrity of the originally conceived grass-roots
project of civil society can be retrieved, developed, and maintained.

This requires an engagement with obvious and difficult questions and paradoxes thrown up by contemporary peacebuilding praxis.

So many private, regional, and international actors are now engaged in developing peacebuilding as the main praxis for dealing with conflict and building a self-sustaining peace in so many contexts, impinging on the lives of so many people, that this has become not just an ideal but an imperative. While the latest phase of development has shown that the 'technology' exists to build institutions and states, the next big step, which will also retain the integrity of the original conflict resolution and peacebuilding project, is to connect this with a really existing social contract (in more classical liberal terms), or, more importantly, to open up to the cultural, customary dynamics of the local environment concerned, and to have a beneficial impact on the everyday lives and needs of the post-conflict individual. Here there is much room for improvement. This may lead either to an enhanced form of a liberal state, which focuses more clearly on the many aspects of the everyday, or to the ability of existing liberal states to develop stable relations with non-liberal entities that are assisted to develop their own variation of the everyday peace, which by necessity has the widest support from its own subjects. This local–liberal hybrid (or liberal–local hybrid, depending on how the relationship is defined in terms of significance, power, and influence) offers, in my own view, a far more plausible approach for the development of peacebuilding than the mere modification of liberalism, or the wholesale dismantling of the liberal peacebuilding system.

A 'peacebuilding' that is not localised, cannot engage with the non-liberal subject, fails to build a liberal social contract or develop customary and hybridised understandings of what is viable, or is not context–driven but rather internationally or donor–driven, will not lead to a sustainable process or outcome.[58] Indeed, the recent elision of the two terms 'peacebuilding' and 'statebuilding' has legitimated statebuilding practices of a top-down, externally driven nature, whereupon their problems have actively discredited the broader agendas of peacebuilding at the expense of the local, its everyday context, the customary, and hybridity. Thus, a necessary rethinking of the relationship between peacebuilding and the contemporary project of statebuilding, and a debate on the relationship between liberalism and the contextualisation and representative capacities of both the local and the everyday, must take place. This requires international personnel, actors, officials, diplomats, peacekeepers, and aid workers to reflect on the baggage they bring to 'peace' activities, and to work as enablers for localised dynamics of peace rather than enablers for an international architecture of peace that has effectively treated the people on the ground as guinea pigs in international engineering projects. This may involve very difficult choices and conversations in a transitionary moment between war and peace, and also a reflection on the liberal project itself, as well as the nature of the liberal state, as it also necessitates localised reflection and reform to avoid repeating the dynamics that led to the conflict in the first place, as well as undermining hard-won rights or needs. Between these two dynamics, there is space for a hybridised form of peacebuilding that can develop international approaches and consensus for peace while also developing and assisting the localised dynamics for peace. This hybridised evolution must occur in a close relationship rather than with the two elements divorced from each other. Otherwise, the dynamics of an international praxis of peace from Cambodia to East Timor, and now Afghanistan and Iraq, will continue to lead to the creation of the empty shells of states, which have little impact during the transitions from violence on the everyday lives of the vast bulk of their populations.

What is needed is the development of a praxis of post-liberal peacebuilding (potentially utilising the eirenist approaches to IR and to peacebuilding that I have detailed elsewhere).[59] These would be designed to capitalise on the core of the original conflict resolution and peacebuilding agendas, addressing needs and root causes, connecting the new liberal state or polity with older, locally recognizable and contextual, customary, political, social, and economic traditions, and engaging with grass roots and the most marginalised members of post-conflict polities. This would require a mediation between the local and the international over peacebuilding praxis and social, political, and economic practices that both deem plausible and acceptable, rather than a wholesale top-down imposition of an only putatively universal liberal model. This would enable the development of a post-liberal form of peacebuilding which would counterbalance the core of liberal peacebuilding with the local as well as its needs and cultural patterns. This would not be to romanticise the local and its capacity for conflict resolution or its dysfunctionality, but rather to enable it to engage in 'unscripted conversations' about what peacebuilding might entail.[60] Rather than representing either an international or even a local bias towards the interests of local elites, this would instead be predicated upon an intimate understanding of everyday life in each context, and how a peaceful everyday life might be facilitated. This might involve liberal peacebuilders facing up to some unpalatable truths about how bias towards geopolitical interests and limited understandings of peace undermine peacebuilding and replicate violence, and would entail some radical shifts of emphasis, not least from a blind faith in the power of political rights and the market for the provision for everyday needs and a better understanding of customary practices.[61] This post-liberal peace, including a liberal–local hybrid and an interface between the two, would also be constantly called upon to reflect on its own interests and assumptions, and not to distance itself ethically and materially from the local, but quite the reverse.

conclusion: an agenda for peacebuilding

Critical approaches and policies for a post-liberal form of peacebuilding might thus engage with the following:[62]

1. A detailed understanding (rather than co-option or 'tolerance') of local culture, traditions, and ontology; and acceptance of peace-building as an empathetic, emancipatory process, focused on everyday care, human security, and a social contract between society and the polity, which acts as a provider of care rather then merely security;
2. in addition, a peacebuilding contract between internationals and local actors which reflects the social contract within the polity;
3. thinking about peace beyond the liberal state mechanism (rather than using peace to propagate liberal states);
4. 'local–local' ownership of a local, regional and global process of peacemaking, or of an agreement (as opposed to international–local elite ownership);
5. local decision-making processes to determine the basic political, economic, and social processes and norms to be institutionalised;
6. international support for these processes, guidance on technical aspects of governance and institution-building without introducing hegemony, inequality, conditionality, or dependency;
7. an economic framework, focusing on welfare and empowerment of the most marginalised, should be determined locally. Internationals may assist in free market reform and marketisation/privatisation not on the basis of external expert knowledge but by local consensus, but they should also immediately introduce a socio-economic safety

net to bind citizens and labour to a peaceful polity (rather than to war-making, a grey/black economy, or transnational criminal activities). Otherwise, neoliberalism clearly undermines any social contract and leads to a counterproductive class system;

8. any peacebuilding process must cumulatively engage with everyday life, custom, care and empathy, as well as institutions;

9. 1–8 should result in a process whereby an indigenous peace is installed that includes a version of human rights, rule of law, and a representative political process that reflects the local groupings and their ability to create consensus, as well as broader international expectations for peace (but not alien 'national' interests).

This reflects the liberal peace in a localised, contextual, and hybridised form. It might also be said to prioritise the local. It emphasises the need to construct local consensus before its development and intervention, and so the emergence of a hybrid and post-liberal peace. What this also means is that peacebuilding actors themselves must be subject to a set of requirements to prevent them from treating every case as the same, and to actualise or at least simulate a social contract between internationals and local populations of post-conflict areas resting on contextuality, locality, and engaging with custom to provide the emerging polity with authenticity with the groups who matter to it most – its citizens and inhabitants. The above agenda requires the following from peacebuilding actors:

(1). A recognition of care, empathy, welfare, and a consideration of everyday life, as the basis of a social contract required between societies, emerging post-conflict polities, and internationals;

(2). peacebuilding actors should not work from blueprints but should develop strategies based upon multilevel consultation in each case. They should develop relations with local partners which reach as far as possible in a local society, enabling grass-roots representation. They should endeavour to see themselves as mediatory agents (the interface between the liberal and the local), whereby their role is to mediate the global norm or institution with the local norm before it is constructed. Hence, academics and peacebuilding policymakers should avoid overstating the applicability of blueprint-type models, but instead engage more with local knowledge in an empathetic manner;

(3). peacebuilding actors should also operate on the basis of the norms and systems they are trying to instil, such as democracy, equality, social justice, etc. Theorists and policymakers cannot ever be beyond ethics, and must acknowledge the reflexive qualities and responsibilities of peacebuilding;

(4). theorists and peacebuilding actors need to move from an institutional peace-as-governance agenda to an alternative, or at least additional, everyday agenda. Putting communities first entails a rethinking of the priorities of peace. In terms of peacebuilding, this would place contextual human needs, particularly economic and security needs, before free market reform, and parallel to democracy, second generation human rights, and a rule of law that protects the citizen and not just wealth and property. This would probably require the creation of social welfare-oriented peacebuilding institutions and the recognition of customary governance and support institutions.

notes

1. This section draws heavily on Chapter 5 of my *Peace in IR* (Routledge, 2008).
2. See debate between C.S. Gray and K. Booth in C.S. Gray, *Modern Strategy,* Oxford: Oxford University Press, 1999.
3. See J. Galtung, 'A Structural Theory of Imperialism', *Journal of Peace Research,* Vol. 8, 1971, pp. 81–117.
4. See S. Tadjbakhsh and A.M. Chenoy, *Human Security: Concepts and Implications*, London: Routledge, 2006.
5. J. Burton, *World Society,* Cambridge: Cambridge University Press, 1972.
6. E.A. Azar, 'Protracted International Conflicts: Ten Propositions', *International Iteractions,* vol. 12, No. 1, 1985, pp. 59–70.
7. D.J. Dunn, *The First Fifty Years of Peace Research,* Aldershot: Ashgate, 2005, p. 78.
8. For more on this elision, see O.P. Richmond and J. Franks, 'Introduction' in O. P. Richmond and J. Franks (eds), Liberal Peace Transitions: Between Statebuilding and Peacebuilding, Edinburgh: Edinburgh University Press, 2009, pp. 1–17.
9. See, for example, the range of essays included in M. Pugh, N. Cooper and M. Turner (eds), *Whose Peace? Critical Perspectives on the Political Economy of Peacebuilding,* London: Palgrave, 2009.
10. See O.P. Richmond, *Maintaining Order, Making Peace,* London: Palgrave, 2002.
11. See my *Transformation of Peace,* Palgrave, 2005, or Roland Paris, *At War's End,* Cambridge: Cambridge University Press, 2004.
12. Ibid., Richmond or Paris? Chapters 2, 3 and 5.
13. *United Nations Charter,* Chapter 2, Article 3.
14. *United Nations Charter,* Article 33 (para. 1 and 2).

15. For a review of these approaches see, among others, J. Bercovitch (ed.), *Resolving International Conflicts: The Theory and Practice of Mediation*, London, Boulder, CO: Lynne Rienner, 1996; J. Bercovitch and J.Z. Rubin, *Mediation in IR: Multiple Approaches to Conflict Management*, Basingstoke: Macmillan, 1992; A. James, *Peacekeeping in International Politics*, I.I.S.S., Macmillan, 1994.

16. On neutrality and partiality see T. Princen, *Intermediaries in International Conflict*, Princeton, NJ: Princeton University Press, 1992; on ripe moments and the hurting stalemate, I.W. Zartman, *The Practical Negotiator*, New Haven, CT: Yale University Press, 1982. See also O. Richmond, 'Devious Objectives And The Disputants' View Of International Mediation: A Theoretical Framework', *Journal of Peace Research*, Vol. 35, No. 6, 1998, pp. 707–722.

17. I.W. Zartman, 'The Timing of Peace Initiatives', in J. Darby and R. Mac Ginty, *Contemporary Peacemaking*, London: Palgrave, 2003, p. 19; On peacekeeping, see A. James, *Peacekeeping in International Politics*, I.I.S.S., Macmillan, 1994.

18. A. Linklater and J. Macmillan, *Boundaries in Question*, London: Pinters, 1995, p. 5.

19. See D. Hammarskjold, *Summary Study UN doc. A/3943*, 9 October 1958.

20. For a superb discussion of this set of approaches see Dunn, *The First Fifty Years of Peace Research*.

21. See W. Isard, *Understanding conflict and the science of peace*, Cambridge: Blackwell, 1992, esp. chapters 2, 4 and 5.

22. See Azar, 'Protracted International Conflicts', p. 29; T.R. Gurr, *Why Men Rebel?*, Princeton, NJ: Princeton University Press, 1970.

23. T.R. Gurr, ibid.; D. Dollard, M. Miller, and Sears, *Frustration and Aggression*, New Haven, CT: Yale University Press, 1939. See also W. Runciman, *Relative Deprivation and Social Injustice*, London: Penguin, 1972, esp. chapters 2 and 3; L. Berkowitz, *Aggression: Its Causes, Consequences and Control*, New York: McGraw-Hill, 1993.

24. Azar, 'Protracted International Conflicts', p. 29.

25. E.E. Azar, *The Management of Protracted Social Conflict*, Hampshire, UK: Dartmouth Publishing, 1990, pp. 9–12, 155.

26. For more on this linkage see O.P. Richmond, 'Rethinking Conflict Resolution: The Linkage Problematic between "Track I" and "Track II"', *Journal of Conflict Studies*, Vol. 21, No. 2, 2001, pp. 109–132.

27. J. Macmillan, 'Whose Democracy, Which Peace?' *Paper presented at ECPR, Marburg*, September 2003, pp. 1, 19.

28. For more on this see D. Jones, *Cosmopolitan Mediation? Conflict Resolution and the Oslo Accords*, Manchester: Manchester University Press, 1999.

29. For a good overview, see Dennis J.D. Sandole, 'John Burton's Contribution To Conflict Resolution Theory And Practice: A Personal View', *International Journal of Peace Studies*, Vol. 6, No. 1, 2001. Available from http://www2.gmu.edu/programs/icar/ijps/vol6_1/cover_1.htm, accessed on 16 October 2009.

30. H. Schmid, 'Peace Research and Politics', *Journal of Peace Research*, Vol. 5, No. 3, 1968, pp. 217–232.

31. For excellent analysis of these approaches see A. Bellamy and P. Williams, *Peace Operations and Global Order*, Abdingdon: Frank Cass, 2005;

E. Cousens and C. Kumar, *Peacebuilding as Politics*, Boulder, CO: Lynne Rienner, 2001; Darby and Mac Ginty, *Contemporary Peacemaking*, p. 19.
32. J.P. Lederach, *Building Peace*, Washington DC: United States Institute of Peace, 1997, p. 39; see also J. Lederach, *Preparing for Peace: Conflict Transformation Across Cultures*, Syracuse: Syracuse University Press, 1995.
33. J.P. Lederach, ibid., pp. 60–1.
34. B. Boutros-Ghali, *An Agenda for Peace: Preventive diplomacy, peacemaking and peace-keeping*, A/47/277-S/24111, 17 June 1992.
35. M.S. Lund, *Preventing Violent Conflicts*, Washington: USIP, 1996, p. 87.
36. J. Chopra, 'The Space of Peace Maintenance', *Political Geography*, Vol. 15, No. 3/4, 1996, p. 338.
37. J. Chopra, 'The UN's Kingdom of East Timor', *Survival*, Vol. 42, No. 3, 2000, pp. 27–40; see in particular the *Report of the Secretary-General's High Level Panel on Threats, Challenges, and Change*, United Nations, 2004; *Carnegie Report on Preventing Deadly Conflict*, 1997, pp. 2–3.
38. For more on this development, see C.T. Call and S.E. Cook, 'On Democratisation and Peacebuilding', *Global Governance*, Vol. 9, No. 2, 2003, pp. 233–46.
39. Ibid., p. 235.
40. Ibid., p. 238.
41. For more on this see C. Sriram, 'Revolutions in Accountability', *American University International Law Review*, Vol. 19, No. 2, 2003, pp. 301–429; C.O. Lerche, 'Truth Commissions and National Reconciliation: Some Reflections on Theory and Practice', in Peace and Conflict Studies, Vol. 7, No. 1, 2000, pp. 2–23.
42. See B. Pouligny, *Peace Operations Seen From Below*, London: Hurst, 2006.
43. For different aspects of this body of thinking see in particular M. Pugh, 'The political economy of peacebuilding: a critical theory perspective', *International Journal of Peace Studies*, Vol. 10, No. 2, pp. 23–42: M. Duffield, *Global Governance and the New Wars: The Merging of Development and Security*, London: Zed Books, 2001; V. Jabri, *Discourses on Violence*, Manchester: Manchester University Press, 1996; V. Jabri, *War and the Transformation of Global Politics*, London: Palgrave, 2007; K. Booth, 'Security and Emancipation', *Review of International Studies*, Vol. 17, No. 4, 1991, pp. 313–26; R. Bleiker, *Popular Dissent, Human Agency and Global Politics*, Manchester: Cambridge University Press, 2000. For a discussion of this fourth generation in more detail see also Richmond, *Maintaining Order, Making Peace*, chapters V and VI.
44. R. Gilpin, *War and Change in World Politics*, Cambridge: CUP, 1981, pp. 42–3.
45. M. Foucault, 'Governmentality', in G. Burchell, C. Gordon and P.Miller (eds), *The Foucault Effect: Studies in Governmentality*, Hemel Hempstead: Harvester Wheatsheaf, 1991, p. 103.
46. See M. Foucault, *The Birth of the Clinic*, London: Routledge, 1976.
47. See for example Preface to F. Debrix and C. Weber (eds), *Rituals of Mediation*, Minneapolis, MN: Minnesota, 2003, p. xv.
48. U. Beck, 'War is Peace: On Post-National War', *Security Dialogue*, Vol. 36, No. 5, pp. 6–9.
49. See among others UNDP *Development Report* 1994; R. Paris, 'Human Security: Paradigm Shift or Hot Air?', *International Security*, Vol. 26, No. 2,

2001, pp. 87–102; Vol. 7, No. 3, Jul–Sep 2001; Y.F. Khong, 'Human Security: A Shotgun Approach to Alleviating Human Misery?', in *Global Governance*, Vol. 7, No. 3, Jul–Sep 2001.

50. See in particular J. Keane, *Global Civil Society?*, Cambridge: Cambridge University Press, 2003.

51. W. Reinicke, *Public Policy*, Washington DC: Brookings, 1998, p. 259.

52. N. Reindorp, 'Global Humanitarian Assistance', *Humanitarian Exchange*, No. 18, London: ODI, March 2001, p. 31.

53. J. Chopra and T. Hohe, 'Participatory Intervention', *Global Governance*, Vol. 10, 2004, pp. 289–305.

54. See in particular O.P. Richmond, 'The Culture of Liberal Peacebuilding' and other contributions on this matter in R. Bleiker and M. Brigg (eds), *Mediating Across Difference: Asian/Approaches to Security and Conflict*, Hawaii University Press, 2010.

55. I am indebted to Roger Mac Ginty's work for this critique. See his piece in Darby and Mac Ginty, *Contemporary Peacemaking*, p. 19.

56. J. Bentham, 'Panopticon', in M. Bozovic (ed.), *The Panopticon Writings*, London: Verso, 1995, pp. 29–95.

57. See for example H. Patomaki, 'The Challenge of Critical Theories', *Journal of Peace Research*, Vol. 38, No. 6, 2001, p. 732; P. Bourdieu, *Outline of a Theory of Practice*, trans. R. Nice, Cambridge: Cambridge University Press, 1977.

58. This draws upon Richmond and Franks, 'Conclusion'.

59. See O.P. Richmond, 'Eirenism and a Post-Liberal Peace', *Review of International Studies*, Vol. 35, No. 3, 2009, pp. 557–580.

60. M. Duffield, *Development, Security and Unending War*, London: Polity, 2007, p. 234.

61. For a very interesting project on this in the context of the Pacific, see V. Boege, M.A. Brown, K.P. Clements and A. Nolan, 'States Emerging from Hybrid Political Orders – Pacific Experiences', *The Australian Centre for Peace and Conflict Studies (ACPACS) Occasional Papers Series*, 2008.

62. This section draws upon Richmond, 'Eirenism and a Post-Liberal Peace'.

part 1
critical agendas: theories, concepts, and methods

2

war, government, politics: a critical response to the hegemony of the liberal peace

vivienne jabri

Locations as diverse as East Timor and Sierra Leone, the Congo and Iraq, Liberia and Afghanistan might be conceived as targets of what is now constructed in discourse as the liberal peace project – interventionist, cosmopolitan, and largely in the hands of Europeans and North Americans – despite the diversity of practices deemed applicable to each case. Ranging from invasion and occupation, to institutional transformation, to the rebuilding of social infrastructures, and varying combinations thereof, the project is clearly multiple in its modes of articulation, has involved a number of agencies, from states to international institutions to non-governmental organisations, and is driven by the desire to realise social transformation beyond violent conflict.

There are clear dividing lines constitutive of the 'liberal peace': that the liberal is to be distinguishable from the illiberal, that peace is the name of the game rather than war, that liberal societies are the paramount agents of transformation. This is a particular reading of peace, however, and is suggestive of a departure from traditional modes of intervention, the aim of which was conflict resolution. In place of resolution, a process which assumes the equal voice of all concerned, the idea of a liberal peace assumes transformation as a means towards achieving an end to violence, but, more importantly, an end to any politically defined conflict. The vehicle for transformation is distinctly institutional, so that the liberal peace is one of design, or put more accurately redesign, of entire social formations so that they are indeed transformed into 'liberal' societies. By definition, therefore, the project requires not just militaries, but an international civil service at large engaged variously in the building of institutions from schools to departments of justice, and reinforced by armies of 'trainers' who in turn engage the local population in such pedagogical exercises as gender awareness, human rights training, budgetary probity and so on. The liberal peace project is hence self-defined as a 'peacebuilding' and indeed a statebuilding project, a form of social engineering internationally rendered.

The arguments for liberal interventions centre on the premise that societies prone to violent conflict, specifically of the kind that suggests societal breakdown, rampaging militias targeting civilians, warlordism and the dissolution of state institutions, and consequent large-scale violations of human rights, are suggestive of 'failure' and can hence no longer claim rights to sovereignty and hence non-intervention. The limits that sovereign statehood provides, guaranteed in international law, should no longer, according to advocates, be applicable when the state as such loses its viability as a governing institution, and, more importantly, subjugates its own population to mass atrocity. In the realm of practice, former UN Secretary General Boutros Boutros-Ghali set the interventionist tone when he published 'An Agenda for Peace', a tract that clearly lays the institutional ground on the side of humanity and against sovereignty as the ultimate limit.[1]

The argument against the liberal peace project might start from the premise that to intervene at all into other societies is by definition colonial, suggestive of dispossession, racialised domination, and subjugation. Clearly, the historical record of the forms of intervention mentioned above directly points to resource dispossession, as witnessed in Iraq. However, the primary form of dispossession relates to the dispossession of agency, the capacity to determine what constitutes political identity. This form of dispossession primarily derives from the view that the liberal peace project is one of protection and hence of security; what is now referred to as 'human security'. In other words, practices that come under the definition of the liberal peace are deemed to serve target populations in terms of 'rescue', 'care', 'protection'. The language of the liberal peace is a language centred on a distinct notion of humanity serviced by an apparatus of security.

The aim of this chapter is to develop an understanding of the liberal peace firstly as a project of war, and distinctly war that has the element of 'humanity' as its organising principle, and secondly as a project of war the purpose of which is the management of populations. Drawing on Michel Foucault's analytics of power, and specifically liberal governmentality, the argument presented is that, while the liberal peace governmentalises post-colonial societies, it at the same time depoliticises social conflict in these societies. Far from being an emancipatory project, therefore, the liberal peace project might be seen as reinforcing a hierarchical conception of subjectivities premised on the primacy of the European liberal self as against others whose modes of articulation remain 'other'. The challenge is hence to formulate ideas relating to responses to violence that place primacy on a critical conception of what it means to be 'self-determining' in a late modern era that appears to defy historic understandings of political subjectivity, and specifically modern political subjectivity based on the emancipatory ideal of 'self-determination'. Where the liberal cosmopolitanism of the liberal peace sees the global within its purview of operations and as such seeks to somehow defy limits while instantiating them in the everyday and the corporeal, the critical moment is to reclaim the limit space, and to reinstantiate the right to politics and political subjectivity.

in the name of humanity

The realm of the international is, according to realist and liberal thinking in International Relations, defined primarily in terms of the interstate system, underwritten respectively by distributions of capability and the mechanics of power in relation to the former and international law and institutions with respect to the latter. The state, in both perspectives, is the organising principle in a modern system that confers limits to political community, that juridically frames diversity through the ideal of sovereignty, and that contains populations within rationalised and regulated spaces subject to the imperatives of government. The historical trajectory of the modern state is clearly rife with violent practices aimed at redesigning diverse populations into coherent, pacified entities amenable to government. Participation in the realm of the international could no longer be guaranteed by ecclesiastical right, but shifted towards a conception of sovereign right, one that made its claims in relation to other states and mediated the interests of clients internationally.

The international as a realm of operation was hence never confined to interactions between sovereign states – for this was also a realm of commerce and trade – but its regulation gradually came under the purview of the state, embodying territorially defined and bounded political authority legitimised gradually through emergent nationalist, as opposed to class collective, loyalties. The consolidation of power internally and its projection externally came to define the modern European state, its place in the international arena guaranteed not just by power, military and economic, but by a system of mutual recognition.[2] While historical sociologies of the state recognise the constitutive role that violence plays in the emergence of the modern European state, the story of the European state in International Relations is one that assumes the state as a given, taken-for-granted entity, so sanitised of the historical record that it is all too easy to divide the world into two simplistic categories, 'states' and 'failed states' or even 'quasi-states'.[3] The model state is hence the European state which, colonialism and the Holocaust notwithstanding, is presented in liberal discourse as the model to emulate. Such is the normative commitment to liberalism that the actuality of its operations of power globally is left aside so that other societies may be brought into the liberal remit.

The system of mutual recognition that underpins the European state's claim to the international as a distinct zone of politics is also the basis upon which authorship of that very system is conferred on the European state. The modern European state and the modern international system of states hence provide the conceptual schema and the institutional architecture that receive the post-colonial world in the aftermath of the anti-colonial struggles of the twentieth century.

The institutional structure of the international sustains, therefore, the international system of states with sovereignty as its defining moment, and a capitalist international political economy that is historically related to the emergence of the state and that forms a constitutive element of the realm of the international and its rules of exchange. There is, however, a third element that defines the international, namely humanity at large, encompassing the interaction and movement of individuals and groups within and across state boundaries, expressive of claims not just in relation to their respective states, but related somehow to the institutional and normative architecture of the international. Each of these three elements of the international, the interstate, the international political economy, and the 'human', historically stands in a tense relationship with the other elements: the state might impose regulatory limits on the movement of capital and peoples, the markets might limit the sovereign manoeuvrability of state capacities, human beings as individuals and as members of groups might make claims in relation to the other two formations. The human element is institutionalised in the form of human rights conventions, the laws of war, and humanitarian law, all as constitutive of the modern legacy as the state and the capitalist system.[4]

The liberal peace project sees itself as championing the human in the realm of the international. The human in this context is defined positively through a juridical understanding of human rights, so that being human in this modernist rendition is to be in possession of human rights, claims that are not just sociologically or normatively framed, but juridically underpinned in relation to the state and international institutions. Sovereign right and human right are hence often interpreted in oppositional terms, so that a gain for sovereignty is deemed a loss for humanity and vice versa. Given this distinctly modernist conception of the human, any invocation of humanity, such as the one seen in Boutros-Ghali's *Agenda for Peace* and subsequent advocacies of so-called humanitarian intervention, hails forth a very distinct framing of being human, one that is situated in relation to the international, one that inhabits a universal terrain of institutionalised discourses and practices, and, crucially, one that transcends the sovereign limits of the territorial state.

If we accept that the liberal peace project indeed champions the 'human' as such, any engagement with the project must seek to delve into its understanding of the human and how such understanding informs its practices. The ontological baseline of liberal thought, specifically a Kantian informed liberal cosmopolitanism, takes as its starting point the autonomous rational individual taken to be the author of a rationally defined public order that serves the interests of the individual and the collective alike. The normative commitment is the primacy of the individual self and any protections thereof must be conceived not just in relation to the sovereign state of which the autonomous self is citizen, but in relation to the realm of the international, conceived as a universal space of humanity at large.[5] When Habermas looks to Kant's conception of the *Perpetual Peace*, he discovers what he interprets as an incomplete project of cosmopolitan modernity, namely one that seeks to retain a conception of the modern state and its sovereignty while imagining a developmental shift towards a form of cosmopolitanism that, in terms of responsibility, transcends the state and sees the human within its purview of duty. For Habermas, the human as such is positively constituted in a juridical framing that then defines the necessary conditions wherein the human self is recognised in terms of rights distinct from those conferred by any sovereign entity other than an emergent form of cosmopolitan law.[6]

Clearly, the Habermasian vision seeks to transcend the state and its juridical limits in the name of servicing the realm of the human, a realm protected in law and hence subject to enforcement. Placed in relation to the international, the enforcement of cosmopolitan law, and indeed its inauguration, comes to be instantiated through interventionist wars fought in the name of humanity, wars proclaimed as responsive to humanitarian crisis situations. Where Kant was distinctly reluctant to extend enforceable law into cosmopolitan space, Habermas calls for the constitution of the human through the force of law, and indeed sees its instantiation in the moment of intervention, as became evident in his support of the first Gulf War and in relation to Kosovo. Importantly, in Habermas, the state as such is considered the primary location in relation to which a citizenry might make its claims; for example, in the provision of welfare or basic infrastructural requirements. However, placed in the context of the international, state sovereignty comes to acquire a distinctly secondary status juridically. However, such a reconception of the international is also constitutive of a political move, in that any transformation of locations of sovereignty is at the same time suggestive of a shift beyond *the* formative moment in modern understandings of politics and political space.

What is significant in this brief engagement with Habermas's juridically informed reconception of the international so that the 'human' element is conferred primacy is that it reveals what Habermas sees as the apotheosis of modernity, namely the post-conventional stage of human development towards the autonomy of the individual self. Placed in relation to questions of war and peace, the post-conventional society comes to guarantee the conditions of possibility for a peace defined in terms of a regulated and indeed 'domesticated' realm of the international. The fully 'human' is then realised in relation to cosmopolitan right, which in turn is positioned in opposition to sovereign right. However, the very constitution of cosmopolitan right, in the instantiation of cosmopolitan law, relies on a certain articulation of sovereign authority, which, in Habermas, clearly originates in societies he refers to as the post-conventional; that is, the liberal societies of the West, though others might aspire to this status in due course.

The liberal peace project might then be seen as derivative of this Habermasian reframing of the Kantian cosmopolitan ideal. Where Habermas seeks to provide a juridical conception of the cosmopolitan so that the space of the international might be redefined in terms of cosmopolitan right, the liberal peace project is the operationalisation, 'on the ground' so to speak, of this cosmopolitan remit. Crucially, authorship of this cosmopolitan space, its juridification as well as its operationalisation, lies with the liberal self, conceived as being in possession of the moral and material resources to realise an ideal the origins of which are, in liberal discursive formations, very clearly located in the European Enlightenment.

Any critical engagement with the liberal peace project is therefore compelled to unravel its reliance on a conception of the 'human' that is distinctly post-conventional and hence developmental. The human in this context is not an empty space, but is rather inscribed juridically as being in possession of rights conferred by the realm of the human, the space of the cosmopolitan as such. While the cosmopolitan constitutes every human in terms of rights, so too the construct of 'human right' comes to be constitutive itself of a post-sovereign space named the cosmopolitan. However, the constituting moment itself lies elsewhere, in the enforcement of law through the decision to use force in the name of the human. According to Habermas, the cosmopolitan moment is the realisation of 'World Spirit', as conceived by Hegel, a distinctly universal moment that is at the same time historical.[7]

What is clear in this Habermasian world view, one that gives philosophical form to the practices encompassed by the liberal peace project, is that the envisaged 'World Spirit', which sees its moment in cosmopolitan law, has an author, a sovereign voice that brings it into form. The constitutive moment is hence a distinctly political one wherein the authority to act is at one and the same time representative of the authorial voice, the voice in whose remit lies the power to inscribe the human as such. The liberal peace project constitutes the practical instantiation of 'world spirit' articulated in global form and its driving agency lies in the West and its institutions. Membership of 'historical mankind', as Hannah Arendt so saliently highlights, happens to be a matter of where power lies at particular junctures of history.[8] Hence, invocations of the human are in actuality always invocations of particular humans.

The liberal peace project is hence constitutively framed in a discourse of modernisation that assumes developmental lines of demarcation that differentiate between the fully rational/liberal societies and those that strive to reach this point, defined primarily as one that is rational, and hence beyond cultural determination, and one that is institutionally implemented and discursively legitimised. The epistemological and ontological underpinning of the liberal peace project is precisely based upon a rationalist construction that is universal in its articulation. Such is the hegemonic standing of the project that to challenge it is to steer discourse back to conceptions of the international that stress the element of political self-determination while acknowledging that such a discourse is itself of modernity and its (post) colonial legacies.

My primary argument is that the liberal peace project is not a project of peace as such, one that would recognise the self-determination of others, but is rather a project of dispossession, one that seeks to depoliticise the temporal and spatial articulation of selfhood in place of a globally affirmed, institutionalised discourse that seeks conformity to a liberal international political economy that is, in late modernity, total in its manifestation.[9] It assumes the right to declare the exception to the rule, to define necessity, and to determine the capacities requisite of such agency. In directing its power at the government of populations through military and pedagogical means, it aims to shape societies so that they become self-governing entities within distinctly liberal lines.

in the name of security

The act of inscribing interventions from Kosovo, to Iraq, to Afghanistan as 'liberal peace' seems to deny the violence that is constitutive of such interventions. Within such inscriptions, distinctions disappear, so that peace and progress, peace and humanity, peace and war, peace and security, are formative and indeed performative dualities that confer agency to some while denying it to the rest. The populations of these regions and their complex diversities come to be reduced to technocratic problems to be solved, rationalised, calculated, and ultimately disciplined. While it is always difficult to place military intervention along the same spectrum of intervention as pedagogical training programmes, nevertheless each is premised, as Oliver Richmond points out, on the idea of 'peacebuilding'; that conditions in certain regions of the world might be transformed from violence to some form of sustainable peace.[10]

What is striking about the liberal peace project is its discursive construction as a benign project of modernisation the remit of which is the accrual of benefit to recipient societies. Variously described as a 'civilising mission', as an expression of the 'responsibility to protect', as a cosmopolitan project geared towards a shift in emphasis away from sovereign right and towards human right, the project is at once both normatively framed and operational in its orientation. Seen in the context of state breakdown and the targeting of civilian populations as a systematic strategy of war, it is difficult to overestimate the legitimacy of interventionist practices geared towards the rescue of individuals and communities targeted, usually by militia groups and gangs of youth engaged in the intimidation of civilian populations.

If the liberal peace project is interpreted as one of security as opposed to peace, we may begin to understand its workings on individuals, populations, and their government. Specifically, the constitutive elements of the project, that it seeks the protection of populations rendered vulnerable, that it does so through establishing structures of governance, and that it is primarily pedagogically defined, may be reinterpreted in relation to technologies of control informed by distinct epistemological and ontological assumptions. Interpreted as a project of security, the primary focus of intervention is a recognition of target societies not so much as distinct political entities, but as spaces open to policing operations.

The epistemological and ontological commitments of the liberal peace project are all too apparent in interpretations of such diverse locations of intervention as Afghanistan, Iraq, the Balkans, and sub-Saharan African conflicts such as Sierra Leone or the Sudan. There is, in each of these, a wholesale disregard for the political sociology of the locality, the distinct identity formations and relations of power that inform local agents, or the complex interplay of history and the present in the formation of ideas and interests relating to political society. Rather, all such complexity is reduced to the identification of culprits and victims, and the operational rationalities that inform what are generally seen as cosmopolitan policing operations. Epistemologically, the sources of violence and social breakdown are confined to what come to be labelled as insurgencies accorded somewhat paradoxically the agency to at once create and destroy, while the rest of society is reduced to a biopolitical mass in need of rescue.

Nowhere is the epistemological construction highlighted above more apparent than in Afghanistan, which seems to represent all that is at once revealing of both the aspirations of the liberal peace project and its limits and paradoxes. This is also the case that, again more than any other, is challenging to the critics of the liberal peace, including the author of this chapter. For Afghanistan seems to be the apotheosis of a late modern articulation of the oppositional forces that are, on the one hand, modernity and all its emancipatory potential, and, on the other, the forces of reaction, those who proclaim and indeed celebrate death in the service of divine right, who kill women in the name of dogma and tradition, and who prohibit all expressions of aesthetic desire. Any progressive politics would seek the defeat of the latter precisely in the name of distinctly modern struggles that have sought the emancipation of societies from oppressive practices. However, if we look closely into the operational modes of the intervention in Afghanistan we see that it might well be defined in terms of the 'liberal peace'. What it does not constitute, however, is a progressive politics of emancipation.

Clearly the Afghanistan context covers the array of intervention-ist practices that define the spectrum of liberal interventionism; from the use of military force to development goals led by civilians from international institutions, both governmental and non-governmental. While Afghanistan forms part of the so-called 'war against terrorism' initiated by the Bush Administration in the aftermath of the events of 11 September 2001, and hence is a constitutive part of the space of operations, from warfare to incarceration and detention, that links the theatre of war to places of incarceration elsewhere across the world, recent re-evaluations of strategy seem to have shifted emphasis, not so much away from war as, perhaps, to a balance of military and civil-ian options. The recent Obama plan for Afghanistan reveals the liberal peace underpinnings of policy, exemplified in this statement made by Michelle Flournoy of the Department of Defence:

> I would say what we're doing is stepping up to more fully resource a counterinsurgency strategy in Afghanistan that is designed to first reverse Taliban gains and secure the population, particularly in the most contested areas of the south and east; second, provide the Afghan national security forces with the training and mentoring they need to expand rapidly and to take... ultimately take the lead in providing security for their nation; and finally to provide a secure environment that will enable governance and development efforts to take root and grow.[11]

The epistemological framing of the analysis contained in this state-ment is exactly within the parameters of the liberal peace pro-ject. There is, firstly, the identification of the source of the problem, namely the Taliban, who are clearly accorded the agency to determine events on the ground; they are, in other words, conferred a distinctly political standing – they are the enemy to be defeated. Just as the 'counter-insurgency' seeks to destroy the Taliban, so too it reconstitutes the Taliban as a distinct political organisation. Rather paradoxically and worryingly for NATO, defining the Taliban as enemy redefines this group as a political organisation that has to be reckoned with. The unintentional consequence is that a mobilising power is conferred on the enemy that it distinctly lacked in the immediate aftermath of the war against the Taliban and Al-Qaida in 2001. The inadvertent logic of the liberal peace in Afghanistan is the instantiation of the Taliban as the only political game in town, so to speak. Consider this statement by Bruce Riedel, former CIA officer and Obama campaigner:

> Let me comment on the Taliban ... We know that the core Taliban leadership, led by Mullah Omar, is determined not to negotiate with anybody. They want to take Afghanistan back to the medieval hell that they created in the 1990s. But there are many of the ... those involved in the insurgency who may not be so committed as that, and if we see the momentum of the Taliban broken this summer and over the course of the fighting season, we may see some fractures within that movement. And I suspect that the core Taliban leadership is very, very worried about just that kind of thing happening.[12]

This might be contrasted with the International Crisis Group's analysis of the Taliban as a loose network, with no clear-cut basis of support: 'While it has made military gains, the Taliban today enjoys little support among an Afghan public tired of war. Its leadership does not command a significant standing army; indeed the Taliban is a disparate network of groups using the name as they pursue different agendas.'[13] However, the ICG's framing is also within the parameters of the liberal peace, so that 'representative government', 'resilient institutions', the 'rule of law', and 'development assistance' are given priority as means for the defeat of the Taliban. This imaginary does not, in other words, extend to forms of political mobilisation that might recognise the Afghan population as forming a political society containing the potential for mobilising progressive political forces against the Taliban or any other grouping defined in religious terms.

Secondly, and most importantly, the other category used in this context is the Afghan 'population' that has to be 'secured'. The Afghan population is hence merely the target of security operations, including the provision of welfare needs, such as health and education. That there might be political allegiances within the Afghan population that are not Taliban does not enter the frame, other than in relation to warlords and their relationship with the Afghan government. While there are a multiplicity of political groups that have participated in Afghan elections, nevertheless, these tend to merge into a diffuse collection, variously defined as offshoots of the old warlord system, as tribal leaders, defined solely in relation to their support or otherwise of the regime. It is as if the political as such cannot be an aspect of democratic transformation in Afghanistan, a perspective that directly stems from representations of the Afghan population in distinctly biopolitical terms.

The political cannot enter the frame when security is the paramount imperative of the government of populations. When the liberal peace project is recognised as a security project, its ultimate remit is to build a security apparatus through the direction of power at the shaping and reshaping of populations. Nevertheless, what should not be forgotten is that war plays a major part in the government of populations, such that it becomes simply another technology in the government of populations now globally rendered. While there might be a local nominally sovereign government, sovereign power, the power to decide who lives and who dies, where the limits are defined, how enemies are constituted, lies elsewhere, with the agencies of intervention, both state and non-state.

The liberal peace project is hence part and parcel of what I have referred to elsewhere as the global 'matrix of war', a complex array of interconnected practices that include the use of military force, policing operations, and statebuilding institutionalising measures geared at the control of populations. The use of overwhelming aerial bombardment of civilian targets in pursuit of insurgents is hence constitutive of both 'collateral damage' *and* the performance of sovereign power that serves to discipline populations. Within the matrix of war, distinctions relating to the inside and the outside, war and security, war and peace, policing and war disappear 'in a complex array of discourses and practices where the political is somehow banished in the name of governmentalising practices the remit of which is global in reach and defiant of limits, boundaries, and distinctions'.[14]

The liberal peace project is also constitutively built on certain ontological commitments informed by a hierarchical conception of subjectivity, so that the liberal self as such is seen as representative of cosmopolitan reach, in possession of agency, and having the capacity to protect. Those on the receiving end of such agency are the 'protected' and hence thoroughly lacking in agency, and indeed expected, in a protectionist discourse, to abdicate any sense of a distinct subjectivity that is not already defined by the sovereign; that is, the liberal self, the author and legislator of the liberal peace. This hierarchical conception of subjectivity is indeed a reinscription of an imperial past that now has a late modern manifestation in the forms of interventions fought in the name of humanity. While the liberal peace project defines itself in terms of institution-building and governance, relocating it in the matrix of war reveals its workings as a twenty-first-century form of colonisation that sees itself expressed in the form of military force, carceral power, confinement of populations to spaces subject to surveillance, administration, acquisition and the dispossession of populations, and the 'training' of locals into societies amenable to self-discipline, self-regulation, and ultimately self-government limited to the parameters of the liberal project. Nowhere have these excesses of liberal interventionism been more apparent than in Iraq and Afghanistan, where the acquisitive logic of domination is distinctly expressed in racialised terms reminiscent of the colonial past.

The hierarchical framing of subjectivity feeds in interesting ways into the conception of security, in the name of which interventions are sustained and legitimised. Analysed in terms of relations of power, and borrowing from Michel Foucault, the matrix of war I describe above is expressive of sovereign power revealed through disciplinary and governmentalising practices. This last element, namely 'governmental management', Michel Foucault highlights, 'has population as its main target and apparatuses of security as its essential mechanism.'[15] While Foucault's analytics are confined mainly to the Western modernity, when the West's remit of operations is directed elsewhere, at other populations, we witness the governmentalisation of other societies precisely through liberal cosmopolitan interventions; what are called, in the current context, liberal peace projects. Given that the directionality of these projects of intervention is indeed from the liberal societies of the West and into other, mainly post-colonial, regions across the globe, they cannot but be framed in terms of new, late modern cartographies of imperial rule, a form of rule that directs its military and civilian resources towards the government of populations enacted precisely through apparatuses of security.

Michel Foucault writes of the 'governmentalisation of the state'[16] when he refers to the liberal occidental state. What I am arguing in the present context is that liberal rule over other societies, enacted through practices constitutive of the 'matrix of war', might be understood as the 'governmentalisation of the post-colonial state'. Where Michel Foucault sees a shift in trajectories of power, away from sovereignty and towards the management of populations through governmentality, what I am arguing is that sovereign power is paramount in that its articulation through military force, through carceral power, through capacities to confine populations is intricately related to other practices of administration and the provision of welfare.

Security is hence the ultimate imperative of the liberal peace project. From Afghanistan to Iraq to other locations of intervention, the primary definition of peace is in relation to security, the security of populations achieved through building a complex assemblage of policing practices and their associated knowledge systems.[17] The governmentalisation of the post-colonial state requires a conceptual shift away from conceptions of the state as the location of political expression and towards one that reads the state and its institutions in terms of capacities to govern the conduct of populations. State failure is hence a failure to govern populations conceived as mass, so that extension of resources in the name of humanity at the same time defines its remit in terms of the imperative to govern. That liberal interventionism is centred around, on the one hand, military and carceral power, and, on the other, around pedagogical power, is reflective of its operational remit to shape recipient societies in accordance with a globally manifest liberal political economy wherein the post-colonial state is simply another participant.

conclusion

The argument formulated in this chapter is that the liberal peace project might be conceived as constitutive of a 'matrix of war' wherein war as a practice is simply another technology in the government of populations. Such interventions, while varying in the degree to which military force is used, seek precisely the governmentalisation of the state in the service of 'humanity' and are premised on the operationalisation of an extended apparatus of security that, in late modernity, has global manifestations. The limits of the state, and indeed of political community as such, are no longer limits to the imperatives of security and its multiform agencies, but might be called forth in the name of practices of government.

If the liberal peace project is interpreted as a project of governmentalisation, it becomes complicit in the banishment of politics and political agency, so that societies targeted for liberal intervention come to be reduced, in discourses and institutional practices, to a division between culprits and victims, where the former come to be defined as the enemy while the latter constitute the biopolitical mass to be protected or rescued. The liberal peace therefore presents a particular conception of cosmopolitanism based on particular epistemological and ontological commitments that assume a universal consensus over the causes of conflict and remedies based on liberal renditions of self and of governance. As argued above, such commitments are generative of a hierarchical conception of subjectivity that places primacy with the liberal European self, the author and adjudicator of knowledge systems on populations, how these might be categorised and recorded, and what constitutes acceptable institutional frameworks for government. There is in this scheme of things not so much a right to politics, which assumes agency and distinct subjectivity framed in the contingencies of social and political life, but a life lived as mass, simply one element in a category inscribed elsewhere and by others.

Any critique of the liberal peace project must in itself provide alternative conceptions of how to respond to conditions that precisely target populations and categories thereof. As I state at the outset of this chapter, the liberal peace project, being a project geared towards the reshaping of other societies, specifically the governmentalisation of the post-colonial state in the shape of liberalism, is a project that appears to primarily dispossess target societies of self-determination and the agency required for the capacity to author political subjectivity. The liberal project is one that expresses both epistemological and ontological universalism, somehow banishing limits and distinctions.

Any critical post-colonial response might see itself as redrawing limits, re-establishing political spaces and subjectivities that draw on the experiences of the past, including post-colonial struggles that generated conceptions of political community, but also ones that, in the post-colonial era, recognise the complex sets of conflicts and grievances emergent from inequalities of access to material and authorial resources. The 'right to politics', a term I borrow from Etienne Balibar,[18] is insurrectionary in ethos and collective in articulation. This is hence a right that is not conferred from the outside, but is framed in struggle and contestation. This is ultimately a progressive politics, not so much external to modernity, but enabled by modernity's discourses and institutions, including the secular state, as the location enabling of an abstracted subjectivity that has a capacity to emerge out of traditional affiliations and into political society, in all its contested forms. Returning to the example that framed the critique of the liberal peace project, namely Afghanistan, the critical response would absolutely reject the imposition from the outside, and through military and carceral power, a regime of governmentality that targets the population in order to somehow redesign it. It would, moreover, not define that particular context in terms of an enemy to be defeated and a population to be protected, for this latter move empowers the forces of reaction, namely the Taliban, defined inadvertently as a political force to be reckoned with, while the rest of the Afghan population is reduced to a depoliticised biopolitical mass in need of rescue, and hence denied political agency.

A progressive response to Afghanistan is one that recognises, and indeed extends solidarity to, progressive forces of emancipation in that society. This is then an alternative distinctly *political* articulation of cosmopolitanism, one that recognises that to be political is to take sides, so that, *contra* the former CIA operative quoted above, the options are not reduced to talking to the Taliban or not, but rather to the extension of solidarity to progressive voices that reject the reduction of Afghan society to the Taliban or indeed other forms of traditional affiliation. However, this is a form of solidarity that at the same time rejects the reduction of Afghan society to a biopolitical, indistinguishable mass of population subject to an apparatus of security, and hence governed so that others might be secure.

notes

1. B. Boutros-Ghali, *An Agenda for Peace: Preventive diplomacy, peacemaking and peace-keeping*, A/47/277-S/24111, 17 June 1992.
2. For historical sociologies of the European state, see especially Tilly, Mann, and Giddens.
3. From Mary Kaldor to Robert Jackson, the notion of the 'failed state' appears variously as both 'cause' and 'consequence' of violent conflict in the post-colonial world.
4. For this triadic conception of the international, see V. Jabri, *War and the Transformation of Global Politics*, London: Palgrave, 2007. For discussions of the implications for conceptions of sovereignty, see R.B.J. Walker, 'Lines of Insecurity: International, Imperial, Exceptional', *Security Dialogue*, Vol. 37, No. 1, 2006, pp. 65–82; and M. Hardt and A. Negri, *Empire*, Cambridge, MA., and London: Harvard University Press, 2000.
5. Two essays formative of the liberal cosmopolitan ideal are Immanuel Kant's 'Perpetual Peace: a Philosophical Sketch' and 'Idea for a Universal History with a Cosmopolitan Purpose', both in Kant, *Political Writings*, ed. H. Reiss, trans. H.B. Nisbet, Cambridge: Cambridge University Press, 1970.
6. Habermas's reframed Kantian cosmopolitanism in terms of cosmopolitan law appears in his essay 'Kant's Idea of perpetual Peace, with the benefit of

Two Hundred Years' Hindsight', in J. Bohman and M. Lutz-Bachmann (eds), *Perpetual Peace: Essays on Kant's Cosmopolitan Ideal*, Cambridge, MA: MIT Press, 1997.

7. J. Habermas, *Inclusion of the Other*, Cambridge, MA: MIT Press, 1998, p. 178.
8. H. Arendt, *Men in Dark Times*, New York, London: Harcourt, Brace and Co., 1968, p. 92. For a discussion of Arendt's critique of Hegel's notion of 'world spirit', see Jabri, *War and the Transformation*.
9. For another powerful critique of Habermasian cosmopolitanism and its (imperial) consequences, see C. Douzinas, *Human Rights and Empire: The Political Philosophy of Cosmopolitanism*, Routledge, 2007.
10. O.P. Richmond, *The Transformation of Peace*, London: Palgrave, 2005.
11. Quoted in R. Dreyfuss, 'Obama's Afghan Plan Could Be Worse', http://www.thenation.com/blogs/dreyfuss/422005/obama_s_afghan_plan_could_be_worse. Accessed 31 March 2009.
12. Ibid.
13. International Crisis Group, 'Afghanistan: New U.S. Administration, New Directions (13 March 2009). http://www.crisisgroup.org/home/index.cfm?id=6007. Accessed 31 March 2009.
14. Jabri, *War and the Transformation*, p. 59.
15. M. Foucault, *Security, Territory, Population*, London: Palgrave, 2007, p. 108.
16. Ibid., pp. 109–10.
17. The use of biometric identification as a technology of surveillance in Iraq, used to record and track the movement of thousands of Iraqi citizens, is just one instance of the reach of security in the government of populations. See reports published by EPIC, the Electronic Privacy Information Centre, Human Rights Watch, and Privacy International.
18. I draw on Etienne Balibar's notion of a right to politics to define a 'political cosmopolitanism' that I distinguish from the 'liberal cosmopolitanism' that I see as underpinning the liberal peace project. See Jabri, *War and the Transformation*, chapter 6, and Jabri's 'Solidarity and spheres of culture: the cosmopolitan and the postcolonial', *Review of International Studies*, Vol. 33, 2007, pp. 715–28. Balibar's notion of a 'right to politics' appears, among other places, in his *Politics and the Other Scene*, London: Verso, 2002.

3

reconstruction: the missing historical link

introduction: the definitional imprecision of 'reconstruction'

This chapter will suggest that the expression and practice of what is widely referred to as 'reconstruction' is now submerged under such a lot of ideological and historical baggage that we ought to try and think of another term altogether to attempt to rescue what is perhaps the most important task of the agenda known as the 'liberal peace' from ridicule and contempt. Some writers have already consigned reconstruction to the dustbin of history. Christopher Cramer has dubbed it the 'Great Post-Conflict Makeover Fantasy' and 'the continuation of war by other means'.[1] I myself have defined it as a 'form of (perhaps enlightened) liberal imperialism'.[2]

Others have been more neutral – it 'is predicated on the assumption that peace will be encouraged through the promotion of liberal-democratic political structures and market liberalization'.[3] But it is, as Tony Addison and Tilman Brück put it, 'a subject fraught with ambiguity: Do societies ever become truly "post-conflict"? Should we be looking to "reconstruct" societies or to "transform" them?'[4] So one inclusive definition (with which I find it hard to disagree) has it thus:

> [R]econstruction encompasses short-term relief and longer-term development. It extends far beyond physical reconstruction to include the provision of livelihoods, the introduction of new or reformed types of governance, and the repairing of fractured societal relationships. Thus reconstruction is not merely a technocratic exercise of rebuilding shattered infrastructure. Instead, it is an acutely political activity with the potential to effect profound social and cultural change. Post-war reconstruction holds the capacity to remodel

the nature of interaction between the citizen and the state, the citizen and public goods, and the citizen and the market.[5]

What all these definitions, and discussion along similar lines by others like Feargal Cochrane,[6] do is to place the idea and practice of reconstruction squarely within the debate on the 'liberal peace'.[7] That in turn places reconstruction within the discourse of 'peacebuilding', so we get a kind of matrioshka doll of logic tying reconstruction to the historical experience of the West in its dealing with the 'Rest' over a period that can easily be traced back a couple of hundred years, and in some cases further.[8]

But, as many others in this book have pointed out, the conceptualisation and practice of peacebuilding reflect the confusion about what the 'international community' is trying to achieve in its reordering of the planet and of specific areas of the world after the end of the Cold War. Knight rightly suggests that peacebuilding is more 'described than defined'; Galtung defines it as 'building structural and cultural peace' possibly as vague as his core idea of 'structural violence'; John-Paul Lederach as encompassing the 'full array of processes, approaches and stages needed to transform conflict towards more sustainable, peaceful relationships'.[9] The whole field is seemingly subject therefore to definitional chaos. So what elements of certainty do we have in answer to any of the above questions and definitional differences?

Given the current concerns of the post-Cold War international community, we could argue that central to the linked logic of both peacebuilding and reconstruction in current IR mythology is the idea of the 'failed state'. Much of the literature on peacebuilding and reconstruction stresses the duty of the 'international community' to do something to remedy this, up to and including international administration, what used to be called under the League of Nations the 'Mandate' system and in the early years of the United Nations 'Trusteeship'.[10] The logic is fairly simple – we have in the West to collectively help our less fortunate neighbours in the Third World, either out of humanitarian impulses, now defined as the 'responsibility to protect',[11] or because to ignore state failure would provoke huge displacements of population in our direction as they seek to escape the chaos.

Ghani and Lockhart define this in terms of a 'sovereignty gap' – the gap 'which exists between the de jure sovereignty that the international community affords such states and their de facto capabilities to serve their populations and act as responsible members of the international community'.[12] As we have already noted, how peacebuilding connects with 'reconstruction' is conventionally explained by implicit reference to liberal peace ideology. Ho-Won Jeong provides us with one further example: '[t]he practice of peacebuilding originally evolved out of an institutional adjustment to peacekeeping and humanitarian intervention responding to internal conflict situations'. It 'involves a wide range of sequential activities, proceeding from cease-fire and refugee resettlement to the establishment of a new government and economic reconstruction'.[13]

This linking of the statebuilding and peacebuilding processes can be criticised in many ways, of course. In other books I have suggested that there has been an inextricable confusion between statebuilding and peacebuilding.[14] Other writers have done likewise.[15] But, more profoundly, we have to make it clear that the state itself is a historically contingent reality. Writers from Charles Tilly[16] to Martin Van Creveld[17] have shown how the state emerged out of a set of political necessities that themselves shifted as the West moved from feudalism, through mature capitalism and into the 'post-modern' world that it now dominates through its control of communications, trade and many other levers of power. In that sense what we have noted as Cramer's dismissal of reconstruction (as part of that state discourse) and 'the continuation of war by other means'[18] is a correct summary of the situation. The West's assumption that its own history of state formation is the 'only way to go' is as familiar as the ideas that there are defined 'stages to growth', as Alexander Gerschenkron stated in the 1960s.

The state is also a self-evidently imposed category in much of the world, often without a great deal of understanding of what is being transferred and what effect that can have on local populations that do not have the same state-building or historically contingent background as the populations of the West. Bertrand Badie has coined the very useful notion of the 'imported state'.[19] Indigenous forms of political organisation are written off as 'tribal', 'clan-based' and lacking in modern functionality, 'unfit for purpose' as the dreadful audit Stalinist vocabulary now has it.

Western commentators and policymakers have difficulty imagining any other form of viable political community than the state as it is understood in the West. The international organisations only deal with established states, even when, for example, in the space known as 'Somalia' there are three entities, of which the best known are Somaliland and Puntland. Other non-states exist practically everywhere. Equally, these writers and policymakers might just about accept that the linked idea of 'reconciliation' after wars necessitates allowing primitive, 'local', practices as the natives cannot quite understand the intricacies of civilised 'War Crimes Tribunals', but that is as far as it can be allowed to go. Democratisation might come before or after institution-building, but both have to happen.[20] The practices of peacebuilding and therefore reconstruction are also usually set in stone. However, it is worth reflecting that we in the West are often unhappy when we are told that our forms of state are no longer 'fit for purpose' and that we must now move on to the 'next stage', for example the 'post-modern state'[21] as incarnated by, for example, the European Union. At least we have the right to vote on it, though when the Irish people seemingly rejected such a model in 2007 they were asked to vote again until they got it 'right'. When the Palestinian people of Gaza did the same in 2006 by electing Hamas, or the Algerian people the Islamists in 1990,[22] they were either smashed into agreeing with The Powers That Be or (as is currently happening, in early 2009) being bombed into quiescence. What is the fundamental difference between a group of Irish democrats opposing the extension of alien rule (from Brussels) and a group of 'insurgents' opposing the same process in Iraq? They were not given the choice of a vote, just to come out with their hands up and submit. The choice, says Robert Cooper, a key advisor to the EU and Tony Blair, is between 'order and chaos'.[23]

So one of the key, and simple, arguments that could be made here is that the reason for this vagueness is because 'reconstruction' is a concept and practice that has changed in line with historical context, both in the 'target' areas where conflict is a problem, and also in the institutional reaction to these areas. It has historically been a changing palette of different policies and rationalisations for action, with thinking and practice made 'on the hoof' by policymakers who were not at all sure what they were trying to do, or how, before they started. To read the tomes of American think tanks since the invasion of Afghanistan and Iraq, one is given to believe that historical examples and templates are at the heart of current thinking. However, I would suggest that any attempt to artificially define and use reconstruction in such a way for all time is doomed to disaster. I will also suggest that many of the problems we now have with it are because we are attempting to use historical templates for new and evolving situations. The international community now needs to realise this, stop trying to 'do a Germany' (or whatever example we care to take), and look instead at the potential for locally generated 'reconstruction' programmes that may well fall short of the standards that we now place on them, especially in terms of their fitting a narrow-minded definition of the 'liberal peace'.

the debate on reconstruction

The Rand Corporation's 'A Beginner's Guide to Nation-Building' gives a kind of 'flat-pack', do-it-yourself manual of how reconstruction is viewed by many policymakers.[24] It has useful graphs and chapters on every conceivable aspect of the task and warns that '[e]ach nation to be rebuilt may be unique, but the nation-builder has only a limited range of instruments on which to rely'. These 'instruments' are item-ised as various kinds of military and administrative personnel, as well as 'experts in political reform and economic development'.[25] The pro-cess tends to exclude the 'locals' at the expense of outside 'experts', and books like Dobbins et al. do tend to put such an emphasis on the out-side agents concerned.

Those who go along with the basic model will allow for many vari-ations on the basic theme. The main underpinnings are that war is by definition dysfunctional and that 'at the individual level, participants in war often pursue a mixture of economic, political and social object-ives'.[26] These have been variously designated as being due mainly to 'greed', though also to 'grievance'.[27] The wars in which they fight are due not only to local issues but also to the effects of globalisation.[28] The initial problem in the reconstruction of any developing country, he notes, is the lack of basic security. In successful states the monopoly of power is held by the state; in states that have experienced a civil war this is certainly not the case. So 'the first task of peacebuilding is to restore the monopoly as a foundation and precondition for all further institution-building efforts'.[29]

'Disarmament, Demobilisation and Reintegration' (DDR) is usu-ally seen as the main initial vector for reducing immediate levels of violence. This is described by Ozerdem as 'becoming civilian',[30] and helping to create a working democracy by changing the civil/military relationship, a feature in many coup-prone countries (as with Fiji or Pakistan), or in countries where dictators have an unhealthy relation-ship with their armed forces, as for example in Zimbabwe, which is arguably worse in the long run for local and regional prospects for peace and prosperity alike. Analogous to this is 'Security Sector Reform' (SSR), where the army and police are reformed to make them more reflective of democratic norms and practices, not mere protectors of the elite and their own livelihoods.

Some of the underlying arguments for the above logic have been undermined by the discussion of exactly how 'new' these wars are.[31] But the actors in these wars clearly do often have distinctly economic motivations, such as the extraction of commodities for their own enrichment.[32] Equally, giving up war has certain disadvantages for such actors.[33] One other key problem is still that 'spoiler violence' (by unsuccessfully disarmed and demobilised militias, for example) seems attendant on most, if not all, post-conflict situations. It has been defined as 'violence that deliberately attempts to undermine peacemaking processes and peace accords'[34] and it has a major impact on attempts at post-conflict reconstruction. However, as John Darby has put it, 'although substantial research attention has been paid to the origin and dynamics of ethnic violence, to the first moves towards negotiations, and to spoiler violence, the threat to post-accord reconstruction is underresearched'.[35]

Critical voices include those who accuse the reconstruction formulas outlined above as being destructive of the very targets that they wish to help, even in some case accusing national and international players of 'deconstructing' societies, in both the metaphysical and actual senses of the term.[36] They also include those who see reconstruction as a vehicle for the capitalist aims of states or transnational corporations.[37] The idiom of these attacks puts them in a different register from the other theorists named above. But this writer, for one, thinks capitalism is a resilient category of action and not likely to be dismantled any time soon. The *way* in which capitalist actors (including transnational corporations and even non-governmental organisations) feather their own nests in post-conflict reconstruction does nonetheless need more critique along the lines of that undertaken by Mark Duffield and David Keen.[38] But, more fundamentally, we still need to address the mismatch between *what* we are examining and *how* we do that – and the missing link, I would strongly assert, is in the lack, most of the time, of any historical perspective.

the 'history' of 'reconstruction'

Addison and Brück acknowledge the importance of history in thinking about post-conflict reconstruction, for 'income and asset inequality generally have deep historical roots'.[39] But there is also a 'history' of reconstruction itself that needs more understanding – it has a long past as a concept and practice. It began in essence as a term and practice after the American Civil War. 'Reconstruction' in that case meant in effect the misappropriation of the defeated.[40] This was illustrated graphically in the 1939 film 'Gone with the Wind'. The character of Scarlet O'Hara (played by Vivien Leigh) is condemned therein not just for her perfidy and behaviour towards Rhett Butler (played by Clark Gable) but also because she collaborates with the invader and helps his cause. It was equally worryingly portrayed in Griffith's 'Birth of a Nation' (1915) as justifying the emergence of the Ku Klux Klan as a liberation movement who were getting their own back on the 'carpetbaggers', in some instances by lynching the main beneficiaries of Northern 'emancipation', the negro (black) population of the South. This latter title is worryingly similar to the aims of Iraqi, Afghan or other insurgents who claim to be liberating their people from foreign oppression and nation-forming by similarly illiberal methods such as shooting teachers, burning down schools and denying women the right to literacy. The old adage that 'people fight for what is theirs' holds irrespective of what good liberals may believe is good for that same people.

The literature on the next great period of the stage of reconstruction, that of 1945–55 in Europe and Japan, is equally blind to its own contradictions. There are marvellous studies of this massive exercise.[41] In tune with what might be called the 'Great Man' thesis in history, Michael Beschloss's standard work on the United States' creation of a new Germany after 1945 gives much of the credit for the success of the enterprise to the inspired leadership of Presidents Roosevelt and Truman. He puts this down to their insistence that 'after victory, the German system that had produced Hitler and his depraved movement should be so transformed that Germany would never again threaten the world'.[42] The operative word here is 'transformed'. However, it is clearly the case that the United States Government of George W. Bush saw this heroic period of successful reconstruction as being the inspiration for what they tried to make happen after the invasion of Iraq in 2003, even though the two eras and cases were totally different. Then, as more recently, the armed forces were de-Nazified/ de-Baathised. The organs of Government in both cases were decapitated and replaced by interim administrations. The leaders in both cases were tried as war criminals. But, whereas in the German and Japanese cases the armed forces were thoroughly decimated and delegitimised, in the 2003 situation that has not been the case and chaos has ensued.[43]

The botched reconstruction of Iraq has shown up many of the problems of the 'one-size-fits-all' model of reconstruction promoted by organisations like Rand based on partial (in both senses of the word) reading of historical cases. Quite apart from the ethical considerations of being responsible, indirectly or directly, for well over a quarter of a million deaths in the aftermath of the war, the United States Government now has its own decades-long cross to bear as a direct result of its miscalculation that the Iraqi people would welcome the invaders of 2003 with open arms. The monetary cost of this debacle alone is estimated by Stiglitz at three trillion dollars.[44] So the invasion of Iraq shows up most clearly the dangers of Badie's 'imported state', for the importers and the exporters.

the perils of historicism

In its analysis of the international reconstruction of Germany, as well as many other examples (Japan, Somalia, Haiti, Bosnia, Kosovo and Afghanistan), and the 'lessons' for the same process in Iraq, the Rand Corporation lists the 'Challenges' and 'What Happened' in the following order: Security; Humanitarian; Civil Administration; Democratisation [and] Reconstruction. This is much in line with Jeong's above sequential explanation of how peacebuilding should generally be seen as having to be undertaken. The authors of the Rand study themselves acknowledge that '[t]he cases of Germany and Japan set a standard for postconflict nation-building that has not since been matched'.[45] So how might we analyse the problems that were faced and how they might be better dealt with in future?

The key overall theme is the need to underpin reconstruction efforts with a credible security apparatus. In 1945 such an apparatus clearly existed; in all of the post-Cold War examples it has not. Moreover, we could cite other, non-American examples, such as where the African Union or the UN has been the central actor, where the security apparatus has been a minimalist adaptation of existing peacekeeping practices. In most, if not all, of these the credibility of the forces deployed has been near to zero. As any reader of a newspaper on what has been happening in Eastern Congo will know, the UN is viewed with utter contempt by the local populations, who are subject to daily murder, rape and mayhem by their own army or 'rebels' while the UN troops stand by in impotence. To them is it as if Peacekeepers just take over city parks and do nothing for those excluded.

Other problems of reconstructing societies and polities have also slowly emerged as key. The reconstruction of Eastern Europe, including Russia, in what were known as 'Big Bang' operations, consisted of a shock therapy of rapid privatisation of economies that had previously been totally state-controlled, usually by issuing shares to all those who worked there, a process that often led to the concentration of power in the hands of a few 'oligarchs', such as the men who now control Norilsk and, until recently, the Russian oil Majors. This process was usually coordinated by the World Bank and the IMF, led by prominent Western economists like Jeffrey Sachs of Harvard, and has often been stressed as 'successful' in that these countries are now capitalist and 'democracies'. The European Union has likewise been active in the Former Yugoslavia.[46] But there is much evidence that the polities thus created are very fragile, the standard of living of the population has suffered, in some cases catastrophically, and the resulting political structures are, to put it mildly, at risk. A recent study in the premier British medical journal, *The Lancet*,[47] looks at the result of the policies of 'Big Bang' in Russia and concluded that there is a direct correlation between the policies employed and 'devastating mortality surges' – the life expectancy of Russian males dropped from the mid-70s to the high 50s in a decade.

The authors of the *Lancet* study conclude that a ' "British-style" case-by-case method' of privatising small chunks of the economy and then letting the effect consolidate is far better than the 'shock therapy' imposed on Russia. The debate rumbles on in the columns of the financial press.[48] However, it is worth remembering that we have been here before. As Cramer rightly points, out the 'reconstruction' that happened after 1945 in Europe was not monolithically similar.[49] Different countries took different paths with the resources provided by the United States in probably the greatest example of self-interested (and wholly beneficial) generosity in the history of the West. And the peoples were trusted to distribute and use their own 'gifts' in their own way so that they felt that they 'owned' the process. How many Iraqis, for example, feel that way about the billions that have been managed in their direction by the reconstruction agencies of Washington? These funds are the functional equivalent of the pipelines that run through the Nigerian Delta – a resource to be stolen with no feelings of bad conscience.

There are other evident historical differences between the models of 1945–55 and those since the end of the Cold War alluded to in other chapters of this book. Private security firms and NGOs now subcontract reconstruction work and have further alienated local populations.[50]

Much more could now be said about the above issue of 'spoilers'.[51] The role of women in post-conflict reconstruction is now very different, both in providing potential leadership and as victims.[52] These would all merit at least a solid chapter each.

think culturally and be honest about history?

Do we therefore need different analytical structures to determine how we should think about such policy options as reconstruction in the future, with all the internal matrioshka dolls that this implies we should also consider? If so, what are they? There is one obvious candidate for consideration. It is now widely accepted that culture is the big blind spot in the analytical viewing apparatus of IR.[53] In point of fact, we have rather forgotten what we once knew in our rush to impose a false equality in the name of eliminating cultural relativism (the doctrine that peoples are different and should be allowed to have their own peculiar, and probably 'illiberal', practices). This liberal belief in equality, justice and the like was probably a necessary reaction to what went before. Before the First World War, as Julie Reeves points out, what 'culture' meant in IR was to do with whether or not a person, or a people, was successfully 'civilised'. This civilisation was both vertical (between nations and races) and horizontal (between classes). So when 'China and Japan went to war in 1894, the incident was not seen as a proper war in the West as neither party could be counted as "civilised" under the general terms of definition. Japan won the war and declared victory in the name of "civilization"…, ensuring (but not entirely securing) Japan a foothold in the civilization camp'.[54]

However, with the new Wilsonian liberal doctrine of equality of peoples (but, it must be noted, only up to a point; people of colour need not apply), it became necessary to change the stress of what 'civilization' meant.[55] In the 1920s it came to mean 'peaceful'. Reeves quotes the influential liberal Leonard Woolf as writing in 1916 that 'public war shall be as impossible between civilised States as is private war in civilised States'.[56] This was later reinforced internationally by the revelations of what was happening in Soviet Russia and Nazi Germany. Such barbarism was rightly described as an affront to all civilised behaviour, but after 1945 it no longer came to be possible just to write off such activity, as would have been the case before 1914, as not really being barbarism since it did not occur between or within 'proper' states. Now it was the domain of concern to all – as Michael Walzer put it, if it 'shocks the moral conscience of mankind' then mankind must deal with it.[57]

This has now developed into a doctrine of a 'responsibility to protect'.[58] The slippery slope had many humanitarian and other worthwhile impulses to lubricate it, but it has undoubtedly led us a long way from the ideas of Woolf, indeed way past the point of deforming them. The reason is also comprehensible, for, as Reeves indicates, there was a genuine fear that 'civilization' itself had been put at risk by the Soviet Union and the Nazis – we could never again let such forces free to roam the Earth. If civilisation was in danger, an idea that, say, Norman Angell would have thought preposterous before 1914, then it must be vigorously defended, wherever it was attacked. The reason for a more militant liberalism was thus, in fact, because it felt that for the first time it was under serious threat, a feeling that has paradoxically just got stronger as liberal states have arguably themselves got stronger.[59] We can see the result of this in the Middle East. If a few hotheads based in Afghanistan fly a plane into your towers in New York, well, obviously, you 'take them out' and destroy a 'primitive' but effective state structure. You cannot negotiate with 'terrorists'; you need to 'reconstruct' their state in the image of your own virtue.

There is evidence that a few isolated voices are now becoming heard in IR to form a necessary corrective to such over-egging of the liberal omelette as it applies specifically to post-war reconstruction. Patrick Chabal and Jean-Pascal Daloz point to an embedded ethnocentricity in many of the conventional statements in the peacebuilding discourse, an unwillingness to accept that we need to take cultural and historical context into account in condemning local practices or trying to impose 'a linear, when not a singular, form of modernisation resulting in Westernisation'.[60] So, where a liberal peace interpretation might well be to say that there is a need for better institutional responses.[61] Chabal and Daloz would point to the need for a root and branch rethinking of the underlying episteme of what we mean by 'politics'.

One main start might be a dose of true humility, what has been termed 'getting out of the "Imperial City"'.[62] What is meant by this is the evident separation that usually exists between 'peacekeepers' and NGO workers and those they are allegedly there to help.[63] Reconstruction teams are seen as living in security bubble while the population does not. There is anecdotal evidence that national and international agencies are beginning to listen, but there is still a long way to go, as anyone who has spent any time in proximity to IGOs and NGOs in developing countries will be able to attest.

some conclusions

The first conclusion to this necessarily brief and impressionistic overview of what is wrong with 'reconstruction' has to do with the state-building that the international agencies, working under the rules of Western liberalism, now impose on developing countries. Capitalism and political liberalism are thus tied into a *danse macabre* in which the main victims are not the much publicised American or British servicemen and women (tragic as their deaths are) but the citizens of developing countries who are on the wrong end of our muddle-headed attempts to state- or nation-build. We thus need a much clearer understanding of both what we are trying to do and how we hope to achieve it. The alternative is yet more Iraqs and Afghanistans.

A second conclusion is that expressed above, the need to be far more sensitive to cultural specificities in our reconstruction efforts. We maybe need to accept that there is not much we in the West can do and leave it to the 'locals' entirely. Such conclusions may well lead to the previously unthinkable conclusion that, for example, we should leave post-conflict reconstruction in Gaza to Hamas and to Hizbollah in Lebanon.[64]

The third conclusion is to listen more to the 'prompting of history', a term used by the late Christopher Thorne in his neglected study of 'Border Crossings' in IR.[65] For IR has been an appallingly ahistorical subject for many years, and particularly in the 1990s. The 'End of History' was taken far too seriously by many scholars, particularly in the United States where formal theories rule supreme and brown bag lunches compare 'models' and theorems that remind most people of the magic tricks of Wall Street, and are now held to be responsible for practically destroying the global financial system. This modelling now runs the same risk of doing terminal damage to our theoretical understanding of politics as it has to that of economics. These same ideas and their attendant hubris have in particular permeated the policymaking community known as the 'neo-cons', but more accurately the 'ultra-liberals'. If the idea of the liberal peace 'is the nearest thing that we have to a law in international relations', then can we be surprised that this law is used to justify conclusions that are also definitive? The problem is that such risk-taking, revealed as it has been to be systemically disastrous on Wall Street, is also being so revealed in the political and military spheres. We need a re-regulation in the latter areas as much as in the former. As Keynesian economics are brought back to recreate the successful parameters of what John Ruggie called 'structural liberalism' (a balanced and regulated capitalism that configured both public and private sectors), so we also need a more sober view of what 'reconstruction' can be expected to do. This is not to jettison liberalism at all. John Stuart Mill would not have been surprised to limit the potential of intervention, to have asserted that 'people get the governments they deserve', and to have understood the limits of imperialism. To remind ourselves of these basic truths we merely need to realise that the frenetic liberalism in the economy was as much a mistake as that of the similar impulses in the political sector. And we need to go back to that basic law of politics – that it is to realise the limits of the possible.

notes

1. C. Cramer, *Civil War Is Not a Stupid Thing: Accounting for Violence in Developing Countries*, London: Hurst, 2006, pp. 245, 249.
2. A.J. Williams, 'Reconstruction: The Bringing of Peace and Plenty or Occult Imperialism?' *Global Society: Journal of Interdisciplinary International Relations*, Vol. 21, No. 4, 2007, pp. 539–51.
3. F. Cochrane, *Ending Wars*, Cambridge: Polity, 2008, p. 168.
4. T. Addison and T. Brück, 'The Multi-Dimensional Challenge of Mass Violent Conflict', in Addison and Brück (eds) *Making Peace Work: The Challenges of Social and Economic Reconstruction*, London: Palgrave Macmillan, 2009, p. 1.
5. R. Mac Ginty, 'Reconstructing Post-War Lebanon: A Challenge to the Liberal Peace', *Conflict, Security and Development*, Vol. 7, No. 3, 2007, pp. 457–82, quote at p. 458.
6. Cochrane, *Ending Wars*, pp. 167–9.
7. Ibid.
8. Cramer, *Civil War Is Not a Stupid Thing*, pp. 245, 249.
9. W.A. Knight, 'Evaluating recent Trends in Peacebuilding Research', *International Relations of the Asia-Pacific*, Vol. 3, No. 2, 2003; J. Galtung, *Peace by Peaceful Means: Peace and Conflict, Development and Civilization*, London: Sage, 1996; J. Lederach, *Building Peace: Sustainable Reconciliation in Divided Societies*, Washington, DC: United States Institute of Peace Press, 1997.
10. R. Caplan, *International Governance of War-Torn Territories: Rule and Reconstruction*, Oxford: Oxford University Press, 2005.
11. A. Bellamy, *Responsibility to Protect: The Global Effort to End Mass Atrocities.* Oxford: Polity, 2008.
12. A. Ghani, and C. Lockhart, *Fixing Failed States: A Framework for Rebuilding a Fractured World*, Oxford: Oxford University Press, 2008, pp. 3–4; R.H. Dorff, 'Failed States after 9/11: What Did We Know and What Have We Learned?', *International Studies Perspectives*, Vol. 6, 2005, pp. 20–34.

13. H.W. Jeong, *Peacebuilding in Post-Conflict Societies: Strategy and Process*, Boulder, CO and London: Lynne Reinner, 2005, p. 1.

14. A.J. Williams, *Liberalism and War: The Victors and the Vanquished*, London: Routledge, 2006; R. Mac Ginty, and A.J. Williams, *Conflict and Development*, Routledge, 2009.

15. D. Ekbladh, 'From Consensus to Crisis: the Postwar Career of Nation-Building in U.S. Foreign Relations', in F. Fukuyama, (ed.) *Nation–Building: Beyond Afghanistan and Iraq*, Baltimore, MD: John-Hopkins, 2006, pp. 19–41.

16. C. Tilly, *The Formation of National States in Western Europe*, Princeton, NJ: Princeton University Press, 1975; C. Tilly, 'War Making and State Making as Organized Crime', in P. Evans, D. Rueschmeyer and T. Skocpol (eds) *Bringing the State Back In*, Cambridge: Cambridge University Press, 1985, pp. 169–91.

17. M. Van Creveld, *The Rise and Decline of the State*, Cambridge: Cambridge University Press, 1999.

18. Cramer, *Civil War Is Not a Stupid Thing*, p. 249.

19. B. Badie, *The Imported State: the Westernization of the Political Order*, Stanford: Stanford University Press, 2000.

20. R. Paris, *At War's End: Building Peace After Civil Conflict*, Cambridge: Cambridge University Press, 2004.

21. Cooper, R., *The Breaking of Nations: Order and Chaos in the Twenty-First Century*, New York: Grove Press, 2003.

22. L. Martinez, (trans. Jonathan Derrick), *The Algerian Civil War 1990–1998*, London: Hurst & Co., 1998.

23. Cooper, *The Breaking of Nations*.

24. J. Dobbins, S.G. Jones, K. Crane and B. Cole DeGrasse, *The Beginner's Guide to Nation-Building*, Santa Monica: Rand Corporation, 2007.

25. Ibid., p. vii.

26. Addison, and Brück, 'The Multi-Dimensional Challenge', p. 3.

27. P. Collier, and A. Hoeffler, 'On the Economic Causes of Civil War', *Oxford Economic Papers*, Vol. 50, 1998, pp. 563–73; P. Collier, *Economic Causes of CivilConflict and Their Implications for Policy*, Washington, DC: The World Bank, 2000; P. Collier, 'Doing Well Out of War: An Economic Perspective', in M. Berdal and D. Malone (eds), *Greed and Grievance: Economic Agendas in Civil Wars*, Boulder, CO: Lynne Rienner, 2000, pp. 91–111.

28. M. Kaldor, *Old and New Wars: Organized Violence in a Global Era*, Cambridge; Malden, MA: Polity Press, 2006.

29. Paris, *At War's End*, pp. 206–7.

30. A. Ozerdem, *Becoming Civilian: Disarmament, Demobilisation and Reintegration*, London: I.B. Tauris, 2008; V. Gamba, 'Post-Agreement Demobilization, Disarmament and Reintegration: Towards a New Approach', in J. Darby (ed.), *Violence and Reconstruction*, Notre Dame, IN: University of Notre Dame Press, 2006.

31. S. Kalyvas, ' "New" and "Old" Civil Wars – A Valid Distinction?', *World Politics*, Vol. 54, No. 1, 2001, pp. 99–108; H. Münkler, *The New Wars*, Cambridge: Polity Press, 2005.

32. M. Pugh and N. Cooper, with J. Goodhand, *War Economies in a Regional Context: Challenges of Transformation*, Boulder, CO: Lynne Rienner, 2004; C. Nordstrom, *Shadows of War: Violence, Power, and International Profiteering in the Twenty-First Century*, Berkeley, CA: University of California Press, 2004; C. Nordstrom, 'Casting Long Shadows: War, Peace and Extralegal Economies', in J. Darby and R. Mac Ginty (eds), *Contemporary Peacemaking: Conflict, Peace Processes and Post-War Reconstruction*, Basingstoke: Palgrave, 2008, pp. 289–9; C. Mayrood and J. Katunga, 'Coltan exploration in Eastern Democratic Republic of the Congo (DRC)', in J. Lind and K. Sturman (eds), *Scarcity and Surfeit: The Ecology of Africa's Conflicts*, Pretoria: Institute of Security Studies, 2002, pp. 159–85.

33. C. Nordstrom, *Shadows of War: Violence, Power, and International Profiteering in the Twenty-First Century*, Berkeley, CA: University of California Press, 2004. For more on this see Mac Ginty, and Williams, *Conflict and Development*.

34. R. Mac Ginty, *No War, No Peace: The Rejuvenation of Stalled Peace Processes and Peace Accords*, London: Palgrave, 2006.

35. J. Darby (ed.), *Violence and Reconstruction*, Notre Dame, IN: University of Notre Dame Press, 2006, p. 6.

36. D. Campbell, *National Deconstruction: Violence, Identity and Justice in Bosnia*, Minneapolis: University of Minnesota Press, 1998.

37. D. Chandler, 'Back to the Future? The Limits of Neo-Wilsonian Ideals of Exporting Democracy', *Review of International Studies*, Vol. 32, No. 3, 2006, pp. 475–94; D.Chandler, 'EU Statebuilding: Securing the Liberal Peace Through EU Enlargement', *Global Society*, Vol. 21, No. 4, 2007, pp. 593–607; T. Jacoby, 'Hegemony, Modernisation and Post-war Reconstruction', *Global Society: Journal of Interdisciplinary International Relations*, Vol. 21, No. 4, 2007, pp. 521–37.

38. M. Duffield, *Global Governance and the New Wars: The Merging of Development and Security*, London: Zed Books, 2001; M. Duffield, *Development, Security and Unending War: Governing the World of Peoples*, Cambridge: Polity Press, 2007; D. Keen, *Complex Emergencies*, Cambridge: Polity Press, 2008.

39. Addison, and Brück, 'The Multi-Dimensional Challenge', p. 3

40. Cramer, *Civil War Is Not a Stupid Thing.*; E. Foner, *Reconstruction: America's Unfinished Revolution, 1863–1877*, New York: HarperCollins, 1989; Williams, *Liberalism and War.*

41. M. Hogan, *The Marshall Plan: America, Britain and the Reconstruction of Western Europe, 1947–1952*, Cambridge: Cambridge University Press, 1987; J. Killick, *The United States and European Reconstruction, 1945–1960*, Edinburgh: Edinburgh University Press, 1997.

42. M. Beschloss, *The Conquerors: Roosevelt, Truman and the Destruction of Hitler's Germany, 1941–1945*, New York: Simon and Schuster, 2002, p. ix.

43. A. Allawi, *The Occupation of Iraq: Winning the War; Losing the Peace*, Yale University Press, 2007; T. Dodge, 'Iraq: the Contradictions of Exogenous State-Building in Historical Perspective', *Third World Quarterly*, Vol. 27, No. 1, 2006, pp. 187–200.

44. J. Stiglitz with L.J. Bilmes, *The Three Trillion Dollar War: The True Cost of the Iraq Conflict*, New York: W.W. Norton, 2008.

45. Dobbins et al., *The Beginner's Guide.*

46. Williams, *Liberalism and War*, pp. 130–6.
47. D. Stuckler, L. King and M. McKee, 'Mass privatisation and the post-communist mortality crisis: a cross-national analysis', *The Lancet*, Early Online Publication, 15 January 2009, doi:10.1016/S0140–6736(09)60005–2, accessed 26 January 2009.
48. For example, *Financial Times*, D. Stuckler, L. King and M. McKee (2009), 'Rapid Privatisation worsened unemployment and death rates', Letters page, 22 January.
49. Cramer, *Civil War Is Not a Stupid Thing*, p. 248.
50. O. Richmond and H. Carey, (eds), *Subcontracting Peace: the Challenges of NGO Peacebuilding*, Aldershot: Ashgate, 2005.
51. Darby, *Violence and Reconstruction*; J. Darby and R. Mac Ginty, 'Introduction: What peace? What process?', in J. Darby and R. Mac Ginty (eds), *Contemporary Peacemaking: Conflict, Peace Processes and Post-War Reconstruction*, 2nd edn, Basingstoke: Palgrave, 2008, pp. 1–9.
52. For a good summary see Anderlini, *Women Building Peace: What They Do; Why It Matters*, Boulder, CO: Lynne Reinner, 2007; M.E. Greenberg and E. Zuckerman, 'The Gender Dimensions of Post-Conflict Reconstruction', in Addison and Brück, 'The Multi-Dimensional Challenge'.
53. T. Väyrynen, *Culture and International Conflict Resolution*, Manchester: Manchester University Press, 2001; J. Reeves, *Culture and International Relations: Narratives, Natives and Tourists*, Abingdon, NY: Routledge, 2004.
54. Reeves, *Culture and International Relations*, p. 27.
55. A.J. Williams, *Failed Imagination? The Anglo-American New World Order from Wilson to Bush*, 2nd edn, Manchester: Manchester University Press, 2007.
56. Woolf, in Reeves, *Culture and International Relations*, p. 31.
57. M. Walzer, *Just and Unjust Wars*, 4th edn, New York: Basic Books, 2006.
58. N. Wheeler, *Saving Strangers: Humanitarian Intervention in International Society*, Oxford: Oxford University Press, 2000; Bellamy, *Responsibility to Protect*.
59. Reeves, *Culture and International Relations*, p. 38.
60. P. Chabal and J.P. Daloz, *Culture Troubles: Politics and the Interpretation of Meaning*, London: Hurst and Company, 2006, p. 9; P. Chabal and J.P. Daloz, *Africa Works: Disorder as a Political Instrument*, Oxford: James Currey, 1999.
61. For example, Gamba, 'Post-Agreement Demobilization', and Paris, *At War's End*
62. R. Chandrasekaran, *Imperial Life in the Emerald City: Inside Baghdad's Green Zone*, London: Bloomsbury, 2007.
63. D. Keen, *Complex Emergencies,* Cambridge: Polity Press, 2008.
64. Mac Ginty, 'Reconstructing post-war Lebanon'.
65. C. Thorne, Border Crossings: Studies in International History, Oxford: Basil Blackwell, 1988.

4

method: theory and ethnography in peace and conflict studies

jevgenia viktorova milne

introduction

The large number of seemingly intractable – despite multiple efforts at resolution – violent conflicts across the world is a testimony to our poor understanding of issues, dynamics and processes involved in both waging conflicts and terminating them. The critique of interventions concerns, in particular, the inability to transcend the 'fixation' with the state and top-level politics in analysing conflict dynamics and attempts to influence them. While the imperative to resuscitate dysfunctional states is perhaps understandable (if not unproblematic) in the context of the Westphalian states-system, this preoccupation with the state effectively obscures the importance of other levels at which conflicts are waged, their impact on societies at large and on individual people, as well as the stakes that actors not bent on 'capturing the state' may have in the continuation of violence. On the flip side, the interveners also underuse the local potential for peace, as the process of state reconstruction often sets into motion dynamics that disempower existing 'peace constituencies' and thwart, rather than capitalise upon, local 'resistances' to violence.[1] The unaccounted 'local' is thus left to clash with the overall framework of liberal peace.

The noted bias, however, is hardly down to the lack of attempts to theorise conflict: there are a plethora of theories dedicated to analysing various aspects and types of conflict, as well as related recipes for resolution.[2] And, while a large proportion of 'conflict theory' is indeed concerned with powerful actors and top-level politics (for instance, 'track one' mediation), there are also well-known approaches focusing on the group and individual levels that are concerned with the 'trickle-up' effects of pacification directed 'upwards' from the grassroots level.[3] Among the latter, there have been abundant examples of innovative use of ethnographic research for gaining valuable insight into the local ideas about what constitutes legitimate goals and means of conflict, and permissible conflict behaviours and levels of violence, as well as pathways out of conflict.[4] The need to grasp the realities of violent conflict and how it affects daily lives, before proceeding towards 'peacebuilding', has been emphasised in a strand of literature pursuing 'anthropologies of war'.[5] A wider body of critique has emphasised the necessity to account for different standards (as well as expressions) of 'rationality' guiding conflict behaviours, as well as the importance of non-material factors serving as both impetus for conflict and assets in its course – aspects that often evade systematic consideration and attention of the more 'traditional' conflict theory.[6] Yet, despite this wealth of insight about the importance of the unsystematic, sometimes uniquely 'local', features that may be largely responsible for the 'intractability' of conflicts, the dominant practise of addressing conflict persistently favours top-down and one-size-fits-all solutions.[7]

As such, the idea that the social and local matter (in the form of group dynamics, economic support networks, or indigenous authorities) is not entirely absent from the awareness of peacebuilding practitioners.[8] However, these aspects are often viewed as an extension of the traditional set of concerns with restoring a functioning state, and presumed to submit to the same instruments of research and policy. Whether the top-level dynamics responds favourably to these instruments is in itself a pertinent question,[9] but there is increasing evidence that, at the substate level, local needs are assumed rather than seriously researched, and local mechanisms of representation supplanted (for example, by habitual 'civil society' frameworks) rather than nurtured.[10] In short, from a local perspective, the frameworks designed for enabling people access to the state and governance are not perceived as neutral and all-accommodating, but rather as restrictive, requiring a rare brand of social capital for their successful use (manifested in the fact that NGOs often become one of the fastest growing industries in (post)conflict settings, often changing their objectives in line with the transient 'fashions' of the donor community),[11] and, as such, become yet another competitor in the flux of post-conflict power relations. Therefore, invoking the notions of 'local needs' or 'social capital' in the rhetoric of major peacebuilding agents does not guarantee in-depth engagement with the local: more often than not, such concepts are applied mechanistically, in a top-down fashion, from a position of 'latest wisdom' in the fields of conflict analysis and development.[12]

How to explain this marginal position of the much needed focus on the 'local'? Why do instances of constructive critique appear to fall on the deaf ears of the 'mainstream'? And why, given that ethnography is hardly a novel practice (dating back, if one considers its pre-anthropological genres, to Herodotus),[13] has this acknowledged source of insight about the ways of life different from the habitual – or even of a fresh, defamiliarised outlook on our everyday – remained largely unrecognised in conflict studies? These are the questions that this chapter seeks to illuminate, as it sketches out the general tension between 'theory' and 'ethnography' as modes of thinking and engagement with the world, examines the kinds of knowledge that ethnography can yield about violent conflict, and considers possibilities of 'cross-fertilisation' between ethnography on the one hand, and conflict theory and peacebuilding practice on the other.

theory versus ethnography: outlining the tension

The challenge of 'capturing the local' seems to be more complex than simply appending ethnography to the existing frameworks of conflict theory and peacebuilding. Although, conventionally, ethnography is understood as a research methodology,[14] a closer look at its history suggests greater 'baggage' than befits the hollow notion of method espoused by social sciences (in the sense of the neutral, technical side of research). Of course, the latter is in itself a crude ideal-type approximation, while in reality methods develop close associations with particular theoretical orientations and epistemologies and come to share their ontological and axiological 'allegiances', which has been known to inspire heated debates.[15] Thus, even a casual glance reveals that the 'theoretical leanings' of ethnography and the 'methodological predispositions' of conventional conflict theory are pulling in opposite directions.

The problem is not so much in the lack of connection between conflict theory and ethnography (although a latent tension is also present there), but rather in the kind of conflict theory that informs practices of addressing conflict. Individually, the generalising tendencies that obtain in 'theory', and the preferences that peacebuilding policy displays for uncontested, coherent, and general theoretical constructs (whose premise of universality and timelessness is assumed to validate the effort of engaging with conflict and underlies the very idea that, as interveners, we know what 'lasting peace' entails),[16] may not seem wholly compelling. However, combined, they effectively eclipse the insights that ethnographic research could contribute.

Concerned as it is with the study of particular human collectives, ethnography does not easily lend itself to generalisation, which (at least as defined in stricter methodological rulebooks) is the basis of conventional 'theory'.[17] Although generalisation is an inevitable part of trying to establish recurrent patterns of social organisation, custom, ritual, belief etc., ethnographic generalisations are relatively small-scale and resist being taken out of context for fear of charges of ethnocentrism;[18] moreover, their scale has undergone a resolute downsizing with the advent of post-structuralism in anthropology, as realisation of the scope of internal cultural variation increased.[19] The ethnographic focus on particularism is also apparent in attempts to preserve not only proper names[20] – which is a stated antithesis of 'theory'[21] – but also 'proper voices': it has been argued that ethnography 'entails... listening to ... [ordinary people] on their terms', rather than 'through the medium of our survey forms, ... our sensitization workshops'.[22] Doubtless, in all this, ethnography relies on a certain degree of 'translation' – otherwise it would be indistinguishable from the 'reality on the ground' and just as invisible to us with an ethnographer in the field as without. Bauman's anecdote about an anthropologist whose field reports increased in detail as he became progressively 'native', until he was accepted as a full member of the tribe and stopped sending any reports at all, is very instructive in showing how the very possibility of serving as a conduit of local voices is premised upon the separateness of the ethnographer's agency.[23] Although translation also involves a degree of generalisation (if only via re-mediation of the 'immediate' field experiences into the terms of habitual – everyday or academic – categories of the ethnographer's own world), this type of generalisation does not bring ethnography closer to the conventional 'theory': on the contrary, the addition of the partiality of individual interpretation to the particularity of the preserved 'proper voices' exacerbates the opposition.

The 'atomistic' nature of ethnographic findings also makes them difficult to employ in peacebuilding as a policy discourse relying on cumulative and general knowledge (epitomised in the wide currency of the concept of 'best practices'). Because of regional and temporal variation, specific ethnographic insights are not easily generalised in the framework of a single intervention, let alone across peace operations.[24] Furthermore, the largely inductive nature of ethnographic research clashes with the problem-solving economy of peacebuilding interventions. Not only are time horizons of a fruitful ethnographic study something of an 'unknown' (in stark contrast to the limited time frame allotted to policy planning and implementation), but so are the precise criteria of such 'fruitfulness', since the focus and terms of ethnographic research sometimes emerge in the course of fieldwork, as a result of a 'free rein' given to the ethnographer's perception of (and participation in) the local dynamics. Such open-endedness does not fit comfortably with the dominant 'project management' approach of peacebuilding with its preconceived terms of engagement, language of 'objectives' and 'milestones', and proliferation of guidelines, checklists, and inventories.[25] It is also doubtful that ethnography, as a largely individual enterprise, could be accommodated in the institutionalised peacebuilding machinery, which not only undermines local particularity but often presents it as the source of conflict[26] (exemplified in references to 'harmful' local practices which involve violations of human rights or perpetuate gender inequality).[27]

Conceptualising the tension between the approaches of ethnography and conventional (albeit diverse) conflict analysis, one can make use of Toulmin's opposition between local, particular, and 'timely' applied knowledge vs. general, universal, 'timeless', and abstract theoretical wisdoms associated with Cartesian-style rationality;[28] or Bakhtin's celebration of dialogue and (sometimes unchecked) polyphony vs. orientation towards monological orderliness.[29] Such conceptualisations could explicate, for instance, the 'monological' predispositions of the contemporary mainstream conflict resolution theory and peacebuilding practice, evident in its inability to surpass the limitations of a rationalist epistemology[30] and engage in a constructive conversation with either competing theoretical perspectives or its professed ultimate referents, 'people on the ground'.[31] But, perhaps even more fruitfully, for the present purposes, this opposition could be cast in terms of the difference between 'explanation' and 'understanding' (Weberian 'Verstehen') as the principal ends of respective enquiries in theory and ethnography.

Distinctly hermeneutic connotations of 'understanding' dialectically link it with a humble resignation to incomprehension, which spurs on the never-ending labour of making sense, asymptotically approaching the 'other' and yet never merging with it completely. But they also alert us to the fact the meanings are not 'there' waiting to be discovered, but are rather 'constituted in retrospect' as part of the effort at understanding, in which the biases of whoever attempts it will be readily and invariably apparent.[32] Furthermore, such hermeneutic understanding is not limited to the 'other' but extends also to oneself, whose meanings are unveiled through very much the same processes.[33] Unsurprisingly, ethnography's 'concern to understand the "other"' also brought about commitment 'to an understanding of the self',[34] and, like its discovery of the 'other' whom it makes the subject of study, ethnography's knowledge of its own disciplinary boundaries and techniques is never fully complete. It can be debated to what extent 'explanation' is oriented towards uniformitarian and regular patterns, as opposed to the orientation of 'understanding' towards particularity and deviance. More saliently, perhaps, 'explanation' entails absorbing the observable phenomena into one's own terms of discourse, while 'understanding' presupposes acceptance of multiplicity of positions and broadening, if not transcendence, of one's own perspective.

The universalising effect of theory is also clear in that 'applying theory' (to a case study) implies casting the observed phenomena in terms of a pre-existing set of ideas, which places limitations on what would qualify as relevant information, as well as on our ability to see beyond the established horizon.[35] Ethnography, although not free from some core methodological assumptions, makes them an explicit focus of scrutiny and review[36] and, ultimately, celebrates the possibility that field observations can challenge and overthrow even the most fundamental assumptions of the researcher.[37] Although theory can also be challenged and amended, it soon returns to its 'monological' stability;[38] while ethnography is rather conceived as a dialogue which can develop in uncharted directions.[39]

Needless to say, this opposition is seldom absolute, since the sheer variety within what could be called 'conflict theory' makes it likely that, while some of its strands will indeed gravitate towards the 'explanation', 'universality', and 'monologism' pole of the outlined continuum, others will be comparatively more orientated towards 'understanding', 'particularity', and 'dialogue'. There is a world of difference, in this respect, between 'traditional' conflict theory and the theory of a more 'reflective' kind, from critical to constructivist to post-structuralist approaches. Terminology and conceptual apparatus will also vary accordingly; for example 'conflict transformation', in contrast to the much-criticised objective of conflict 'resolution',[40] allows for recognition that conflict is instrumental for constructive change and development[41] and implies the possibility of leaving the direction of change to the care of local visions and debate.[42] However, as evident from a marginal position of the bulk of critical literature on peacebuilding, the kinds of conflict theory that are able to benefit from ethnographic insights are precisely those that are banished by the uniform style of peacebuilding practice, and thus unlikely significantly to influence the mainstream.

negotiating the difference: 'meeting points' in ethnography

The inductive orientation of ethnography and the deductive nature of conflict theory make even contemplating a meeting point between them look like an impossible task. However, the dilemma of overcoming such seemingly insuperable dichotomies is not novel for social sciences. Scholars in many disciplines have grappled with bridging the apparent methodological hiatus between 'macrosocial structures and microsocial behaviours',[43] with discourse and practice theories bringing out the problematic of interrelation of individual agents and collective structures especially acutely.[44] Furthermore, 'generalising' and 'particularising' tendencies, as two irreducible aspects of knowledge and comprehension, have been shown to coexist in the organisation of human consciousness,[45] and it is incontestable that, empirically, people variously negotiate their meeting points in daily lives.

As a discipline that arose from enquiry into unfamiliar ways of organising human affairs, ethnography should be well placed to illuminate the points of coalescence between the 'downward' tendency to particularise and the 'upward' drive to generalise, which could serve as a source of inspiration in the quest for meeting points between conflict theory and ethnography. Indeed, ethnography itself, as gleaned from the history of its disciplinary development, has had to deal with the task of negotiating the opposing pulls of particularising and generalising tendencies within its approaches and methods. And although this negotiation has not, for the most part, been even-handed, the problems encountered by ethnography in this matter may prove as illuminating as its successes.

While the particularising tendency is dictated by the nature of ethnography's subject matter, the pressure to generalise has been exacerbated by decades of harbouring aspirations to provide a tool for 'scientific' study of cultures. This pressure proved truly formative for the bulk of academic ethnography, since ideas about what constituted appropriate objects for scientific enquiry and the kinds of knowledge attainable about them have imposed considerable restrictions on what could be seen as 'valid' ethnographic interest and insight. The array of methods viewed as the legitimate means for distilling 'mere' field observations into reliable 'data'[46] reflected this bias, effectively privileging the systematic and repetitive in ethnographic portrayals of cultures. Accounts of uncharacteristic cultural dynamics or disruptive occurrences were relegated to the domain of subjectivity and chance – and the margins of the discipline.[47]

Such implicit privileging of the traditional methodological devices of 'theory' in the domain supposedly attuned to the perspectives of the subjects has led to a critical re-examination of the very character of ethnographic enquiry, which produced a series of uncomfortable admissions. Thus, while there is a clear sense that ethnographic fieldwork liberates one from preconception by putting the 'subject' first and, consequently, anything happening to the ethnographer in the field is 'fieldwork', preconceived ideas about the proper way of conducting field research can be shown to dominate the approaches of many ethnographers of renown, leading, for instance, Evans-Pritchard to lament how organisational clashes with the 'local' ways effectively held him back from fieldwork.[48] James Clifford also comments on entrenched ideas about what qualifies as a worthy ethnographic observation, noting that the implicit privileging of 'sight' is evident in the absence of odours from most ethnographic accounts.[49]

Preconception, which effectively orders the 'unmediated' field experiences, is also manifest in the selection of subjects for ethnographic study, which is mostly defined by a focus on the powerless.[50] Historically, this is perhaps understandable, given that exoticism, this magnet for ethnographic gaze, could hardly be attributed to peoples occupying highly visible positions in international power configurations. But this also raises uncomfortable questions about political and ethical implications of the 'production' of ethnographic 'subjects', with suspicions that connotations of weakness are imparted to the subjects by the very methods of ethnographic studies. Contrary to the early anthropological sentiments of egalitarian oneness based upon rediscovery of common humanity underneath the superficial differences of custom and conduct,[51] present-day anthropologists draw attention to how the very references to 'culture' as a category of ethnographic discourse inevitably produce hierarchical structuring of relations with 'others'.[52]

The idea that local cultures are 'contaminated' through previous contacts with the outside world runs through many a classic ethnography.[53] However, the preference for pre-contact cultures[54] is especially problematic given that contamination also comes from exposure to prior ethnographic attention. A token account of this is offered by Marjorie Shostak, who, revisiting a fieldwork site explored some five years previously by Richard Lee and Nancy Howell, finds herself faced with 'others' that 'are fallen, corrupted not only as non-Europeans, but specifically as ethnographic informants'.[55] Ultimately, such an encounter undermines the self-image of 'the anthropologist preserver-of-the-culture', casting the ethnographer, instead, as the 'interventionist corrupter-of-the-culture'.[56] In Vidich and Lyman's words,

> [t]he postmodern sociologist-ethnographer and his or her subjects are situated in a world suspended between illusory memories of a lost innocence and millennial dreams of a utopia unlikely to be realized. From such position, not only is the standpoint of the investigator problematic ... but also that of the people to be investigated.[57]

In short, critical introspection reveals preconceptions that defy even the most careful 'bracketing' in ethnographic praxis. This is persuasively demonstrated by Crapanzano's analysis of Geertz's 'Deep Play', which is found guilty of the same charges as the dominant approach to peacebuilding – objectifying the local and preoccupation with reasserting one's own identity over the troublesome 'otherness'. In this light, ethnography's credentials in putting the 'local' first or approaching it on its own terms appear to rest on a shaky foundation.[58] Should ethnography, then, be condemned alongside the bulk of conflict theory and peacebuilding practice as yet another 'corrupt' framework? Can it offer no guidance to conflict theory with a view to the impossible dream of fusing 'objective and subjective practices'?[59] Or is there, perhaps, something that could keep these unhelpful biases in check?

It appears that the danger of regression into 'monologism' – of unethical 'digestion' of the 'other'[60] – is ever-present even in those paradigms that are explicitly orientated towards respect for otherness. However, the never-ending supply of 'unsystematic' ethnographic material, as well as the shift towards epistemological privileging of 'rupture' rather than continuity,[61] associated with the advent of post-structuralism in anthropology, may help even out the imbalance. In addition, acknowledgement of the wider scope of the problematic of opposition between generalising and particularising tendencies allows one to see beyond the constraints of the scientific paradigm in ethnography. As noted by Pratt, the two general styles of ethnographic writing – the 'narrative' style, conveyed in the present tense, and concerned with 'impersonal' observation of repetitive features of social organisation, and the 'descriptive' style, distinguished by past-tense reflections upon the ethnographer's personal experiences in the field – predate 'the rise of modern science'.[62] Their coexistence in travel writing, missionaries' reports and prescientific ethnography suggests that the tendency to generalise and 'objectify' – whether biologically or culturally determined[63] – is part of the 'human' cognitive repertoire as much as attention to deviance and detail. Significantly, the descriptive style, however marginalised by 'formal ethnographic description', has not been 'killed by science'.[64]

Furthermore, unlike peacebuilding agents in their majority, ethnographers have, over the past few decades, tried to explicate the hidden assumptions of their approaches and field practices and to remain watchful of the unintended power implications of their work.[65] This has led ethnography away from 'totalist' writing and imagination towards the acknowledgement of subjectivity and partiality, evident in attempts to explicate the impact that the ethnographer's perception and experiences will have on his/her portrayal of ethnographic realities. Thus, however beset it may be with dilemmas arising from the logical incompatibility of the upward (inductive) and downward (deductive–theoretical) orientations, ethnography manages to convene them both on a single plane of ethnographic writing.

While there have been numerous attempts to bestow similar realisations upon peacebuilding, whether this can produce a 'paradigmatic shift' in the dominant approaches to conflict and peace is debatable. The literatures exposing the problematic aspects of organised peacebuilding are varied and vast, but the critique has a limited impact because the agency of the critics and practitioners of peacebuilding remains more separate than in ethnography, where the majority of critics are also practicing ethnographers. Superficially, there is a growing sense of 'humility' on the part of peacebuilding practitioners faced with crude 'reality checks' of their grand assumptions, which is supported by their increasing awareness of peacebuilding critique.[66] But this is largely offset by the unwavering righteousness regarding certain cornerstones of peacebuilding, such as human rights and democracy, whose presumed timeless universality is seen as justifying the problematic practice of top-down enforcement.[67] Furthermore, the institutional inertia of peacebuilding makes it difficult to act upon the critical self-awareness that is emerging, as well as to consider instances of peacebuilding that fall outside the conventional image.[68] While it would be wrong to assume that ethnography is not constrained by some institutional frameworks, field-work remains very much an individual experience which balances this out. Peacebuilding, even in its less orthodox forms, is a collective enter-prise and, as such, predisposed towards generalisation.

cross-fertilisation: ethnography and violent conflict

While ethnography has been shown to struggle with reconciling the upwards and downwards-directed modes of enquiry, these struggles are symptomatic of how a meeting between such opposing drives can be envisaged. Clearly, it does not produce an unproblematic fusion, since the opposing tendencies do not cancel each other out, but coexist in the actual instances of ethnographic knowledge in a state of suspended contradiction. Furthermore, the discovery of the generalising 'under-current' in ethnography suggests that unaccounted 'dissident' dynamics accompany even the established disciplinary self-images. Application of this insight to conflict theory leads me, if somewhat paradoxically, to question its advantages as the habitual framework for explaining con-flict, before proceeding to scrutinise the kinds of knowledge about con-flict that are enabled by an ethnographic perspective.

Although conflict theory has gone a long way trying to identify regu-larities and causal connections in conflict behaviours and respective structural environments, a number of post-Cold War conflicts, which have been branded as barbaric, irrational, or even 'mindless',[69] appear to have disrupted the cumulative effort at such 'normalising' analysis. Despite the professed neutrality of the metalanguage of theory, its very propensity to systematise and regularise on this occasion clearly clashes with the character of its object. The liberal peacebuilding paradigm, for its part, is not best equipped for understanding conflict either: after all, the liberal ideology hinges on conflict avoidance,[70] and, as liberal models of governance are presumed to have a 'built-in quality of peace-ful conflict resolution',[71] their export can be seen as a mission to elim-inate violent conflict altogether. Thus, for the liberal peace, war itself becomes the enemy.[72]

'Analysing' conflicts involves more than offering troubled peoples the benefit of an impartial perspective on their misfortunes: what is at stake is dictating the terms in which their condition should be perceived and addressed (which, of course, limits both the role allo-cated to local agency in conflict or its resolution, and the scope for open-minded understanding of issues involved). Quite apart from charges of hegemonic imposition and symbolic 'appropriation' effected by inclusion into our cognitive space, this invites a reconsideration of the ideas of order and chaos in the 'liberal' mentality, coupled with the apparent need to subjugate the experienced turbulence of conflict into the controlling regularity of rational and causal models. Conflict, it appears, presents the ultimate challenge to our compelling need to make sense, but, by trying to squeeze its 'deviant' dynamics into the moulds of rationality and predictability, we risk missing precisely that which makes conflict appear irrational and deviant in the first place. This is where conflict theory is let down by its scientific aspirations, and where approaches venturing to use 'the eccentric... to explain the central'[73] can make a constructive contribution.

Ethnography, it has to be noted, is not the only such approach; nor is it the most radical one in terms of its use of 'the eccentric': art and aesthetic approaches generally can be used to convey uniqueness of events without even committing themselves to their mimetic repetition.[74] However, ethnography may be best positioned to achieve an understanding of the place that violent conflict occupies in the totality of social processes and interactions. Paul Richards claims that 'anthropologies of war' can achieve a better understanding of violent conflict through recontextualising it as a social project among others, (often) organised and regulated by the same social agents and through the same avenues as 'peace'.[75] Thus, denying war a privileged analytical status is a way to demonstrate its place in, and entwinement with, other aspects of social reality. Paradoxically, it is often the removal of constraints of analytical privilege that allows for a consideration of violence in 'its own right' – its societal functions, its dynamics of constitution and the symbolism with which it engages and which it generates.[76] Although such 'undue' attention to violence often causes moral unease on the part of the peace-loving international community bent on presenting violence as something external to 'normal' conditions, ethnography can show how violence may play an important role in structuring the very idea of the conditions of normality (or otherwise) as seen from a local perspective.[77]

Such recontextualisation of violence can take many paths, and need not remain within the confines of what could be considered ethnography proper (although its input in the form of careful study of communal practice and ways of life is often a requisite starting point). Many studies associated with ethnography in this way are variously concerned with the effects of socialisation on the formation of norms and expectations with regard to violent and peaceful behaviours in society,[78] or with instrumental uses to which violence can be put for preserving the sense of self, community and identity[79] – or simply for achieving goals recognised by the community as 'rational', if not always legitim-ate.[80] Close scrutiny of symbolic and social contexts in which violence unfolds also allows consideration of the reasons why the instrumental function it fulfils has taken this particular form (violent as opposed to non-violent), and how its expressions are connected with other fea-tures making up the people's idea of their cultural self. Studies such as Stephen Ellis's[81] reveal how violence perceived as directed against cer-tain cultural norms and institutions may originate in the same cultural 'substrate' and rely on the same symbolic constructs that it appears to defy (as in the case of attacks on figures of authority in the Liberian civil war). Yet, ethnographies of violence need not be perceived as advo-cating deterministic militarism, for they can equally unveil practices of (non-violent) resistance and reconciliation that evolve in response to violence, and explore their origins and place in the same cultural con-texts.[82] Ethnography can not only show how 'cultures of violence' are created and perpetuated, but also illuminate the processes and prereq-uisites of their 'un-making',[83] thus refashioning the unfruitful policy discourse on the 'destruction of the social fabric' by violent conflict[84] into the terms of cultural contestation.

Useful revelations about conflict that ethnography can provide are not limited to the issue of violence. For instance, the understandings accompanying interindividual relations among the Mende of Sierra Leone – which Ferme describes in terms of 'being *for* someone'[85] – can be seen to support the notorious institute of neopatrimonialism that argu-ably damages the viability of multi-party democracy in sub-Saharan Africa.[86] Relatedly, the cultural expectation that 'big men' would be foolish not to abuse their office for personal enrichment, since for 'cli-ents' their status is communicated through displays of affluence,[87] sheds an interesting light on the prospects of the fight against corruption in Liberia. A wealth of specifically conflict-related insight is provided by studies of mechanisms that local cultures develop to respond to typ-ical conflict situations, and the adaptation of those mechanisms to new types of violence.[88] Yet other studies help recontextualise what appear to be unprecedented determinants in contemporary violent conflicts, such as the links to transnational shadow economies,[89] in terms of local historical experiences of the links with the outside, such as the slave trade for the Atlantic coast of Africa.[90]

Yet the ethnographic perspective also seems to experience discomfort with regard to some forms of 'deviance' brought about by conflict, and thus recontextualisation of war has its limitations. In their excellent ethnographies of Mende and Temne parts of Sierra Leone, respectively, Ferme and Shaw uncover memories of past violence embedded in spatial and social organisation, as well as coping strategies that local cultures have devised to adjust to, or subvert, unfavourable power relations.[91] And, while the uncovered continuities convincingly link the present ways of life to the turbulent past, they mostly fail to incorporate the beginnings of the rebel war which was gathering pace during the later phases of both Shaw's and Ferme's fieldwork. While some features of the RUF war tactics were shown to originate in the same social processes that have obtained throughout the post-colonial history of Sierra Leone, many more were perceived as representing marked departures from the established local ideas about permissible ways of waging conflict. The perception that the rebel war brought about a radical breach with the earlier practices is perhaps understandable, given that, superficially, post-colonial Sierra Leonean history may appear relatively 'peaceful'.[92] However, as ethnographers, both Ferme and Shaw have shown that violence had been a prominent feature of both pre- and post-colonial history, so their perception of this discontinuity raises interesting questions.

In ethnography's own terms, the issue of violent conflict appears to bring out the tension between what Marcus calls 'the salvage mode and the redemptive mode' for 'self-consciously fixing ethnography in historic time':

> In the salvage mode, the ethnographer portrays himself as 'before the deluge,' so to speak. Signs of fundamental change are apparent, but the ethnographer is able to salvage a cultural state on the verge of transformation. … In the redemptive mode, the ethnographer demonstrates survival of distinctive and authentic cultural systems despite undeniable changes.[93]

The conflict between these modes is apparent in Ferme's and Shaw's different treatment of the effects of past and present violence on the Sierra Leonean 'everyday':[94] having failed to derail culture in the past (the 'redemptive mode'), violence is now threatening to engulf and destroy it (the 'salvage mode'). The ability to relate change to the past continuities apparently hinges on its 'consummated' character, which is inconceivable when change unfolds in one's presence and thus becomes part of what Bakhtin termed the 'I' mode of perception.[95] One might argue that ethnographic experience of conflict as a rupture limits ethnography's ability to recontextualise war. On the other hand, the habit of 'juggling' with the possibilities of outside vs. inside, repetitive vs. unique, and regular vs. unruly brings ethnography closer to the realisation that, in some instances, multiple experiences of rupture may form a basis for continuity of a different kind,[96] and, albeit being perceived as transcendental to the 'normal' conditions, they can perpetuate a sense of cultural self-identity just as effectively as gradual and imperceptible change.[97]

conclusions: the promise of ethnography

Ethnography cannot offer 'final truths' – to aspire to use it for 'stripping away' the layers of subjectivity would imply joining in the eternal positivist quest for absolute knowledge. Furthermore, the local and 'timely' knowledge which it yields may not always be soothing or complimentary, as it is likely to expose clashes between rhetorical aspirations of peacebuilding and the 'illiberal' realities. Still, the charge that ethnography offers 'partial truths' and participates not in 'representation' but in 'the invention' of cultures[98] appears more of an advantage than a limitation in the light of the present purposes: the practice of 'invention' (and periodic 'reinvention') is better suited to grasping the uncertain, unpronounced, mutable, and variable character of 'cultures', which presents bearers and observers alike with many more latent guises and possibilities than can be recorded in any one representation.[99] Crucially, admitting the partiality of any 'truths' could be an important step away from the presumed omniscience of the 'non-perspective'[100] assumed by both conventional conflict theory and peacebuilding. Allowing ethnography to uncover what 'makes sense locally'[101] can help peacebuilding practitioners to tailor practice to local expectations and needs.

As has been pointed out, ethnography is not the only source of 'local and timely' knowledge, but it may be unique in terms of offering a truly dialogical experience which marks self-transcendence not only on the part of the researcher, but also for his/her research 'subjects.' Peter Just shows how a conflict about betrothal obligations in a Dou Donggo village was resolved through a cathartic realisation of the deeper principles that guided its somewhat rigid and obsolete customs, bringing about a renewed sense of dignity and self-respect for the community:

> Ompu Camba's argument ... spoke to this fundamental moral value, one too deeply seated and ramified to obtain of an orthogenic transformation into determinate rules, but tremendously powerful for its very indeterminacy.[102]

The indeterminacy of the deep-seated cultural possibilities can also unfold through redefinition of important symbols (polysemous by definition) towards non-violence in the post-conflict setting. Just's example indicates that the presence of an ethnographic other is not strictly necessary for the need for such redefinition to become actualised; in a sense, being faced with unprecedented social situations can in itself set these processes in motion. Experiences of violent conflict, in this respect, offer possibilities for reassessment of one's cultural 'baggage' – although this is not to deny the blatantly debilitating effects of violent conflict in many cases.

In this regard, what promise does ethnography hold for overcoming violent conflict? It has been noted that reproduction of antagonistic identities paves the way for a renewal of open violence; if this is to change, a certain transcendence of exclusive identities is required.[103] The potential for self-transformation contained in the ethnographic approach, manifested in the readiness to question one's initial assumptions and categories, the ability to be 'surprised',[104] could be of enormous value for mapping the possibilities of un-closure of identities. Of course, the relationship between an ethnographer and his/her 'subjects' will differ in many important ways from the daily encounters between former adversaries in a post-settlement setting. But if the experience of self-transcendence (or self-rediscovery) – through redefining him- or herself with respect to an unfamiliar 'other' of the ethnographer – can play some role in illuminating, for the subject, the processes involved in identity construction generally, there is a very different sense in which the traditional roles of the 'third parties' in conflict resolution can be understood.[105] An ethnographic encounter thus enables a redefinition and reinvention of local identities vis-à-vis a non-adversarial other, exploring the non-antagonistic potential of the sense of self that can be subsequently redirected to re-evaluate the 'otherness' of former adversaries in conflict. In terms of Levinasian ethics, ethnography potentially enables an encounter with *autrui* – that 'wholly other' which is not substitutable, appropriable and 'digestible' by the sameness of the self.[106] In part, it is this ultimate recognition of otherness and its 'unknown' nature that compels ethnography to redraw anew the contextual horizons of every enquiry, which can prove invaluable for understanding conflict.

Unsurprisingly, this is also what makes ethnography uncomfortable for inclusion in any organised practice of conflict analysis (given the difficulty of producing a 'blueprint' of necessary procedures). To remain true to itself, ethnography needs the freedom to proceed in unsystematic ways; but, unless the peacebuilding practice changes accordingly, this freedom will also exile ethnography to the margins of conflict resolution theory and practice. On the other hand, by offering insight into the 'local', ethnography can support attempts at rediscovering the 'original' ambitions of peacebuilding, conceived as a bottom-up, emancipatory and empowering process.[107] This would not be synonymous with elevating the 'local' to an undisputable reality, complete, as many critics point out, with problematic structures and 'harmful' practices perpetuating conflict and violence. For a conscientious ethnographer, the 'local' hardly ever represents a clear-cut, finite 'system', for even a limited fieldwork experience presents the researcher with a polyphony of versions and interpretations of lived reality. Also, hardly anyone *in situ* is entirely happy with the local 'ways', and visions of a different future and aspirations for change are part and parcel of the 'local' culture as much as the actual social practices and power structures.[108] It is with getting beyond the dominant narratives and 'teasing out' these latent possibilities that ethnography can assist, just as it can help explicate hidden cultural assumptions that are left implicit because, for members of a given culture, they may appear 'unacceptable at the explicit level'.[109]

notes

1. M. Kaldor, *New and Old Wars: Organised Violence in the Global Era*, Cambridge: Polity Press, 1999; A.B. Fetherston, 'Peacekeeping, Conflict Resolution and Peacebuilding: A Reconsideration of Theoretical Frameworks', in T. Woodhouse and O. Ramsbotham (eds), *Peacekeeping and Conflict Resolution*, London: Frank Cass, 2000, pp. 190–218.
2. For representative overviews and analyses of conflict theory, see, for example, M. Brown, *Theories of War and Peace: An International Security Reader*, Cambridge, MA: MIT Press, 1998; O.P. Richmond, *Maintaining Order, Making Peace*, Basingstoke: Palgrave, 2002; O. Ramsbotham, T. Woodhouse and H. Miall, *Contemporary Conflict Resolution*, 2nd edn, Cambridge, UK; Malden, MA: Polity Press, 2005.

3. E. Azar and J. Burton (eds), *International Conflict Resolution: Theory and Practice*, Sussex: Wheatsheaf, 1986; J.P. Lederach, *Building Peace: Sustainable Reconciliation in Divided Societies*, Washington, DC: US Institute of Peace Press, 1997.
4. K. Avruch, P.W. Black and J. Scimecca (eds), *Conflict Resolution: Cross-Cultural Perspectives*, London: Greenwood Press, 1991; M.H. Ross, *The Culture of Conflict: Interpretations and Interests in Comparative Perspective*, New Haven, CT: Yale University Press, 1993; N.L. Whitehead (ed.), *Violence*, Santa Fe: School of American Research Press, 2004; M. Brigg and R. Bleiker (eds), *Mediating Across Difference: Indigenous, Oceanic and Asian Approaches to Conflict Resolution*, Hawaii University Press, forthcoming, 2008.
5. See, for example, C. Nordstrom, *Warzones: Cultures of Violence, Militarisation and Peace*, Canberra: Australian National University, Peace Research Centre, 1994; C. Nordstrom and A.C.G.M. Robben (eds), *Fieldwork under Fire: Contemporary Studies of Violence and Survival*, Berkeley: University of California Press, 1995; P. Richards (ed.), *No Peace No War: An Anthropology of Contemporary Armed Conflicts*, Oxford: James Currey, 2005.
6. Such as R. Fisher and W. Ury, *Getting to Yes*, 2nd edn, Arrow Books Ltd., 1997; O. J. Bartos and P. Wehr, *Using Conflict Theory*, Cambridge: Cambridge University Press, 2002.
7. M. Duffield, *Global Governance and the New Wars*, London: Zed Books, 2001.
8. Author's interviews with a member of the UNDP's Bureau for Crisis Prevention and Recovery, New York, 13 March 2007, and with J. Large, of NGO Crisis Management Initiative (CMI), Brussels, 15 May 2007.
9. See, for example, R. Paris, *At War's End*, Cambridge: Cambridge University Press, 2004.
10. R.C. Kent, 'Security and Local Ownership: Rhetoric and reality', in T. Tardy and R. Mani (eds), *Pursuing Security in the Post-Conflict Phase: Implications for Current and Future Peace Operations*, Report from a workshop of the Geneva Centre for Security Policy, 12–13 June 2005, Geneva: GCSP; B. Helander, 'Who Needs a State? Civilians, Security and Social Services in North-East Somalia', in P. Richards, *No Peace No War*, pp. 193–202.
11. Helander, 'Who Needs a State?'; R. Shaw, 'Rethinking Truth and Reconciliation Commissions: Lessons from Sierra Leone', USIP Special Report No. 130, 2005. http://www.usip.org/files/resources/sr130.pdf, accessed 16 october 2009; author's interview with a member of the World Bank's Development Research Group, Washington DC, 15 March 2007.
12. Duffield, *Global Governance and the New Wars*.
13. J. Clifford, 'Introduction: Partial truths', in J. Clifford and G.E. Marcus (eds), *Writing Culture: The Poetics and Politics of Ethnography*, Berkeley: University of California Press, 1986, pp. 1–26.
14. For example, University of Pennsylvania web page defines ethnography as 'two things: (1) the fundamental research method of cultural anthropology, and (2) the written text produced to report ethnographic research results. Ethnography as a method seeks to answer central anthropological questions concerning the ways of life of living human beings. Ethnographic questions generally concern the link between culture and behaviour and/or how

cultural processes develop over time. The data base for ethnographies is usually extensive description of the details of social life or cultural phenomena in a small number of cases.' http://www.sas.upenn.edu/anthro/anthro/whatisethnography, accessed 16 October 2009.

15. See, for example, J.A. Tickner, 'What Is Your Research Program? Some feminist answers to International Relations methodological questions', *International Studies Quarterly*, Vol. 49, 2005, pp. 1–21; C. Cramer, '*Homo Economicus* Goes to War: Methodological individualism, rational choice and the political economy of war', *World Development*, Vol. 30, No. 11, 2002, pp. 1845–64; K.M. Fierke, 'Meaning, Method and Practice: Assessing the new security agenda', in S. Lawson (ed.) *The New Agenda for International Relations*, Cambridge: Polity Press, 2002, pp. 128–44.

16. See, for example, M. Berdal and D. Keen, 'Violence and Economic Agendas in Civil Wars: Some Policy Implications', *Millennium*, Vol. 26, No. 3, 1997, pp. 795–818.

17. For instance, S. Van Evera, *Guide to Methods for Students of Political Science*, Ithaca, NY: Cornell University Press, 1997.

18. C. Geertz, *The Interpretation of Cultures*, New York: Basic Books, 1973, pp. 24–5.

19. Clifford, 'Introduction: Partial truths'; T. Förster, 'The Transformation of Violence and Civil Security in Northern Côte d'Ivoire 1979–2002: Rethinking statehood from the local perspective', paper given at COST Action A24 'The Construction of Threats' workshop in Brussels, 20–21 September 2004.

20. M.C. Ferme, *The Underneath of Things: Violence, History and the Everyday in Sierra Leone*, Berkeley, CA: University of California Press, 2001; R. Shaw, *Memories of the Slave Trade: Ritual and the Historical Imagination in Sierra Leone*, Chicago, IL: University of Chicago Press, 2002.

21. Van Evera, *Guide to Methods*.

22. Shaw, 'Rethinking Truth and Reconciliation Commissions'.

23. Z. Bauman, *Culture as Praxis*, 2nd edn, London: Sage Publications, 1999, p. 20.

24. See, for example, Mats Utas's work on regional variation in the applicability of reintegration programmes in Liberia: M. Utas, 'Building a future? The Reintegration and Re-marginalisation of Youth in Liberia', in P. Richards (ed.) *No Peace, No War: An Anthropology of Contemporary Armed Conflicts*, Ohio University Press, 2005, pp. 137–54.

25. R. Mac Ginty, 'The Role of Symbols in Peacemaking', in J. Darby and R. Mac Ginty (eds), *Contemporary Peacemaking: Conflict, Violence and Peace Processes*, Basingstoke: Palgrave Macmillan, 2003, pp. 235–44. For examples of 'project-management-style' approaches to conflict analysis, see the 'European Commission Check-list for Root Causes of Conflict', http://ec.europa.eu/comm/external_relations/cfsp/cpcm/cp/list.htm, accessed 26 April 2007, or UNDP, *Inter-agency Framework for Conflict Analysis in Transition Situations*, November 2004, http://www.undp.org/cpr/documents/prevention/integrate/Interagency_framework_for_conflict_analysis_in_transition_situations.doc, accessed 11 February 2007. In contrast, what Mac Ginty, in his 5 March 2007 seminar talk at the School of International Relations, University of St Andrews, has termed 'Post War Reconstruction the Hezbollah Way' is characterised by marked aversion to bureaucratic accountability.

26. Duffield, *Global Governance and the New Wars*.
27. Author's interview at UNDP Bureau for Crisis Prevention and Recovery.
28. S. Toulmin, *Cosmopolis: The Hidden Agenda of Modernity*, Chicago, IL: University of Chicago Press, 1992, and *Return to Reason*, Cambridge, MA: Harvard University Press, 2001. Toulmin's distinction is ultimately between 'theoretical' vs. 'applied' science, and he places a lot of hope in the latter's ability to develop relevant, necessary, 'timely' kinds of knowledge matching the actual issues with which humankind is grappling at every particular moment in time. Among these applied sciences he lists clinical disciplines. While he convincingly outlines the differences between the two kinds of scientific practice and the benefits of the latter, I am sceptical of Toulmin's optimism with regard to clinical science as the flagship of the 'timely' and 'particular' knowledge. It is suggestive, in this regard, that reliance on quasi-medical 'diagnosis', as well as the abundance of medicinal metaphors, usually characterises conflict theory of the 'general' and 'uniform' type as well as social and political theory with unhelpfully essentialising biases (see, e.g. V. Pupavac, 'Human Security and the Rise of Global Therapeutic Governance', *Conflict, Security and Development*, Vol. 5, No. 2, 2005, pp. 161–81, or M. Luoma-Aho, 'Body of Europe and Malignant Nationalism: A Pathology of the Balkans in European Security Discourse,' *Geopolitics*, Vol. 7, No. 3, 2002, pp. 117–42). Crucially, this also invokes dangers associated with Foucaludian implications of identifying 'sicknesses' and appropriate institutional 'remedies' (see M. Foucault, *Madness and Civilization: A History of Insanity in the Age of Reason*, New York: Random House, 1965, and *Discipline and Punish: The Birth of the Prison*, New York: Pantheon, 1977).
29. M.M. Bakhtin, *Problems of Dostoevsky's Poetics*, ed. and trans. by C. Emerson, introduction by W.C. Booth, Minneapolis, MN: University of Minnesota Press, 1984; *Speech Genres and Other Late Essays*, trans. V.W. McGee, ed. C. Emerson and M. Holquist, Austin: University of Texas Press, 1986; 'Author and Hero in Aesthetic Activity', pp. 4–256 in M. Holquist and V. Liapunov (eds), *Art and Answerability: Early Philosophical Essays by M. M. Bakhtin*, trans. V. Liapunov, Austin: University of Texas Press, 1990; *Toward a Philosophy of the Act*, trans. with notes by M. Holquist and V. Liapunov, Austin: University of Texas Press, 1993[1986]. See also M. Holquist, *Dialogism: Bakhtin and His World*, New York: Routledge, 1990; J. Viktorova, 'Identity and Alterity: An Apologia for Boundaries,' in H. van Houtum and E. Berg (eds), *Routing Borders between Territories, Discourses and Practices*, Aldershot: Ashgate, 2003, pp. 141–60.
30. A.B. Fetherston, 'From Conflict Resolution to Transformative Peacebuilding: Reflections from Croatia', Centre for Conflict Resolution, Department of Peace Studies, University of Bradford, working paper no. 4, 2000.
31. Kent, 'Security and Local Ownership'.
32. Z. Bauman, *Hermeneutics and Social Science: Approaches to understanding*, London: Hutchinson, 1978, pp. 180–95. See also S. Critchley, *The Ethics of Deconstruction: Derrida and Levinas*, Oxford: Blackwell, 1992, p. 23.
33. Bauman, *Hermeneutics and Social Science*, p. 181; A. Schutz, *Collected Papers*, Vol. 2, The Hague: Martinus Nijhoff, 1967.

34. A.J. Vidich and S.M. Lyman, 'Their History in Sociology and Anthropology', pp. 37–84 in N.K. Denzin and Y.S. Lincoln (eds), *Handbook of Qualitative Research*, Thousand Oaks, CA: Sage Publications, 2000, p. 38.

35. P. Chabal and J.-P. Daloz, *Culture Troubles: Politics and the Interpretation of Meaning*, London: Hurst & Co., 2006.

36. I. Dey, *Qualitative Data Analysis: A User-Friendly Guide for Social Scientists*, London: Routledge, 1993; A. Massey, ' "The Way We Do Things Around Here:" The culture of ethnography,' paper presented at the Ethnography and Education Conference, Oxford University Department of Educational Studies, 7–8 September 1998, http://www.geocities.com/Tokyo/2961/waywedo.htm, accessed 28 February 2008.

37. Avruch et al., *Conflict Resolution*.

38. This point could perhaps warrant a longer philosophical discussion, invoking, as it does, the tension immanent in the positivist principle of falsifiability on which the credibility of any scientific theory must rest (see, e.g., L. Kolakowski, *Positivist Philosophy: From Hume to the Vienna Circle*, trans. N. Guterman, Harmondsworth: Penguin, 1972). However, as pointed out by numerous critics of positivist research methodologies, such self-imposed limitations on claims that can be made with the help of rationalist modes of theorising – just as the limitations of a positivist approach to theory as such – are easily forgotten (see, for instance, J. George, *Discourses of Global Politics: A Critical Reintroduction to International Relations*, Boulder, CO: Lynne Rienner, 1994; Toulmin, *Cosmopolis*; or M. Oakeshott, *Rationalism in Politics and Other Essays*, London: Methuen & Co., 1962).

39. This tension is well articulated in anthropology in terms of 'emic' vs. 'etic' approaches, where the former privilege actor-centred understandings, while the latter represent an outsider's perspective, seeking to draw 'emic' findings into broader conceptual horizons spanning cases and cultures under study (see, for instance, K. Avruch, *Culture and Conflict Resolution*, Washington, DC: United States Institute of Peace Press, 1998, pp. 60–1). While the emic perspective naturally falls into the province of field ethnography, etic approaches form the part of anthropology perhaps better known to conflict theorists – such as Douglas's grid-group theory (M. Douglas, *Natural Symbols: Explorations in Cosmology*, New York: Pantheon Books, 1970), or Hall's low vs. high-context cultures (E.T. Hall, *Beyond Culture*, New York: Anchor Books, 1976) – although in this case, as well, universal applicability of these frameworks comes with the price of hollowing out what can be 'known' about the local with their help.

40. Fetherston, 'From Conflict Resolution to Transformative Peacebuilding'.

41. A.B. Fetherston and C. Nordstrom, 'Overcoming Habitus in Conflict Management: UN peacekeeping and war zone ethnography', *Peace and Change*, Vol. 20, No. 1, 1995, pp. 94–120; J. Echavarria, 'EU's Global Battles: Conflict prevention and management in Third World countries', paper given at COST A24 'Social Construction of Threats/ The EU as A Global Actor' workshop in Tallinn, 28–29 June 2007.

42. Lederach, *Building Peace*.

43. L. Thévenot, 'Pragmatic Regimes Governing the Engagement with the World,' pp. 56–73, in T.R. Schatzki, K.K. Cetina and E. von Savigny (eds),

The Practice Turn in Contemporary Theory, London and New York: Routledge, 2001, p. 58.

44. See R. Bleiker, *Popular Dissent, Human Agency and Global Politics*, Cambridge: Cambridge University Press, 2001 for an innovative take on the problem of agency in discourse. Bourdieu's work on habitus explores the 'middle-range' connections between the distant poles of structure and agency (see P. Bourdieu, *Outline of a Theory of Practice*, trans. R. Nice, Cambridge: Cambridge University Press, 1977 and *The Logic of Practice*, trans. R. Nice, Cambridge: Polity Press, 1990), while de Certeau's conceptions of tactics vs. strategies are concerned with the processes of subversion of established macro-structures of hierarchy by micro-practices of resistance and evasion (M. de Certeau, *The Practice of Everyday Life*, trans. S. Rendall, Berkeley, CA: University of California Press, 1984).

45. Y. Lotman, *Universe of the Mind: A semiotic theory of culture*, trans. A. Shukman, London: Tauris & Co., 1990.

46. G. Spindler and L. Spindler, 'Cultural Process and Ethnography: An Anthropological Perspective', *The Handbook of Qualitative Research in Education*, London: Academic Press, 1992, p. 65.

47. M.L. Pratt, 'Fieldwork in Common Places', in J. Clifford and G.E. Marcus (eds) *Writing Culture: The Poetics and Politics of Ethnography*, Berkeley, CA: University of California Press, 1986, pp. 27–50.

48. E. Evans-Pritchard, *The Nuer*, Oxford: Oxford University Press, 1940; see Pratt, 'Fieldwork in Common Places', pp. 39–41.

49. Clifford, 'Introduction: Partial Truths', p. 11.

50. I.B. Neumann, 'European Identity, EU Expansion, and the Integration/Exclusion Nexus', *Alternatives: Social transformation & humane governance*, Vol. 23, No. 3, 1998, pp. 397–416.

51. C. Jenks, *Culture*, London: Routledge, 1993, pp. 8–9.

52. For example, L. Abu-Lughod, 'Writing against culture', pp. 137–62 in Richard G. Fox (ed.) *Recapturing Anthropology: Working in the Present*, Santa Fe: School of American Research Press, 1991; D. Scott, 'Culture in Political Theory', *Political Theory*, Vol. 31, No. 1, 2003, pp. 92–115.

53. Pratt, 'Fieldwork in Common Places', pp. 40–1; D. Maybury-Lewis, *Akwe-Shavante Society*, Oxford: Clarendon Press, 1967, p. xxiii.

54. C. Brumann, 'Writing for Culture: Why a Successful Concept Should not be Discarded', *Current Anthropology*, Vol. 40, Supplement, 1999, pp. S1–S27.

55. Pratt, 'Fieldwork in Common Places', pp. 42–5; M. Shostak, *Nisa: The Life and Words of a !Kung Woman*, Cambridge, MA: Harvard University Press, 1981.

56. Ibid.

57. Vidich and Lyman, 'Their History in Sociology and Anthropology', p. 59.

58. V. Crapanzano, 'Hermes' Dilemma: The masking of subversion in ethnographic description', in J. Clifford and G.E. Marcus (eds) *Writing Culture: The Poetics and Politics of Ethnography*, Berkeley, CA: University of California Press, 1986, pp. 51–76; C. Geertz, 'Deep Play: Notes on a Balinese Cockfight', *The Interpretation of Cultures*, New York: Basic Books, 1973. The ethnographic ideal of treating 'the beliefs and habits of another man from his point of view' is expressed already in B. Malinowski's *Argonauts of the Western Pacific*, London: Routledge, 1922, p. 518. For instances of peacebuilding

critique, see Kent, 'Security and Local Ownership' and Echavarria, 'EU's Global Battles'.

59. J. Clifford, 'On Ethnographic Allegory', in J. Clifford and G.E. Marcus (eds) *Writing Culture: The Poetics and Politics of Ethnography*, Berkeley, CA: University of California Press, 1986, pp. 98–121.

60. See Critchley, *The Ethics of Deconstruction*, p. 6.

61. Shaw, *Memories of the Slave Trade*, p. 226.

62. Pratt, 'Fieldwork in Common Places', p. 34.

63. See, for example, Lotman, *Universe of the Mind*, and R. Brubaker, M. Loveman and P. Stamatov, 'Ethnicity as Cognition', *Theory and Society*, Vol. 33, 2004, pp. 31–64.

64. Pratt, 'Fieldwork in Common Places', p. 32.

65. For example, J. Clifford and G.E. Marcus (eds), *Writing Culture: The Poetics and Politics of Ethnography*, Berkeley, CA: University of California Press, 1986; N.K. Denzin and Y.S. Lincoln (eds), *Handbook of Qualitative Research*, Thousand Oaks, CA: Sage Publications, 2000; Scott, 'Culture in Political Theory'; M. Brigg, *Asking After Selves: Knowledge and Settler-Indigenous Conflict Resolution*, PhD thesis, University of Queensland, 2005.

66. Author's interviews at UNDP and CMI Bureau for Crisis Prevention and Recovery,.

67. This is not to claim that ideas embodied in for example 'human rights' are inherently wrong (after all, it is hard to imagine anyone who would wish their 'human rights' violated), but to question their uncritical privileging and sweeping application. It appears that the political framing of human rights is often extremely counterproductive with regard not only to their observance but also to peacebuilding objectives generally. One of my interviewees working with the UN Peacebuilding Commission noted that the rhetoric of human rights often hinders substantive discussion of conflict, since, due to the contentious nature of human rights, country representatives get caught up in debating claims and counterclaims regarding their country's record on this issue (deeply 'nationalist' mentality pervading debates in UN representative bodies was something noted by another UN-related interviewee with lengthy experience of representing his country in UNGA). Another interviewee at UNDP commented that enforcing human rights was perfectly legitimate given their legal endorsement by most countries, and that by extension this made democracy as unequivocally legitimate since, arguably, it is the only regime capable of guaranteeing human rights. In the view of scholars of peacebuilding, not only is such interlinking of 'good intentions' problematic (see, e.g., Karen Smith's analysis of EU's foreign policy in her *European Union Foreign Policy in a Changing World*, Cambridge: Polity Press, 2003), but also their increasing swamping in the uniform 'technical' frameworks devised for their application: thus, 'governance' as a priority of post-conflict interventions has gradually displaced even formal concerns with the establishment of democratic rule (see B. Baker, 'Post-settlement Governance Programmes: What is being built in Africa?', in O. Furley and R. May (eds) *Ending Africa's Wars*, Aldershot: Ashgate, 2006, pp. 31–46).

68. V. Boege, 'Bougainville and the Discovery of Slowness: An unhurried approach to state-building in the Pacific', Occasional Paper No. 3, The Australian Centre for Peace and Conflict Studies, 2006; Lederach, *Building Peace*, and 'Of Nets, Nails and Problems: The folk language of conflict resolution in a Central American setting', in Avruch et al., *Conflict Resolution*, pp. 165–86; C. Nordstrom, 'The Tomorrow of Violence', in Whitehead (ed.), *Violence* pp. 223–42.
69. See, for example, R.D. Kaplan, *The Coming Anarchy: Shattering the Dreams of the Post-Cold War*, New York: Vintage, 2000; S. Ellis, 'Interpreting Violence: Reflections on West African wars', in Whitehead (ed.), *Violence*, pp. 107–24; P. Richards, 'New War: An Ethnographic Approach', in Richards (ed.), *No Peace No War*, pp. 1–21.
70. Although see Paris, *At War's End*, on inherent conflictiveness of the liberal norms of both political and economic competition.
71. R. Rummel, *The Common Foreign and Security Policy and Conflict Prevention*, London: International Alert and Saferworld, 1996, p. 21.
72. Richards, *New War: An Ethnographic Approach*.
73. Toulmin, *Return to Reason*, p. 30.
74. R. Bleiker, 'The Aesthetic Turn in International Political Theory', *Millennium: Journal of International Studies*, Vol. 30, No. 3, 2001, pp. 509–33.
75. Richards, *New War: An Ethnographic Approach*.
76. Whitehead, (ed.), *Violence*.
77. Brigg, *Asking After Selves*.
78. Ross, *The Culture of Conflict*; E. Boulding, *Cultures of Peace: The hidden side of history*, Syracuse, NY: Syracuse University Press, 2004.
79. R. Girard, *Violence and the Sacred*, trans. P. Gregory, London: The Athlone Press, 1988.
80. D. Riches (ed.), *The Anthropology of Violence*, Oxford: Basil Blackwell, 1986.
81. Ellis, 'Interpreting Violence' and *The Mask of Anarchy: The Destruction of Liberia and the Religious Dimension of an African Civil War*, London: Hurst and Co., 1999.
82. Nordstom, *Warzones*; Fetherston and Nordstrom, 'Overcoming Habitus in Conflict Management'.
83. Nordstom, *Warzones*.
84. See, for example, Duffield, *Global Governance and the New Wars*, for critique.
85. Ferme, *The Underneath of Things*.
86. P. Chabal and J.-P. Daloz, *Africa Works: Disorder as Political Instrument*, Bloomington: Indiana University Press, 1999.
87. Ellis, *The Mask of Anarchy*.
88. Avruch et al., *Conflict Resolution*; Brigg and Bleiker, *Mediating Across Difference*; P. Uvin and C. Mironko, 'Western and Local Approaches to Justice in Rwanda', *Global Governance*, Vol. 9, No. 2, 2003, pp. 219–31.
89. C. Nordstrom, 'Contested Identities/Essentially Contested Powers', in K. Rupesinghe (ed.) *Conflict Transformation*, Basingstoke: Macmillan, 1995, pp. 93–115; Kaldor, *New and Old Wars*.
90. Shaw, *Memories of the Slave Trade*.
91. Ibid; Ferme, *The Underneath of Things*.

92. Author's informal interview with a staff member of the British High Commission in Sierra Leone, Freetown, 19 September 2006.
93. G.E. Marcus, 'Contemporary Problems of Ethnography in the Modern World System', in Clifford and Marcus, *Writing Culture*, pp. 165–93.
94. Ferme, *The Underneath of Things*; Shaw, *Memories of the Slave Trade*.
95. Bakhtin, *Speech Genres and Other Late Essays*, pp. 39, 117; Holquist, *Dialogism*, p. 22; Viktorova, 'Identity and Alterity'.
96. Shaw, *Memories of the Slave Trade*, p. 226.
97. Lotman, *Universe of the Mind*.
98. Clifford, 'Introduction,' pp. 7, 2.
99. Lotman, *Universe of the Mind*.
100. J. Häkli, 'Discourse in the Production of Political Space: Decolonizing the symbolism of provinces in Finland', *Political Geography*, Vol. 17, No. 3, 1996, pp. 331–63.
101. Chabal and Daloz, *Culture Troubles*.
102. P. Just, 'Conflict Resolution and Moral Community among the Dou Donggo', in K. Avruch et al., *Conflict Resolution,* pp. 107–44, p. 132.
103. V. Jabri, *Discourses on Violence: Conflict Analysis Reconsidered*, Manchester: Manchester University Press, 1996; C. Coker, 'How Wars End', *Millennium Journal of International Studies*, Vol. 26, No. 3, 1997, pp. 615–30; S. Buckley-Zistel, 'In-Between War and Peace: Identities, boundaries and change after violent conflict', *Millennium Journal of International Studies*, Vol. 35, No. 1, 2006, pp. 3–21.
104. P.W. Black, 'Surprised by Common Sense: Local understandings and the management of conflict on Tobi, Republic of Belau', in K. Avruch et al., *Conflict Resolution,* pp. 145–64.
105. See J.S. Murer, 'Countering the Narratives of Simplification: Embracing complexity as a means of conflict resolution and understanding identity formation', CPCS paper series in Peace and Conflict Studies, November 2008, http://www.st-andrews.ac.uk/intrel/media/Murer_violence_of_simplification.pdf, accessed 25 March 2008. That such redefinition of one's identity, when faced with an inquisitive ethnographer, does take place is suggested by the difficulty people experience when asked to define themselves in interviews. Originally, I attributed this to the fact that definition (or delimitation), as a practice, belongs to the realm of otherness, whereas one's perception of oneself is always in flux and unfinished (see Bakhtin, *Speech Genres and Other Late Essays*, p. 117; Viktorova, 'Identity and Alterity'). But if we take Barth seriously (see F. Barth (ed.), *Ethnic Groups and Boundaries*, Oslo: Norwegian University Press, 1969), then the explanation that ethnographic encounter lifts the fixed terms of identity and alterity, usually reproduced through recurrent social situations, seems even more pertinent.
106. Critchley, *The Ethics of Deconstruction*, pp. 16–18, 28.
107. Lederach, *Building Peace*; Nordstrom, 'The Tomorrow of Violence'; Fetherston, 'From Conflict Resolution to Transformative Peacebuilding'.
108. A. Appadurai, 'The Capacity to Aspire: Culture and the Terms of Recognition', pp. 59–84 in V. Rao and M. Walton (eds) *Culture and Public Action*, Stanford, CA: Stanford University Press, 2004.
109. Spindler and Spindler, 'Cultural Process and Ethnography', p. 73.

5

challenging statebuilding as peacebuilding – working with hybrid political orders to build peace

m. anne brown, volker boege, kevin p. clements and anna nolan

Since the end of the Cold War, agencies responsible for international peacebuilding operations have explicitly linked the restoration of security, development and peace to statebuilding and governance. The medium of the state, and in particular the liberal democratic, free market state, has been understood as providing the fundamental framework for the achievement of stability, sustainable conflict management, and development.[1] By contrast, 'state failure' and 'state fragility' have been identified as establishing and entrenching conditions for violent conflict and widespread impoverishment within, but also beyond, the borders of the state in question. The topic of fragile states gained particular prominence when it was framed in the context of the security discourse of the industrialised states of the Global North following the terrorist attacks of 2001 and the 'war on terror'. Fragile states came to be seen 'through the dominant lens of Western security interests', and through this lens they appear as breeding grounds and safe havens for terrorism and hence as a matter of international security – which is, above all, the security of the industrialised states.[2] Thus fragile states are represented in much of the peacebuilding and development policy-related community as 'the crux of today's development challenge and an increasing source of potential threats to global security', with USAID, for example, identifying 'no more urgent matter'.[3]

As a result of these intermeshing trends, strengthening states through statebuilding programmes has come to be regarded by major donors as a central response to violent conflict and insecurity and a core element of peacebuilding programmes (and of development assistance). In the post-colonial states of the Global South, external peacebuilding operations are often faced not only with responding to the effects of violent division, but with the reality of weak (or virtually non-existent) state institutions coexisting with other logics of authority, power, and order (customary, societal) as well as societal fragmentation in various forms (ethnic, tribal, religious, criminal etc.). Such states are pre-eminently amongst those categorised as fragile, failed or failing.

This chapter challenges conventional statebuilding approaches as an appropriate response to the demands of either peacebuilding or state formation. Rather than the category of the fragile state, we put forward the concept of hybrid political orders as an analytical instrument that helps to understand and engage with the deeply challenging processes of state formation and sustaining social peace in states of the Global South. By 'hybrid political orders' we refer to the (often uneasy and vulnerable) coexistence of very different orders of governance and government. In regions characterised by hybrid political orders, diverse, sometimes competing, sometimes complementary authority structures, logics of order and claims to power interact and pull against each other, combining elements of introduced Western models of governance and elements stemming from local indigenous traditions of governance and politics, with further influences exerted by the forces of globalisation and associated societal fragmentation (in various forms: ethnic, tribal, religious ...). From such processes of interaction and mutual permeation, new hybrid institutions and political orders emerge.

We also posit that the dominant discourse of statebuilding, derived from 'ideal model' accounts of Western developed states, is shaped by overly narrow conceptions of what constitutes a state as a working political community. The models of the state that have dominated international peacebuilding (and broader state-strengthening) operations fundamentally misconstrue key dimensions of the nature of political community, and particularly of participatory, democratic political community. These models are therefore often poorly adapted to supporting the emergence of viable political community, especially in societies struggling with the aftermath of violent division. Nor are these models oriented towards acknowledgement of, or interaction with, the forms of societal governance or the sources of legitimacy that may be at work in the countries in which the external peacebuilding operations are in train.

Reconceptualising so-called 'fragile states' as hybrid political orders allows for a more neutral and nuanced understanding of the complex domains of power and authority in these societies, by widening the frame of reference from the functions and capacities of state institutions to also include the operation of customary and other non-state institutions in providing sources of social peace, justice, political representation, and participation. This approach enables exploration of the nature and quality of interactions between formal state institutions and customary and other non-state institutions, and potentially identifies processes of positive mutual accommodation between these various domains of governance, from which new forms of statehood may be discernible.

By contrast, statebuilding responses to 'state fragility' are ordered around negatively highlighting the discrepancy between the reality of state institutions in the country in question in contrast to a narrowly conceived 'ideal model' of an OECD-style state. They are not organised around understanding the broader reality of the society and so repeatedly fail to grasp the significance of the strengths that may also be present. Alternatively, we argue that the political hybridity of post-colonial societies of the Global South offers forms of governance – often, but not only, based in customary and community life – that carry significant social legitimacy. Such local societal forms of governance are likely to be a necessary part of the emergence of any broader national order capable of underpinning social peace and providing working democratic government.

The concept of hybrid political orders is not put forward as an alternative to the state. Rather, it is an analytical instrument that seeks greater conceptual and practical openness to governance mechanisms that may be in operation on the ground. For post-colonial states and societies struggling with violent conflict or its aftermath, this approach enables a different logic of engagement from that afforded by categories of state failure. Instead of the assumption that the complete adoption of Western state models is the most appropriate avenue for peacebuilding and conflict prevention, there is a need for more flexible and richer models of governance and of the state as political community that are capable of recognising the strengths of the social order and resilience embedded in the communal life of societies within the Global South. Processes of state formation in hybrid political orders may, however, also have things to teach us about the ongoing work of making political community and creating social peace, and about the evolving reality of states more generally.

hybrid political orders

The modern, Western-style Weberian state, towards which much of the statebuilding as peacebuilding policies and the fragile states discourse is oriented, hardly exists in reality outside the OECD. Many states in the 'rest' of the world are political entities that do not closely resemble that model state. In much of the Global South, the locus of social order and effective governance resides in non-state forms of customary rule rather than in government institutions. Despite colonialism and post-colonial statebuilding, traditional actors and institutions, customary law, and indigenous knowledge have shown considerable resilience and continue to persist and coexist with introduced state institutions.

Contemporary 'customary institutions', 'customary ways', etc. are of course *not* the institutions and ways of the pre-contact and precolonial past. Traditional societies everywhere in the world have come into contact with outside influences; they have not been left unchanged by the powers of – originally European – capitalist expansion, colonialism, evangelism, imperialism, and globalisation. This holds true even for the most remote parts of the Global South. In practice, therefore, there are no clear-cut boundaries between the realm of the exogenous 'modern' and the endogenous 'customary'; instead processes of assimilation, articulation, adoption, and transformation are at the interface of the global/exogenous and the local/indigenous.[4] Nevertheless, the use of the terms 'custom', 'customary institutions', etc. is helpful because they indicate specific local indigenous characteristics that distinguish them from introduced institutions that belong to the realm of the state and civil society. It is also important to note that 'custom' or 'tradition', especially where it exists as a living form of governance, is not fixed but remarkably dynamic and adaptable.

Formal state institutions in the Global South often lack roots in their own cultures and in the patterns of authority and legitimacy that have weight at the (often rural) grassroots. Western state forms were 'delivered off the rack' to many parts of the Global South in a relatively short time span during decolonisation. In many of the newly independent states there was no history of precolonial unitary rule and no processes by which national identity could arise. Whether or not they were democracies at home, colonial powers by and large had acted as authoritarian and coercive regimes in their colonies – there was generally little interest in the emergence of multiple connections between state institutions and society, and little preparation for sustainable statehood.[5]

So-called fragile states lack the core element that, since Max Weber, has been seen as the decisive criterion of statehood, namely, the monopoly over the legitimate use of physical violence. The state authorities cannot effectively enforce the laws of the state or the domination of state institutions against the will of non-state actors. Conventional statebuilding approaches perceive these states as 'incomplete', 'not yet' properly built, 'fragile', 'failing', or 'failed' because government has not yet penetrated throughout society. However, a narrow focus on failure to match the OECD model state, without also looking at sources of strength or social resilience in the societies in question, generates a distorted perspective on the state, and has locked international peacebuilding operations into statebuilding programmes that endeavour to shore up central state institutions at the expense of social context.

It is important to look at what actually constitutes social and political order in these regions. Informal, non-state institutions and actors form an integral and important dimension of local governance in many places – all the more so as the state's 'outposts' are mediated by 'informal' indigenous societal institutions that implement their own logic and their own rules within or alongside state structures. In such circumstances, 'the state' is only one actor among others, and state order is only one of a number of orders claiming to provide frameworks for conflict regulation and social services. In particular, security is not primarily delivered or provided by state institutions, but by non-state actors (who may be operating implicitly and to varying extents in conjunction with formal security, or in competition with it).[6] Customary law, indigenous knowledge, and traditional societal structures – extended families, clans, tribes, village communities – traditional authorities such as village elders, headmen, healers, etc. and other societal mechanisms continue to determine the social reality of large parts of the population in the Global South. At the local level it is often these structures that underpin food security, land arrangements, welfare, and conflict management. At the same time, customary norms and practices may provide the context for collective and individual senses of meaning and value.[7]

In many instances state institutions work through the utilisation of kin-based and other traditional networks, which means that they are mediated by 'informal' indigenous societal institutions that implement their own logic and their own rules within the ('incomplete') state structures. This leads to their deviation from the ideal type of 'proper' state institutions in the Weberian sense. They may be captured by social forces that make use of them in the interest of traditional, mostly kinship-based, entities. Electoral processes, for example, may operate in this way. State institutions – not only at the periphery, but also in the very centre of the state – become the subject of power struggles between competing social groups and their leaders and are utilised by those groups and leaders for their own benefit, regardless of the needs of the 'nation' or the 'citizenry'. Much of the debate about neopatrimonialism, clientelistic networks and patronage, for example, in postcolonial African states revolves around this usurpation and reconfiguration of imported formal governance structures by indigenous informal societal forces.[8]

On the other hand, the intrusion of state agencies impacts on nonstate local orders as well. Customary systems of order are subjected to deconstruction and re-formation as they are incorporated into central state structures and processes. Customary institutions and customary authorities do not remain unchanged; they respond to and are influenced by the mechanisms of the state apparatus. They adopt an ambiguous position with regard to the state, appropriating state functions and 'state talk', but at the same time pursuing their own agenda under the guise of the state. Taking state functions and state talk on board, however, also involves a change of processes and approaches. Some governments deliberately incorporate traditional authorities in order to strengthen state capacities and legitimacy.[9]

Particularly in regions which have suffered protracted war, the complex nature of governance is further fractured by the emergence of movements and formations that often have their origins in the effects of, and reactions, to entrenched conflict, large-scale displacement and negative globalisation, including warlords and their militias in outlying regions, gang leaders in townships and squatter settlements, vigilante-type organisations, ethnically based protection rackets, millenarian religious movements, transnational crime networks, or new forms of tribalism. Where state agencies are unable or unwilling to deliver security and other public goods, or are themselves predatory, and customary orders have been eroded, people will turn to other social entities for support. Some of these new formations manage to seize power in certain regions of a given state or across states. These movements have the capacity to exert significant violence and control within their respective strongholds. Their presence and competition has undermined or substituted the state's claimed monopoly over the legitimate use of violence and often supplanted customary or community-based orders. As a consequence, in some states 'oligopolies of power' emerge.[10] The break-up of states into the fiefdoms of competing warlords is the most extreme and destructive form of the inability to exercise the monopoly on the use of violence. More often than total state collapse and the complete replacement of state structures by a warlord-type order, the emergence of a delicate structure of horizontally organised para-statal and intermediary institutions and actors occurs; the 'rule of the intermediaries' substitutes for the rule of the central state.[11]

Under such conditions, combinations of forces from the customary sphere – such as chiefs, traditional kings, religious authorities and their constituencies – and forces from the sphere of the new formations – such as warlords and their militias, ethnic or millenarian movements, or organised crime – can emerge. The new formations can be linked to traditional societal entities and attempt to instrumentalise them for their own goals such as new forms of power and profit – as they can also be linked with arms of the state. Customary checks to corruption, misuse of power, and violence then become seriously undermined. The protagonists of the traditional societal entities such as lineages, clans, 'tribes', or religious brotherhoods, on the other hand, pursue their own agendas (which are often not reducible to aims such as political power, or to economic considerations such as private gain and profit) which may include concepts such as 'honour', or the need to fulfil ritual requirements. Thus non-state traditional actors and institutions, their motives and concerns as well as their ways of doing things, can blend with private actors and their motives. Clan leaders might become warlords (or warlords might strive for an authoritative position in the customary context) or tribal warriors might become private militias, and a political economy based on extensive use of violence might emerge. The new formations can also merge with state agencies, particularly around the security sector. Customary authorities may also resist the new warlords, however, with non-compliant traditional leaders becoming a target of violence.[12] Even in the face of war, local forms of authority may themselves be striving to create peace or maintain viable community, as Carolyn Nordstrom's exploration of Mozambique during its civil war underlines.[13]

There is not one single form of hybrid political order: customary authorities may be working for social peace in Bougainville, for example, while warlords are leading powerful armed forces in Afghanistan. In addressing the problematic forms of hybrid political order, we acknowledge the profoundly difficult and long-term challenges for peacebuilding in many of these societies. Nevertheless, we posit that engagement with local sources of legitimacy and authority will provide avenues supporting positive mutual accommodation between state and non-state institutions, which in turn contributes to the building of viable political community, providing security, peace and a framework for the non-violent conduct of conflicts.

statebuilding as peacebuilding

State-strengthening programmes in peace-building operations have focused on how to build liberal democratic, free market states, where the components of that state are taken as already known in advance. There has been far less attention, in some cases none at all, paid to questions about what political order or community might mean in the society in question, what forms of governance might already be in operation and how they interact, what forms of harm, violence or suffering those forms of governance might sustain and which they might restrain, what processes might support or repress participative political community, or how the formal state institutions might interact with other, societal sources of power or authority. What attention there has been to such questions tends to throw all customary or other societal governance mechanisms into the one category – as obstacles or threats to proper state institutional practice, which must be suppressed or at best ignored. In practical and policy terms, the goal of supporting the emergence of peaceful political community in many states struggling with violence and division thus becomes the mechanistic (but nevertheless extraordinarily difficult) effort to establish institutions identified as key to the management of liberal states and the process of elections (party political structures, a security structure, a legal system, a financial system, and the bureaucracies associated with some key services such as health or education). This approach is conceptually authorised by the models of the state dominant in current discourses of international statebuilding, which have identified the state with its centralised, formal institutional and legal apparatus and then conceptualised it as existing in a realm distinct from society.[14]

A viable state, however, is a complex political community that is far from reducible to a set of institutions that can be delivered like a product. While central government institutions are of critical significance, the formal dimensions of the state are intermeshed with, and to varying degrees dependent, upon the social, political, economic, and cultural lives of the population. This is most notably the case in democratic or participatory political orders. Fundamental political, legal, and economic institutions work in large part because they are embedded in networks of social practice, patterns of values, and frameworks of meaning that underpin interactions and enable trust. Political community more broadly depends also upon the quality of the processes linking different arms of government, government and people, and different levels of governance. 'To pluck out of this dense thicket of institutions, cultures, traditions, mores and practices, merely the formal rules or architecture of legal [or other] institutions is simply to pick at leaves'.[15]

participation, citizenship and legitimacy

The emphasis on central state institutions and the reduction of state formation to institutional transfer in dominant statebuilding practices has meant that there has been relatively little focus on questions of citizenship, participation, and legitimacy – that is, on questions of the state as political community. Rapid institutional transfer can result in central government institutions and, perhaps even more important, processes that are significantly disconnected from prevalent social practices and values and divorced from the actual socio-political and economic dynamics shaping people's lives. Under these conditions there is little chance for government structures to establish legitimacy within their own populations and cultures. The political life of a population becomes cut off from the 'state' and a gulf is created between the new, technical version of state institutions and the forms and language of political community that make sense to people. While central government institutions are of great significance, institutional transfer does not of itself enable the vital connections between government, forms of societal governance, and people, in which legitimacy is embedded and citizenship is possible. Legitimacy, however, is crucial to sustained social peace. State fragility is a problem not only of capacities, resources, institutions, and powers of enforcement and implementation, but also of legitimacy.

Not only does the 'lack of fit between local political culture and imported political institutions' work against legitimacy;[16] it also creates incentives for corruption, rule-breaking, self-enrichment, poor accountability and other dimensions of bad governance, and means that the interactions between these new, technical forms of the 'state' and the actual political dynamics driving the country are more likely to be working at cross purposes. Political debate or struggle at the local or national level is likely to occur through channels that have largely

opportunistic relationships with the institutions of governance, contributing to the mystification and corruption of the dynamics of power.
This creates or enlarges conditions for the emergence of warlordism or
other forms of entrenched political violence.

Indeed, state institutions may be more responsive to external agencies
than to the communities within their own borders. This dynamic can
engender amongst the population a deep alienation from state systems
of governance and law, and in effect disenfranchise the local population. 'The state' is perceived as an alien external force, 'far away' not
only physically (in the capital city), but also psychologically. Individuals
are loyal to their group (whatever that may be), not the state; they obey
the rules of their group, rather than the state.

Genuine processes of participation and inclusion need to engage with
the social values and practices of people on the ground; engagement
does not always or necessarily entail endorsement, but it requires listening, interaction, and exchange. Participation and citizenship have
predominantly been conceptualised according to highly individualised
modes of political agency. Such models have little relevance to many
non-OECD states, where the primary basis for identity, leadership, and
power is often derived through affiliations to local places, membership
of language groups, clans or lineages, and residence in particular communities. Partly because of individualised models of political participation, the resilience of community or of more corporatist identities is
often highlighted by external commentators as an obstacle to the emergence of real citizenship. 'The direction of development, it was assumed,
is away from the primordial (biological criteria of attachment) towards
attachment to the larger territory'.[17] Discussions of citizenship in the
context of statebuilding thus tend to set the goal of building citizenship
in opposition to the existence of local identities, which are often seen
reductively as merely contributing to violence, or simply as parochial.

Trying to 'build' citizenship in blanket opposition to the forms of
sociality that already exist is very unlikely to be successful. In subsistence economy societies, the extensive breakdown of clan and village
identities would entail the breakdown of relationships that maintain
the available levels of security and resilience.[18] The erosion of those
forms of social order that have survived violent conflict can expand
the scope for the emergence of the 'new tribalism'. Acknowledging and
working with the multiple nature of people's identities may enable a
more nuanced approach to citizenship. If local communities are working as the basis of social cohesion and identity, then efforts to support

citizenship need to engage with the village, or the clan, or the local community, rather than reject them as merely the source of clientelism, parochialism, and division. Local communities can also provide scope for participative politics and decision-making. The disjunction and fragmentation between state and societal forms of governance may be a greater challenge to the emergence of effective participation and citizenship than particularism, as it undermines the potential for participation and legitimacy.

positive mutual accommodation and political community

Peacebuilders and statebuilders have often overlooked or ignored endogenous political orders, seeing them as irrelevant to modern political community and to be overtaken by the way of the future. Often they have categorised them as a threat to statehood that needs to be repressed, seeing traditional norms and values as the problem to be expunged (and so setting themselves an extremely ambitious, disruptive, indeed revolutionary goal). Non-Western forms of societal organisation and modes of governance are very much alive in many regions, however, and are here to stay.[19] In the interests of peacebuilding it is important to recognise the hybridity of political orders in these regions and to search for ways of generating positive mutual accommodation of state institutional governance with customary non-state as well as civil society mechanisms and institutions – which in real life are not isolated domains, but elements of a particular 'messy' local socio-political context.[20] We have argued the possibility and necessity of the emergence of 'indigenised' forms of statehood through positive mutual accommodation. Such indigenised forms of statehood might look very different from the Western ideal of 'the state'. Forms that might appear 'weak' or 'fragile' in the eyes of outsiders through lack of institutional capacity and effectiveness could nevertheless have significant legitimacy in the eyes of the people on the ground through constructive interaction with peaceful forms of local order.[21]

The main problem is not the fragility of state institutions as such, but the lack of constructive linkages between communities and state institutions and between introduced modes of institutional governance and local practice – hence the problem of legitimacy and citizenship.[22] Engaging with communities and non-state customary institutions, therefore, is as important as working with central state institutions and governments.[23] 'If the weaknesses of many state institutions are in significant part the result of their lack of grounding in society, then focusing on the interface between state and society is at least as important as focusing on the institutions alone.'[24] Through underestimating the positive potential of non-state indigenous institutions and practices for forming political community, external actors (working with local elites) have unwittingly opened the door to deeply violent forms of political order.

Positive mutual accommodation, however, does not apply only to the interactions between community and customary governance mechanisms on the one hand and state institutional forms on the other hand. It applies also to the international agencies and associated bodies engaged in peacebuilding and statebuilding, and to the broader political dynamics within which the relationships between national and international peacebuilding agencies and states and societies grappling with violent conflict or its aftermath take shape. This also means to challenge the belief, articulated decades ago in the form of modernisation theory, that all societies have to progress through linear stages of state–society development to arrive at the ideal of 'proper' Western-style states. Despite decades of critique, the underlying assumptions of modernisation theory remain deeply embedded in statebuilding policy and practice, which still works as if the task were for 'the West' to teach 'the rest' how to do liberal state institutions better. This approach to peacebuilding is entrenched in much of the *modus operandi* of international development; it is itself a form of epistemic violence. Richer, more flexible models of, and approaches to, the state as political community need to be embedded in the economy of policy and administrative action, and not simply have an abstract or rhetorical existence.

This is not to question that there is much of great value that can be learnt from the accumulated history of state practice; nor is it to suggest that the broad structures of formal statehood already in place in the Global South be abandoned, although the processes of exchange and interaction in many cases need to change profoundly. Except perhaps at the most general level, the answers to questions about the nature of political community in societies struggling with a complex legacy of violence are not, in practical and concrete terms, already given in advance. To consider that they are is to overlook the critical significance to state formation of processes of participation and exchange across difference and division. For an external peacebuilding agency to imagine that it is the bearer of answers to the inadequacy and failure of the other is to step away from the potential for dialogue and mutuality within which constructive coexistence and the emergence of participative political community are possible.

Statebuilding through institutional transfer has yielded poor results with regard to building sustainable peace. Conceptualising the state as a matrix of central institutions overlooks the state's existence as political community; that is, it overlooks both the complex relationships between government institutions and the many dimensions that make up society, and the role of people as agents of governance and in 'enacting' the state. Significant dimensions of legitimacy, participation and coherent governance, however, depend upon how these relationships play out in practice. The circle of exchange and interaction that, however imperfectly, links government with the diversity of society and its forms of governance constitutes political community and enables its emergence.

These comments do not entail the rejection of the notion of the state, but rather call for a more encompassing approach to the state as political community. The state understood as political community is not given content simply by ethnic or cultural identity as a nation or by institutional structures as an idealised model of civic rationality, but is shaped by the ongoing processes of mutual accommodation across the profound differences of culture and identity, of institutional and customary or other societal forms of governance. Understanding states as political community has relevance not only to states struggling with a legacy of violent conflict but to all states faced with the challenges of holding difference together – between ethnic or religious groups, between indigenous and settler peoples, across histories of grievance – without embedded violence or marginalisation.

future research directions

More detailed work on the actual interactions between state institutional, customary, and other forms of governance in specific regions and states and specific sectors is needed to gain a more grounded understanding of the potential for greater constructive relations between them. Are there inherent limits to constructive interaction, imposed by the reality of often profoundly different world views or regimes of practice, or are the possible limits rather a reflection of different economic and political agendas?

Much of the field research that has shaped these arguments has been drawn from the Pacific Island region, East Timor and Somaliland, where forms of customary community life remain vibrant and in large part underpin social order and well-being. While we are confident that the insights from this research apply to societies with more significant surplus economies or to other states in Asia, Africa, or Latin America where forms of community order have been more completely broken down by war and displacement, what are the limits of its application and what can more difficult cases, where hybridity is dominated by forms of violent 'order', teach us? What is the role of various transnational forces in the interactions between societal and state institutional modes of order? What might international peacebuilding responses that are able to interact more constructively with local mechanisms for social peace look like and how might they work? What implications would this more dialogic orientation have for the political economy of peacebuilding and development, for the ways that decisions and directions are taken and accounted for, and for the relationship between policy and practice? These directions for exploration could provide for a deeper understanding of what really contributes to building peace and political community in 'fragile' situations of the Global South, and in the broader context of evolving forms of the state.

notes

This chapter draws upon an earlier paper 'On Hybrid Political Orders and Emerging States: State Formation in the Context of "Fragility". See V. Boege, M.A. Brown, K. Clements and A. Nolan, *On Hybrid Political Orders and Emerging States: State Formation in the Context of 'Fragility'*, Berghof Handbook Dialogue No. 8, (Online version), Berlin: Berghof Research Center for Constructive Conflict Management, 2008. Available at: http://www.berghof-handbook.net/uploads/download/boege_etal_handbook.pdf (accessed 30 March 2009).

1. This orientation has been detailed and in different ways critiqued by R. Paris, *At War's End: Building Peace after Civil Conflict*, Cambridge: Cambridge University Press, 2004; O. Richmond, *The Transformation of Peace*, Basingstoke: Palgrave Macmillan, 2005.
2. M. Boas and K.M. Jennings, 'Insecurity and Development: the Rhetoric of the "Failed State"', *The European Journal of Development Research*, Vol. 17, No. 3, pp. 385–95, quote on p. 388.
3. K. Brown and S. Patrick, *Greater than the Sum of its Parts? Assessing 'Whole of Government' Approaches to Fragile States*. New York: International Peace Academy, 2007, p. 1; USAID, *Fragile States Strategy*. US Agency for International Development PD-ACA-999, Washington, DC, 2005, p. 1.
4. A. Rumsey, 'The Articulation of Indigenous and Exogenous Orders in Highland New Guinea and Beyond', in *The Australian Journal of Anthropology*,

Vol. 17, No. 1, pp. 47–69; G. White, *Indigenous Governance in Melanesia*, State Society and Governance in Melanesia Discussion Paper, Research School of Pacific and Asian Studies, Canberra: Australian National University, 2006; R. Mac Ginty, 'Indigenous Peace-making versus the Liberal Peace', *Cooperation and Conflict*, Vol. 43, No. 2, 2008, pp. 139–63.

5. See Boege et al., *On Hybrid Political Orders*; S. Dinnen, 'The Solomon Islands intervention and the instabilities of the post-colonial state', *Global Change, Peace & Security*, Vol. 20, No. 3, 2008, pp. 339–55; T. Kelsall, *Going with the Grain in African Development?*, Power and Politics in Africa Discussion Paper No. 1, London: ODI, 2008.

6. 'Evidence suggests that in some fragile states more than 80–90% of security and justice services are provided outside the state'. See OECD-DAC, *Concepts and Dilemmas of State Building in Fragile Situations. From Fragility to Reslience*, OECD-DAC Discussion Paper, Paris: OECD, 2008, p. 72.

7. Boege et al., *On Hybrid Political Orders*; Dinnen, 'The Solomon Islands'; R. Nixon, 'The Crisis of Governance in New Subsistence States', *Journal of Contemporary Asia*, Vol. 36, No. 1, 2006, pp. 75–101.

8. For an overview of the state of the discourse on neopatrimonialism see U. Engel and G. Erdmann, 'Neopatrimonialism Reconsidered: Critical Review and Elaboration of an Elusive Concept', *Commonwealth and Comparative Politics*, Vol. 45, No. 1, 2007, pp. 95–119.

9. The problematic of incorporating traditional leaders in the framework of government is discussed by White, *Indigenous Governance*, pp. 12–13.

10. A. Mehler, *Legitime Gewaltoligopole – eine Antwort auf strukturelle Instabilitaet in Westafrika?*, IAK Diskussionsbeitraege 22, Hamburg: Institut fuer Afrikakunde, 2003.

11. T. von Trotha, 'Die Zukunft liegt in Afrika. Vom Zerfall des Staates, von der Vorherrschaft der konzentrischen Ordnung und vom Aufstieg der Parastaatlichkeit', *Leviathan*, Vol. 28, 2000, pp. 253–79, quote on pp. 277–8.

12. S. Schmeidl with M. Karokhail, *The Failure of 'Pret-a-Porter States': How the McDonaldisation of State-building Misses more than just the Story in Afghanistan*, Berghof Handbook Dialogue Series, no 8, Berlin: Berghof Research Center for Constructive Conflict Management, 2009; C. Nordstrom, *A Different Kind of War Story*, Philadelphia, PA: Pennsylvania University Press, 1997.

13. Nordstrom, ibid.

14. For a critique, see J. Migdal, *Strong Societies and Weak States: State-Society Relations and State Capabilities in the Third World*, Princeton, NJ: Princeton University Press, 1988.

15. M. Krygier and W. Mason, *Interpersonal Violence, the Rule of Law and its Enforcement*, Paper presented at the Global Development Network Conference, Brisbane, January 2008, p. 5.

16. Kelsall, *Going with the Grain in African Development?*, p. 11.

17. J. Migdal, *State in Society*, Cambridge: Cambridge University Press, 2001, p. 200.

18. Nixon, 'The Crisis of Governance'.

19. It is worth noting that the OECD-DAC most recently has come to acknowledge the positive role that local non-state actors can play. 'A growing interest

in and willingness to work with local institutions of governance – such as *shuras* in Afghanistan – is also welcome. Traditional systems, which may not be recognisable in western states, may still perform the same functions and generate the same outputs as formal state institutions. Respect and willingness to accommodate such systems (...) can be helpful in restoring governance', OECD-DAC, *Concepts and Dilemmas*, p. 36.

20. Kelsall, *Going with the Grain in African Development?*. With regard to Africa, Goran Hyden gives an insightful account of the 'curious mixture' of formal and informal institutions, behaviours and norms 'which are often contradictory, but sometimes complementary' (G. Hyden, *Institutions, power and policy outcomes in Africa*, Power and Politics in Africa Discussion Paper No. 2, London: ODI, 2008, p. 11).

21. Somaliland and Bougainville (Papua New Guinea) are examples of indigenous state formation based on positive mutual accommodation of introduced Western and local customary institutions of governance. At the same time they are success stories of peacebuilding and formation of political community. For Bougainville see V. Boege, *Bougainville and the Discovery of Slowness: an Unhurried Approach to State-Building in the Pacific*, ACPACS Occasional Paper No. 3, Brisbane: ACPACS, 2006, and V.Boege, *A promising liaison: kastom and state in Bougainville*, ACPACS Occasional Paper No. 12, Brisbane: ACPACS, 2008; for Somaliland see M.V. Hoehne, *Traditional Authorities in Northern Somalia: Transformations of Positions and Powers*, Halle/Saale: Max Planck Institute for Social Anthropology Working Paper No. 82, 2006, and K. Menkhaus, 'Governance without Government in Somalia. Spoilers, State Building, and the Politics of Coping', *International Security*, Vol. 31, No. 3, 2006, pp. 74–106; for a brief comparison of Bougainville and Somaliland see Boege et al., *On Hybrid Political Orders*.

22. A more recent publication that was elaborated in the context of the OECD-DAC Fragile States Group also acknowledges this point: 'We place particular emphasis on state-society negotiation and the fact that state-building strategies need to appreciate that states are comprised of more than formal institutions.' See OECD-DAC, *Concepts and Dilemmas*, p. 14.

23. Examples are provided by swisspeace-Afghanistan's Tribal Liaison Office in the Loya Paktia area of Afghanistan and ACPACS's cooperation project with the National Council of Chiefs in Vanuatu. The TLO's starting point is that for working on governance and security in Afghanistan the cooperation with traditional institutions and leaders 'is not just beneficial, it is essential'. See M. Karokhail and S. Schmeidl, 'Integration of Traditional Structures into the State-Building Process: Lessons from the Tribal Liaison Office in Loya Paktia', in Heinrich Boell Foundation (ed.) *Afghanistan*, Publication Series on Promoting Democracy under Conditions of State Fragility, Issue 1, Berlin: Heinrich Boell Foundation, 2006, pp. 59–78, quote on p. 66. Its mission is 'to facilitate the formal integration of communities and their traditional structures with Afghanistan's governance framework. The project strategy relies on the cooperation with and the involvement of the tribal structures ...' (ibid., p. 65). On ACPACS's work in Vanuatu see P. Westoby and M.A. Brown, 'Peaceful Community Development in

Vanuatu: A Reflection on the Vanuatu Kastom Governance Partnership', *Journal of Peacebuilding and Development*, Vol. 3, No. 3, 2007, pp. 77–81.

24. M.A. Brown, 'Conclusion', M.A. Brown (ed.), *Security and Development in the Pacific Islands: Social Resilience in Emerging States,* Boulder, CO; London: Lynne Rienner, pp. 287–301, quote on p. 289.

6

human security and the legitimisation
of peacebuilding

shahrbanou tadjbakhsh

introduction

One of the most dramatic turns in international relations since 1945 has been the recent legitimisation of interventions by the international community under the Responsibility to Protect (R2P) doctrine, which, since its first conception in the 2001 Report of the International Commission on Intervention and State Sovereignty (ICISS), seems to have posed an ethical responsibility for the international community to act on behalf of individuals in cases where states are unable or unwilling to protect them. For critical theorists, the R2P norm has become an instrument for legitimising and giving moral authority to new, more direct forms of Western intervention and regulation.[1] For post-colonial critics, external intervention, under any name, can hardly create a just world order, for it sustains the existing asymmetry of power in international relations. After all, the South can never in conceivable imagination muster the resources or the confidence to intervene in the North, even though a number of industrialised states, plagued by the downturns of economic globalisation, are failing in their responsibilities to protect the jobs, welfare, social security, and health care of their populations. But advocates of utilitarianism and liberal internationalists counterclaim that the alternative of disengagement, or non-action, is not a viable solution. From a utilitarian viewpoint, a potential relapse to war could have more negative consequences than the potential side effects of intervention.

Instead of further engaging in the ethical debate about whether or not to intervene, this chapter ponders on the aftermath: when interventions do happen, whether in the name of responsibility to protect, or for strategic interests and regime changes, what happens afterwards? As Liden argues, 'The damage of imperialistic colonialism is done, and a postcolonial ethic of non-hegemonic engagement rather than retreat must follow in its wake.'[2] To engage with the ethics of peacebuilding means channelling the question from whether peacebuilding should be done to how to do it in a legitimate manner.[3] The question is therefore posed as to whether applying a particular type of human security framework can help in the legitimisation of the peacebuilding that supposedly comes after interventions, and, ultimately, in the development of this 'ethic of non-hegemonic engagement'.

in defence of human security: which and whose dog is it anyway that did not bark?

First, however, there is a need to clarify which human security framework is still valid, after the meat-grinding debate that the concept has solicited since it made its foray into international relations through the UNDP Human Development Report in 1994 by describing it as 'freedom from fear' and 'freedom from want'.[4]

Although there is no widely accepted universal definition of human security, there are two different conceptual precepts that institutions engaging with human security framework operationally follow. The first school insists on limiting it to a narrow definition focusing on 'freedom from fear'. Such a minimalist approach is adopted by Canada, the Report of the International Commission on Intervention and State Sovereignty *A Responsibility to Protect* (2001), and the EU doctrine for Human Security (2004). It concentrates on factors that perpetuate violence and direct threats to individuals' safety and to their physical integrity: armed conflict, genocide, public insecurity, and organised crime. A second approach follows a broad definition, based on 'freedom from want, freedom from fear and freedom from indignity' as an essential tool for understanding contemporary crises. The maximalist approach is adopted by the UNDP, by the Government of Japan, and by the Commission on Human Security (2003). It concentrates on threats, both direct and indirect, both objective and subjective, which come from traditional understandings of insecurity, but also from underdevelopment and human rights abuses.

In the academic world, in the meantime, gargantuan debates around human security have saved the *raison d'être* of critical writing.[5] For those from the realist and neo-realist tradition, human security lacks analytical rigour, is not an analytically useful paradigm but a political agenda and not a new or acceptable subject worthy of study. Proponents and critics of human security have, curiously, both tried to claim terrain within critical theory. Proponents argue that by shifting focus on the individual as the referent object of security, and broadening the range of threats to their security, the concept introduces a radical challenge to state-based security theories. Critics, however, lament that by not engaging enough with deconstructing the politics of securitisation, and by simply 'grafting on' the need to protect individuals to existing international practices,[6] proponents are missing opportunities at best to completely deconstruct or reformat existing security approaches.[7] They act in essence, say the critics, as collaborators of state-based international organisations and mostly Western powers in keeping the status quo in international relations and reinforcing dominant power relations and structures within the international system.[8] Given the dominant liberal paradigm under which international institutions currently operate, proponents of the human security approach are supposedly reinforcing hegemonic international liberalism. What is more, they have even created a justification for even deeper and more invasive forms of interpenetration, as a form of biopower.[9] And to think that scholars tend to see themselves as powerless in influencing, let alone shaping, global political agendas!

The crosstalk between the various communities seems to stem from whether human security *explains* or at least *identifies* problems or *proposes* solutions, whether it is a framework for description or prescription. The tendency to conflate these, by both proponents and critics, has arguably added to conceptual confusion. The underlying misunderstanding, however, is in the different types of human security approaches that proponents and critics use, mirroring closely the narrow and broad approaches of the operational world. What so far has been agreed is that there is no one human security approach in the singular.[10]

In his critical review of a book published by this author with Anuradha Chenoy in 2007,[11] for example, David Chandler claims that human security is a 'dog that did not bark'.[12] His main contention is that human security advocates did not directly engage with a contestation of power relations, leaving the approach open to co-option by political elites.[13] As a result, it is the 'universalist interest of power rather than cosmopolitical ethics of empowerment that drive the discourse of human security'.[14]

He posits three propositions as evidence that the human security 'dog didn't bark', or, in other words, not only fails to provide a radical alternative to interest-based and state-based security theories but is also co-opted by political elites. First, he claims that human security advocates exaggerate post-Cold War security threats and their independence as a ploy for action and attention, in other words, playing up to 'realist calculations of self-interest' instead of posing an 'ethical normative challenge'.[15] Second, Chandler claims that, by locating new security threats in the developing world, human security advocates ride the bandwagon with realists and liberals in constructing imaginary dangers of the 'other', the so-called failed states.[16] The human security framework is said to facilitate the 'problematisation of the non-Western state',[17] feed into the fears of Western elites which have 'lost their sense of purpose and social connection',[18] and further secure the rich consumerist West by containing the circulatory problems of world market inequalities and exclusion within the post-colonial South.[19] Third, Chandler claims that discussions around urgency facilitate short-term policymaking at the expense of strategic foreign policy visions.

I contend, however, that Chandler's own bias towards power, as it exists and currently operates, may be betraying his reading into what human security advocates are trying to do. A narrow read of the narrow approach to human security misses the point of complexity. On the first point, that human security advocates exaggerate threats, the question is why the mere recognition of menaces to welfare, dignity, and everyday life beyond bare life (survival) is automatically associated with the imperative that something must be done by political elites and existing institutions. Such recognition may bring realists to understand the question of interdependence and mutual vulnerability, but it does not diminish the need to focus on the actual existence of these threats and the fact that individuals and communities are the ones bearing the brunt of them. The act of recognition becomes associated with action only by those who believe in their own power. But power obviously operates within its own narrow contextual logic, and is locked into the world of those wanting to take monopoly over the act of securitisation for extending more of their limited but inflated perception of power. The proponents of the narrow approach, who argue for a workable definition restricted to threats under the realm of tangible violence,[20] measured, for instance, by the number of battle-related deaths,[21] are automatically accepting the efficacy and interest-based morality in disguise of those holding on to power. Recognition of larger factors that hamper emancipation is not, in Roland Paris's words, making a 'laundry list' of threats which 'effectively means nothing'.[22] Threats to human dignity need to be identified as such, even if they may or may not solicit action by political elites. Far from an instrumental ploy to solicit action, this recognition seems a logical position, if not an ethical imperative. Engaging with the politics of problem-solving and the powerlessness of power is a worthy, but *separate*, exercise.

The curiosity of Chandler's second otherwise noble criticism, that human security approaches objectify other spaces by relegating threats to the post-colonial South, is that the critic seems to have accepted the so-called power of the North in shaping discourses and action. The critique buys into the presumed validity of the Grand Bargain: that the North provides development assistance to an underdeveloped South, while the South assures traditional security in exchange, by refraining from developing weapons, by curbing conflicts, etc. In this constellation, human security seems to read as a good that Western countries seem to provide and countries of the South seem to lack. But human security threats are 'located' in the developing world only by those who believe in a liberal and non-liberal division of the world based on countries that can 'act' (hence project their power) in other spheres, and those that are mere recipients of such benevolence/malevolence. This too is a narrow conception of the liberal human security approaches which believe that problems of the developing world of the South can and should be solved through interventions, financial assistance, human rights sanctions, democratisation, marketisation etc., all precepts for making liberal. The broad approach would instead argue for the universal applicability of the subject, conceived with regard to people's daily concerns – no matter where they live geographically. Relational, objective, and subjective perceptions of insecurity persist as much, if differently, among inhabitants of Parisian suburbs as they do in Darfur.[23] The urban violence, job insecurities, health epidemics, privatisation of social delivery, militarisation of societies, etc. that plague industrialised societies of the North are as much human insecurities as the famine, wars, poverty, and genocides that characterise extreme situations of some countries, notably in the developing or post-colonial world. That is why the broader approaches may not agree with some academic attempts to propose a threshold of degree of severity of threats to human life,[24] which would then fail to recognise the insecurity felt by people in Western welfare societies.

Contextual analysis, instead of quantitative absolute measurements, better reflects the full meaning attributed to a life worth living. What people consider vital varies across individuals, societies and cultures.[25] The narrow approach to human security discourses, when insisting on a threshold approach that distinguishes urgent threats, such as those to survival, that require immediate action, may forego strategy for short-term action depending on the currency and will available for politicians to act, perpetuating conditions that allow Chandler's third criticism. Yet, for advocates of broad human security approaches, the mere recognition of structural violence[26] and threats to dignity require, *de facto*, strategic planning, root cause analysis, preventive action, etc. Dignity-related threats are certainly not to be dealt with through short-term problem-solving approaches. They invite critical assessment of structural causes. In this regard, Chandler is categorically mistaken in his read of the two chapters of our book that look at interventions: instead of basing ourselves on the benefits of R2P, as he claims,[27] we instead opted out for a practice of prior engagement by the international community, long before interventions are supposed to take place in front of *fait accompli* in the name of responsibility to protect, and in full recognition of the contributions of negative global politics and power asymmetries for the development of crisis in post-colonial and developing countries.

The misdiagnosis of the ability of the 'dog to bark' is perhaps because Chandler, like many Western critics, engages with a partial reading of human security that neglects dignity and emancipation, as opposed to bare life, as a principle to protect. Chandler's invitation for proponents, critiques and counter-critiques to answer why and how human security approaches become co-opted by power and why there is supposedly little contestation of it as the most important (or only) field of research worthy of query, and to base the realm of possibility within empirical research only, betrays a partial understanding of the narrow liberal interpretation of the idea of human security, the one that happens to be projected onto the international system as the model to follow. Such partiality stems from bias towards the comfortable materialist/empiricist trend in Anglo-Saxon academia to relegate non-material, ideational factors to intermediary roles. The critique, therefore, instead of recognising the full range of possibilities that the question of dignity and emancipation raise around values of the good life, and alternative spaces for their fulfilment, satisfies itself with what becomes a postmodern engagement with the power and politics of current academic and political practices. In a sense, it limits itself geographically to the vertical dialogue in the institutional North, by the North and for the North, relegating other spheres to oblivion at best and objectification at worst.

The problem is not that critical discourses serve the policy needs of the so-called powerful, but the underlying assumption of complicity that exists between the supposed power of Western political circles, engulfed in their perceptions of responsibility vis-à-vis others, and that of critical academics, assuming only the responsibility to debunk the power of the powerful. The problem is not only the misuse of such concepts by political elites, but the limited exercise of debunking proposed by Western critiques that only follow the scent of power. In this complicity, human security shifted from its original descriptive and universal concept, concerned with global justice and equity in the mid-1990s writings of Mahbub Ul Haq, who at the time was very much concerned about the North–South divide, to a prescriptive tool in international relations, 'for others' and 'by others' in foreign policy and aid policy. And critiques accept this shift uncritically.

towards genuine emancipation from dogs and suchlike

Ultimately, though, it does not matter whether the limited kinds of human security frameworks that have been understood and accepted through Western bias in political and academic circles have reinforced rather than challenged power relations. What matters is that engaging and using the broad lens of human security allows an identification of the range of referent objects of threats, the nature of a broad scope of menaces (whether to existence, welfare, or emancipation), and the variety of subjects for possible responses.

When pluralism is accepted, there is no need to wait for empirical measurements to demonstrate whether human security has served the needs of emancipation or the interests of power.[28] In this framework, idealism rules, normative speech acts rule, and so does prescription, because anything less would succumb to Western or particularly Anglo-American preference for empiricism (knowledge being inferred only from observable characteristics of reality) and for materialism (causation being sought only in material factors). Once in the realm of normative theorising that surrenders to the spirit of ideas and ideals, the confusion between description and prescription, empirical analysis and normative advocacy is not a detriment, but an imperative. Otherwise, succumbing to the limiting but standard practice of empirical analysis, from which theorising can take place (ascending from earth to heaven, the opposite of what Chandler accuses human security advocates of doing), not only limits the realm of the ethical and desirable, but also fails to take heed of the opening that Robert Cox provided when he unveiled the basic truism that 'all theory is for someone and for some purpose'.[29]

Ultimately, the (mis/ab)use of the human security approach by institutions and Western powerful states does not detract from the viability of the framework for recognising alternative perspectives. That is why the broad emancipatory, as opposed to narrow liberal, approaches to human security present more spaces for contention and pluralist voices.[30] In liberalism, critics contend, when 'rational consensus' and agreement are the only way in which peaceful relations can be created, disagreement and conflict are ultimately divisive and can lead to violence.[31] Emancipation, by contrast, requires accepting difference and deviation, alternative values, and negotiating new relationships. Regardless of whether or not it is successful in displacing *existing* power-based interests, the human security approach, in its broad emancipatory notion, is also an ethical framework because of its focus on the broad needs and aspirations of individuals *qua* persons. It extends the notion of 'safety' to a condition beyond mere existence (survival and bare life) to a life worth living: hence, welfare, well-being and dignity of human beings.[32] As such, it can be a useful framework to engage with the ethical concerns around the legitimisation of contemporary peacebuilding.

legitimacy, peacebuilding, and human security

The emancipatory approach to human security allows a new engagement with the dominance of liberal peace as the basis of contemporary practice of peacebuilding, in contrast with the tendency of liberal approaches to oppose dissent against their dominant views and impose, sometimes through force and sometimes in the name of cosmopolitan norms and ethics, their own narrow version of peace.[33] That such an emancipatory human security approach can be used for critically examining ideology and hegemony, and for opening up to pluralistic views, is interpreted by some as being 'superior' to the liberal view of human security, which is presumably bent on imposing a limited, Western-based assertion of hegemonic values and norms.[34]

This essay is ultimately interested not in the questions of efficiency of peacebuilding, based on whether there are enough resources, enough institutional capacity, enough coordination and coherence among international actors and between international and local actors,[35] but in concerns around the problematic of legitimacy: whether there is consensus, hence legitimacy, among different actors on the supremacy of the model of liberal peace. The question is how the broad emancipatory approach to human security could potentially contribute to the legitimisation of alternative peacebuilding approaches.

Theoretical critiques that engage with questions of legitimacy of peacebuilding come from a variety of different angles,[36] and whether liberal peacebuilding is the best modality for post-conflict reconstruction has been debated at length in literature. Peacebuilding in general, because it usually involves external actors, is deemed, for example, as illegitimate from a post-colonial perspective. Post-colonial critics contend that external actors violate internal norms and traditions in the name of peace and development. The fact that interventions and external statebuilding always take place by the North in the South reinforces the asymmetry in international relations.

For critical theorists, the uncritical imposition of Western models of governance based on political and economic liberalisation on non-Western war-torn societies has seen more or less consensus.[37] Critics, however, are split between those who ponder whether the liberal peace model is legitimate but should be reformed in terms of priorities and timing,[38] and those who reject the reformist notion, questioning the underlying assumptions that neoliberalism is better than welfare in post-conflict situations, for example,[39] or that liberal values are or should be shared by all.

For one set of critical theorists, the liberal model is right but conditions in post-conflict situations are not ripe. To them, liberal, assumed cosmopolitan, principles of universalism, egalitarianism, human rights, and democracy form the core of individual moral freedom which is shared by all. Rethinking the mechanisms through which liberal peace is delivered, such as sequencing, prioritisation or local participation, could in principle provide solutions for the failures.

Others, however, doubt the very essence of the model of liberal peace imposed in post-conflict, non-Western societies, questioning, for example, the benefits of neoliberal development models or competition-based democracies as reconstruction strategies after conflicts. Liberalisation is not necessarily peace-inducing, and may even exacerbate conflict by opening up fragile societies to competition. Democratisation, in principle, poses an alternative to violence, by encouraging the resolution of disputes through the political process. But in practice democratic institutions have often failed to resolve conflicts, and in some cases have

even aggravated them.[40] Such criticisms question the theoretical premises of liberal peacebuilding based on the efficiency of proven record.
The model is not bad because it is liberal, but because it is hegemonic,
imposed to reinforce international liberalism and used instrumentally.
The problem is not the assumption of values of liberalism, of liberty,
freedom and human rights, but how and why it is imposed.

A subset of critical voices are increasingly questioning the legitimacy
of liberal peacebuilding from the point of view of assumptions made
around the universality of norms and values by hegemonic liberalism.[41]
In this regard, they are closer to communitarian critics who argue that
reconstruction efforts destroy indigenous knowledge and sometimes
lives and that peacebuilding disregards local politics, informal institutions, values and cultures. Communitarianism concerns itself with
the fact that the universalisation of liberal values, such as democracy,
capitalism, and secularism, undermines the traditions and practices of
non-Western cultures. 'Because morality is seen as embedded in local
culture, this culture itself acquires a moral value to communitarians. It
cannot be normatively assessed on outside premises, and the imposition
of an international ideological agenda that does not take the local conditions of the host-country as its moral and political point of departure
violates the intrinsic moral value of the communities affected'.[42]

Legitimacy-oriented, as opposed to efficiency-oriented, queries into
peacebuilding ultimately have at their root an engagement with ethics.[43]
In the ethical framework, legitimacy does not matter from a functional,
utilitarian point of view to improve the efficiency of peacebuilding
operations by mustering up to a certain extent local consent for success,
such as through heart and mind operations conducted by the military,
for example. In such instances, the criticism that peacebuilding does
not treat the subjects of peacebuilding as aims in themselves but as
objects or means to the preservation of an international order where the
peacebuilders themselves are the primary subjects may be valid. Ethics-
based legitimacy centres instead on discussions over what is right and
wrong, with reference to norms and values rather than to instrumental
calculations for self-seeking purposes.[44]

From an ethical perspective, something is legitimate if it is considered
as such by unanimous opinion, or consensus around a common good,
presumably that of peace. In peacebuilding settings, the idea of shared
norms and values becomes more problematic. The question of ethics in
legitimacy is framed by understanding what this common goal is and
who should be defining it.[45] The ethical question is the tension that

exists between the answer to these processes: Why peace? How peace? Whose peace? and Which peace?

- *Why peace?* For instrumental, utilitarian reasons (like international security or the security of systems and regimes) or for the emancipation of individuals and communities?
- *How peace?* Through force and coercion, through imposition/instalment of liberal institutions of the state and the market, or through welfare, participation, inclusion, and plurality? Through changing local culture along universal norms or preserving diversity? Through adhering to international law, to domestic norms in the home country of the peacebuilding practitioners, or to the norms of the people affected by these actions?
- *Whose peace?* That of external actors engaged in peacebuilding or that of local beneficiaries?
- *Which peace?* One that responds to local people's understandings of culture or to the culture of hegemony, or for the security of institutions, power, etc.? An institutional peace or an emancipatory peace?

the convergence of legitimacy, emancipatory human security, and communitarianism

From the ethical point of view, the underlying dilemma for a legitimate model of peacebuilding is between a liberal peace that corresponds to internationally recognised norms and principles, and the communitarian peace, which may be embedded in potentially non-liberal cultures and traditions.[46] Communitarianism and pluralism seek to root ethics in local values, culture and traditions, while cosmopolitanism and solidarism emphasise universal norms as a precondition for cultural difference. The dilemma centres around the debate in moral and political theory between liberals and moral universalists, or communitarians and moral particularism. As Lidén puts it, followers of liberal schools of thought, such as Kantian, utilitarian and contractarian, derive 'legitimacy and universal applicability of substantive social, economic and political arrangements from abstract rational (liberal) principles.'[47] For communitarians, morality has to be defined in concrete and particular terms based on local experiences and local responses, sometimes in adoption, sometimes in rejection, and sometimes coming up with a hybrid model accepting in part cosmopolitan values.

The debate is similarly echoed in questions surrounding the legitimacy of the ultimate end state assumed in statebuilding exercises. The nation state is caught between legitimacy from the outside and from inside.[48] Legitimacy to adhere to international norms and be recognised as a 'stable democracy' worthy of its name by the international community of nations requires the state to play by certain criteria: open and liberal institutions, overruling of corruption, the monopoly over the use of force and neutralisation of deviant non-state actors, defending sovereignty, etc. But legitimacy is also and especially viewed from inside: whether the state can provide, protect and empower its own citizens, how it responds to them and upholds the social contract. Far from the Weberian concept of the state, such a foundation of legitimacy comes from the fulfilment of expectations and needs of the population. The state finds its meaning and moral legitimacy, its *raison d'etat,* only in its response to the people. Legitimacy is eroded when a state is highly dependent on foreign aid and answers to the needs of external institutions instead. It is also eroded when the state relinquishes its power to other actors, such as international organisations, NGOs, and private companies, out of weakness or force. In an ideal world, the two should coincide, but the challenge of statebuilding in post-conflict situations is precisely the tension that exists around the universal demands on a centralised, rule-creating state with modern institutions and perceptions from local, traditional and fragmented societies manned by populations with large expectations of the state to provide and protect. Combining what can be called universal legitimacy with local legitimacy is the challenge.

From an emancipatory human security point of view, the emphasis is on the perceptions of people within a state rather than the existence, power, or nature of the state itself. The legitimacy comes, therefore, not from the institutions of leadership, good governance, or social capital, but from perceptions of justice, of the capacity and results of delivery of public goods, and of the space provided for diversity of opinions, and from the degree of the population's satisfaction of basic and strategic needs. By human security definition, a weak state is one which cannot exercise its primary function of social protection and therefore fails in its duty to protect and care for its citizens.[49] A 'failed state', therefore, is one that is weak primarily in the eyes of its own citizens. Fragility is 'dangerous' not because it menaces international security or challenges

the institutions of liberal governance and markets, but because it threatens the survival, livelihood, and dignity of the population.

As to what type of peace peacebuilders are supposed to build, defenders
of the narrow, liberal human security position would argue for a kind of
cosmopolitan peace that is recognised externally. The broader emancipatory approach, with its focus on dignity taking meaning at the local level,
would be more inclined towards a communitarian position. Emancipation,
in this sense, is tied to local meaning and values for moral life, the life
worth living. Communitarianism converges with emancipatory human
security and the ethical critique of liberal peacebuilding as founded on
the premises of external liberal actors rather than on local premises.[50]

In this sense, understanding what peacebuilding means to the persons affected is crucial to ethical reasoning.[51] In post-conflict situations,
the ethical focus is based on what those who have suffered (individuals) perceive as morally valuable instead of the cost/benefit rationale
made by external peacebuilding. The perception of beneficiaries then
becomes the legitimising factor. Legitimacy, then, from the emancipatory human security point of view, depends on the consensus around
the validity of the models and their content used in peacebuilding by
local populations, as well as how populations perceive the success of
changes in improving people's everyday lives.

By putting its focus on individuals' perceptions of needs, aspirations,
and opportunities, as opposed to models, states, and institutions as referent objects and subjects of peace, emancipatory human security can
answer the legitimacy problem of peacebuilding. The more populations
and their perceptions of the common good are included, the more difficult it would be to simply impose particular ideals, values, or models
deemed universally applicable but proven problematic. But this does
not mean a mere adherence to the principles of participation, as utilitarianism would see it, to improve the success of reforms or to prevent
inertia at best and hostile response at worst. Perceptions count, not
because sentiments of mistrust against 'imposition or broken promises
can result and spark a local backlash that undermines the legitimacy of
reforms and may even result in violence'.[52] They count because perceptions respond directly to moral judgements by populations of affected
countries, whether they are liberal, illiberal or aliberal. The local gains
moral ownership by virtue of being the primary subject and object of
insecurity, in its broad form.

The emancipatory approach to human security, then, would answer
the ethical questions raised above with a focus on the individuals and

communities living the everyday perceptions. Peace becomes a synonym, not of an end of violence, but of a condition that allows for emancipation from insecurities in the broad sense:

- *Whose security/peace?* That of people whose security is at stake and who need to feel secure, as opposed to that of external actors in a peacebuilding situation, or of hegemony, power, and institutions (including the state, the international system, and lso models and ideas such as liberal democracy, market economy).
- *What type of security/peace?* A peace that responds to emancipation from insecurities in everyday life, be they basic threats to survival and bare life, functional threats that hamper livelihoods, or those concerned with dignity. The emancipatory, everyday peace which has local meaning, as opposed to the cosmopolitan, liberal, individualistic peace focused on the validity of institutions or the neorealist preoccupation with international stability.
- *Security/peace – how?* Through empowering people, transforming them into agents of change, protecting them, and providing welfare. A departure from viewing the liberal state as the precondition to peace and international security, by focusing not on the existence or otherwise of such a state, but on its responsibilities.

bringing it down to the local meaning: who are the people and what do they want?

Undoubtedly bringing down the query to the level of the local raises a host of new questions, not the least of which is who the people are and what they value. While discourses on local ownership have increasingly become part of the vocabulary of post-conflict peacebuilding, any query that turns to the actual content of the local becomes inevitably condemned for 'romanticising' the local or sentimentalising about local needs and aspirations.

From a purely utilitarian, functional position, the 'local voice' is supposed to matter, for it brings: (1) *legitimacy over the ownership* of the peace process, or as Richmond puts it: 'internal legitimisation of perspectives to justify the governance of the unruly other';[53] (2) *effectiveness* by inserting local know-how. As Tore Rose puts it, 'while the assumption is not that internal actors will always develop better policies than external actors, externally driven peacebuilding, much like externally driven development strategies, often generates resentment, inertia and resistance';[54] (3) *sustainability of reforms*. Critical studies have long argued that the reason that peacebuilding does not work is that local content, including culture and informal institutions, is not incorporated enough into the institutions to give them local meaning; and (4) *appeasement,* for they can spoil the external peace if they do not 'buy into' the reforms proposed by the peacebuilding agenda.

Richmond argues that 'romanticisation of the local' is a cultural project of the liberal international community and its agencies, organisations, institutions and NGOs. The 'romanticised local relegated to a zone of incivility in which new wars occur and corruption, lack of capacity, and "primitive" political, social, and cultural practices are present'.[55] Romanticisation of the local consists of four key types. The first is Orientalism, in which locals are seen as exotic and unknowable, thus justifying top-down blueprints and illiberal approaches rather than local engagement. The next approach lies in an assertion of a lack of capacity, in which locals are seen as unable to play a role because they are effectively helpless. This is again used to justify top-down illiberalism. The third is an assertion of local deviousness and incivility. In the fourth approach the local is seen to be a repository of indigenous capacities that internationals might co-opt. In these frameworks, difference is only acceptable when it operates within the liberal framework, and, instead of equitable engagement, the liberal culture of peacebuilding objectifies the local for its hegemonic aspirations. For Richmond, liberal peacebuilders seek to propagate a specific neoliberal practice and to defer responsibility for the welfare of the local. Engagement with culture, when it exists, is therefore little more than instrumental.[56]

Under such utilitarian engagement with the local, the question about how to reconcile the liberal consensus with a respect for the cultural integrity of the host countries becomes superfluous. What is more, the question misses the point from a communitarian ethical perspective. William Boyce, Michael Koros and Jennifer Hodgson, for example, pose the dilemma as '... how to promote liberal values in post-conflict situations, without taking advantage of the compromised position of those individuals and groups who are trying to rebuild their lives'.[57] The question, posed this way, tries to put the query on the powerlessness of internal actors, but it fails to consider why it is assumed that liberal values are coveted by local populations as morally superior to other value systems.

The emancipatory human security framework does not stop at local ownership and participation.[58] Instead of satisfying itself with the modality of improving peacebuilding (through participation and inclusion), it seeks to open up the more contentious question of compatibility of cultural and value systems. As such, it is not a neoliberal tool that emphasises individual rights and freedoms for the sake of cosmopolitan values. Instead, and unlike the narrow liberal approach, it seeks to bring down meaning to the local level, to the meaning of everyday life as perceived by communities. In this approach, assumptions are not made about the coveting of political liberty at the expense of rights to development, as is the case for the liberal view. The inquiry must essentially begin on the one hand with a scrutiny of the assumptions made about the value (in both senses of the word) of liberalism and its assumed universality, and hence supremacy, and engage on the other hand with the local meanings that values have in local contexts. In this sense, Richmond validly argues that the 'local' ultimately consists of not only actors and agencies such as government/nation, society, groups, communities, and individuals, but also values, culture, identity, and informal institutions in themselves.

Apart from anthropological studies, the literature on why culture matters in political sciences and development literature has been scant, essentialist and prescriptive in nature. Harrison and Huntington, for example, argue that the reason why some countries and ethnic/religious groups have done better than others, not just in economic terms but also with respect to consolidation of democratic institutions and social justice, is because some cultures are better than others at creating freedom, prosperity, and justice.[59] This line of thinking follows Alexis de Tocqueville, who concluded that it was the congeniality to democracy of the American culture that made the political system work there, and Max Weber, who explained the rise of capitalism as essentially a cultural phenomenon rooted in religion. From this scrutiny, however, neoconservative scholars have concluded that cultural values can, and indeed should, be modified in order to achieve democracy and development. Left in the hands of proponents of interventions, regime changes, aid conditionality, and neoliberal policies, such conclusions have taken queries around culture in the wrong direction.

Left in the hands of liberal peacebuilders, assumptions are made about the universality, compatibility, and moral value of liberalism for everyone. However, communitarianism would argue that domestic actors may have different understandings of what is valued as a good life. The local and the external actor may have different cultural and value systems which form their understandings of normative concepts, be they peace, well-being, etc., or ideologies such as liberalism. In the emancipatory approaches to human security, then, assumptions cannot be made about the legitimacy of liberal politics over socio-economic well being as a priori. That is why the broad approach puts equal emphasis on development rights as much as political freedoms. What is prioritised comes directly from local experiences. When assumptions are made that principles of individualism, egalitarianism, and universalism are accepted and valued everywhere, when declaring that the urge for individual freedom as it is expressed in human rights is inherent in all people, liberal peacebuilders more easily objectify and 'orientalise' the other over whom they can rule and for whom they can bring political liberty from their supposed evil regimes.

The entry of culture into the peacebuilding literature should ultimately not limit itself to whether local values and culture could be factors that hamper or support peacebuilding efforts. Instead, intellectual integrity would require the scrutiny to begin with how the (often externally imposed) liberal peacebuilding is a culture in itself – with its own set of assumptions, prejudices, perceived 'universal good', and value judgements about its universality. Otherwise, assuming that liberal culture is universal, as propagated by liberal peacebuilding, would be subjugating the entire notion of culture as intersubjectivity restricted to the domain of dominant ideology,[60] a marked departure from Gramsci's understanding of culture as a complex ensemble of materialist, symbolic, and interpretative practices.[61] If culture is to be studied as the currency of hegemonic practices (such as externally imposed liberal peacebuilding), scholars must also avoid falling into the trap of neglecting the transformed and transformative nature of both hegemony (the external project) and the local setting (internal actors, processes, institutions). The local culture does not simply respond as a counter-hegemonic resistance, native, local, and particularistic, in reaction to the Liberal Peace for example, but expresses its 'otherness' through mere existence/persistence, on the one hand, and transformation and hybridity on the other. The Liberal Peace project may also not be as static, homogenised and hegemonic as it seems: it too is shaped and consolidated through the dynamic of interaction.

conclusion

The challenge for contemporary peacebuilding practices raises the question as to whether problems lie in the way that externally led liberal peacebuilding is imposed from the outside, sometimes in a coercive manner and often in the absence of negotiations between external and internal actors in the guise of adherence to universal common goods such as peace, or in value-based peacebuilding which induces a clash of culture and values between liberalism and other values/ideologies/cultures of local populations (such as collectivism, socialism, religious ethics, a variety of traditionalism, etc.).

A broad emancipatory approach to human security, by suggesting the articulation of ideas, culture, and perceptions in peacebuilding as opposed to the dominance of institutional, state-centric frameworks, contributes to the legitimisation of peacebuilding in theory and practice. Such an approach would combine ethical queries, social constructivist opening to ideas, norms, knowledge, and culture,[62] and the communitarian imperative to ground and evaluate meanings in local experiences. Local meaning, in both its material and perceptive senses, becomes more important than power or cosmopolitan notions of common good as propagated by realist or liberal approaches to peace. Rather than seeking a common political framework that the agents of peacebuilding should follow, the politics of peacebuilding should spring organically from the agency of the people involved. This should prevent peacebuilding from becoming an instrument for the imposition of Western hegemony.[63]

Although a shift towards a more transformative and emancipatory approach is needed, even proponents of the emancipatory view of human security may agree that the liberal approach is dominant and used as a rhetorical and practical tool in current practices of peacebuilding. Yet, an ethical idea can never travel too far from its original source, especially for instrumental reasons. There is hope for a return.

notes

1. D. Chandler, 'The Responsibility to Protect? Imposing the Liberal Peace', *International Peacekeeping*, Vol. 11, No. 1, 2004, pp. 59–81.
2. From abstract of K. Lidén, 'Peace, self-governance and international engagement: A postcolonial ethic of pragmatic peacebuilding', Paper presented at the annual meeting of the International Studies Association, *Exploring The Past, Anticipating The Future*, New York, 15 February 2009.
3. K. Lidén, *Whose Peace? Which Peace? On the Political Architecture of Liberal Peacebuilding*, MA thesis in Peace and Conflict Studies, University of Oslo, Norway, 2006, p. 102.
4. See a summary of the variety of definitions used, critiques and counter-critiques in Chapters 1 and 2 of S. Tadjbakhsh and A. Chenoy, *Human Security: Concepts and Implications*, London: Routledge, 2007.
5. On 20 March 2009, Google Scholar gives 22,700 hits when Human Security is entered with brackets, although all may not be critical writing *per se.*

6. P. Kerr, W.T. Tow and M. Hanson, 'The utility of human security agenda for policy-makers', *Asian Journal of Political Sciences*, Vol. 11, No. 2, 2003, pp. 89–114.

7. J.H. Peterson, 'Creating political spaces to promote human security: A solution to the failings of the liberal peacebuilding?', paper presented at the annual meeting of the International Studies Association, *Exploring The Past, Anticipating The Future*, New York , USA, 15 February 2009.

8. Ibid.

9. M. Duffield, *Development, Security and Unending War: Governing the World of Peoples*, Cambridge University Press, 2007; O. Richmond, *The Transformation of Peace*, New York: Palgrave Macmillan, 2005.

10. See parts of the debate in O. Taylor, 'The Critique that Doesn't Bite: A Response to David Chandler's "Human Security: The Dog that Didn't Bark"', *Security Dialogue*, Vol. 39, No. 4, 2008, pp. 445–53; D. Chandler, 'Human security II: waiting for the tail to wag the dog – A rejoinder to Ambrosetti, Owen and Wibben', *Security Dialogue*, Vol. 39, No. 4, 2008a, pp. 463–9.

11. Tadjbakhsh and Chenoy, *Human Security*.

12. D. Chandler, 'Human Security: The Dog that Didn't Bark', *Security Dialogue*, Vol. 38, No. 4, 2008b, pp. 427–38.

13. Ibid, p. 431.

14. Chandler, 'Human Security II', p. 468.

15. Chandler, 'Human Security' p. 431.

16. Ibid, p. 435.

17. Ibid.

18. Chandler, , 'Human Security II' p. 468.

19. Duffield, *Development, Security*.

20. T. Owen, 'Human Security – Conflict, Critique and Consensus: Colloquium Remarks and a Proposal for a Threshold-Based Definition', *Security Dialogue*, Vol. 35, No. 3, 2004, pp. 373–87; G. King and C. Murray, 'Rethinking Human Security', *Political Science Quarterly*, Vol. 116, No. 4, Winter 2001–2002.

21. See for example the Human Security Report Project produced by the Simon Fraser University.

22. R. Paris, 'Human Security: Paradigm Shift or Hot Air?', *International Security*, Vol. 26, No. 2, 1992, p. 91.

23. For Mahbub Ul Haq, writing in the UNDP 1994 *Human Development Report*, 'The threats to their security may differ – hunger and disease in poor nations and drugs and crime in rich nations – but these threats are real and growing.'

24. Owen, 'Human Security, p. 374; T. Owen, 'Measuring Human Security: Overcoming the Paradox', *Human Security Bulletin*, Vol. 2, No. 3, 2003.

25. Commission on Human Security, *Human Security Now*, 2003, p. 4.

26. J. Galtung, 'Violence, Peace and Peace Research', *Journal of Peace Research*, Vol. 6, No. 3, 1969, pp. 167–91.

27. Chandler, 'Human Security', p. 431.

28. D. Ambrosetti, 'Human Security as Political Resource: A Response to David Chandler's "Human Security: The Dog that Didn't Bark"', *Security Dialogue*, Vol. 39, No. 4, 2008, pp. 439–44.

29. R.W. Cox, 'Social Forces, States and World Orders: Beyond International Relations Theory', *Millennium: Journal of International Relations*, Vol. 10, No. 2, 1981, p. 128.
30. O. Richmond, 'Emancipatory Forms of Human Security and Liberal Peacebuilding', *International Journal*, Vol. 62, No. 3, pp. 459–78.
31. C. Mouffe, *The Return of the Political*, New York: Verso, 1993, pp. 139–40.
32. Tadjbakhsh and Chenoy, *Human Security*, p. 1.
33. Peterson, 'Creating Political Spaces'.
34. Ibid.
35. See E.B. Eide A.T. Kaspersen, R. Kent and K. von Hippel, *Report on Integrated Missions: Practical Perspectives and Recommendations*. Independent study for the expanded UN ECHA core group, May 2005; A.J. Bellamy and P. Williams, 'Peace Operations and Global Order', *International Peacekeeping*, Vol. 10, No. 4, 2004; R. Paris, *At War's End: Building Peace After Civil Conflict*, Cambridge: Cambridge University Press, 2004, where Paris focuses on building a liberal democratic state and the role of institutions, rather than on the question of the legitimacy of the model.
36. See a full discussion in Lidén, *Whose Peace? Which Peace?*; also see J. Brassett and D. Bulley, 'Ethics in World Politics: Cosmopolitanism and Beyond?', *International Politics*, Vol. 44, 2007, pp. 1–18.
37. Among the many works see Paris, *At War's End*; Richmond, *The Transformation of Peace*; A.J. Bellamy and P. Williams, *Peace Operations and Global Order*, London: Routledge, 2004; see also M. Duffield, *Global Governance and the New Wars: The Merging of Development and Security*, London: Zed Books, 2001.
38. Paris, *At War's End*.
39. M. Pugh, 'The political economy of peacebuilding: a critical theory perspective', *International Journal of Peace Studies*, Vol. 10, No. 2, 2005; M. Pugh, N. Cooper and M. Turner (eds), *Whose Peace? Critical Perspectives on the Political Economy of Peacebuilding*, London: Palgrave Macmillan, 2009; S. Tadjbakhsh, 'Economic Woes of Liberal Peace', *ConflictINFOCUS* Issue No. 22, July 2008.
40. R. Luckham, A.M. Goetz and M. Kaldor, 'Democratic institutions and democratic politics', in S. Bastian and R. Luckham (eds) *Can Democracy be Designed?*, London: Zed Press, 2003; F. Stewart and M. O'Sullivan, 'Democracy, conflict, and development – three cases', in G. Ranis, S.-C. Hu and Y.-P. Chu. (eds) *The Political Economy of Comparative Development into the 21st Century*, Cheltenham: Edward Elgar, 1999.
41. Peterson, 'Creating Political Spaces'. See also S. Tadjbakhsh, H. Kubo and D. Asta, proceedings of the conference 'Liberal Peace: Value-Based, External Models and Local Alternatives in Peacebuilding' organized by the CERI Program for Peace and Human Security at Sciences Po, Paris, 16–17 June 2008, accessed at http://www.peacecenter.sciences-po.fr/pdf/conf_report_160608.pdf on 20 March 2009.
42. Lidén, *Whose Peace? Which Peace?*, pp. 47–8.
43. A new project of the Peace Research Institute of Oslo (PRIO) project on *Liberal Peace and the Ethics of Peacebuilding: Towards the Integration of Ethics in Peacebuilding* focuses on various theoretical and ethical inquiries, including legitimacy, in liberal peacebuilding.

44. Lidén, *Whose Peace? Which Peace?*, pp. 47–8.
45. K. Lidén, 'Introduction on the Ethics of Liberal Peacebuilding', presented at The Ethics of Liberal Peacebuilding and the Cyprus peace process, PRIO, Nicosia, Cyprus, 12 November 2008.
46. Ibid.
47. Lidén, *Whose Peace? Which Peace?*, p. 47.
48. An argument pursued, albeit in a different format, in terms of the clash between tribalism and globalism in the context of terrorism and its threats to democracy in B. Barker, *Jihad vs. McWorld: How Globalism and Tribalism Are Reshaping the World*, New York: Ballantine Books, 1996.
49. S. Tadjbakhsh, 'State failure through the human security lens', in J.M. Chataigner and H. Magro (eds) *Etats et Sociétés Fragiles*, Paris: Karthala, 2007.
50. Lidén, *Whose Peace? Which Peace?*
51. K. Lidén, 'What is the Ethics of Peacebuilding?' Lecture prepared for the Kick-off Meeting of the PRIO Liberal Peace and the Ethics of Peacebuilding project, 18 January 2007.
52. A.K. Talentino, 'Perceptions of Peacebuilding: The Dynamic of Imposer and Imposed Upon', *International Studies Perspective*, Vol. 8, No. 2, 2007, 152–71.
53. O. Richmond, 'The Romanticisation of the Local: Welfare, Culture and Peacebuilding', *International Spectator*, Vol. 44, No. 1, 2009.
54. T. Rose, 'Reflections on Peacebuilding and the United Nations Development Assistance Framework', *Journal of Peacebuilding and Development*, Vol. 2, No. 3, pp. 64–77.
55. Richmond, 'The Romanticisation of the Local'.
56. Ibid.
57. W. Boyce, M. Koros and J. Hodgson, 'Community Based Rehabilitation: A Strategy for Peace-Building', *BMC International Health and Human Rights*, Vol. 2, No. 6, 2002, p. 5. Accessed at http://www.pubmedcentral.nih.gov/picrender.fcgi?artid=139991&blobtype=pdf 20 March 2009.
58. J. Chopra and T. Hohe, 'Participatory intervention', *Global Governance*, Vol. 10, No. 3, 2004, pp. 289–305; V. Jabri, *War and the Transformation of Global Politics*, London: Palgrave Macmillan, 2007; O. Richmond, *Peace in International Relations*, London: Palgrave Macmillan, 2008.
59. L.E. Harrison and S. Huntington (eds), *Culture Matters: How Values Shape Human Progress*, New York: Basic Books, 2001.
60. R. Cox, *Production, Power and World Order: Social Forces in the Making of History*, New York: Columbia University Press, 1987.
61. A. Gramsci, *Prison Notebooks*, Vol. 1, ed. by J.A. Buttigieg, trans. by J.A. Buttigieg and A. Callari, New York: Columbia University Press, 1992; A. Gramsci, *Prison Notebooks*, Vol. 2, ed. and trans. by J.A. Buttigieg, New York: Columbia University Press, 1996.
62. E. Conteh-Morgan, 'Peacebuilding and Human Security: A Constructivist Perspective', *International Journal of Peace Studies*, Vol. 10, No. 1, 2005, pp. 9–86.
63. Mouffe, The Return of the Political, p. 126.

7
gender and peacebuilding

tarja väyrynen

introduction

Peacebuilding has become one of the mantras of conflict resolution theory and practice. It is often treated uncritically, and its disciplinary and institutional roots are neglected. An early academic usage of the word 'peacebuilding' can be found in the Scandinavian tradition of Peace Research, where the structural theory of violence held a prominent position for decades. At the institutional level, on the other hand, the term gained prominence in the 1990s, when UN Secretary-General Boutros Boutros-Ghali launched 'An Agenda for Peace' (1992) that defined the UN agenda for conflict resolution and peacebuilding. Very recently, a corpus of critical literature has emerged that criticises the non-reflexive use of the term 'peacebuilding'. Despite the emerging critical research agenda on the topic, the connection between gender and peacebuilding remains a little-studied subject.

Critical and reflexive writing on peacebuilding seeks to demonstrate the underlying ideology of peacebuilding. The very core of the critique is the critical reading of modernity and its instrumental reason that leads to problem-solving and social engineering in conflict management. A trend in the reflexive study of peacebuilding coincides with post-structuralist feminist scholarship. Feminist scholars argue that knowledge claims based on instrumental rationality and the coupling of war with men and women with peace – deeply embedded in modernity – need to be deconstructed in order to gain a better understanding of peacebuilding and its gendered dynamics.

The aim of this article is to point out the problems that emerge from essentialist and standpoint feminist understandings of peacebuilding.

It is argued that, by essentialising the notion of women and by uncritically relying on the concept of 'women's experience', feminist thinking
constitutes women as a homogeneous group best suited for civilian roles
in peacebuilding. Furthermore, 'local women' are constituted as Others
who need protection from the first world (masculine) actors. In order to
establish the argument, the article first examines the traditional understanding of peacebuilding and its recent critique. It then moves to the
feminist thinking on gender and peacebuilding, points out its problems
and proposes an alternative research agenda that critically examines
the interconnections between gender, peace and war.

mainstream views on post-conflict peacebuilding

Johan Galtung argues that peacebuilding, unlike conflict management and
resolution strategies, is based on an associative approach that aims at the
abolition of structural violence (oppression and domination), not just direct violence (warfare). According to Galtung, peacebuilding differs fundamentally from dissociative strategies of dealing with conflict because they
do not deal with the root, namely structural, causes of conflict. Transition
from violent conflict to post-conflict peacebuilding and nation-building is
seen to form a continuum where new institutions and structures replace
old ones. According to Galtungian thinking, in order for sustainable and
positive peace to emerge, structural transformation is needed.[1]

A group of peacebuilding theories suggests not only that structures
matter, but that there is an overlap of structural and procedural elements in peacebuilding. For example, Paul Lederach argues that conflict
transformation and peacebuilding include four interdependent elements: individual (emotional, perceptual and spiritual), relational (communication and mutual understanding), structural (underlying causes
of conflict), and cultural.[2] Not all scholars accept the Galtungian structural theory of violence that underpins his definition of peacebuilding.
In less structurally oriented definitions peacebuilding is associated, for
example, with 'laying down a foundation for social harmony supported
by measures which foster cooperation among adversarial communities'.[3] This entails a wide range of activities, from demobilisation of
paramilitary groups, to refugee resettlement, to economic reconstruction, to community-building. It is notable that none of these theories
discuss the gendered dynamics of peacebuilding.

In more practice-oriented definitions, peacebuilding is often
defined as consisting of three main objectives. It means creating and

strengthening democratic political institutions, encouraging sustainable, poverty-reducing development, and fostering collaborative, non-violent social relations. Roland Paris, on the other hand, relates peacebuilding to external interventions that aim at creating the domestic conditions for durable peace within countries just emerging from civil wars. He speaks about international peacebuilding missions that seek to transform war-shattered states into liberal market democracies. At the core of the modern peacebuilding missions there is, according to Paris, the ideology of liberalisation that implies democratisation and marketisation of post-conflict societies.[4]

The United Nations' discourse on peacebuilding emerged in the 1990s when Secretary-General Boutros Boutros-Ghali launched 'An Agenda for Peace', in which post-conflict peacebuilding is defined as 'action to identify and support structures which will tend to strengthen and solidify peace in order to avoid a relapse into conflict'.[5] Thus, the Galtungian structural orientation to peacebuilding forms a basis for the UN approach in the 1990s. In the document, peacebuilding is thought to aim ultimately at economic and political development, but this is not yet seen to require economic liberalisation.[6] States are, rather, encouraged to seek functionalist solutions to their economic and social problems, including joint agricultural projects and joint resource management that would spill over to such areas as cultural exchange and youth and educational projects.

The most recent institutionalisation of the UN peacebuilding work can be found in its Peacebuilding Commission, which aims at helping to build effective public institutions within constitutional frameworks and the rule of law for post-conflict societies. In the inaugural session of the Commission, UN Secretary-General Kofi Annan states that the problem of these societies is often the problem of legitimacy, since the citizens do not trust state institutions. He claims that when exclusionary social, economic, and political structures are left untouched, perpetuated, or inadvertently strengthened in societies emerging from conflict it causes a legitimacy crisis. The Peacebuilding Commission is expected to support the development of peacebuilding strategies that tackle the above-mentioned structural dimensions of peace.[7]

Liberalisation efforts have become an important component of new generation UN peacebuilding. The World Bank and International Monetary Fund are an integral part of the peacebuilding missions. These international fiscal institutions advocate the generation of economic growth and market democracy in war-torn societies. Their practices of cutting back on taxes and government social spending, eliminating tariffs and other barriers to free trade, reducing regulations of labour markets, financial markets, and the environment, and focusing macro-economic policies on controlling inflation rather than stimulating the growth of jobs are based on a neoliberal theory of economics. In short, they produce liberal modes of governance in parts of the world where international peace and security are seen to be threatened.[8]

peacebuilding as a form of modern governance

The scholarly and more practice-oriented peacebuilding discourses have been a target of criticism. As indicated earlier, peacebuilding has gained wide acceptance among peace scholars and practitioners, and the critical, reflexive literature is in a minority. Few writers and practitioners have scrutinised the assumptions that underlie peacebuilding. This emerging literature is vital from the perspective of gender and peacebuilding too, because it shares the critique of modernity with post-structuralist feminist thinking on gender, peace, and war.

Critical social theory argues that modern societies are dominated by instrumental rationality. Instrumental rationality is characterised by technical control and the efficiency and success of goal-directed actors. Jürgen Habermas writes about instrumental rationality, and claims that it marks the self-understanding of the modern era. It 'carries with it connotations of successful self-maintenance made possible by informed disposition over, and intelligent adaptation to, conditions of a contingent environment'.[9] This type of rationality aims at instrumental mastery of the world. Furthermore, instrumental reason encounters ready-made subjects and systems without questioning their foundations.

The critique of modern instrumental rationality has also been targeted at the ideology of modern peacebuilding. According to the criticism, instrumental rationality expresses itself in attempts to improve the utility of peacebuilding operations. Instrumental approaches to peacebuilding and their emphasis on improving peacebuilding utility are seen to leave significant normative assumptions unexplored. These include the assumptions that international peace and security represent moral good, that violent conflict represents a breakdown of normal social relations, and that good post-conflict governance is equivalent to Western-style statehood, democratisation, neoliberal economics, and the existence of civil society.[10] In non-reflexive thinking, peacebuilding is considered to be a positive and universally acceptable form of action, and therefore the problems emerging during peacebuilding processes can be treated as technical problems and with expert knowledge. Problems are tackled using instrumental reason without questioning the ideology of peacebuilding itself.

Peacebuilding is, thus, criticised for being based mainly on problem-solving theory that treats problems as pre-given and ready-made, gives preference to hegemonic and dominant theories and practices, and seldom seeks alternatives. As pointed out earlier, problem-solving approaches tend to offer largely technical solutions to problems that are ultimately normative dilemmas.[11] Problem-solving theory aims at maintaining the existing structures and world order.[12] Paris argues that peacebuilding interventions in post-conflict societies are nothing less than enormous experiments in social engineering that reproduce hegemonic forms of power in global politics.[13]

What kind of peace, then, is created by modern peacebuilding missions? The critical theorising on peacebuilding has tried to map out the constitutives of the liberal peace that is created through peacebuilding missions. Peace is seen to imply the restoration of 'law and order' and return to 'normal conditions'. The opposite, war and violence, is conceptualised in terms of societal pathology that plagues societies. Critical theorising argues that the liberal hegemony underlying modern peacebuilding produces and preserves the contemporary world, state-centric, order without aiming at alternative orders. The order it seeks to preserve is the Westphalian state-centric order characterised by a territorial form of governance, fixed boundaries and population. Oliver Richmond sees this type of peace as peace-as-governance, where the ideology of democratic peace guides the institutionalisation of social, political, and economic order. Peace-as-governance often takes the form of external governance, as in Kosovo, where the region is largely dependent on outside visions of peace. Liberal peace dismisses the social and human consequences of the process of constructing peace.[14]

gender and peacebuilding: three feminist views

There are three alternatives that feminist scholarship on peace and war has offered for the quest in reflexive thinking and for more self-sustaining peace postulated by critical theorising. Essentialist feminism argues that including women in peacebuilding makes a difference, because women are more peaceful than men. Standpoint feminism urges us to look at women's experiences of war and peace in order for more sustainable peace to emerge from the processes of peacebuilding. Post-structuralist feminism, on the other hand, calls for the understanding of the process of the construction of masculinities and femininities that takes place during the formative moment of peacebuilding.

At the very core of essentialist feminist thinking there is a view that women are peace-oriented while men are war-oriented. The difference between women and men is drawn either from biology or from social-isation theory. In its most simplified form, the essentialist thinking argues that women are born to be more peaceful, caring and consensus-seeking than men. This biologically founded argument has been replaced by socialisation theory, which sees women as being socialised in 'relational thinking', i.e. women become more capable than men of think-ing of relationships and the social consequences of actions.[15] For Sara Ruddick, women are also capable of 'maternal thinking', which naturally arises out of their caring relationship to the world. Maternal thinking includes care, protection of all forms of life, and peace education and, therefore, it also leads easily and naturally to political peace work.[16]

The implication of relational and maternal thinking is that there is an organic relationship between feminism and pacifism. Women's way of thinking and relating to the world makes them nurture understanding, build consensus, prioritise open communication and dialogue, and aim at equal distribution of resources.[17] These qualities can be seen to be the prerequisites of peacebuilding. The essentialist argument claims that women's participation in peacebuilding efforts would lead to a more self-sustainable peace that means eliminating the structural causes of violence and the emergence of a just society. All Lederach's criteria for successful peacebuilding will be met, according to the essentialist point of view, since structural, individual (including emotions and percep-tions), and relational elements of peace will be tackled by including women in peacebuilding processes.

Although essentialist thinking seeks to offer an alternative view of peacebuilding, it remains within the framework of modern thinking. It is based on immutable differences between men and women derived from permanent biological or social factors. A form of determinism is embedded in essentialism. All men are seen to be masculine in the sense that they are less relational, less caring, and more war-oriented than women. The 'true' nature of women includes caring, relational capacities, and maternal thinking, and these are thought to be univer-sal. From women's 'true' nature peaceful action is seen to follow nat-urally. Jean Bekthe Elshtain criticises all simplified views that couple femininity with peace and masculinity with war. She argues that this type of thinking postulates women as 'pacifist Others' and that, in turn, reinforces the image of militaristic masculinity. Thinking that is based on simple binary oppositions leads to strict and unchangeable social roles.[18] Ultimately, the logic underlying essentialist views contributes to the 'feminisation of peace' and the 'masculinisation of war' that justifies taken-for-granted patterns of behaviour and fields of action.[19]

Standpoint feminism tries to answer this critique by emphasising the notion of experience. The starting point for standpoint thinking is the observation that war affects women differently from men. It is noted that women are not only the victims of war; they also take a variety of roles in war, including combatant roles. Furthermore, it examines within the standpoint frame how the borderline between masculinity and femininity is blurred in warfare. Women are not 'Beautiful Souls' who are pure and innocent when it comes to matters of war and men 'Just Warriors' who protect their womenfolk and their nation. These roles become blurred in war: there are militaristic women, and men take a variety of caring and relational roles in wartime.[20]

An example of standpoint thinking on peacebuilding can be found in Elisabeth Rehn's and Ellen Johnson Sirleaf's report 'Women, War, and Peace', commissioned by the United Nation's Development Fund for Women (UNIFEM) in 2002. Rehn and Sirleaf base the report largely on first-hand data and the testimonies of women who have experienced war. The style of writing in the report supports the primacy of experience when discussing women, peace, and war; namely, it relies heavily on observation, witnessing, and personal narration. The authors seek to demonstrate that the 'experiences [of women] are not country-specific, but global'.[21] They do not argue that women are more peaceful than men, but emphasise the different roles assigned to women and men in peace and war. Neither do they consider women to be mere victims of war. Rather, they stress the multiple roles women actively take in wartime. The report notes that the main focus should be on gender roles (i.e. socially constructed roles that are assigned to men and women when making war and peace) rather than biologically determined sex and the impact of war on men and women.[22]

According to Rehn and Sirleaf, the problem from the perspective of peacebuilding is that, although women often organise locally for peace, their activities are not included at the official level. In other words, women have difficulties in getting to the official negotiation tables. Societal and political structures may prevent women from participating fully in peace processes, women's safety is particularly vulnerable in post-conflict situations, women do not have funds to organise themselves efficiently, and women have less access than men to political decision-makers. Furthermore, according to the report, women's needs are seldom addressed during peace negotiations and the phase of post-conflict reconstruction. The report concludes that women's voices are not fully integrated into peacebuilding processes.[23]

If 'An Agenda for Peace' and later the Peacebuilding Commission established the institutional frameworks for mainstream thinking on peacebuilding, the Security Council Resolution 1325 on Women, Peace and Security (2000), and some months prior to this the Windhoek Declaration and the Namibia Plan of Action on Mainstreaming a Gender Perspective in Multidimensional Peace Support Operations (2000), are the institutional expressions of essentialist and standpoint feminisms and their ways of seeing the relationship between gender and peacebuilding. In the UN discourse on gender and peacebuilding as it is expressed in these documents, the starting point is that women have not had equal access and participation in peace support operations and peacebuilding, although 'civilians, particularly women and children, account for the vast majority of those adversely affected by armed conflict'.[24] Women have been denied their full role in multidimensional peace support operations both nationally and internationally, and the 'gender dimension in peace processes has not been adequately addressed'.[25]

It is argued that women do have an important role in the prevention and resolution of conflicts. Therefore, gender equality must permeate these processes. According to the documents, there is an urgent need to mainstream a gender perspective more generally into peacebuilding. Resolution 1325 urges participants to adopt a gender perspective when negotiating and implementing peace agreements. Measures that support local women's peace initiatives should be taken, and women should be involved in all of the implementation mechanisms of the peace agreements.

The UN discourse adopts the strategy of mainstreaming when encouraging gender equality. The ways of mainstreaming gender into the UN peace activities vary from specialised training to increased representation of women in conflict management and resolution. In my earlier work, I have demonstrated how the UN discourse on gender and peacebuilding constitutes peacebuilding as a form of governance and how it follows modern problem-solving logic. The aim of the UN discourse is not to think anew or critically at the structures that have rendered gender silent in the first place. The aim is rather to add the gender element

to the existing state-centred and patriarchal practices of conflict resolution and peacebuilding. By demanding the inclusion of women in
peacebuilding, the discourse assumes that women's participation in the
missions would create a new kind of knowledge that is needed in the
governance of post-Westphalian conflicts and in the creation of liberal
peace. The quest for adding women to the existing structures is, therefore, based ultimately on an objectivist epistemology that characterises
modernity and its instrumental reason.[26]

emerging post-structuralist research questions on gender and peacebuilding

In order to overcome the problems arising from essentialist and standpoint feminism in relation to peacebuilding, it is important to ask how
we can address the issue of gender and peacebuilding in investigating social and global power and the interconnection between gender,
peace, and war. Such a research question aims at avoiding the problems of modern epistemologies and instrumental reason. It challenges
the taken-for-granted knowledge on gender and peacebuilding, offers
a critical stance towards the existing logic of peacebuilding, and provides foundations for alternative practices. It shifts the focus from the
unquestioning acceptance of presumably ungendered peacebuilding
to the gendered micropractices of power that take place during peacebuilding processes.

A starting point for contemplating these interconnections can be
found by closely studying the processes of nation-building and the
symbolic functions women have in these processes. Post-conflict peacebuilding is an intensive moment in nation-building. Erik Ringmar calls
this intensive moment a 'formative moment', when new narratives are
being told and submitted to the public forum, and new demands for recognition presented. In formative moments meanings are contested and
fought over with the help of all sorts of rhetoric.[27] Furthermore, formative moments of peacebuilding are gendered moments. Kavita Daiya's
observation that 'women's bodies bear often the symbolic burden of
community building – national or otherwise'[28] rightly emphasises the
corporeal, symbolic, and gendered elements of constructing the nation
state. For example, women's honour is seen to work as a foundation
for the morality of the whole community. Similarly, women's role in
rearing children and acting as ideal mothers constitutes the essence
of the modern (imagined) nation state.[29] The use of women's bodies

intensifies during times of violent political conflict and during peace-building when the community has to be renarrated and reconstructed. However, the state – or any other agency capable of providing hege-monic narratives – tries to discipline and normalise the experiences of violent political conflicts and traumas embedded in violence.

The intimate connection between gender and nation-building after violent conflict is highlighted in Inger Skjelsbaeks's comparative study on Yugoslavia, El Salvador and Vietnam. Through these three case studies she examines the roles women take and are assigned in peace-building and national reconstruction. For women, the wars in Croatia and Bosnia were characterised by mass rape, torture and sexual vio-lence. The everyday lives of women changed radically. These societies had not experienced war for decades and all of sudden apparently irrational violence became prevalent. In addition to violence against women, women lost husbands, sons, fathers and other family members. There was a massive absence of men in many communities. According to women, their vulnerability increased. Ethnicity became a mode of being and ethnic identities became vital points of reference. Skjelsbaek's interviews demonstrate how women and women's bodies came to sym-bolise ethnic groups and their boundaries as well as violence against ethnicities. A form of victimised and ethnicised femininity emerged in post-conflict Croatia and Bosnia.

The cases of El Salvador and Vietnam differ from the case of the former Yugoslavia. Women's political mobilisation has a long history in Latin America. Women have organised strikes and demonstrations and joined political parties. According to a rough estimate, 30% of the com-batants of the FMLN (Farabundi Martí National Liberation Front) in El Salvador were women. The conflict did not appear sudden, but rather it was seen to be an inevitable consequence of the gap between rich and poor. Both women and men participated in the conflict, and, in com-parison with Croatia and Bosnia, women were active participants who also took combatant roles. A new unity of women and men emerged in El Salvador due to the conflict experience. The ideology of liberation, including women's liberation, came to characterise the conflict and post-conflict reconstruction. Although machismo prevails, according to the study, more equal opportunities exist for women in post-conflict El Salvador than before the conflict. The female agency is not that of a victim, but of an active member of post-conflict society.[30]

The war in Vietnam resulted in a massive mobilisation of women's par-ticipation in warfare. Skjelsbaek's material shows how women's fighting in this case did not change the gender roles in the post-conflict society, and thus it represents a form of conservative feminism where there is a strong loyalty to the family, the husband, and the state.[31] Skjelsbaek's study is important, because it opens up new research agendas. It offers a contextualised reading of a variety of gendered roles in post-conflict societies and gendered micropractices that shape peacebuilding after violent political conflict. Furthermore, it can be expanded to cover the issue of agency, namely, the research framework allows us to ask what the forms of gendered agency are that constitute the foundations for post-conflict societies.

It might be also worth examining how international peacebuilding missions contribute to the disciplinary and normalising gender practices that are at the core of nation-building. International missions contribute to the practices by producing certain types of femininities and masculinities. For example, in the UN discourse on gender and peace-building women are seen largely as victims of war, and therefore in need of protection. In peace support missions women are invited to take civilian roles and posts rather than combatant or peace-enforcement roles. The special need to protect women's security in conflict zones is noted, for example, by calling 'all parties to armed conflict to take special measures to protect women and girls from gender-based violence, particularly rape and other forms of sexual abuse'.[32] Resolution 1325 also urges the 'Secretary-General to seek to expand the role and contribution of women in United Nations field-based operations, and especially among military observers, civilian police, human rights and humanitarian personnel'.[33]

In these discursive strategies of the UN documents and the gender practices that derive from them, women are coupled with conflict resolution and peace. Their civilian roles in promoting conflict resolution and peace are emphasised and, thereby, the binary pairs of women/ victim/protected/peace and men/aggressor/protector/war are normalised. Through the discursive strategies, women are assigned a particular type of agency and identity: the dominant form of femininity is that of civilian, protected, and passive, whereas the hegemonic masculinity reconfirms the roles of combatant, protector and active actor. Research on gender and peacebuilding needs, therefore, offers a critical reading of these taken-for-granted discourses and practices.

What about the 'local women'? Does the above-mentioned gendered peacebuilding logic touch them? The UN discourse, as well as the mainstream writing on gender and peacebuilding, insists on including local

women in peacebuilding.[34] The inclusion of local women is seen to offer
a voice for marginalised groups that are seen to be vital for peacebuilding and, therefore, a key to self-sustaining peace. Yet, who are these
'local women' who should be included and whose voice is more authentic than the voice of women representing 'international community'?
Gyatri Spivak's question 'can the subaltern speak?' and Judith Butler's
question 'what can we hear?' can open up a perspective to examine the
dilemma of 'local women', who seem to occupy a large part of mainstream discourse on gender and peacebuilding.

In her essay 'Can the Subaltern Speak?' Spivak examines the possibility of speaking of and for the subaltern women as well as the question
of representation. For Spivak, subaltern refers to a colonial subject who is
cast to the margins and whom the Western epistemic violence constitutes
as Other. She argues that the 'ideological construction of gender keeps
the male dominant' and that 'in the context of colonial production, the
subaltern has no history and cannot speak, the subaltern as female is
even more deeply in the shadow'.[35] It is exactly these subaltern subjects
Western peacebuilding interventions tries to deal with when it insists
on including the local women. Spivak warns us strongly against solutions that assume a monolithic collectivity of oppressed who can speak
for themselves in the way we in the West understand speech and who
can be included in political dialogue. She considers it to be a dangerous
path to take, where the first world intellectual (or policymaker, activist,
etc.) masquerades as an absent non-representer who lets the oppressed
speak for themselves. For Spivak, the colonised subaltern subject is irre-
trievably heterogeneous and cannot speak. The standpoint feminism
outlined above offers the solutions Spivak criticises. It suggests the inclusion of local women's experiences, considers concrete experiences to be
something authentic, and relies on uncritical acceptance of the ideology
underlying the formation of colonial subjects it seeks to include.[36]

Following Spivak's inquiry, it is important to examine how the
Western peacebuilding interventions participate in the production
of colonial subaltern subjects. It is worth examining whether peacebuilding is a form of imperialist subject-constitution that renders the
subaltern women as mute as ever. Spivak's essay also gives rise to a
research problematic that asks how the protection of women becomes
a signifier of a good society and how the imperialist project of establishing good societies is marked by the espousal of woman as an object
of protection from her own kind ('white men seeking to save brown
women from brown men', as Spivak calls it).

As important as Spivak's question is Butler's question, 'what can we hear?' Butler examines the means by which some lives become grief-worthy while others are perceived as not meriting grief in current world politics. According to her, our human existence is ultimately dependent, vulnerable, and sociable. Despite some shared foundations of being human, some names, images, and narratives are erased from public representation of war and violence as if they were less human while others are celebrated, mourned, and grieved. The ultimate question for Butler is what counts as a liveable life and a grievable death. Her critique coincides with Paris's critique when she argues that the first world elite is unable to think about the grounds and causes of current conflicts. Our frame of understanding of violence precludes certain types of questions and historical inquiries, as well as functioning as a justification of action and inaction. Our capacity to hear is limited unless we question this very frame of understanding.[37]

Butler also cautions us against assuming a single coherent womanhood. She refers to Chandra Mohanty, who maintains that the Western views of the oppression of the 'third world women' falsely produce a monolithic conception of who they are and what they want. For example, single-minded condemnation of the use of the veil or burkha constitutes the first world as a site of authentic feminist agency and limits the very possibilities of agency that are relevant for third world women.[38] Similarly, peacebuilding interventions with their insistence on engaging 'local women' run the risk of assuming a monolithic set of women whose needs and security the mission should take care of, whose voice should be integrated into the process, and whose (feminist) agency should follow the Western models.

In order to combine Spivak's and Butler's inquiries, one needs to ask what we can hear if and when the subaltern speaks. In terms of gender and peacebuilding, it is vital to examine our own constitution in relation to the 'local and subaltern women' as Other who should be included in peacebuilding processes. Can we really hear them? Are we constituting them as a part of our own fantasy of being members of a good and moral international community? We are keen to discuss the suffering of others as well as our responsibility to protect, but can we really hear the voices we so eagerly want to protect in our peacebuilding missions? More general, it is equally important to study our frame of understanding of conflicts and the justifications for peacebuilding interventions they offer as well as the frames of understanding we hold on gendered agency in post-conflict situations.

conclusions

The mainstream understanding of peacebuilding sees it to be ungendered universal practice that leads to just social, political, and economic arrangements in post-conflict societies. The critical literature, however, urges us to examine the underlying logic of peacebuilding. It argues that peacebuilding is largely founded on a modern problem-solving attitude that employs instrumental reason and relies on expert knowledge. It also argues that peacebuilding is a form of governance where Western models of society, politics, and economy are imposed on war-torn societies at different locations in the world. Yet, even this critical literature on peacebuilding leaves the interconnections between gender and peacebuilding unexamined.

Feminist scholarship has offered three ways of looking at the interconnections between peace, war, and gender. Essentialist and standpoint feminism leave the modern foundations of peacebuilding unexamined and thereby run the risk of repeating and reproducing mainstream thinking and practices. By arguing that women are more peaceful or by insisting on including women in peacebuilding missions, this thinking constitutes women as a homogeneous group and couples women with peace. Women's agency becomes limited and remains within the binary oppositions established by modernity.

An alternative research agenda can be established by looking at women's role in nation-building. Women's bodies bear the symbolic burden of nation-building, and the use of female bodies intensifies in post-conflict societies, where the nation has to be renarrated. International peacebuilding missions contribute to the construction of masculine and feminine agencies in post-conflict societies by importing, supporting, and creating a limited range of agency available. An unquestioning acceptance of the hegemonic forms of agency leaves a wide variety of gendered agency untapped, and thereby limits the potential for self-sustaining peace.

Similarly, it is important to examine the constitution of 'local women' and the function this discursive constellation has in modern peacebuilding missions. It is argued in this chapter that 'local women' serve the construction of Western agency as protector, human, and ethically active. The wish to hear the voices of 'local women' is distinctly problematic and opens up a critical research agenda that seeks to examine the role of colonial and subaltern subjects in the construction of first world agency. Our capacity to hear these voices is limited and, therefore, a single-minded attempt to include local women in peacebuilding should be scrutinised with care by taking into the account both the global macropractices and local micropractices of power that shape the formation of subjectivity.

Institutional discourses, and practices embedded in them, change slowly, and thereby peacebuilding practices that do not reproduce gendered victimhood by making local subjects complicit in their essentialisation, marginalisation or bio-governance are in the making. In general, policymakers and researchers should conduct themselves in their work so that they are sensitive to dangers of projecting and being complicit in liberal hegemony. Seen from the perspective of 'local women', 'speaking', and 'hearing' that is opened up by Spivak's and Butler's inquiry, peacebuilding should engage with the local in the form of translation,[39] not in the form of integration. It should be accepted that 'international' policymakers, peacebuilding practitioners and local subaltern subjects play different language games (assuming that the subaltern can speak). They often have disparate interpretations of the post-conflict situation as well as gendered agency, which means that there is no mutual definition of peacebuilding and its gendered dynamics either. The games tend to become enclosed and schematic. Local gender focus groups can act as 'gender translators' between peacebuilding missions and locals. The local gender focus group can convey meaning from one game to the other, and by doing this interprets the situation for the parties. The goal of the 'gender translation group' is to act as a translator who translates meaning from one language game to another and to allow the parties at the same time to examine the porous borders between 'us' and 'them', 'international' and local', as well as 'feminine' and masculine'.

notes

1. J. Galtung, *Peace, War and Defense, Essays in Peace Research*, Vol II, Copenhagen: Christian Ejlers' Forlag a-s, 1976, pp. 286–304.
2. J. Lederach, *Building Peace: Sustainable Reconciliation in Divided Societies*, Washington, DC: United States Institute of Peace Press, 1997.
3. H.W. Jeong, 'Peacebuilding: Conceptual and Policy Issues', in Ho-Won Jeong (ed.) *Approaches to Peacebuilding*, Houndsmill, Basingstoke, New York: Palgrave, 2002, p. 5.
4. R. Paris, *At War's End: Building Peace after Civil Conflict*, New York: Cambridge University Press, 2004, pp. 1–5.
5. B. Boutros-Ghali, *An Agenda for Peace: Preventive Diplomacy, Peacemaking and Peace-Keeping*, A/47/277-S/24111, 17 June 1992, para. 21.
6. Ibid., para. 56.

7. K. Annan, 'Opening First Session of Peacebuilding Commission', http://www.un.org/News/Press/docs/2006/sgsm10533.doc.htm, accessed 30 May 2008.
8. For a critical study of international monetary institutions and peacebuilding see P. Williams, 'Peace Operations and the International Financial Institutions: Insights from Rwanda and Sierra Leone', in A. Bellamy and P. Williams (eds) *Peace Operations and Global Order*, London and New York: Routledge, 2005, pp. 103–23.
9. J. Habermas, *The Theory of Communicative Action, Reason and the Rationalization of Society*, Vol I, Oxford: Polity Press, 1991, p. 10.
10. For a summary see A. Bellamy, 'The 'Next Stage' in Peace Operations Theory?', in A. Bellamy and P. Williams (eds) *Peace Operations and Global Order*, p. 19. See also M. Duffield, *Global Governance and New Wars: The Merging of Development and Security*, London: Zed Books, 2001;. R. Paris, 'Mission Civilisatrice', *Review of International Studies*, vol. 28, no. 4, 2002, pp. 637–56.
11. A. Bellamy, *Peace Operations and Global Order*, pp. 18–19.
12. R. Cox, 'Social Forces, States and World Orders', *Millennium: Journal of International Studies*, vol. 10, no. 2, 1981, pp. 126–55.
13. R. Paris, *At War's End*, p. 4.
14. O. Richmond, 'UN Peacebuilding Operations and the Dilemma of the Peacebuilding Consensus', in A. Bellamy and P. Williams (eds), *Peace Operations and Global Order*, p. 92; O. Richmond, 'The Dilemmas of Subcontracting Liberal Peace', in O. Richmond and H. Carey (eds) *Subcontracting Peace, The Challenges of NGO Peacebuilding*, Aldershot: Ashgate, 2005, pp. 28–31. See also R. Paris, *At War's End*, pp. 5–8.
15. B. Brock-Utne, 'Feminism, Peace and Peace Education, *Bulletin of Peace Proposals*, Vol. 15, no. 2, 1984, p. 149.
16. S. Ruddick, *Maternal Thinking: Towards a Politics of Peace*, London: The Women's Press, 1989.
17. B. Reardon, *Women and Peace, Feminist Visions of Global Security*, New York: State University of New York Press, 1993.
18. J.B. Elshtain, *Women and War*, Brighton: Harvester Press, 1987, p. 4.
19. J. Goldstein, *War and Gender*, Cambridge: Cambridge University Press, 2001, p. 331; A. Tickner, 'Why Women Can't Run the World', *International Studies Review*, Vol. 1, no. 3, 1991, pp. 1–11.
20. Elshtain, *Women and War*.
21. E. Rehn and E.J. Sirleaf, *Women, War, Peace: The Independent Experts' Assessment on the Impact of Armed Conflict on Women and Women's Role in Peace-Building*, UNIFEM, 2002, p. viii.
22. Ibid., p. 2.
23. Ibid., pp. 75–87.
24. Security Council Resolution 1325 on Women, Peace and Security (2000), S/RES/1325, 31 October 2000.
25. The Windhoek Declaration and the Namibia Plan of Action on Mainstreaming a Gender Perspective in Multidimensional Peace Support Operations (2000), A/55/38, S/2000/693, 31 May 2000.
26. T. Väyrynen, 'Gender and UN Peace Operations: The Confines of Modernity', in A. Bellamy and P. Williams (eds) *Peace Operations and Global Order*, pp. 125–42.

27. E. Ringmar, *Identity, Interest and Action. A Cultural Explanation of Sweden's Intervention in the Thirty Years War*, Cambridge: Cambridge University Press, 1996, pp. 83–7.
28. K. Daya, '"Honourable Resolutions": Gendered Violence, Ethnicity and the Nation', *Alternatives*, Vol. 27, no. 2, 2002, p. 235.
29. See N. Yuval-Davis, *Gender and Nation*, London: Sage, 1997.
30. I. Skjelsbaek, 'Is femininity Inherently Peaceful? The Construction of Femininity in the War', in I. Skjelsbaek and D. Smith (eds) *Gender, Peace & Conflict*, London: Sage, 2001, pp. 47–67.
31. Ibid., pp. 58–61.
32. S/RES/1325.
33. Ibid.
34. See, for example, ibid.
35. G. Spivak, 'Can the Subaltern Speak?', in C. Nelson and L. Grossberg (eds) *Marxism and the Interpretation*, Basingstoke: Macmillan, 1988, p. 287.
36. Ibid., pp. 271–313.
37. J. Butler, *Precarious Life, The Powers of Mourning and Violence*, London and New York: Verso, 2004.
38. Ibid., p. 47.
39. On Spivak and translation see J. Maggio, '"Can the Subaltern Be Heard?": Political Theory, Translation, Representation, and Gyatri Chakravorty Spivak', *Alternatives*, Vol. 32, no. 4, 2007, pp. 419–44. For a Gadamerian-inspired view on conflict resolution and translation see Tarja Väyrynen, 'A Shared Understanding: Gadamer and International Conflict Resolution', *Journal of Peace Research*, vol. 42, no. 3, 2005, pp. 349–57.

8

liberal peace, liberal imperialism: a Gramscian critique

ian taylor

In the current epoch of an increasingly integrated – 'globalised' – world, the global capitalist order is undergoing a profound reconfiguration and transformation. Neoliberalism has, over the past three decades, emerged as the hegemonic political and economic project, with a transnational elite class increasingly important in the attempted reordering of the global political economy. This global elite is comprised of transnational executives and their affiliates; globalising state bureaucrats; capitalist-inspired politicians and professionals; and consumerist elites.[1] Transnational class formation has spread from the North to the South, linking an emergent fraction of Southern-based elites with their Northern counterparts at the core of a concentric circle of social, economic, and political power.[2]

Those inhabiting this core increasingly possess a considerable degree of class consciousness and view their interests as being outwardly linked to the wider transnational sphere.[3] As Williams notes regarding the United Kingdom's elite, 'Britain, increasingly, has an elite whose attitudes are "offshore" and disconnected from the business of being British'.[4] They 'have largely lost any sense of Britain as a national project and are largely disengaged from it'. It is the transnational, rather than the purely domestic milieu, that such elites now look towards, entailing a 'subordination of domestic economies to the perceived exigencies of a global economy. States willy nilly [have now] become more effectively accountable to a nebeleuse personified as the global economy'.[5]

Elites, both in the North and in the South, actively construct the domestic and external political, bureaucratic, and constitutional frameworks that permit the operation and consolidation of the global capitalist order. Global linkages found within the International Financial Institutions (IFIs), United Nations (UN) system and other elite meeting points 'tighten the transnational networks that link policy-making from country to country'.[6] This overall process is conducted by a 'powerful phalanx of social forces ... arrayed ... behind the agenda of intensified market-led globalisation'.[7] Crucially:

> The ideas of the ruling class are in every epoch the ruling ideas, i.e. the class which is the ruling material force of society, is at the same time its ruling intellectual force ... The ruling ideas are nothing more than the ideal expression of the dominant material relationships, the dominant material relationships grasped as ideas; hence of the relationships which make the one class the ruling one, therefore, the ideas of its dominance.[8]

Obviously, the assertion of neoliberalism as the hegemonic discourse has not just occurred: 'it is a social system that has [had] to struggle to create and reproduce its hegemonic order globally, and to do this large numbers of local, national, international and global organisations [were] established' to promote the new organising norms.[9] The role of such bodies (organic intellectuals in Gramscian parlance) is to advance 'a uniform conception of the world on an increasingly transnational society'.[10] The agents of the increasingly integrated global economy are a new transnational elite, who currently occupy the positions of power where decisions vis-à-vis global governance are made. The power of this transnational elite class has been dramatically strengthened as global integration has accelerated in the contemporary period. Indeed, there has been a wholesale shift in the balance of forces between classes within each national state, with the outwardly linked transnational elite in each state enjoying unprecedented power. It is accurate to assert that, at present, it is to this transnational elite and their locally situated representatives with their specific interests (frequently posturing as the 'national interest') that the administrations of nation states respond to, with all the wider contradictions that this spawns.

This transnational elite has sought to bring into being the environment most advantageous to the unimpeded operation of capitalism on a global scale. In pushing this vision, they have been engaged in a veritable 'transnational agenda' which seeks to establish specific economic and political ingredients right across the globe.[11] Indeed, this 'requires a stable global system of multiple states to maintain the kind of order and predictability that capitalism – more than any other social form – needs'.[12] Since 'capitalism encompasses the entire globe, its architects require a universal vision, a picture of a globally conceived society, to join classes in different countries... [in order] to institutionalise global capital accumulation by setting general rules of behaviour and disseminating a developmentalist ideology to facilitate the process'.[13] This 'universal vision' is neoliberalism. I suggest that an exceptional opportunity for such processes to be unleashed in the developing world can be found in post-conflict spaces.

Neoliberalism aims to 'expand the scope for capital accumulation through privatisation, and replac[e] collective welfare by entrepreneurship and individualism as the legitimating values of liberal democracy'.[14] In short, 'neo-liberalism has become the predominant ideology legitimating the privatisation of the state-controlled economy and the substitution of the market for the social provision of basic welfare'.[15] This has profound implications for state governments in the South, where:

> The more dependent countries become dependant on the goodwill of investors, the more ruthless must governments be in favouring the already privileged minority who have sizeable assets. Their interests are always the same: low inflation, stable external value of their currency, and minimum taxation of their investment income... [Yet the] financial short-circuit between different countries forces them into a competition to lower taxes, to reduce public expenditure, and to renounce the aim of social equality.[16]

Post-conflict spaces are of interest in this process as it is here that we might observe – via the imposition of the liberal peace project – the imperialist nature of neoliberalism at its most naked. Here, imperialism 'is defined not by the export of capital, but by the export of *capitalism*: the social relations of production that define it and institutions devised to promote and sustain them. Second, as the central role of the UN suggests, it is led not by states but by international organisations committed to capitalism *as a global project*'.[17]

shock and awe: post-conflict spaces and liberal imperialism

It is quite apparent that current peacebuilding efforts are grounded in the advancement of the liberal peace, reflecting the hegemony of liberal values that reigns in global politics. As Pugh remarks, 'The liberal peace has promoted transformation through macro-economic stability, reduction of the role of the state, the squeezing of collective and public space, a quest for private affluence, and a reliance on privatisation and on exports and foreign investment to stimulate economic growth'.[18]

As I have noted elsewhere,[19] all intergovernmental organisations, as well as OECD states and other donor agencies, more or less accept as common-sense the self-evident virtuosity and truth of the liberal peace project. This hegemony is reinforced and amplified by the fact that the liberal peace is the foundation upon which the International Financial Institutions (IFIs) operate. This normative agenda is equally dominant within the UN system, with a broad consensus on what peacebuilding is, as well as what constitutes the fundamentals of any sustainable peace. All of this fosters an intellectual climate at the policy level in which the basic assumptions of the liberal peace go unproblematised, indeed, are hegemonic.

This is extremely important given that, historically, the UN has been the international body charged with and practised in dealing with post-conflict rebuilding. Until the end of the Cold War, the ability of capitalist elites to use their structural power (via states and/or the UN) to advance a reordering of the global political economy along neoliberal lines was limited. However, post-1989 the unbridled hubris associated with the End of History has led to a far more aggressive position in advancing neoliberal values in spaces where they have been seen as foreign and unwelcome.[20] Regarding the United Nations, 'systematic institutional reform pursued by Kofi Annan after he became UN Secretary-General at the beginning of 1997 ... effected a shift from security through peace-keeping (Annan's previous remit) to security through capitalist hegemony, and succeeded by 2005 in transforming the UN into the lead agency for the global dissemination of capitalist values and imperatives'.[21] In the post-Cold War era, it has been possible for the advocates of neoliberalism even to reframe the very underpinning of what constitutes peace and post-conflict re-building (the 'liberal peace') in quite explicit directions. The UN's understanding of what peace and security is underscores this point:

In the post-Cold War era, peace and security can no longer be defined simply in terms of military might or the balance of terror. The world has changed. Lasting peace requires more than intervention of Blue Helmets on the ground. Effective peace-building demands a broader notion of human security ... In today's world, the private sector is the dominant engine of growth; the principal creator of value and wealth; the source of the largest financial, technological, and managerial resources. If the private sector does not deliver economic and economic

opportunity – equitably and sustainably – around the world, then
peace will remain fragile and social justice a distant dream.[22]

The whole point of the liberal peace is to construct the institutional
framework that will allow the private sector to 'deliver' and work its
magic in post-conflict spaces.

Global restructuring along neoliberal lines is, then, 'an explicit project at the heart of recent World Bank-IMF activity, aimed at the "completion of the world market" and the global imposition of the social
relations and disciplines central to capitalist reproduction. This is
pursued through the promotion of a "sound" macro-economic framework, along with structural reforms – national and global liberalisation, and privatisation – and associated regulatory innovations'.[23] The
liberal peace project cannot be divorced from such structural realities.
However, they are hidden by various discourses, which seek to mask
their own partialities and present as wholly commonsensical the components contained within peacebuilding projects. 'The effect is to present a set of policies infused with the disciplines and class logic of
capitalism as if they were inspired by disinterested benevolence. The
purposive action of human agents bent upon establishing the hegemony of a particular social form of organisation of production is presented as if it were the natural outcome of abstract forces too powerful
for humanity to resist.'[24]

The current agenda advanced by the main actors in any multilateral
peacebuilding initiative is premised on the notion that liberalisation –
that is, liberal democracy and the free market – will facilitate positive
peace (see below). In this formulation, external actors are granted a pivotal role in this wholesale attempt at societal transformation. Boutros
Boutros-Ghali indeed asserted that 'UN [peace] operations now may
involve nothing less than the reconstruction of an entire society and
state.'[25] Thus, in the current times, 'peacebuilding is in effect an enormous experiment in social engineering – an experiment that involves
transplanting Western models of social, political, and economic organisation into war-shattered states in order to control civil conflict: in other
words, pacification through political and economic liberalisation'.[26]

However, it must be stated that the sort of policies being advanced by
the global elites cannot readily be implemented on willing populations
in normal circumstances where popular resistance might disturb the
process. Two twin processes in post-conflict spaces are often required:
first, a deeply traumatised population and secondly, a form of politics

that insulates elites and dissipates resistance. I shall first discuss the former element before moving onto how 'democratic politics' in post-conflict spaces is the actual antithesis to self-realisation by societies emerging from war.

Naomi Klein's *The Shock Doctrine* makes a compelling argument that societies staggering out of traumatic experiences, be they natural disasters, wars, or major economic crises, are more prone to the implementation of neoliberalism.[27] Klein asserts that, because of the intrinsic social contradictions inherent within neoliberal policies, political turmoil and a disoriented citizenry that springs from processes such as war are coercive pretexts for implementing neoliberal reforms, the type of which most of the affected public would in general reject under 'normal' conditions. Klein demonstrates that neoliberalism has continually been applied in the absence of the compliance of the governed by taking advantage of a range of types of national 'shock therapy'. In post-conflict spaces, it might be argued that what is presented to the IFIs and UN system is a tabula rasa upon which the promoters of neoliberal capitalism believe their programmes can be implemented. Klein uses the examples of Chile under Pinochet, Argentina under the military juntas, post-apartheid South Africa, post-Solidarity Poland, Russia under Yeltsin, 'reconstruction' of Iraq post-US invasion, Sri Lanka after the tsunami, and New Orleans post-Katrina.

I suggest that we might also regard post-conflict spaces as fitting with Klein's thesis and as offering the proponents of neoliberalism a great opportunity to reconstitute society along approved lines. What we see in such countries is a de-patterning of societies caused by war, and this facilitates attempts to remake them from scratch. After all, Milton Friedman wrote in his preface to *Capitalism and Freedom* that 'Only a crisis – actual or perceived – produces real change... our basic function [is] to develop alternatives to existing policies, to keep them alive and available until the politically impossible becomes politically inevitable'.[28] As part of the attempt to remake societies in crisis along neoliberal lines, as per Klein's thesis, there is a need to insulate the elites imposing such programmes from popular resistance. This is where 'democracy' comes in.

the inconsistencies of the liberal peace and the ostensible 'answer': polyarchy

As is evident to all observers, neoliberalism stimulates deep contradictions, for a project based on liberalisation and privatisation and representing the dislocating effects of globalisation has little chance of becoming hegemonic. Indeed, a hegemonic project in the Gramscian sense needs a 'politics of support' as well as a 'politics of power', however mighty transnational capital and its class allies may be.[29] This consensual element in the neoliberalist project is 'polyarchy'. Polyarchy, as per Robert Dahl,[30] is the form of elitist democratic government first implemented in the United States and now advanced as the only 'practical' form of democratic governance. Indeed, Dahl does not argue that polyarchy is the ideal system, rather that it is the only 'realistic' model workable in modern capitalist societies. Of note here is Wood's critique of the American model of democracy, whose 'main purpose – and we should have no illusions about this – was not to strengthen democratic citizenship but, on the contrary, to preserve elite rule in the face of an unavoidable mass politics and popular sovereignty. The objective [at the time of American Independence] was to depoliticise the citizenry and turn democracy into rule by propertied classes over a passive citizen body, and also to confine democracy to a limited, formal sphere'.[31] Importantly, mainstream academic literature initially 'understood [democracy] in terms of reformist ideals, and the science of politics was viewed as a servant of those ideals. Against the backdrop of the Cold War [however] democracy came to be defined in procedural terms, and the science of politics was reconfigured as an ideal-free science appropriate for an ideal-free democracy'.[32]

Polyarchy aims to soothe the social and political pressures that are created by the transnational elite-based neoliberal order and create a state of 'low intensity democracy'.[33] Such an analysis echoes the assertion that 'the construction of a corporate-dominant order ... require[s] the neutralisation of social forces precipitating persistent and effective questioning of the established order'.[34] By its very nature, polyarchy dissipates the energies of those marginalised by the ongoing order into parliamentary procedures that in themselves are acted out by political fractions whose power and prestige are dependent on the polyarchical model. In short, polyarchy expresses 'not the fulfilment of democratic aspirations, but their deflection, containment, and limitation'.[35] Furthermore, polyarchy is based on a separation of the economic from the political, ignoring the reality that 'the so-called economic realm is inseparable from its political and ideological effects'.[36] And polyarchy ignores and obscures the fundamental fact that 'political power, properly so called, is merely the organised power of one class for oppressing another'.[37]

However, abstract conceptualisations of what constitutes 'democracy' are currently dominant – certainly within the literature on 'democratisation' in the South.[38] Yet, as Wood points out, 'Both capital and labour can have democratic rights in the political sphere without completely transforming the relations between them in a separate economic sphere; and much of human life is determined in the economic sphere, outside the reach of democratic accountability.'[39]

In contrast to conceptualisations of popular democracy,[40] theorisations of this kind consciously divorce 'economics' from 'politics', for, in this abstraction, the former responds only to the logic of 'the market', whilst the latter is restricted in its role of permitting that logic to proceed without obstruction.[41] By doing so, the polyarchical process limits itself to the 'purely political', consciously excluding any qualitative degree of socio-economic redistribution. This limited understanding of democracy, however, serves to provide protection and confidence to the established elites in countries undergoing transition from conflict. However, as Hobsbawm asserts:

> We are at present engaged in what purports to be a planned reordering of the world by the powerful states... The rhetoric surrounding this crusade implies that the system is applicable in a standardised (Western) form, that it can succeed everywhere, that it can remedy today's transnational dilemmas, and that it can bring peace rather than sow disorder. It cannot.[42]

civil society: winning hearts and minds

Critical analysis of why the sort of policies promoted by the liberal peace – and not others – are readily adopted in post-conflict spaces is generally lacking. Most post-conflict transitions today obviously replicate Western-style parliamentary democracy and not alternative models. It is as if the Westminster model were the only option. Clearly it is not, but why it became viewed as such is an intriguing part of any discussion of the imperialist logic behind the liberal peace.

According to Cammack, 'the leaders of the [neoliberal] project, in their efforts to embed and legitimize it, have worked as much through NGOs and "civil society" as through governments.'[43] 'Specialists, operating out of policy groups, foundations, think-tanks, university research institutes, and government agencies, bring long-range political considerations and issues concerning social stability to the attention of the dominant classes and their inner core in the corporate community.'[44] By doing so, such activities constitute the vital mediating link between agency and structure in the development of policy and the building of hegemony. By acting within the realm of civil society, these activities are engaging the territory where hegemony is contested and (eventually) achieved, for 'in times of crisis the institutions of civil society remain as the primary site of the cohesion of new political forces that may create a new order'.[45]

This understanding tends to undermine the naïve belief that civil society is in itself a 'good thing', which mechanically enhances democracy and accountability. Instead, such a scenario can actually strengthen the position of the economic/political elites whilst providing a useful façade of legitimacy in the form of 'civil society'. As one analyst wrote on the tactic by the West of strengthening civil society in Africa, 'Assisting [elements within civil society] will lead to better economic decisions as well as strengthen governance: letting a hundred flowers bloom on the capitalist side of the civil society will help establish the rule and norms enabling societies to run themselves along the lines required by capital'.[46]

Of course, in many developing world contexts, the bourgeois-like 'autonomous agentic individual' described by the dominant paradigm, the essential prerequisite in the making of civil society itself, is absent.[47] This is where donor funding of 'acceptable' organisations and/or the outright manufacture of such bodies is crucial as a means of informing and directing public debate towards neoliberal solutions to postconflict crises. Such bodies can also serve as helpful mediating agents (organic intellectuals) for establishing a hegemonic project.

This is integral both to the closure of debate during post-conflict transitions and to shaping the discourse around which post-war policies are formulated. The importance of this aspect of civil society is 'that the consensus forged by these experts over the identification [and solution] of problems shapes the way that interests of states are defined'.[48] By acting thus, and in the absence of any strong alternative, business-aligned and donor-friendly elements within civil society – invariably donor-funded – contribute to the marginalisation of any contrary impulses during the transition.

This is essential for the elite classes, as many of the conflicts that the advocates of liberal peace are seeking to resolve were predicated at the grass-roots level around a form of resistance to, and revulsion from, the anodyne form of democracy previously practised and abused by incumbent elites. In the absence of even nominal democracy, very often revolts were based on a deep antipathy towards the extant social order. Installing a popular democracy would in either situation pose a real threat to the ongoing capitalist order and the wider class interests that benefit from such a milieu.[49] Indeed, very often, amongst the rebel factions fighting in conflicts, capitalism and elitist forms of government were viewed as aggregate aspects of oppressive systems. Liberation rhetoric in such circumstances may be consciously anti-capitalist. Yet, as a result of such aspirations, a means by which struggles can be undermined and privileged interests defended becomes imperative for the local elites, acting in tandem with their senior partners in the North. In such milieux, local groups within civil society that can marshal impressive international allies to contest the definition and uses of democratic institutions impose boundaries within which the discourse on what constitutes 'democracy' is defined, discussed, and promoted.[50]

These parameters are invariably defined as the 'middle ground', and space may be opened up for various contenders to negotiate themselves *within* this framework – a framework that is predicated upon variants of liberal democracy as the 'common sense' model upon which any post-conflict dispensation may be based. Hence, 'prevailing philosophical and theoretical consensus legitimates some forms of "theoretical" inquiry and *de-legitimates* others'.[51] Noam Chomsky illustrates this general point when discussing the state of Economics in the United States:

> When [a] Nobel Prize winner in Economics considered the range of possible economic systems, he saw a spectrum with complete *laissez-faire* at one extreme and 'totalitarian dictatorship of production' at the other. Assuming this framework, 'the relevant choice for policy today' is to determine where along this spectrum our economy should lie…. There are other dimensions, however, along which [his] polar opposites fall at the same extreme: for example, the spectrum that places direct democratic control of production at one pole, and autocratic control, whether by state or private capital, at the other. In this case, as so often, the formulation of the range of alternatives narrowly constrains 'the relevant choice for policy'.[52]

By doing so the 'natural' and 'superior' explanations that neoliberalism provides are advanced. After all, the superiority of the neoliberal ideology and its evident common sense has emerged from an ostensibly 'free' debate (the mythical free market of ideas, central to the liberal delusions about how politics is practised), where alternative viewpoints must surely have been proffered and shown to be lacking upon inspection. This process in fact has seen the elevation of neoliberalism as *la pensée unique* and the market as the ultimate arbiter of what is or what is not acceptable, economically, politically, and, increasingly, socially. As Bukovansky notes

> Liberal democracy is often presented as a technical prescription for curing a host of ills, rather than as a political value to be debated and adapted to particular conditions. Use of the term 'technical assistance' to describe a broad array of policies designed to disseminate proper institutional forms from the liberal core to the non-liberal or quasi-liberal periphery is symbolic of the prevailing wisdom. Sending advisors who show local authorities how to set up elections or courts or banking systems is presented as a *technical* rather than a *political* act. Calling such dissemination of ideas 'technical' links them to science and engineering, rather than politics and ethics. It gives them an aura of value-neutrality and scientific validity.[53]

Similar attempts to create 'realistic' options for post-conflict policy choices are part and parcel of interventions into civil society by advocates of the liberal peace, facilitating ideological conditions and fit between power, ideas, and institutions for the construction of hegemony.[54] Such activities need not stem from a restricted intellectual base – indeed, diversity is important as a self-legitimising device; 'narrow orthodoxy or exclusiveness would be a self-defeating criterion', and thus the ideas within the ranks of the organic intellectuals 'reach the outer boundaries of what might be ultimately acceptable'.[55] In many respects, it is the *quantity* of advice and the message that is given within a particular remit from a particular epistemic community that count, as well as the negative shaping of what is *not* possible.

Yet we must avoid the reductionist tendency to see this process simply as a manufactured conspiracy emanating from the North. Although such processes coincide with Northern imperialist interest, the development is more accurately a 'complex convergence of interests among an increasingly cohesive transnational elite headed by a US-led Northern bloc' but also 'incorporating elite constituencies in the South'.[56] This process explicitly aims to thwart the demands and aspirations of the popular classes within a historical juncture where crisis and a traumatised population emerging from war facilitate the introduction of previously intolerable policies.

the liberal peace as common sense

At the global structural level, interesting processes of legitimisation are apparent whereby local cooperative fractions are incorporated into the wider transnational class alliance in support of the hegemonic project. This not only grants the ongoing global order greater legitimacy but also serves as a means by which local elites in the South may be anointed as 'responsible' leaders who understand the common sense realities of neoliberalism. Common sense here is used in the Gramscian meaning.

According to Gramsci, ideology can appear either as seemingly abstract theorisations derived from individualist activities – 'philosophy' – or, in its basest and most popular form, as 'folklore'. Common sense is a mediating position, taking on attributes of both. As such it is fragmentary, often logically inconsistent, and is the conception of the world which has been uncritically adopted by the masses.[57] It is not the obtuse theorisations of philosophers (which indeed may be more coherent and satisfactory), but is the philosophy of 'real men, formed in specific historical relations, with specific feelings, outlooks [and] fragmentary conceptions of the world'.[58] This common sense is the result of a specific historical scenario vis-à-vis material production combined with the 'agglomeration within it of disparate social elements'.[59]

Though this common sense may be contradictory, it is nonetheless a conception of the world and has a material basis in presenting the world as 'natural' and 'the way of doing things' to those who share in this common sense. Common sense facilitates a situation where 'we rarely question why we think and act in a certain way, but rather, regard our ways of thinking and acting as absolutely objective and eternal and, as such, as needing no deep study into their origins or consequence'.[60] To wit, 'common sense shapes our ordinary, practical, everyday calculation and appears as natural as the air we breathe. It is simply "taken for granted" in practice and thought, and forms the starting-point (never examined or questioned) from which every conversation begins'.[61]

So how does this relate to the notion of hegemony? It is surely not argued that the elite class gains hegemony by spreading its ideology throughout society until all succumb to it. Such a totalitarian project can never fully succeed, even in an Orwellian nightmare. For Gramsci, the degree of hegemony is not simply equivalent to the ability of its philosophy to displace common sense (actually to transform, as common sense is made up of a synthesis of previous generations' historical relationships that continue to perpetually form and reformulate a society's common sense). No, the ideology promoted by the elites and its intellectuals operate in a manner to thwart the development of common sense into 'good sense' (the positive empirical nuclei of common sense). Hegemony 'implies the struggle to contest and disorganise an existing political formation'.[62] It is this disorganising of alternatives that lies at the core of common sense and the ongoing construction of hegemony. And it is in this disorganising of alternatives that the advocates of the liberal peace have been most successful.

In short, the potential for critical reason against the elite ideology intrinsic to the prescriptions of the liberal peace is cut off, and a scenario of Thatcherite 'TINA' is realised. 'The main strategy in recent years has been to treat the global capitalist economy as an impersonal, natural phenomenon and a historical inevitability, an idea nicely conveyed by conventional notions of globalisation'[63] As one commentator has noted vis-à-vis policy advice to African regimes, 'liberalism... is not an ideology; it is the ideology'.[64] Such a process does not and cannot shape common sense, however. This is not the aim. Rather, as Gramsci points out, a limitation of 'the original thought of the masses in a negative direction [is attempted], without having the positive effect of a vital ferment of interior transformation of what the masses think... about the world and life', that is common sense.[65] In short, things appear as self-evident: 'Untrammelled international competition, the celebration of the market, of wealth and self, anti-communism and anti-unionism; all these are no longer propagated as "revolutionary" in the sense of challenging a prevailing consensus of a different content, but they are now part of normal every day discourse; self-evident, near impossible to contradict or even doubt.'[66] 'We are given to understand that the laws of the market will inevitably embrace the whole world, so there is really no point in fighting them.'[67]

Yet, in the early days of the neoliberal renaissance, the monetarist ideology was perceived as beyond the pale of the welfare nationalist consensus that had been constructed post-1945. For sure, 'capitalism does not just happen', and the assertion of neoliberalism as the hegemonic discourse similarly did not simply 'occur'. 'It is a social system that has to struggle to create and reproduce its hegemonic order globally, and to do this large numbers of local, national, international and global organisations [were] established' to promote the new organising norms.[68] Post-conflict spaces, where the general population is disorganised and in shock, arguably provide the most receptive arena for such policy impositions.

The ultimate result of this process (which remains ongoing, and of which post-conflict liberal peace prescriptions can be seen as constitutive parts) was 'a sea change in the intellectual zeitgeist: the almost universal acceptance by governments and markets alike, of a new view about what it takes to develop'.[69] As Mao noted, 'When the superstructure (politics, culture, etc.) obstructs the development of the economic base, political and cultural changes become principal and decisive.'[70] This development vis-à-vis neoliberalism has 'set free-market ideas up as the only sensible response which political leaders and policy-makers [can] possibly make to a wide range of economic problems'.[71] This has been accomplished by a strategy aimed at constructing a new common sense based on neoliberal norms. A vast array of agents (including the IMF, the World Bank, WTO, OECD and regional development banks, influential think tanks and foundations) all either directly fund post-conflict 'rebuilding' or, via academic actors, fund 'research' which arrives at the conclusion that more liberalism in the economic and political realm is what the world needs, particularly if in a post-conflict situation. 'Economic development compatible with the "free market" rather than social organisation for social change becomes the dominant item on the funding agenda' once the immediate crisis is over.[72]

This is not to say that such a process is simply 'top-down' imparting of the received wisdom. The process is dialectical, where certain groups of intellectuals 'inspired by the promise or actual achievements of global capitalism, articulate[d] what they perceive[d] to be its essential purposes and strategies' as the material conditions of globalised capitalism underwent a transformation.[73] For sure, they are supported with moral and financial largesse from the already established transnationalised hegemonic elite, and this is frequently manifested via the agents of the corporate foundations and think tanks. Certainly, state and non-state elites in the South are 'lectured and advised...insistently...on the virtues of the free market, privatisation, and foreign investment'.[74] 'Civil society' is intrinsic to such a process. This (ongoing) re-educative project has been remarkably successful.

In this context Kees van der Pijl's discussion of fetishism and neoliberalism may be usefully deployed. Fetishism is the ascription of vital spirit and mysterious powers to dead objects – the animation of the inanimate. Clearly, van der Pijl's analysis borrows from Marx's notion of fetishism, which he saw as a form of cultural imagination that endows processes and things with agency, or a life of their own.[75] According to van der Pijl, neoliberalism and 'the market' have increasingly become fetishised, creating a scenario whereby 'professional economists serve to keep alive the idea that the workings of the market economy are only interfered with at one's peril. Even obviously inhuman conditions of production, such as child labour, are declared beyond regulation in the name of the free market'.[76]

This fetishisation of 'the market' is invariably externalised, hanging like the sword of Damocles over any administration that, in Margaret Thatcher's phrase, dare 'buck the markets'. For countries in post-conflict situations desperate for 'rebuilding' and/or with elites eager for legitimisation, this can act as a useful alibi to be deployed in defence of administrations that intend to embark on neoliberal restructuring and can serve to bolster the consensual element of hegemony. This fetishisation has not yet reached the level of common sense, but the incantations sounded by those elements of 'civil society' tied to this project whenever criticism is raised make its almost hallowed status quite clear. At the same time, this fetishisation of the market acts, as Gramsci suggests, to stifle debate. Thus, in spite of the hardships that neoliberalism has created in post-conflict spaces, no coherent alternative counter-hegemonic project has yet emerged as the ideology of neo-liberalism appears as 'natural'.

Essentially, discussion has been limited to debate as to how best to ameliorate such outcomes or 'ride through' the crises, that is the discussion becomes exclusively preoccupied with 'problem-solving'. But the fundamentals of 'the market' dare not be tampered with, lest 'the market' punish such transgressors – a neat tautology that heads off counter-hegemonic impulses at birth. In such an environment, those who oppose neoliberalism being implemented upon countries emerging from conflict are 'extremists' or 'peace spoilers' who advocate 'bad policies' in the face of 'reality' where there is 'no option'. Meanwhile, neoliberalism is posited as self-evident 'to reasonable men who understand the workings of an economy'.[77]

Interestingly, as apartheid drew to a close in South Africa and post-liberation policies were being discussed, the business press asserted that 'private property and freedom of contract ... are values that are absolutely necessary to peace, prosperity and liberty. That is not a theory. It is a matter of observable fact'.[78]

Yet it needs to be said that prior to the neoliberal counter-revolution, the type of policies that neoliberalism espouses were way beyond the pale of 'normal' economic thinking, be it Keynesianism or socialist – indeed, Hayek's theories were seen as 'stupid' and leading down the 'road to reaction' when they were first publicised.[79] It is a reflection of the immense success that this ideology has had in achieving hegemony that it is now put forward as the common sense 'centre', in relation to which all other policy prescriptions must be judged accordingly and in the light of their compatibility with its prescriptions. It is indeed a testament to the immense success that the ideology's advocates have achieved in placing dead centre to any post-conflict rebuilding project the core tenets of an ideology as if they were 'natural', if not God-given. Indeed, the fixed certainties that surround neoliberalism have achieved the status of a dogma against which only crazed heretics may venture.

conclusion

Within the wider context of an increasingly integrated world economy, advocates of the ongoing hegemonic ideology – neoliberalism – demand a profound harmonisation and deepening of fiscal and political policies across the globe in order to facilitate the mobility of capital demanded by transnational elites in their search for profit and capital aggregation. 'The new imperialism of the twenty-first century features the export of *capitalism* to politically independent states within a comprehensive regulatory framework governed by co-operating international organisations and aimed at imposing the "fundamental characteristics of capitalism in general" across developed and developing states alike'.[80] This project, as Marx and Engels noted, 'compels all nations, on pain of extinction, to adopt the bourgeois mode of production'.[81] The specifically American-derived origins of this model are highlighted by Eric Hobsbawm who noted that 'today's ideologues see a model society already at work in the US: a combination of law, liberal freedoms, competitive private enterprise, and regular contested elections with universal suffrage. All that remains is to remake the world in the image of this "free society"'.[82]

Hence, the move in supporting 'democracy' and economic 'common sense' in the South in spaces recovering from conflict is of profound importance. This is not to say that in many cases a move to polyarchy does not represent a considerable advance for the popular masses. But we should not be under any illusions as to the limitations that the post-conflict transitions under this guiding paradigm have engendered for any further advance in the socio-economic situation for the popular classes, particularly when combined with an erosion of state capacity under conditions of economic liberalisation.

Equally, as I have noted elsewhere,[83] there is a profound disjuncture between the hegemonic support neoliberalism and its manifestation as the liberal peace enjoy at the global level and the general absence of hegemony locally in most post-conflict spaces. Such a reality militates against any triumphant application of the liberal peace and calls into question the very viability of most of the project's policy prescriptions, expectations and basic assumptions. What is left then is a virtual peace, generally satisfactory to donors and external actors, and also to the connected domestic elites, but not broadly sustainable or able to enjoy hegemonic support. Certainly, in many parts of the developing world where the liberal peace is presumed to work its magic, the non-hegemonic nature of domestic ruling classes has forced them to take direct charge of the state itself. However, such leaders have generally relied on effected control and patronage rather than through building a hegemonic integral state. They control the state, but it is a state which their own practices continually undermine and weaken. This is deeply problematic, for, as Hobsbawm notes,

> Even within the ranks of territorial nation-states, the conditions for effective democratic government are rare: an existing state enjoying legitimacy, consent, and the ability to mediate conflicts between domestic groups [i.e. a hegemonic integral state]. Without such consensus there is no single sovereign 'people' and therefore no legitimacy for arithmetical majorities. When this consensus – be it religious, ethnic or both – is absent, democracy has been suspended (as is the case with democratic institutions in Northern Ireland), the state has split (as in Czechoslovakia), or society has descended into permanent civil war (as in Sri Lanka). 'Spreading democracy' aggravated ethnic conflict and produced the disintegration of states in multinational and multi-communal regions after both 1918 and 1989.[84]

This is the historical context within which the advancement of the liberal peace must be situated. Understanding this, and how ideas are promoted and integrated until they become 'natural' and 'unquestionable', helps us analyse the situation that has developed when and where the liberal peace project is advanced in post-conflict spaces. The theoretical

work of Gramsci and other Marxists helps us comprehend such processes and developments.

notes

1. L. Sklair, 'Social Movements and Global Capitalism', *Sociology*, Vol. 29, No. 3, 1995, p. 503.
2. A. Hoogvelt, *Globalisation and the Post-Colonial World: The New Political Economy of Development*, Baltimore, MD: Johns Hopkins University Press, 1997.
3. K. Van der Pijl, 'The International Level', in T. Bottomore and R. Bryan (eds) *The Capitalist Class: An International Study*, Hemel Hempstead: Harvester Wheatsheaf, 1989.
4. H. Williams, *Britain's Power Elites*, London: Constable, 2006, p.18.
5. R. Cox, 'Global Perestroika', in R. Miliband and L. Panitch (eds) *The Socialist Register, 1992*, London: Merlin Press, 1992, p. 27.
6. R. Cox, 'Problems of Power and Knowledge in a Changing Global World Order', in R. Stubbs and G. Underhill (eds) *Political Economy and the Changing World Order*, London: Macmillan, 1994, p. 49.
7. M. Rupert, 'Contesting Hegemony: Americanism and Far-Right Ideologies of Globalisation', in K. Burch and R. Denemark (eds) *Constituting International Political Economy*, Boulder, CO: Lynne Rienner, 1997, p. 117.
8. K. Marx, *German Ideology*, London: Lawrence Wishart, 1970 [1845–6], p. 39.
9. L. Sklair, 'Social Movements for Global Capitalism: The Transnational Capitalist Class in Action', *Review of International Political Economy*, Vol. 4, No. 3, 1997, pp. 514–15.
10. O. Holman, 'Transnational Class Strategy and the New Europe', *International Journal of Political Economy*, Vol. 22, No. 1, 1992, p. 13.
11. W. Robinson, *Promoting Polyarchy: Globalisation, U.S. Intervention, and Hegemony*, Cambridge: Cambridge University Press, 1996.
12. E. Wood, 'Democracy as Ideology of Empire', in C. Mooers (ed.) *The New Imperialists: Ideologies of Empire*, Oxford: Oneworld Publications, 2006, p. 14.
13. J. Mittelman and M. Pasha, *Out From Underdevelopment Revisited: Changing Global Structures and the Remaking of World Order*, Basingstoke: Macmillan, 1997, p. 51.
14. C. Leys and L. Panitch, 'The Political Legacy of the Manifesto', in C. Leys and L. Panitch (eds) *The Socialist Register, 1998*, London: Merlin Press, 1998, p. 20.
15. H. Overbeek and K. van der Pijl, 'Restructuring Capital and Restructuring Hegemony: Neo-liberalism and the Unmaking of the Post-war Order', in H. Overbeek (ed.) *Restructuring Hegemony in the Global Political Economy: The Rise of Transnational Neo-Liberalism in the 1980s*, London: Routledge, 1993, p. 1.
16. H. Martin and H. Schumann, *The Global Trap: Globalisation and the Assault on Democracy and Prosperity*, London: Zed Books, 1997, p. 61.

17. P. Cammack, 'UN Imperialism: Unleashing Entrepreneurship in the Developing World' in C. Mooers (ed.) *The New Imperialists: Ideologies of Empire* Oxford: Oneworld Publications, 2006, p. 230.
18. M. Pugh, 'The Political Economy of Peacebuilding: A Critical Theory Perspective', *International Journal of Peace Studies*, Vol. 10, No. 2, 2005, p. 2.
19. I. Taylor, 'What Fit for the Liberal Peace in Africa?', *Global Society*, Vol. 21, No. 4, 2007.
20. M. Bukovansky, 'Liberal States, International Order, and Legitimacy: An Appeal for Persuasion over Prescription', *International Politics*, Vol. 44, Nos 2–3, 2007.
21. Cammack, 'UN Imperialism', pp. 229–30.
22. K. Annan, 'Secretary-General, in Address to World Economic Forum, Stresses Strengthened Partnership between United Nations, Private Sector', Press Release SG/SM/6153, 1997, www.un.org/News/Press/docs/1997/19970131.sgsm6153.html, accessed 15 October 2009.
23. P. Cammack, 'The Governance of Global Capitalism: A New Materialist Perspective', *Historical Materialism*, Vol. 11, No. 2, 2003, p. 38.
24. Ibid., p. 48.
25. B. Boutros-Ghali, '"Beyond Peacekeeping"', *New York University Journal of International Law and Politics*, Vol. 25, Fall, 1992, p. 115.
26. R. Paris, 'Peacebuilding and the Limits of Liberal Internationalism', *International Security*, Vol. 22, No. 2, 1997, p. 56.
27. N. Klein, *The Shock Doctrine: The Rise of Disaster Capitalism*, London: Allen Lane, 2007.
28. M. Friedman, *Capitalism and Freedom*, Chicago: University of Chicago Press, 1962.
29. A. Gamble, *The Free Economy and the Strong State: The Politics of Thatcherism*, London: Macmillan, 1988.
30. R. Dahl, *Polyarchy: Participation and Opposition*, New Haven, CT: Yale University Press, 1971.
31. Wood, 'Democracy as Ideology', p. 17. See also E. Wood, *Democracy Against Capitalism: Renewing Historical Materialism*, Cambridge: Cambridge University Press, 1995.
32. I. Oren, *Our Enemies and Us: America's Rivalries and the Making of Political Science*, Ithaca, NY: Cornell University Press, 2003, p. 176.
33. B. Gills, J. Rocamora and R. Wilson, *Low Intensity Democracy: Political Power in the New World Order*, London: Pluto Press, 1993.
34. J. Harrod, 'Social Forces and International Political Economy: Joining the Two IRs', in S. Gill and J. Mittelman (eds) *Innovation and Transformation in International Studies*, Cambridge: Cambridge University Press, 1997, p. 108.
35. K. Good, 'Development and Democracies: Liberal Versus Popular', *Africa Insight*, Vol. 27, No. 4, 1997, p. 253.
36. M. Burawoy, *The Politics of Production: Factory Regimes Under Capitalism and Socialism*, London: New, 1985, p. 63.
37. K. Marx and F. Engels, *Manifesto of the Communist Party*, Moscow: Foreign Languages Press, 1967 [1850], pp. 60–1.
38. See for example L. Diamond, J. Linz and S. Lipset, *Democracy in Developing Countries*, Boulder, CO: Lynne Rienner, 1988; G. di Palma, *To Craft Democracies*,

Berkeley, CA: University of California Press, 1990; S. Huntingdon, *The Third Wave: Democratisation in the Late Twentieth Century*, Norman: University of Oklahoma Press, 1991.

39. Wood, 'Democracy as Ideology', p. 11.
40. See for example C. Pateman, *Participation and Democratic Theory*, Cambridge: Cambridge University Press, 1970; C. Gould, *Rethinking Democracy: Freedom and Social Co-operation in Politics, Economy and Society*, Cambridge: Cambridge University Press, 1988.
41. M. Neufeld, 'Globalisation: Five Theses', paper presented at the conference 'Globalisation and Problems of Development', Havana, Cuba, January 1999, p. 4.
42. E. Hobsbawm, *Globalisation, Democracy and Terrorism*, London: Little, Brown, 2007, p. 115.
43. Cammack, 'UN Imperialism', p. 230.
44. Robinson, *Promoting Polyarchy*, p. 27.
45. C. Murphy, *International Organisation and Industrial Change*, Cambridge: Polity Press, 1994, p. 31.
46. D. Moore, 'Reading Americans on Democracy in Africa: From the CIA to "Good Governance"', *European Journal of Development Research*, Vol. 8, No. 1, 1996, p. 140.
47. R. Fatton, 'Civil Society Revisited: Africa in the New Millennium', *West Africa Review*, Vol. 1, No. 1, 1999, p. 3.
48. J. Mittelman, 'Rethinking Innovation in Internal Relations: Global Transformation at the Turn of the Millennium', in S. Gill and J. Mittelman (eds) *Innovation and Transformation in International Studies*, Cambridge: Cambridge University Press, 1997, p. 255.
49. S. Friedman, *Building Tomorrow Today: African Workers in Trade Unions, 1970–1984*, Johannesburg: Ravan Press, 1987.
50. T. Koelble, *The Global Economy and Democracy in South Africa*, New Brunswick, NJ: Rutgers University Press, 1999, p. 10.
51. R. Tooze, 'Understanding the Global Political Economy: Applying Gramsci', *Millennium: Journal of International Studies: Journal of International Studies*, Vol. 19, No. 2, 1990, p. 273.
52. N. Chomsky, *Problems of Knowledge and Freedom*, London: Barrie and Jenkins, 1972, p. 53.
53. Bukovansky, 'Liberal States', p. 181.
54. S. Gill and D. Law, 'Global Hegemony and the Structural Power of Capital', *International Studies Quarterly*, Vol. 33, 1989, p. 488.
55. R. Cox, 'Ideologies and the New International Economic Order: Reflections on Some Recent Literature', *International Organisation*, Vol. 33, No. 2, 1979, p. 260.
56. Robinson, *Promoting Polyarchy*, p. 653.
57. A. Gramsci, *Selections From the Prison Notebooks*, London: Lawrence and Wishart, 1971, p. 419.
58. Ibid.
59. Ibid., p. 198.
60. E. Augelli and C. Murphy, *America's Quest for Supremacy and the Third World: A Gramscian Analysis*, London: Pinter Publishers, 1988, p. 18.

61. S. Hall, *Thatcherism and the Crisis of the Left: The Hard Road to Renewal*, London: Verso Press, 1988, p. 9.
62. Ibid., p. 7.
63. Wood, 'Democracy as Ideology', p. 15.
64. T. Young, ' "A Project to be Realised": Global Liberalism and Contemporary Africa', *Millennium: Journal of International Studies*, Vol. 24, No. 3, 1995, p. 529.
65. Gramsci, *Selections From the Prison Notebooks*, p. 420.
66. Overbeek and Van der Pijl, 'Restructuring Capital', p. 2.
67. Wood, 'Democracy as Ideology', p. 15.
68. Sklair, 'Social Movements for Global Capitalism', pp. 514–15.
69. P. Krugman, 'Dutch Tulips and Emerging Markets', *Foreign Affairs*, July–August 1994, p. 28.
70. Z. Mao, 'On Contradiction' in *Selected Readings from the Works of Mao Tsetung*, Beijing: Foreign Languages Press, 1971 [1937], p. 116.
71. M. Berger, 'Up From Neo–Liberalism: Free Market Mythologies and the Coming Crisis of Global Capitalism', *Third World Quarterly*, Vol. 20, No. 2, 1999, p. 454.
72. J. Petras, 'A Marxist Critique of Post-Marxists', *Links: International Journal of Socialist Renewal*, no. 9, 1997, p. 47, links [online], available at: http://links.org.au/node/189, accessed on 2 November 2009.
73. Sklair, 'Social Movements for Global Capitalism', p. 515.
74. A. Hirschmann, 'The Political Economy of Latin American Development: Seven Exercises in Retrospect', *Latin American Research Review*, Vol. 22, March 1987, pp. 30–1.
75. K. Marx, *Capital*, London: J.M. Dent and Son, 1951 [1867].
76. K. Van der Pijl, *Transnational Classes and International Relations*, London: Routledge, 1998, p. 13.
77. N. Bruce, 'No Easy Road', *Leadership*, Vol. 11, No. 3, 1992, p. 18.
78. *Financial Mail*, December 14, 1990.
79. H. Finer, *Road to Reaction*, Chicago, IL: Quadrangle Books, 1963, p. 67.
80. Cammack, 'UN Imperialism', p. 234.
81. Marx and Engels, *Manifesto of the Communist Party*, p. 6.
82. Hobsbawm, *Globalisation*, pp. 116–17.
83. Taylor, 'What Fit for the Liberal Peace in Africa?'.
84. Hobsbawm, *Globalisation*, pp. 117–18.

9

the ideology of peace: peacebuilding and the war in iraq

mikkel vedby rasmussen

There is a tendency to reduce peacebuilding, in theory as well as in practice, to a technocratic question. Academics and policymakers in Western capitals, as well as military officers and aid workers from Liberia to Afghanistan, ask themselves how to make a durable peace. The question of 'how to make peace?' is the subject of endless number of books and articles, as well as manuals and consultancy reports, that try to describe the best techniques for making peace. However, this focus on how to make peace might have turned our attention away from what kind of peace is actually being made. Perhaps, and this is more troubling, this inattention to the nature of the peace which one strives to achieve is the reason why peace all too often remains unattainable, as well as the reason why the price other people pay for the schemes of the academics, policymakers, officers and aid workers is at times so terribly high.

Instead of asking 'how peace?', I will ask 'why peace?' Why is it that peace has become the end as well as the means for the most central issues of foreign and security policy? Needless to say this essay does not offer the definite answer to that question, but it does suggest that if we study peace as an ideology rather than as a state of affairs we get one explanation as to why peacebuilding has become such a pivotal policy area. Taking my point of departure in Clifford Geertz's anthropological notion of ideology, I shall define peace as an ideology which is based, firstly, on a discourse which rejects military victory as an end in itself in favour of a peace settlement that transcends the conflict in favour of a liberal community. Secondly, the ideology of peace is based on a practice of peacebuilding which assumes that the Western 'custodians of peace' know best how to build it.

Geertz's concept of ideology is a way to study what one might term the culture of politics. Studying peace as an ideology enables one to move beyond the theoretical debate about the nature of peace and focus on how the concept of peace informs action. This anthropological framework is by its very nature more limited than many of the other approaches adopted in this book, since it is grounded in a specific cultural practice of peacemaking. This chapter thus focuses exclusively on the modern Western culture of peace, arguing that its conceptual foundation can be found in the Enlightenment discourse on the subject, which is presented most insightfully in Kant's writings. A culture is not only made up of ideas, however, and the modern ideology of peace only fully developed when it became the basis for political discourse in the twentieth century.

The ideology of peace defines the approach to peace within our political culture. In order to demonstrate the pervasiveness of the ideology of peace, this chapter focuses on the debate surrounding the Iraq war. The war has been a widely debated and truly divisive issue in the Western world. This debate brings a number of politically marginal and alternative conceptions of peace into the open, and the controversial nature of the conflicts forces policymakers to engage with these statements. If there is such a thing as an ideology of peace, then those in power and those who criticise them ought to share it. The present study uses policy statements as well as Harold Pinter's Nobel lecture and a wide range of other sources to demonstrate that this is indeed the case. The two elements of the ideology of peace are very clearly represented on both sides in the debate about the war in Iraq. The war in Iraq is used to illustrate how the ideology works in practice and the policy options the ideology offers with respect to the use of military force to produce victory and with respect to 'winning the peace' by building a new Iraqi society.

The first section begins with an outline of the conceptual foundation of the ideology of peace. It briefly describes Kant's notion of perpetual peace and how this concept developed from a critical, marginal view held by philosophers to declarations by presidents. This leads to an analysis of how this concept of peace is an ideology in Geertz's definition of the term. The second section shows how the ideology of peace informed the criticism of the Iraq war as well as the Western leaders' response. The third section describes how the ideology of peace set such high standards for what to achieve in Iraq that it in fact made an exit strategy a near impossibility. The third section is followed by the con-clusion. We begin, however, with a joke.

Kant's joke

Immanuel Kant begins his *Zum ewigen Frieden* with a joke. It might not be much of a joke, but by the standards of the philosopher from Königsberg it is actually quite funny. Kant opens the book by telling how a Dutch inn displays a sign with the picture of a graveyard with the caption 'perpetual peace'.[1] By choosing this phrase as the title of his book Kant uses irony to put his carefully crafted treaty for a 'pacific federation' into perspective: peace is an ideal and even the most practic-ally minded suggestions for how to achieve it will be hard to realise. So the graveyard may be the surest way to achieve perpetual peace, but it is also, from a real world perspective, the only alternative. For Kant the irony of peace is the relative ease by with one can define it a priori at the same time, as it is so difficult to realise. Thus Kant was being funny at his own expense; because he knew that in the final analysis peace was not a pure concept which he could define and provide the recipe for how it should be realised. Peace was by its very nature an ideology in the sense that it was about the realisation of an idea, rather than a description of the idea which in turn described a certain reality.

Kant's notion of peace thus fits Clifford Geertz's definition of an ideology. What Kant in fact did was to provide a liberal recipe for peace which made the pursuit of peace as a goal in itself possible.[2] According to Geertz, this is exactly the function of ideology: 'The function of ideology is to make an autonomous politics possible by providing the authoritative concepts that render it meaningful, the assuasive images by means of which it can be sensibly grasped.'[3] Augustine remarked that one makes war in order to attain a certain peace, but by that Augustine surely meant that warfare was a means to achieve something. The peace Augustine referred to was a certain state of affairs which was some-how better for the victor because of the war. Kant's point is much more radical because he removes victor and vanquished from the equation. Instead of regarding peace as an outcome of a conflict, peace is regarded as a discrete phenomenon. Peace is not the by-product of war and therefore always defined by the nature of a particular war. Peace is a phenomenon in and of itself. When peace becomes an end in itself it follows that there is a distinct path to peace which can be followed without involving war, or at least by avoiding the traditional notions of winning and losing in war. Kant's recipe for a pacific federation is thus a peaceful way to achieve a world state, as opposed to the numerous unpeaceful attempts to achieve hegemony which had defined the international history Kant knew about. Kant constructs an ideology of peace because he identifies it as a cure for a world at war.

By making peace an ideology Kant is redefining it from something which is either ideal (belonging to the afterlife, as symbolised in the graveyard) or the by-product of war to a goal in its own right. That peace became an ideology did not make it less real or less desirable. Geertz notes that ideologies have a bad press, and points out that by labelling an idea or system of thought as an ideology one is already discrediting it. It is an 'intellectual error' which should be studied in order to show where its adherents went wrong.[4] The holistic world view of the ideology is regarded as something that stands in the way of looking at the facts.[5] From Geertz's anthropological perspective, however, it is clear that ideologies do not so much stand in the way of a rational political process as enable a political process to take place. 'It is through the construction of ideologies, schematic images of social order,' Geertz argues, 'that man makes himself for better or worse a political animal.'[6] To Geertz, the idea of politics comes before politics as practice. Man learns how to do things; he is not driven by instincts, and this is also the case with politics, where ideologies instruct on how to do politics.

The fact that peace becomes an ideology thus gives it a different ontology. It becomes a malleable phenomenon which can be shaped according to political wishes rather than just the by-product of a war. Peace thus functions in the same way as 'freedom' does in Liberalism and 'equality' does in Socialism. These concepts too may objectively define a state of affairs (are incomes distributed equally among citizens?), but in ascertaining whether or not a certain income distribution is equal the ideological assessment kicks in; and it does so by the notion that equality is something worth striving for. And, just as people continue being liberals even if 'freedom' is curtailed or keep working for social justice even if inequality is rising, people work for peace even if the goal seems elusive. In 1914, when Norman Angell had to face up to the fact that major war was not a 'grand illusion', his response was not that he had been wrong – he had merely been 'unsuccessful'. Another element of Kant's joke is that people, without much success, will strive for peace until they reach the graveyard. The fact that peace is an ideology explains why they keep going. 'Ideology bridges the emotional gap between things as they are and as one would have them be,' Geertz writes, 'thus insuring the performance of roles that might other wise be abandoned in despair or apathy.'[7]

If one studies peace as an ideology it becomes easier to understand how the notion of peace, which Kant did so much to frame, was transformed from being a politically marginal view held by those who criticised power to become the dominating discourse on peace. Few have spoken more eloquently about the Kantian ideology of peace than US President Woodrow Wilson, when he assured Congress that the United States did not enter the First World War in order to win in the traditional sense of the word:

> Victory would mean peace forced upon the loser, a victor's terms imposed upon the vanquished. It would be accepted in humiliation, under duress, at an intolerable sacrifice, and would leave a sting, a resentment, a bitter memory upon which terms of peace would rest, not permanently, but only upon quicksand. Only a peace between equals can last, only a peace the very principle of which is equality and a common participation in a common benefit.[8]

War was no longer about victory; Wilson argued that it was about achieving lasting peace. Michael Howard describes how peace is 'a modern invention' that came to dominate our notion of what war should be all about.[9] Perhaps one can argue that the ideology of peace became truly hegemonic when the UN Charter in 1948 outlawed war as a means of policy in its own right – from then on states were only allowed to wage war if they could justify it with regard to the ideology of peace. Self-defence was justified as a means to maintain domestic peace and deter aggression, and the UN Security Council was able to authorise war in the name of international 'peace and security'. Peace was no longer the exception; it had become the rule. The ideology of peace was thus setting the rules even for how wars were to be fought. Wars should, as Wilson had argued, not be concerned only with the achievement of military victory but also with the achievement of lasting peace. 'Humanitarian interventions' are perhaps the conceptually perfect version of this conception of war. Here, military force is used not to achieve a decisive outcome, but to ensure the peaceful resolution of a conflict. Armed force may be used coercively, but it is not used by the logic which officers learn at staff colleges. The soldiers are not to use force to achieve a decisive victory; they are to use force to make sure that the conflict cannot be settled by military means.[10] This is an example of what John

MacMillan describes as 'liberalism's pacificistic orientation...in relations with non-liberal states'.[11] It is true that the liberal agenda in Kant's
notion of peace transforms peace into a guiding principle of foreign
policy, but, as the number of humanitarian interventions in the 1990s
demonstrates, this does not mean that following the ideology of peace
means that one eschews the use of the armed force – just as Wilson's
rejection of victory was followed by the shipment of American army
divisions to Northern France. Peace becomes the concept that guides
the use of force rather than the concept that rejects it.

If peace is an ideology, how should you study it? When studying
ideology, Geertz argues, 'you should look in the first instance not at
its theories or its findings, and certainly not at what its apologists say
about it; you should look at what the practitioners of it do'.[12] If one
regards ideology as the culture of the political, then one should be
studying the practice of ideas rather than the ideas themselves. Ann
Swidler defines culture as the 'tool kit' enabling agents to form strategies of actions.[13] Swidler sees 'culture's casual significance in providing cultural components that are used to construct strategies of
action'.[14] Cultural studies describe *how* actors act rather than why and
for what purpose. If one regards the actions of people following the
ideology of peace – from Woodrow Wilson onwards – I think there is
reason to argue that their ideology results in a practice based on two
pillars:

(1) The rejection of military victory as a goal in itself. Victory does not
matter as much as the ability to transcend the conflict which led to war
in the first place. This is what Wilson means by 'war without victory'.
Followers of the ideology of peace want to win. They do not merely
want to win on the battlefield; they want to win the hearts and minds
of the opponents. They want the vanquished party to join them in
Kant's pacific federation.

(2) From this follows the insistence on peace as something which is
built rather than achieved. Military victory is only the stepping stone
to the real work of building a durable peace. It follows from this that
the vanquished party does not have any inherent interests different
from those of the victor. Making peace is thus about remaking a society
according to a certain recipe for peace. In the following section I will
demonstrate how these two elements of the ideology of peace worked
out in the case of Iraq.

not in our name

On both sides of the Atlantic the slogan for the opposition to the war in Iraq has been 'not in our name'. Parading that slogan on banners and t-shirts, protesters have demonstrated their belief that winning this war was not necessary and that it was not fought in a legitimate way. Only President Bush, Prime Minister Blair, and other government leaders believed in the legitimacy of the war, according to the protesters, who wanted to make sure that the Western leaders would be held accountable for what was actually done in their name.

The protests against the Iraq war illustrate how victory in itself has become a problematic concept. 'The West,' Edward Luttwak observes, 'has become comfortably habituated to defeat. Victory is viewed with great suspicion, if not outright hostility.'[15] Luttwak made this observation in 1986, and perhaps one should think that Western victory in the Cold War and various conflicts in the 1990s means that things have changed. But they have not. This anti-victory discourse is a part of the ideology of peace. It was the notion behind Wilson's assertion in 1917 that victory was standing in the way of peace. It follows that a war which does not offer the prospect for transcending conflict in favour of a lasting peace is merely slaughter. On 3 September 1939, when the House of Commons was about to decide to go to war with Germany, George Lansbury – pacifist and former Labour leader – felt he had to remind the House of the futility of the enterprise:

> The cause that I and a handful of friends represent is this morning, apparently, going down to ruin, but I think we ought to take heart of courage from the fact that after 2,000 years of war and strife, at last, even those who enter upon this colossal struggle have to admit that in the end force has not settled, and cannot and will not settle anything.[16]

Lansbury did not want the Second World War to be fought in his name. The very idea that war could 'settle anything' (that is, produce a decisive victory) would remove the focus from the suffering of war. According to the ideology of peace, war cannot achieve anything in and of itself because military victory is simply not the stuff peace is made of. Peace is about accepting a new order; not about coercion. 2005 Nobel laureate Harold Pinter thus found that President Bush's and Prime Minister Blair's talk of victory obscured the truth: that war is slaughter. Thus he

echoed Kant, who wondered whether the graveyard was the only place
where kings would be peaceful because they 'can never have enough of
war'.[17] In his Nobel lecture, Pinter passionately wanted to speak truth to
power, but he had more to say about the people in power than the truth
of war. While Pinter offers an analysis of the reasons why the United
States and Britain went to war, war is oddly reified in his account.
Neither considerations on military technology nor the nature of the
campaign is offered in his Nobel lecture, nor is an analysis of exactly
how much Iraqi soldiers and civilians suffered. Thus the cruelty of war
remains absolute and abstract in Pinter's account. Nevertheless, it is the
cruelty of war which in Pinter's eyes delegitimises any justification or
reasons for going to war. He thus writes in his Nobel Lecture: 'We have
brought torture, cluster bombs, depleted uranium, innumerable acts of
random murder, misery, degradation and death to the Iraqi people and
call it "bringing freedom and democracy to the Middle East".'[18]

By winning, or believing the war could be won, the coalition forces
had done things which in themselves removed any justification for victory. 'At the time of writing, the hospitals of Baghdad are overflowing
with the wounded and dying, as the city is pieced apart by American
tanks,' Tariq Ali wrote in the New Left Review; ' "We own it all," declares
a US colonel, surveying the shattered capital in the spirit of any Panzer
commander in 1940.'[19] Ali's repeated comparisons between Hitler's
armies and the US forces advancing on Baghdad suggest that any use of
military force turns you into a Nazi – or at least the functional equivalent.[20] Where Hegel argued that success on the battlefield proves the
superiority of a nation's values,[21] Pinter and Ali argue the opposite. This
echoes Wilson's notion that no true peace can come from a mere military victory.

One reason why the use of military power seems illegitimate is the
asymmetrical nature of the fighting during the invasion of Iraq and the
subsequent insurgency. What Herman Kahn noted with respect to the
Vietnam War seems to be true of the Iraq war as well:

> There appears to be an encounter between a seemingly depersonal-
> ized technological arsenal of war and defenders who are perceived
> on a human scale – as individuals in a backward society compelled
> to endure punishment without proportionate defenses (although
> using terrorist methods of offence which, paradoxically, seem to
> some people almost legitimized by the perceived disproportion in
> the material means of conflict).[22]

When Pinter describes the way US forces and their allies fight in Iraq, advanced weapons like cluster bombs or depleted uranium shells are mentioned on par with torture and 'random murder'. Thus, in Pinter's view, advanced military technology is cruel and unusual punishment in itself. Following this line of argument, Mary Kaldor suggests that the purpose for using military force ought to be to protect people's rights rather than to achieve victory.[23] If the very means by which their forces try to defeat the enemy undermines the legitimacy of victory, then the British and American governments not only have to defend the conduct of their troops; they also have to defend the entire possibility of achieving victory. Tony Blair was surely mastering the British art of understatement when he described the situation as 'ironic':

> That to me is the painful irony of what is happening. They [the insurgents in Iraq] have so much clearer a sense of what is at stake. They play our own media with a shrewdness that would be the envy of many a political party. Every act of carnage adds to the death toll. But somehow it serves to indicate our responsibility for disorder, rather than the act of wickedness that causes it. For us, so much of our opinion believes that what was done in Iraq in 2003 was so wrong, that it is reluctant to accept what is plainly right now.[24]

What was ironic to Blair was the way in which the Kantian concept of peace made it impossible for him to explain what was at stake in Iraq for the public. The interception of a letter from Al-Qaida leader Ayman al-Zawahiri to the insurgent leader Abu Musab al-Zarqawi in Iraq reinforced the British and American governments' belief that their enemy understood what was at stake in Iraq much better than their own publics. In the letter Zawahiri outlines how victory in Iraq should be used to 'extend the jihad wave'. So arguing, Zawahiri adopts a view of religious geopolitics where Iraq is in the centre of the Middle East. The US cannot hold that centre, the Al-Qaida leader believes, and he goes on to argue that if the jihadists gain power in Iraq they will be able to bring down the non-Islamic regimes of the region.[25] Zawahiri's belief in the ability of the force of arms to change the world actually mirrors the second concept of victory – the crucial difference being that Zawahiri has no ambition to transcend the hostility that defines his attitude to the West.

It is worth noting that Zawahiri apparently is eager to discuss with Zarqawi how the US perceives the prospects of victory. 'Things may develop faster than we imagine,' Zawahiri writes; 'the aftermath of the collapse of American power in Vietnam – and how they ran and left their agents – is noteworthy.'[26] In other words, the Western debate on the possibility of victory makes Zawahiri speculate that the United States and its allies will give up – as the United States did in Vietnam. The debate about if and when the United States and its allies can win the war in Iraq thus becomes a centre of gravity of the conflict. The United States cannot be defeated by arms, but, as in Vietnam, it can be brought to believe that victory is either impossible or carries too high a price. It all depends on the prospect of victory, and the irony – to use Blair's phrase – is that the West cannot win if victory is measured in purely military terms. The Western public demands a peace without victory that delivers a kind of Iraq which is not only peaceful but has transcended the present conflict.

winning the peace

The ideology of peace transfers much of the valour and heroism traditionally associated with warfare to the fight for peace. Peace is thus something which has to be forged by 'those who assume custody of a peace'.[27] This is the term used by Richard Solomon in an introduction to an anthology on peacemaking published, tellingly, by the US Institute for Peace in cooperation with the Army War College. Solomon goes on the to describe the duties of the 'custodians of peace': 'to forge a sustainable peace, the authors explain, one must transform the sources of violent conflict; the motivations and means for conducting a destabilizing insurgency must be recognized, and overcome'.[28] It is clear that forging peace is not in itself a peaceful enterprise. 'Winning the peace' is something that is put on a par with winning the war.[29] While it may sound nicer, this approach is in many ways more combative than a traditional concept of victory because it leaves no option for conflict to settle a dispute. The vanquished party not only has to lose; it also has to like it. This is exactly the problem the United States has been confronted with in Iraq. While the US forces clearly were able to achieve a decisive victory, Saddam's regime denied the United States victory by not accepting defeat and the new order that followed but simply fought on. As the insurgency was joined by Al-Qaida and others, the United States was not able to impose the transformed relationship between victors and vanquished which would render a peace without victory.

Thus President Bush argued that 'when the history of these days is written, it will tell how America once again defended its own freedom by using liberty to transform nations from bitter foes to strong allies.'[30] The 'national strategy for victory in Iraq', which the White House published in 2005 in order to counter the charges of 'muddled thinking about strategy',[31] thus emphasised that 'victory in Iraq will not come in the form of an enemy's surrender, or be signalled by a single event...The ultimate victory will be achieved in stages'.[32] To the Bush administration, the insurgency pales in comparison with the fact that the Iraqi government has turned from being an enemy to 'a partner in the global war on terror'.[33] Because the fight against the insurgents is seen in the context of the 'war on terrorism', establishing an Iraqi democracy is the central element of the strategy. When Iraq becomes a democracy it will assume its rightful place in the phalanx of democracies, it is argued. What used to be the United States' fight will then become the Iraqis' fight as well. It follows that victory should not be measured by the number of insurgents who are defeated but rather by the number of Iraqis who share the United States' values and political goals in Iraq. Senator Joe Lieberman stresses this point when he argues:

It is a war between 27 million and 10,000; 27 million Iraqis who want to live lives of freedom, opportunity and prosperity and roughly 10,000 terrorists...who know their wretched causes will be set back if Iraq becomes free and modern. We are fighting on the side of the 27 million because the outcome of this war is critically important to the security and freedom of America.[34]

Politicians acting according to the ideology of peace do not merely seek victory; they seek peace – a peace which the vanquished as well as the victors can accept as their own. From this perspective the insurgents have no legitimate claims. The Iraqi insurgents are not the enemies of an occupying power; they are, in words of Prime Minister Blair, 'rejectionist groups'.[35] They reject the peace the British and American governments are trying to make in Iraq. By defining the insurgents as the enemy of the British and the Americans as well as the Iraqi people, the British and American governments are setting themselves a very high standard for victory, while at the same time arguing that this standard has actually already been met. National Security Advisory Stephen Hadley thus argues that 'it is our belief that most Iraqis share the president's definition of victory in Iraq.'[36] The Iraqis have transcended their enmity towards the Americans and Iraq has become a fellow democracy (albeit new and struggling). This analysis underscores the American commitment to help the Iraqis – after all, helping democracies in distress is a foreign policy doctrine which goes back at least to Truman, but Hadley's claim is also a claim that in the process towards victory the most important threshold has been passed already. Transcendence has been achieved; values are shared. One is left with the impression that implementation is all that is left.

This rather technocratic approach to peacemaking follows from the notion that peace is not something which needs to be negotiated as a conclusion to the outcome of a war, but that military victory negates any demands or designs the erstwhile enemy might have for the future. The definition of the content of peace belongs squarely to the Western 'custodians of peace', and anyone who rejects their notion of peace is acting against the true interests not only of the Western occupiers but also of the Iraqi people. The ideology of peace thus conceptually denies the Iraqis the possibility of formulating unique Iraqi interests in favour of a universalist claim on democratic peace.

conclusions

Peacemaking is not a technocratic question, but the Enlightenment terms by which peace is most often conceived in the West mean that we deal with it as if it was. This is true of politicians and academics in Western capitals and this is true of those with their boots on the ground. At least one reason why the West has such a poor record for making peaceful and stable societies in the wake of a military intervention is this particular focus on how to make peace. Thus, if we keep debating how to make peace in Darfur, Iraq or Afghanistan, we should not be surprised if nothing much comes of it – because we are asking the wrong question. We should realise that the peace the West furthers is an ideology rather than an objective state of affairs. There we should be asking 'why peace?' rather than 'how peace?'

Asking why we want peace at all and what kind of peace we want is not another way of saying that there is no such thing as peace; rather, the anthropological approach to peace is a way of illustrating that, while peace may be a common aspiration for all mankind, it can be practised in many different ways. For instance, it makes no sense from an anthropological point of view to discuss whether Swedes or Samoans have the 'best culture'; it makes little sense to search for the 'perfect peace'. Peace is not a recipe; it is a practice. Realising this is a crucial first step in coming to grips with the way peace shapes current Western strategy.

Ideology always comes with a price. While an ideology is necessary and perhaps even desirable as a foundation for formulating a policy, ideology also results in a narrow conception of what the situation at hand is, as well as the means and ends needed to rectify that situation. It is because of their inability to see the situation in a way other than that which serves their ends and preferred means that ideologues have made a bad name for themselves. In the case of peacemaking, however, the price is mostly being paid by the non-Western countries in which peace is supposedly made. From 2005 to 2008 41,000 Iraqi civilians and 6,700 Iraqi security forces were killed, while the US-led coalition debated how to make peace in Iraq.[37]

So, while the West debated in whose name (if anyone's) the war should be fought and went over the strategic options, the adversaries in Iraq skilfully used the ideology of peace against the US-led coalition. Exactly because the war was ideology by other means, the insurgents could be surprisingly effective by waging war against Iraqi civilians with the intention of destroying the symbols of peace and stability which the West needed in order to achieve peace. By 2008 many people were thus asking how peace was to be made in Iraq at all. But perhaps they were asking the wrong question.

notes

1. I. Kant, 'To Perpetual Peace. A Philosophical Sketch', in H. Reiss (ed.) *Kant's Political Writings*, Cambridge: Cambridge University Press, 1970, p. 93. See also Kant's 'Idea for a Universal History with a Cosmopolitan Purpose', in *Kant's Political Writings*, ed. by Hans Reiss and trans. by H.B. Nisbet, Cambridge: Cambridge University Press, 1970, pp. 41–53.
2. M.V. Rasmussen, *The West, Civil Society and the Construction of Peace*, London: Palgrave, 2003, pp. 29–30.
3. C. Geertz, *The Interpretation of Cultures. Selected Essays*, New York: Basic Book, 1973, p. 218.
4. Ibid., pp. 196–7.
5. Ibid., p. 198.
6. Ibid., p. 218.
7. Ibid., p. 205.
8. *The World War*, Papers Relating to the Foreign Relations of the United States, 1917, Supplement I, Vol. I, Washington, DC: United States Government Printing Office, 1932, p. 26.

9. M. Howard, *The Invention of Peace*, New Haven, CT: Yale University Press, 2000.
10. C. Coker, *Humane Warfare*, London: Routledge, 2001.
11. J. MacMillan, *On Liberal Peace. Democracy, War and the International Order*, London: Tauris Academic Studies, 1998, p. x.
12. Geertz, *The Interpretation of Cultures*, p. 5.
13. A. Swidler, 'Culture in Action: Symbols and Strategies', *American Sociological Review*, Vol. 51, 1986, p. 273.
14. Ibid.
15. E. Luttwak, *On the Meaning of Victory*, New York: Simon and Schuster, 1986, p. 289.
16. Quoted in J. Black, *War in the New Century*, London: Continuum, 2001, p. 2.
17. Kant, 'To Perpetual Peace', p. 93.
18. H. Pinter, *Art, Truth and Politics*, Nobel Lecture, 7 December, Stockholm: The Nobel Foundation, 2005.
19. T. Ali, 'Re-Colonizing Iraq', *New Left Review*, May–June 2003, p. 21.
20. After the invasion Susan Watkins kept the World War II metaphor going by referring to the Iraqi government installed by the US in 2004 as the 'Vichy on the Tigris'. Watkins argued that anyone who opposes US hegemony should support the 'the Iraqi maquis'. S. Watkins, 'Vichy on the Tigris', *New Left Review*, July–August 2004, p. 17.
21. G.W.F. Hegel, *Elements of the Philosophy of Right*, ed. by Allen W. Wood, Cambridge: Cambridge University Press, 1991, p. 361.
22. H. Kahn, W. Pfaff and E. Stillman, *War Termination: Issues and Concepts*, Croton-on-Harmon, NY: The Hudson Institute, 1968, p. 63.
23. M. Kaldor, 'From Just War to Just Peace', pp. 255–73, in C. Reed and D. Ryall (eds), *The Price of Peace. Just War in the Twenty-First Century*, Cambridge: Cambridge University Press, 2007, p. 269.
24. T. Blair, *Victory for Democracy in Iraq and Afghanistan is Vital if Global Terrorism is to be Defeated*, to The Foreign Policy Centre in association with Reuters, 21 March 2006, London: Office of the Prime Minister, §54.
25. A. Al-Zawairi, *Letter to Abu Musab al-Zarqawi*, English translation 12 December 2005, posted at www.weeklystandard.com, accessed 12 April 2006, §10–25.
26. Ibid., §43.
27. R.H. Solomon, 'Foreword', in J. Covey, M.J. Dziedzic and L.R. Hawley, *The Quest for Viable Peace. International Intervention and Strategies for Conflict Transformation*, Washington, DC: United States Institute for Peace, 2005, p. xi.
28. Ibid.
29. Rasmussen, *The West*, pp. 97–8.
30. G.W. Bush, *President Discusses Iraqi Elections, Victory in the War on Terror*, 14 December 2005, The Woodrow Wilson Center, Washington, DC: The White House, Office of the Press Secretary, §45.
31. R.B. Killebew, 'Winning Wars', *Army*, 55, 2005, p. 27.
32. National Security Council, *National Strategy for Victory in Iraq*, November 2005, Washington, DC: The White House, p. 3.

33. Ibid.
34. J. Lieberman, 'Our Troops Must Stay', *Wall Street Journal*, 29 November 2005.
35. Blair, *Victory for Democracy*, §37.
36. S. Hadley, *Victory in Iraq*, Center for Strategic and International Studies, Washington, DC, 20 December 2005, §33.
37. Iraqi civilian casualties are much disputed. The numbers mentioned here are based on news-reporting; see http://icasualties.org/oif/, 24 March 2008.

part 2
key agendas: institutions, issues, and themes

10

the institutionalisation of peacebuilding: what role for the Un Peacebuilding Commission?

alex j. bellamy

There is broad agreement nowadays that the international community has a responsibility to help states and societies rebuild after war.
One of the main reasons for this is that peacebuilding *after* violent
conflict tends not to arouse the same sorts of concerns about interference in sovereign affairs that preventive action *prior* to conflict and
reactive intervention *during* conflict provoke. This is because there
is a clear link between assistance in rebuilding state institutions and
capacity, the rule of law, shattered economies and basic infrastructure and the strengthening of state sovereignty. In short, post-conflict
rebuilding is chiefly about enabling and empowering states and societies in order to establish sustainable and legitimate peace, not about
impinging and overriding their sovereignty. This point was made most
clearly by Donald Steinberg, Vice-President of the International Crisis
Group, in an address on Burundi to the UN's Peacebuilding Commission
(PBC). Steinberg maintained that:

> Some may worry that these measures would undercut Burundi's sov-
> ereignty. Instead, the exact opposite is the case. The PBC can empower
> the Burundian people and government to harness the good will and
> hard resources of the international community to end the cycle of
> violence, political unrest, and economic upheaval that has shadowed
> Burundi for most of the past half-century.[1]

There is much less agreement, however, on what form that responsibility should take and what types of policies are needed to build

sustainable peace. Many of these differences are canvassed in other con-tributions to this volume. It has been well documented elsewhere that there is a broad neoliberal consensus among the key agencies involved with post-conflict reconstruction (especially the World Bank), which holds that the key to long-term peace lies in rapid processes of democra-tisation and market liberalisation designed to attract foreign investment and stimulate growth. In recent years, though, it has become increas-ingly clear that this model is deeply problematic. Rapid democratisa-tion can provide triggers for renewed violence and might inadvertently legitimise those very elites that caused conflict and state collapse in the first place. Market liberalisation can weaken already fragile states and exacerbates economic inequalities, one of the key causes of civil war.[2] In addition to these questions about the most appropriate path to take are questions about the way in which international assistance is delivered. Some espouse a large and highly directive international engagement, typified by the transitional administrations set up in Kosovo and East Timor, whereby the UN assumed the role of both peacebuilder and sov-ereign.[3] Others argue that these are impractical and expensive endeav-ours that deliver uncertain results and deny local ownership. They prefer the 'light footprint' approach developed as a strategy for post-war Afghanistan by Lakhdar Brahimi. Finally, there are myriad practical questions about how the international community can best support the transformation of war-torn societies into havens of stable peace.

There are three things we do know about peacebuilding, however. First, peacebuilding is critically important for the *prevention* of war. The single most important contributing factor to the outbreak of civil war is a past history of civil war, especially in the previous five years. A recent history of war can increase the likelihood of further war by as much as 40%. Indeed, almost 50% of peace agreements collapse within the first five years.[4] What is more, recent studies have shown that, whilst inter-national engagement with countries in crisis can improve levels of dem-ocratisation, gains made are quickly reversed and authoritarian politics re-emerge once engagement is downsized.[5] Effective peacebuilding is therefore a necessary component of prevention.

Second, we know that, for all its other faults, the UN is relatively good at peacebuilding when it is given adequate resources and pol-itical support. The UN has a significantly better track record than the US when it comes to nation-building. According to RAND, of 16 prominent cases of post-conflict rebuilding, 11 enjoy stable peace today. Of the eight UN-led endeavours (Congo, Namibia, El Salvador,

Cambodia, Somalia, Mozambique, Eastern Slavonia, Sierra Leone and East Timor), seven enjoy relatively stable peace today (Congo being the obvious exception). The American record is much more mixed. Only four of the eight US-led missions resulted in stable peace (West Germany, Japan, Bosnia, and Kosovo), though two of those (West Germany and Japan) were immense successes owing primarily to the extraordinarily high levels of political and financial support and local consent to the statebuilding project. The other four US-led missions have not produced successful outcomes (Somalia, Haiti, Afghanistan, and Iraq).[6] Of course, a more stringent test might add Sierra Leone and East Timor to the list of failures and would certainly raise concerns about progress in Cambodia and El Salvador. Indeed, if the benchmark is taken as something more substantive than the absence of widespread violence, the UN's record looks much less impressive. Charles Call and Susan Cook argued that, of 18 countries in which the UN was involved between 1998 and 2002, 13 were still classified as 'authoritarian' in 2002.[7] Likewise, Roland Paris argues that only two of the aforementioned missions (Eastern Slavonia and Namibia) could be described as 'unqualified successes'.[8] In a separate study including all countries that had played host to UN missions, including small peacemaking missions, Call concluded that countries that played host to a UN mission in the post-conflict setting were no less likely to revert to war than countries that had not hosted a UN mission.[9] However, when these figures are controlled for the size and scope of the UN's engagement with a particular crisis, it becomes clear that the better resourced, mandated and politically supported a peacebuilding endeavour, the more likely is a stable peace.[10]

Finally, as mentioned earlier, although the practice of rebuilding is highly controversial, it is much easier to build international consensus on the need to actively engage in rebuilding after armed conflict than it is to forge consensus on prevention or reaction. However, rebuilding is a long and costly endeavour and it has proven very difficult to persuade states to provide the necessary resources over a long enough period of time. This problem is perhaps best exemplified by the fact that whilst the world was quick to embrace the proposed new PBC in 2005 – at least once its mandate was limited to post-conflict settings – it has proven less eager to provide the Commission with the resources and funds necessary to effectively fulfil its role.

This chapter evaluates an important contemporary effort to improve the international community's ability to make a positive contribution to peacebuilding – the creation of the UN's PBC. It investigates the politics behind its creation and explores what role it might best fulfil. My argument is that, contrary to the expressed intentions of those who work for the Commission, the early indications suggest that the PBC is unlikely to play a leading role in constructing and executing peacebuilding plans and that attempts to make it fulfil this role might prove counterproductive, as this would involve duplicating work already underway. As presently conceived, the PBC is heavily politicised but lacks the bureaucratic clout, technical expertise, and financial resources to make a significant difference to the UN's efforts to support the consolidation of peace and prevent the all-too frequent backsliding into war and authoritarianism that follows a peace operation in the near term. However, the PBC can play an important role in marshalling political support for peacebuilding and providing a forum for donor consultation. More importantly, perhaps, it represents high-level political recognition of the need for the UN to support peace consolidation in the long term and creates an institutional setting for the advancement of new, better resources and more effective strategies.

the genesis of a commission

By early 2005, the idea of establishing a PBC was widely perceived by UN members as an 'idea whose time has come'.[11] The Commission enjoyed broad political support, especially in Africa. Although the idea of establishing a PBC was first mooted by the High Level Panel established by Kofi Annan to make proposals for reforming the UN, the idea of creating a Peacebuilding Unit within the UN's Department of Political Affairs (DPA) to support the UN's field operations had been put forth many times in the past and had suffered a similarly negative fate to proposals for an early warning unit. A majority of General Assembly members, in particular those associated with the Non-Aligned Movement, worried that initiatives such as this would strengthen the capacity of the Secretariat vis-à-vis the member states.

Nonetheless, Kofi Annan recognised the need to develop a capacity to better manage the transition from war to peace in his 2001 report on the exit and closure of peace operations. Annan noted that 'more than once during the last 10 years the United Nations has withdrawn a peacekeeping operation, or dramatically altered its mandate, only to see the situation remain unstable, or sink into renewed violence'.[12] The 'ultimate purpose' of UN peace operations, Annan argued, was 'the achievement of a sustainable peace'. In the aftermath of civil wars, peace 'becomes sustainable, not when all conflicts are removed from society, but when the natural conflicts of society can be resolved peacefully through the exercise of State sovereignty and, generally, participatory governance'. He continued, advocating a mixture of heavy involvement and 'light footprint': 'to facilitate such a transition, a mission's mandate should include peace-building and incorporate such elements as institution-building and the promotion of good governance and the rule of law, by assisting the parties to develop legitimate and broad-based institutions'.[13] To achieve sustainable peace, the Secretary-General argued, it was necessary to fulfil three objectives: consolidate internal and external security; strengthen political institutions and good governance; and promote economic and social rehabilitation and transformation.[14]

Although at this time Annan stopped short of advocating institutional reforms to make the secretariat more able to provide guidance to the Security Council about how best to achieve these objectives, there were moves to improve the UN's capacity in this area on an ad hoc basis. In October 2001, the UN established its first full-time Integrated Mission Task Force (IMTF) in New York to facilitate joint planning among UN bodies and agencies for the new mission in Afghanistan. Unfortunately, the task force lasted only six months and was disbanded in February 2002, before the mission had been fully deployed and Brahimi's plan for Afghanistan fully developed.[15] At the same time, the Department for Peacekeeping Operations (DPKO) attempted to improve coordination between peacekeepers and peacebuilders by developing an 'Integrated Mission Planning Process' involving other UN agencies.[16] In the absence of a body designated to take the lead in developing peacebuilding strategies, progress was painfully slow, prompting calls from some quarters for institutional reform. As Jehangir Khan, a former senior official in the DPA, put it: 'We desperately needed a high-level political body to support political processes and help countries implement peace accords. Historically, the DPA had been the lead UN body for peacebuilding, but it is not set up to be operational.'[17] These calls were echoed outside the UN. In October 2004, a meeting of NGOs and officials hosted by the International Peace Academy called for the UN to create an institutional 'home' for peacebuilding, where decisions could be taken and implemented.[18]

Recognising this need, the High Level Panel called for the establishment of a PBC supported by a Peacebuilding Support Office (PBSO) provided by the secretariat. The Panel recognised the critical relationship between peacebuilding and the prevention of future wars identified at the beginning of this chapter. It argued that there was 'no place in the United Nations system explicitly designed to avoid State collapse and the slide to war or to assist countries in their transition from war to peace', maintaining that this was no surprise given the Charter's focus on relations between states. Nevertheless, the Panel noted a clear international obligation to assist states in developing the capacity to perform sovereign functions effectively and legitimately.[19] This, it argued, should be the task of the PBC.

Thus, the High Level Panel conceived that the PBC would have broad-ranging tasks. The Commission should be charged with enabling the UN to act in a 'coherent and effective way' on a broad continuum of measures ranging from early warning and preventive action to post-conflict reconstruction. The PBC would identify countries at risk, organise and coordinate assistance, and oversee the transition from war to peace and peacekeeping to peacebuilding.[20] Importantly, it would fulfil the twin roles of conflict prevention and post-conflict reconstruction. In so doing, the PBC would facilitate joint planning across the UN system and beyond, would provide high-level political leadership (thus utilising peacemaking), and would increase the funds available for prevention and rebuilding.[21]

The proposed PBC was broadly welcomed. Within the US State Department, there was some initial resistance to the creation of 'another UN bureaucracy' but the proposal's backers prevailed, helped in no small part by the United States' abject failure to build peace in Iraq. From around autumn 2004, therefore, the US administration supported the proposal – though not without some important reservations.[22] Kofi Annan endorsed both the PBC and the Support Office, agreeing that the absence of such a body constituted 'a gaping hole in the United Nations institutional machinery'.[23] Unsurprisingly, however, given traditional hostility to granting the UN a role in early warning, there was no support for giving the PBC a broad mandate covering everything from early warning to post-conflict reconstruction as recommended by the High Level Panel. Some – especially the five permanent members of the Security Council – worried that these provisions impinged on the Council's prerogatives in this area. In order to protect the core proposal for the establishment of a PBC from the political fallout, Annan moved to distance himself from the prevention of the proposal, tying peacebuilding squarely to *post-conflict* reconstruction. Indeed, the first iteration of Annan's reform agenda – a report entitled *In Larger Freedom*, issued on 21 March 2005 – omitted reference to the whole question of prevention. However, after informal consultations with member states, Annan addressed the question of prevention in

an explanatory note issued in May as an addendum to *In Larger Freedom*.
Rather than a standing capacity to monitor member states as a way of
identifying those in need of support, Annan preferred a voluntary system
whereby the UN might provide preventive assistance on request. Thus, in
the addendum, he maintained that 'there are other mechanisms in the
United Nations for what has become known as "operational prevention"'.
He continued:

> I do not believe that such a body [PBC] should have an early warning
> or monitoring function, but it would be valuable if Member States
> could at any stage make use of the Peacebuilding Commission's
> advice and could request assistance from a standing fund for peace-
> building to build their domestic institutions for reducing conflict,
> including through strengthening the rule-of-law institutions.[24]

It is important to recognise that, in addition to the obvious political
problems associated with the proposed prevention role for the PBC, there
were also some serious practical and institutional difficulties. Annan
maintained that the UN already had functions designed to address early
warning and conflict prevention, not least the organisation's peacemaking and preventive deployment capabilities. It would be better to
strengthen these capacities, Annan argued, than to overlay them with
new offices. The Secretary-General insisted that the development of additional offices dealing with conflict prevention might lead to inadvertent
duplication and unhelpful interference in politically sensitive peacemaking activities.[25] It would be difficult, analysts concluded, for the DPA to
conduct quiet diplomacy on behalf of the Secretary-General when an
issue was before an intergovernmental body like the PBC.[26] Then there
was the risk of duplication with the Special Adviser on the Prevention
of Genocide, a position currently held by Francis Deng. Finally, Annan
argued that his proposed PBC model contained within it the capacity to
act in support of prevention efforts through its advisory function. Thus,
as Jessica Almqvist concluded, although there were serious deficiencies
in the strength of the PBC's mandate and capacity, it would have been
difficult for the new body to contribute to conflict prevention without
duplicating and interfering in the work of other arms of the UN.[27]

Even this modest proposal for the PBC to play a consent-based role in
assisting member states in capacity-building proved too much for the
General Assembly. In its final form, the PBC's mandate was limited to
bringing together 'all relevant actors to marshal resources and to advise

on and propose integrated strategies for post-conflict peacebuilding and recovery'.[28] The 2005 World Summit also supported the creation of a PBSO, but insisted that it be funded and staffed out of existing resources. The key driver of this restriction was the US, which argued against increased assessed contributions to fund the PBC/PBSO and insisted that the PBC's membership reflect the financial contributions it received from member states.[29] The General Assembly did, however, support the creation of a new fund to support peacebuilding.

Arguably, the most significant political dispute over the PBC concerned the question of where the Commission would be situated institutionally. The High Level Panel envisaged the PBC as a subsidiary of the Security Council, calling for its establishment by the Council under Article 29 of the Charter. The Security Council would 'consult' with the Economic and Social Council (ECOSOC) on the formation of the PBC but would have ultimate responsibility for the new body. Tellingly, the High Level Panel omitted the General Assembly from its proposed schema.[30] This proposal was not well received by many General Assembly members. India argued that the PBC should be entirely autonomous of the Security Council to make it easier for states to seek the Commission's assistance.[31] Others – most notably Iran – took this argument a step further and expressed concern at the expansion of the UN's capacity for interfering in the domestic affairs of states. Iran argued that the Commission should only conduct country-specific meetings at the request of the member state concerned. The proposed link to the Security Council would give the PBC potentially far-ranging powers of interference in sovereign affairs on a non-consensual basis. Even Switzerland expressed doubts about the connection between the PBC and the Security Council, though for different reasons. Switzerland lamented that the prominence given to the Security Council would further undermine the relevance of ECOSOC.[32]

Partly in response to these concerns, Annan rejected the proposal for the PBC to be a subsidiary of the Security Council. Instead, he proposed a structure whereby the Commission would be an 'intergovernmental' organ, comprising an equal number of members from the Security Council and ECOSOC, which would be subsidiary to both the General Assembly and the Security Council.[33] Unsurprisingly, this failed to stem the arguments, which dragged on into 2005. The Bush administration tempered the State Department's earlier enthusiasm for the PBC by insisting that the Commission be controlled by the Security Council in that the Council should be responsible for determining when and where the PBC should become involved in post-conflict reconstruction. In particular, the US argued that the PBC should be subsidiary to the Security Council on matters with which the Council is involved but that the Commission could continue its work after the Council has completed its dealings.[34] This position was strongly opposed by African governments especially. Africa's common position on UN reform (the 'Ezulwini consensus') insisted that the PBC be closely related to the ECOSOC and General Assembly as well as the Security Council. This position was endorsed by other key members of the Group of 77 (G77), including Indonesia and – we noted earlier – Iran.[35] The views of other states generally sat somewhere between these two poles. Sweden supported the US position on the grounds that the PBC would need to coordinate its efforts with the UN's peace operations and that this would require a close relationship with the Security Council and DPKO. On the other hand, Brazil used instrumental arguments to reject Security Council primacy, insisting that peacebuilding 'is best implemented by means of a core social and economic approach, rather than one based almost exclusively on political and security considerations'.[36]

The end-product was a framework almost identical to that proposed by Annan, comprising the General Assembly, ECOSOC and Security Council. The PBC would be subsidiary to the General Assembly and Security Council and would act as an 'advisory body' for the Assembly and two Councils. It would report, however, only to the General Assembly. This model paved the way for complex negotiations about membership. In addition to equal representation from the Security Council and ECOSOC, the Non-Aligned Movement insisted upon strong representation for the General Assembly itself. On the other hand, many Western states joined the US and argued that representation should be based on the level of financial contributions. After much wrangling, a compromise was reached granting the General Assembly equal representation with the Security Council and ECOSOC, plus membership rights for the top five financial contributors and top five troop contributors to UN peace operations.

the tripartite system: commission, support office, fund

The PBC was formally established by concurrent Security Council (Resolution 1645, 20 December 2005) and General Assembly (Resolution 60/180, 30 December 2005) resolutions. Created as an intergovernmental body, it was described by the Vice-President of the International Peace

Academy, Necla Tschirgi, as 'a very unusual and unique experiment'.[37]
As set out in the two resolutions, the PBC was given three primary purposes:

1. To bring together all relevant actors to marshal resources, to provide advice, and propose integrated strategies for post-conflict peacebuilding.
2. To focus attention on the necessary reconstruction and institution-
   building efforts to ensure post-conflict recovery and sustainable
   development.
3. To provide recommendations and information to improve coordination of all relevant actors.

The PBC's formal status is as an 'advisory body' answerable to the
General Assembly and ECOSOC, and to the Security Council on request.
It operates on the basis of consensus among its 31 state members. The
Commission organises 'country specific meetings' to assess the needs of
individual states that come onto its agenda. Countries may come onto
the PBC's agenda at the request of the Security Council, the ECOSOC
or General Assembly with the consent of the state concerned, in exceptional circumstances at the request of the concerned state, or at the
request of the Secretary-General.[38] Even where consensus between PBC
members and UN agencies is possible, the PBC lacks the formal authority to ensure the envisaged level of coordination between UN bodies
and agencies. As one commentator put it, 'its influence within the UN
stems entirely from the quality of its recommendations, the relevance
of the information it shares, and its ability to generate extra resources'.[39]
Of course, the PBC is not operating in a 'policy vacuum' but in an area
already crowded with UN agencies and bodies, regional organisations,
individual government donors, and NGOs. Finding a place within this
context and within the limitations set by the General Assembly is the
single greatest challenge facing the new body.

As conceived by Annan, the PBSO would be given the role of preparing substantive inputs for Commission meetings, providing inputs
for the planning process, and conducting best practice analysis and
policy guidance where appropriate.[40] It would be staffed by 21 new
appointments funded by the regular budget. Once again, however, the
UN membership had a more circumscribed view, limiting the PBSO's
role to 'gathering and analysing information relating to the availabil-
ity of financial resources, relevant United Nations in-country planning

activities, progress towards meeting short and medium-term recovery goals and best practices'.[41] Most notably absent was the policy guidance role envisaged by the Secretary-General. Nor, as noted earlier, were the members convinced by Annan's case for new appointments to staff the PBSO in part due to financial concerns (on the part of the US) and in part due to concerns among the G77 that a strong and effective PBSO might interfere in the domestic affairs of states.

Under pressure from these two directions, the UN's budget committees insisted that the PBSO's needs be met from existing resources. To accomplish this goal, PBSO was placed under the leadership of Carolyn McAskie (Canada), assigned seven staff members, three seconded personnel and five UN employees redeployed from other areas. The reduction from 21 to 15 staff was achieved by cutting Professional and General Services posts, leaving a relatively 'top-heavy' office. The use of redeployed rather than newly recruited employees also provoked concerns in some quarters. Speaking on behalf of the G77, South Africa expressed apprehension about the impact of redeployment on the releasing department.[42] Others have raised the possibility that redeployment might encourage turf struggles between departments and observed that releasing departments might refuse to release high-quality professionals. In addition to salaries and associated personnel costs, the PBSO receives an annual operating budget of $1.2 million sourced from the DPA.[43]

The third element of the UN's new peacebuilding capacity is the Peacebuilding Fund (PBF). At the behest of the US, the fund was created as an alternative to increased assessed contributions and is managed by the head of the PBSO and administered by the UNDP. The decision-making process associated with the fund's distribution is quite cumbersome and involves country-level reports, steering committees comprising UN agencies, bilateral donors, NGOs, and the host government, and requests by the PBC and/or Secretary-General. Initially, it was envisaged that the fund would be used to support projects in countries under consideration by the PBC and other post-conflict states.[44] This was subsequently narrowed as a result of the relatively low level of donations actually received. According to a 2007 PBSO briefing, the PBF is now intended to fill an important funding gap between the conclusion of a peace treaty and the commencement of fully fledged peacebuilding measures. Rather than providing substantive funding, the PBF envisages its role as 'catalytic' – helping to stimulate further funding by other agencies and donors.[45] The Secretary-General set a target of $250 million per year; by May 2007 governments had formally pledged $221 million and the Fund had actually received $137 million. Many of these pledges, however, were multi-year, making the actual annual fund far lower than the target. To date, the largest single donor to the fund is Norway, which has contributed $30 million.[46] By mid-2007 the fund had begun dispersing a small amount of this income on projects in Sierra Leone and Burundi – the PBC's two priority cases. A little over $5 million (of a projected total of $25 million) had been assigned to Sierra Leone for capacity-building measures in the police service and youth enterprise development. Burundi fared somewhat better, receiving $15.5 million for projects on resolving land disputes, anti-corruption measures, national reconciliation, supporting the role of women in the peace process, creating a national human rights commission, improving the judicial system, the disarmament of small arms, and barracking the national army.[47]

the commission at work

It is too early to make definitive judgments about the extent to which the PBC, PBSO and PBF have improved the UN's capacity for rebuilding. Tschirgi maintained that the PBC model 'will have little money and authority' and 'will therefore be a much less effective body than what many had wished for'.[48] Gareth Evans, meanwhile, argued that, despite these constraints, the PBC could play an important role in improving the UN's peacebuilding capacity – though only if member states embraced the Commission as a 'full partner' in peace and provided it with adequate resources.[49] The PBC's first six months were characterised by diplomatic wrangling conducted in a 'climate of suspicion' over procedures and membership.[50] It was not until October 2006 that the Commission began substantive work, beginning country-specific meetings on Sierra Leone and Burundi at the request of the Security Council. Sounding a note of optimism, however, Carolyn McAskie maintained that, once the Commission came to address substantive matters, 'the whole tone of the discussions and atmosphere changed 180 degrees. All members of the Commission were engaged on the issues of peacebuilding'.[51]

The initial focus on Burundi and Sierra Leone has been described in some quarters as emblematic of the PBC's 'cautionary and limited capacities' because neither has recently emerged from conflict and both had established peace agreements and post-conflict reconstruction efforts.[52] Another thing Sierra Leone and Burundi have in common is that the PBC was asked to play a role at precisely the moment that UN peace operations wound down, suggesting the possibility of a smooth transition from peacekeeping to peacebuilding orchestrated by the new Commission.

The Commission's first country-specific meetings identified the critical challenges facing the two countries. In relation to Sierra Leone, those challenges were identified as social and youth empowerment and employment, consolidating democracy and good governance, and justice and security sector reform. In Burundi, the main priorities were identified as promoting good governance, strengthening the rule of law and security sector, and ensuring community engagement. Following up on these meetings, the PBC/PBSO worked with the respective governments to develop plans to address these challenges. Specific measures were identified and $25 million allocated from the PBF (discussed earlier). Significantly, the World Bank and IMF agreed to cooperate with the PBC and extend credit to both countries.[53]

In relation to Sierra Leone, the Commission has encouraged the international community to increase its overall commitment to the government and has called on donors to broaden the donor base, provide secure assistance, relieve government debt, and meet consolidated peacebuilding objectives.[54] In the first half of 2007, the Commission focused on preparations for the country's presidential elections. In particular, the PBC served as a forum for UNDP and Sierra Leonean officials to identify potential risks to the election and those that might be generated by the election, along with members of the UN's Integrated Office in Sierra Leone (UNIOSIL). The PBC hosted discussions on the development of strategies to reduce those risks, including measures to ensure that the election itself was managed fairly, transparently, and effectively; a process of dialogue and confidence-building involving the electoral commission and political parties; measures to ensure freedom of speech in the media whilst also guarding against hate speech through the instigation and supervision of a government-sponsored Code of Conduct for the media; and measures to uphold the recommendations of the Truth and Reconciliation Council in order to discourage opposition spoilers. In addition to these measures already adopted by the government of Sierra Leone, the PBC advocated a range of other initiatives aimed at reducing the risks related to elections. The PBC argued that the government should establish a National Human Rights Council to address grievances raised by political parties and individuals, develop a strategy for decentralising public policy and the electoral commission to make them both better able to respond quickly and effectively to regional concerns, and initiate a process of dialogue with political parties that would continue after the election.[55] Taken together, these measures constitute a reasonably comprehensive plan for dealing with the inherent risks associated with the holding of elections identified in the first part of this chapter. Indeed, indications from Sierra Leone's presidential elections suggest that they succeeded in ensuring a largely free, fair, and non-violent process.

In the case of Burundi, the PBC followed up on its identification of the key challenges for peacebuilding by initiating a wide-reaching programme of activities, described earlier. In addition, the Commission has continued to monitor and comment on the development of a strategic plan for peacebuilding. In mid-2007, the government of Burundi, in partnership with key national figures and international donors, developed a draft 'Strategic Framework for Peacebuilding in Burundi' aimed at identifying objectives and specific tasks designed to achieve those objectives, as well as clear measures that could be used to ascertain progress. The PBC acted as one partner in this process, making a series of recommendations drawn from informal 'country-specific meetings'. Some practical and political tensions were evident, however, in the dialogue between the government of Burundi, other sponsors of the framework and the PBC. On the practical level, some PBC delegates argued that the framework should be 'action-oriented' and liable to revision as circumstances changed. This contrasted with the Burundian view – and that of several agencies working in Burundi – that the framework should *not* be an action plan but should instead set out an overarching strategic vision. These actors argued that individual programmes already had specific action plans and that the framework would simply add an extra layer of bureaucracy without making much of a concrete contribution to the peacebuilding effort in Burundi. Two types of political tension were also in evidence. Some delegates expressed concern about the way in which the proposed framework referred to neighbouring states. For example, the draft text referred to refugees in Tanzania as a 'threat to peace', drawing calls for revision from the PBC. Others, keen to avoid the *de facto* expansion of the PBC's remit, voiced concerns that some aspects of the proposed framework were broader than the scope of the PBC.[56]

Early signs, therefore, suggest that the PBC's political character makes it better suited to acting as a catalyst to attract government donations for UN operations than to providing operational guidance. Indeed, some commentators have noted that PBC meetings have already taken the form

of pledging conferences, helping to focus attention on specific countries and measures in need of support.[57] The early indicators also suggest
that the PBC is unlikely to play a clear or decisive role in coordinating
UN agencies. The PBC lacks the constitutional clout (it does not have a
mandate to coordinate UN agencies), bureaucratic capacity, or financial
power (its programmes are dwarfed by those run by the UNDP, UNHCR,
UNICEF, WFP, etc.) to be an effective coordinator. Its coordination role
is therefore more one of providing a forum for agencies, donors, and the
states concerned to identify peacebuilding priorities, develop strategic
plans, and initiate relatively small but high-profile programmes.[58] The
danger, then, is that the PBC might simply 'duplicate, confuse and divert
scarce resources' already dedicated to particular countries.[59]

Some members have insisted that the PBC should work with the states
concerned to develop Integrated Peacebuilding Strategies. Indeed, there
is broad agreement that it is in the development of such strategies that
the PBC will make its primary contribution. Speaking on behalf of the
EU, Thomas Matussek insisted that 'promoting the development of a
viable peacebuilding strategy which has broad ownership is where the
Commission can really add value'. The NAM broadly agreed, calling for
the PBC to develop 'holistic, coherent and inclusive' approaches to post-
conflict reconstruction.[60] There is clear merit here, and at the time of writing the PBC is developing Integrated Peacebuilding Strategies for Burundi
and Sierra Leone. However, without the constitutional, bureaucratic, or
financial wherewithal to coordinate even UN agencies in the realisation of those strategies it is hard to see how duplication can be avoided.
As Richard Ponzio notes, Sierra Leone already has a Poverty Reduction
Strategy, Medium-Term Expenditure Framework, a Peace Consolidation
Strategy, and bilateral strategies with the UK and EU on security and justice sector reform. It would be hard to disagree with Ponzio's view that
these context-specific and locally negotiated strategies developed by indigenous authorities and actors actively engaged on the ground are likely
to prove more effective than centralised strategies developed by political
figures in New York on the advice of a tiny support office.[61]

However, even with the narrow confines of its mandate and resourcing,
there are ways in which the PBC could make an effective contribution to
post-conflict rebuilding. First, it could embrace its political nature and
become an engine for augmenting donations and resources in support of
programmes already in place. From Afghanistan to Angola, post-conflict
reconstruction efforts are woefully under-resourced, and the PBC could
play a useful role as a focal point for persuading governments to provide

the necessary resources. The PBC could also play an important role in
ensuring that states deliver on their pledges of assistance. In Burundi, for
example, by early 2006 only 66% of the $1.1 billion pledged by donors
in 2000 had actually been disbursed.[62] The PBC's high profile and political standing make it ideally suited to fulfilling this role. In addition,
the PBC also builds an important bridge between the Security Council
and the World Bank. All too often, the security and economic wings of
the UN have acted at cross purposes – the latter using economic coercion to instil neoliberal marketisation and the retreat of the state whilst
the former sought to improve and develop state capacity. Sometimes,
as in the cases of Sierra Leone and Rwanda, World Bank policies have
directly contributed to political instability and violence.[63] In both of
those cases, the World Bank and IMF promoted market-driven growth
and focused on the collection of debt repayments, largely ignoring the
destabilising political and social effects of their policies. In both cases,
marketisation stimulated economic growth at the expense of widening
economic inequalities, which sharpened political and ethnic differences.
The focus on debt repayment contributed to cuts in vital services, weakening already fragile states.[64] By bridging the gap between security and
economics, the PBC could not only work to mitigate these effects; it could
also provide a forum for the articulation of consolidated peacebuilding
strategies whereby the security, governance, and economic dimensions
reinforced one another rather than operating at cross purposes.

Second, working alongside the DPKO, which significantly strengthened its civilian component by establishing a separate office on the
Rule of Law, the PBC/PBSO could explore ways of improving the organisation's capacity to augment peace operations with civilian capabilities
in areas such as the rule of law, electoral management, parliamentary
oversight, economic management, and government effectiveness.[65]
Ideally, the PBC should also play a key role in coordinating multi-agency
programmes of support to post-conflict societies, but there seems to be
little political support for this.

conclusion

The emergence of the PBC is testament to the fact that there is a clearly
emerging consensus on the importance of post-conflict reconstruction
and the contribution that the international community can make to
that process. There is also evidence of a less tangible consensus about
how best to go about transforming shattered communities after war.

Whilst democratisation and market-led growth are important, there is growing recognition that both can also sow the seeds of future conflict and, therefore, of the need to develop strategies to reduce the risks associated with them. It is telling in this respect that one of the earliest issues to come before the PBC was the development of 'risk reduction strategies' for Sierra Leone's 2007 presidential elections. The emerging consensus combines elements of the trusteeship mentality that underpinned the UN's transitional administrations in the Balkans and East Timor with basic ideas from the 'light footprint' approach. Thus, it is widely recognised that only local elites and civil societies can build sustainable peace but that the international community has an important role to play in helping to develop the necessary capacities to facilitate locally managed peacebuilding.

The main problem in relation to post-conflict rebuilding is not so much the proclivity towards neocolonialism identified by critics of the UN's transitional administrations, but the international community's relatively short attention span. Peacebuilding is an expensive and long-term endeavour involving myriad agencies. One of the primary reasons for establishing the PBC was the hope that an institutional 'home' for peacebuilding might help to capture and hold the world's attention. Given the broad support it enjoyed, we might have expected the PBC to be relatively immune from some of the political disputes that have dogged efforts to improve the UN's capacity for prevention and intervention. This proved not to be the case. Agreeing to the Commission in principle, states disagreed about its role and its place in the wider UN organisation. These debates reflected differences of opinion over the nature of peacebuilding itself and the appropriate locus of authority within the UN. At the risk of overgeneralising, Western governments typically see peacebuilding as a political and security-led endeavour closely associated with the work of the Security Council. They are also relatively comfortable with enlarging the Security Council's remit to cover peacebuilding. By contrast, many states in the global South remain deeply concerned about the increasing dominance of the Security Council and sought to use the PBC to reassert the authority of the General Assembly and ECOSOC. Moreover, as Brazil argued, they typically see peacebuilding as an economic and socially led activity.

Both sides of the debate were united by two considerations, however: they both supported the PBC in principle and neither wanted it to develop a strong institutional capacity. As a result, the PBC has a narrow advisory role and lacks the authority or capacity to coordinate

UN agencies, conduct planning, or develop consolidated strategies. This has led some to doubt that the PBC will be able to develop a useful role that avoids duplicating and interfering in the work of other organisations. These very real concerns notwithstanding, the PBC can play an important role in holding the attention of world leaders and providing a catalyst for funding, in encouraging broad dialogue on lessons learned, and in identifying ways of improving the UN's civilian capacity to promote peace. In the longer term, the PBC provides a high-level institutional venue for the further development of the UN's capacity to support the consolidation of peace. The danger, however, is that if an under-resourced PBC fails to stem the backslide into war in high-profile cases it will be seen as a failure by states and civil society groups alike, closing off its potential future development and expansion.

notes

This chapter draws arguments and some text from Alex J. Bellamy, *Responsibility to Protect: The Global Effort to End Genocide and Mass Atrocities*, Cambridge: Polity, 2009.

1. D. Steinberg, 'Peacebuilding Commission: Enhancing the Sovereignty of Burundi', presentation to the UN Peacebuilding Commission, 11 December 2006.
2. Set out superbly by R. Paris, *At War's End: Building Peace After Civil Conflict*, Cambridge: Cambridge University Press, 2004.
3. As described by R. Caplan, *International Governance of War-Torn Territories: Rule and Reconstruction*, Oxford: Oxford University Press, 2005.
4. P. Collier, V.L. Elliott, H. Hegre, A. Hoeffler, M. Reynal-Querol, and N. Sambanis, *The Conflict Trap*, New York: Oxford University Press for the World Bank, 2003, p. 7.
5. V. P. Fortna, 'Peacekeeping and Democratization', in A.K. Jarstad and T.D. Sisk (eds) *From War to Democracy: Dilemmas of Peacebuilding*, Cambridge: Cambridge University Press, 2008, p. 71.
6. J. Dobbins, S.G. Jones, K. Crane, A Rathmell, B. Steele, R. Teltschik and A. Timilsina, *The UN's Role in Nation-Building: From the Congo to Iraq*, Santa Monica: RAND, 2005, pp. xxv–xxvii.
7. C.T. Call and S.E. Cook, 'The Democratisation of Peacebuilding', *Global Governance*, Vol. 9, No. 2, 2003, p. 240.
8. R. Paris, *At War's End*, p. 151.
9. C.T. Call, 'Institutionalizing Peace: A Review of Post-Conflict Peacebuilding Concepts and Issues for DPA', unpublished paper, 31 January 2005, p. 8.
10. M.W. Doyle and N. Sambanis, *Making War and Building Peace: United Nations Peace Operations*, Princeton, NJ: Princeton University Press, 2006.

11. J. Almqvist, 'A Peacebuilding Commission for the United Nations', Fundación para las Relaciones Internationales y el Diálogo Exterior (FRIDE) policy paper, Madrid, June 2005.
12. S/2001/394, 20 April 2001, para. 4.
13. S/2001/394, 20 April 2001, paras 8 and 10.
14. S/2001/394, 20 April 2001, para. 20.
15. R. Ponzio, 'The United Nations Peacebuilding Commission: Origins and Initial Practice', Disarmament Forum working paper, 2007, p. 7.
16. DPKO/HMC/2004/12, 23 January 2004.
17. Interviewed by Ponzio, 'Peacebuilding Commission', p. 7.
18. N. Gibbons, 'An Expert View on the Peacebuilding Commission: A Unique and Unusual Experiment', Center for UN Reform Education, 21 December 2005.
19. UN High Level Panel on Threats, Challenges and Change, *A More Secure World: Our Shared Responsibility*, A/59/565, 2 December 2004, p. 83.
20. Ibid., p. 83.
21. Ponzio, 'Peacebuilding Commission', p. 8; S.C. Breau, 'The Impact of Responsibility to Protect on Peacekeeping', *Journal of Conflict and Security Law*, Vol. 11, No. 3, 2007, p. 455.
22. S. Patrick, 'The Peacebuilding Commission and the Future of US-UN Relations', comments to the Annual Meeting of the UN Association of the USA, 9 June 2006.
23. K. Annan, *In Larger Freedom: Towards Development, Security and Human Rights for all*, A/59/2005, 21 March 2005, para. 114.
24. Ibid., para. 115.
25. Annan, *In Larger Freedom*, addendum, A/59/2005/Add.2, 23 May 2005.
26. Almqvist, 'Peacebuilding Commission', p. 7.
27. Ibid.
28. World Summit Outcome Document, para. 98.
29. S/PV.5187, 26 May 2005.
30. HLP, *A More Secure World*, para. 263.
31. A/60/PV.66, 20 December 2005, pp. 9–10.
32. A/60/PV.66, 20 December 2005, pp. 10–17. Also see S. Chesterman, 'From State Failure to State-Building: Problems and Prospects for a United Nations Peacebuilding Commission', *Journal of International Law and International Relations*, Vol. 2, 2005, pp. 155–69.
33. Annan, *In Larger Freedom*, paras 114–17.
34. S/PV.5187, 26 May 2005.
35. Common African Position on the Proposed UN Reform, para. 4. Also see Almqvist, 'Peacebuilding Commission', p. 5; Ponzio, 'Peacebuilding Commission'.
36. Sweden and Brazil's positions are set out in summary form at www. reformtheun.org. These quotes are taken from Almqvist, 'Peacebuilding Commission', p. 5.
37. N. Gibbons, 'An Expert View on the Peacebuilding Commission: A Unique and Unusual Experiment', Center for UN Reform Education, 21 December 2005.
38. General Assembly Resolution 60/180, 30 December 2005, para. 15.

39. Ponzio, 'Peacebuilding Commission', p. 8.
40. Annan, *In Larger Freedom*, addendum 2, para. 21.
41. General Assembly Resolution 60/180, 30 December 2005, para. 23.
42. See C.S.R. Murthy, 'New Phase in UN Reforms: Establishment of the Peacebuilding Commission and Human Rights Council', *International Studies*, Vol. 44, No. 1, 2007, p. 52.
43. Ponzio, 'Peacebuilding Commission'; Henry L. Stimson Centre Peace Operations Fact Sheet Series, 2007, p. 3.
44. Ponzio, 'Peacebuilding Commission', p. 3.
45. 'The UN Peacebuilding Fund (PBF)', presentation by the Peacebuilding Support Office, 3 July 2007.
46. C.S.R. Murthy, 'New Phase in UN Reforms', p. 48.
47. 'The UN Peacebuilding Fund (PBF)', presentation by the Peacebuilding Support Office, 3 July 2007.
48. Gibbons, 'Expert View'.
49. G. Evans, 'What Difference Would the Peacebuilding Commission Make: The Case of Burundi', presentation to EPC/IRRI Workshop on the Peacebuilding Commission and Human Rights Council, Brussels, 20 January 2006.
50. See Security Council Report, 'Special Research Report: Peacebuilding Commission', 13 June 2006.
51. Interview with Assistant Secretary-General Carolyn McAskie, Center for UN Reform Education, 4 June 2007.
52. G. Thallinger, 'The UN Peacebuilding Commission and Transitional Justice', *German Law Journal*, Vol. 8, No. 7, 2007, p. 704.
53. Murthy, 'New Phase in UN Reforms', p. 53.
54. Chairman's Summary of the Country-Specific Meeting of the Peacebuilding Commission, 13 December 2006, para. 14.
55. 'PBC Update: First Lessons Learned on Sierra Leone', Center for UN Reform Education, 20 February 2007.
56. 'PBC Country-Specific Meeting Discusses Draft of Burundi's Strategic Framework', Center for UN Reform Education Briefing, 11 June 2007.
57. Ponzio, 'Peacebuilding Commission', p. 10.
58. 'The UN Peacebuilding Commission: Benefits and Challenges', background paper prepared by the International Peace Academy for the Regional Seminars organized by the Friedrich-Ebert-Stiftung, 6 June 2006.
59. Ponzio, 'Peacebuilding Commission', p. 10.
60. A/61/PV.86, 6 February 2007, pp. 6–8.
61. Ponzio, 'Peacebuilding Commission', p. 10.
62. G. Evans, 'What Difference Would the Peacebuilding Commission Make: The Case of Burundi', presentation to EPC/IRRI Workshop on the Peacebuilding Commission and Human Rights Council, Brussels, 20 January 2006, p. 5.
63. P.D. Williams, 'Peace Operations and the International Financial Institutions: Insights from Rwanda and Sierra Leone', in A.J. Bellamy and P.D. Williams (eds) *Peace Operations and Global Order*, London: Frank Cass, 2005, pp. 103–23.
64. Ibid., p. 118.
65. These are suggested by Ponzio, 'Peacebuilding Commission', p. 10.

11
democratisation and development: a difficult relationship

dirk kotzé

introduction

The relationship between political democratisation and socio-economic development in the context of conflict resolution and peace processes is increasingly debated as part of an evolving concept: post-conflict reconstruction and development.[1] It is also related to terms such as 'liberal peace',[2] 'developmental peacekeeping'[3] and 'multidimensional and integrated peace operations' (MIPO).[4]

Examples of programmes in which it received prominence are Boutros Boutros-Ghali's 'An Agenda for Peace' (1992) and its Supplement (1995), the African Union's 'Policy Framework for Post-Conflict Reconstruction and Development' (2006) and the 'African Post-Conflict Reconstruction Policy Framework' (2005) designed by the AU's New Partnership for Africa's Development (NEPAD). The UN's involvement in El Salvador, Timor Leste, Cambodia, Kosovo and Sierra Leone are examples of post-conflict reconstruction in the past two decades. The role that democratisation and development played in these cases has to be researched in much more detail.

One of the earliest examples of post-conflict reconstruction was the Marshall Plan after the Second World War. It focused mainly on Western Europe, Greece, Turkey, and Japan, and its main emphasis was on economic reconstruction. Japan is a good example where economic development received preference, while Gen. MacArthur acted as the governor of Japan between 1945 and 1948. For the purpose of this discussion it is noteworthy that the democratisation of Japan commenced only after the American period.

Today the question of the place of democratisation and development in peace processes is complex and influenced by many exogenous factors. Many of the views about it are not informed by empirical research but clouded by ideological commitments to liberal democracy or the free market. Intellectual activism promoting the moral and indispensable value of democracy does not allow for critical questions about its role in peace processes. Professional interests or ideological commitments to a global free market (Fukuyama's 'the end of history' was an example), such as those of researchers associated with the World Bank, find any doubt about the socio-political primacy of the economy indefensible. Paul Collier is an example of a highly influential scholar in the discipline of conflict resolution, whose work is symbiotically influenced by the logic of the free market. His influence on the democracy–development debate has to be understood in the context of his World Bank association. The purpose of this chapter is to make a contribution to this debate by focusing specifically on a number of African experiences.

Another introductory remark is about the powerful influence of the Pacific Rim ('Asian Tigers') states on development theory. Since the transitions in the early 1990s in Africa and Latin America, the examples of territories such as South Korea, Singapore, Taiwan, and Hong Kong have presented a model of statist economic development with high growth rates. Such a development path is shielded from pluralistic political pressures by a one-party dispensation. Only after an extended period of economic growth do evolving social pressures open space for political democratisation. This model postulates that development should start with economic growth, followed much later by political democratisation. In this model the cascading effect of growth is believed to be the dynamo for development. African states were undeniably influenced by these thoughts. How they apply to peace processes have, however, not yet been intensively explored.

In view of these introductory considerations, this chapter is concerned with the following three questions:

- Is there a sequential progression from democratisation to development, or vice versa, or do they unfold concurrently? Several arguments – including some based on the Pacific Rim examples – assume that democratisation and economic development cannot be implemented at the same time. In some instances causality is assumed: development inevitably leads to democratisation, or democratisation is a necessary precondition for development. Other arguments – especially those by the AU, the South African government and even the World Bank – are that practical political pressures do not allow the luxury of a sequential progress but demand concurrent implementation. The question then is: is there any sequence in which results in the two areas (democratisation and economic development) start to appear?

- Which process (democratisation or development) is the most likely to be implemented as part of a peace process; which of them is/are most appropriate for conflict resolution and peacebuilding; and which of them has the best chance of success? Conflict resolution and post-conflict reconstruction are about dealing with the root causes of the conflict. This question relates to whether democratisation and/ or development are the most appropriate and successful means to address these root causes. Can we consider them as a generic package for post-conflict rehabilitation?

- How appropriate is economic development primarily driven by the private sector for post-conflict reconstruction and development? Does private sector development address the economic/social factors which caused the conflict or caused a relapse of the conflict? Economic reconstruction is most of the time substantially influenced by the dogma of international financial institutions, major banks and international NGOs. Given the weak capacity of most post-conflict states, the private sector (both domestic and external) is treated as the institution with the best capacity and motivation to drive a development process. A related question, which will not receive much attention in this chapter, is whether aid (humanitarian and longer-term donor aid) contributes to real economic development. Is aid an initial alternative for development by the private (or public) sector, or is it a necessary supporting mechanism for the private sector? It should be noted that in Africa aid has not been a long-term approach to economic development in the 1990s, but has been replaced relatively quickly by externally induced economic structural adjustment programmes with a strong neoliberal orientation.

This chapter first looks at research conclusions already reached about the relationship between democratisation and development, and how it is relevant for conflict resolution. The second main focus in this chapter is on existing policy practises or statements in which the relationship plays an important part. It looks at pronouncements by UN leaders and in the NEPAD policy framework.

In the third main theme in this chapter the focus shifts to the African context. Four states which experienced conflict have been selected for the purpose of the discussion: South Africa, Mozambique, Rwanda, and Burundi. Their experience with post-conflict reconstruction and development is considered in relation to the abovementioned research conclusions and the questions raised above. The purpose of their inclusion is to use a limited number of empirical cases as reference points to test the general assumptions about the role of democratisation and development in conflict resolution and post-conflict reconstruction.

existing research about the relationship

This discussion is an extension of the research conclusions on the implications of the democracy–development relationship for conflict resolution already reviewed in another publication.[5] The main conclusions were as follows. Post-conflict reconstruction and development assumes that a combination of political democratisation and socio-economic development is the panacea for conflict. Regarding the correlation between democratisation and conflict resolution, the conclusion is that it depends on the constructivist understanding of democracy. If the understanding is procedural in nature (i.e. that democracy is essentially about regular elections, separation of powers, the rule of law, bill of rights, and other procedural matters) and if the root causes of the conflict are about political discrimination, a dysfunctional social contract, or human rights violations, then a direct correlation between democratisation and conflict resolution exists. If, however, the root causes are about identity matters (such as the Banyamulenge in the DRC, Ivoirité in Côte d'Ivoire, or authenticity in Darfur) and democracy is understood as predominantly substantive in content (i.e. about socio-economic equity and moral considerations), then democratisation is less appropriate as an instrument for conflict resolution. The correlation between democratisation and conflict resolution is therefore a contingent relationship, depending on the constructivist understanding of democracy in each context.

The second conclusion is concerned with the correlation between socio-economic development and political democratisation. The research done by a wide range of scholars, notably Adam Przeworski and his colleagues,[6] concluded that democratic regimes are more sensitive to economic development than to the impact of their political legacy, religious and ethno-linguistic diversity, or even the international political environment, on their democratisation. They also concluded that in developing states economic growth is directly and positively correlated with freedom. Personal income is strongly correlated with the degree of democratic stability, and in developing states a decline in income increases the probability of democratic decline. A number of African case studies, however, question the unqualified validity of a theoretical correlation between democracy and economic development. The view that high growth rates cause political volatility is qualified by the fact that relatively low real growth, but with substantial and visible impact on an economy (which is relatively well developed), can cause more volatility and democratic instability than a high growth rate with less of a social impact (if the economy is less developed). Patterns of income distribution (i.e. concentration of wealth in different strata, and therefore the rich/poor gap) do not have an impact on democratic (or non-democratic) stability. The human development index (HDI) also does not show a consistent correlation with democratic (in)stability. Overall, it can be concluded that economic development factors are not necessarily a catalyst for democratisation.

The third conclusion addresses the assumption that a combination of democratisation and socio-economic development (as part of 'liberal peace') provides a necessary structural basis for resolving deep-rooted conflicts. The fact that the correlations between democratisation and conflict resolution, and between democratisation and development, are not unqualified implies that this assumption cannot be verified. The only correlation not yet addressed here is between economic development and conflict resolution (in either democratic or non-democratic conditions). The question is whether economic development on its own can reduce the potential for conflict, or resolve a conflict, irrespective of the type of political system. Its implication would be that economically less developed states are more prone to conflict than more developed states. In a UN Security Council debate in January 2007 the Lithuanian representative and then-President of the Economic and Social Council made the statement that there is a strong correlation between low levels of development and conflict. According to him, nine of the 10 states with the lowest human development indices have experienced conflict in the past 16 years. The World Bank calculated that conflict reduces the GDP growth of the local economy by 2.2% each year.[7] These are not yet conclusive evidence of a correlation between economic development and conflict, and therefore the impact of development still requires more attention.

In the next section we look at policy practices in which the democracy–development relationship plays an important part in the context of conflict and peacebuilding. It is included in the discussion to elucidate the practical relevance of this relationship as ostensibly a popular point of departure for UN-assisted peace processes, and to identify how international diplomats and policymakers understand this nexus.

the democracy–development nexus in policy frameworks

Both Boutros Boutros-Ghali and Kofi Annan developed frameworks for the UN in which political democratisation and socio-economic development are symbiotically linked to conflict resolution and peacebuilding.
     In 'An Agenda for Peace' Boutros-Ghali made the following observation:

> There is a new requirement for technical assistance which the United Nations has an obligation to develop and provide when requested: support for the transformation of deficient national structures and capabilities, and for the strengthening of new democratic institutions. The authority of the United Nations system to act in this field would rest on the consensus that social peace is as important as strategic or political peace. There is the obvious connection between democratic practices – such as the rule of law and transparency in decision-making – and the achievement of true peace and security in any new and stable political order.[8]

Boutros-Ghali also referred to structures 'which will tend to consolidate peace and advance a sense of confidence and well-being among people'. He referred explicitly to democratic institutions, such as monitoring elections, advancing efforts to protect human rights, referring or strengthening governmental institutions, and promoting formal and informal processes of political participation.[9]
     In his original formulation the UN Secretary General paid more attention to the political–democratic dimension of post-conflict peacebuilding than to the socio-economic developmental dimension. It is significant that he concentrated on the procedural aspects of democracy (elections, human rights) and on institutions. It provides insight into his understanding of the core issues in conflict resolution and post-conflict peacebuilding, which appear to be mainly structural in nature.
     Three years later, in his Supplement to the 'Agenda', he continued with a similar approach but included socio-economic development as well. According to him, the measures of post-conflict peacebuilding include demilitarisation, the control of small arms, the monitoring of human rights, electoral reform and social and economic development.[10]

'An Agenda for Peace' is a good proponent of the (neoliberal) 'liberal peace' paradigm in which democratic institutions play an important part. The role of market-driven development as a complementary component is, however, less prominent in the UN plan than in other proponents of this paradigm. 'Social and economic development' is presented in the 'Agenda' in neutral terms, but if we consider it in conjunction with deficient 'national structures' then a structural approach to development is usually suggested with a strong neoliberal bias.

Kofi Annan has been even more explicit about the role of democratisation in conflict resolution. He made the following remarks:

Democratic principles provide the essential starting point for implementation of such settlements, which usually involve not only democratizing the state but also giving more power to civil society. Once political actors accept the need for peaceful management of deep-rooted conflicts, democratic systems of government can help them develop habits of compromise, co-operation and consensus-building.[11]

If both Annan's and Boutros-Ghali's sentiments are considered, the general approach in the UN is to rely on democratisation and development as a paradigm for conflict resolution and peacemaking. This paradigm's ideological or philosophical content is not always clear, but its approach to conflict resolution is mainly a structural and institutional one. This appears to be the UN's main approach. The organisation does not present alternative resolution frameworks. The question is, therefore, whether it suits all, or most, conflicts.

Should we move the focus to Africa, NEPAD's policy framework can be used as an example for determining whether the same nexus of a structural relationship is also utilised. In its Executive Summary the following perceptive observation is registered:

The nexus between development, peace and security have become a central focus of post-conflict reconstruction thinking and practice over the last decade. The key policy tension in the post-conflict setting appears to be between economic efficiency and political stability.[12]

Economic efficiency and political stability are juxtaposed in this statement, while a nexus between development and peace–security is observed. Arguably, a correlation between development and economic efficiency, and between peace–security and political stability, is established. In view of the fact that post-conflict reconstruction is understood by NEPAD as 'addressing the root causes of a conflict and to lay the foundations for social justice and sustainable peace[13] the nexus should also address the root causes.

The NEPAD policy framework operationalises the nexus in the following five dimensions: (1) security; (2) political transition, governance, and participation; (3) socio-economic development; (4) human rights, justice, and reconciliation; and (5) coordination, management, and resource mobilisation.[14] Their proportional contributions to post-conflict reconstruction are analytically separated into three phases: the emergency, transition, and development phases. The transition phase concentrates on political matters, such as a transitional government, constitution-making, and ultimately an election. The development phase – four to 10 years long – includes reconciliation, socio-economic reconstruction, and ongoing development programmes.

NEPAD summarises all these aspects in the following table:

Goals within each element during the three phases of post-conflict reconstruction

	Emergency phase	Transition phase	Development phase
Security	Establish a safe and secure environment	Develop legitimate and stable security institutions	Consolidate local capacity
Political transition, governance, and participation	Determine the governance structures, foundations for participation, and process for political transition	Promote legitimate political institutions and participatory processes	Consolidate political institutions and participatory processes
Socio-economic development	Provide for emergency humanitarian needs	Establish foundations, structures, and processes for development	Institutionalise long-term developmental programme
Human rights, justice and reconciliation	Develop mechanisms for addressing past and ongoing grievances	Build the legal system and processes for reconciliation and monitoring human rights	Established and functional legal system based on accepted international norms
Coordination and management	Develop consultative and coordination mechanism for internal and external actors	Develop technical bodies to facilitate programme development	Develop internal sustainable processes and capacity for coordination

Source: NEPAD[15]

Two of the five operational dimensions, which are particularly important for this discussion, are 'political transition, governance, and participation' and 'socio-economic development'. For the sake of presenting them as authentically as possible, the relevant paragraphs in the policy framework are quoted here.

Paragraph 40 (page 11) represents the political and democratic dimension:

> The **political transition, governance and participation** dimension involves the development of legitimate and effective political and administrative institutions, ensuring participatory processes, and supporting political transition. Aside from facilitating elections, programmes include strengthening public sector management and administration; establishing a representative constituting process; reviving local governance; strengthening the legislature; broadening the participation of civil society in decision-making process, and building the capacity of political parties and civil society for effective governance while giving former rebel groups a chance to turn themselves into viable political parties if they so wish. There is typically a focus on engendering a culture of rule of law based on existing or newly formulated constitutions, by supporting justice sector reform and related institutions. The transition phase should focus on the need to ensure plurality and inclusiveness, dialogue and the participation of all constituencies and stakeholders. During the development phase it is important to encourage and develop broad-based leadership at all levels; to build a shared purpose for the nation; to develop national capacity in terms of skills, mobilisation of resources and reviving national infrastructure; to promote good political and economic governance; develop checks and balances to measure progress; and finally, to institute a culture of long-term assessment of the impact of post-conflict reconstruction activities and programmes.

This articulation of the political dimension differs significantly from the Annan formulation. It reaches beyond a structural view of democracy to one involving leadership, political culture, the rule of law, and an important role for civil society. Even good economic governance is included in the NEPAD formulation.

Paragraph 41 (pages 11–12) in the NEPAD document deals with socio-economic development:

> The **socio-economic development** dimension covers the recovery, rehabilitation and reconstruction of basic social and economic services as well as the return, resettlement, reintegration and rehabilitation of populations displaced during the conflict including refugees and IDPs. This dimension needs to focus on an approach that ensures effective dynamic linkages between activities related to the provision of emergency humanitarian needs and longer-term measures for economic recovery, sustained growth and poverty reduction. It is also crucial that balance is struck on the relationship between social capital and social cohesion at all stages of the post-conflict reconstruction process. Programmes to be implemented in this dimension include emergency humanitarian assistance; rehabilitation and/or reconstruction of physical infrastructure; provision of social services such as education, health, and social welfare; and enhancing economic growth and development through employment generation, trade and investment, and legal and regulatory reform.

The NEPAD articulation is a relatively narrow view of socio-economic development, because it does not demonstrate an appreciation of the ravages of conflict and how deep-rooted the destruction or paralysis in the economy often is. Transformation from a war economy to a post-conflict economy, post-conflict social rehabilitation and linking economic development to it, is often one of the most daunting challenges. How to delink politics from the economy in a conflict (e.g. 'blood diamonds' in Angola and Sierra Leone or the linkage between the war in the DRC and multinational involvement in mining and the timber market), while at the same time establishing a new link between democratisation and socio-economic development, is a Herculean task for post-conflict reconstruction. NEPAD appears not to fully incorporate all these aspects in its strategy.

the nexus in the African context

In this part of the chapter four cases from Africa will be used to continue analysing the correlation between democratisation and development in the context of conflict resolution. The vast literature on this correlation, already summarised in a previous section, is mainly concerned with the relationship between democratisation and development, and does not generally distinguish post-conflict from relatively peaceful but undemocratic conditions. Uncertainty exists, therefore, as to whether the democratisation-development nexus manifests itself differently in post-conflict than in peaceful circumstances. In this chapter the focus is only on post-conflict peacebuilding.

A methodological uncertainty is where to start with the empirical investigation: with democratisation, and thereafter proceeding to determining its effect on economic development, or vice versa? The independent variable in both possibilities will be the absence of widespread political conflict in the peacebuilding process. In this study the exception is Burundi, which serves as the control case in which democratisation and economic development are implemented under conditions of intermittent conflict.

For the purpose of this study a choice has been made about the methodological approach in line with Kekic's[16] argument that the standard modernisation thesis (i.e. economic development leads to democracy) has been replaced by a causal direction leading from democracy to development (operationalised as income). The focus is therefore, in the first instance, on democratisation in South Africa, Mozambique, Rwanda and Burundi. The progress made with democratisation in the four cases has to be established. Thereafter the same will be done with socio-economic development. In the following section the main objective is to investigate how possible it is for democratisation to commence soon after a conflict. Is it therefore realistic to include it in the initial peacemaking and peacebuilding package?

democratisation as a post-conflict tool

In the absence of a consensus on defining and measuring democracy, a range of indicators and measuring tools will be used, including those of Freedom House, the *Economist* Index of Democracy, Afrobarometer, Transparency International's Corruption Perception Index, and the Mo Ibrahim Foundation's Index of African Governance (IAG). The intention is to determine whether a general consensus about democratisation in the four cases does exist.

Freedom House focuses on political rights and civil liberties, and releases an annual assessment based on a seven-point scale, with 1 as the best rating. The four cases were rated as follows:

Year	South Africa		Mozambique		Rwanda		Burundi	
	PR	CL	PR	CL	PR	CL	PR	CL
1993	5	4	6	5	6	5	7	7
1994	2	3	3	5	7	7	6	7
1995	1	2	3	4	7	6	6	7
1996	1	2	3	4	7	6	7	7
1997	1	2	3	4	7	6	7	7
1998	1	2	3	4	7	6	7	6
1999	1	2	3	4	7	6	6	6
2000	1	2	3	4	7	6	6	6
2001	1	2	3	4	7	6	6	6
2002	1	2	3	4	7	5	6	5
2003	1	2	3	4	6	5	5	5
2004	1	2	3	4	6	5	5	5
2005	1	2	3	4	6	5	3	5

PR = political rights; CL = civil liberties ;
Source: Freedom House[17]

The first factor of significance in these ratings is the possible impact of the first election after a conflict: the elections held in 1994 in South Africa and Mozambique, in 2003 in Rwanda, and in 2005 in Burundi. The Freedom House ratings indicate that in all four cases they marked an improvement in the political rights and freedoms, but not necessarily in civil liberties – only in South Africa did the election produce such results. Another characteristic is that the initial elections did not introduce a deepening of democracy – except in South Africa. Though Mozambique has a strong opposition, in the form of Renamo, it does not translate into a gradual improvement in the quality of either political rights or civil liberties.

Rwanda and Burundi, with comparable histories up to 1994, also look quite similar in the Freedom House ratings after 1994, despite Rwanda's relative peace for almost 10 years and Burundi's ongoing civil strife. President Paul Kagame's approach in Rwanda to postpone elections until 2003 has meant that the post-conflict reconstruction process did not include democratisation. Since 2003 it does not appear as if Rwanda has entered a period of democratisation. With its election in 2005, violence-torn Burundi has actually overtaken Rwanda in the area of political rights. Burundi is now quite similar to a democratising Mozambique in terms of both categories of ratings.

The Freedom House score card appears to suggest no correlation between democratisation and conflict, except for South Africa. At this stage of the analysis it suggests the absence of any correlation between peacebuilding and democratisation; in other words, (procedural) democratisation does not necessarily address the deficits in political rights and civil liberties. A speculative explanation is that the deep-rooted causes of the conflict in Mozambique and Rwanda might have been less about political rights and civil liberties than in South Africa and Burundi. (The similarities of the conflicts in Rwanda and Burundi, however, make such an explanation not entirely plausible.)

The *Economist* Index of Democracy is based on five categories: the electoral process and pluralism, civil liberties, the functioning of government, political participation, and political culture. The four cases are rated as follows for 2007:

	Overall score	Electoral process	Functioning of government	Political participation	Political culture	Civil liberties
South Africa	7.91	8.75	7.86	7.22	6.58	8.82
Mozambique	5.28	5.25	5.71	4.44	6.58	4.12
Burundi	4.51	4.42	3.29	3.89	6.25	4.71
Rwanda	3.82	3.00	3.57	2.22	5.00	5.29

Source: Kekic[18]

The overall scores for the four states confirm the pattern established by Freedom House. The latter's ratings of political rights are also more or less in line with the Index's patterns. Regarding civil liberties, the two ratings do not correspond. In all other respects, the conclusions about democratisation and peacebuilding are supported by the Index.

The Mo Ibrahim Foundation's Index of African Governance (IAG) is another indicator.[19] Its main focus is on 'good governance' and not only democratisation, but for the purpose of this discussion its indicators (based on 58 measures) can be compared for the four cases:

	Burundi			Rwanda			South Africa			Mozambique		
	2000	2002	2005	2000	2002	2005	2000	2002	2005	2000	2002	2005
Safety and security	40.8	49.6	60.4	64.4	73.5	76.2	61.1	61.1	61.1	86.1	86.1	86.1
Rule of law, transparency, corruption	47.3	47.3	48.8	49.6	53.3	47.6	76.5	73.8	75.2	39.8	43.1	43.8
Participation, human rights	29.6	32.3	41.9	34.6	35.3	69.7	87.4	88.5	81.1	71.0	76.7	71.0

Source: Mo Ibrahim Foundation[20]

These scores underline the effects of elections in Burundi (2005) and
Rwanda (2003) on safety and security in Burundi (less in Rwanda) and
on participation and human rights in both. The rule of law, transparency and corruption did not improve in either after their elections – in
Rwanda it actually declined (which is confirmed by Freedom House).
In Mozambique, the rule of law, transparency, and corruption are
gradually improving, while in South Africa they remained constant.
In both South Africa and Mozambique, ratings on public participation
and human rights have declined between 2002 and 2005, ostensibly
because of their lower voter participation in the 2004 general elections.
This tendency is not registered in the Freedom House ratings. The level
of participation (as articulated in the IAG) is not similar to the quality of democracy (as articulated by the Freedom House and *Economist*
Index). In proportional terms the IAG follows most of the tendencies
registered in the other rating systems.

Though corruption is not a direct indicator of democracy (see e.g. Italy
and Japan), it negatively influences a sense of good governance and the
public credibility of elected institutions. Transparency International is a
leading agency which uses its Corruption Perception Index (CPI) to track
corruption in states. The following is a table of the four cases plus a few
comparable states (the higher the score, the less corrupt is the state):

	1998	1999	2000	2001	2002	2003	2004	2005	2006	2007
Botswana	6.1	6.1	6.0	6.0	6.4	5.7	6.0	5.9	5.6	5.4
Namibia	5.3	5.3	5.4	5.4	5.7	4.7	4.1	4.3	4.1	4.5
South Africa	5.2	5.0	5.0	4.8	4.8	4.4	4.6	4.5	4.6	5.1
Rwanda								3.1	2.5	2.8
Mozambique			2.2			2.7	2.8	2.8	2.8	2.8
Burundi								2.3	2.4	2.5
Tunisia	5.0	5.0	5.2	5.3	4.8	4.9	5.0	4.9	4.6	4.2

Source: Transparency International[21]

Certain of the tendencies identified in the IAG are supported by these
gradings: in South Africa the perceived worsening of corruption between
2000 and 2001, and improvement between 2003 and 2004; the worsening in Rwanda after 2005, and the improvement in Burundi after 2005,
are examples of corroboration.

A significant feature of this table is that corruption is endemic in conflict situations (like Burundi's) but that democratisation (in the form

of elections) does not necessarily improve the situation. A comparison between Rwanda and Burundi indicates that conflict is not the deciding factor in the prevalence of corruption. Mozambique's high levels of corruption, despite a decade of peace, also bring into question a correlation between democratisation and a reduction in corruption – even South Africa's relative increase in corruption supports this notion.

The last indicator of democratisation is Afrobarometer. It consists essentially of opinion surveys, in which the difference between the procedural and substantive notions of democracy plays an important part. As a general premise, substantive democracy assumes that political democratisation and socio-economic development should occur concurrently. Procedural democracy, on the other hand, implies prioritisation of political democratisation ahead of economic development.

Afrobarometer reported on surveys conducted in Botswana, Zimbabwe, Zambia, Malawi, Lesotho, Namibia, and South Africa between 1999 and 2000. Of the four cases used in this chapter, only South Africa is included in these surveys, and hence the surveys have limited comparative value. The importance of the studies is that they significantly deviate from the standard practise which looks at democratisation and democratic consolidation mainly from an institutionalisation or procedural point of view. It quoted Richard Rose and his colleagues,[22] who argued, that if political institutions are the 'hardware' of a democratic system, what people think about democracy and those institutions is the 'software' of that system.[23] For the purpose of our discussion, it adds a perceptional/ experiential dimension to democracy in addition to the rights-based and institutionally based dimensions. How has democracy fared in South Africa since the election in 1994? Can interaction between the political and socio-economic dimensions of democratisation and development be detected in these studies?

The results of the surveys are that the citizens of Lesotho, Namibia, and South Africa are the least likely in Southern Africa to consider the political elements as the most important components of democracy. They insist on the inclusion of important substantive components of economic delivery.

While South Africans exhibit the greatest awareness of democracy as a concept in Southern Africa, elected and representative institutions enjoy less trust with them than more purely state institutions. South Africans are also more likely to emphasise the realisation of socio-economic outcomes as crucial for democracy, rather than key procedural components (such as elections, multiparty competition, and the separation of powers).

In conclusion, the expected correlation between post-conflict peace and democratisation is not confirmed by the case studies as necessarily correct. Absence of conflict, in comparison with conflict situations, does not automatically correlate with higher levels of political rights or civil liberties, or reduction in corruption.

Though not yet confirmed, the case studies suggest that the general dictum that peace leads to democratisation has to be qualified. A more appropriate approach might be to look for a correlation between *specific causes* of the conflict and democratisation, and not conflict in general. If the causes were specifically factors violating democracy in a political sense, then a post-conflict peace might be conducive for democratisation. South Africa is a good example. Sudan is not a good example. Resolution of other types of conflict (e.g. territorial disputes, resource conflicts, and even conflicts about identities) might not necessarily lead to, or require, democratisation. The same applies to support for substantive democracy as part of a post-conflict package. It appears to depend on the nature of the conflict.

In this section we looked at one part of the nexus (democratisation) in Africa. In the next section the focus is on socio-economic development.

socio-economic development as a post-conflict tool

The purpose of this section is to determine whether there is any relationship between socio-economic development and post-conflict reconstruction in the four case studies. For many reasons it is exceptionally difficult to operationalise socio-economic development, especially in circumstances ravaged by conflict. Mindful of this qualification, our operationalisation in this discussion consists of three elements, namely the Human Development Index (HDI) as determined by the UNDP, economic growth articulated as the Gross Domestic Product (GDP), and the Gini coefficient as an indicator of economic inequality. The three indicators encompass the debate between 'modernisation' (growth) and 'development' in the sense that development is not only measured by growth but also by the effect of growth on reducing the income gap, and improving quality of life in terms of literacy and life expectancy.

The first step is to address the Human Development Index.

(1) Hdi and conflict

The UNDP (2007, p. 225) explains the HDI as 'a composite index that measures the average achievements in a country in three basic dimensions of human development: a long and healthy life; access to knowledge; and a decent standard of living'. The table below provides us with the statistics of the four case studies (the closer to 1.000, the better is the HDI):

	1975	1980	1985	1990	1995	2000	2005
South Africa	0.650	0.670	0.699	0.731	0.745	0.707	0.674
Rwanda	0.337	0.385	0.403	0.340	0.330	0.418	0.452
Mozambique	–	0.304	0.291	0.317	0.335	0.375	0.384
Burundi	0.290	0.318	0.352	0.366	0.347	0.368	0.413

Source: UNDP[24]

In South Africa the HDI increased from 1975 to 1995 and thereafter started to decline. In Rwanda, the HDI also systematically increased between 1975 and 2005, except for the period 1990–2000. A similar systematic increase can be seen in Burundi, except for the period 1995–2000. In Mozambique the HDI declined between 1980 and 1990 but thereafter also increased systematically.

The tendencies in the HDI indicate that protracted conflict does not necessarily inhibit human development. Dramatic violent events, like the Rwandese genocide in 1994 and the ethnic violence in Burundi during the same period, do have a negative effect on HDI, but thereafter recover relatively quickly, while conflict continues at lower intensity.

A post-conflict situation does not, therefore, necessarily contribute to human development. Countries in conflict might even have higher levels of human development than those with relative peace – compare Burundi with Mozambique. South Africa's decline in HDI is partially ascribed to the effects of HIV/AIDS on life expectancy (0.430 in 2005 compared with 0.47 in 1998).

Economic growth, in the form of GDP, is the next indicator.

(2) GDP and conflict

Paul Collier is of the opinion that conflicts reduce a country's annual GDP growth by an average of 2%. This implies that in a post-conflict situation an increase in growth could be expected. Collier is, however, of the opinion that after a conflict considerable attention is paid to new political designs, but the same does not apply to economic policies and institutions. In his view, 'economic development is the *sine qua non* of achieving a major reduction in the global incidence of civil war'.[25]

What can the four case studies tell us about GDP growth in Africa? The following table provides statistics, albeit incomplete:

	South Africa	Mozambique	Rwanda	Burundi
1993			−10.0	
1994			−49.0	
1995		1.5		
1996	4.3	6.4		
1997	2.6	11.3		
1998	0.5			
1999	2.4		7.6	
2000	4.2		6.0	−0.9
2001	2.7		6.7	
2002	3.6		9.9	
2003	2.8	8.0	4.0	−1.2
2004	4.5	7.0	3.5	4.8
2005	5.1	8.2	0.9	0.9
2006	5.0	7.5	5.2	5.1
2007		7.9	5.8	

South Africa adopted a macroeconomic policy in 1994 (Reconstruction and Development Programme) based on socio-economic fundamentals. It did not attract significant foreign direct investments, which served as one of the reasons for the policy change in 1996 to the neoliberal Growth, Employment and Redistribution (GEAR) policy. Up to 2003 growth was volatile and averaged 2.7% per year. In 2004 (coinciding with the third general election since 1994), growth entered an accelerated phase. It therefore took about 10 years before the peace dividends reached the economic sector.

Mozambique followed almost the same political trajectory as South Africa, starting with democratic elections also in 1994. Growth responded much more quickly to the political situations: the average growth in 1993–99 was 6.7%, and in 1997–99 it was 10.0%. Between 2003 and 2007 the average was 7.7%. Mozambique therefore differs from South Africa in terms of both growth level and a quicker response to political changes.

Five years after Rwanda's genocide its growth rate was 7.6%, compared with –49.0% in 1994. This growth rate was maintained until 2002. Rwanda held its first presidential and parliamentary elections after the genocide in 2003. At the time of the election its economic growth rate declined by 3–5%, but started to recover in 2006. Between 2004 and 2006 the growth rates of Rwanda and Burundi were comparable.

In summary, the case studies present two growth patterns after a conflict: the first is South Africa's, in which growth responded relatively slowly to the political changes, but entered a high growth path after about 10 years. Mozambique and Rwanda followed comparable trends as the second pattern. They responded more quickly to the post-conflict situation and their growth rates were impressive in the first years after the conflict. After 3–4 years the growth slowed down and consolidated at a level which South Africa only reached after 10 years.

Burundi's example is even more responsive to conflict resolution. In 2003 its GDP was –1.2%. In the same year a ceasefire was signed by the Government and one of the main rebel groups, while the other groups continued with the war. In 2004 the GDP was 4.8%. The next year a new constitution was implemented and the first election held. GDP increased to 5.1% (the same as South Africa's and Rwanda's) though some rebel groups remained outside the peace process.

A general conclusion, therefore (though based on a small sample of case studies), is that GDP growth appears to respond positively to post-conflict situations or even a significant reduction in conflict. GDP growth, therefore, does not depend on the *absence* of conflict, as Burundi indicated. In the absence of a large number of case studies or a large sample it is impossible to determine whether South Africa is an exception to this conclusion or represents another category.

As indicated earlier, the Gini coefficient can also be used in determining the nature of socio-economic development.

(3) Gini coefficient and conflict

In view of the previous discussion of GDP growth, the question is whether socio-economic development in a post-conflict situation also addresses economic, income or wealth inequalities. The statistics are summarised in the table below:

	South Africa	Mozambique	Burundi
1991	0.68		
1995	0.596		
1996	0.69	0.396	
1998	0.59		0.424
2000	0.578		
2001	0.64		
2002	0.635	0.42	
2003	0.593		
2004	0.578		
2007	0.593	0.396	0.333

Mozambique's example is significant in the sense that, though it attained impressive levels of GDP growth, the Gini coefficient neither increased nor decreased. In Burundi it decreased after 1998. No statistics for Rwanda are available. South Africa is, once again, problematic in the sense that its pattern is volatile. Up to 2004 no correlation existed between GDP growth and the Gini coefficient. The general opinion is that, with the significant increase in GDP growth since 2004, income and wealth inequality also increased.

A general conclusion is that post-conflict economic development does not improve the situation of economic inequality. Economic growth is often impressive but it does not address structural inequalities. It appears to benefit the formal economy more than the informal economy. Compared with a politically unstable and not yet democratic situation (like Burundi's), economic development in more stable post-conflict situations does not necessarily provide a basis for a better quality of economic life for the population as a whole. On the other hand, the business class experiences a significant difference.

general conclusion

We can now combine the conclusions regarding democratisation and socio-economic development as post-conflict tools, and return to the question of whether a combination of the two is an appropriate model for post-conflict reconstruction and development.

All the case studies suggest that post-conflict peace or stability on its own cannot be positively correlated with guaranteed increased levels of democratisation or socio-economic development. Similar levels of civil liberties, political rights, or corruption can also be present in unstable and conflict-prone situations. A direct correlation between peace and a combination of democratisation and development could not be confirmed by this study.

Another question is whether a combination of democratisation and socio-economic development, to be implemented simultaneously, should or could constitute a post-conflict reconstruction package. The four case studies suggest that in practise the two elements are prioritised differently. In the case of South Africa, the economic dividends appear only after about 10 years. The first decade was a period of radical political changes and consolidation of the constitutional dispensation. GDP growth was relatively slow. Rwanda and Mozambique represent another scenario: delay in democratisation or political restructuring while economic development and security stabilisation were prioritised. Only 9 years after the genocide did Rwandese President Paul Kagame authorise the first multiparty election.

The study concludes that the case studies deviate from the policy documents (UN and NEPAD) but support the theoretical discomfort with the notion that democratisation and socio-economic development can be implemented concurrently and with the same levels of success. A preference for the one or the other as the first priority after a conflict is, however, not yet clear from the research. While it is easier to quantify early economic successes than political successes (as South Africa has shown), the policy choices will depend on the leaders' political judgements and not on scientific political theory.

notes

1. D. Kotzé, 'Post-Conflict Reconstruction: New Discourse, Old Theories', in D. Kotzé and H. Solomon (eds), *The State of Africa: Post-Conflict Reconstruction and Development*, Pretoria: Africa Institute of South Africa, 2008, p. 107.
2. O.P. Richmond, *The Transformation of Peace*, Basingstoke: Palgrave Macmillan, 2007.
3. N. Madlala-Routledge and S. Liebenberg, 'Developmental peacekeeping: what are the advantages for Africa?', Paper presented to the Africa Defence Summit, Midrand, 13 July 2004 (www.issafrica.org/pubs/ASR/13No.2/Contentpdf.html)
4. E.J. Munro, *Multidimensional and Integrated Peace Operations: Trends and Challenges*, GCSP Geneva Papers, Norwegian Ministry of Foreign Affairs, 2008.
5. D. Kotzé, 'Implications of the Democracy-Development Relationship for Conflict Resolution', *African Journal on Conflict Resolution*, Vol. 5, No. 1, 2005, pp. 85–7.
6. A. Przeworski, M.E. Alvarez, J.A. Cheibub and F. Limongi, *Democracy and Development: Political Institutions and Well-Being in the World, 1950–1990*, Cambridge: Cambridge University Press, 2000.

7. Security Council SC/8945, 31 January 2007. Security Council holds day-long debate on post-conflict peacebuilding; focus on early efforts of new Peacebuilding Commission (www.un.org/News/Press/docs/2007/sc8945. doc.htm, accessed 2 August 2007). See also P. Collier, L. Elliot, H. Hegre, A. Hoeffler, M. Reynal-Querol and N. Sambanis, 'Civil war as development in reverse', *Breaking the Conflict Trap: Civil War and Development Policy*, Oxford: Oxford University Press, 2003.

8. B. Boutros-Ghali, *An Agenda for Peace: Preventive Diplomacy, Peacemaking and Peace-Keeping*, Report of the Secretary-General pursuant to the statement adopted by the Summit Meeting of the Security Council on 31 January 1992, A/47/277-S/24111, 17 June 1992, para. 59.

9. Ibid., para. 55.

10. B. Boutros-Ghali, *Report of the Secretary-General on the Work of the Organization: Supplement to an Agenda for Peace*, Position paper of the Secretary-General on the occasion of the fiftieth anniversary of the United Nations, A/50/60-S/1995/1, 3 January 1995, para. 47.

11. K. Annan, in P. Harris and B. Reilly (eds) *Democracy and Deep-Rooted Conflict: Options for Negotiators*, Stockholm: IDEA, 1998, pp. vii–viii.

12. NEPAD, *African Post-Conflict Reconstruction Policy Framework*, Midrand: NEPAD Secretariat, 2005, para. 6, p. v. (www.iss.co.za/AF/RegOrg/nepad/pcrpoljun05.pdf), accessed 19 October 2009.

13. Ibid., para. 3, p. iv.

14. Ibid., para. 38, p. 11.

15. Ibid., p. 8

16. L. Kekic, The Economist Intelligence Unit's index of democracy (*The World in 2007*), pp. 2, 6.

17. Freedom House, *Freedom in the World* (www.freedomhouse.org/template. cfm?page=15/), accessed on 27 March 2008.

18. Ibid., pp. 2–5.

19. Mo Ibrahim Foundation, *Index of African Governance* (www.moibrahimfoundation. org/en/section/the-ibrahim-index/scores-and-ranking), accessed 28 March 2008.

20. Ibid., Index of African Governance.

21. Transparency International, *Corruption Perceptions Index* (www.transparency.org/policy_research/surveys_indices/cpi), accessed on 25 March 2008.

22. R. Rose, W. Mishler and C. Haerpfer, *Democracy and Its Alternatives: Understanding Post-Communist Societies*, Baltimore, MA: John Hopkins University Press, 1998.

23. R. Mattes, C. Keulder, A.B. Chikwana, C. Africa and Y.D. Davids, 'Democratic Governance in South Africa: The People's View', Afrobarometer Working Papers, No. 24, pp. i, 1.

24. UNDP, *Human Development Report 2007/2008. Fighting Climate Change: Human Solidarity in a Divided World*, New York: UNDP – Palgrave Macmillan, 2007, pp. 236–7.

25. P. Collier, 'Development and conflict', Paper presented to the Centre for the Study of African Economies, Oxford University, 2004, p. 10.

12
Ngo dilemmas in peacebuilding

henry f. chip carey

Scholarly interest in transnational advocacy networks, government networks, and 'networked networks' of NGOs, states, and IGOs has continued.[1] NGOs have shown states that the latter are not the only actors in town. By initiating lawsuits, such as that which denied Pinochet head of state immunity from torture, they illustrate this power. Along with intergovernmental organisations (IGOs), NGOs have begun to decentralise world power. Are NGOs a panacea? Clearly NGOs are not. Is the proverbial glass half-empty or half-full? Both. Yet, with a gap between formal and actual practice, with power not federated locally, NGOs face the choice between advocating where power is actually located or where it is supposed to be.

The failure of peacebuilding in Haiti and the troubled situations in Cambodia, Bosnia, Kosovo, Afghanistan, and Iraq have made it difficult for international and any local NGOs to be effective. The lack of security is not the only restriction on NGOs; government policy can make it very difficult for them to exist or operate. States also control NGOs through regulations, infiltration, and dishonesty. Press controls imposed by Pervez Musharaff's Pakistan in May 2007 and Vladimir Putin in Russia since 2000 have also been applied to foreign NGOs. Putin has targeted opposition or advocacy NGOs and news media, with arbitrary use of administrative measures and indifference to the rule of law by officials; most often, the officials perpetrating such abuses have kept out of the spotlight.[2] Putin has referred to a 'new threat, as during the Third Reich', against which he has created and provided military training to mobilise paramilitary groups, such as the 15,000-member Nashi Army and Police, the Young Guards, and Walking Together.[3] Virtually no opposition or independent NGO voices have appeared on

Russian television since the 2007–8 elections.[4] Similarly, during the 2008 Zimbabwe elections, President Robert Mugabe halted food distribution by humanitarian NGOs (HINGOs).[5] Under the military junta in Burma/Myanmar, the government largely restricted French and US ships from unloading supplies and foreign and domestic NGOs from distributing aid after Cyclone Nargis in May 2008 killed 100,000 people. The storm also coincided with a constitutional referendum campaign, which was dubiously declared approved. The country's monks and a few domestic NGOs provided a modicum of survival assistance, even if the majority of dispossessed were left on their own.[6] In the past decade, a DONGO mass youth organisation, USDA, has harassed and infiltrated pro-democracy movements and NGOs, as well as killing members of Aung San Suu Kyi's entourage on a rural road in 2003.[7]

Pessimism has also resulted because some illiberal NGOs, such as paramilitary groups, have instigated conflicts. Unlike in the Cold War, when regimes and ideologies were the target of geopolitical competition, in the apocalyptic 'age of terrorism' since 11 September 2001 some 'NGOs', otherwise depicted as terrorists, have not differentiated between militaries, governments, and their citizens as targets of armed attack and genocidal propaganda. Civic and liberal NGOs have had their commitment tested by the assassination of NGO staff, as in East Timor, Sierra Leone, Chechnya, Bosnia, and Afghanistan. Globalisation has helped induce the rise of anti-civic NGOs opposed to Western-led globalisation, based on Manichean narratives and categories of evil infidel versus the true religion. For its part, the West, especially the US, has sacrificed individual rights, particularly of immigrants,[8] despite complaints of violations from human rights NGOs, because 'We are at war Stupid!'[9]

NGOs of these different types have transformed, reformed, and undermined peacebuilding, though they have been controversial in applications and heterogeneous in goals, capabilities, and sympathies. Even in seemingly, uncontroversial tasks, such as clearing land of mines and unexploded munitions, for example, controversies emerge because of concomitant tasks requiring the fostering of economic conditions that lead to peace. System reform is needed if demining is to become a productive part of peacebuilding.

types of Ngos

In an idealistic definition, NGOs are 'self-governing, private, not-for-profit organisations that are geared towards improving the quality of life of disadvantaged people'.[10] NGOs can also be domestic and/or international. As Aggestam writes, 'NGOs are often the first actors to become aware of the risks of conflict escalation and tend to be the ones who remain in conflict areas the longest.'[11] NGOs serve as watchdog groups to monitor situations; they provide humanitarian services in conflict-ridden areas; they provide logistical support in post-conflict states; and they provide relief goods in conflict and post-conflict situations. NGOs play a very important and large role in prevention, which is roughly half of the theory of peacebuilding, but hardly half of the practical and actual efforts of peacebuilding. NGOs should represent unpopular causes; if they can make sure that those groups are not abused by others, whether the state, the majority, or the minority, that is sufficient. No NGO has to respond to typically right-wing criticism that they do not have the right to advocate, because that is essential to any right to assemble, speak, or associate.

However, if Clausewitz is correct, that war is not really categorically different from ordinary politics, then private armies and mercenaries should also not be excluded from the category of NGOs just because they are attempting different political goals from those of the liberal peace or civil society. For that reason and for the purpose of this study, we define NGOs[12] broadly. An NGO is defined as any association, liberal or illiberal, not part of the government and in society (excluding states and parties), whether civil or not. This broader definition more clearly reflects the reality that permitting associations does not necessarily make them beneficial to peace. Illiberal NGOs are more likely to emerge during illiberal or authoritarian regimes. We should not be naïve about NGOs. They are self-interested groups with a set of views, who make truth claims on the basis of their expertise. NGOs are not supposed to be 'representative' in the sense of being elected to their positions. They do not have to represent any large groups because they protect the minority if need be. NGOs do not represent constituencies, in the sense of being elected, and certainly do not represent majorities. If anything, they are needed to represent minorities against majoritarian tyranny, since most countries lack a judicial branch to protect minorities or majorities against tyranny. However, NGO advocacy can lead to minority interests being advanced, which could be equally tyrannical if no democratic process can accommodate or induce compromises on issues of greatest intensity. NGOs offer democratic participation, not democratic representation. However, the distinction is not that clear, because one participates in part in order to gain better representation.

Barnes suggests a typology with just three types of NGOs: NGOs that are not tied to the conflict, for example the Church; those which get involved; and those NGOs which are tied to the conflict. The third category is the most numerous and just tends to reproduce the existing cleavages in a conflict.[13] This typology is distinguished from those based on funding and autonomy dimensions, such as Gordenker and Weiss's distinctions between NGOs, QUANGOs (quasi-NGOs because of dependency on government support), and DONGOs (donor-created NGOs).[14] Many scholars make various distinctions within NGOs, such as between international and domestic, profit and non-profit, human rights NGOs and humanitarian NGOs, etc. The International Committee of the Red Cross (ICRC) has been called a QUANGO (a quasi-non-governmental organisation, because it relies to a very high degree on public resources),[15] and the International Finance and Reconstruction Corporation (IFRC) a DONGO (donor-NGO),[16] which is not considered to be an NGO. This distinction may not be particularly meaningful, since more than half of the NGOs in New York City are dependent on public resources.[17] Yet this distinction is not perfect, since both the IFRC and ICRC provide services and resources, in the case of the latter to refugees in complex humanitarian emergencies.[18] Sikkink notes that most human rights organisations are NGOs, but Amnesty International is not only an NGO but can also be considered a social movement because part of its work also involves independent volunteer groups to set priorities.[19] Yet Weiss and Gordenker depict the ICRC as the 'oldest, most disciplined, and best organised as an organization' of the NGOs lobbying or utilising the UN.[20] Within the social movement literature in sociology and political science, NGOs would fit the type of social movement organisation, though not all NGOs would be a type of social movement. Yet what Tocqueville stressed as necessary to protect civil society included any type of NGO, including the press, business, and religious associations, well before the emergence of the 'Beltway Bandit' phenomenon.

The number and quality of NGOs vary in different civil societies. NGOs also vary in terms of five contextual arenas of peacebuilding in which they operate: quality of civil society, political society, market economy, the extent of the rule of law, and the quality of state effectiveness. The US has been adept at utilising QUANGOs and DONGOs for its own purposes. The most notorious have been the CIA fronts that ran arms sales to the Iranians and transferred the profits to the Contras in the mid-1980s. More recently, the US has used Blackwater USA and other private military companies, or what detractors would call 'mercenaries', to protect diplomats and other military operations that involve, probably deliberately, operations outside international humanitarian law (IHL). Since IHL binds US forces, Blackwater USA can operate with impunity from, for example, either Iraqi or US law, for its killing of civilians in Iraq.

The UN Department of Public Information has approved 1,523 NGOs with whom it is associated.[21] The DPI Committee on NGOs 'disassociated' a substantial number of NGOs 'because they no longer meet the criteria for association', including Catholic Relief Services, the US Catholic Conference, the Lesotho Program, Lesotho, the US Chamber of Commerce, and the Council on International Educational Exchange, USA.[22]

Sudan serves as a cautionary example of a state with numerous HINGOs that have been and are continuing to be manipulated. Despite the need for goods and services of the multiple HINGOs operating in Sudan, many are exploited by warring parties. As De Montclos explains:

> The country of Sudan is extremely poor, and international assistance therefore has played a major role in shaping the local war economy. Humanitarian aid [is] siphoned off by combatants for military and strategic ends. By unwittingly furnishing supplies for the combatants, international assistance has even been blamed for prolonging the conflict.[23]

In Sierra Leone, once security was established, NGOs were able to successfully operate and provide aid and assistance in coordination with the peace process. As Jackson writes, '*Medicins Sans Frontieres* began to effectively operate again.'[24] Furthermore, 'by 2002, the United Nations High Commissioner for Refugees (DONGO funding), announced that fifteen INGOs, four local NGOs and two UN agencies would work together and coordinate their efforts to reintegrate refugees into society'.[25] Major NGOs such as Amnesty International aided in the efforts to establish an independent judiciary, as well as a special court for the prosecution of war crimes and the creation of a Truth and Reconciliation Commission to enable reconciliation.[26] The special courts began 'holding trials in 2004 of those deemed primarily responsible for war crimes and human rights abuses'.[27]

Late in the communist regime in Yugoslavia, there were many so-called 'independent' agencies that were officially working without government control and were considered to be NGOs. Actually they were controlled and operated by the communist party and government officials and were funded from the state budget. They were a market-ing tool for (mis)representing liberties and freedoms within an unfree society. Another type, independent NGOs, were opposed to Milosevic: groups such as the 'Independent Association of Journalists of Serbia', 'Forum for Ethnic Relations', various student organisations, unions of lawyers, etc. After the 1999 NATO bombing, the police and the secret police started to arrest and prosecute the members and sympathisers of groups such as the Forum for Ethnic Relations, including the coordinator of the Forum, Professor Dusan Janjic, and try them as traitors. The gov-ernment fight against the student lead organisation *Otpor* (Resistance) was even more aggressive. These kinds of organisations were the key players in helping to oust Milosevic out of power after the 2000 elec-tions. These NGOs were funded from abroad and collaborated with for-eign NGOs, mostly from the US and Western Europe. $3 million came from government foundations to be spent in Serbia from the September of 1998 to 2000. *Otpor Resistance*, which led the successful overthrow of the Milosevic regime, following training in Hungary and Banja Luka, Republic of Bosnia *Srpska*, received the largest share.

nature of dilemmas

Dilemmas result in part from paradoxes arising from contemporary phenomena, which have been noticed by scholars of modernisation nation-building and statebuilding, but which have not been integrated into a theory of peacebuilding. Studies of NGOs have drawn attention to these dilemmas, such as: (a) NGO neutrality in the face of evil, trad-ing off access for principle; (b) prolonging war, by providing humani-tarian relief, which either feeds those who might otherwise give up the fight or is stolen by the more powerful for a profit, or which induces the more powerful to be more harsh because its opposition is suffering less; or (c) actively building peace, which increases conflict and violence in practice in order to achieve an end state of a just peace. There can also be a conflicting logic in practice between long and short-term peace-building, because the latter causes conflict. The confrontation by NGOs and other actors to establish a just and therefore a stable peace requires the acceptance of common standards and practices of human rights, as well as a consensus on a type of capitalist economics.

Peacebuilding approaches would work brilliantly if both sides trusted each other and behaved rationally. Actors, however, are rational over the short run, but not in the long run, where complex interdependence and trust would pay off. The problem is that attempting to gain the trust of the other side makes him or her less trustful, not more. This can be because each side feels that they will be cheated and have less relative power.

Why might the efforts of NGOs to build peace backfire? The plausible hypotheses include that, first, NGOs are relatively impotent to affect or inhibit other, more powerful, causes. If one looks at the various books published in the conflict resolution series, for example, by several important commercial, academic presses, such as Lynne Reinner or Palgrave Macmillan, one will see NGOs active, to some, however limited, extent, in every country with violent political conflicts, low-intensity warfare and/or war itself. Clearly, the NGOs may be achieving some good for peace, over the short and/or the long term. Even assuming they have no negative, unintended externalities, such NGOs may be too insignificant to make much of a difference, in the face of political parties, interior ministries, terrorist cells, army-backed conspiracies, independent militias, and armed forces, any of which may be mobilised to use force. More directly, former UN Secretary General Kofi Annan used to assert that peacebuilding is an essentially political process. This profound observation has many ramifications. However, the most direct statement would be that the political process must achieve a high degree of consensus, particularly over the formulation of a constitution and formal (such as including opposition party members in a cabinet) and informal (such as working together in drafting legislation committees) mechanisms of power-sharing. While NGOs can make suggestions as to how to achieve consensus, as well as to criticise those who do not support it, or criticise the terms of any consensus that appears unethical, secret, or exclusive, they are largely out of the loop of influence. If political adversaries choose to remain polarised, then peacelike politics will be difficult to achieve.

Second, NGOs themselves may contribute to systemic polarisation, even though they may be asserting democratic and/or human rights. NGOs in El Salvador, such as *Tutela Legal*, and in the Philippines, such as Task Force Detainees (TDF), openly sided with the Marxist, FMLN, and NPA insurgents in both countries. Whether or not they were front groups for the insurgents, they did champion their cause, if only by reporting on veritable human rights violations committed by government forces. Other NGOs in both countries were certainly NGO fronts for guerilla groups, while others were ideological and partisan, even if not linked to insurgents. Such polarised NGOs, which essentially ignored the legitimacy of other NGOs' views, have continued in both countries, which have been able to sustain a relative peace of sorts since 1991 and 1986, when democratic regime changes were inaugurated. This is probably because these were ideological and economic conflicts, rather than racial ones (though there are certainly racial implications, given the mestizo/near European domination in both countries).

Third, some NGOs are illiberal or even violent. Pakistan is filled with terrorist NGOs, which have covers as student or religious or party-based groups. Some of these are militia as such and others are bona fide groups, with paramilitary wings, such as the party student groups at campuses such as the University of Sindh, which have committed many murders; the various Shia and Sunni groups that have committed terrorist, tit-for-tat attacks against each other; or the Mohajir Qaami Movement (MQM) or the Jamaat Islaami political parties' armed wings. In Northern Ireland, prior to their April 2007 commitment to disarmament, the Irish Republican Army's relationship with the *Sinn Fein* political party was ambiguous and led in the short term to increased violence until several years after the Palm Sunday accords of 1997, when the former finally persuaded most of the latter to opt for the political process. The Norway II peace agreement of 1993, mediated partly by a Norwegian NGO headed by Jan Egeland, led to the unprecedented, suicidal terrorism by Palestinians beginning in the mid-1990s and then culminating in the greater suicidal attacks by the Al Aqsa Martyrs Brigade and Hamas in the *Intifadah* II uprising of 2001.

In Latin America and elsewhere, one of the greatest obstacles to peacebuilding is a non-state actor, criminal gangs. They appeared in Baghdad immediately after the liberation and contributed to the widespread looting. They remain a fixture in Port-au-Prince, Caracas, Rio de Janeiro, and especially San Salvador. As in post-conflict economic rackets, prevention is as important as law enforcement. Once created, such gangs are very hard to control.

Fourth, NGOs may participate in election monitoring where the results are not accepted, either because they are not acceptable, or because neither side is prepared to accept them. Thus, we have the exemplar of Angola, where Jonas Sivimbi was opposed to any electoral process where he would not win. In Liberia, Charles Taylor virtually coerced voters into accepting him because he was clearly ready to attack the election process if they did not. The same accusation was made by some Sandinista supporters in 1990, when the Contras were still mobilised. NGOs have played important, track-II roles in making and sustaining peace. NGOs helped to bring peace, by promoting free elections that were generally accepted in Nicaragua (1990), Philippines (1986), Haiti (1990), Romania (1996 and 2004), El Salvador (1991), and Pakistan (1988), among many examples. Usually, these are cases where the results are not close. Close elections, whether really so, or where the figures are manipulated to produce a short victory margin, are likely to have an opposite effect, particularly when you have suspicion of fraud and mobilisation. Of course, there are cases of well-founded suspicions of fraud, but a flat civil society, such as in Romania in 1992, led to no palpable reaction to rigging at all, as also occurred in Pakistan in 1990.

Fifth, NGOs can be terrorist groups, which are less defensive than paramilitary rebels or party militia, and more offensive in their indiscriminate attacks on civilians in order to advance radical political changes. The US has begun a 'war on terror' as a military solution to a much more complicated struggle. British Member of Parliament, Hilary Benn, has argued that this only strengthens various militant groups into a large cause, 'by making them feel part of something bigger',[28] what Huntington referred to as the 'clash of civilisations'. Terror and terrorism are tactics of states and radical non-state actors. There are *jihadists* in various locations, some of which are linked internationally through states and religious affiliations that lead them to unify. The US is also not focused on non-Islamic terrorists such as the Tamil Tigers, and less concerned with Shia-terrorists like Hizbollah, primarily of Lebanon. Of course, secularist and nationalist terrorists tend to be less destructive and less threatening to the US. Such groups also benefit from the anti-US attitude resulting from US foreign policies, such as regarding Israel and Palestine on the one hand or the invasion and occupation of Afghanistan and especially Iraq on the other.

Finally, ostensibly liberal NGOs may not want peace because they want armed intervention to stop human rights violations. For example, in 1999, important INGOs like Human Rights Watch did not publicly call for an armed intervention to stop Serbia's ethnic cleansing in Kosovo. Yet, according to David Reiff, the leading officials in that INGO, presumably Ken Roth and Areyeh Neier, gave a collective sigh of relief when the US did intervene militarily.[29]

Scholars have searched for ways to minimize or avoid such dilemmas of conflict mitigation and post-conflict reconstruction. One approach has been to reduce the conflicting pressures on the state-centric geopolitical system by relying on transnational and domestic civil society. One component of this admittedly inchoate concept, NGOs have obviously not proven a panacea, but they have offered alternative strategies for states in peacebuilding. Still, NGOs have not avoided many dilemmas of states, since NGOs face some of the same issues, collaborate with states, and often are merely subcontractors for the same functions. NGOs have also produced some dilemmas of their own, ironically resulting from their relative independence from geopolitics, which also limits their leverage compared with states in regards to some of the warlike orientations of actors. It is useful to categorise dilemmas resulting from how NGOs operate in practice.

a. procedural dilemma: illiberal Ngos, movements, and parties produce illiberal outcomes, and illiberal civil societies may render liberal Ngos impotent

We cannot assume that they are only liberal because a free environment only means no government censorship. While J.S. Mill assumed that the best arguments would win out in a free environment, it is not clear that this is the historical record. And many environments which begin as free may become closed afterwards to all but those who support the state. *People Building Peace II* is the rare book dedicated largely to presenting helpful lessons learned, especially from NGO success stories, which warns of all the dangers from NGOs and other civil society groups, because either can act uncivilly. Or, even if one only looks at the genuinely civil actors, their freedom also opens the door to uncivil NGOs.[30]

Fundamentalist Muslim NGOs have several goals and methods. Their goals include opposing secularism, especially from the West, as well in the military governments. They want to establish states run according to and by religious authorities.[31] Fundamentalists favour democracy, albeit illiberal versions with censorship and religious establishment, because they are popular and can win elections. The fundamentalists often begin by establishing NGOs that provide humanitarian relief. Their methods include a militia, because they do not trust an army that has run secular states, be they democratic or authoritarian. They also establish subsidiary NGOs running schools and hospitals managed by the clergy. Their ideology favours violence and exploits anger over poverty, which is so common in the Arab Middle East. NGOs' fighting extreme poverty with services leads to new alliances with angry young Muslim men, who take on the military establishments of their country, from whom many in the public are alienated. It would be very difficult, though not impossible, to establish a consensus with those who want to oppose capitalism and liberal democracy, and seek to go back to what the *Qu'ran* says is the way to live, in obedience to Allah's representative leaders on earth. The NGOs favouring Shar'iah law and no separation between religion and government can make maximalist demands that those in power must find ways to accommodate with reality and their own desire to maintain power.

Oppositions to dictators are full of would-be democrats who represent every illiberal political ideology. Furthermore, oppositions rarely stay united against dictatorship, putting their own power above the cause of uniting against tyranny. NGOs committed to democracy might avoid this tendency, but they too are often split into particularist causes. Since such states often lack democratic experience, there is little or no reference point for the claims to prior legitimacy of democracy by NGOs or others. Political leaders may also demand elections as part of a democratic claim, whether or not there is any likelihood that the conditions for democratic contestation are likely to be free, let alone permit the kind of vigorous contestation that certain political currents would regard as necessary for a democratic contest. Oppositions can also include radical elements, if they stay united, which invites the state counterterrorism units and other state security groups to arrest part or all of the opposition and to raid the rest, as the Russians did to the United Civil Front's Office in December 2006 because of the presence of the National Bolsheviks in the Other Russia coalition.

b. procedural dilemma: officially neutral Ngos usually favour one side

NGOs, ranging from formal small professional units to more broad-based social movements, encompass the variety of non-state actors outside political and economic society. Whether international or domestic in orientation and resources, INGOs and domestic NGOs have the potential of assuring that society will not be dominated. Yet they usually represent some particular set of interests, whether enlightened or not. Peace processes, whether dominated by states and IGOs or oriented towards alternative tracks managed by civil society, can also take on a set of interests of their own. The dynamics of peace, as well as the activities of NGOs and INGOs, are all as political as high politics. Each type of peace process involves a different set of NGO, INGO, and state interests, each seeking the moral high ground, but resorting to the realities of power and position.

NGO peacebuilding involves political action to improve institutions that protect rights that are supposed to be legally guaranteed, and therefore apolitical. As Elizabeth Cousens writes: '... the proximate cause of internal violence is the fragility or collapse of political processes and institutions. The defining priority of peacebuilding thus becomes *the construction or strengthening of authoritative and, eventually, legitimate mechanisms to resolve internal conflict without violence'.*[32] However, advocating political improvements, inherent in peacebuilding, makes NGOs seem partisan. And, often, if not usually, they have private partisan feelings that are manifest in their actions. This bias can be left or right-wing, secular or religious. However, the aura of apolitical entities is belied in perception, as well as in fact, by the realities of political action to achieve institutional reforms and government policy changes.

NGOs are more apt to complain about the dangers of the other side. Some NGOs have played a polarising role during the high-intensity phases of these conflicts. As conflicts move into transition to the stages of either low-intensity or less violent political conflict, NGOs can play polarising roles, if necessary, in documenting human rights abuses: polarising because violations are usually documented by only the other side to a conflict; necessary because violations need to be identified for them to stop. Identity conflicts rarely have multicultural NGOs. Instead, they identify with one side. In Pakistan, the Human Rights Commission has supported the Pakistan People's Party. The ethno-religious conflicts, Sunni–Shia in the Punjab, Sindhi–Mohajir in Sindh, Balochistan secessionism, and Pathan *jihadist* attacks on the Pakistan Army have all been analysed by partisan NGOs. Similar patterns exist in the Philippines (the various insurgencies that have sought Muslim separatism in Mindinao and other southern islands), as well as the NPA communist army in Luzon, which has ethnic dimensions.

The practice of one-sided human rights evaluations was common. Task Force Detainees in the Philippines has focused only on the Armed Forces of the Philippines; the supposedly autonomous, governmental, Human Rights Commission of the Philippines, headed by Mary Concepcion Baptista, ignored the AFP and focused only on the communist New People's Army. From the 1980s to the mid-1990s, the Nicaraguan Human Rights Commission, headed by Lino Hernandez, focused only on violent human rights violations of the Sandinista Popular Army and the pro-Sandinista equivalent headed by Wilma Nunez, while the INGO, Witness for Peace, focused only on the *Contra*. In El Salvador, all NGOs were either pro-FMLN, such as the Tutela Legal NGO of the Catholic Church, which focused only on army or death squad activities, but never the violations of the FMLN, or the 'autonomous' government human rights commission, which largely focused on FMLN violations and not those of the military, the latter of which it attempted to educate on human rights. The supposedly autonomous, but pro-governmental NGO focused only on violations of human rights law by the FMLN and educated Salvadoran troops. In Haiti from 1991 to 1994, the Platform for Human Rights in Haiti examined only the violations of the coup regime of President Emile Jonaissant and the Prime Minister, while the best NGO prior to the coup exonerated the regime and continued to focus on the violations of the deposed Aristide government. In Pakistan, the Human Rights Commission of Pakistan, headed by former Justice Dorab Patel, was pro-Pakistan People's Party. In Romania, the two NGO communities were divided into those funded by US-AID, several German political foundations, and the European PHARE programmes, all of which were pro-Western and explicitly pro-opposition, and those funded by the Romanian state headed by Ion Iliescu, which were largely former communist institutes.

While there are conservative NGOs, most human rights NGOs are progressive or left-wing politically. There is no point in denying the obvious, which is that human rights standards are not met by any country; human rights NGOs are critics of violations and proponents of reform and change in the direction of compliance. This reality does not justify the false critique from 'right-wing' NGOs that most NGOs are illegitimate. It is true, however, that human rights NGOS usually undervalue and are less interested in values other than human rights, such as peace, stability, national sovereignty and security, etc. There are conservative human rights NGOs, such as Freedom House and NGO Monitor, who do balance these values.

The ICRC faces the dilemma of maintaining neutrality in the face of evil. It appears to have modified its past stance of never passing judgment publicly, as it has criticised the US for Guantanamo and for bombing its supply warehouse in Kabul, as well as the Sudanese government for attacking its refugee camps and for the genocide. There are overlap and interaction effects among these four dimensions. One dilemma is between domestic NGOs that attempt to be pragmatic, if this leads to consternation and warnings by foreign foundations or INGOs with different agendas.

c. procedural dilemma: context and regimes matter

Not every situation will be the same. Methods of peacebuilding require the ability to adapt procedures and processes to accommodate local conditions. As such, 'Careful, critical exploration of traditional and non-traditional alternatives to a "cookie-cutter" post-conflict political package seems warranted.'[33] Although there are overall goals that must be carried out in every situation, each instance must be analysed individually due to differences such as culture. Cultural aspects can affect the way peacebuilding is achieved, and therefore not every state should be treated in exactly the same manner.

For starters, there must be a legal framework to protect NGO activity from censorship and other forms of legal intimidation, as well as to forbid violence against NGO activity, or by NGOs for that matter. Prior to the age of NGOs, the US Congress passed laws for eight years to forbid vigilantes like the KKK, until Reconstruction ended. In 1883, Congress struck down the ch-1875 *Civil Rights Act* and the Courts held that the 14th Amendment to the US Constitution did not forbid private discrimination, only state discrimination.

NGOs are powerless unless the average person cares. If a groupuscle articulates eloquently about injustice or peace and the regime can easily ignore the complaints, because there is no resonance in civil society, the NGO might as well be from Mars. Civil society was the great concept of NGOs in the communist and post-communist world, particularly in the stronger regimes that had moved into a post-totalitarian phase, such as Hungary and Poland, and to a lesser extent East Germany and Bulgaria and the last-minute leadership changes prior to their revolutions. The concept was exported without acknowledging early on that those regimes that were still totalitarian but had a relatively strong civil society in 1989 amounted to one case, Czechoslovakia, while Romania and the rest of the former Soviet Union had a flattened civil society that required much more time to become active enough for NGOs to have any liberalising effect. Similarly, most post-colonial states in Africa and Asia have been characterised by a largely inactive society, except in the urban centres, and there only among the middle and elite classes. The urban and rural poor remain only occasionally mobilised, largely economically vulnerable, and politically unaware. Demagogues are more able to mobilise the masses for either war or violence than for the hard steady work of democratisation. Occasionally, weak societies may mobilise for a democratic regime change, either through popular demonstrations and/or internationally monitored elections, particularly if the international sector pressures vulnerable regimes requiring international support to survive, such as in the Philippines in 1986, South Korea in 1987, Nicaragua in 1990, Romania in 1996, Georgia in 2003, and the Ukraine in 2004. What is remarkable, despite these dramatic 'crowd symbols', is how many bogus elections were held before and often after the democratic regime change. Civil society's awareness of the regime's opaqueness and chicanery seems generally low and its ability to monitor and demand transparency weak. Instead of building peace based on law, NGOs and the political class often acquiesce to opaque regimes holding elections with either a dominant or hegemonic party on the one hand or alternating weak parties on the other, as Carothers aptly explained. The NGOs are so weak that they effectively add to the legitimacy of domination through pseudo-liberal rule. Of course, reform is a long-term project in such environments, but the dilemma is whether the distortion of politics to make the erroneous seem normal tends to institutionalise practices that subvert the rule of law and peacelike politics.

NGOs have very little meaning in tribal societies, where individuals do not count, only groups (marriages reflect the combining of two families, for example, not the matrimony of two individuals). NGOs are collections of like-minded individuals, who share common goals, not collections of groups seeking to maintain group interests against other groups, as such, with no room for individual disagreements. Tribal leaders command what NGOs and other followers do, preventing any other interests from coming forth that have different priorities from those of the tribal leader claiming to represent his group.

Some societies have many cross-cutting cleavages and NGO affiliations, while others have segmented cleavages. Civil society is more than public-minded NGOs, but even the latter include many organisations of diverse views, including illiberal ones. If the political system is unable to process and channel the disagreements into viable political outcomes, then the politics of NGO interest articulation will likely be violent. Even if the NGOs are civil and practice civility, that is no guarantee that other political institutions will be civil as well.

Among the critical facts that NGOs must advance is to counterbalance the prejudices of the statist, mass or corporate media, with all its biases towards public irrationality, national interest, and racial and elite orientations or obsessions. As a BBC reporter once put it, 'To get on the BBC, there must be 5000 Bengalis drowning, 5000 Egyptians shot, one-hundred British soldiers killed, or two Buckingham palace guards caught kissing.' What drives media and public policy interest in the developed world follows these racially and nationally driven biases of the dominant states. The needs of peace that threaten peoples removed from the interests of the West can be best addressed by the NGO community, with the support of UN departments in coalition against the permanent members of the Security Council, who have decisive authority over peace issues.

d. procedural dilemma: local Ngos can reduce fear and encourage collaboration with state institutions in the short to medium term, if they can participate in peacemaking. collaborating with the state may compromise Ngo independence and objectivity

Scholars have generally argued that peacebuilding is possible and desirable, though disagreed as to whether states, NGOs, and international governmental organisations (IGOs) can alter their behaviour and act, either in their enlightened self-interest or altruistically, in pursuit of peace. Yet even the constructivist paradigm, emphasising how ideas, identity and reputation can change behaviour, has largely only presented examples constituting exceptions that prove the rule of self-serving, risk-averse and even aggressive states, NGOs, and IGOs.

Most instances of peacebuilding take place in countries without a reliably free press. NGOs could help alleviate this need, but, even then, their discoveries have to be published rather than ignored, or, failing that, ridiculed. Many great efforts at large political and economic cost have been undertaken in the name of peace. However, what is stated for public relations may reflect stagecraft more than statecraft or NGO-craft. The 2003 US invasion was called Operation Iraqi Freedom, though real US motives and consequences have been far different from the start. While NGOs may have sought to bring greater idealism to peacebuilding, many accounts have shown their often mixed motives, from pleasing their government benefactors to assuring their contracts are renewed. The notion of 'nothing ventured, nothing gained' for NGO involvement deserves an empirical test. What is their actual track record? Anecdotal evidence seems to suggest that outsiders can achieve both wonderful and terrible outcomes, the latter unforeseen, but quite predictable.

Daniel Gilbert asserts that we usually remember that which is unusual or exciting or newsworthy, in effect, that which is not typical or characteristic. Furthermore, defence mechanisms lead to denial syndromes or happy spins on experiences. 'Intense suffering is one factor that can trigger our defenses and thus influence our experiences in ways we don't anticipate.'[34] Thus, some peoples are more likely to risk peace if their defence mechanisms are working than those who were only mildly touched by war. Thus the French and the Germans, and the Serbs and the Croats, got along relatively well after the Second World War, but the children and grandchildren of the Yugoslavs fought terrible wars in the 1990s. The imagination helps to select facts, along with coaching. If humans rely on others who have had experiences that may await them in the future, they are more likely to make better decisions about the future. However, most humans rely on their imagination, which may often make mistakes, rather than relying on the NGOs and others with the direct experience involved. Thus, coaching is often not followed carefully, even when it is helpful. If the coaching is helpful and is followed, then the narrative can be based on something other than reinforcing the selective memories and biases of memory and imagination. If the coaching by NGOs is based more on what is really typical and representative, which is that neighbours are generally peaceful or that their leaders took them to war, then there is a chance that the space for peace can be filled with demands for peace.

e. procedural dilemma: domestic autonomy (principle) versus international control (power)

Peacebuilding has been initiated and coordinated by foreign states and organisations that have agendas different from securing long-term peace. They often opt out of intense engagement and responsibility in the majority of crises that could utilise effective peace enforcement and peacekeeping, let alone peacebuilding. However, where the international community has been resolved to act, it has not occasionally worked wonders in establishing and maintaining peace. The jury is still out on longer-term peacebuilding, though efforts undertaken are plentiful by historical standards. If past is precedent, however, the peace will likely fail within 10–15 years in most cases. The optimistic view is that these efforts may still bear fruit, delaying the outbreak of violence in some cases and preventing it in others, because such efforts to build the institutions, practices, and culture of a positive peace have never been undertaken until recently. The pessimistic view is that the nature of politics has not been radically altered either by UN Charter-based initiatives or by the new, human rights culture fostered by leading Western powers. A closer look might reveal some important challenges that the new efforts must face, but which policymakers and scholars have apparently ignored.

The attempt of the West to build Western-style liberal democracy in countries that either lack the institutions and economic development, or who are ethnically divided, or whose culture is quite opposed to Western values and/or prior colonial experience, is unlikely to succeed, especially under alien military occupation. Thus, it remains for NGOs to oppose such imperial missions, since it is unlikely that these countries will benefit from such misguided 'peace missions'. History shows that

there are Western approaches that are never going to succeed in ethnically polarised, divided countries, except through 'negative peace', in
which power-sharing agreements are replaced by military dominance of
populations otherwise determined not to live with their ethnic antagonists. NGOs can attempt to overcome the arrogance of Western power
thinking that it cannot abide threats to its own sense of omnipotence.

f. procedural dilemma: Ngos can also limit perceptions that reform is based on inappropriate western constructs or ideals

There is a large peacebuilding dilemma faced by the international community in general and NGOs in particular, which is the desire to put
a legitimate government in charge as soon as possible, even though a
state is not ready for self-government. This is similar to the dilemma
faced by post-colonial states, for which a period of transition had been
planned, but which usually gained independence very quickly. The
world was misled by the partition and independence of the Indian subcontinent in 1947 because the former 'Jewel in the British Crown' was
much better prepared for independence than any other post-war, newly
independent state. In the case of post-conflict polities, the international
community does not recognise many transitional regimes as legitimate,
other than those rare cases, like Haiti from 2004 to 2006, sanctioned by
the UN Security Council.

In theory, democracies permit, promote, or require an independent
civil society, which leads to a more open society, better and more independent journalism, better quality of information, decision-making
and political participation, and ultimate public checks or vetoes of warlike politics. In reality, democratic regime changes do not automatically lead to open societies, even if there is no official censorship, even
though this may be the easiest goal and consequence of democratisation, compared with institution-building.

Democracy alone cannot ensure a sustainable peace. Economic considerations must be addressed simultaneously with the democratisation
process. Resources must be available, most likely provided by donors
through NGOs, to assist in the overall transition period with the
provision of goods and services and in order to stimulate the economy.[35]
The provision of food is essential in preventing resurgence of violence.
As de Montlos explains, 'war and famine are related in two ways: as
war provokes famine, famine also incites conflict.'[36] Resources are also
important in helping aid the transition from combatants to civilian
workers, which is crucial for security purposes.[37] Economic progression,

or lack thereof, can hinder the democratisation process greatly. As Jeong explains, economic instability is one of the main obstacles to democracy. In particular, peace would not be durable without equitable development that benefits the majority of people in the society combined with income-creating opportunities for the poor. Thus, development activities need to be geared towards mitigating economic hardships and reintegrating the society across ethnic, racial, religious, and other divisions.[38] Therefore, in order to ensure democratic achievements, economic considerations must be included in the peacebuilding process. These processes must all be implemented simultaneously in order for a peace agreement to succeed, and in order to prevent governments and rebels from manipulating NGOs.

g. procedural dilemma: legitimate complaints can lead to endless finger-pointing

Assertions of injustice can lead to a 'chicken and egg' problem. For example, the Israeli settlements on Palestinian territories or the terrorist bombs, or the occupation by Israel or earlier by Jordan. Why is the former so much more objectionable? Because of an intolerant clash of civilisation or the appearance of neocolonialism – even though Israeli territory was colonised?

One can see this tendency dramatically in using religion to cite injustice. Established religions often find themselves with the dirty hands of everyday politics. At the same time, adherents of religion can use the ideology or apparatus of organised religion for war or warlike ends or means. Yet all religions preach a message of peace as a primary tenet – even as they also can teach *jihad* as meaning organised, violent struggle, or Jesus 'coming with a sword'.[39] Unfortunately, religion itself and its believers (and non-believers) have contributed or been used, often falsely, to cause or sustain war. Religions can induce both desire for reform and change, and violence. It is plausible that different religious thought can produce contradictory outcomes, such as exclusivity and superiority in doctrine inducing war, while its call for peace, inducing non-violent approaches to conflict resolution. However, there is also evidence of a range of outcomes. Religious assertiveness or differences, for example, can be feared and attacked, or acknowledged and embraced. Yet practising the sermon may prove unsuccessful in practice.

Religious ethics are more easily applied to human relations than politics. Justice is foundational, but defining it is conflictual in particular circumstances. To achieve the potential of love and compassion, one has not to fear an enemy that is quite frightening. The hand of peace requires one side to take the risk of vulnerability and the other to respond in kind. This requires one side to move beyond their own pain, when it is sometimes that pain which moves people to religion in the first place. Then people have to transcend their own preoccupations and consider the worries of the other side. In so doing, it helps to evaluate one's own record of possible missteps, a level of public candour which might tend to undermine confidence in one's leaders were they to admit they do not monopolise virtue and wisdom. In warlike environments, the tendency is to demonise the other side as uniquely flawed, rather than 'loving one's enemy'.

h. procedural dilemma: the confidence versus criticism dilemma

A dilemma arises over what combination of pressure and persuasion strategies should be used by NGOs in confrontation or mere support for states. If a more minor, subordinate role is undertaken, NGOs may be able to provide crucial intellectual and legal expertise, information and communication technologies. More adversarial postures, while closer to normative positions, may have less influence if their advocacy and campaigns alienate the state interlocutors. If parties to negotiations are less complicated, complex and intransigent, domestic NGOs and INGOs may be able to offer their own unique and innovative outcomes, including implementing negotiated accords. This could involve the democratisation of negotiated settlements. Alternatively, if NGOs insist on maximalist positions and influence, they could just as easily jeopardise these potentials for opening peace plans to greater civil society involvement and responsibilities.

Human rights NGOs are the bearers of bad tidings. To some extent, reporting on problems undermines the confidence needed to keep a delicate peace process, requiring trust, moving forward. The criticisms may be valid, but they may also corrode the belief in the integrity of one's interlocutors. By analogy, when various sports have been undermined by doping scandals, they are punished for 'doing right' by engaging in vigorous testing of athletes.

A Good friend will always tell you where you have gone wrong. But Bush told Blair where to go into Iraq rather than the reverse. Furthermore, Blair tried to fight the war in Iraq 'on the cheap', whereas Bush eventually spent huge amount of funds to fight – even if it came late. (General Sir Michael Rose).

i. procedural dilemma: striving for desired end-states, especially democracy and development, leads to turbulent transitions of interests, power and values

While governments are generally focused on short-term results, peace-building generally requires longer-term investments in institutions as well as facilitating changes in the values of a political culture towards empathy and reconciliation and away from bitterness and resent-ment. In theory, if not in practice, NGOs are better suited to longer-term investments than are states, for which a variety of distracting, self-interested goals are likely to deflect peacebuilding from the slow painstaking efforts needed. Still, NGOs have not proven to be a pana-cea to the wages of war. NGOs are needed to develop structures likely to divert war as the tactical temptation of folly in most cases. Even in good or necessary wars, the tactics chosen by states tend to deepen resolve to resist or get vengeance at a later juncture, after wounds have healed. Unfortunately, NGOs have often imitated the folly of states or have been unable to direct attention to the wages of peace.

There is a tradeoff between short-run and long-run NGO objectives and strategies. Conflicts emerge when foreign actors focus on short-run approaches, reflecting their priorities, while domestic NGOs may lack the power and resources, despite often greater legitimacy, to insist on long-term approaches. Donors often exclude them from negoti-ations over the peace agreements that determine who will become active under a new regime. Security considerations are primary for for-eign governments, who also may not assist viable new police forces and new civilian-led armies in the long run. The failure to build the Haitian National Police led to chaos five years later, by 2000, and the collapse of the state in just three weeks of rebel activity in February 2004. NGOs were not involved in training this force, but human rights groups did cite its violations. In Cambodia, most DANGOs and QUANGOs have been impotent to stop violence since the 1993 elec-tions, during and after the 1997 coup. In Bosnia and Kosovo, NGOs have advocated respect and equal treatment for different ethnic groups from international police forces, which have not yet been effectively replaced by national forces. In these cases, local NGOs have had minimal involvement compared with the QUANGOs and DANGOs contracted on the scene.

Most peace processes aim to establish or re-establish democratic regimes, despite the very long odds of democratic stability, particularly in post-conflict situations with failed states and/or very low human development. Despite exhortations to democracy, NGOs will tend to follow existing, local ideologies, some of which may have been partly responsible for the previous war. Societies with low development and high inequality, and with high dependency on foreign resources, have been the typical cases of formal peace processes. Their low democratic potential has only been heightened by the confluence of peace processes in step with the war on terrorism. Even where NGOs sincerely seek to promote the democracy project, the congeries of conflict resolution *cum* democracy promotion, NGOs must complexify their capabilities from monitoring to active consultation and implementation. This requires not only more resources, but the will to avoid the 'briefcase temptation' to orient NGOs towards professional status and future contracts. Those peace processes lacking sufficient foreign resources are free from this scourge of 'overnight NGOs-for-travel', but suffer a capability gap.

j. procedural dilemma of weak States lacking authority and institutionalisation

The emphasis on NGO peacebuilding emerged from civil society theorists, who focused on societal conquest of authoritarian and totalitarian regimes to prompt democratic transitions. More recent emphasis by some analysts, like Francis Fukuyama and Fareed Zakaria, on state-building[40] would contradict civil society theories, while actual practice suggests foreign support for both processes.

In the new democracies of the developing world, the non-governmental factions have yet to be developed; the courts, which evolve most slowly among new democratic institutions, lack significant power; and the majority are most likely to experience intense feelings. Tocqueville noted the greater rapidity with which NGOs formed in the United States in its first 70 years of existence, but these were actually a form of counterbalance to the weight of factions. Except for the issue of slavery, whose dangers were noted by Tocqueville, the US was not a 'house divided', but a multi-layered house. The danger in the new democracies, as was true in Madison's day, was the fear of the dominant majority and the dominant legislative branch.

National resources make it unprofitable for groups to accept reform. Their trafficking provides not only personal profits, but the means to continue wars. Unique resources (oil for Sudan and diamonds for

Sierra Leone) have enabled the violence to continue at horrific levels, which has complicated the situations in numerous ways. Since they are located on the same continent, they both also deal with the same geographical and regional considerations, and contain somewhat similar cultural challenges. It would be more difficult to compare two states that have nothing in common culturally, historically, and geographically, due to many other variables that could affect the conclusions. We will now consider some substantive dilemmas that NGOs face in particular issue areas.

conclusions

To succeed, NGO actors involved must exhibit patience. Peace does not happen quickly, so much time must be invested by all in the peace-maintenance process. Second, there is no one specific method for peacekeeping and peacebuilding. Some aspects may need to be altered in order to accommodate differences in each case. Third, all aspects of peacekeeping and peacebuilding must allow the indigenous population to remain in control of the process. Fourth, security must be established, both within the country and regionally. Fifth, governance issues must be addressed. Sixth, democratisation must be initiated, and eventually consolidated. Finally, economic improvements must occur. If the above requirements are not fulfilled in conjunction with NGO aid and/ or assistance, then NGOs will not be successful in supporting the peace process and will actually become counterproductive or self-defeating. Since it is so difficult to accomplish all of these goals, the question remains whether, realistically, NGOs should be involved in trying to do the difficult or impossible on the basis that trying is always better than not trying. In fact, we may lose hope if trying does not succeed.

These are not the only requirements to be satisfied. Careful attention must be paid to the conditions that must be satisfied by the United Nations and other international interveners. Their roles in the peace-keeping and peacebuilding processes are extremely important as well. While the requirements analysed here are not exhaustive, they must all be fulfilled, minimised, or managed, depending on the circumstances of each element, in order for NGOs to avoid manipulation and operate effectively, and for peacekeeping and peacebuilding to be successful. As Donini writes, 'If one element is left out of the equation then the whole peace process is compromised.'[41] If the requirements described above are left out of the process, then NGO efforts will be open to manipulation, thus failing to be successful in their effort to support the overall peace project.

Dilemmas of NGO peacebuilding result from the contradictory or conflicting logics emerging out of the multitudinous, perhaps inordinate, number of peacebuilding tasks. In attempting to do seemingly everything, peacebuilding needs the support of NGOS to reduce the risks of accomplishing little or nothing, or, worse, producing counterintuitive results that backfire into war. While there is not yet an NGO with a name like Peacebuilding Watch, we need to begin to oversee how, long-term, NGO peace projects are developing.

States have increasingly recognised their need to rely on NGOs in state, political society, and civil society-building. They have passed responsibility for these extremely difficult and complex tasks to NGOs and others, even including the privatisation of security functions. Transfer of responsibility from states to NGOs, in order to overcome state bias or bureaucratic lethargy or to exploit comparative advantages, does not have to mean less accountability from utilised NGOs, though that is the frequent consequence. Unlike many states in many situations, NGOs can mediate or induce discussions among enemies, deliver humanitarian services, and cross international boundaries, etc. State–society relationships are deemed fundamentally changed.

The way out of the dilemmas in weak states in a world of powers, or within a sovereign, if weak, state, might be to rely on non-governmental organisations, business development, and any other force that might inspire the development of a more robust civil society. Such a strong alternative to a weak state may not be preferable to a functional state, but with a dysfunctional state the only alternative is to develop strong society relations and rules that can be self-enforced to a high degree. The difficulty is that weak states are unlikely to emerge into, or to foster, strong societies. Business development is one, maybe the only, alternative, where society grows strong by dint of private enterprise, either alone or in conjunction with a strengthening state. Such private economic development, in theory, could make the warlike states and societies, in theory, become immersed in the business of business rather than of war or warlike politics. Of course, the development of NGOs in weak states is usually bought on the cheap by outside powers seeking a quick fix, by subsidising the development of what really amounts to a liberal project theory, but a foreign-owned and sponsored project of societal development for the interests of outside powers.

Thus, NGOs are one of the only answers, but they cannot be reasonably seen as a panacea for warlike politics because they are not indigenous or genuine expressions of domestic demands and supplies, with resources supplied by those in the society with stakes and interests in the long-term development of that market and society. Instead, what may have emerged in the development of the international liberal project is an artificial sponsoring of civil society institutions that reflect the corporatist interests of outside powers, seeking to sponsor some local autonomy, but serving the ultimate interests of outside powers. This form of authoritarian, exclusionary corporatism is only worsened in highly polarised settings, where the NGOs reflect the segmented ethnic, class and social cleavages of society in a politicised state society in a politicised state, where interests become the basis for unending clashes, rather than the aggregation of interests. While it is possible for NGOs to serve important roles in articulating interests of those who have been unrepresented, they may also aggravate existing conflicts by mobilising opposing forces without providing avenues of conflict resolution. In pursuit of the liberal project, foreign-sponsored NGOs, while establishing important new institutions for the development of civil society, risk polarising rather than resolving conflicts.

notes

1. On advocacy networks, c.f. M.E. Keck and K. Sikkink, *Activists Beyond Borders: Advocacy Networks in International Politics*, Ithaca, NY: Cornell University Press, 1998; on government networks and networked networks, c.f. A. Slaughter, 'Governing the Global Economy through Government Networks', in M. Byers (ed.) *The Role of Law in International Politics: Essays in International Relations and International Law*, Oxford: Oxford University Press, 2001, pp. 177–205. For a critique, c.f., A. Riles, *The Network Inside Out*, Ann Arbor: University of Michigan Press, 2000.
2. S.E. Mendelson, 'The Putin Path: Civil Liberties and Human Rights in Retreat', *Problems of Post-Communism*, Vol. 47, no. 5, September/October 2000, p. 4.
3. O. Matthews and A. Nemtsova, 'Putin's Shock Forces: Young Militants Provide new Muscle for the Kremlin', *Newsweek*, 28 May 2007, p. 38.
4. C.J. Levy, 'It Isn't Magic: Putin Opponents Vanish From TV', *The New York Times*, 3 June 2008, p. A1.
5. C.W. Dugger, 'In a Crackdown, Zimbabwe Curbs Many Aid Groups', *The New York Times*, 4 June 2008, pp. A1, A10.
6. E. Schmitt, 'Gates Accuses Myanmar of "Criminal Neglect"', *The New York Times*, 2 June 2008.
7. J. Kurlantzick, 'The Survivalists: How Burma's junta hangs on', *The New Republic*, 11 June 2008, pp. 7–8.

8. H.F. Carey, 'Immigrants, Terrorism, Counter-Terrorism and Social Peace', *Peace Review*, Vol. 14, no. 2, 2002.

9. K. O'Beirne, 'It's a War, Stupid: Understanding and Misunderstanding the Detainees', *National Review*, 16 September 2002, pp. 22–4.

10. P. Van Tuijl, 'NGOs and Human Rights: Sources of Justice and Democracy,' *Journal of International Affairs*, Vol. 52, no. 2, 1999, p. 495, pp. 493–512.

11. K. Aggestam, 2003. 'Conflict Prevention: Old Wine in New Bottles?', *International Peacekeeping* Vol. 10, no. 1, p. 16, pp. 12–23.

12. Common abbreviations are NGOs (non-governmental organisations), INGOs (international non-governmental organisations), IGOs (intergovernmental organisations). Here, we collapse NGOs and INGOs into NGOs generally.

13. C. Barnes, 'Weaving the Web: Civil Society Roles in Working with Conflict and Building Peace', in P. van Tongeren, M. Brenk, M. Hellema, and J. Verhoeven (eds) *People Building Peace II: Successful Stories of Civil Society,* Boulder, CO: Lynne Rienner, 2005, p. 7.

14. T.G. Weiss and L. Gordenker (eds) in Weiss and Gordenker (eds) *NGOs, the UN and Global Governance*, Boulder, CO and London: Lynne Rienner, 1996, p. 21.

15. Weiss and Gordenker, 'Pluralizing Global Governance: Analytical Approaches and Dimensions', in Weiss and Gordenker, 'Introduction', p. 21.

16. Ibid., p. 28.

17. *The New York Times*, 18 November 1998.

18. Weiss and Gordenker, 'Introduction', p. 67.

19. K.A. Sikkink, 'Nongovernmental Organizations, Democracy, and Human Rights in Latin America', in T. Farer (ed.) *Beyond Sovereignty: Collectively Defending Democracy in the Americas*, Baltimore, MD: Johns Hopkins University Press, 1996, p. 151.

20. Weiss and Gordenker, 'Pluralizing Global Governance: Analytical Approaches and Dimensions', in Weiss and Gordenker (eds), *NGOs, the UN and Global Governance*, Boulder, CO and London: Lynne Rienner, 1996, p. 73

21. UN Document NGO/551-PI/1630 (20 December 2004).

22. Ibid.

23. Marc-Antoine Perouse De Montclos, 'A Crisis of Humanitarianism', *Forum for Applied Research and Public Policy*, Vol. 16, no. 2, 2001, pp. 95–100, quote on p. 99.

24. M.G. Jackson, 'A Necessary Collaboration: NGOs, Peacekeepers and Credible Military Force – The Case of Sierra Leone and East Timor', in O.P. Richmond and H.F. Carey (eds), *Subcontracting Peace: The Challenges of NGO Peacebuilding*, Burlington: Ashgate Publishing Company, 2005, p. 111.

25. Ibid.; UN Department of Public Information, 'Major Peacekeeping Operations – Sierra Leone: A Success Story in Peacekeeping', 2006, http://www.un.org/Depts/dpko/dpko/pub/year_review05/sierra_leone.htm accessed 26 October 2009.

26. Jackson, 'A Necessary Collaboration', p. 111.

27. Graduate Paper, Rachel Collis, Georgia State University, (2004); Freedom House. 'Freedom in the World – Sudan (2006)'. http://www.freedomhouse.org/template.cfm?page=70&release=789, "Arab Leaders Urged to Press Al-Bashir on ICC Warrant, Darfur Aid Ban" accessed on 26 October 2009.

28. 'Benn criticizes "war on terror"', BBC, 16 April 2007, http://news.bbc. co.uk/2/hi/uk_news/politics/6558569.stm accessed on 26 October 2009.
29. D. Reiff, *The New York Times Magazine, ca.* August 1999.
30. P. van Tongeren, M. Brenk, M. Hellema, and J. Verhoeven (eds), *People Building Peace II: Success Stories of Civil Society,* Boulder, CO: Lynne Reinner, 2005.
31. As with Christian fundamentalists, their theology emphasizes belief and the afterlife, but differs in espousing fatalism toward the present life. Churches in secular societies tend to emphasize values, ethics and other worldly concerns.
32. E.M. Cousens, 'Introduction', in Cousens and C. Kumar (eds) *Peacebuilding as Politics: Cultivating Peace in Fragile Societies,* Boulder, CO: Lynne Reinner, 2001, p. 4. Emphasis in the original.
33. C.T. Call and S.E. Cook, 'On Democratization and Peacebuilding.' *Global Governance* Vol. 9 (2003), p. 243, pp. 233–46.
34. D. Gilbert, *Stumbling on Happiness,* New York: Alfred A. Knopf, 2006, p. 183.
35. J.J. Hamre and G.R. Sullivan, 'Toward Postconflict Reconstruction', *The Washington Quarterly,* Vol. 25, no. 4, 2002, pp. 91, 85–96.
36. De Montclos, 'A Crisis of Humanitarianism', p. 97.
37. R.I. Rotberg and E.A. Albaugh, *Preventing Conflict in Africa: Possibilities of Peace Enforcement,* Cambridge, MA: World Peace Foundation, 1999, p. 87.
38. H.W. Jeong, *Peacebuilding in Post-Conflict Societies: Strategy and Process,* Boulder, CO: Lynne Rienner, 2005, p. 124.
39. *Matthew* 10:34: 'Do not think that I have come to bring peace on earth; I have not come to bring peace but a sword.'
40. F. Zakaria, *The Future of Freedom: Illiberal Democracy at Home and Abroad,* New York: W.W. Norton, 2004; F. Fukuyama, *State-Building: Governance and World Order in the Twenty-First Century,* Ithaca, NY: Cornell University Press, 2004.
41. A. Donini, 'Asserting Humanitarianism in Peace-Maintenance.', in J. Chopra (ed.), *The Politics of Peace Maintenance,* Boulder, CO: Lynne Rienner, 1998, p. 94.

13

welfare in war-torn societies: nemesis of the liberal peace?

michael pugh

Every State has an inalienable right to choose its
political, economic, social and cultural system, without
interference in any form by another State.[1]

Global management is replete with declarations upholding domestic
state autonomy that have been ignored. External economic interventions in Bosnia and Herzegovina, Kosovo, Afghanistan, and Iraq are
some of the most pronounced examples of foreign-determined economic policy in current war and post-war environments. They replicate
the generalised infractions of sovereignty that affect war-torn societies
under the auspices of peacebuilding led by core capitalist states and the
international institutions that these states dominate. In a double movement, however, the goal of interventionists has been to rebuild states
according to a hollowed-out model of statism. Consequently, not only
is peacebuilding co-opted by statebuilding, but the idealised state to be
built is one that functions as an 'executive committee of capitalist class
interests'.[2] This chapter has two main contentions. First, liberal peacebuilding as practised since the 1990s has broadly favoured entrepreneurship over employment and commercial over social contracts in welfare
policy. Second, in attempting to cure strangers of their strangeness, international actors have failed to respect socially and historically embedded
welfare arrangements as the basis for negotiating change in social contracts. Nevertheless, the limitations of liberal hegemony suggest that a
paradigmatic shift in thinking about welfare in peacebuilding would
help to foster local conceptions of peace. The chapter begins by defining

262

welfare and its relevance in war-torn societies. Next it indicates that in this sphere the dominant 'liberal' ideology in peacebuilding diverges significantly from earlier interpretations of 'liberal'. The analysis then turns to the assumptions and practices of commercial, self-reliant welfarism. The limitations of liberal hegemony are then discussed, and last the chapter outlines an alternative approach to welfare that potentially breaches the problem-solving intellectual frameworks. The arguments draw partly upon critical analyses of capitalist developmentalism,[3] and partly upon critical work on the peace differend: economic injustice arising from well-intentioned (perhaps even ill-intentioned) interference in reconstructing war-torn societies. The universalising concept of peace that produces a differend between policy and outcome has been summarised by Oliver Richmond in the following way:

> peace is often little more than a chimera, a superficial implant, camouflaging illiberalism, transplanted into a soil without water, dependent upon foreign resources, and subject to uncertainty about the longevity of external commitment. It suffers from both a cultural disconnection with its local hosts and offers little in the way of direct and immediate socioeconomic support for individuals during that all-important transition period while the liberal peace is taking root.[4]

The analysis here develops an immanent critique of the 'liberal' project in relation to welfare in war-torn societies, highlighting the gulf between peacebuilding promises and everyday life. It also pinpoints the global instability of capital flows as one of the main forces behind this contradiction.

meanings of welfare

Welfare is an ill-defined term with a variety of meanings in different temporal and geographical contexts. Varieties of welfare reflect class, gender, and ethnic struggles (such as the welfare societies established by workers), but also forms of state or monetised control and discipline through conditionalities imposed on populations.[5] In some parts of the world, notably in Europe, welfare is associated with state provision of universal public goods and services paid for by taxation. In the United States it connotes 'hand-outs' and dependency on the part of the indigent and uninsured citizenry. In advanced capitalist economies the commercialisation of public goods and the vulnerability of welfare provision to capital accumulation have grown to an advanced stage and led ineluctably to a 'welfare apartheid': the wealthy insured and the poor uninsured, each group receiving highly divergent standards of access and support.[6]

A pluralistic conception is adopted here, following Bob Deacon and Paul Stubbs, whereby welfare incorporates social value, altruism, and human agency.[7] It is used here in a broad sense to mean individual and community-fostered well-being that embodies a functional social contract. It may be provided by state, local administrations, class or clan leaders. But the key defining feature is not the sovereign institution providing welfare – for Kantian liberals the enlightenment state – but its socially integrative contribution to everyday life. This requires the means to maintain public goods and confidence in the system, not necessarily through representative democracy, but through a balance between consent and coercion that is sufficiently flexible to manage change. Indeed, social policy is traditionally distinguished from economic policy by its objective of building an individual's well-being and identity around a community through appeals to integration that can entail unilateral transfers as varieties of public goods.[8] In brief, the role of welfare with roots in local societies is significant in the quest for identity, social cohesion, and viable and legitimate social contracts with governing polities, whether states or non-state providers. However, state welfare requires institutions and bureaucracies that war-torn states are unable to construct readily. War-torn societies are characterised by a blurring of informal and formal economies; an 'official' residual welfare sometimes available for the poorest while the powerful are privately served and secured; a denial, by both 'insured' and 'uninsured', of reliance on audited provision.

classical and social liberalism

The term 'liberal' is an essentially contested concept marked by great variation. Classical liberalism, associated with John Stewart Mill, Richard Cobden, and Adam Smith, and drawing on Locke's conception of property as a natural right, reifies protection of property, entrepreneurship, the idealised free market, and free trade as the most efficient means of bringing about prosperity and peace. Although the ideology of *laissez-faire* implied a non-interventionist state, a huge exception to this was state protection of property and state assistance to capital accumulation and trade. It defined the classical movement. While liberals trumpeted a moral philosophy of reward for effort and invention, in practice state assistance to capitalism and trade also relied on crony-ism and colossal levels of corruption. In the eighteenth century, the venality of the UK's first 'prime minister', Sir Robert Walpole, was as profound as his support for capitalist development.

After the Second World War a central European school, represented by Friedrich Hayek and Joseph Schumpeter, added a morally persuasive bonus. Individuals could be liberated through individual freedom from state interference and collective welfare. This chimed well with a power-ful ethos in the United States – the Horatio Alger myth of social mobil-ity. Since the 1960s, the systemic influence of the Chicago School and its symbiotic relationship with authoritarian politics rendered everyday life and welfare, including health care and education, subject to mon-etary rather than social value. This ideological thrust married the clas-sical and liberationist schools to produce a 'neoliberalism' which, until the crash of casino capitalism in 2007–08, pitted the market against the state. The state relinquished control over economic development, except to subcontract state functions. In his critique of neoliberalism, Ioannis Glinavos contends that 'the state is no longer an impartial arbi-ter and social guardian, but an organisation catering to self-interested politicians and bureaucrats, who are not acting in the general wel-fare but to the benefit of their client groups'.[9] Welfare comes from the individual's purchasing power in a context where state functions are privatised, including the privatisation of privatisation processes.[10] To maintain the validity of their ideology, the neoliberal economists and policymakers ignored the history of developmental capitalism or, as in the case of Milton Friedman, intentionally reinvented the social trans-formations since the Second World War as triumphs of the free market. They simply denied that states in Western Europe, North America, and Asia had expanded through economic nationalism and state direction, ownership and control.[11] Many of their kind, though, were first in line to claim state welfare at tax-payers' expense for financial bail-outs in the crash of 2007–08.

While classical liberals had made an exception to *laissez-faire* in requiring state support for capital accumulation, social liberals made an equally significant exception in recognising that unregulated cap-italism produced social unrest which threatened the contract between state and individual. Consequently, capitalism had to be managed to contain popular revolt, as the arch-realist, Otto von Bismarck, under-stood in providing social insurance in Germany, ahead of any other country. As suggested by Ellen Wood, 'the state must help to keep alive a propertyless population which has no other means of survival when work is unavailable, maintaining a "reserve army" of workers through the inevitable cyclical declines in the demand for labour'.[12] The social contract stripped to its essentials had meant that the state would protect citizens if they submitted to industrialisation, law and order, and the call to fight for 'King and Country'. It could contribute to 'national efficiency', a prevalent policy orientation in industrial capitalism.[13] Richard Titmuss, the pioneer of British social policy and a prominent member of the Eugenics Society, had noted that state welfare was progressively extended from the care of soldiers on the battlefield to support for their dependants, and then expanded to welfare for the masses whose cooperation was essential for war mobilisation.[14]

For Titmuss and Scandinavian welfare theorists, the link with development was also unmistakable; welfare was partial compensation for bearing the social costs and insecurities of industrialisation and social dislocation.[15] However, a contract was not exclusively bestowed by the state in exchange for obedience in order to reduce the costs of policing or to fight wars efficiently. As Karl Polanyi noted in 1944, social unrest was inherent in the demands of capital, obliging entrepreneurs and politicians to yield to the resistance of labour against exploitation and to popular demands for political and socio-economic rights.[16] In the social liberal vision, the unstable cycles of capitalism and war raised issues of social justice for society as a whole. Thus Titmuss regarded welfare as an instrument to achieve social integration, identity, and participation in society.[17] He was nevertheless bound by precepts that co-opted the needy into a contract with the state, whether under a capitalist or a command economy, and conditional on acceptance of its disciplinary and social engineering functions. He identified categories of welfare according to stages of capitalist development, cultural norms, and the diversity of social relations and resources available (state safety nets when other sources failed; corporatist benefits from paid work; social democratic redistribution). Nevertheless, his models were distinctive to western states. Only from the 1980s, with the revival of a critical literature on 'globalisation', have post-colonial welfare systems received serious attention: systems in Asia, for example, required compulsory savings.[18]

With regard to conflict and instability, the divergence of neoliberals from social liberals is quite stark. For neoliberals, the social chaos caused by disasters, regime change, or civil war acts as a kind of asset-stripping that provides opportunities to break the state's restraints on private capital accumulation, and to reconfigure politics by removing democratic control over the economy. Thus, as Glinavos demonstrates, law and constitutional reforms have often been driven by an economic management that is frequently entrusted to consultants and so-called independent bodies, which divorce economic decision-making from political legitimation.[19] The polarisation of politics and economics results in entire classes and sectors of society being disempowered and marginalised.

The neoliberalism that, at least until the end of 2007, informed the political economy of peace and stability was thus quite different from the sort of peace articulated by social liberals. The trio of John Maynard Keynes, Richard Titmuss, and Sir William Beveridge, who severally advised on the kinds of policies British society would welcome in the aftermath of the Second World War, were highly sceptical of the free market and self-reliance. 'Peace consolidation' was the post-war priority for Beveridge, but then:

> [t]he second thing we need is that each man and woman, so long as he or she is able to work and serve and earn, shall have an opportunity to do so. The third thing we need is that each man and woman shall be assured of an income sufficient for honourable subsistence and maintenance of any dependants when for any reason he or she is unable to work.[20]

Such principles, summed up by Titmuss as 'full employment in a free society', drew upon long-standing social liberal demands, including the Liberal Party's 1929 election manifesto for a programme of public works.[21] The searing experiences of depression and war had reinvigorated the social contract between individual, community, and state in many other countries, Franklin D. Roosevelt's New Deal (which founded the Fanny Mae and Freddie Mac mortgage corporations, nationalised when they collapsed in 2008) was a prime example.

Unsurprisingly, surveys conducted by international organisations such as the UNDP find that the principles of this social liberalism are also highly significant for post-intervention populations.[22] They have not, however, figured in the priorities of the interventionists.

the liberal welfare paradigm in post-intervention societies

Social policy is integrally connected to the form of political economy directed by interventionists and donors as the condition for their peacebuilding assistance. After emergency relief has been provided and refugee returns have been stimulated, the neglect by the international actors of what Mark Duffield calls 'the uninsured' population in post-intervention contexts[23] is a characteristic of the liberal peacebuilding paradigm. Welfare is its nemesis. As Richmond argues, 'neoliberal policies fail to provide welfare, undermine what little substitution strategies there are and infantilise local culture', largely because institutionalised welfare is anathema, ideologically speaking, to market incentives and individual freedom from state control.[24] The intended or unintended exacerbation of 'bare life' through policies that stress a future based on self-reliance in a globally integrated political economy has the effect of expanding the class of uninsured and its dependence on informal economic activity. Liberalisation does not benefit the majority because they cannot claim compensation for trade adjustments and income losses from a state whose economic functions are shrinking.

A fundamental contradiction in the liberal peace is that the 'social liberalism' and humanitarian impulses that spawned the 'responsibility to protect' and save strangers, so as to bring them 'individual freedom', is then assaulted by a determination to cure their strangeness. Promises of global integration, export-led growth, and trickle-down redistribution, as well as freedom of choice through self-reliance, have been a central component of liberal peace and crisis management techniques in the last 20 years.[25] The rationale advanced is a seductive one: that 'illiberalism' brought about the violence (and cries for help) in the first place. There is no room in the explanation for the wealth of evidence that neoliberal demands on developing economies, globally and imposed by international institutions such as the IMF and WTO, also played a role in destabilising societies.[26]

Transformation trajectories for developing countries, generally, are mapped by external agencies (and their domestic allies in the entrepreneurial and political classes) to implant institutions and policies that privilege 'free and open market' measures, such as subsidising the private sector, eliminating protectionism and relying on foreign direct investment to stimulate growth.[27] The state's role in providing jobs and welfare is subject to monetary and fiscal discipline, not simply because securing internal revenue is problematic in the aftermath of war. The 'market mantra' also means that the economy is vulnerable to adverse trade balances, while counter-cyclical deficit spending is ruled out by donors and the IFIs who restrict state budgets. The governed are expected to welcome or tolerate radical experiments with their economic environment that usually entail policies and institutional mechanisms to achieve macroeconomic stability and self-reliance. Populations have limited say in devising a social contract, though they are capable of ignoring, resisting, co-opting and adapting the new circumstances of capital accumulation.[28]

Social contracts between external actors and communities are initially fashioned out of high levels of dependency on humanitarian relief aid. In societies assumed to be completely broken by conflict, interventionists necessarily start by prioritising safety nets, often instituted by non-state actors. Indeed, a strong characteristic of international social policy, generally, has been the array of welfare providers mobilised to supplement the state, often suggesting a degree of welfare solidarity across borders that feeds aspirations for transnational advocacy and global citizenship.[29] It also feeds the appetites of the assemblages of non-state providers, including powerful Western international NGOs which claim to be empowering societies undergoing reconstruction, but whose representation of aid recipients 'maintains a gulf between themselves, the people that they seek to "aid" and the indigenous partners that they fund, perpetuating an international systemic hierarchy of "benefactors" and "beneficiaries", rule-makers and those that have to play the game'.[30] The game in this account is a neoliberal one, its players failing to interrogate the paradigm that makes aid necessary while perpetuating predominantly 'Western' knowledge and values.

Economic policies introduced to a variety of post-intervention contexts result in further social dislocation and increased inequality – the (re)creation of social atomisation rather than cohesion – for which local leaders are then bequeathed responsibility by unaccountable interveners.[31] The ideological reification of economic self-reliance is backed by and supports a technology of governance to maintain elite control, and through command of global finance to which war-torn societies need access. Official, audited welfare is thus contingent, not only on foreign agenda-setting, policy transfer, and limited domestic revenue, but also on conditional external subsidy. The attempt at replicating individualistic, self-reliant welfare in war-torn societies has uneven outcomes, as resistance exacerbates the socially divisive, atomising effects of conflict, namely capital accumulation by dispossession,[32] reorientations of patronage, and fragmentation of authority.

hegemony resisted?

Interventions by global social movements, norm entrepreneurs, transnational policy communities, and the voluntary and private sectors contribute to a complex pattern also ensured by conflict end-games, porous borders, competition between international organisations, and the resistance, adoption, and co-option strategies of local communities and elites. For example, aggressive neoliberalism is most likely to be facilitated when the end-game allows foreign actors to exert unaccountable sovereignty, as in Iraq and Afghanistan. In their analysis of social policy transfers, Bob Deacon and Paul Stubbs contend that explanations cannot be reduced to a simple dichotomy of hegemonic imposition by the powerful and meek absorption by recipients. Political entities are not fixed, policy processes are fluid, impacts are multilayered, multiple actors are engaged in a series of encounters, and the effects of historical resilience and social resistance create 'policy assemblages' that undermine hegemonic ideology and cushion the impact of raw neoliberalism.[33] Accordingly, the 'liberal' project is not a homogeneous concept, linear in its impact.

Everyday negotiations, characterised as 'tricks of everyday life' by Béatrice Pouligny, have a fundamental bearing on local adaptations that promote welfare, social relations, and social inclusion.[34] In societies affected by dislocation and low rates of formal employment, the non-audited economies provide a welfare function, including access to goods, services, and income. Informal employment is such a significant aspect of the labour market (in the region of 50% of all employment in the Balkans) that it is clearly an essential element in household consumption, as are remittances by diasporas and transfers by expatriate visitors. Such activity, not to be equated with morally heinous people-trafficking, continues a tradition in which volatile issues, such as ethnic difference, are marginalised.[35] It keeps people above the poverty line, offers a form of social and economic inclusion for the uninsured, helps to sustain resistance to the social alienation entailed in economic liberalisation and takes advantage of the public spaces unfilled or abandoned by the state.[36] Everyday life does not conform to the rationalism of the liberal engineers. The 'tricks' signal traditional quests for sufficiency and subsistence quite independent of constructed transitions to a particular future. They enable people to participate in 'free markets' *par excellence*, in the sense that they are not regulated by authority but offer 'daily reinvented social norms around the claim to subsistence'.[37] In sum, people arrange their welfare not because of the benefits of an international presence, but often in spite of the socially corrosive disparities of wealth under liberalisation.

Furthermore, there is competition and discord among and within agencies – and switches in policy. Longer-term reform and reorganisation of welfare can be welcomed by domestic reformers, social workers and institutionalised 'patients'. For example, in some central and eastern European communities the treatment of disabled, orphaned, and other vulnerable people has been reformed, with UNICEF support, to supplant harsh institutional treatment and to engender respect for disadvantaged citizens.[38] Indeed, perhaps the most significant flaw in the romanticisation of domestic versus imposed universalist transformation is the assumption that the domestic context is unreceptive to external norms and stratagems.

Some intergovernmental institutions have also budged. The UN Conference on Trade and Development (UNCTAD) has proposed a huge investment in welfare in Africa, commensurate with the MDGs and with long-standing reviews by the UN Research Institute for Social Development (UNRISD).[39] The UN's Peacebuilding Commission has engaged in negotiations with civil society groups in Sierra Leone, Burundi, and Guinea. The World Bank's *World Development Report* for 2006, echoing Amartya Sen, incorporated 'equality of opportunity' for individuals to pursue a life of their choosing into its conceptualisation of development.[40] Rifts within and outside the Bank were marked in 2006 by the UK government's proposal to temporarily withhold a £50 million contribution to the Bank until the latter relaxed conditionalities on its loans. The Bank promotes accessible public provision for basic health care and primary education. Similarly, the IMF supports access to basic social services, and claims that its programmes of public provision have made a difference to poverty.[41] A consensus reached by the World Bank, IMF, and OECD privileges free primary education and basic health (notably reproductive health) in line with the Millennium Development Goals. The self-reliance ideology of the IFIs and donors has frayed at the edges with the attention to public service for reproductive health and primary education.

Nevertheless, the case for diffusion and against hegemony is contentious because it underestimates the framing of welfare by economic rather than social policy goals. UNCTAD, UNRISD, and even the OECD lack the clout of the WTO and G8. Nor does the modified orientation of the Bretton Woods institutions represent abandonment of commodification and self-reliance. The donors and lenders foster a hierarchy of welfare, with mixed private and public provision for higher education but wholesale privatisation for pensions.[42] Increased social spending either cannot occur because of weak revenue-gathering capacity or cannot keep pace with increasing demand. Moreover, the World

Bank's quest to 'make services work for the poor' cements discriminatory international support and social divisions based on the wealthy
buying welfare while the poor rely on public provision that is condi-
tioned by foreign insistence on restrictive monetary and budgetary policies.[43] The commodification of welfare through market mechanisms
has been integral to a hegemonic engagement with society. As Peter
Alcock points out, classical economic ideology has 'simply redistrib-
uted benefits in favour of private welfare and exposed the individual
to greater hazard', for example, in terms of access to safe medicines.[44]
The dominant framework reinforces a hierarchy of power relations that
configure inequalities and subjugate systems that are incompatible with
that dominance, and assumes either the existence of a tax base, service
infrastructures, and bureaucracies able to operate welfare, or that these
things can be readily created.[45] Assistance is predicated on macroeconomic conditionalities that specify a limited economic role for the state
and a major role for entrepreneurs, manifested in the fetish for privatisation, microcredit, and business incentive schemes. These simply fail to
provide employment on scales sufficient to generate transformation in
household income, aggregate purchasing power, and tax revenue.[46] As
Thomas Koelble and Edward LiPuma argue, the mechanics of the global
financial and trading systems 'imposes a myriad of hidden constraints
on their economic policy, which, in turn, constrains the possibility for
creating the foundation for the realisation of these critical [democratic]
values'.[47] Finally, as Oliver Richmond contends, liberal peacebuilding
marginalises local definitions of peace and well-being, and its agents
assume that resistance and reliance on informal economies are illegitimate.[48] Indeed, lack of economic sovereignty in 'undeveloped' societies
means that local politicians are less accountable to their own people
than to external agencies and, in the case of international administrations in war-torn societies, to foreign purveyors of 'good governance'.

    Certainly, the crisis of casino capitalism, and global uncertainties
with regard to food and energy resources and environmental sustainability, may see the demise of neoliberal ideology. It seems probable
that there will be greater regulation of financial speculation and a re-
establishment of the role of the state. A global slump could also prompt
a restoration of protectionism. However, claims that the 'Washington
consensus' of 1989 has evaporated in favour of support by international
agencies for 'mixed economies' was not blindingly obvious in 2009.
US economic advisers in Afghanistan were urging the government to
end a system of rationing that was enabling the poorest to survive, and

foreign companies were free to plunder Iraqi oil by a US-devised law that removed democratic control from the oil industry. Besides, the crisis in global finance is the kind of 'shock', commonly endured by war-torn societies, that effectively results in asset-stripping, enabling predators to buy up assets cheaply, leaving debt burdens to be borne by future taxpayers, hobbling state budgets, and tempting governments to cut public welfare even further in years to come.[49]

conclusion

The peace differend is nowhere starker than in the liberal assault on public welfare as a social contract, even though, as Titmuss pointed out, entrepreneurs have much to gain from a skilled, well-educated and healthy population with purchasing power. If welfare has been the nemesis of the liberal peace it is because the lessons of the social liberal contractarians were forgotten in the late twentieth century. But even these lessons would not suffice to exculpate liberalism. The emphasis on improvement of the 'other' – curing strangeness – is practised without local ownership or political roots. Well-being and welfare are as varied as forms of social integration. Local responses to external projects lead to adoptions, adaptations and resistances, creating a mottled welfare space that might be labelled 'hybridity' or 'multiplicity', to modulate the asymmetries of power that securitise welfare.

Reformist approaches may promote 'local stakeholding', 'capacity-building', 'empowerment', and 'shared sovereignty' through deliberative processes that allow people to determine the good life and how to achieve it for themselves.[50] But, as Pablo Leal contends, the mantra of participation has served not to facilitate the agency of the poor and reduce their subjugation by the state and its international backers, but to create 'a populist justification for the removal of the state from the economy and its substitution by the market'.[51] Liberation from an interventionist state and participating in the market was cast as 'inherently empowering'. The incorporation of participation into the discourse of welfare disempowers those without money to pay for privatised welfare and basic needs such as water. Thus empowerment through 'participation' can be considered as a governmentality, in the Foucauldian sense, that reinforces the power of those facilitating participation to 'contain it within the bounds of the existing order'.[52] The neoliberal version of liberalism also ensures that control of the process is beyond political accountability. This is not to say that peacebuilding invariably carries the assumption of an idealised, liberal, free market, since convergence with the liberal order is hardly a feasible goal in many contexts.[53] In practice interventionists promote something rather different – reduction in security risks to themselves but also rendering war-torn societies open to potential capital accumulation and destruction of difference. Reforms aim to keep a lid on disorder rather than seeking a fundamental shift in the prevailing paradigm of the global economy.

For Richmond and Duffield, such a shift would require non-prescriptive negotiations with local communities. Engagement and dialogue between heterodoxies would need to be more profound than hitherto practised. From such critical perspectives, the historically embedded exertions of class, gender, and identity can be resourced to ferment a non-securitised counter-discourse that would take local voices seriously, engage with heterodoxy, and in many cases reconceptualise atomised societies as collectives. However, it is not clear how the reformulation of social contracts and expressions of solidarity with the governed would address the factors that facilitated the breakdown of contracts or avoid romanticising local abusive power elites. A sole focus on domestic sovereignty would also leave the operations of the global economic structures unproblematised. For Robert Cox, a necessary correlative shift would encompass a world order 'in which different traditions of civilisation could co-exist, each based on different intersubjectivity defining a distinct set of values and a distinct path towards development'.[54] This envisages a political transformation of the structures and institutions that underpin the disempowerment of subaltern societies and that securitise 'welfare as poor relief'. It would likely entail the wholesale regulation of finance capital and radical reform or replacement of the global financial and trade system. In practice, however, could the system be revolutionised without liberals committing the equivalent of hara-kiri?

Perhaps opportunities to escape from the liberal nemesis may yet arise from turmoil in the financial system and shifts in the distribution of global power. Emancipatory peacebuilding might be reconfigured to take advantage of trends that lend purchase to more diffuse sovereignties. States, international agents, and their subcontracted organisation will not be the only safeguards against injustice and ill-being. Resistance to the sullied liberal project can produce a different set of actors, perhaps with greater concern for everyday life. Transnational and domestic actors, peace movements, human rights movements, welfare and labour organisations, with *sans frontières* as a guiding principle, would be positioned to participate in and construct welfare independent of the current ideological orthodoxy.

This would not be a cosmopolitan and universalising replacement for the liberal peace, but would need to create room for alternative, tailored concepts of welfare as socially-contracted forms of identity and politics. Organisationally and financially, this might not be as far-fetched as might be imagined. Alternative forms of transition and welfare can be discerned in the collective resistances organised locally, from the Zapatistas to the Democratic Alliance movement headed by Ibrahim Rugova in Kosovo. In the event that the stresses in the international system create space for non-predatory forms of political economy, such as producer-owned cooperatives and (re)mutualised savings and lending institutions (credit unions being an obvious example), then there is potential for more balanced intersubjective politics in peacebuilding. In place of self-reliance, asset-stripping and the 'state as agent of capital', the interfaces of external and local interests would potentially demonstrate a greater concern for the welfare of everyday life.

acknowledgements

This research benefited from a grant by the UK Economic and Social Research Council (Res. 223.25.0071) for research on the Transformation of War Economies (www.brad.ac.uk/acad/twe).

notes

1. UN General Assembly Resolution 2131, on 'The Inadmissability of Intervention in the Domestic Affairs of States and their Independence and Sovereignty', UN doc., A/6014 (5), 1965.
2. D. Harvey, *Spaces of Global Capitalism: Towards a Theory of Uneven Geographical Development*, London: Verso, 2006, p.106.
3. Deriving from the work of K. Polanyi's *The Great Transformation: The Political and Economic Origins of Our Time*, Boston: Beacon Press, 1957 [1944] and contemporary critiques by Ellen Wood, David Harvey and Ha-Joon Chang.
4. O.P. Richmond, 'Critical Research Agendas for Peace: The Missing Link in the Study of International Relations', *Alternatives*, Vol. 32, 2007, pp. 247–74 (on p. 269). See also N. Cooper, 'On the Crisis in the Liberal Peace', *Conflict, Security & Development*, Vol. 7, No. 4, 2007, pp. 605–16; D. Chandler, 'Post-Conflict State-building: Governance Without Government', in M. Pugh, N. Cooper and M. Turner, *Whose Peace? Critical Perspectives on the Political Economy of Peacebuilding*, Basingstoke: Palgrave, 2009, pp. 337–55.
5. B. Deacon, *Global Social Policy and Governance*, London: Sage, 2007, p. 7.
6. As exposed by Hurricane Katrina in Louisiana in 2005. See N. Klein, *Shock Doctrine: The Rise of Disaster Capitalism*, New York: Metropolitan Books, 2007, pp. 406–22.

7. B. Deacon, M. Hulse and P. Stubbs, *Global Social Policy: International Organisations and the Future of Welfare*, London: Sage, 1997. See also A. Deacon, *Perspectives on Welfare* (Buckingham: Open University Press), 2002, p. 14.

8. K.E. Boulding, 'The Boundaries of Social Policy', *Social Work*, Vol. 12, No. 1, January 1967, pp. 3–11; *Beyond Economics: Essays on Society, Religion, and Ethics*, Ann Arbor, MI: University of Michigan Press, 1968, p. 67.

9. I. Glinavos, 'Neoliberal Law: Unintended Consequences of Market-Friendly Law Reforms', *Third World Quarterly*, Vol. 29, No. 6, 2008, pp.1087–99.

10. B. Hibou (ed.), *Privatising the State*, London: Hurst, 2004.

11. As demonstrated by: H. Chang, *Bad Samaritans: The Guilty Secrets of Rich Nations and Their Threat to Global Prosperity*, London: Random House Business Books, 2007; UNDP/Kamal Malhotra, *Making Global Trade Work for People*, London: Earthscan, 2003; J. Stiglitz, *Globalization and its Discontents*, London: Penguin, 2002; B. Morvaridi, *Social Justice and Development*, Basingstoke: Palgrave, 2008.

12. E.M. Wood, *Empire of Capital*, London: Verso, 2005 [2003], p.18; I. Lødemel and H. Trickey, 'A New Contract for Social Assistance', in Lødemel and Trickey (eds) *An offer you can't refuse. Workfare in International Perspective*, Bristol: The Policy Press, 2000, p. 26.

13. G.R. Searle, *The Quest for National Efficiency: A Study in British Politics and Political Thought, 1899–1914*, Oxford: Blackwell, 1971. On Bismarck see C.W. Guillebaud, *The Social Policy of Nazi Germany*, Cambridge: Cambridge University Press, 1941, pp. 2–3.

14. R.M. Titmuss, *Essays on the Welfare State*, London: Allen & Unwin, 2nd edn, 1963 [1958], pp. 75–87; Titmuss, 'The Welfare State: Images and realities', in P. Alcock, H. Glennerster, A. Oakley and A. Sinfield (eds) *Welfare and Wellbeing: Richard Titmuss's Contribution to Social Policy*, Bristol: The Policy Press, 2001, p. 51.

15. Titmuss, *Commitment to Welfare*, London: Allen & Unwin, 2nd edn, 1976, pp. 131–3; G. Esping-Andersen, *The Three Worlds of Welfare*, Cambridge: Polity Press, 1990.

16. K. Polanyi, *The Great Transformation: The Political and Economic Origins of Our Time*, Boston, MA: Beacon Press, 1957 [1944].

17. Titmuss, *Commitment to Welfare* (note 15), p. 21; Titmuss, *The Gift Relationship: From Human Blood to Social Policy*, London: Allen & Unwin, 1970, p. 224. The unconditional, non-commodified norm of donating blood and body parts to the UK's National Health Service means that even the bare life of the individual can serve as a public good.

18. Deacon, *Global Social Policy and Governance*, pp. 6–7; Deacon, Hulse and Stubbs, *Global Social Policy*.

19. Examples are the task force in charge of rebuilding Sri Lanka after the 2004 tsunami and the inability of the elected representatives in the UK parliament to determine interest rates. See Glinavos, 'Neoliberal Law'; R.W. Cox, 'Globalization, Multilateralism, and Democracy', J. Holmes memorial lecture to the Academic Council on the United Nations System (ACUNS), 1992 (www.igloo.org/community.igloo?r0=community&r0_script=/scripts/folder/view.script&r0_pathinfo=%2F%7Bdb9ad9e0–7451–46aa-8726–8fc85f098b64%7D%2FJohn%20Holmes%20Memorial%20

Lectures%2FHolmes%20Lectures%2FCox&r0_output=xml),   accessed on
25 December 2008. For an apocalyptic interpretation of social breakdown
as a marketing opportunity see Klein, *Shock Doctrine*.

20. W. Beveridge, *Full Employment in a Free Society*, 1944, preface.
21. D.L. George, *We Can Conquer Unemployment*, Liberal Party manifesto, 1929.
    Titmuss moved into the Labour Party during the war.
22. Klein cites a US-conducted poll in Iraq which suggests that 49 percent of
    Iraqis would have voted for a party promising government-created jobs, as
    opposed to 4.6 percent hoping for private sector jobs (Klein, *Shock Doctrine*,
    p. 364; UNDP in Bosnia).
23. M. Duffield, *Security, Development and Unending War, Governing the World of
    Peoples*, Cambridge: Polity Press, 2007, pp. 19–24, 228.
24. O. Richmond, 'Welfare and the Civil Peace: Poverty with Rights?', in Pugh,
    Cooper and Turner (eds), *Whose Peace?*, pp. 290–1.
25. See, notably, the effort to get refugees to look after themselves in *Handbook
    for Self-Reliance*, Reintegration and Local Settlement Section, Division of
    Operational Support, UNHCR, Geneva, August 2005.
26. As noted *inter alia* by Joseph Stiglitz, Amy Chua, Carl-Ulrik Schierup, Naomi
    Klein.
27. Evidence is to be found in M. Spoor (ed.), *The 'Market Panacea': Agrarian
    Transformation in Developing Countries and Former Socialist Countries*, London:
    Intermediate Technology, 1997; R. Paris, *At War's End: Building Peace After
    Civil Conflict*, Cambridge: Cambridge University Press, esp. ch. 7; M. Pugh
    and N. Cooper with J. Goodhand, *War Economies in a Regional Context:
    Challenges of Transformation*, Boulder, CO: Lynne Rienner, 2004.
28. See C. Cramer, *Civil War is Not a Stupid Thing: Accounting for Violence in
    Developing Countries*, London: Hurst, 2006.
29. See Deacon, *Global Social Policy and Governance*, pp. 7, 175–7. See also the
    'Globalism and Social Policy Programme' website, University of Sheffield
    (http://gaspp.stakes.fi/EN/index.htm), accessed on 25 December 2008.
30. Niomi Turley, 'British Humanitarian Aid NGOs and Tamilnadu after the
    Tsunami', unpublished PhD thesis draft, University of Bradford, 2008. See
    also Z. Marriage, *Not Breaking the Rules, Not Playing the Game: International
    Assistance to Countries at War*, London: Hurst, 2006; R. Apthorpe, 'Alice in
    Aidland: A Seriously Satirical Allegory', in D. Mosse, *Travelling Rationalities:
    The Anthropology of Expert Knowledge and Professionals in International
    Development*, Oxford: Berghahn, in press; K. Pawlowska, 'Humanitarian
    Intervention: Transforming the Discourse', *International Peacekeeping*,
    Vol. 12, No. 4, 2005, pp. 487–502.
31. On atomisation see Z. Bauman, *Liquid Modernity*, Cambridge: Polity Press, 2000.
    See also the remarkably frank admission by Paddy Ashdown, former High
    Representative in Bosnia and Herzegovina, *Swords and Ploughshares: Bringing
    Peace to the 21st Century*, London: Wiedenfeld and Nicholson, 2007, p. 83.
32. D. Harvey, *The New Imperialism*, Oxford: Oxford University Press, 2002, p. 210.
33. B. Deacon and P. Stubbs (eds), *Social Policy and International Interventions in
    South East Europe*, Edward Elgar: Cheltenham, 2004, pp. 3–9.
34. B. Pouligny, *Peace Operations Seen from Below: UN Missions and Local People*,
    London: Hurst, 2006.

35. L. Jašarević, 'Everyday Work: Subsistence Economy, Social Belonging and Moralities of Exchange at a Bosnian (Black) Market', in X. Bougarel, E. Helms and G. Duijzings (eds) *The New Bosnian Mosaic: Identities, Memories and Moral Claims in a Post-War Society*, Aldershot: Ashgate, 2006, p. 274 (n. 2) and p. 284.
36. Cramer, *Civil War is Not a Stupid Thing*.
37. Ibid., p. 292.
38. V. Bošnjak and P. Stubbs, 'Towards a New Welfare Mix for the Most Vulnerable: Reforming Social Services in Bosnia-Herzegovina, Croatia and Serbia', in Ž. Lovrinčević, Z. Marić and D. Mikulić (eds) *Social Policy and Regional Development: Proceedings*, Zagreb: Zagreb Institute of Economics and Friedrich Ebert Stiftung, 2007, pp. 139–65.
39. UNCTAD, 'Doubling Aid. Making the *Big Push* Work', Geneva, 2006.
40. See Morvaridi, *Social Justice and Development*, ch. 5; A. Sen, *Development as Freedom*, Oxford: Oxford University Press, 1999.
41. Deacon, *Global Social Policy and Governance*, p. 44.
42. Ibid., p. 49.
43. World Development Report 2004, *Making Services Work for the Poor*, Washington DC: World Bank, 2003.
44. Alcock, Glennerster, Oakley and Sinfield, *Welfare and Wellbeing*.
45. Morvaridi, *Social Justice and Development*, ch. 3.
46. See the stringent critique of microcredit by M. Bateman, 'Microfinance and borderlands: Impacts of "Local Neoliberalism"', in Pugh, Cooper and Turner (eds) *Whose Peace?*, pp. 245–65.
47. T.A. Koelble and E. LiPuma, 'Democratizing Democracy: A Postcolonial Critique of Conventional Approaches to Democracy', *Democratization*, Vol. 15, No. 1, 2008, pp. 1–28, on p. 4. See also D. Chandler, *Empire in Denial: The Politics of State-Building*, London: Pluto, 2006; R. Shilliam, 'Hegemony and the Unfashionable Problematic of "Primitive Accumulation"', *Millennium, Journal of International Studies*, Vol. 32, No. 1, 2004, pp. 59–88.
48. O.P. Richmond, 'The Romanticisation of the Local: Welfare, Culture and Peacebuilding', *International Spectator*, Vol. 44, No. 1, March 2009, pp. 149–170.
49. Klein, *Shock Doctrine*, pp. 375–6; Glinavos, 'Neoliberal Law'. See M. Pugh, 'Post-war Economies and the New York Dissensus', *Conflict, Security & Development*, Vol. 6, No. 3, 2006, pp. 269–89.
50. M. Barnett, 'Building a Republican Peace: Stabilizing States after War', *International Security*, Vol. 30, No. 4, 2006, pp. 87–112, on p. 90.
51. P.A. Leal, 'Participation: the ascendancy of a buzzword in the neo-liberal era', *Development in Practice*, Vol. 17, Nos 4–5, 2007, pp. 539–48, on p. 541.
52. Ibid., p. 545.
53. R. Kiely, 'Poverty reduction through liberalisation? Neoliberalism and the myth of global convergence', *Review of International Studies*, Vol. 33, No. 3, 2007, pp. 415–34.
54. R. Cox, 'Structural Issues of Global Governance: Issues for Europe', in S. Gill (ed.) *Gramsci, Historical Materialism and International Relations*, Cambridge: Cambridge University Press, 1993, p. 265; O.P. Richmond, 'Emancipatory Forms of Human Security and Liberal Peacebuilding', *International Journal*, Vol. 62, No. 3, 2007, pp. 459–77, on p. 477.

14

resolving conflicts and pursuing accountability: beyond 'justice versus peace'

chandra lekha sriram

introduction

Over the past 25 years, domestic polities and the international community alike have increasingly confronted a vexing problem: how to deal with perpetrators of past abuses, particularly where those perpetrators cling to power or otherwise may disrupt the peace. This challenge was one primarily faced initially by societies emerging from authoritarian rule or civil war through domestic processes, with or without support from the international community. Later it became a challenge for the international community – how to enforce human rights and humanitarian norms in the wake of gross human rights violations, war crimes, crimes against humanity, or genocide? With the rapid growth of peacekeeping and peacebuilding missions, international assistance has increasingly involved support not only to transitional justice and accountability processes, but also to rebuilding rule of law in societies.

Yet more recently domestic courts have again taken up the challenge, but domestic courts far from the original site of the crime, through universal jurisdiction, or civil cases. Recently we have seen the creation of a hybrid tribunal in Cambodia, the first arrest warrants and arrest of the International Criminal Court, and cases before Spanish courts involving crimes alleged to have occurred in Rwanda. Addressing justice at a national, international, or hybridised level has become almost routine. The rapid proliferation of practice has meant that we have seen a shift in the practice of transitional justice, involving both what might be seen as a 'return' to international approaches, with the Nuremberg and Tokyo Tribunals

279

as reference points, and the development of new models, through trans-national and hybrid justice. In this chapter, I consider the evolution of transitional justice, and some contemporary critiques and challenges. I turn first to what I will term 'traditional' transitional justice.

traditional transitional justice debates

There is a vast literature on transitional justice, and thus this is but a brief overview.[1] The academic literature about transitional justice describes and assesses a range of political and institutional responses which have developed to address a political, moral, and legal dilemma.[2] Citizens of countries that have experienced authoritarian rule, internal armed conflict or transboundary conflict, or some combination of the three, will often also have suffered significant human rights abuses or violations of international humanitarian law. Violations may include torture, extra-judicial execution, disappearances, torture, war crimes, crimes against humanity, forced labour or enslavement, and genocide. They may have been committed by state security forces, rebel groups, militias, and private persons, many of whom may retain significant military, political, or economic power. Victims, members of civil society, transnational and international actors are also likely to call for some form of 'justice', whether juridical or not. The dilemma emerges because calls for justice are likely to generate tensions and exacerbate conflicts that have the potential to undermine peacebuilding. There has thus developed a vast literature debating how to respond to past abuses and analysing the complex practice that has emerged.

Traditional debates about appropriate responses to past abuses have taken several forms. These have been both normative–philosophical and empirical, driven by case studies, with some work attempting to merge the two approaches. Much of the normative work in transitional justice considers claims about what is good for societies or victims, or simply what is 'right'.[3] These are essential debates to be had within a conflict-affected society, and those who seek to support transitional justice from outside should also carefully consider the trade-offs involved. However, normative discussions only occasionally offer insights into the prerequisites for peacebuilding.[4] This may be in part because considerations of stability are perceived to be at odds with justice, rather than necessary for and complementary to it. Empirical studies do seek to address this gap, identifying challenges of pursuing justice while making peace or implementing peace agreements in a range of countries, from El Salvador to Sierra Leone. This research has provided important insights about not only the goals of domestic transitional justice actors, but also the goals, role, and impact of international peacekeeping and peacebuilding actors.[5] Through an examination of a range of comparative experiences, scholars have developed a range of arguments about what is feasible or appropriate with regard to accountability. Some scholars will argue that truth commissions are essential in mediating at least in part the peace/justice divide, because they help to out the truth and promote public dialogue. Others will argue that some form of legal accountability is essential for a range of reasons, including promoting peace, while yet others will argue that amnesties may be necessary in some instances. There remains no consensus in the academic literature, although there is a growing recognition of the range of options which may be more or less appropriate for specific situations.[6]

Transitional justice is, however, more than an academic literature. It is also an active area of policymaking, practised by the UN, and supported by regional organisations, international financial institutions, bilateral donors, and specialised NGOs such as the International Center for Transitional Justice.[7] While such organisations engage in the practice of transitional justice, they may differ significantly in their views as to its appropriate scope, and may be as divided as the academic work discussed as to the necessity of legal accountability. Yet if we consider recent political transitions and negotiated peace accords, as well as international peacebuilding efforts, we can see that a debate about accountability, and usually some efforts to prosecute, almost inevitably accompanies such transitions. Some may be considered more legitimate, or may be more or less accepted internationally – relatively recent examples include the referral of crimes committed in Sudan and the Democratic Republic of Congo to the International Criminal Court, the creation of the Special Court for Sierra Leone, and the creation of the Iraqi Special Tribunal and the Special Tribunal for Lebanon. Meanwhile, the trials at the ad hoc tribunals for the former Yugoslavia and Rwanda are set to be completed, with unfinished cases referred in some instances to domestic courts.[8] Oftentimes decisions about accountability are not only explicitly enshrined in peace agreements (and may include decisions to impose amnesties), but may also be addressed through peacebuilding operations (particularly through rule of law programming), and through new institutions that emerge alongside peacebuilding operations.[9]

However, despite the proliferation of peacebuilding and transitional justice practice, a rather narrow debate over 'peace vs. justice' continues in some quarters. Some, therefore, argue that legal accountability is absolutely necessary so that democracy and the rule of law can be rebuilt, and future crimes prevented, while others claim that, for the sake of stability, accountability ought to be eschewed.[10] In reality, the option is seldom *either* peace *or* justice: rather, there is a range of tools that may be utilised, such as trials (in the formal or informal justice sectors), truth commissions, lustration or vetting, reparations, and amnesty and pardon, selective or otherwise.[11] Transitional justice entails the careful weighing, and context-specific balance, of these tools and processes, which may also compete with a range of peacemaking and peacebuilding incentives, such as power-sharing arrangements.[12] Regimes emerging from violent conflict or state repression, often with the support of the UN, regional organisations, and/or bilateral donors, must make choices about whether, and if so how, to address the crimes of the recent past.

However, transitional justice involves more than these specific choices, which constitute traditional transitional justice. In contemporary practice, transitional justice also involves broader strategies to address the sources of past and potential future violence. In practice, transitional strategies, including tools of accountability or amnesty, are now closely linked to a range of reforms and processes which are not in the first instance about accountability for past abuses, including reform of the justice sector and reform of the security sector, including both the police and the military. This may entail a range of activities that are not obviously about justice for past crimes, but are more or less essential to it. These may include institutional reform of judiciaries, training of judges, reformulation of military and other security doctrines, and reformation of security institutions themselves, which are indistinguishable from peacebuilding efforts. Further, they are necessarily connected with activities essential to peacebuilding but not at first blush at all related to justice, such as inclusion of former rebels in new security structures, and disarmament, demobilisation and reintegration (DDR) of ex-combatants.[13] Attempts at justice can have direct effects upon activities such as DDR. For example, in conducting research in Sierra Leone, I learned from court officials that fighters in Liberia were afraid to demobilise due to rumours that their ID benefits cards would be used to allow the Special Court for Sierra Leone to identify, locate, and prosecute them.[14] Contemporary transitional justice is a broader set of activities that includes not only those specific measures that pertain to victims and perpetrators, involving accountability or the decision not to pursue it, but also a set of activities that have traditionally been 'peacebuilding' activities, which address restoration of the rule of law and security.[15] It also involves a range of activities, including trials, at a significant distance from the countries affected by conflict and human rights abuses.

evolution of contemporary practice

Contemporary practice of transitional justice has become far more complex than initially conceptualised, as a set of difficult choices about amnesty or accountability to be made by a country emerging from conflict or repression, largely on its own terms. It is increasingly internationalised, and inextricably linked with a range of institutional reforms and peacebuilding activities. International involvement in these processes has become more extensive and complex, whether addressing abuses in-country, or at a very great distance. As a result, new challenges and risks have emerged.

international engagement with past abuses, in-country

Of course, traditional transitional justice was in reality something that few transitional regimes addressed completely on their own. Instead, transitional processes, including accountability mechanisms and truth commissions, were supported with financial and technical assistance from the United Nations and bilateral donors, and often received support from international NGOs in a variety of ways as well. However, contemporary transitional justice is not only more complex, it is much more tightly linked to complex peacekeeping and peacebuilding processes. It also creates new objections and challenges.

Where once transitional justice, human rights, and responses to mass atrocities might have been viewed as being in competition with peacekeeping, peacemaking, and peacebuilding, they are now often an integral part of peacebuilding activities conducted by bilateral donors, regional organisations, and international institutions such as the United Nations and the World Bank. Thus in the autumn of 2004, the United Nations Secretary-General issued the first report of its kind for the organisation, on *The rule of law and transitional justice in conflict and post-conflict societies*.[16] Perhaps most important to note about the report is that it treats the rebuilding of the rule of law, and specific mechanisms of transitional justice, both as intertwined with each other and as central to post-conflict peacebuilding. Work that might previously have been treated as purely legal is now viewed as part of the work of numerous departments, funds, and agencies across the organisation. For example, the United Nations Development Programme's Bureau for Crisis Prevention and Recovery (BCPR), the focal point of the UN's development arm for post-conflict peacebuilding, engages in programming that entails and often links transitional justice and security sector reform.[17] Its programmatic work treats judicial reform and reconstruction, along with corrections and police reform, as integral, and linked to efforts at post-conflict justice. Rule of law programming is now regularly built into many large UN peacekeeping operations, and transitional justice and human rights are included as part of the mandate of the missions as a whole, or rule of law sections specifically. Thus for example, the UN Mission in the Democratic Republic of Congo, MONUC, includes in its UN Security Council-authorised mandate responsibilities for human rights and a rule of law generally, including explicit roles in rebuilding rule of law and support to transitional justice/accountability processes.[18]

Other international actors similarly encompass transitional justice activities within their peacebuilding and reconstruction work. While the primary focus of World Bank programming in post-conflict reconstruction and conflict prevention remains reconstruction and development activities generally, work on capacity-building may encompass development of the rule of law and judicial reform.[19] The UK Foreign and Commonwealth Office treats human rights as integral to democracy-building in unstable places, and the reform of justice generally as integral to post-conflict development.[20] In short, concerns for post-conflict reconstruction have become integrally linked with a wide range of rule of law programming – in the judiciary, in criminal justice, in policing – and tied to efforts at post-conflict justice.[21]

However, as we shall see with internationalised processes addressing past abuses, international supporters of domestic processes of accountability and rule of law are not without their detractors. In particular, they may be accused of promoting a Western concept of human rights and rule of law that is historically or culturally inappropriate. The accusation of cultural inappropriateness may have particular traction where the majority of the population have only had limited access to the formal justice system, and rely upon customary, traditional, or 'non-state' justice. This objection may give rise to concerns about not only the introduction of new laws and institutions, but also the use of trials for accountability. Some may instead promote the use of traditional justice, such as the *mato oput* ritual in northern Uganda or cleansing rituals in Sierra Leone.[22] Such mechanisms have their own limitations, but peace-building policymakers may ignore these concerns at their peril.

international engagement with past abuses, extraterritorially

Just as international actors have increasingly engaged, in the last few decades but at an accelerated rate in the last few years, in the promotion of internal transitional justice and accountability mechanisms in post-conflict or transitional states, there has also been a rapid increase in international or transnational accountability processes. These have developed in part because, even with international support, states emerging from conflict have often still been unwilling or unable to pursue accountability. Domestic responses were also often necessarily limited, where they did occur, as many leaders gave themselves amnesty as they exited power, or continued to maintain significant influence and the capacity to disrupt a nascent democracy. Thus while trials have been pursued in numerous 'transitional' countries, most of these were limited in scope, and often arrived at compromise solutions including amnesties and commissions of inquiry. As a result, processes to address past abuses have been increasingly internationalised, seeking to fill so-called impunity gaps where national actors cannot or will not. These may be categorised as being of at least three types: purely international, transnational, and hybrid. The first two involve the promotion of proceedings addressing past abuses in a country, outside the country, while the last involves a greater degree of local action and access, but has a heavily international element.

Internationalised justice perhaps only became possible again following the end of the Cold War, following a 50-year hiatus after the Nuremberg and Tokyo tribunals. The atrocities in the former Yugoslavia and the genocide in Rwanda prompted the unprecedented creation, by the UN Security Council, of international criminal tribunals.[23] These were, of course, isolated institutions, covering only a delineated territory and time period. They have also had serious institutional flaws, such as lack of significant outreach, which meant that they were often unable to achieve many of the goals sought by prosecution, such as reconciliation or the reinstatement of the rule of law. Further, their limited resources have meant that they have had limited effect, able to prosecute only a very few perpetrators until recently. Most recently, the creation of the International Criminal Court holds out the prospect that impunity for certain crimes will diminish globally. It remains to be seen whether it will, with its more expansive ambit, be more successful.

At the same time, punishment for past crimes has occurred in domestic courts, but this time not in courts of territories where crimes occurred, but in distant locales through the exercise of universal jurisdiction. These prosecutions have addressed situations that the ad hoc tribunals were unable to address, from persecution in Chile to genocide in the DRC.[24] Civil cases have also been pursued in the United States through the use of the Alien Tort Claims Act, where abuses have been committed in other countries, by foreign nationals and against foreign nationals. However, I will argue that these developments carry with them a range of risks, including the risks of external imposition of norms, and impeding upon delicate transitional decisions. External processes may also suffer from other flaws, such as a lack of legitimacy, or failure to have real effect upon the societies where the crimes initially occurred.

Finally, there has been an attempt to fuse domestic and international aspects of transitional justice, through the innovation of hybrid tribunals. Hybrid tribunals are tribunals which take place in the territory of a country which experienced mass atrocities such as war crimes, genocide, and crimes against humanity, but which involve national and international judges and staff, and which punish international crimes but may also utilise some domestic law. Examples include the Special Court for Sierra Leone, the Special Panel for Serious Crimes in Timor Leste, and the Extraordinary Chambers in the Courts of Cambodia.[25] Proceedings in mixed tribunals may be seen as an attempt to combine the virtues of domestic and international prosecutions and avoid some of the vices. It is hoped that they might, through careful combination of international and domestic legal standards and judges, be more impartial and professional than many domestic prosecutions, but more legitimate and relevant domestically than distant international proceedings. However, I will argue that they may suffer the flaws of both domestic and international justice. I turn now to the risks of internationalised and hybrid accountability mechanisms in a bit more detail.

current practice, new risks

I argue that the proliferation of accountability mechanisms and activities may have some positive dimensions, including the punishment of at least a few persons responsible for truly appalling violations of international human rights and humanitarian law, but that there are significant limitations to these. Specifically, I argue that external judicial processes, in particular those carried out through the exercise of universal jurisdiction or civil accountability, should be pursued cautiously, precisely because they take place far away and the affected communities may have very little access to the processes.[26] I suggest that caution is essential because externalised processes may not take sufficient account of local needs and in extreme cases may even undermine them. In so doing they may not only fail to address many of the purposes for which we often argue trials are useful, but may also undermine post-conflict peacebuilding.

Transnational accountability mechanisms, whether prosecutions through the exercise of universal jurisdiction, or civil accountability abroad, seek to offer a remedy where national courts of a state affected by conflict are unwilling or unable to address past violations. National courts may have been barred from pursuing cases because of amnesties, pardons, or a settlement in a peace agreement. They may, alternatively, choose not to hear cases (or national prosecutors may choose not to pursue them) out of concerns about renewed conflict and instability. In such instances, the bringing of cases very far from the locus of the crime may seem to be the only viable alternative. Furthermore, there may be a ready population of former victims and refugees pressing the courts of another country to pursue cases.

There is a clear benefit of pursuing cases abroad when they cannot be pursued at home – it may provide relief to some victims, and serves to uphold principles of human rights. However, there are some reasons for concern. First, because cases pursued under the exercise of universal jurisdiction take place at great remove, the vast majority of victims may be simply unaware that they are taking place. Thus, the expected benefits of vindication are unlikely to be met, and broader goals, such as re-education of society, support to national reconciliation, or the promotion of the rule of law at home, are often not imputed. Only a very few members of the country affected are likely to have significant access to the trial proceedings, particularly in poor countries where literacy is low and other modes of media are also limited. It is for this reason that, when the trial of Charles Taylor before the SCSL was transferred to The Hague, plans were put in place to bring local journalists from Liberia and Sierra Leone to attend sessions of the proceedings.[27] The limitations of distant accountability mechanisms are not new: this critique was raised quite strongly against the International Criminal Tribunal for Rwanda. A key failing of the Tribunal has been its distance from Rwandan society; it is not only physically separated from Rwanda, but has been limited in its capacity to communicate with that society.

There are few televisions in Rwanda and little radio coverage as well. This means that average Rwandans are not involved in the work of the tribunal; without such involvement, active or passive, it is unclear that there can be much in the way of pedagogy, reconciliation, or deterrence produced by the Tribunal's work.[28] This is a limitation that trials at a distance may often share.

However, distant justice can also have the reverse problem – the very fact of its being received in country may serve to upset local compromises and strengthen hardliners. This is of course more likely to be the case where a greater proportion of the population have access to media, and also where the local media are biased or politically controlled and manipulated. Thus, for example, Slobodan Milosevic used the platform of his trial before the ICTY to defend himself, and in the process make propagandistic statements which were broadcast in Serbia, potentially strengthening hardliners.[29] Saddam Hussein sought to do the same during his trial before the Iraqi Special Tribunal. In both cases they sought to present their trials as illegitimate external impositions; Hussein managed to do so even though his trial was before an essentially Iraqi, if deeply flawed, institution.

Many of the flaws of externalised justice may mean that it is not always the best option to address past abuses. This does not mean that it never is, but there are remedies beyond the use of international tribunals, and universal jurisdiction, and even civil accountability. External actors who still wish to help societies that have experienced gross human rights violations, war crimes, etc. may turn to mixed or hybrid tribunals, or 'externalisation reversed', setting up quasi-international processes in the country where the events of concern took place.[30] This may in part remedy the concerns created by distance, though some lingering legitimacy objections are likely to remain. Mixed tribunals such as those developed for Cambodia, Sierra Leone, and elsewhere have sought in design, at least, to remedy some of the concerns about external justice raised here. However, they themselves have a number of flaws that are in part quite similar to those of distant trials, and do not entirely surmount problems with domestic trials.

First, hybrid tribunals may share, in common with domestic trials, significant resource constraints, and the risk or perception of politicisation. Thus, for example, in Timor Leste many citizens felt that the use of the hybrid model was not a useful innovation, but a choice by an international community unwilling to invest in a proper international tribunal. In Sierra Leone, the limited budget and mandate of the court has affected its operations and its capacity to compel the execution of arrest warrants. The court in Sierra Leone may well be a neutral, impartial one, but many inside the country as well as outside believe it to be politically manipulated or constrained. Of particular concern have been controversies over the unsealing of the indictment of Charles Taylor, the trials of members of the Civil Defence Forces, and the exclusion from jurisdiction of former President Kabbah and other members of his government.[31] Security concerns and fears of conflict have loomed large over the court's operation, prompting the move of the trial of Taylor to The Hague.[32] In addition to concerns that the trial of Taylor might upset peacebuilding, there were also concerns that CDF trials would destabilise Freetown.

Second, hybrid tribunals may share some of the flaws of internationalised or distant justice already noted. Despite including local judges, lawyers, and administrative staff, they may be viewed as essentially foreign impositions; indeed, there are concerns that the Special Court for Sierra Leone is viewed locally as a 'spaceship phenomenon'.[33] Hybrid courts may be viewed not only as externally imposed, and therefore having little to do with the people affected, but also as a product of the agenda of outside countries. If this is the case, it may be all the easier for hardliners, whether defendants or not, to propagate propaganda deriding the institutions as illegitimate or even neocolonial. In such instances, courts may fail to have the desired local effects, and may even run the risk of being counterproductive.

conclusions

Contemporary responses to past abuses are far more complex and internationalised than traditional transitional justice. Not only are there a wide range of policy options within countries, ranging from amnesty to vetting to prosecutions, but these are also inextricably linked to a wider range of peacebuilding policies, including reform of the judiciary and rule of law generally, and of the security sector. Further, transitional justice and peacebuilding processes have become far more internationalised, as they are promoted over extended periods of time by the United Nations in both peacekeeping (particularly integrated) missions and peacebuilding missions, as well as by a range of bilateral donors and international NGOs. And processes of accountability are often not solely the province of the states emerging from conflict, but may take place at a great distance, in the domestic courts of other nations or in international and internationalised tribunals. While these developments may be hailed as progress, and in many ways they are positive developments for both accountability and peacebuilding, they are not without their limitations. In particular, the very internationalisation of these processes means that they may seem, or actually be, disconnected from the individuals and societies they are designed to benefit, or be viewed as externally imposed and illegitimate by some of the putative beneficiaries. Practitioners of contemporary transitional justice need, therefore, to be attentive not only to the traditional debates and trade-offs I noted at the beginning, but to a wide range of new options but also new risks with internationalised transitional justice.

notes

1. Key sources from which this discussion is drawn include P. Hayner, *Unspeakable Truths: Confronting State Terror and Atrocity*, London: Routledge, 2001; C. Hesse and R. Post (eds), *Human Rights in Political Transitions: Gettysburg to Bosnia*, Zone Books: New York, 1999; J. Malamud-Goti, *Game Without End: State Terror and the Politics of Justice*, Norman, OK: University of Oklahoma Press, 1996; M. Minow, *Between Vengeance and Forgiveness: Facing History after Genocide and Mass Violence*, Boston: Beacon Press, 1998; A. Neier, *War Crimes: Brutality, Genocide, Terror, and the Struggle for Justice*, New York: Times Books, 1998; M. Osiel, *Mass Atrocity, Collective Memory, and the Law*, New Brunswick, NJ: Transaction Books, 1997; R. Mani, *Beyond Retribution: Seeking Justice in the Shadows of War*, Cambridge: Polity Press, 2002; N. Roht-Arriaza (ed.), *Impunity and Human Rights in International Law and Practice*, Oxford: Oxford University Press, 1995; R.I. Rotberg and D. Thompson (eds), *Truth v. Justice: The Morality of Truth Commissions*, Princeton, NJ: Princeton University Press, 2000; C.L. Sriram, *Confronting Past Human Rights Violations: Justice vs. Peace in Times of Transition*, London: Frank Cass, 2004; P.R. Williams and M.P. Scharf, *Peace With Justice? War Crimes and Accountability in the Former Yugoslavia*, Lanham, MD: Rowman and Littlefield, 2002; N.J. Kritz (ed.), *Transitional Justice: How Emerging Democracies Reckon With Former Regimes*, 3 vols, Washington, DC: United States Institute of Peace Press, 1995. I have considered the development of transitional justice literature and debates over the past few decades in Chandra Lekha Sriram, 'Transitional Justice Comes of Age: Enduring Lessons and Challenges', *Berkeley Journal of International Law*, Vol. 23, No. 2, 2005, pp. 506–23.

2. *Rule of law and transitional justice in conflict and post-conflict societies. Report of the Secretary-General*, UN Doc. S/2004/616, 23 August 2004, para. 8, defines transitional justice as 'the full range of processes and mechanisms associated with a society's attempts to come to terms with a legacy of large scale past abuses, in order to ensure accountability, serve justice, and achieve reconciliation. These may include both judicial and non-judicial mechanisms, with

differing levels of international involvement (or none at all) and individual prosecutions, reparations, truth-seeking, institutional reform, vetting and dismissals, or a combination thereof'.

3. Neier, *War Crimes*; M. Osiel, *Mass Atrocity*; M. Minow, *Between Vengeance and Forgiveness*.

4. See E.M. Cousens and C. Kumar, with K. Wermester (eds), *Peacebuilding as Politics: Cultivating Peace in Fragile Societies*, Boulder, CO: Lynne Rienner, 2001; J.P. Lederach, *Building Peace: Sustainable Reconciliation in Divided Societies*, Washington, DC: US Institute of Peace Press, 1997; compare a critique of the traditional assumptions of peacebuilding in Roland Paris, 'Peacebuilding and the Limits of Liberal Internationalism', *International Security*, Vol. 22, 1997, pp. 54–89.

5. I. Johnstone, *Rights and Reconciliation: UN Strategies in El Salvador*, Boulder, CO: Lynne Rienner, 1995; J. Malamud-Goti, *Game Without End*.

6. P. Hayner, *Unspeakable Truths*; R. Rotberg and D. Thompson (eds), *Truth v. Justice*; M. Osiel, *Mass Atrocity*.

7. *Rule of law and transitional justice in conflict and post-conflict societies. Report of the Secretary-General*, UN Doc. S/2004/616, 23 August 2004; see also www. ictj.org, accessed on 16 October 2009.

8. C.L. Sriram, *Globalizing Justice for Mass Atrocities: A Revolution in Accountability*, London: Routledge, 2005, chapter 6, and conclusion; M.H. Arsanjani and W.M. Reisman, 'The Law in Action of the International Criminal Court', *American Journal of International Law*, Vol. 99, April 2005, pp. 385–403; D.A. Mundis, 'Closing an International Criminal Tribunal While Maintaining International Human Rights Standards and Excluding impunity', *American Journal of International Law*, Vol. 99, April 2005, pp. 142–58. Compare C. Eckart, 'Saddam Hussein's Trial in Iraq: Legitimacy and Alternatives, a Legal Analysis', Ithaca, NY: Cornell Law School Paper Series, 2006, at http://lsr.nellco.org/cornell/lps/papers/13; UN Security Council Resolution S/RES/1757, 30 May 2007, mandated the Lebanon tribunal. Clearly these responses have been taken by very different sets of actors and have differing degrees of legitimacy, which for reasons of space I do not address here.

9. On rule of law in conflict prevention and peacebuilding, see Sriram, 'Prevention and the Rule of Law: Rhetoric and Reality', in A. Hurwitz with R. Huang (eds), Civil War and the Rule of Law: Security, Development, Human Rights, Boulder, CO: Lynne Rienner, 2008.

10. These are not the full range of reasons offered: others, such as the needs of victims, may be adduced for accountability, and the need to entrench a nascent democracy may also be offered as a reason to abandon accountability. See C.L. Sriram, *Confronting Past Human Rights Violations*, introduction and chapter 2, for a discussion of these and illustrations from myriad cases.

11. In many instances, countries choose several of these options simultaneously, or serially. See C.L. Sriram, *Confronting Past Human Rights Violations*, chapter 2.

12. Sriram, *Peace as Governance: Power-Sharing, Armed Groups, and Contemporary Peace Negotiations*, London: Palgrave, 2008.

13. C.L. Sriram, *Confronting past human rights violations*, chapter 1 and conclusion, discusses these strategies. This recognition is clearly enshrined in the newly developed United Nations *Integrated DDR Standards* (December 2006), available online at http://www.unddr.org/iddrs/, accessed on 16 October 2009.

14. C.L. Sriram, *Globalizing Justice for Mass Atrocities*, chapter 6, discusses this in more detail.

15. On the restoration of the rule of law and conflict prevention and peace-building policies, see C.L. Sriram, 'Discourses of Prevention and Rule of Law: Rhetoric and Reality', in A. Hurwitz with R. Huang (eds), *Rule of Law Programming in Conflict Management*, Boulder, CO: Lynne Rienner, 2008.

16. *Rule of law and transitional justice in conflict and post-conflict societies. Report of the Secretary-General* UN Doc. S/2004/616, 23 August 2004.

17. See BCPR's transitional justice page at http://www.undp.org/cpr/we_do/trans_justice.shtml, accessed on 16 October 2009.

18. See MONUC Mandate, http://www.un.org/Depts/dpko/missions/monuc/mandate.html, accessed on 16 October 2009. See also UN Security Council Resolution 1628, 30 September 2005, UN Doc. S/RES/1628. Similar mandates exist within many missions, including UNMIL in Liberia and UNMIS in Sudan; I am currently directing a British Academy-funded research project on such rule of law programming activities.

19. For example, a recent in-house summary of work in conflict prevention and reconstruction primarily included work in development, reconstruction and mine clearance, but it also included work on rule of law. See World Bank, Conflict Prevention and Reconstruction (CPR) Unit, 'CPR and Related Publications on Conflict and Development', at: http://siteresources.worldbank.org/INTCPR/Publications/20812069/CatalogSep7.05.pdf, accessed on 16 October 2009.

20. See descriptive page at: http://www.fco.gov.uk/servlet/Front?pagename=OpenMarket/Xcelerate/ShowPage&c=Page&cid=1007029393564, accessed on 1 May 2008.

21. See generally R. Huang, *Securing the Rule of Law: Assessing Strategies for Post-Conflict Criminal Justice* (New York: International Peace Academy policy report, November 2005) at http://www.ipinst.org/media/pdf/publications/ipa_e_rpt_securingrol.pdf, on accessed 16 October 2009.

22. See UK Department for International Development, 'Non-state Justice and Security Systems', May 2004; L. Huyse and M. Salter (eds), *Traditional Justice and Reconciliation After Violent Conflict*, Stockholm: International IDEA, 2008; B. Baker, 'Who do people turn to for policing in Sierra Leone?', *Journal of Contemporary African Studies*, Vol. 23, No. 3, September 2005, pp. 371–90.

23. http://www.un.org/icty/ and http://69.94.11.53/ are the sites of each institution.

24. N. Roht-Arriaza, *The Pinochet Effect: Transnational Justice in the Age of Human Rights*, Philadelphia, PA: University of Pennsylvania Press, 2005, argues that this is a positive progression with important demonstration effects.

25. Sriram, *Globalizing Justice for Mass Atrocities* and Kai Ambos and Mohamed Othman (eds), *New Approaches in International Criminal Justice: Kosovo, East Timor, Sierra Leone, and Cambodia*, Freiburg: Max Planck, 2003, discuss these further.

26. However, Madeline Morris raises concerns about the impact of the ICC on non-party states in this issue in Morris, 'The Disturbing Democratic Defect

of the International Criminal Court', *Finnish Yearbook of International Law*, Vol. 12, 2001, pp. 109–18, and in Morris, 'High Crimes and Misconceptions: The ICC and Non-Party States',*Law and Contemporary Problems*, Vol. 64, 2001, pp. 13–67.

27. 'Press conference by prosecutor of Special Court for Sierra Leone', 22 January 2008, at http://www.un.org/News/briefings/docs/2008/080122_Rapp.doc. htm, accessed on 16 October 2009.

28. M.A. Drumbl, 'Juridical and jurisdictional disconnects', *Finnish Yearbook of International Law*, Vol. 12, 2001; Morris, 'The Trials of Concurrent Jurisdiction', p. 360.

29. See M.P. Scharf, 'Making a Spectacle of Himself', *The Washington Post*, 29 August 2004, reposted at: http://www.publicinternationallaw.org/publications/editorials/Milosevic_Spectacle.htm, accessed on 16 October 2009.

30. C.L. Sriram and B.R. Roth, 'Externalization of Justice: What Does it Mean and What is at Stake?', *Finnish Yearbook of International Law*, Vol. 12, 2001, pp. 3–6.

31. Sriram, 'Wrong-Sizing International Justice'

32. Sriram and A. Ross, 'Trying Charles Taylor: Justice Here, There, Anywhere?', *The Jurist*, 4 April 2006, at http://jurist.law.pitt.edu/forumy/2006/04/trying-charles-taylor-justice-here.php, accessed on 16 October 2009.

33. T. Perriello and M.Wierda, 'The Special Court for Sierra Leone Under Scrutiny', March 2006, at http://www.ictj.org/static/Prosecutions/Sierra.study.pdf, p. 2, accessed on 16 October 2009.

15

reconciliation (reflections from Northern Ireland and South Africa)

john darby

a troublesome term

It is unfortunate that the term reconciliation has become imbedded into discussion about social reconstruction. It is the wrong word. It implies a prior state of conciliation, just waiting to be reinstated were it not for the inconvenient intervention of violence. It panders to a nostalgia myth, common in violently divided societies, that the conflicting groups had enjoyed at worst an uneasy peace and at best some golden age of harmony and fairness before the violence, a condition that only existed in the imaginations of the mythmakers.[1] The danger in this view is that it suggests that the violence itself, rather than the underlying disputes that led to it, is the main problem. Whatever new relationships might emerge from a peace agreement, there is one certainly: that they will be different from how relationships operated in the past.

a different species?

The distinctions between interstate wars and internal armed conflicts take on an added relevance after the violence ends. When interstate wars end the combatants retire behind their national frontiers. The immediate post-war priority is the establishment of regional stability and security between the ex-combatants, and this can be approached in a variety of ways: the 1965 Indo-Pakistan war and the Korean war (1950–53) were followed by armed stand-offs; after the Second World War the victors preferred to support economic reconstruction in

Germany and Japan. At all points along this spectrum of approaches, regional stability requires an international understanding as well as operational procedures to deal with post-war disputes. Anything beyond this is a bonus. It does not require reconciliation.

Communal wars are a quite different species. When a violent internal conflict comes to an end, the combatants continue to occupy the same contested arena. Their daily lives are often intermeshed with those of their enemies. Withdrawal behind a recognised frontier is not an option, although opponents may continue to operate within increasingly segregated communities. If the fighting is not to resume in the future, the disputes that had caused it in the first place must be tackled. Arrangements are needed to deal with communal disagreements, which are likely to recur on a regular basis – over jobs and resources, culture, religion, status – and the arrangements must be negotiated between groups who distrust and fear each other. Reconciliation is a fundamental requirement for long-term stability. To apply a more domestic analogy, when a dispute develops between neighbours, the disagreements, although vexatious, are usually occasional and specific; but when a dispute breaks out within a family, it erodes the very fabric of the household on a day-to-day basis. Interstate wars are neighbourhood disputes. Internal armed conflicts are family breakdowns.

Reconciliation, then, ought to be the central concern of internal peace negotiations, but it rarely is. Successful peace processes may look like courtship rituals between ex-combatants. They are not. They are primarily contests between competing interests and actors, horns locked as concessions are reluctantly agreed, bluffs attempted and called, and compromises reached in the interest of peace and stability. Respect, or even trust, may grow during the process, but the distrust that led to war in the first place does not erode quickly either for the negotiators or, more importantly, for their followers. While the fighting was still going on, combatants were encouraged to demonise and hate their opponents. A ceasefire or peace agreement does not change that.

A peace process is not only a contest between opposing groups. It is also a contest between competing agendas: how can negotiations be initiated, organised, and completed? Which parties should be participating in the negotiations? How can acts of violence, which will certainly occur during negotiations, be prevented from undermining the talks? Can common institutions be agreed? How can the post-war society be policed and defended? What about war crimes – should these be overlooked or addressed through a Truth Commission? These questions and others jostle for attention within the narrow space of peace negotiations. Some are in direct competition with others. Uganda is a case in point. In 2006 the government of Uganda began negotiations with the Lord's Resistance Army (LRA) in an attempt to end the vicious war there. The LRA leaders insisted that they should be granted amnesty for crimes committed during the war, as a precondition for entering negotiations. The government was prepared to concede amnesty in order to secure peace. Further, the Acholi community, which had suffered the worst atrocities from the LTTE, also supported amnesty. The problem was that the International Criminal Court (ICC), on behalf of the international community, had issued arrest warrants against six leaders of the LRA, including Joseph Kony. Morris Ogenga-Latigo, the head of Uganda's parliamentary opposition, summed up the dilemma well: 'The ICC has become an impediment to our efforts. Should we sacrifice our peacemaking process here so they can test and develop their criminal-justice procedures there at the ICC? Punishment has to be quite secondary to the goal of resolving this conflict.'[2] The dilemma was stark. To overturn the warrants might save many lives and bring some stability. To overturn the warrants would overlook some appalling crimes. How is the dilemma to be resolved? Not every peace process faces such a stark confrontation between peace and justice as that in Uganda, but all of them have to confront the issue at some level.

Even if it is generally acknowledged that all the questions on the agenda for negotiations must be addressed eventually, some are perceived to demand immediate priority, or the negotiations will collapse; these usually include agreement on the negotiating parties and the agenda, and confidence-building measures like demilitarisation or the early release of prisoners. Others, by implication, can be deferred until later.

In practice, reconciliation generally falls into the latter category. In South Africa and Northern Ireland, as in most negotiations, the problem of reconciliation did not receive much attention during the early stages of the peace processes. In South Africa, the management of the negotiations dominated the peace process until the agreement was signed in 1994, and the Truth and Reconciliation Commission only started its work in 1996, delivering its final report in 2001; during this time it investigated 14,000 cases of political killings and granted 127 applications for amnesty. Around 22,000 one-off payments of $4,600 are being paid out by the state. This process was greatly assisted by a series of magnanimous acts by Nelson Mandela and the ANC, and by the successful adoption by followers of all groups of a new South African anthem, an agreed national flag and other symbols representing an agreement between all major parties to advance as a united country. South Africa as a state has been accepted and even welcomed by the conflicting parties, but it is less reconciled on matters of socio-economic transformation.[3] The underlying social inequalities remain, and may become a greater threat to post-war reconstruction unless addressed more radically. Nevertheless any objective audit would still support Timothy Sisk's assessment that 'the TRC has mostly succeeded in putting the past to rest, as least in terms of transitional justice'.[4]

In Northern Ireland the delay between the agreement and reconciliation was even greater. The refusal by Protestant Unionists to redress the systematic economic and social disadvantages facing Catholic nationalists fuelled minority discontent in the 1960s and provided the stimulus for the resurgence of the IRA and the 25 years of violence known as the Troubles. Within a decade of the 1998 Good Friday agreement, however, the feeling among Catholics that they suffered from severe disadvantage had largely disappeared. A 2003 review found that only 18% of Catholics perceived their own cultural tradition as 'the underdog', compared with 29% of Protestants.[5] However, the issue of reconciliation, which had been so openly confronted in South Africa, had hardly been tackled at all in Northern Ireland. No Truth and Reconciliation Commission had been established. Demographic segregation between Catholics and Protestants had grown significantly during the years of fighting, and no significant integrative moves emerged in the decade following the Good Friday Agreement; in fact the number of 'peace lines', most of them built at the request of local communities to protect them from perceived threat from the other ethno-religious community, had increased since the Good Friday Agreement was signed; in 2008 around 40 still stood, about half of them in Belfast. The establishment of a power-sharing executive led by the Democratic Unionist Party (DUP) and Sinn Fein, traditionally the two most intransigent parties, has attracted international praise; but the only major attempt to tackle the problem of reconciliation – a consultation exercise on community relations called *A Shared Future*, which indicated a wide concern about the levels of division in the community and expressed wide support for stronger measures to encourage reconciliation – has been allowed to wither away.[6] In 2002 62% of the population believed that community relations had worsened in the eight years since the 1994 ceasefires.[7] A heavily segregated society remained heavily segregated. There has been little appetite for tackling this issue, and less invention.

So both the South African and Northern Irish peace processes can point to considerable successes, but in different aspects of post-war reconciliation. In general terms, South Africa has managed to forge a sense of common purpose among white and black South Africans, but the continuing and growing disparities within South Africa may breed future disaffection, especially from the poorest elements in society. In Northern Ireland the balance of success and failure lies in the opposite direction. Northern Ireland's civil rights campaign was fuelled by the institutional bias against Catholics, but there is no longer a strong perception of such bias; indeed, some Protestants argue, rather unconvincingly, that the balance has swung in the opposite direction. The point is that the inequalities that dominated debates in the 1970s and 1980s are no longer a matter of political dispute. On the other hand, there is a growing perception that, despite the amelioration of these equity issues and the evident success of the top-level peace process, relationships between Catholics and Protestants remain suspicious and nervous, and have not been sufficiently addressed during, or in the decade following, the Good Friday agreement.

clarifying reconciliation

The academic literature on peace processes acknowledges the importance of reconciliation as an objective, but struggles to provide concrete guidance for policymakers on how it might be achieved. In 2006 David Bloomfield pointed to a parallel growth in both interest in reconciliation and confusion about what it actually means.[8] The growth is easily demonstrated; reconciliation projects now rank third in value of all peacebuilding initiatives receiving support from donors, after political development and socio-economic assistance.[9] Yet confusion still abounds about the meaning of the term. 'Is it an individual, psychological, even "theological" process? Is it a process at all, or does it describe a state of relationships at the end of a process? .... For many people, especially since the South African Truth and Reconciliation Commission, 1995–2003 – certainly not the first of its kind, but definitely the most high-profile of all – the term is closely related to "truth" and "forgiveness", even if those also both remain disputed terms in themselves'.[10]

Endorsing the IDEA definition of reconciliation as 'a process through which a society moves from a divided past to a shared future',[11]

Bloomfield identifies eight 'ongoing debates from scholarship as well as policy and practice'. These include:

- the tendency for some commentators to see reconciliation primarily as a process, while others emphasise an 'end-state of harmony';[12]
- the promotion of reconciliation as an umbrella term subsuming a range of themes including 'the search for truth, justice, forgiveness, healing';[13]
- the relationship between reconciliation and politics, including the evidence that past violence is unlikely to disappear spontaneously unless it is openly acknowledged and addressed; and
- the possibility that coexistence is a more achievable target than reconciliation, and perhaps might become a stage on the path to reconciliation.

Across a broad spread of conflict situations, two aspects of reconciliation have proven to be particularly troublesome. First, the relationship between reconciliation and justice: most commentators see justice as central to reconciliation, as the Uganda case illustrates, but others believe that justice sometimes needs to be traded off in the interests of a peace by amnesties, especially if the trade-offs are strongly advocated by local rather than international actors. Second, the relationship between reconciliation and forgiveness: the Christian ideals underpinning the South African Truth and Reconciliation Commission raise the question of whether forgiveness is necessary for reconciliation, or an unrealistic and sometimes unachievable aim. 'Reconciliation', as Susan Dwyer put it, 'is conceptually independent of forgiveness'.[14]

active and passive reconciliation

Some scholars[15] have emphasised the distinction between active and passive reconciliation, active reconciliation being the dominant approach currently used internationally, with its emphasis on determining the truth about past events, on responsibility, on apology and on reparations. They argue that reconciliation can also result from passive reconciliation, defined as a process in which parties to a protracted conflict passively form or restore genuine peaceful relations. Passive reconciliation is achieved without deliberate policies aimed at reconstructing positive relations, but through the simple passage of time and from utilitarian acts carried out without any overt attempt to improve community relations. The effects of time and cooperation, through the emergence of a new generation not harmed by the war, may gradually undermine the collective negative memory of the past and advance reconciliation without conscious or active effort.

The value of this argument lies in its emphasis on the essentially long-term nature of reconciliation. Close to the core of reconciliation is its requirement for changes in traditional attitudes and behaviour. Attitudinal changes in particular cannot be achieved in the short term. However, they cannot be achieved at all unless the necessary foundations are laid and unless structured policies are introduced and implemented as early as possible in a peace process. Relying on time to do the job flies in the face of evidence that time is just as likely to reinforce differences and lead to a resumption of violence. There is no guarantee, nor much evidence, that the next generation will become peacemakers rather than troublemakers. Strategies are necessary to make this happen.

equity versus harmony

How can a path be navigated through this morass? The focus should be firmly fixed on two principal tasks – building an equitable society and building a harmonious society. Far from being complementary tasks, they are often in direct conflict with each other. The changes needed to produce an equitable society will inevitably highlight the divisions between communities by setting out to remove existing disadvantages in employment, social conditions, and access to power. The changes needed to build a harmonious society will highlight society's common values and aspirations, and will aim to put past differences behind and to start afresh. Both sets of changes are carefully scrutinised by all groups in the nervous and hostile atmosphere that follows armed conflicts. Initiatives are interpreted, not on their own merits, but according to group perceptions of gain or loss.

In Northern Ireland the conflict between equity and harmony resurfaced in 2008 over the question of symbols in public spaces; during the years of the Troubles, some Unionist-controlled local council offices, taking the view that the country was under siege, exhibited the artefacts and signs of national defence: memorials to soldiers of policemen who had been killed; plaques presented by the police and British regiments; the Union flag. When the power-sharing executive was established in 2007, some Nationalists demanded the removal of these symbols to create a neutral working environment, a right monitored by an Equality

Commission. To some Unionists this seemed to be an attack on their history and culture. A letter handed in on behalf of 50 Orange lodges described the removal of a painting and RUC plaques from public display in Banbridge as 'utterly devastating', and accused the Equality Commission of engaging in 'a long-term strategy to wipe the face of Britishness from Northern Ireland'. Councillor Cathal Hassan defended Sinn Fein's insistence on removing a Royal Engineers paperweight and a toy dragon presented by the Welsh Guards from Limavady council thus: 'In the absence of inclusivity, neutrality is really our only option.'[16] As soon as this debate became public, compromise became more difficult. Both of the possible alternatives – the removal of all political artefacts, or the augmentation of existing ones with artefacts representing the other community – were ruled out as unacceptable.

How might this apparently trivial, but actually damaging, confrontation have been avoided? There is some merit in looking to South Africa for insights, and envying its wisdom in anticipating the importance of creating common symbols like an anthem and a flag; the realisation that majority rule was inevitable allowed a level of black magnanimity to the white minority, and also encouraged white acceptance. Black magnanimity and white acceptance were the midwives of reconciliation in South Africa. In post-war societies like Northern Ireland where these conditions do not apply, a more calculated sequencing of change is a better option. Rather than debating the relative effectiveness of active and passive approaches to reconciliation, more thought needs to be applied to how their distinctive contributions could be better coordinated within a strategic framework. The different elements required to create both equity and harmony need to be identified and disaggregated, and implemented through a reciprocal and orchestrated strategy for change.

choreographing change: a reconciliation sequence

It is not enough for the negotiating parties to agree on a strategic framework, although that is not an easy task. The sequence of implementing the elements of the framework is equally important. It includes three discrete sets of tasks: the sequence should start with the removal of existing structural practices of inequity; the early moves towards building formal and informal social structures acceptable to all groups cannot wait until the first phase is completed, but must start in parallel with it; the third task is the construction of a common society to accommodate the rights and aspirations of all groups. Although generally sequential, there is often considerable overlap between these phases.

clearing the ground

The first step to reconciliation is to clear the ground by removing any remaining discriminatory practices – an essential component of any comprehensive peace agreement. Hard issues like economic, social, cultural, and political discrimination were often the main causes for violence in the first place, so peace negotiations are conditional on these grievances being rectified. In Northern Ireland a substantial start had already been made in this direction while the fighting was still going on, through the introduction of fair employment legislation, recognition of cultural diversity, and educational and housing reforms. However, the redress of these grievances is often bitterly contested during negotiations. Regardless of the objective reality, equity is perceived differently by contesting parties who have just emerged from a violent conflict.

Failure to deal adequately with equity issues is not the only cause of simmering post-war discontent. Equally contentious, and even more difficult to tackle, are war crimes. It has become rare for a new peace process not to consider the creation of a truth commission to address the violence of the past. The arguments for this are powerful: the need for victims' families to claim their dead; the need for perpetrators to admit to their crimes; the demands of justice. There is plenty of evidence that atrocities committed during wars will not wither away of their own accord. Seventy years after the ending of the Spanish Civil war in 1939 the discovery of mass graves resulting from war atrocities can still lead to outrage and dissension. Consequently, it is argued, national reconstruction requires the establishment of a truth commission to address war crimes, as attested by the very name of the South African Truth and Reconciliation Commission.

This is far from an uncontested view. In some post-war societies, it is suggested, such an investigation will rekindle the fires that have just been extinguished, and may seriously hamper moves towards reconciliation. The dominance of the argument favouring truth commissions has somewhat steamrollered this debate since the early 1990s, but the two key questions are legitimate ones, and can only be answered in relation to individual cases: under what circumstances would a truth commission contribute to reconciliation, and under what circumstances would it obstruct it? And, if a truth commission is to be established, what should be its mission?

laying the foundations

Laying the foundations of a shared society should not have to wait for the removal of all the discriminatory practices, although their removal can provide a firm platform for an equitable society. Social structures that were strongly contested before the war must be reformed and reconstructed during peace negotiations and implemented after them, so as to deliver a fair and agreed electoral system, equality before the law, fair access to employment and housing, fair policing, equal access to education *and housing*, and language and religious rights. The creation of acceptable structures includes the encouragement of cross-cutting cooperation and contact between opposing groups, and cultural initiatives to challenge the heritage of past hostility.

This cannot be achieved without moving well beyond elite negotiations into informal social relationships. 'It is important to recognise', as Ben-Tal and Bennink put it, 'that although the reconciliation process may begin either with the leaders or with the grass roots, to be effective it must always proceed top-down and bottom-up simultaneously'.[17] Sisk and Stefes put it more strongly: 'As the South African experience illustrates, limiting power sharing to formal political institutions described in an initial peace settlement is not enough; practices of inclusiveness, compromise, and moderation must expand and deepen into myriad informal bargaining arenas beyond the political elite that negotiate the formal political arrangements.'[18] Ten years after the Good Friday Agreement, the Northern Ireland experience illustrates the need for a comprehensive approach by providing such a stark contrast between a functioning power-sharing executive at the top and continuing social segregation between the communities.

building a common future

While the first moves in any reconciliation sequence are likely to be biased towards the removal of discriminatory practices and structures, the aim from the start is to move rapidly into a more constructive mode through the establishment of a political, economic, cultural, and social structure that sets down an agreed framework of equal opportunity for post-war society. Symbolic gestures between the two sides are important in building confidence, but symbols will not work without substance. Balancing the need to keep minorities on board, while delivering results to the majority, is a difficult act.

Success in a reconciliation process should not be regarded as an end position. It is, rather, a set of evolving relationships where the confrontational violence of the past has transmuted into one where the terms 'peace process' and 'reconciliation' are no longer used because they are no longer necessary. A reconciled society is one where the institutions of the state are functioning to the general satisfaction of its citizens. It is not a society without conflict – an unachievable and undesirable condition in any case – but one where conflict is handled without recourse to violence through an elected government, a representative society, and fair and acceptable courts. Perhaps most of all, the eventual measure of success is the creation of a society where primary allegiances are to the state rather than to communities imprisoned within it.

the neglect of reconciliation

The reluctance to address sufficiently the issue of reconciliation, both in the academic literature and during peace negotiations, is driven by the perception among negotiators that their energy should be concentrated on more immediate and important tasks. Two types of argument are often presented to counter this view. The first and most common – that it is right and fair to involve all the community rather than its political and security elites in peace processes – cuts little ice with negotiators. Mac Ginty, Richmond and others have argued that the Western neo-liberal emphasis on security, economic viability and institutional state-building has undervalued the need to build functioning relationships between conflicting communities on the ground, where progress will take longer and evaluation is more difficult.[19] According to this stance, reconciliation is a worthy but vague aspiration, a bone to be thrown to churchmen, civil society and do-gooders; it will keep them occupied while we get on with the real business of negotiations.

The second, and stronger, argument for moving reconciliation to centre stage is the demonstrable reality that reconciliation has the potential to derail or overturn a peace agreement. The view that peace agreements are the products of negotiations between political leaders is an accurate, but incomplete, view. Neither agreement nor reconciliation can be delivered without the approval of the community, as demonstrated by recent peace processes. In the last decade negotiations initiated by governments and opposition leaders in Sri Lanka, East Timor, Lebanon, the Basque Country and Kosovo have stalled or failed. The post-agreement experiences of many recent processes further reinforce the danger of neglecting relationships on the ground. Even in those cases regarded as successful, like South Africa and Northern Ireland, the completion of the processes has been hampered by their failure to deal with, respectively, inequality and reconciliation. There is little doubt that the ten-year delay in securing a level of political stability following the Good Friday Agreement could have been significantly shortened if the Agreement had set in motion processes to reduce the mutual suspicion and fears that expressed themselves concretely through issues like disarmament and policing reform. In South Africa, too, it was not difficult to forecast that a failure to address fundamental social inequalities would lead to social discontent and instability. Agreement to negotiate between leaders is not enough. A peace accord will not deliver peace or reconciliation if it does not include a strategy that reaches down into the community.

Nor can the peace process sequence be completed in a single generation. It took nine years after the Good Friday Agreement for a functioning power-sharing administration to be established in Northern Ireland, and it will take much longer than that for people on the streets to become reconciled. In South Africa, majority rule was deferred for five years after the 1994 Agreement, and reconciliation still has some distance to travel. Reconciliation is a long-term project.

notes

1. J. Darby, *Intimidation and the Control of Conflict in Northern Ireland*, Dublin: Gill and Macmillan; New York: Syracuse University Press, 1986.
2. H. Cobban, 'Uganda: When International Justice and Internal Peace are at Odds', *Christian Science Monitor*, 24 August 2006.
3. J. Gibson, *Overcoming Apartheid: Can Truth Reconcile a Divided Nation?* New York: Russell Sage Foundation, 2004.
4. T.D. Sisk, *Bargaining with Bullets*, Abingdon and New York: Routledge, 2008.
5. R. Mac Ginty and P. du Toit, 'A Disparity of Esteem: Relative Group Status in Northern Ireland after the Belfast Agreement', *Political Psychology*, Vol. 28, No. 1, 2007, pp. 13–31, on p. 26.
6. J. Darby and C. Knox, *'A Shared Future': A Consultation Paper on Improving Community Relations in Northern Ireland*, paper commissioned by the Office of the First Minister and Deputy First Minister (OFMDFM), Northern Ireland, Belfast: OFMDFM, 2004.
7. P. Brown, 'Peace but No Love as Northern Ireland Divide Grows Even Wider', *The Guardian*, London, 4 January 2002.
8. D. Bloomfield, *On Good Terms: Clarifying Reconciliation*, Berlin: Berghof Center for Constructive Conflict Management, 2006.
9. D. Smith, *Towards a Strategic Framework for Peacebuilding: Getting the Act Together*, Oslo: Royal Norwegian Ministry of Foreign Affairs, 2004.

10. Bloomfield, *On Good Terms*, p. 5.
11. D. Bloomfield, T. Barnes and L. Huyse (eds), *Reconciliation after Violent Conflict: A Handbook*, Stockholm, IDEA, 2003, p. 3.
12. Ibid., p. 6.
13. Ibid., p.11.
14. S. Dwyer, 'Reconciliation for Realists,' in C. Prager and T. Govier (eds) *Dilemmas of Reconciliation: Cases and Concepts*. Waterloo, ON: Wilfrid Laurire University press, 2003, pp. 91–110, on p. 106.
15. See G. Ben-Porat (ed.), *The Failure of the Middle East Peace Process?*, London: Palgrave Macmillan, 2008; R. Nets-Zehngut, 'Passive Reconciliation in the Context of the Israeli-Palestinian Conflict', in Ben-Porat, *The Failure of the Middle East Peace Process?*; D. Ben-Tal and G. Bennink, 'The Nature of Reconciliation as an Outcome and a Process', in Y. Bar-Simon-Tov (ed.) *From Conflict Resolution to Reconciliation*, Oxford: Oxford University Press, 2004.
16. *The Irish Times*, 16 February 2008.
17. Ben-Tal and Bennink, 'The Nature of Reconciliation'.
18. T.D. Sisk and C. Stefes, 'Power Sharing as an Interim Step for Peacebuilding: Lessons from South Africa', in P.G. Roeder and D. Rothchild, *Sustainable Peace: Power and Democracy after Civil Wars*, Cornell: Cornell University Press, 2005, pp. 293–317, on p. 294.
19. R. Mac Ginty, *No War, No Peace: The Rejuvenation of Stalled Peace Processes and Peace Accords*, Basingstoke: Palgrave, 2006; O. Richmond, *The Transformation of Peace*, Basingstoke: Palgrave Macmillan, 2005.

16
training goldfish (in a desert): transforming political economies of conflict using voluntarism, regulation and supervision

neil cooper

'... many international workers ... speak privately about the futility of their missions; of having impacts as lasting as training goldfish'.[1]

introduction

One of the features of the post-Cold War era has been a remarkable growth in academic and policy attention devoted to the role played by economic actors and economic agendas in the inception and perpetuation of civil conflicts as well as in shaping the prospects for post-conflict peacebuilding. This has incorporated a large and diverse range of themes ranging from the trading of specific conflict goods, the conflict dynamics resulting from the interaction of greed, feasibility, and grievance factors at the local level, the broader economic and governance challenges arising from what has been labelled the 'resource curse', and the even broader challenges produced by the interaction of local, regional, and global economic structures.[2]

This diversity of themes has also been reflected in the production of a rather disparate set of policies aimed at transforming economies of conflict. Indeed, a feature of these policies is that they have mostly been produced as subsets of other initiatives (environmental sustainability, good governance, poverty reduction, anti-corruption, corporate social responsibility [CSR], etc.). One of the first observations to be made about the challenge of transforming war economies, then, is that, whilst it is widely recognised as a vital element in resolving conflicts, the universe of potentially relevant policy action is so diffuse and so disaggregated into other policy arenas that there is a sense in which it does not really exist as a discrete field of policy in its own right.

In one view, this dissipation into other policy frameworks does not really matter, as issues of good governance, anti-corruption, etc. are all integral elements of a broader liberal peace project capable of transforming war economies via the export of democracy, rights, and free markets. There is also a sense, even in much of the more critical literature, that, whilst the technicalities of specific policies may need refinement, the broad reform agenda on issues such as ethical trading or anti-corruption is nevertheless part of a progressive liberal history of ethical global regulation under which the range of issues tackled has gradually widened and the frameworks of ethical regulation have become ever deeper or more substantive. The remainder of this chapter will be devoted to challenging these assumptions. In particular, I will examine three sets of initiatives that are most closely associated with the task of transforming war economies: voluntary ethical trading schemes, formal or *de facto* regulation to promote ethical trading or good resource governance, and economic supervision schemes.

The mainstream literature is characterised by a heated debate over the relative weight that should be given to these approaches, with voluntarism and formal regulation, in particular, often characterised as mutually exclusive options. In essence, however, this represents a debate over what constitutes the best strategy to achieve a common goal: to set a framework that balances the pursuit of business (whether conducted to make profit, make war or simply make do in situations of acute poverty) against the broader economic and non-material needs of individuals, societies, states, and the global system as a whole, and to do so in a context that takes liberal market precepts as a given. In short, the aim is deemed to be the creation of a more harmonious and pacific liberal political economy. Thus, the task of voluntarism, regulation, or economic supervision is simply to get economic actors operating under the imperatives of market logic to remember they have a broader social responsibility rather than succumbing to the regular temptations of narrow profit-making and the functional amnesia it can generate. As in the quote at the start of this article from William Reno's critique of economic supervision in Liberia, the common task is assumed to be akin to training goldfish to remember. To the extent that there is a disagreement, it is principally over how widespread and how profound the predilection for amnesia is, how easy it is to bring back memory, and of course exactly where the point of harmony in a political economy of peace is located. In contrast, the final section of this chapter will suggest that what is more striking from a critical political economy perspective is the way in which discourse and practice effectively work to obscure the recycling of failed policies, the retreat from more ambitious forms of ethical regulation, and the absence of substantive action.

voluntary ethical trading schemes

The post-Cold War era has witnessed an explosion in voluntary ethical trading schemes. These include initiatives undertaken under the aegis of multilateral organisations such the UN Global Compact, initiatives specific to particular industry sectors such as the Extractive Industries Transparency Initiative (EITI), and countless numbers of CSR initiatives undertaken by individual companies. Proponents of voluntarism emphasise the difficulties involved in persuading states and companies to agree binding regulation, noting that the non-binding nature of voluntary initiatives makes them more attractive to such actors and thus far more likely to be adopted. At the same time, they also adopt an essentially optimistic view of both the scale of ethical amnesia to be addressed and the ease with which memory can be restored. Thus, voluntarism assumes that the peer and civil society pressure exerted via non-binding commitments is sufficient to remind the majority of companies and governments of the need to trade responsibly. Voluntary approaches also assume that it is relatively easy to reconcile the demands of profit-making with some kind of ethical trading framework. Indeed, on this view, making profits, and thus adding to taxes and growth, represents a public good that should not be dismissed, whilst ethical trading represents a form of enlightened self-interest on the part of economic actors who have just as much interest as consumers in ensuring strong states, law and order, wealthy customers, and brand loyalty.[3] For example, a number of empirical studies have suggested a positive relationship between socially responsible behaviour and the financial performance of companies.[4] Thus, it is possible to envisage the norms promoted in voluntary initiatives ultimately becoming socially embedded features of the global system.

Critics, on the other hand, highlight the way in which voluntary initiatives tend to be characterised by either non-existent or anaemic monitoring of compliance, and that even where forms of monitoring do exist there is little in the way of formal sanction for non-compliance. Moreover, the voluntary nature of such initiatives means that membership can lack the universality that would make such initiatives really meaningful.

One of the better examples of voluntarism is the EITI, which includes donor governments, civil society, producer countries, and companies in the extractive sector. The aim of EITI is to promote revenue transparency in the extractive sector through double parallel disclosure of payments by both host governments and companies.[5] The underlying assumption is that transparency will deter the corrupt use of resource payments, thus ensuring that money is used for the benefit of local populations and in ways more likely to maximise the developmental impact of natural resource wealth. EITI includes 37 of the world's largest oil, gas and mining companies and 23 EITI candidate countries. The latter are required to implement EITI processes, which include publishing information on state revenues from the extractive sector and engaging with a national stakeholder group. If certified as compliant by an EITI Validator, a country is then labelled as an EITI Compliant country. At the time of writing no country has yet been validated by EITI, although it is expected that Azerbaijan and Nigeria will achieve this status quite soon. In response to criticism that the EITI focuses on just one part of the revenue chain – company payments to governments – the World Bank has, in addition, sponsored a separate programme, labelled EITI++, which aims to cover the entire resource chain, including extraction, processing, managing revenues, and promoting sustainable utilisation of resource wealth.

Despite such notable strengths, however, the voluntary nature of EITI means that membership remains patchy – only one of the world's top ten oil producers (Norway) and only one OPEC country (Nigeria) are members of EITI.[6] Moreover, the record of many candidate countries is not inspiring – Nigeria has failed to comply with legal requirements to audit 2006 and 2007 extractive industry revenues, and in 2008 the former head of the company Kellogg Brown and Root (now KBR) pleaded guilty to providing $180 million in bribes to Nigerian officials between 1995 and 2004.[7] In Iraq, another EITI country, Judge Rahdi, a leading anti-corruption official, has fled the country in fear of his life, whilst only Burma and Somalia have a worse ranking in Transparency International's Corruption Perception Index.[8] Furthermore, whilst the World Bank may have sponsored EITI++, one 2008 survey found that it only designated transparency as a programme benchmark in 19% of country lending programmes and that 90% of World Bank operations in resource-rich countries failed to promote contact disclosure.[9]

The key problem with the EITI, however, is that it can be understood as a voluntary – and thus weaker – alternative to calls for more rigorous formal regulation – in particular the 'publish what you pay' (PWYP) campaign to make the listing of companies on stock markets contingent upon transparent publication of all payments to national governments.[10]

formal regulation

The perceived failings of voluntarism have spurred calls for more formal regulation and/or *de facto* regulation via the creation of strong international regimes to address the different dimensions of war economies. Such calls have largely come from an NGO sector that has tended to hold a pessimistic conception of both the scale of ethical amnesia on the part of economic actors and the severity of the tension deemed to exist between the pursuit of profit and the broader economic and social responsibilities of such actors. For these proponents of formal regulation, market logic creates particularly strong imperatives for amnesia that require equally strong mechanisms of monitoring and enforcement if economic actors are to be persuaded to resist the siren temptations of functional forgetfulness.

Formal regulation is usually viewed, both by supporters and opponents alike, as an ethical high-water mark – even where commentators advocate some mix of voluntarism and regulation as the most pragmatic and effective means of promoting responsible business practices.[11] Examples of formal regulation include national regulations such as the US Alien Torts Claims Act, which allows companies to be sued at home for their behaviour abroad, and UN commodity sanctions imposed on actors in conflict, multilateral initiatives such as the OECD Convention on Combating Bribery (1997). An example of a relatively strong regime is the Kimberley Process Certification Scheme (KPCS), agreed in 2002 to prevent the trade in conflict diamonds. At the heart of the scheme is a requirement for participating governments to issue a certificate for each parcel of rough diamond exports, declaring them to be conflict-free, and for importing countries to accept rough diamonds only when accompanied by such certificates. Although Kimberley is a voluntary multi-stakeholder initiative, it nevertheless involves members enacting domestic legislation to support the scheme and can punish non-compliance by expulsion. Given that the scheme involves all the major rough diamond-producing, exporting and importing companies and countries, this is, in theory at least, quite a severe sanction. Indeed, for supporters this means that 'in real terms it is compulsory'.[12]

Nevertheless, even formal and *de facto* regulatory approaches suffer from a number of weaknesses. For example, they can – like action on conflict trade more generally – be criticised as shaped by a 'drugs, thugs and rocks' bias that primarily targets non-state actors such as rebel groups, specific rogue states and particular pariah goods (drugs, conflict diamonds) rather than the phenomenon of conflict trade or war economies *per se*. Thus, one study examining 26 conflicts involving resources in the period 1989–2006 found UN commodity sanctions were used on only seven occasions.[13] Formal regulation and regime development also tends to occur within a security (e.g. anti-terror) or policing and law and order framework that fails to address the political economies driving involvement in shadow trade and underpinning civil conflict.

More generally, initiatives have also been criticised as being shaped by the interests of developed world actors, predominantly aimed at the developing world and underpinned by crude representations of post-colonial states as arenas of poor governance and endemic corruption.[14] Moreover, even where initiatives are actively promoted by developed world actors, they often have the power and resources to ignore their requirements when they are deemed to interfere with more fundamental economic and security interests. For example, despite its membership of the OECD Convention on Combating Bribery, the UK government cancelled a Serious Fraud Office investigation into allegations of corruption involving the defence company BAE and officials of the Saudi government. The decision (widely reported as a response to Saudi threats to pull out of a large defence contract and to cease anti-terrorist intelligence cooperation if the investigation continued[15]) neatly illustrates the goldfish-like capacities of even those states apparently most committed to ethical standards of business. It also illustrates the implementation gap that can occur even with formal regulation – another case in point being the generally poor enforcement of UN arms and commodity sanctions.

The Kimberley Process Certification Scheme to prevent the trade in conflict diamonds embodies many of the criticisms levelled at formal regulation and strong ethical trading regimes. For example, whilst the regime, which came into operation in January 2003, is ostensibly designed to prevent the trade in conflict diamonds, it operates under a restrictive definition that describes them as 'rough diamonds used by rebel movements or their allies to finance conflict aimed at undermining legitimate governments as described in relevant United Nations Security Council (UNSC) resolutions'.[16] Consequently, whilst Kimberley aims to prevent the trade in 'conflict diamonds', it does not necessarily prevent the trade in diamonds from conflicts – either because the definition excludes both the trade in polished diamonds and trade conducted by 'legitimate governments' or because the trade has not, in any case, been subject to UN sanction. As Kimberley has evolved, however, actual practice has tended to exacerbate such definitional problems even more.

For instance, diamond sanctions imposed on Charles Taylor's Liberia in 2001 were continued not only for 4 years after his eviction and the formation of a Transitional Government in 2003 but for over a year after a new democratically elected government came to power in January 2006. This was on the grounds that, although conflict was over, it was necessary to keep sanctions in place until Liberia improved governance of the diamond sector. Consequently, Liberian diamonds were effectively treated as conflict diamonds by the Kimberley Process. With the ending of sanctions on Liberia the only remaining example of 'conflict diamonds' as defined by Kimberley are those exported from the rebel-held areas of Cote d'Ivoire. This trade, currently under UN sanction since 2005, has been valued at between $12 and $21 million annually,[17] thus allowing the Kimberley Process to claim that conflict diamonds account for less than 0.1% of world production.[18]

In contrast, the Israeli government recorded net exports of polished diamonds (after returns) of $6.6 billion in 2006 and net exports of rough diamonds of $2.7 billion.[19] Separate Kimberley Process data recorded a slightly higher figure for rough diamond exports of $3.5 billion, making Israel the world's largest exporter of rough in 2006 according to KP data.[20] In total, official net diamond exports accounted for almost 15% of goods and services exported from Israel in 2006, thus making a significant contribution to the Israeli war economy.[21] Yet, despite the ongoing Israeli–Palestinian conflict, Israel's continued breach of UN resolutions and its 2006 war in Lebanon, neither its polished or rough diamond exports were (or are) deemed to be conflict diamonds by either the UN or the Kimberley Process. Instead, Israel has been elected as Deputy Chair of the Kimberley Process for 2010.

A further problem with regard to Kimberley is that it was primarily established to address the issue of conflict diamonds via a system of policing and monitoring, rather than to address the broader political economies of diamond production that contributed to the production of conflict economies in the first place. For supporters, Kimberley has, nevertheless, produced important developmental benefits. For example, whilst Kimberley only came into being after the end of conflicts such as those in Sierra Leone or Angola, it is argued that NGO campaigns on conflict diamonds and the subsequent negotiations on Kimberley provided a deterrent effect that restricted the ability of rebel groups to raise funds – thus contributing to the peace necessary to spur development.[22] It is also argued that certification has produced marked rises in official exports from such states, thus raising the tax revenue also necessary to promote development.[23] Moreover, the absence of a formal development component in Kimberley itself has been addressed via the creation in 2005 of the Development Diamond Initiative (DDI), a separate but complementary multi-stakeholder initiative involving many of the same industry and NGO actors associated with Kimberley. The aim of the DDI is to 'optimize (sic) the beneficial development impact of artisanal diamond mining to miners and their communities'.[24] In addition, donors such as the UK and US have promoted various initiatives (e.g. the creation of cooperatives in Sierra Leone) aimed at addressing the exploitation of diggers and improving governance of the diamond sector in post-conflict states.

However, the experience of post-conflict Sierra Leone illustrates the development deficiencies in this broader conflict/development diamond regime. First, donor initiatives to address the pay and conditions of diggers have mostly been tokenistic and short-term – thus only five cooperative projects involving 50 to 70 people were implemented in an industry estimated to involve at least 120,000 diggers, and even these have now ceased.[25] Similarly, whilst the DDI has produced a number of reports on the conditions of diggers, etc., it has, to date, resulted in few concrete projects. Diggers in Sierra Leone therefore continue to earn an estimated $1–2 a day, whilst in 2005 the country's top three exporters officially transferred diamonds worth $105 million.[26] Second, although the government's tax take from diamond exports has risen, this amounted to just $5.2 million in 2004[27] and is constrained by the fact that higher taxes stimulate shadow trade across porous borders. In neighbouring Liberia, government revenue from the now sanction-free diamond sector is predicted to be just $500,000–750,000, enough to cover the costs of implementing Kimberley but little else.[28] Third, whilst smuggling certainly remains a problem for countries like Sierra

Leone, its principal problem is arguably the phenomenon of capital flight, which has meant 'hardly any of the profits generated by the diamond sector are reinvested in Sierra Leone'.[29] Fourth, neither Kimberley nor the DDI addresses the fact that the economic returns from Sierra Leone's diamond sector are limited as a result of the way value is added elsewhere in the global diamond economy. For example, one estimate for 2007 calculated that, whilst the global value of rough diamond production amounted to $12.5 billion, the value after polishing was $19 billion, after going through the jewellery wholesale pipeline it increased further to $30 billion and finally amounted to some $70 billion in the jewellery retail sector.[30]

A combined conflict/development diamond regime that responds to the structural exploitation inherent in the global diamond industry with acts of ethical tokenism is perhaps best understood as a simulation of an ethical trading regime rather than a substantive manifestation of one. Similarly, a conflict diamond regime that permits Israeli diamond exports in the middle of its war in Lebanon whilst simultaneously proscribing diamond exports from post-conflict Liberia is best described as a disciplinary tool directed against non-state actors and weak and pariah states, rather than one aimed at the phenomenon of conflict diamonds *per se*.

China bribing

A key issue that has emerged in the debate about ethical trading initiatives in general has been over the implications of the quite significant growth in Chinese trade with regions such as Africa.[31] This stems largely from the perception that Chinese companies essentially use their willingness to overlook human rights abuse and corruption in weak states as a form of comparative advantage in the search for market share. For example, commentators point to the way Chinese investment in the Angolan oil industry allowed the government to turns its back on IMF funding that would have imposed conditionalities linked to revenue transparency in a state where as much as $4 billion in oil revenues may have been lost to corruption in the last five years.[32]

Whilst such critiques are certainly not without foundation, the crude representation of Chinese firms as especially amoral (or profoundly amnesiac) is problematic on a number of grounds. First, the critique is far too modest about the ability of Western governments and corporations to embrace the amoral. For example, despite declaratory policies to the contrary, the US actually provides more of its aid to more corrupt countries[33] and more of its arms transfers to human rights-abusing states.[34] Second, as illustrated above, the critique is also far too immodest about the success of ethical trading initiatives. Third, it assumes that Chinese companies are uniquely immune to the costs arising from corruption and poor governance. In contrast, the evidence suggests they experience many of the same frustrations as Western companies. In Nigeria, for example, they have expressed concerns regarding corruption, the integrity of contracts, poor infrastructure and attacks on Chinese workers.[35] In Sierra Leone, they have even complained of being disproportionate victims of low-level corruption (e.g. by customs officials) in comparison to European firms.[36] Fourth, Chinese companies may simply be operating with a different (rather than non-existent) conception of CSR. For example, a recent survey of 25 Chinese firms by the UN's Special Representative for Business and Human Rights found that, whilst Chinese firms tended to recognise fewer rights than firms in general, they expressed more frequent support for the right to development and were more likely to recognise social and economic rights. Moreover, the survey also found that state-owned companies and major global companies were more likely to have published human rights policies, suggesting that both government and major Chinese firms were susceptible to the same pressures around brand image as Western firms have experienced.[37] Fifth, it is not clear that Chinese investment is ultimately antithetical to good governance and development. Indeed, there is some evidence to suggest that intensified trade links with China have produced higher growth rates, better terms of trade, increased export volumes, and higher public revenues for states in Africa.[38] Finally, Western governments and NGOs have tended to preach the language of local ownership whilst practising anti-corruption and good governance initiatives that have extended formal and informal conditionalities on developing world states – often with little positive effect. As will be noted below, practising real local ownership and effecting real change may, ironically, require an embrace of more heterodox approaches to governance and economy, as well as a move from top-down conditionality to a more equal negotiation on issues such as ethical trading. This will require a shift from mutual scapegoating to mutual learning between Chinese and Western externals as well as local actors – one example being the joint evaluation and follow-up seminar on Chinese, Norwegian, and Nigerian perspectives on the risks associated with the petroleum sector in Nigeria.[39]

economic supervision: amnesia meets polyphasia

The third approach to the interrelated problems of conflict trade, the resource curse, and the challenge of transforming war economies has been to use various forms of economic supervision to address the economic agendas of actors during conflict or to improve economic governance during peace. This has most commonly occurred when donors have been able to take advantage of a state's permanent or temporary dependence on external funds or troops to impose forms of oversight or guidance that significantly undermine the sovereign powers of a particular aid or security supplicant – albeit with the aim of transforming war economies. Such initiatives are underpinned by acutely pessimistic assumptions about the willingness of local political elites to engage in ethical amnesia. Indeed, there is often an assumption that corruption and exploitation are so widespread and ingrained as to be intrinsic to the political economy of society – in short, that there is not much in the way of ethics to forget in the first place. At the same time, however, it is also assumed there is a latent demand amongst the general population for liberal forms of political and economic governance that is simply waiting to be released. The solution advocated, therefore, is emergency external oversight to deter and detect abuse combined with radical projects of societal transformation (capacity-building, civil society empowerment, etc.) aimed at reforming elites, releasing pent-up demand and thus preventing or demobilising war economies.

The most cited example of economic supervision is the way in which the need for World Bank support of the Chad/Cameroon oil pipeline was used as a lever to impose a range of governance conditionalities on Chad, most notably the passage of a Revenue Management Law that specifies how funds from the pipeline will be spent (e.g. 80% of oil royalties were to be spent on poverty reduction programmes[40]). Another example is the Governance and Economic Management Assistance Programme (GEMAP) introduced in post-conflict Liberia in an attempt to address the pervasive corruption that has dogged successive Liberian governments. A key element in this programme is the placing of international experts (or 'foreign corruption spotters'[41]) in key positions inside major ministries and economic agencies such as the forestry commission and the Central Bank of Liberia to prevent the misuse of resources.

However, local actors are often quite adept at deploying strategies of obstruction, evasion or co-option of such initiatives. Moreover, a decline in dependence on external support may lead to renegotiation or outright rejection of supervision, particularly in a context where externals place rhetorical emphasis on both sovereignty and local ownership – and tend to suffer from a limited attention span anyway. Thus, once the oil came on tap in Chad the government passed a new law in 2005 (ultimately accepted by the World Bank) permitting revenues to be spent on security and administration. In 2008 the World Bank finally withdrew from the project, having concluded it would not achieve its original aims. Chad's total oil revenue from the beginning of the project to the first half of 2008 amounted to $3.3 billion, less than 1,000 Chad citizens work in the oil sector, average life expectancy is 50.5 years, and NGOs have concluded 'oil has brought more misery to the south, more AIDS, more alcoholism and more family problems'.[42] Similarly, whilst GEMAP has achieved some short-term successes, Reno has noted how it is merely the latest in a succession of similar initiatives that ultimately had little effect – in 1998, for instance, the US sponsored an initiative that also put foreigners into government agencies.[43] Goldfish-like Liberians, it would seem, are adept at sitting out emergency projects of social engineering and relying on the equal facility of donors to forget both their current ambitions for reform and the fact they have already been tried and failed anyway.

Moreover, projects of economic supervision are framed as exceptional responses to local manifestations of pathologies supposedly common to all non-liberal forms of political economy – and which in their local form threaten the security of citizens and externals alike. Thus, economic supervision depends for its legitimisation on a one-size-fits-all problematisation (and securitisation) of local governance and economy whilst also proffering a one-size-fits-all solution in the form of the liberal peace. Indeed, both the problematisation of war economies and the emphasis on the imperative of transformation can be understood as speech acts that securitise and pathologise the local in order to legitimise the extraordinary measures deemed necessary to bring about liberal governance.[44]

However, the crude representations of both the problem and the solution are equally flawed. For example, certain forms of corruption may actually facilitate growth or provide stability,[45] and even certain features of war economies can be engines of development.[46] Part of the task of transforming political economies of conflict, then, is to avoid dismissing them as wholly dysfunctional and instead to identify the building blocks of peace and development existing inside local war economies. Furthermore, liberal projects of societal transformation imposed on post-conflict societies can actually exacerbate features of poor governance – for example by introducing new opportunities for corruption linked to electoral or privatisation processes – which can be further fanned by the unwillingness of donors to critique key economic or security allies.[47]

For some commentators the attempt to transform or prevent war economies via economic supervision has echoes of imperial imposition or can be understood as a strategy of biopolitics[48] that *aims* to regulate the actions and transform the sensibilities of target populations – albeit under a simulacrum of empowerment[49]. Such analyses provide important insights into the politics underpinning economic supervision strategies. However, it is also important to recognise that the multiple strategies of co-option and resistance employed by local actors combine with selective strategies of accommodation on the part of externals to *actually* create hybrid forms of the liberal peace that, at least partly, frustrate the aims of external engineers. Moreover, these hybrids are often as problematic as the modes of governance and economy they replace – with only temporary external instruments of pacification (troops and increases in aid) concealing this fact. However, rather than concluding that local ownership and accountability therefore represent a prerequisite for the successful transformation of war economies, advocates of liberal intervention often view dysfunctional hybridity as a reason for even more extensive attempts to engineer liberal mimesis in the societies of the 'other'.[50]

The combined effect is to leave projects of economic supervision looking more like examples of cognitive polyphasia on the part of externals who simultaneously invent more ambitious projects of reform whilst fetishising sovereignty and local ownership, engaging in serial accommodation with local actors and forgetting that their strategies have often been tried (and failed) before anyway.

the production of forgetting

In many respects the problem-solving debates over the appropriate balance between voluntarism, regulation, and economic supervision are fierce – as is the discussion on how best to reform the technicalities of initiatives such as EITI or Kimberley. Underpinning these fierce debates, however, is a shared understanding of the goal and direction of action. The goal is deemed to be the creation of frameworks that will transform economic actors capable of evincing the moral memory of goldfish into ethical elephants – who never forget their broader obligations to state, society, and the international system. Moreover, whatever the nature of temporary setbacks, the direction of action is assumed to be ever onwards and upwards to the production of more extensive and more substantive ethical frameworks.

From a critical political economy perspective, however, the frameworks of voluntarism, regulation, and supervision – and indeed the dominance of the consensus – are better understood as cornerstones in an architecture of forgetting that functions in a number of ways and has a number of features.

First, the assumption of linear advancement in ethical initiatives requires (and reinforces) extensive amnesia over the extent to which contemporary policies have either been recycled from past failures or actually represent a retreat from ethical regulation. In the first instance, programmes of monitoring in Liberia or, as in Sierra Leone, cooperative experiments that echo the Child's programme of the 1950s are presented as elements of a new, more progressive architecture of liberal intervention to transform war economies, rather than examples of history rhyming. Moreover, the ballooning of voluntary multi-stakeholder ethical trading initiatives in the post-Cold War era is best understood as actually working to mask the general failure of attempts in the 1970s to impose meaningful constraints on corporate power and rebalance the relationship between the developed and developing world as part of Southern demands for a New International Economic Order. Thus, the 1974 *UN Charter of Economic Rights and Duties of States* had little effect, as it was resisted by those countries with most jurisdiction over TNCs; the UN Center on Transnational Corporations (UNCTC), also established in the mid-1970s, was disbanded in the 1990s under pressure from Northern governments; the development of a *Draft Code of Conduct on Transnational Corporations* had stalled by the 1980s. A similar initiative in the forms of NGO pressure to make the 2003 UN *Draft Norms on the Responsibilities of Transnational Corporations* legally binding has been equally fruitless. In the main, those initiatives that have survived from the 1970s have tended to be the weaker, non-binding agreements that emerged, such as the OECD's *Guidelines for Multinational Enterprises* or the ILO's *Tripartite Declaration of Principles Concerning Multinational Enterprises*. Consequently, the formal regulation of companies is principally left to negotiations between companies and national governments – yet a feature of contracts signed with non-OECD countries is that they constrain the host state's regulatory powers significantly more than those signed with OECD countries.[51] Furthermore, as Utting has noted, the current framework of mainly

voluntary ethical trading initiatives can be understood as forms of global branding and corporate control of the supply chain that are actually integral to the successful functioning of companies rather than an
imposition of ethical memory.[52]

Second, the impression of frenetic ethical activity produced by the current plethora of initiatives obscures the failure to meaningfully address
the various iniquities in the global trading system. These include declin-
ing terms of trade for low-income countries predominantly dependent on
commodities for export and limited in their ability to add value in global
trading systems such as that for diamonds – agricultural prices, for example, declined by 70% between 1961 and 2001.[53] This problem has been
further compounded by the adoption of various strategies to restrict market access to OECD countries. For instance, developing countries exporting to OECD countries face tariff barriers four times higher than those
experienced by rich countries, at a cost to the developing world of $100
billion a year.[54] At the same time, subsidised goods from developed world
economies are dumped on the economies of aid supplicants required to
open up their markets. Initiatives such as the Doha development round
or the EU's Everything But Arms (EBA) programme – designed to provide
LDCs with preferential access to EU markets – are either serially stalled,
as in the case of Doha, or anaemic anyway. In addition, the failure to
circumscribe capital flight from the developing world and to take effective action against tax havens means that developing countries lose three
times the value of aid provided by the developed world.[55] At the same
time, poverty reduction initiatives inside the developing world essentially
constitute a relabelling of neoliberal macroeconomic policies emphasising deregulation, privatisation, lowering company taxes, reducing government wage bills, and integration into global markets. In contrast,
in 2006 just $88 million out of a total $103 billion of aid from OECD
countries was dedicated to tax-related tasks.[56] The combined effect on the
political economies of vulnerable post-conflict societies, in particular, is
akin to rubbing salt into war wounds.[57]

Third, the simulation of ethical action on both trade and war economies effectively functions as form of misdirection that obscures the way
current initiatives combine a problematic cocktail of disciplinary action
aimed at particular pariah actors or goods with either ethical tokenism or
simple neglect. Thus, whilst post-conflict Liberia struggled with the legacy
of diamond sanctions for 4 years, the reality is that most forms of conflict
trade remain unregulated, uncertified, and unsanctioned. Indeed, there
is not even an agreed international definition of what constitutes conflict

trade. At the same time, however, the multiplication of tokenistic initiatives gives the impression that a high point of formal and informal ethical regulation has been reached. It is instructive, however, to compare
the panoply of weak ethical trading initiatives with the regulatory frameworks deployed to defend the core principles of neoliberalism. For example, both states and firms face significant penalties for breaching free trade
and competition requirements. Thus, the WTO permits states to impose
quite substantial sanctions on other countries deemed to be engaging in
anticompetitive practices; the EU has imposed a series of fines amount-
ing to €1.7 billion on Microsoft for breaching competition policy, whilst
Shell had total fines of £85 million imposed on it by authorities in the
United Kingdom and the United States for overstating its oil reserves and
€161 million for its role in a cartel designed to fix the price of synthetic
rubber.[57] It might be argued that such fines are not that substantial when
compared with the global sales of the firms involved. However, with the
possible exception of Kimberley, they provide an embarrassing contrast
to current action on the phenomenon of conflict trade.

conclusion

Whilst the goal of transforming war economies during or after conflict
has been thoroughly incorporated into the lexicon of peacebuilding,
actual action is notable for the way it has been disaggregated as components of other initiatives (anti-corruption, CSR, environmental sustainability, etc.). In many respects, there is no specific focus on, and thus no
policy for, transforming war economies *per se*. The goal is deemed to be
central to peacebuilding; the task is subsumed within or subcontracted
out to a myriad of disparate initiatives. In one view this does not matter, as these different initiatives combine to realise the generic panaceas
of the liberal peace – markets, democracy and good governance – capable of solving what are framed as the generic pathologies of the non-
liberal. Moreover, the mix of voluntarism, regulation, and economic
supervision generally identified as elements in this panacea are deemed
to constitute a high-water mark of ethical regulation designed to facilitate memory amongst economic actors predisposed to forgetting their
broader responsibilities to states, society, and the global system.

   In contrast, the analysis presented here suggests that the current mix
of voluntarism, regulation, and supervision is characterised by a drugs,
thugs, and pariah bias that serves to discipline various weak, pariah,
and non-state actors rather than imposing regulation to transform war

economies *per se*. Thus, on the one hand, the problematisation of war economies serves to securitise the presumed pathologies of local governance and economy in order to legitimise the application of extraordinary measures designed to induce liberal mimesis inside weak and post-conflict states – measures that are resisted in ways that actually produce dysfunctional hybrids of the liberal peace. On the other hand, on the outside of the weak and post-conflict state, the apparent profusion of ethical action on conflict trade, etc., masks not only the failure to undertake substantive action to reform global structures that promote economies of conflict but also significant elements of retreat from this goal. This is not to suggest that initiatives such as Kimberley or EITI are totally without merit; rather, it is to suggest that, even where individual initiatives achieve limited successes, the broader structures of the global economy and the application of one-size-fits-all neoliberal prescriptions inside the weak and post-conflict state militate against any substantive transformation. If the aim of action really is to encourage economic actors with a tendency for ethical amnesia to remember their broader responsibilities beyond narrow profit-making, then current action is more akin to training goldfish in a desert – however good individual training programmes might be, the broader context in which they occur means they are ultimately destined to fail.

notes

This research benefited from a grant by the UK Economic and Social Research Council (res. 223.25.0071) for research on the Transformation of War Economies (www.brad.ac.uk/acad/twe)

1. W. Reno, 'Anti-Corruption Efforts in Liberia: Are they Aimed at the Right Targets?', *International Peacekeeping*, Vol. 15, No. 3, 2008, p. 390.
2. K. Ballentine and H. Nitzschke, *Profiting from Peace: Managing the Resource Dimensions of Civil War*, Boulder, CO: Lynne Rienner, 2005; M.L. Ross, 'How Do Natural Resources Influence Civil War? Evidence from Thirteen Cases', *International Organization*, Vol. 58, No. 1, pp. 35–67; P. Collier, A. Hoeffler and D. Rohner, 'Beyond Greed and Grievance: Feasibility and Civil War', *Oxford Economic Papers*, Vol. 61, No. 1, pp. 1–27; M. Pugh and N. Cooper with J. Goodhand, *War Economies in A Regional Context: The Challenges of Transformation*, Boulder, CO: Lynne Rienner, 2004.
3. K. Schwab, 'Global Corporate Citizenship: Working With Governments and Civil Society', *Foreign Affairs*, Vol. 87, No. 1, 2008, pp. 107–18.
4. J.D. Margolis and J.P. Walsh, 'Misery Loves Companies: Rethinking Social Initiatives by Business', *Administrative Science Quarterly*, Vol. 48, No. 2, 2003, pp. 268–305.
5. C. Jakobeit with M. Maier and N. Cooper, 'Addressing the Political Economies of Armed Conflict in Africa', in O. Greene, J. Buxton and

C. Salonius-Pasternak, *Conflict Prevention, Management and Reduction in Africa*, Helsinki: Development Policy Information Unit, Ministry of Foreign Affairs, 2006, p. 169.

6. S. Taylor, Director Global Witness, Testimony for Hearing, 'Resource Curse or Blessing: Africa's Management of its Extractive Industries', Senate Foreign Relations Committee, SubCommittee on Africa, 24 September 2008. See: http://foreign.senate.gov/hearings/2008/hrg080924a.html, accessed on 1 December 2008.

7. *The Guardian*, 'Former head of Haliburton firm faces seven years in jail for bribery', 4 September 2008.

8. Report of the Minority Staff of the United States Senate Committee on Foreign Relations, The Petroleum and Poverty Paradox: Assessing US and International Community Efforts to Fight the Resource Curse (Draft), 9 September 2008, p. 66. See:http://lugar.senate.gov/sfrc/pdf/DRAFT_petroleum_poverty_paradox.pdf, accessed on 1 December 2008.

9. Global Witness and the Bank Information Center, *Assessment of International Monetary Fund and World Bank Group Extractive Industries Transparency Implementation*, 2008, p. 1. See: http://www.globalwitness.org/, accessed on 18 November 2008.

10. M. Turner, 'Taming Mammon: Corporate Social Responsibility and the Global Regulation of Conflict Trade', *Conflict, Security and Development*, Vol. 6, No. 3, 2006, p. 375.

11. L. Lunde and M. Taylor, 'Regulating Business in Conflict Zones: Challenges and Options', in K. Ballentine and H. Nitzschke, *Profiting from Peace*.

12. I. Smillie, *The Kimberley Process Certification Scheme for Rough Diamonds*, Verifor/ Partnership Africa Canada, 2005, p. 4. See: http://www.verfor.org/resources/case-studies/kimberley-process.pdf, accessed on 20 November 2008.

13. P. Le Billon and E. Nicholls, 'Ending "Resource Wars": Revenue Sharing, Economic Sanction or Military Intervention?', *International Peacekeeping*, Vol. 14, No. 5, 2007, p. 620.

14. L. Lunde and M. Taylor, 'Regulating Business in Conflict Zones: Challenges and Options'.

15. For further details see: http://www.guardian.co.uk/world/bae, accessed on 3 March 2009.

16. See http://www.kimberleyprocess.com/documents/basic_core_documents_en.html, accessed on 10 March 2009.

17. Letter dated 8 October 2008 from the Chairman of the Security Council Committee established pursuant to resolution 1572 (2004) concerning Côte d'Ivoire addressed to the President of the Security Council, New York: United Nations, S/2008/598, 9 October 2008, p. 33, para. 133.

18. See http://www.kimberleyprocess.com/faqs/index_en.html, accessed on 10 March 2009.

19. Office of the Diamond Controller, *Facts and Figures: Diamonds, Precious Stones and Jewelry, 2006*, Ministry of Industry, Trade and Labor, Diamonds, Precious Stones and Jewelry Administration, Office of the Diamond Controller, May 2007.

20. See https://mmsd.mms.nrcan.gc.ca/kimberleystats/publicstats.asp, accessed on 10 March 2009.

21. Ministry of Industry, Trade and Labor, *The Israeli Economy at a Glance 2007*. See http://www.moital.gov.il/NR/exeres/C3969F21-C61D-4E23-90E9-5C7486E9029B.htm, accessed on 10 March 2009.
22. Partnership Africa Canada, *Diamonds and Human Security: Annual Review 2008*, p. 22. See http://pacweb.org/e/index.php?option=content&task=v iew&id=42&Itemid=65, accessed on 10 March 2009. Partnership Africa Canada, *Killing Kimberley? Conflict Diamonds and Paper Tigers*, Occasional Paper No.15, rev. edn, Ottawa, 2006.
23. See http://www.ddiglobal.org/pages/ddi_mission.php, accessed on 10 January 2009.
24. N. Cooper, 'As Good As It Gets: Securing Diamonds in Sierra Leone', in M. Pugh, N. Cooper and M. Turner (eds) *Whose Peace? Critical Perspectives on the Political Economy of Peacebuilding*, Basingstoke: Palgrave Macmillan, 2008, p. 103–15.
25. Ibid.
26. Ibid.
27. Partnership Africa Canada, *Land Grabbing and Land Reform: Diamonds, Rubber and Forests in the New Liberia*, Occasional Paper No. 17, Ottawa, 2007.
28. C.E. Zohar, 'Sierra Leone Diamond Sector Financial Policy Constraints', MSI for Peace Diamonds Alliance and USAID, 2003, at www.resourcebeneficia-tion.org/home.asp?id=12, accessed on 10 January 2009.
29. DIB Online, 'Chaim Even-Zohar Addresses Diamond Industry Issues at Mining Indaba Conference', 5 February 2008, see http://www.diamondin-telligence.com/, accessed on 18 November 2008.
30. H.G. Broadman, 'China and India Go to Africa: New Deals in the Developing World', *Foreign Affairs*, Vol. 87, No. 2, 2008, pp. 95–109.
31. I. Taylor, 'China's Oil Diplomacy in Africa', *International Affairs*, Vol. 82, No. 5, 2006, pp. 937–59.
32. P. Le Billon, 'Corrupting Peace? Peacebuilding and Post-Conflict Corruption', *International Peacekeeping*, Vol. 15, No. 3, 2008, p. 354.
33. R. Perkins and E. Neumayer, 'The Organized Hypocrisy of Ethical Foreign Policy: Human Rights, Democracy and Western Arms Sales', 2008 (unpublished manuscript submitted to Geoforum for review).
34. B. Brandtzæg H. Wenping, C. Nwoke, A. Eriksson, O. Agbu, *Common Causes Different Approaches*, Research Report 2008–014, Oslo: Econ Pöry, 2008.
35. Centre for Chinese Studies (undated), China's interest and Activity inAf-rica's Construction and Infrastructure Sectors, Centre for Chinese Studies, Stellenbosch University, p. 39.
36. Human Rights Policies of Chinese Companies: Results from a Survey. Conducted under the mandate of the UN Secretary-General's Special Representative for Business and Human Rights Professor John G Ruggie, Harvard University, September 2007. See: http://www.business-humanrights.org/Documents/Ruggie-China-survey-Sep-2007.pdf, accessed on 1 December 2008.
37. N. Woods, 'Whose Aid? Whose Influence? China, Emerging Donors and the Silent Revolution in Development Assistance', *International Affairs*, Vol. 84, No. 6, 2008, p. 1206.
38. Brandtzæg et al., *Common Causes Different Approaches*.

39. K. Alexander and S. Gilbert, *Oil and Governance Report: A Case Study of Chad, Angola, Gabon, and Sao Tome é Principe*, 2008, see http://www.idasa.org.za/ index.asp,accessed on 10 March 2009.

40. United Nations Integrated Regional Information Network, 'Foreign Corruption Spotters Are Now in Place', 24 May 2006.

41. International Crisis Group, *Chad: A New Conflict Resolution Framework*, Africa Report No. 144, Sept. 2008, p. 5, see http://www.crisisgroup.org/ home/index.cfm, accessed on 1 December 2008.

42. W. Reno, 'Anti-Corruption Efforts in Liberia: Are They Aimed at the Right Targets?', *International Peacekeeping*, Vol. 15, No. 3, 2008, p. 388.

43. K.M. Jennings, 'Securitising the Economy of Reintegration in Liberia', in M. Pugh, N. Cooper and M. Turner (eds) *Whose Peace?*.

44. W. Reno, 'Anti-Corruption Efforts in Liberia'; D. Kang, *Crony Capitalism: Corruption and Development in South Korea and the Philippines*, New York: Cambridge University Press, 2002.

45. C. Cramer, *Civil War is Not a Stupid Thing: Accounting for Violence in Developing Countries*, London: Hurst & Company, 2006.

46. P. Le Billon, 'Corrupting Peace'.

47. M. Duffield, *Development, Security and Unending War: Governing the World of Peoples*, Cambridge: Polity Press, 2007; D. Chandler, *Empire in Denial: The Politics of State-building*, London: Pluto Press, 2006; M. Ignatieff, *Empire Lite: Nation-building in Bosnia, Kosovo and Afghanistan*, London: Vintage, 2003.

48. For example, see S.D. Krasner, 'Sharing Sovereignty: New Institutions for Collapsed and Failing States', *International Security*, Vol. 29, No. 2, 2004, pp. 85–120.

49. Pugh, Cooper and Turner, p. 391

50. Special Representative of the Secretary-General on Human Rights and Transnational Corporations, *Protect, Respect and Remedy: A Framework for Business and Human Rights*, 7 April 2008, pp. 11–12, see http://www.reports-and-materials.org/Ruggie-report-7Apr-2008.pdf, accessed on 1 December 2008.

51. P. Utting, *Rethinking Business Regulation: From Self-Regulation to Social Control*, United Nations Research Institute for Social Development, Technology, Business and Society Programme Paper No 15, Geneva: UNRISD, September 2005, p. 20.

52. S. Willett, 'Trading with Security: Trade Liberalisation and Conflict', M. Pugh, N. Cooper and M. Turner (eds) *Whose Peace?*, p. 70.

53. Ibid.

54. A. Gurría, 'The Global Dodgers', *The Guardian*, 27 November 2008.

55. Ibid.

56. M. Pugh, 'Rubbing salt into War Wounds: Shadow Economies and Peacebuilding in Bosnia and Kosovo', *Problems of Post-Communism*, Vol. 51, No. 3, 2004, pp. 53–60.

57. *The Guardian*, 'EU fines Microsoft record £680m "to close dark chapter" in fight against monopoly', 28 February 2008; *The Guardian*, 'Shell faces new damages claim', 10 January 2006.

part 3
developing agendas

17
culture: challenges and possibilities

morgan brigg

Culture matters for peace and conflict studies. The ways in which individuals and groups make meaning of their social and physical world, and the values, beliefs and processes that are reproduced through this meaning-making, have implications for how conflicts are waged and resolution pursued, and for the ideas and practices that constitute peace. The starkest examples in recent decades relate to how culture can be mobilised to fuel conflict. Equally, local cultural processes are increasingly recognised as valuable ways to manage conflicts, and to reconcile communities in post-conflict peacebuilding efforts. This recognition of the importance of culture has emerged partly through bitter or practical experience, and partly as a result of persistent and coherent arguments by scholars from a range of disciplines about the significance of culture for peace and conflict studies.

At the same time, recognition of the importance of culture in peace and conflict studies means that we must grapple with culture as a vague, political, and notoriously difficult term. Our efforts to know culture raise questions about our current deficit in understanding many cultural processes, the risks of overstating culture's role in conflict resolution practice, and the value of frameworks for knowing cultural difference. Still larger questions about how we form and maintain political community tend to be obscured and under-recognised, with researchers tending to overlook how our understandings of culture have been elaborated through one tradition of scholarship. We have neglected, in other words, the way our knowledge of human difference is itself culturally constructed. Fortunately, the recent move to more dynamic and relational ways of knowing culture offer possibilities for addressing these shortfalls and drawing upon cultural difference to expand our ways of thinking about and dealing with the intersubjective tensions of communal life which generate conflict and challenge peace.

This chapter begins by providing an overview of the relatively recent recognition of culture in peace and conflict studies in relation to first, second, and third generation approaches to peacebuilding. The second section discusses a selection of the puzzles and challenges that accompany our efforts to know culture for peace and conflict studies. The third and concluding section summarises the chapter and argues that advancing peacebuilding beyond current approaches requires disrupting current social science knowledge and democratising our knowledge production as part of taking up the recognition of culture in peace and conflict studies.

recognising culture in peace and conflict studies

The authors of a recent popular textbook surveying the conflict resolution field conclude that culture 'is in the end the most important issue of all'.[1] Indeed, in a globalised and increasingly interconnected world, the task of processing conflict does seem truly cross-cultural.[2] Such statements are likely to be uncontroversial among contemporary scholars and practitioners, but to speak in such terms has only recently become possible.

For most of the modern era the state and its associated institutions have operated as the primary vehicles for achieving and maintaining order and peace. In the thinking and practice of politicians, scholars, lawyers and diplomats, notions of formal governance – particularly law and diplomacy – have served as the dominant means for regulating conflict domestically and internationally. Within these broad first generation approaches to conflict resolution,[3] culture is thoroughly secondary to nationalist projects attached to particular domestic territories and to the dynamics of international interstate rivalry. Indeed, culture has been controlled and subordinated by the (nation) state, as realpolitik approaches have tended to marginalise cultural considerations, particularly in the context of a bipolar Cold War world. In short, culture has been considered broadly irrelevant to mainstream questions of peace and conflict for much of recent history.

Dominant realpolitik approaches to social and political order have, though, also been challenged by peace studies and facilitative approaches to conflict resolution in the post-war period. Well-known peace studies concepts, including structural violence and the distinction between negative and positive peace, discussed elsewhere in this volume, have helped to reveal the violence that is embedded within mainstream institutions and begun to point to the challenges of managing conflict by monopolising and mobilising power through the institution of sovereignty. These second generation approaches to peacebuilding and conflict resolution[4] have attempted to address structural violence and other shortfalls of first generation approaches by emphasising human-centred frameworks (including notions of individual and collective human needs and security), deep-seated societal causes of conflict, and the importance of informal and grass-roots actors rather than the formal institutions of state and diplomacy.[5]

There is much to recommend second generation approaches, not least of which is their often insightful critique of the state-centric orthodoxy of mainstream international relations and security studies. Yet both mainstream international relations and their peace and conflict studies critics have tended to under-recognise culture. Both frequently derive their methodologies from Western social science and develop analyses that generalise on the basis of assumptions drawn from experiences of Western social and political life and the accompanying theoretical frameworks. Prominent examples include influential notions of self-interested rationality and universal needs. In summary of his human needs approach, for instance, John Burton, writes that 'needs are a part of human inheritance and common to all peoples, regardless of culture'.[6] The result, for Burton, is that 'analytical processes, which seek to reveal those needs that are held in common, are applicable to all peoples in all cultures'.[7] The familiar and comfortable subtext at play here is one of benign Western expansionism and, as a corollary, the denial of other traditions and approaches to conflict and its resolution. Increased social science knowledge about the causes and dynamics of conflict, the application of powerful analytical reason through problem-solving workshops, and the spread of these developments around the globe promise to bring to the world new and improved ways of addressing the scourge of conflict. Non-Western approaches to conflict resolution and peace do not appear in this schema.

To criticise Burton's human needs approach is not to say that human universals do not exist, or that there is no community of human being. All humans do seem to reason, and it also seems clear that we have shared basic needs – for security, shelter, and respect, for instance. But it is also the case that variation in what people reason with and about (both of which derive from values) and variation in the concrete ways in which needs are articulated and addressed or otherwise met are at least as significant as abstract notions of reason and need, if not more so. This brings into focus culture and difference rather than the universal. It also points to diverse ways of approaching and processing conflict and the politics of knowing human difference through the concept of culture.

Much of the detailed twentieth-century study of culture and conflict occurs outside mainstream international relations in the discipline of anthropology, predominantly through the practice of studying cultural groups in relative isolation from broader international dynamics.[8] Studies undertaken through the subdiscipline of legal anthropology, a field whose activity peaked in the 1950s and 1960s, provide ethnographic description of the variety of ways in which people process the tensions and conflicts of intersubjective and communal life.[9] This cataloguing of how people process disputes, from avoidance to mediation, and from fighting to warfare, lay the foundation for subsequent cross-cultural comparisons of approaches to negotiation and conflict resolution.[10]

While the comparative theme remains important,[11] legal anthropological research gradually gave way (in the 1970s and 1980s) to more interpretive studies that made greater attempts to understand and analyse conflict processing from insiders' points of view.[12] And, while legal anthropology remains a valuable body of ethnography built upon by others, the explicitly legal orientation fell by the wayside as the processing of conflict and maintenance of order was taken up as part of other ways of studying culture and conflict,[13] including through cross-cultural analyses of mediation.[14]

Anthropological analyses of different approaches to conflict and peace do not support any straightforward conclusions about conflict behaviour over time or among cultures. This is so despite popular imaginings and the conclusions of some scholars. It is not the case, for instance, that traditional and indigenous cultures are more warlike than their modern Western counterparts, or that the latter possess more sophisticated or 'civilized' ways of managing conflict.[15] Nor is it the case that traditional cultures are more peaceful than contemporary Western society. Peaceful and warlike cultures and subcultures exist throughout the world's peoples and societies.[16] The opportunity for generalisation seems to be limited (careful comparative analysis is another matter), other than perhaps noting the apparently broadly shared tendency for many individuals to be sufficiently embedded within their own cultures to readily overlook the fact that their understandings and views are not held by others.

From the 1980s anthropologists and others began to address the fact that anthropological insights about questions of culture, society, and conflict were hitherto rarely available to those outside the discipline. Rubinstein and Foster and their contributors[17] bring the study of other societies, including different approaches to war and conflict processing, to a broader audience, partly by exploring and promoting the potential of anthropology as policy science for guiding approaches to conflict at the national and international levels. In the process they turn a critical analytical lens towards Western societies by attempting to understand 'the underlying reason for our own propensity for international confrontation'.[18] This anthropologising of Western societies, and especially the demonstration that ways of processing conflict are culturally formed, begins an important challenge to the universal claims of much mainstream international relations and political and social science. Cultural analysis shows, for instance, that conventional realpolitik approaches to international relations, such as those pursued in the Iran/American hostage crisis from 1979 to 1981, begin to appear less universal or rational, and more culturally derived.[19]

The recognition that culture has greater importance and influence for conflict and peace than had previously been allowed gathered pace from the late 1980s and into the 1990s. Echoing the goals of Rubinstein and Foster,[20] Avruch and Black brought anthropological insights to the newly formed Institute for Conflict Analysis and Resolution at George Mason University.[21] One of their key arguments is that culture has a constitutive rather than an incidental role in the waging and processing of conflict. That is, culture speaks to how people conceive of conflict, the meanings they take from it, how they process conflict, and so on.[22] The implication of their argument is that conflicts cannot be seen through a single lens. Rather, efforts to manage and resolve conflict should take account of differing interpretive frameworks – sometimes multiple and overlapping frameworks – associated with the culture(s) that individuals and groups bring to conflicts. Avruch and Black, therefore, speak of the need to attend to local understandings of conflict, and the accompanying practices and techniques used to address it, as part of conflict resolution and peacebuilding efforts.[23]

Raymond Cohen's 1990 analysis of the dynamics of Israeli–Egyptian relations[24] provides a striking demonstration of the importance of understanding how approaches to conflict are culturally constituted. He shows how the Israelis pursued a strategy of deterrence throughout the 1950s and 1960s in the expectation that they could extract –

indeed force – a rational calculation from the Egyptians that they must, among other actions, do more to stop cross-border incursions into Israel. Cohen shows that the Israelis held to this approach when it was not working, even going so far as to conclude that their use of military force had not gone far enough.[25] Meanwhile, Cohen demonstrates, the Egyptians remained unresponsive to the measured tones of Israeli statements while themselves communicating in ever more strident and demonstrative statements. Moreover, their experience was of the Israelis breaking, with increasing flagrancy, crucial codes of proportionate violence and revenge – circumstances which saw them honour-bound in Arab tradition to entertain violence regardless of the cost. In short, the actors were not operating from the same register, a situation that Cohen characterises as a dialogue of the deaf which inexorably escalated violence.

Culture frames how people approach conflict and interpret the actions of others in ways which can profoundly influence conflict dynamics, but it can also be used within conflict to mobilise individuals and groups for violent ends. The fact that cultures are powerful and sometimes encompassing frameworks for human action is forcefully demonstrated in violent conflicts from Rwanda to Bosnia to Sri Lanka. The power of ethnocentrism can lead individuals to see those who are different as inferior and a threat – processes that facilitate the dehumanisation of 'others' and justify their domination and even elimination. Once again, though, straightforward conclusions about the role of culture or particular cultures are not possible. Rather, as Jack Eller shows,[26] a key issue is how culture is employed in the context of past, present, and future political and other considerations and calculations. Experiences in Rwanda and elsewhere, then, call for efforts to develop a better understanding of the 'relation between cultural resources and social action'.[27]

Much more positively, recent experience also shows that culture is likely an under-recognised human heritage and resource for processing conflicts. From the Gacaca courts of Rwanda, to the Sulha of the Middle East, Nahe Biti of Timor Leste,[28] and indigenous reconciliation processes in Bougainville, so-called 'grass-roots' processes are being called into service to assist with peacebuilding in intractable and post-conflict situations in the context of third generation approaches to peacebuilding.[29] These approaches value cultural difference to the extent that they include local actors through a realisation that peacebuilding efforts need to be multidimensional and coordinated. Yet it remains the case that the recognition of local approaches remains severely constrained, as a Western-dominated peacebuilding consensus thinking continues to frame and dominate peacebuilding interventions.[30]

It is also true, of course, that local approaches and processes are not a panacea.[31] To note one key challenge, the relationship between these practices and a global human rights framework does require working through. Efforts to understand and draw upon local approaches to conflict are also nascent rather than advanced, and indigenous approaches are not quickly recognised (and can be marginalised) in the context of contemporary global liberal approaches to peacebuilding.[32] But in time, and with the appropriate attention from scholars and practitioners, drawing upon culturally diverse approaches and processes promises to significantly expand both our understanding of conflict and the range of approaches and resources available for managing and resolving it.

The recent recognition of culture within peace and conflict studies has brought attention to the ways in which people's approach to conflict and its resolution is culturally constituted, and to how culture can be mobilised to escalate or manage conflict. In other broad developments, Johan Galtung updated his framework approach to violence to include 'cultural violence",[33] and some international relations scholars discussed the place and influence of culture in foreign policy[34] and the study and dynamics of world politics.[35] The recognition of culture has also facilitated innovative analyses that demonstrate the global connectedness of contemporary conflict. Carolyn Nordstrom's work, for example, shows how war is simultaneously international and localised; how it generates links among diplomatic relations, weapons industries, and the frontline politics of identity and personhood.[36] Such analyses challenge the traditional separation between the international and the domestic, in part by showing that local dynamics and realities are 'as nuanced as the international associations that make war possible'.[37]

The realisation that culture matters for peace and conflict studies represents an important enlargement of the field, generating possibilities for the further development of conflict resolution and peacebuilding beyond first, second and third generations, but it also comes with practical and conceptual challenges which must be grappled with. As Avruch shows, becoming sensitised to the role of culture in conflict dynamics risks overstating the importance of culture, something which can play into the hands of those actors who might be seeking to mobilise culture within conflict.[38] But Avruch's solution to this puzzle – invoking Western social science to decide when actors' use of culture is genuine and when it is political[39] – raises a politico-methodological challenge: is the Western-trained social scientist authorised to make such a decision over and above local 'cultural' actors? If peace and conflict studies has made the move to recognise local cultures, including local approaches to conflict, on what basis can we reassert Western social science knowledge over local ways of knowing?[40] And if we are to talk of culturally constituted ways of knowing, then surely we should logically ask how culture is itself culturally constructed?

Even to ask the question 'what is culture?' throws up potentially embarrassing challenges to those seeking to claim scientific legitimacy. Culture is an enormously broad and complex term, which is used in many different ways across a range of academic disciplines and popular contexts. It embodies a range of sometimes contradictory assumptions and its very meaning is contested because of the way it has been bound with national and (post)colonial struggles over several centuries. One measure of complexity is found in the longstanding problem of definition: a contemporary and admirable cross-disciplinary effort to understand the meanings of culture acknowledges that culture is a moving target and ends with 87 pages of definitions.[41] Serious research and analysis of matters cultural in peace and conflict studies cannot avoid engaging with at least some of the puzzles which accompany this difficult term and our attempts to know human diversity through it. The range and depth of conceptual debates and complexity cannot be covered here, but it is possible to outline a selection of the challenges.

knowing culture: key conceptual challenges

Much of the difficulty accompanying the idea of culture arises because it typically refers to a 'complex whole'. Not only does culture refer to the sum of a people's beliefs, customs, ways of making meaning, values, processes and behaviours associated with them and so on, it also takes in a *wholeness* that 'their coexistence somehow creates or makes manifest'.[42] Problems arise because Western scientific knowledge gains much of its force and standing by isolating and reducing elements of the physical and social world to component parts to undertake more controlled analyses. The idea of a complex whole refers us, in contrast, in the opposite direction. The situation is yet more perplexing, because disciplines such as anthropology, sociology, and psychology have claimed the mantle of science to legitimise their efforts to know. So, even as natural science designated that which it does not study as a remainder which came to be called 'culture' in European thought,[43] social-scientific disciplines emerged to pursue the 'scientific' study of culture.

For those who are comfortable with the complexity associated with 'wholeness' – often scholars pursuing phenomenological or hermeneutic methodological approaches which emphasize experience or interpretation – culture offers a fascinating avenue for exploring the dynamics of human social life, including the multitude of ways in which humans pursue conflict and peace. Those who prefer precise concepts and categories are more likely to find the study of culture frustrating. However, there are also numerous attempts to know culture in more formal and schematic ways. The most well-known of these is Geert Hofstede's cultural dimensions, a series of dyads – including masculinity versus femininity, individualism versus collectivism and short-term versus long-term orientation – which are meant to describe tendencies in national and regional cultural groupings.[44]

Hofstede's categorisations have been used to analyse people's approaches to conflict,[45] but, while such distinctions seem to make common sense and may provide some useful guidance for practitioners about the conflict behaviours they may encounter in different cultures, they have limited analytical value. To assert, for instance, that 'West Africans and Arabs clearly respect authority and are apt to subordinate themselves to the dictum of the collectivity' while 'Swedes and Israelis are much more individualistic and have less concern for formal authority'[46] invites examples of individuals who do not fit these profiles. People are rarely amenable to simplistic ordering. Part of the problem for attempts to know culture in such ways arises from the fact that differences within cultural groups seem to be greater than those among groups. As current analysis shows, levels of intragroup heterogeneity and the associated statistical anomalies suggest, at least at this stage, that individualism and collectivism are 'not meaningful constructs or that we do not know how to measure them'.[47]

A broader and equally telling critique of current efforts to know culture through schematic frameworks or measurement relates to the tendency to rely upon Western cultural and conceptual frameworks. Research and literature on the individualism–collectivism distinction, to continue our example, assumes that this distinction is universally relevant without investigating implications of cultural difference for this framework itself. The individualism–collectivism distinction is simply assumed to be useful and universal. However, while this differentiation may make sense for many Westerners, anthropological research explains that the traits of individualism and collectivism are *mixed* for some peoples.[48] That is, some peoples cannot be placed on an individualist–collectivist continuum because their behaviour and their supporting values and forms of social and political organisation are *simultaneously* individualist and collectivist.[49]

The cultural limitations of the individualism–collectivism continuum point to the broader possibility, noted above, that culture itself is a 'culturally specific' way of interpreting and knowing human difference. A full history of the term cannot be taken up here, but we can note that much of culture's current meaning emerges out of encounters with other peoples and the development of means for describing, grouping, dividing, and ordering human difference through the activities of European travellers, explorers, and colonial administrators.[50] This ordering of human difference is itself a type of 'cultural' invention. As Roy Wagner[51] shows, the analogies the scholar creates in the field to make sense of foreign behaviours and systems of meaning are filtered through the notion of culture. These analogies are extensions of his or her own notions and culture, and of his or her sense-making.[52]

Culture, then, is not intrinsic. Rather, it is a contingent conceptual formulation inflected through European knowledge disciplines, the colonial experience, anthropology, and related endeavours. Such a way of knowing human difference is invariably selective, affirming that our processes of representation are creative rather than simply reflective of pre-existing reality.[53] Cultural differences, as Homi Bhabha points out, 'are not simply *there* to be seen or appropriated'. Rather, the production of cultural differentiation is the *'effect'* of discriminatory practices'.[54] 'Culture' helps to construct, produce and maintain cultural difference even as it seeks to explain and understand this difference.[55]

Although perplexing, this situation should not disable our efforts to understand and know cultural difference for peace and conflict studies and peacebuilding, and nor should it lead us to discard the notion of culture for other terms which may be just as troublesome. Our knowledge is enhanced by reflection and understanding about its epistemological, ontological and methodological assumptions, and the historical, social and political circumstances which give rise to them. One of the results of framing human difference through culture in the colonial era, for instance, is that variation among Europeans tends to be understated while their difference from others tends to be magnified and thereby exaggerated.[56] This facilitates notions of 'us' and 'them'[57] that potentially contribute to conflict and its escalation. Understanding

these and other issues increases our capacity for knowing and working
with difference in peace and conflict studies, particularly when much
contemporary politics and conflict relates to differences in world view
and versions of truth and reality.[58]

Addressing these types of challenges is crucial for peace and conflict
studies because one of the key issues the field must face at the beginning
of the Asian century and amidst ongoing cultural and identity claims
is the question of its relationship to a European colonial heritage. From
the colonial era to contemporary liberal peacebuilding, critical scholarship shows how knowledge disciplines and policy establishments are
integral to the operation of mechanisms for governing and control. To
the extent that it does not critically reflect upon the cultural entail-
ments of its heavily European heritage, peace and conflict studies implicitly privileges modern Europe as the moral, scientific, and political
capital of the world, and risks serving as an agent of the liberal peace.
To do so limits our capacity to develop an interculturally credible body
of knowledge for pursuing peace and resolving conflict.

For these reasons our currently available theoretical frameworks tend
to be insufficient for addressing the challenges of cultural difference
in peace and conflict studies. Take cosmopolitanism, for instance. It is
true that cosmopolitan does have more to offer for working across cultures than realpolitik first generation approaches to conflict resolution.
In addition, the notion, advanced by Ramsbotham and colleagues,[59]
of dealing constructively with conflict beyond particular states, societies, or established centres of power has understandable appeal. Yet
it remains the case that cosmopolitanism is expounded from Kantian
European roots. To invoke cosmopolitanism without self-critical analysis is to be part of a consistent privileging of modern Europe that
involves an implicit claim that European ethnophilosophy is global and
universal.[60] This claim is ultimately untenable for those who want to
strike up a global conversation across difference.

The challenge of knowing culture also generates more familiar
debates and tensions, which, while likely to endure, also offer recent
meaningful compromise for beginning to address the foregoing challenges. Take the longstanding debate between universalism and pluralism, for instance.[61] Scholars have long debated the tension between the
sense that human behaviours and ways of being are universally shared
and the pluralistic sense that human groups exhibit distinctive ways of
behaving and being. In its strongest form, the pluralistic position claims
that cultures are unique and separate, and should be preserved as such,

particularly in the face of the impacts of modernisation and development. Much twentieth-century anthropological scholarship lends broad support to this position because of a tendency to study groups as separate entities. Yet suggestions that cultures are fundamentally different and that there are no human universals cannot hold because this contradicts the very possibility, and achievement, of anthropological and other understandings which generate understandings across cultural difference. At the same time, recent decades have seen the amassing of arguments and evidence that universal approaches often involve the more or less disguised assertion of a *particular* position across and over human difference.

There is no ready solution, then, to this tension. The universalism–pluralism debate is likely to continue, and the accompanying discussions will continue to provide a useful way of thinking through the challenges of working with political community and conflict across difference. Nonetheless, the recent move to more dynamic and relational ways of conceptualising culture provides welcome relief from the straightforward opposition of universalism and pluralism. Increases in movement and interaction of peoples from different cultures and the adoption of more subtle theoretical approaches lead most contemporary culture theorists to avoid notions of static and separate cultures and to instead see different individuals *and* peoples as 'both unique and resonating with the human condition in myriad complex ways'.[62] One of most important accompanying insights is that people tend to articulate their differences *through* relations with others. The corollary, as noted above, is that difference is not pre-existing. Rather, differentiation is *produced* through encounters and interaction. This suggests at least some level of sameness, even in the process of articulating difference. Indeed, some recent and innovative analysis shows that people produce difference in an effort to avoid sameness and that this dynamic generates much conflict.[63]

In this broadly relational approach, questions about the politics of universalism become more grounded and practical: problems arise not with universalism *per se*, but with the operation of universality that is not responsive to difference or the social and cultural conditions to which it is applied.[64] Such an approach is also able to accommodate the fluidity and complexity appropriate to contemporary understandings of culture. In addition to convincingly showing that cultural difference is fluid rather than fixed, relational approaches allow that people's lived experiences of difference are no less real for the fact that they emerge through a shared process. This provides a basis for respecting cultural values and behaviours *and* for their open debate and scrutiny within peace and conflict studies and peacebuilding practice.[65] Furthermore, it demonstrates the possibilities for working across cultural difference in addressing the contemporary challenges of knowing human difference. Of course, to think of culture in a relational sense poses challenges for much mainstream quantitative social science practice, particularly for those who prefer to work with firm categories, but this simply evokes the challenge and possibility of culture.

beyond ethnocentric knowledge and peacebuilding?

Evidence from around the globe suggests that, to survive, all societies must find ways to deal with frustration and aggression, and to manage, govern, or otherwise successfully process the intersubjective tensions of communal life. The resulting political and social institutions, values, and processes often find expression as 'culture'. Recent peacebuilding scholarship and practice may be beginning to realise not only that culture must be understood to enable us to comprehend and intervene in conflict dynamics, but also that it is an under-recognised human heritage and resource for processing conflict and pursuing peace. But to draw upon this resource as a way of moving beyond current approaches to a fourth generation of peacebuilding requires much more than adding to our store of conflict resolution processes or expanding our existing ways of knowing culture and doing social science.

Comfort with mainstream Western ways of knowing continues to lead many to neglect the ways in which our knowledge of conflict and human difference, and the political prescriptions and institutions of current peacebuilding, are imbued with a European and colonial legacy. One of the most notable instances of this problem lies in the way that much current cultural analysis and peacebuilding is subtended by an ethnocentric conceit that the big questions about political community and order are already resolved in favour of globalised liberalism. The implication is that indigenous and marginalised people remain, as in the colonial era, peoples without king, law, or history. Local processes are 'only' local, with the inhabitants cast as people without institutions that can contribute, beyond their immediate cultural milieu, to the sustenance of human community or the broader processing of conflict. This narrow purview deserves to be disrupted, particularly at the beginning of the Asian century. Prevailing assumptions about reason and

selfhood and their extrapolation in, for instance, rational choice theory, deterrence doctrines, and interest-based negotiation must be thoroughly questioned, partly by bringing cultural difference to bear. We
require, then, a democratisation of knowledge as part of taking up the
recognition of culture in peace and conflict studies.

The dynamics of intrasubjective and intersubjective tensions, the way
they interact with social and political institutions, and their aggregation and escalation into large-scale and protracted conflict continue to
puzzle us. Managing these tensions and the accompanying relations in
peaceful ways in the twenty-first century will require drawing upon the
accumulated insights of humanity's diverse ways of forming political
community and processing conflict. The recognition of culture in peace
and conflict studies offers an avenue to a new generation of peacebuilding in which we engage in multiple ways of building peace and political
community to deal with the perennial challenges of communal life. But
this is only possible by approaching local ways of addressing conflict as
ways of thinking about how humans organise being together and dealing with the difficulties of coexistence as well as a means for helping to
deal with the intractability of some conflicts or difficult post-conflict
situations.

In short, challenges and possibilities accompany the relatively recent
recognition of culture within peace and conflict studies. Culture has
implications for how conflicts are waged and resolution pursued, and
for the ideas and practices that constitute peace. It can be mobilised to
fuel conflicts, and it generates truly puzzling conceptual conundrums.
Recognising culture fundamentally challenges first, second, and third
generation approaches to peacebuilding, but it is also a potential avenue
to a fourth generation of peacebuilding. As we face this possibility, the
insights of a scholar writing at a time when culture was little considered
in peace and conflict studies and international relations seem prescient. In 1960 Adda Bruemmer Bozeman notes European disregard for
non-Western modes of governance which nonetheless resonate with
the values that western nations pursue in their own political development.[66] There is a 'considerable cost' associated with bypassing non-
western approaches to political community and conflict because it 'has
been attended by a steady weakening of the separate cultures that now
are being called upon to support a world society'.[67] If we are up to the
task, the recognition of culture within peace and conflict studies provides avenues for remedying this situation and working anew to build
peace across cultures.

notes

1. O. Ramsbotham, T. Woodhouse and H. Miall, *Contemporary Conflict Resolution: The Prevention, Management and Transformation of Deadly Conflicts*, Cambridge, UK; Malden, MA: Polity Press, 2005, p. 302.
2. Ibid., p. 329.
3. O.P. Richmond, 'A Genealogy of Peacemaking: The Creation and Re-Creation of Order,' *Alternatives*, Vol. 26, No. 3, 2001.
4. Ibid. pp. 321–7.
5. J.P. Lederach, *Building Peace: Sustainable Reconciliation in Divided Societies*, Washington, DC: United States Institute of Peace Press, 1997; J.P. Lederach, *A Handbook of International Peacebuilding: Into the Eye of the Storm*, San Francisco: Jossey-Bass, 2002.
6. J.W. Burton, *Conflict Resolution: Its Language and Processes*, Lanham, MD & London: Scarecrow, 1996, p. 23.
7. Ibid.
8. There are limited exceptions. See, for instance, A.B. Bozeman, *Politics and Culture in International History*, Princeton, NJ: Princeton University Press, 1960; A.B. Bozeman, *Conflict in Africa: Concepts and Realities*, Princeton, NJ: Princeton University Press, 1976.
9. P. Bohannan, *Justice and Judgment among the Tiv*, London: For the International African Institute by Oxford University Press, 1968 [1958]; J. Gibbs, 'The Kpelle Moot: A Therapeutic Model for the Informal Settlement of Disputes', *Africa*, Vol. 33, No. 1, 1963; L. Nader and H.F. Todd, 'Introduction: The Disputing Process', in L. Nader and H.F. Todd (eds) *The Disputing Process: Law in Ten Societies*, New York: Columbia University Press, 1978; M. Gluckman, *The Judicial Process among the Barotse of Northern Rhodesia*, Manchester: Manchester University Press, 1955; M. Gluckman, 'African Jurisprudence', *The Advancement of Science*, Vol. XVIII, No. 75, 1962; M. Gluckman, *The Ideas in Barotse Jurisprudence*, New Haven, CT: Yale University Press, 1965.
10. P.H. Gulliver, *Disputes and Negotiations: A Cross-Cultural Perspective*, New York: Academic Press, 1979; L. Nader and H.F. Todd (eds), *The Disputing Process: Law in Ten Societies*, New York: Columbia University Press, 1978.
11. See J.A. Scimecca, P.W. Black and K. Avruch, *Conflict Resolution: Cross-Cultural Perspectives*, New York: Greenwood Press, 1991.
12. S. Roberts, *Order and Dispute: An Introduction to Legal Anthropology*, Harmondsworth, Middlesex, England; New York: Penguin, 1979.
13. P. Caplan, *Understanding Disputes: The Politics of Argument*, Oxford; Providence, R.I.: Berg, 1995; B. Schmidt, I. Schröder and European Association of Social Anthropologists, *Anthropology of Violence and Conflict*, New York: Routledge, 2001.
14. C.J. Witty, *Mediation and Society: Conflict Management in Lebanon*, New York: Academic Press, 1980.
15. B.D. Bonta, 'Conflict Resolution among Peaceful Societies: The Culture of Peacefulness', *Journal Of Peace Research*, Vol. 33, No. 4, 1996; D.P. Fry, *The Human Potential for Peace: An Anthropological Challenge to Assumptions About War and Violence*, New York: Oxford University Press, 2006; D.P. Fry and

K. Björkqvist (eds), *Cultural Variation in Conflict Resolution: Alternatives to Violence*, Mahwah, NJ: Lawrence Erlbaum Associates, 1997.
16. See Fry, *The Human Potential*.
17. R.A. Rubinstein and M. LeCron Foster (eds), *Peace and War: Cross-Cultural Perspectives*, New Brunswick, NJ: Transaction Books, 1986.
18. R.A. Rubinstein and M. LeCron Foster, 'Introduction,' in R.A. Rubinstein and M. LeCron Foster (eds) *Peace and War: Cross-Cultural Perspectives*, New Brunswick, NJ: Transaction Books, 1986, p. xvi.
19. See W.O. Beeman, 'Conflict and Belief in American Foreign Policy', in Rubinstein and LeCron Foster (eds) *Peace and War*.
20. Ibid.
21. K. Avruch and P.W. Black, 'A Generic Theory of Conflict Resolution: A Critique', *Negotiation Journal*, Vol. 3, No. 1, 1987; J.W. Burton and D.J.D. Sandole, 'Expanding the Debate on Generic Theory of Conflict Resolution: A Response to a Critique', *Negotiation Journal*, Vol. 3, No. 1, 1987; P.W. Black and K. Avruch, 'Anthropologists in Conflictland: The Role of Cultural Anthropology in an Institute for Conflict Analysis and Resolution', *Political and Legal Anthropology Review*, Vol. 16, No. 3, 1993.
22. K. Avruch and P. Black, 'The Culture Question and Conflict Resolution', *Peace and Change*, Vol. 16, No. 1, 1991, pp. 31–4.
23. Ibid.
24. R. Cohen, *Culture and Conflict in Egyptian-Israeli Relations: A Dialogue of the Deaf*, Bloomington and Indianapolis: Indiana University Press, 1990, pp. 92–105.
25. Ibid., p. 101.
26. J.D. Eller, *From Culture to Ethnicity to Conflict: An Anthropological Perspective on International Ethnic Conflict*, Ann Arbor: University of Michigan Press, 1999.
27. Ibid., p. 5.
28. D. Babo Soares, 'Nahe Biti: The Philosophy and Process of Grassroots Reconciliation (and Justice) in East Timor', *The Asia Pacific Journal of Anthropology*, Vol. 5, No. 1, 2004.
29. Richmond, 'A Genealogy of Peacemaking'.
30. O. Richmond, *Maintaining Order, Making Peace*, Houndsmills, Basingstoke, Hampshire: Palgrave, 2002.
31. V. Böge, 'Traditional Approaches to Conflict Transformation: Potentials and Limits', *Berghof Handbook for Conflict Transformation*, July 2006.
32. R. Mac Ginty, 'Indigenous Peace-Making Versus the Liberal Peace', *Cooperation and Conflict*, Vol. 43, No. 2, 2008.
33. J. Galtung, 'Cultural Violence,' *Journal of Peace Research*, Vol. 27, No. 3, 1990.
34. V.M. Hudson (ed.), *Culture & Foreign Policy*, Boulder, CO: Lynne Rienner, 1997.
35. J. Chay, *Culture and International Relations*, New York: Praeger, 1990; Y. Lapid and F.V. Kratochwil (eds), *The Return of Culture and Identity in IR Theory, Critical Perspectives on World Politics*, Boulder, CO: Lynne Rienner, 1996.
36. C. Nordstrom, *A Different Kind of War Story*, Philadelphia, PA: University of Pennsylvania Press, 1997, pp. 4–5.
37. Ibid., p. 8.

38. K. Avruch, 'Type I and Type II Errors in Culturally Sensitive Conflict Resolution Practice', *Conflict Resolution Quarterly*, Vol. 20, No. 3, 2003.
39. Ibid., p. 355.
40. For discussion of these and associated issues see M. Brigg and K. Muller, 'Conceptualising Culture in Conflict Resolution' *Journal of Intercultural Studies*, Vol. 30, No. 2, 2009, pp. 121–40.
41. J.R. Baldwin, *Redefining Culture: Perspectives across the Disciplines*, Mahwah, NJ: Lawrence Erlbaum Associates, 2006, pp. 3–24, 139–226.
42. C. Herbert, *Culture and Anomie: Ethnographic Imagination in the Nineteenth Century*, Chicago and London: University of Chicago Press, 1991, p. 5.
43. M. de Certeau, *The Practice of Everyday Life*, Berkeley: University of California Press, 1984, p. 6.
44. G. Hofstede, *Culture's Consequences: International Differences in Work-Related Values*, Beverly Hills: Sage Publications, 1984; Geert Hofstede, *Cultures and Organizations: Software of the Mind*, New York: McGraw-Hill, 1997.
45. For example, see M.R. Hammer, 'The Intercultural Conflict Style Inventory: A Conceptual Framework and Measure of Intercultural Conflict Resolution Approaches', *International Journal of Intercultural Relations*, Vol. 29, No. 6, 2005; P. Trubisky, S. Ting-Toomey and S.-Ling Lin, 'The Influence of Individualism-Collectivism and Self-Monitoring on Conflict Styles', *International Journal of Intercultural Relations*, Vol. 15, No. 1, 1991; D.A. Cai and E.L. Fink, 'Conflict Style Differences between Individualists and Collectivists', *Communication Monographs*, Vol. 69, No. 1, 2002; G.O. Faure and G. Sjöstedt, 'Culture and Negotiation: An Introduction', in G.O. Faure and J.Z. Rubin (eds) *Culture and Negotiation: The Resolution of Water Disputes*, Newbury Park, CA: Sage Publications, 1993.
46. Faure and Sjöstedt, 'Culture and Negotiation: An Introduction,' p. 7.
47. A.P. Fiske, 'Using Individualism and Collectivism to Compare Cultures – a Critiques of Validity and Measurement of the Constructs: Comment on Oyserman Et Al.', *Psychological Bulletin*, Vol. 128, No. 1, 2002, p. 80.
48. See, for instance, F.R. Myers, *Pintupi Country, Pintupi Self: Sentiment, Place, and Politics among Western Desert Aborigines*, Berkeley, CA: University of California Press, 1991; J. Overing, 'In Praise of the Everyday: Trust and the Art of Social Living in an Amazonian Community', *Ethnos*, Vol. 68, No. 3, 2003; E.R. Sorenson, 'Preconquest Consciousness', in H. Wautischer (ed.)*Tribal Epistemologies: Essays in the Philosophy of Anthropology*, Aldershot; Brookfield: Ashgate, 1998, pp. 79–115, especially p. 82.
49. Joanna Overing explains that for the Piaroa the high value placed on 'being able "to live one's life in one's own way" ... is not to be confused with the egoism of a familiar brand of Western individualism' because '*personal autonomy is a social capacity*'. Overing, op. cit. (note 48), pp. 305–6, emphasis in original.
50. N.B. Dirks, 'Introduction: Colonialism and Culture', in N.B. Dirks (ed.) *Colonialism and Culture*, Ann Arbor: University of Michigan Press, 1992, p. 3.
51. R. Wagner, *The Invention of Culture*, Englewood Cliffs, NJ: Prentice-Hall, 1975.
52. Ibid., p. 12.

53. See M. Foucault, *The Archaeology of Knowledge & the Discourse on Language*, New York: Pantheon Books, 1972, p. 49; J. Clifford, 'Introduction', in J. Clifford and G.E. Marcus (eds) *Writing Culture: The Poetics and Politics of Ethnography*, Berkeley; London: University of California Press, 1986, p. 2.

54. H.K.Bhabha, *The Location of Culture*, London and New York: Routledge, 1994, p. 114, emphasis in original.

55. L. Abu-Lughod, 'Writing against Culture', in R.G. Fox (ed.) *Recapturing Anthropology: Working in the Present*, Santa Fe, New Mexico: School of American Research Press, 1991, p. 143.

56. N. Thomas, *Entangled Objects: Exchange, Material Culture, and Colonialism in the Pacific*, Cambridge, MA: Harvard University Press, 1991, p. 3.

57. E. Said, *Culture and Imperialism*, London: Vintage, 1993, p. xxviii.

58. J.S. Docherty, *Learning Lessons from Waco: When the Parties Bring Their Gods to the Negotiation Table*, Syracuse, NY: Syracuse University Press, 2001; R.E. Young, *Intercultural Communication: Pragmatics, Genealogy, Deconstruction*, Clevedon, England: Multilingual Matters, 1996, p. 148.

59. Ramsbotham, Woodhouse and Miall, *Contemporary Conflict Resolution*, p. 250.

60. H. Yol Jung, 'Introduction', in H. Yol Jung (ed.) *Comparative Political Culture in the Age of Globalization: An Introductory Anthology*, Lanham, MD: Lexington Books, 2002, p. 2.

61. Another dualistic tension that has inhabited culture is that between idealism and materialism. For a brief outline in the context of international relations see R.B.J. Walker, 'The Concept of Culture in the Theory of International Relations', in Jongsuk Chay (ed.) *Culture and International Relations*, New York: Praeger, 1990, p. 5.

62. Nordstrom, *A Different Kind of War Story*, p. 6.

63. S. Harrison, *Fracturing Resemblances: Identity and Mimetic Conflict in Melanesia and the West*, New York, Oxford: Berghahn Books, 2007.

64. J. Butler, *Giving an Account of Oneself*, New York: Fordham University Press, 2005, p. 6.

65. See Brigg and Muller, 'Conceptualising Culture in Conflict Resolution', *Journal of Intercultural Studies*, Vol. 30, No. 2, 2009, pp. 121–40.

66. B. Bozeman, *Politics and Culture in International History*, p. 7.

67. Ibid., p. 8.

18

gilding the lily? international support for indigenous and traditional peacebuilding

introduction

Let's begin with an extended analogy. From the mid-1980s, consumers in the United Kingdom (and many other states in the global North) have sparked an organic revolution in choosing foods grown without the use of nitrates and other agrichemicals. Consumers believed that organic fruit and vegetables were tastier, healthier and better for the environment. The organic revolution gathered pace in the face of food scares such as 'mad cow disease' and fears over genetically modified crops.[1] An organic 'perfect storm' developed in the United Kingdom, as the increasing interest in organic farming chimed with a series of other concerns: that an 'obesity time bomb' awaited society; that rural communities were being decimated by factory farming; and that large-scale retailers were exploiting their market dominance to put small producers out of business.[2] By 2006, global sales of organic food had reached £19.3 billion, with the United Kingdom market growing by an average of 27% annually between 1996 and 2006.[3] All things organic became trendy, whether through farmers' markets, growing your own, or the home delivery of vegetable boxes.[4] The BBC may have gone too far by crowning gardening as 'the new sex', but there has been a significant cultural change in that, for much of the post-Second World War period, metropolitans in the United Kingdom had regarded growing your own vegetables as backward or a sign of austerity.[5] Now it had become fashionable.

While many consumers championed organic farming as a way of harking back to a simpler era in which the distance between farm gate and plate was much shorter, major retailers saw the organic revolution as a market opportunity. In fact, they drove demand – enthusiastically supporting campaigns by governments that encouraged citizens to eat more healthily. While sales of organic products rose by 30 % in the United Kingdom in 2005, the major supermarkets were poised to take advantage of this trend: organic food sales at Tesco (Britain's largest retailer) surged by 70 % in that year.[6] In the United Kingdom, consumer demand for organic food outstripped domestic supply. The result? The supermarkets turned overseas to source much of their organic supplies, transporting some of it by air. With frightening irony, a demand that was partially driven by environmental concerns was satisfied by the most polluting form of transport: aircraft. As Joanna Blythman observed, 'when I pick up a carton of organic Chilean blueberries, Argentinian blackberries, or Zambian sugarsnap peas, all air-freighted from their countries of origin, my carefully constructed rationale for buying organic is shot full of holes.'[7] Importantly, consumer demand for organic foods is not necessarily authentically popular – stemming from an educated and self-motivating public. Instead, governments (aided by agricultural and supermarket lobbies) have worked hard to create the demand.[8]

The analogy has relevance to our interest in traditional and indigenous approaches to peacebuilding. Indeed, traditional and indigenous approaches to peace could be labelled as 'organic peacebuilding' in that they have the same perceived advantages: sustainability, independence from expensive and artificial additives in the form of external peace-support interventions, and originating locally. Just as environmentalists fret over 'food miles' or the immense distances of food supply networks, many peace practitioners and scholars have concerns about the artificiality of many peace-support interventions (both ideas and practices) which are imported from overseas. In a sense, they are concerned about 'peace miles' or the importation of artificial ways of making and building peace that may have few connections with local cultural norms. In a number of post-civil war contexts, reliance on local approaches to peacebuilding (often approaches that draw on tradition or indigenous practice) have been increasingly regarded as a way of countering the alien, and often inefficient, Western style of peacebuilding. But, as we will see in this chapter, just like organic farming, attempts to promote or deploy traditional and indigenous approaches to peacebuilding face a number of problems. Significant among these problems are questions about authenticity. If international organisations promote 'traditional' and 'indigenous' approaches to peacebuilding (as is the case in many instances) does this compromise the authenticity of these practices and perhaps detract from the very factors that makes them worthwhile in the first place? The question is not unlike asking: by genetically modifying organic rhubarb, can we still label it as organic?

the advantages of traditional and indigenous peacebuilding

A fuller conceptualisation of traditional and indigenous approaches to peacebuilding has been carried out elsewhere.[9] For our purposes, traditional peacebuilding refers to dispute resolution and reconciliation approaches that draw on long-held practice. Indigenous peacebuilding refers to dispute resolution and reconciliation that draw on local custom. Although the terms 'traditional' and 'indigenous' are not precisely the same, they are often used interchangeably with respect to peacebuilding. At a minimum, we can take them to mean approaches that are locally inspired rather than the increasingly standardised approaches to peacemaking and peacebuilding that are used by international organisations and INGOs in post-civil war environments.

Although traditional and indigenous peacebuilding practices are necessarily rooted in specific communities and thus may have highly localised elements, it is possible to identify a number of common traits.[10] Firstly, many of the practices rest on the moral authority of respected community figures, for example, village elders or other sources of counsel. Often these figures demand a certain level of deference and there is a strong social expectation that their judgements or advice will be adhered to. Secondly, many of the practices have a public element that adds to the transparency of decision-making processes. They are deliberately accessible (perhaps held in a central point in a village or at a location between two disputing villages), with this public dimension providing a visible affirmation of legitimacy. Multiple public witnesses may make it more difficult for disputants to renege on any agreement that is made as a result of arbitration. Sometimes, this public element may take the form of ritual or a public display that symbolises reconciliation or a new understanding. Thirdly, many of the practices have a story-telling aspect. This public articulation of grievances and perspectives is highly accessible and may conform to the dominance of oral traditions. Fourthly, there is often a strong emphasis on relationships rather than a definitive agreement. This stems from a recognition that disputants and their families and communities are likely to continue to share the same resources (e.g. water or routes to a market) over an extended time period. There is thus a sophisticated understanding of the nature of peace and conflict as processes rather than as events. Finally, the peace-building practices often rely on locally derived resources. These may be items with a high material or symbolic value (e.g. green stones in the case of Maoris or cattle in the case of some African pastoralists) or simply items that are close to hand (e.g. leaves from vegetation).[11]

Fundamentally, the principal advantage stemming from traditional and indigenous approaches to peacebuilding lies in its culturally intuitive nature. In theory, such approaches are able to connect with 'cultural memory banks' and conform to popularly held and accepted norms and expectations. They have low start-up costs in that they do not require extensive explanation and the importation of expensive outside expertise or material resources. Instead, their efficacy and legitimacy lies in a near-automatic public understanding and acceptance.

It is worth noting how many of the characteristics of traditional and indigenous peacebuilding listed above (respected local figures, a public dimension, storytelling and an airing of grievances, an emphasis on relationships, and reliance on local resources) differ significantly from peacebuilding as executed by international organisations and INGOs. In reviewing the internationally supported peace processes and post-war reconstruction and reconciliation interventions in the post-Cold War era, it becomes evident that many were top-down processes that involved national elites but ignored local communities, including local elites.[12] Where peacebuilding filtered down to the local level, it was often administered by a newly created peace-support cadre in the Western-funded democracy, 'good' governance, and capacity-building sectors. This cadre often usurped traditional sources of authority and counsel, or co-opted them into liberal peace initiatives through the resources they were able to offer. In other words, the power relations involving local leaders changed: they became agents of the liberal peace – newly empowered by the resources and legitimacy brought to them from outside.

In contrast to the public dimension common in many indigenous and traditional approaches to peacebuilding, internationally sponsored peace processes and peacebuilding exercises can often be characterised by their exclusive character. Peace deals are often made behind closed doors or in locations far removed from the violent conflict.[13] There may be very few avenues through which citizens can voice their opinion. Certainly they will often have very few routes of direct communication with those external actors (regional hegemons, international organisations, international financial institutions, and INGOs) who may hold immense power in shaping the peace accord and any new post-conflict political dispensation. Apparently public aspects of peace processes, such as a referendum on a peace accord or new constitution, are often limiting; restricting citizens to affirming or rejecting a document formulated elsewhere.

The technocratic bias of Western approaches to peacebuilding means that the storytelling and grievance-airing dimensions of peacebuilding often found in indigenous and traditional approaches may be sidelined. Very often, international actors focus on 'striking a deal' and 'moving on'.[14] The peace deal is often highly technical and legalistic and so makes few concessions to the oral traditions through which local communities might discuss and remember. The desire to 'move on' and 'put the past behind us' is especially attractive to many international sponsors of peacebuilding. Technocratic operating procedures that divide peacebuilding into a series of time-limited and target-led programmes and projects mean that many agents of the liberal peace hold an essentially ahistorical world view.[15] In such a culture of external peace imposition, it is easy to dismiss the airing of grievances as 'harking back to the bad old days' and 'failing to move on with the times'. Admittedly, many internationally sponsored peacebuilding operations have constructed forums which allow citizens to narrate their grievances, but externally created 'truth recovery' processes do not always conform to local cultural norms of storytelling. Instead such forums may be heavily influenced by the Western legal tradition and are comprised of transcribed hearings, witnesses supported by lawyers, and a final report: all alien to the culture in which the conflict occurred and the society that is expected to rebuild itself.

The already-mentioned emphasis on securing a peace deal that is evident in many Western-sponsored peace processes can be antithetical to the need for peace processes to stay focused on relationships. Western political culture, seemingly aping corporate culture, emphasises the need for timely, definitive, written deals.[16] Thus, in some cases, a peace deal must be reached by a certain deadline and the aspirations of a community are shoehorned into a legalistic contract or peace accord. The danger is that peace becomes an event rather than a process. The one-off deal is far removed from conceptualisations of peace in which there is a continuing dialogue or understanding between antagonists based on a recognition that they share the same temporal space and will – in all probability – need to rely on each other to manage future conflicts.

Finally, while indigenous and traditional approaches to peacebuilding might rely on local resources, the very nature of externally sponsored peacebuilding means that it introduces external personnel, ideas, and material resources into the post-conflict context. In many cases these external resources may be very worthwhile; for example, a mediator with the energy and skill to facilitate local antagonists to see their situation in a fresh perspective, or the security to allow a minority to return to a particular locality. Yet, the external provision of such resources raises questions of sustainability.

the 'rediscovery' of traditional and indigenous peacebuilding

As the above section shows, Western, technocratic, template-style peacebuilding may differ significantly from indigenous and traditional approaches. There has been a growing academic and policy understanding of the shortcomings of Western approaches to peacemaking. Many actors involved in peace support activities (governments, international organisations, INGOs, and NGOs) have gained more nuanced understandings of the complications of post-war environments.[17] There has been an internalisation in a number of foreign ministries, international organisations, development agencies, and specialist conflict transformation INGOs that post-war reconciliation and reconstruction is often a costly and long-term endeavour. In many cases, peacebuilding interventions have become increasingly complex and comprehensive. Peacebuilding has elided with governance, state building, and development programming and, in the wake of 9/11, with a renewed security imperative.[18] The resulting 'peacebuilding mission creep' has caused many analysts and practitioners to question the utility of some aspects of internationally sponsored peace-support interventions.

Some scholars believe that currently dominant approaches to peacemaking are so fundamentally flawed (and biased in favour of Western sources of power) that a radical revision of the structures and processes of peacemaking and peacebuilding is required.[19] Others take a more timid approach and believe that existing peacebuilding approaches can be salvaged in a modified form.[20] This 'problem-solving' or 'peace-fixing' approach attempts to soften some of the rougher edges of peacebuilding, and over the past decade we have seen the adoption and near-deification of a range of concepts and practices designed to make peacebuilding more acceptable and successful. Thus terms such as 'local ownership', 'participation', and 'sustainability' have gained immense prominence in development and peace-support programming. In a sense, international organisations and INGOs have seized upon these concepts as a rescue package to help stave off the perceived failures of orthodox, Western-supported peace interventions. Crucially, the international peacebuilding agents that regard 'local ownership', 'participation', and 'sustainability' as the saviours of peacebuilding have also identified indigenous and traditional approaches to peacebuilding as a means to promote their peacebuilding agenda.

Advocates of the 'peace-fixing' approach believe that local ownership, participation, and sustainability can all address specific areas of concern associated with orthodox approaches to peacebuilding in the aftermath of civil wars. It was hoped that local ownership of peacebuilding projects could counter criticisms that peace-support operations were the creatures of international agents (or their in-country proxies). A common perception among citizens in post-peace accord societies was that the peace accord and new political dispensation were more popular in international diplomatic capitals than at the on-the-ground level where the most profound effects of the conflict were evident. Certainly, the liberal peace literature makes clear the extent to which external actors often hold power in post-peace accord societies. To the extent that peace could be 'possessed', critics felt that peace was owned elsewhere. International organisations, INGOs, and their in-country proxies (often national elites and local NGOs) sought to counter this perception that peacebuilding was essentially a top-down exercise by stressing the need for the local ownership of peace-support initiatives and institutions.

In relation to participation, many post-peace accord environments and peace-support interventions were criticised for their exclusive character.[21] In many cases, certain actors seemed to have more power and involvement than others. Many of these actors were external, for example, representatives of the international financial institutions or international organisations, who held the keys to resources and in some cases wielded immense power. The European Union's Office of the High Representative in Bosnia-Herzegovina was so empowered that it was likened to a 'European Raj'.[22] More generally, critics in post-war societies often pointed out that a relatively limited number of actors – often national elites with good connections to the international sponsors of the peace – were able to participate in decision-making. This was problematic, since, with a limited number of stakeholders, the community ready to defend peace was likely to be small. Thus international organisations and INGOs have resorted to the language of participation, believing that, through political and economic participation, the pro-peace community in societies emerging from violent conflict can be enlarged. By participating in the building of a peace over which they felt a sense of 'ownership', such internal stakeholders could act as a bulwark against conflict recidivists who might wish to act as spoilers or reignite a civil war.

A key objective of many peace-support interventions by external agents is to stabilise the post-conflict environment in order to hand over control to local agents and expedite the exit of external agents. The reality in many societies emerging from violent conflict has been the growth or continuation of a dependency on external actors. This has been most starkly illustrated in Afghanistan, where President Hamid Karzai's tenure (2002–) could not be sustained by Afghan resources alone. Karzai relied on Western airpower and ground troops to blunt Taliban resurgence, Western bodyguards for his life, and the constant flow of dollars and euros through the government coffers to oil the patronage and clientelist networks that kept him in power. Somewhat paradoxically, given the stated aim of many Western actors to reduce the dependency of post-war societies, many of the structures and processes promoted by international peace-support agents actually increase dependency. For example, many of the financial instruments and practices insisted upon by the International Monetary Fund and World Bank steer post-war economies in particular directions and often prevent the development of indigenous income-generation and export capacity.[23] Many voters and polities in Western societies are acutely sensitive to overseas claims on their budgets and militaries, and so are keen for their governments to promote the idea of sustainability in post-war societies.[24]

Faced with the need to achieve local ownership, participation and sustainability in peace-support operations, a growing number of international organisations, international financial institutions, INGOs, and NGOs have investigated the potential of traditional and indigenous approaches to peacebuilding. In many cases this process has been driven by Western needs rather than conditions on-the-ground in post-war societies or a critical engagement with the opportunities and pitfalls presented by traditional and indigenous approaches to peace. In pragmatic terms, such approaches possess a number of advantages that render them attractive to external peace-support agents.[25] Firstly, they have the potential to achieve local legitimacy; they can be participative, culturally intuitive, and locally based. Secondly, they are often low-cost, since they are often low-tech, are rurally based and need few expensive expatriate personnel. Thirdly, they present a means of passing the responsibility for reconciliation onto local communities and can help absolve external actors of responsibility for failure.

There are multiple examples of external actors promoting traditional and indigenous peacemaking and peacebuilding. In Burundi, UK NGO ActionAid 'has been successfully supporting the rebuilding of the traditional systems of conflict resolution and peacebuilding, the Bashingantahe'.[26] With funding from the UK's Department for International Development, OXFAM has been sponsoring traditional peacebuilding techniques among pastoralist communities in Kenya.[27] The North American-based Mennonite Central Committee has a long history of sponsoring customary dispute resolution among nomadic and semi-nomadic communities in Kenya.[28] For UK-based INGO Practical Action, 'it can be emphatically concluded that customary indigenous governance mechanisms can provide a solid framework for building a community's conflict resilience through strengthening traditional conflict resolution mechanisms, enhancing local people's potential and rediscovering elders' wisdom, knowledge and other resources.'[29] The essential point is that many INGOs (and the international organisations and Western governments that fund them) hold positive views of the potential of indigenous and traditional approaches to peacebuilding to connect with local communities, lower the costs of Western interventions, and produce a better peace.

genetically modifying indigenous and traditional peacebuilding

The last decade has witnessed the 'rediscovery' of indigenous and traditional approaches to dispute resolution by international organisations and INGOs. Many of these techniques were known, to anthropologists at least, but were regarded as being at best quaint or at worst irrelevant given the 'advantages' of more modern and Western approaches to peacebuilding.[30] In an increasing number of cases, international actors have resuscitated traditional and indigenous approaches to peacebuilding. This has often involved encouraging local communities to 'rediscover' or once again use traditional dispute resolution and reconciliation techniques. Often these techniques are modified in order to suit modern Western norms of peacebuilding. So, for example, traditional dispute resolution techniques that were confined to males have – at the behest of Western agents – been made more inclusive and have involved women as active participants. Or techniques that traditionally dealt with local petty cases have been given an extended remit so that they can deal with cases linked to a wider violent political conflict. The result, in some cases, has been the stretching of an original concept to the extent that its traditionalism and indigenousness (the very characteristics that made it so attractive to the external peacebuilding agents in the first place) are compromised. To return to our analogy at the beginning, it is akin to genetically modifying a vegetable in order to preserve or enhance its organic qualities.

The example of the Gacaca, or the community-based courts that have been instituted in the wake of the 1994 Rwandan genocide, is useful in illustrating how the rush to rediscover traditional peacebuilding techniques has – in some cases – been guilty of a romanticisation of the benefits of traditional and indigenous peacebuilding. Given the scale of the genocide (approximately 800,000 people murdered in 100 days), observers can be forgiven for seizing upon 'good news stories' or local initiatives aimed at fostering reconciliation. The Gacaca system, as originally evolved, dealt with local-level or family disputes.[31] The courts operated at the village level, with village elders taking the role of chair and mediator. It was a very simple system that invited disputants to air their grievances publicly and allowed the elders to discuss the case and mediate an outcome, including compensation and/or contrition. The literal meaning of 'Gacaca' is 'grass', referring to a grass location at the centre of the village where the community could gather. In its modern incarnation, the term has resonance because it evokes an attempt to connect with the 'grass' roots of communities. As originally designed, the Gacaca system combined accessibility, localism, simplicity, transparency, cost-effectiveness and timeliness.

In the wake of the genocide, the Gacaca system was revisited in attempts to deal with local-level consequences of the genocide and the need for reconciliation. The attractions of the Gacaca system were enhanced by the fact that the formal judicial system was in disarray and that by 1999 some 120,000 persons had been arrested on genocide-related charges.[32] It was estimated that the formal judicial system would require over a century to work its way through all the cases, and a number of observers voiced concerns about the conditions in which detainees were held and the arbitrary nature of some detentions.[33] In 2001, the Rwandan Government legislated to empower Gacaca courts to deal with genocide-related cases. While a tribunal would deal with elite-level and major perpetrators, it was felt that the Gacaca system would help expedite community-level reconciliation. An 18-month pilot phase, in which the courts were limited to specific localities, was followed by a fine-tuning and extension to the programme nationwide. According to the government, the aims of the Gacaca system were: 'to disclose the truth on the genocide events; to speed up the genocide trials; to eradicate the culture of impunity; to reconcile and strengthen unity among Rwandans; to prove the Rwandan society's capacity to solve its own problems'.[34] President Kagame saw the Gacaca system as a form of restorative justice that could help unite a fractured society: 'If we all rise up and support that gacaca process we will have shown our love for our country and our fellow Rwandans.'[35]

Although the origins and rehabilitation of the Gacaca system lie within Rwanda itself, elements of the international community became strong moral and material supporters of the Gacaca courts. In 1999, for example, the United States spent $3 million to publicise a supposedly indigenous restorative justice system among Rwandans.[36] The European Union has spent €7 million supporting the Gacaca system, the UK's Department for International Development £0.7 million, and the initiative also found favour with UNDP.[37] For a time, the Gacaca system was the darling of the international community; a poster child for local-level restorative justice projects. Yet much of the breathlessly complimentary commentary on the Gacaca system inflated its potential to seal the peace. Amid the romanticisation of the Gacaca methodology, many commentators overlooked the very real problems that attended the system.

Firstly, the resuscitated Gacaca system was not dealing with petty local cases involving disputes over land or grazing. Instead, in their modern incarnation, the courts were an adjunct to a larger process of post-genocide stabilisation and reconciliation. As such, they were caught up in much broader and more complex dynamics connected with the country's emergence from genocide. Secondly, the new Gacaca system was acutely political. It was no longer dealing with village-level petty disputes. Alana Erin Tiemessen referred to the Gacaca system as 'victor's justice', whereby an essentially Tutsi state was able to employ the courts as part of a wider post-genocide statebuilding project. She noted that: 'The nature of "modernised" Gacaca is most dramatically a departure from its indigenous form as it represents a state-imposed model of justice that threatens the community-based principles of restorative justice. The modernised elements of Gacaca serve the interests of a government that can be characterised as a Tutsi ethnocracy.'[38]

This risked compromising the accessibility of the mechanism. No longer was it merely a community-based restorative justice mechanism that was locally based. Instead, it risked becoming 'tainted' by its association with wider national political dynamics. Indeed, given the public nature of the Gacaca courts (whereby judges were elected and members of the public could be prosecutors), there were concerns that some of the trials risked becoming conflict by other means: a means of prosecuting revenge and retribution in a legalised format. There were also concerns that the courts were being used to publicly identify enemies (Hutu or Tutsi) and that retribution would be exacted later and away from the courts.

Thirdly, rather than the courts acting on an ad hoc basis, convening infrequently and only when the need arose, the sheer volume of accused persons in detention meant that the modernised Gacaca process risked becoming an institution rather than a localised norm. It is now possible to speak of a Gacaca 'system', with its trained judges, pilot programme, and pre-trial stages. Fourthly, there have been some criticisms that the state-sponsored reinvigoration of the Gacaca courts will undermine the longer-term statebuilding objective of establishing a transparent and uniform judicial system.[39] While the flexibility of the Gacaca courts is a major advantage in one sense (bringing local accommodations to local problems), in another sense they risk transmitting the message that law enforcement in post-genocide Rwanda will be arbitrary, parochial, and particular to local circumstances.

Fundamentally, the adoption of the Gacaca courts by the central government, and their funding and promotion by external peace-support agents, challenged the very organic qualities that made the Gacaca system so attractive in the first place. By gilding the lily, many of the delicate flower's essential attributes may be lost.

concluding discussion

It is argued here that the adoption or sponsorship of indigenous and traditional peacebuilding by international organisations and INGOs has often been the result of an uncritical interpretation of the potential of localised peacebuilding. Aware of the limitations and costs of their own top-down activities, many international organisations and INGOs saw traditional and indigenous approaches to peacebuilding as a quick fix: a remedy that would lower their own costs and meet donor requirements of localism, inclusiveness, and local participation. There was, of course, a gaping contradiction in this donor stance: their support of local and indigenous approaches to peacebuilding stood in contrast to the donor priorities of transparency and accountability.[40] Across a number of post-conflict environments, international donors were sponsoring a series of technocratic interventions designed to enhance and standardise administrative capability, while at the same time many of these very same donors were sponsoring indigenous and traditional dispute resolution techniques that failed the transparency and accountability tests. To a certain extent this was a function of the sprawling nature of the liberal peace, or Western-sponsored peace-support interventions. A mix of the franchising of peacebuilding to multiple INGOs and NGOs and the target-driven peace programme culture meant that few (if any) actors had a strategic view of peacebuilding in any one location. The result was that peacebuilding contradictions could easily develop in post-conflict environments.

A more thorough analysis of the advantages and disadvantages of indigenous and traditional approaches to peacebuilding may have resulted in a more realistic assessment of their capabilities. Certainly the advantages of local participation, cultural sensitivity, and accessibility are very considerable indeed. Yet, there are also significant drawbacks that demand attention and thus a more circumspect evaluation of these forms of peacebuilding. Firstly, and as the term suggests, many traditional approaches to peacebuilding are essentially conservative. They are designed to reinforce the existing power hierarchy (usually a patriarchy) and uphold the legitimacy of existing norms and practices. Although the label 'participatory' is often attached to traditional and indigenous practices, it is important to note that traditional practices usually privilege the participation of some (elders, warriors, men, members of particular kin groups) more than others (women, non-combatants, minorities).

A second criticism of traditional and indigenous approaches to peacebuilding that was often overlooked by the breathless rush to embrace this 'new' way to build peace was that the sociocultural support structures upon which traditional and indigenous practices depended had often irrevocably broken down. Many of the ethno-national civil wars in the post-Cold War period were so destructive that traditional social structures were unsustainable.[41] Rural–urban migration, the collapse of agricultural economies, the flight of young men to militias, the monetisation of exchanges, and the flood of small arms all helped change the nature of power relations in many societies. Importantly, they also helped change the perception of power relations. Traditional sources of authority and respect may have found their legitimacy eroded (if not obliterated), and so attempts to reconstitute 'traditional' and 'indigenous' processes faced a struggle. In blunt terms, one of the reasons why a number of societies have descended into civil war has been the failure of traditional and indigenous dispute resolution methods to contain the war causation factors. Attempts by international organisations and INGOs to recreate traditional dispute resolution methodologies may be well-meaning, but may also rest on a fundamental misreading of the social changes that have occurred in the society as the result of civil war.

A third critical point is that many indigenous approaches to dispute resolution are deeply violent. Much of this is a result of the already-mentioned breakdown of social structures, and it reminds us of the need to be cautious in embracing all things 'indigenous' and 'traditional'. Contemporary accounts of community responses to crime and violence in a number of Central American and African locations emphasise the power of vigilantes, mobs and lynching.[42] Megan Plyler notes how vigilantism is a popular response to theft in parts of Tanzania and is implicitly legitimised by the state, while the UN reported over 400 cases of lynching in Guatemala in the 1996–2002 period.[43] María Cristina Fernández García notes how, before the Guatemalan civil war, 'communities relied on traditional formulas handed down from generation to generation to solve conflict … After the war it was not possible to rebuild the traditional justice system, as the fabric of society had been irreparably torn. Nor has the official system of justice been able to fill this vacuum.'[44] Civil war had helped brutalise society and rendered certain forms of social violence more acceptable.

A final criticism relates to the enthusiasm with which some international organisations and INGOs have embraced indigenous and traditional approaches to peacebuilding. Specifically, the nature of indigenous and traditional approaches (often small-scale and localised) means that they are unable to challenge the structures of peacemaking and peacebuilding, which are often controlled by international and national elites. Thus they may be able to alter local-level events and attitudes, but they are unable to engage, in an effective manner, with the meta-level processes that often define the post-conflict environment.

None of the above should be interpreted as a universal scepticism of all things indigenous and traditional. It is simply a plea that all peacebuilding techniques should be judged according to their efficacy. Both Western-style peacebuilding and indigenous and traditional techniques hold advantages in certain circumstances. In reality, most post-civil war societies are home to a hybrid of peacebuilding and conflict-avoidance methodologies that draw on both Western and local techniques. The precise nature of the mix will differ from context to context. A key issue, though, is who determines the mix. The nature of many peace-support interventions is that Western actors (and their local proxies in the form of national elites) hold the power and resources that allow them to determine the mix. As a result, traditional and indigenous techniques often operate on the margins: in rural and inaccessible areas or with regard to issues that the liberal peace has difficulty dealing with. One such issue relates to the affective dimension of peacebuilding. Peace, like war, is human. As such, it is invested with emotion: hatred, revenge, empathy, love, loss, solidarity and many other feelings have a role to play. Technocratic peacebuilding that is shoehorned into pre-packed peace projects and programmes is often unable to connect with this affective dimension of the transition from war to peace. Its attempts to deal with such emotions often reveal its ethnocentric bias; for example, through recommending Western notions of therapy and medicalised 'trauma care' to 'victims' in conflict zones. Perhaps the greatest advantage of traditional and indigenous approaches to peacebuilding is that they are able to connect more deeply (and less artificially) with the affective needs and expectations of populations. This is especially the case in terms of 'reconciliation' or developing a widely shared understanding that communities are going to have to continue to share a territory and resources and must strive to find an accommodation that will facilitate that sharing. This is not an easy task, but it requires more subtlety than that mustered by many Western-style peace interventions.

To return to the opening analogy of organic fruit and vegetables, a leading peacebuilding practitioner, John Paul Lederach, has used the metaphor of cultivation in relation to peacebuilding.[45] For Lederach, peace is not about the harvest, or the moment when the fruit and vegetables are ripe. Instead, he notes,

> Over the past two decades, my efforts at peacebuilding and conciliation have led me to the metaphor of cultivator more than harvesters, towards nourishment of soil and plant more than picking the fruit. The images that accompany this metaphor suggest an organic connection to context, the building of relationships, and a commitment to process over time.[46]

We live in an era of regime change by B-52 (as was the case in Afghanistan) and time-limited peace interventions where Western publics suffer from peace fatigue. Western template-style peacebuilding has increasingly objectified peacebuilding into packages (programmes and projects) aimed at producing 'deliverables' or defined outcomes. In many cases, Western 'peace engineers' assume that they have privileged peacebuilding knowledge and take the lead. Yet what Lederach and other prescient practitioners note is the need for patience and a recognition of the importance of local actors and perceptions of peace:

> Cultivation is recognizing that ultimately the change process must be taken up, embraced and sustained by people...The cultivator [external mediator], as a connected but outside element in the system, approaches this soil with a great deal of respect, the suspension of quick judgement in favour of wisdom of adaptation, and an orientation towards supporting the change process through highs and lows, ebbs and flows of violence and thawing of tensions, whether or not the situation appears ripe. The cultivator gives attention to the well-being of the eco-system not just the quick production of a given fruit.[47]

Traditional and indigenous peacebuilding and dispute resolution techniques have enormous potential to help fulfil this cultivation process. But local, national, and international peacebuilders need to be circumspect in their adoption of all peacebuilding techniques (modern or traditional) and subject them to rigorous scrutiny. International peacebuilders might also benefit from considerably more restraint before intervention. Western peacebuilding interventions, although often well-intentioned, may distort local dynamics or stymie local initiatives. As with organic gardening, sometimes less is more.

notes

1. J. Humphrys, *The Great Food Gamble,* London: Coronet Books, 2002.
2. See, for example, J. Chapman, 'The obesity time-bomb', *Daily Mail,* 18 February 2002; B. Marsh and D. Harrison, 'Childhood obesity time bomb explodes', *Daily Telegraph,* 25 February 2006; 'OFT in new supermarket crackdown', BBC News Online, 28 April 2008 or J. Blythman, *Shopped: The Shocking Power of British Supermarkets,* London: Fourth Estate, 2004.
3. Soil Association, *Organic Market Report 2007 – Executive Summary,* p. 1, http://www.soilassociation.org/web/sa/saweb.nsf/89d058cc4dbeb16d80256a73005a2866/efd75fcb51d9029c8025734800579da9/$FILE/Executive%20summary.pdf, accessed on 9 May 2008.
4. A. Simpson, 'Growing trend cuts the size of allotments', *Daily Telegraph,* 14 August 2007.

5. BBC, 'Dig the new gardening', BBC News Online, 24 May 2000, http://news.bbc.co.uk/2/hi/uk_news/761834.stm, accessed on 9 May 2008.
6. F. Lawrence, 'Sales of organic produce up 30% in year', *Guardian*, 2 September 2006.
7. J. Blythman, 'Food miles: The true cost of putting imported food on your plate', *Independent*, 31 May 2007.
8. T. Branigan, 'Government acts to boost organic food', *Guardian*, 30 July 2002.
9. R. Mac Ginty, 'Indigenous Peace-Making Versus the Liberal Peace', *Cooperation and Conflict*, Vol. 43, No. 2, 2008, pp. 139–63.
10. Explanation of specific contemporary and historical indigenous and traditional approaches to peacebuilding and dispute resolution can be found in: A. Al-Krenawi and J. Graham, 'Conflict Resolution through a Traditional Ritual among the Bedouin Arabs of the Negev', *Ethnology*, Vol. 38, No. 2, 1999, pp. 163–74; J. Briggs, 'Conflict Management in a Modern Inuit Community', in P. Schweitzer, M. Biesele and R. Hitchcock (eds) *Hunters and Gatherers in the Modern World*, New York: Berghahn Books, 2000, pp. 110–24; F. Hela, *Tradition and Good Governance*, Research School of Pacific and Asian Studies, ANU Discussion Paper, Vol. 97, No. 3, 1997.
11. A. Vayda, *War in Ecological Perspective: Persistence, Change and Adaptive Processes in Three Oceanic Societies*, New York: Plenum Press, 1976.
12. Discussion of the top-down nature of many contemporary peacebuilding and peace-support interventions can be found in D. Chandler, *Bosnia: Faking Democracy after Dayton*, London: Pluto, 2000; J. Darby and R. Mac Ginty, 'Introduction: What Peace? What Process?' in J. Darby and R. Mac Ginty (eds) *Contemporary Peacemaking: Violence, Peace Processes and Post-War Reconstruction*, Basingstoke; New York: Palgrave Macmillan, 2008, pp. 1–8; R. Mac Ginty, *No War, No Peace: The Rejuvenation of Stalled Peace Processes and Peace Accords*, Basingstoke; New York: Palgrave Macmillan, 2006.
13. See the role of secrecy in peacemaking in J. Egeland, 'The Oslo Accord: Multiparty Facilitation through the Norwegian Channel', in C. Crocker, F.O. Hampson and P. Aall (eds) *Herding Cats: Multiparty Mediation in a Complex World*, Washington, DC: United States Institute of Peace Press, 1999, pp. 529–48.
14. This is reflected in some academic studies of peace processes that tend to concentrate on negotiations and deal-making without considering the quality of any resulting deal or peace.
15. This ahistoricism is made clear in T. Jacoby, 'Hegemony, Modernisation and Post-War Reconstruction', *Global Society*, Vol. 21, No. 4, 2007, pp. 521–37.
16. Mac Ginty, 'Indigenous Peace-Making'.
17. Large numbers of 'lessons learned' publications have been produced, including: A. Galama and P. van Tongeren (eds), *Towards Better Peacebuilding Practice: On Lessons Learned, Evaluation Practices and Aid and Conflict*, Utrecht: European Centre for Conflict Prevention, 2002, or J. Goodhand and H. Atmar, *Aid, Conflict and Peacebuilding in Afghanistan: What Lessons Can be Learned?*, London: International Alert, 2002. Institutionally, the establishment of the UN's Peacebuilding Commission is also significant.

18. C.L. Sriram, *Peace as Governance: Power-Sharing, Armed Groups and Contemporary Peace Negotiations*, Basingstoke; New York: Palgrave Macmillan, 2008. Mark Duffield's work is particularly good on the securitisation of development and peacebuilding in the wake of 9/11. See, for example, M. Duffield, *Development, Security and Unending War: Governing the World of Peoples*, Cambridge: Polity Press, 2007.

19. Much of this 'critical peace studies' literature is European in origin and uses the concept of 'the liberal peace' to capture the interrelated and exploitive aspects of peacemaking dominated by leading Western states, international organisations, and international financial organisations. Examples include: N. Cooper, 'On the Crisis in the Liberal Peace', *Conflict, Security and Development*, Vol. 7, No. 4, 2007, pp. 605–15; R. Mac Ginty, *No War, No Peace*; M. Pugh, 'The Political Economy of Peacebuilding: A Critical Theory Perspective', *International Journal of Peace Studies*, Vol. 10, No. 2, 2005, pp. 23–42; O. Richmond and J. Franks, 'Liberal Hubris? Virtual Peace in Cambodia', *Security Dialogue*, Vol. 38, No. 1, 2007, pp. 27–48; O. Richmond, *The Transformation of Peace*, Basingstoke; New York: Palgrave Macmillan, 2005.

20. The 'problem-solving approach' is most prominent in the reports of INGOs who are seeking to modify their practice. Academic advocates might include R. Paris, *At War's End: Building Peace after Civil Conflict*, Cambridge: Cambridge University Press, 2004, and much of the work emerging from the United States Institute of Peace.

21. There is a good literature on issues of participation, some of it critical. See, for example, J. Chopra and T. Hohe, 'Participatory intervention', *Global Governance*, Vol.10, No. 3, 2004, pp. 289–304; W. Cooke and U. Kothari (eds), *Participation: The New Tyranny?*, London: Zed Books, 2004.

22. G. Knaus and F. Martin, 'Lessons from Bosnia and Herzegovina: Travails of the European Raj', *Journal of Democracy*, Vol. 14, No. 3, 2003, pp. 60–74. See also D. Chandler, 'Introduction: Peace Without Politics?' in D. Chandler (ed.) *Peace Without Politics? Ten Years of International State-Building in Bosnia*, London: Routledge, 2006, pp. 1–15.

23. These issues are discussed in R. Brynen, *A Very Political Economy: Peacebuilding and Aid in West Bank and Gaza*, Washington, DC: United States Institute of Peace Process, 2000.

24. In 1994, for example, the United States Institute of Peace noted how 'A mood of "Afro-pessimism" and "peace fatigue" has prevailed' in the United States following loss of life among US troops in Somalia and the failure of a number of peace initatives. USIP, 'The US contribution to conflict prevention, management and resolution in Africa', USIP Special Report 11 (December 1994), http://www.usip.org/resources/us-contribution-conflict-prevention-management-and-resolution-africa, accessed on 17 October 2009.

25. An interesting academic defence of traditional peacebuilding approaches can be found in S.P. Stobbe, 'Role of traditional conflict resolution processes in peacebuilding in Laos', paper presented to the International Studies Association annual convention, San Francisco, April 2008.

26. ActionAid, 'Traditional peace building in Burundi', ActionAid website, undated media release, http://www.actionaid.org.uk/1338/peace_building_in_burundi.html, accessed 7 May 2008.

27. OXFAM, OXFAM GB-Funded Peacebuilding Initiatives in the Arid Districts of Kenya: Lessons and challenges (March 2003), http://www.oxfam.org.uk/resources/learning/pastoralism/downloads/peacebuildingkenyafinal2004.pdf, accessed 7 May 2008.

28. J. Mbaria, 'Kenya: Peace by local means', *The East African*, 5 May 2008, accessed at http://allafrica.com/stories/200805050106.html, accessed on 9 May 2008.

29. B. Rabar and M. Karimi, *Indigenous Democracy: Traditional Conflict Resolution Mechanisms*, Nairobi: Intermediate Technology Development Group, 2003, p. 93.

30. A summary of anthropological literature on indigenous war and peacemaking can be found in Mac Ginty, *No War, No Peace*.

31. For accounts of the Gacaca courts see: W. Schabas, 'Genocide trials and Gacaca courts', *Journal of International Criminal Justice*, Vol. 3, No. 4, 2005, pp. 879–95; J. Fierens, 'Gacaca Courts: Between Fantasy and Reality', *Journal of International Criminal Justice*, Vol. 3, No. 4, 2005, pp. 896–919.

32. See Rwandan government presentation 'Gacaca Jurisdictions: Achievements, problems and future prospects', http://www.inkiko-gacaca.gov.rw/PPT/Realisation%20and%20future%20persective.ppt#284,1, accessed 8 May 2008.

33. Ibid. and Amnesty International, 'Rwanda, Gacaca – a question of justice', Amnesty International, 17 December 2002, http://www.amnesty.org/en/library/info/AFR47/007/2002, accessed on 17 October 2009.

34. Rwandan government presentation 'Gacaca Jurisdictions'.

35. BBC, 'Rwanda tests genocide courts', BBC News Online, 19 June 2002, http://news.bbc.co.uk/1/hi/world/africa/2053508.stm, accessed 8 May 2008.

36. Human Rights Watch, 'Rwanda: Human Rights Developments', Human Rights Watch, undated, http://www.hrw.org/wr2k/Africa-08.htm, accessed 8 May 2008.

37. UNPO, 'Batwa: European Union gives support to Gacaca tribunals', 12 April 2005, http://www.unpo.org/content/view/2313/236/, accessed 8 May 2008; DFID, 'Evaluation of DFID Country Programmes – Country Report: Rwanda 2000–2005', January 2006, http://www.dfid.gov.uk/Documents/publications/evaluation/ev660-summary.pdf, accessed on 17 October 2009; UNDP, 'Good Governance for Poverty Reduction Phase II – Support for Capacity Building to Ministry of Justice, Supreme Court, and Gacaca Jurisdictions', http://www.undp.org.rw/hiv_aids_project2.html, accessed 8 May 2008.

38. A.E. Tiemessen, 'After Arusha: Gacaca Justice in Post-Genocide Rwanda', *African Studies Quarterly*, Vol. 8, No. 1, 2004, p. 64.

39. S. Ilesanmi, 'So that peace may reign: A study of Just Peacemaking experiments in Africa', *Journal of the Society of Christian Ethics*, Vol. 23, 2002, pp. 213–26.

40. R. Fanthorpe, 'On the limits of the liberal peace: Chiefs and democratic centralisation in post-war Sierra Leone', *African Affairs*, Vol. 105, No. 415, 2005, pp. 27–49.

41. David Keen provides a particularly good account of the nature of modern warfare in *Complex Emergencies*, Cambridge: Polity Press, 2008.

42. See, for example, S. Jensen, 'Security and Violence on the Frontier of the
    State: Vigilant citizens in Nkmoanzi, South Africa', in P. Ahluwalia, L.
    Bethlehem and R. Ginio (eds), *Violence and Non-Violence in Africa*, London:
    Routledge, 2007, pp. 105–23.
43. M.G. Plyler, ' "Keeping the Peace": Violent Justice, Crime, and Vigilantism
    in Tanzania', in P. Ahluwalia, L. Bethlehem and R. Ginio (eds), *Violence
    and Non-Violence in Africa*, pp. 124–40; T. Mansel, 'Mob justice in rural
    Guatemala', BBC News Online, 15 August 2005, http://news.bbc.co.uk/1/hi/
    world/americas/4152632.stm, accessed 9 May 2008.
44. M.C. Fernández García, *Lynching in Guatemala: Legacy of War and Impunity*,
    Harvard University: Weatherhead Center for International Affairs, June
    2004, http://www.wcfia.harvard.edu/fellows/papers/2003–04/fernandez.
    pdf, accessed 9 May 2008.
45. There is an interesting debate on the merits and complementary poten-
    tial of 'ripeness' and 'cultivation' in peacebuilding in I.W. Zartman, 'The
    timing of peace initiatives: Hurting stalemates and ripe moments', and J.P.
    Lederach, 'Cultivating Peace: A Practitioner's View of Deadly Conflict and
    Negotiation', both in Darby and Mac Ginty (eds), 'Introduction', pp. 22–35,
    36–44.
46. Ibid., p. 41.
47. Ibid.

19

kindered peacebuilding: liberalism and beyond

alison m.s. watson

There are more resources now devoted to the pursuit of peace than at any time in the history of the international system. The participating cast of actors – international, regional, state, and non-state – seek to create a peace that is essentially Kantian in spirit, and thus heavily dependent upon the maintenance of an international liberal order through international governmental organisations, such as the United Nations. The resultant peacebuilding strategies are then often justified in terms of the promotion of human rights, democratisation, and 'human security' – concepts that together form the cornerstone of what has come to be termed the 'liberal peace'. Evidence increasingly suggests, however, that the mechanisms used to achieve such a peace typically fail to secure a *sustainable* peace, and in particular that they may not adequately take into account those actors whose claims for peace may prove especially intransigent – such as those with ethnic and identity claims, and those, ironically, for whom the achievement of human security is particularly pertinent.

This impasse encourages an emerging critique regarding the ability of the dominant actors in the prevailing liberal peace approach: first, to adapt to the wide diversity of actors currently making claims for rights; and second, and related to this, to listen to those whose generational, racial, sexual, and even moral language may differ from their own. This is not to say that the aims of the liberal peace are not appropriate. Indeed, the establishment of democratic institutions and an accompanying rule of law is crucial to the promotion of human rights – including children's rights – in any post-conflict environment. However, the liberal peace framework fails to live up to its lofty principles because, despite rhetoric to the contrary, it remains rooted in an institutional rather than 'human' prescription.

The place of children in this morass is particularly pertinent.[1] Arguably, children as a group are among those most affected by contemporary models of conflict. The plight of children, however, is little discussed when it comes to agreeing on the minutiae of a peace proposal, despite the fact that children are widely recognised – even from within the institutions of the liberal peace itself – as significant to the sustainability of peace. Yet, rather than concentrating upon this specific group as a potential conduit for long-term conflict resolution, those attempting to secure peace tend to assume that a programme of post-conflict recovery requires only the redressing of general systemic wrongs that will eventually 'trickle down' to benefit youth along with the rest of the population.

As a result, most approaches to building peace marginalise issues surrounding children: they are little discussed in peacebuilding policies, seldom asked to participate in peacebuilding projects, and peacebuilding strategies are rarely informed by knowledge regarding either their wartime experiences or their post-conflict needs. Yet, given that they are disproportionately affected by conflict, children should be placed centre stage, not only as a motivation for a sustainable settlement, but as actors for peace themselves. Not doing so undermines the potential for successful settlement over the long term and indeed the liberal peace agenda itself. With this in mind, this essay argues for a 'kindering' of peace, such that children are recognised as one of the 'fault-lines of the human condition', which Johan Galtung has argued are so critical to debates regarding the nature of peace.

children and conflict, children and peace

The advent of so-called 'new wars', in which the victims are overwhelmingly civilian, has increased child casualties such that a significant number of all those now killed in conflict are under 18. Children are affected by conflict in a variety of ways. Sometimes they become victims simply because they are in the wrong place at the wrong time, but children may also be deliberately targeted, either because they are representative of the continuity of a particular ethnic and/or religious identity or because they have taken part in hostilities and are thus viewed as justifiable objects of attack. In the aftermath of war, children are the group most likely to suffer the long-term consequences of, among other things, inadequate health care and insufficient access to education. They are also affected by the loss of family members or friends and by forced dislocation. Estimates suggest that there are today some nine million children who have had to leave their homes as a result of war and are currently living either as refugees or as internally displaced persons.[2]

Children may also, of course, be soldiers themselves. According to the most common estimates there are currently around 300,000 children taking part in some 30 conflicts worldwide, although this number can fluctuate. While the phenomenon of 'child soldiers' is not new, an increase in the proliferation of small arms has undoubtedly expanded their numbers. Further, children often play a variety of other roles that amount to logistical support for the war process. These roles could include ferrying supplies, delivering messages, and providing domestic and sexual services. Finally, children may also, more generally, form part of a war effort within a given society, such as when the United States and the United Kingdom called on children during the Second World War to tend victory gardens and to support other domestic elements of the war effort.

Despite this variety of roles that children play, our perceptions of conflict – and indeed of international politics more widely – consign children to a mere footnote, leaving them without sufficient attention or representation in formulations of peace. Certainly, policymakers talk a great deal about creating peace in children's name. For example, Tony Blair, at the climax of his remarks on the declaration made a year after the Good Friday Agreement in Northern Ireland, spoke of 'offering the children...the future they deserve, which is now coming within their grasp'. But the only mention of children in the text of the agreement is in its recognition that 'young people from areas affected by the troubles face particular difficulties' and its promise to 'support the development of special community-based initiatives based on international best practice'.

Equally telling is the omission of any mention of the child, children, youth, or young people in some of the most crucial negotiations between Israel and Palestine. In the statements made at the signing ceremony for the 1998 Wye River talks, US President Bill Clinton, Vice President Al Gore, Israeli Prime Minister Benjamin Netanyahu, PLO Chairman Yasser Arafat, and King Hussein of Jordan all referred to children as a reason for peace. However, in the actual text of the Wye River Memorandum there was no mention of children whatsoever. In fact, no peace treaty has officially considered specific children's rights issues as they relate to a particular conflict. Partly this is a result of ignorance: policymakers often do not realise the extent of the conflict's impact upon children. Partly, too, it stems from the fact that the parties to treaties seldom consider the knowledge and advice of those who advocate on behalf of children, such as non-governmental organisations (NGOs). Rather, NGOs are expected to support already agreed post-conflict strategies.

The exclusion of children from the peace agreement process is also related to the fact that children are easily conceptualised as victims, but very much marginalised as agents. The common view that children lack agency, however, is not necessarily accurate – as has been recognised in other social science discourses. In reality, children may be able to take an active role in creating peace and in ensuring its sustainability. Take, for example, the case of the Children's Peace Movement in Colombia. By the mid-1990s a series of peace negotiations had begun, spearheaded by a Conciliation Commission that was made up of prominent civic and religious leaders. Although, as a civil society effort, it was much more successful than anything that the government had managed to achieve, the Colombian peace movement as a whole remained weak and fragmented – until the creation of the Children's Movement for Peace. Beginning with a number of young people working in isolation, the movement evolved, without a formal structure, into a significant social force whose contributions to the peace process were recognised in its nomination for a Nobel Peace Prize.

Children can, of course, also disrupt peace if inadequate attention is given to their needs. Peace agreements represent only the beginning of the post-conflict process. The solutions to some of the most pressing and long-term issues that post-conflict societies face depend crucially on children and young populations. Those children who have actively taken part in hostilities, for example, must, in the aftermath of war, be reintegrated into their home communities. What, however, is their status? They may be children under international law, but they may be criminals, too. Like any other soldier, they face the societal impact of reintegration; but, whereas most post-conflict policies provide demobilised adult soldiers with a package of benefits designed to aid such integration, there is no such clear-cut policy for child soldiers, and particularly not for older children. For example, former combatants in Sierra Leone do not receive adequate funding for their reintegration, something that was recognised by Kofi Annan in his report prior to Resolution 1389 on the UN Mission in Sierra Leone (UNAMSIL). In some instances, job creation may simply not be a priority for either donors or the presiding government.

Children are also at a disadvantage in terms of land rights in post-conflict societies – a significant issue for those children returning to their homes who find themselves orphaned and perhaps the heads of households. This has been a particular issue in Rwanda, where orphans have been an important class of land claimant and disputant. In general, national legal systems are not yet able to cope with children making such claims, and the result is even more children without a sustainable economic future, something that itself can threaten an already fragile peace. As one recent World Bank study has noted, there is 'robust support for the hypothesis that youth bulges increase the risk of domestic armed conflict, and especially so under conditions of economic stagnation ... [This is] bad news for regions that currently exhibit both features, often in coexistence with intermediary and unstable political regimes, in particular Sub-Saharan Africa and the Arab World'.[3] In Kosovo young people (between the ages of 15 and 20) were identified as the greatest potential source of civil unrest. A report by the Women's Commission for Refugee Women and Children argues that young people should be viewed as critical to the foundation of development and a sustainable peace in Kosovo, although in actuality they were denied a place in reconstruction efforts.[4]

a life beyond childhood

The current liberal peace approach puts in place a set of norms when negotiating settlement and its aftermath that are very much dependent upon states, NGOs, and international organisations for their realisation. These include the encouragement of a democratic political system and the rule of law alongside a liberal market system as a means of achieving economic development. These are very much 'top-down' approaches, however; they require that the necessary institutions and mechanisms are already in place to ensure that such norms can be achieved. Arguably, a more comprehensive solution would encourage the promotion of human rights and human security by fully taking into account grass-roots concerns. Recognising children as agents in their own right would thus become inherent to a successful strategy of conflict resolution, where the root causes of conflict are addressed, all aspects of human security are taken into consideration, and the process of negotiation becomes an inclusive one. The question remains, however, as to how this might occur, and in this there are some fundamental difficulties.

We could, for example, argue for far more representation of the interests of children when concluding the terms of peaceful settlement.
This could take place in a couple of obvious ways. NGOs advocating
for children could consistently be asked their views at the time of the
negotiations towards peaceful settlement, rather than it being assumed
that their role is important only as administrators of the welfare programmes that are instituted in post-conflict zones. This would require
policymakers to consider the effect of the settlement upon children's
lives, rather than treating it simply as an afterthought. In addition, children themselves could be consulted regarding the nature of the peace,
and of their requirements in it. One problem with involving children
in decision-making processes, however, is in the framing of the boundary between childhood and adulthood. The question of children's
agency has become a significant site of negotiation between those who
interpret children as fully competent social actors, able to make legitimate claims for the realisation of their rights, and those who interpret children as 'still developing' social actors for whom rights claims
can only be realised by adult actors on their behalf. Onora O'Neill has
even questioned the use of the language of rights when approaching
ethical issues as they relate to the child, arguing that a focus on obligations may be more relevant. Because children are dependent (unlike
other 'oppressed social groups' in a plea for rights) and vulnerable, she
argues that the focus should change from the rights of children to the
obligations that adults have to them. This is not an uncommon view;
indeed, it characterises much of the language of those measures that
have been designed to address the 'rights' of the child within the international system, such as the UN Convention of the Rights of the Child
(UNCRC). Nevertheless, O'Neill concedes that the boundary between
childhood and adulthood is blurry. The variety of experiences that
children under the age of 18 may have means that some children, notably those O'Neill terms 'mature minors', may find themselves as a
group in a position partly analogous to that of other oppressed social
groups.

Childhood, as much as it is a social construct, presents conceptual and practical challenges for policymakers attempting to negotiate a sustainable settlement. The experiences of children affected by
conflict do not constitute the ideal that appears to be fundamental
to the Western liberal model. These are not children who have been
under parental behest until the age of 18, who have had the chance to
play, to develop a network of friends, to feel safe within a secure local

environment, to plan for their education. These are children who may have been heads of their households from the age of 12, who may have had to journey far to achieve their version of safety, who may have been forced to take part in the worst forms of child labour to secure some sort of income, and who may have had to kill as a way to survive. Giving them back an ideal childhood is not an option, and so they cannot be treated as if they will revert to being children once peace has been achieved. Rather, children should be seen in the aftermath of war as actors whose opinions are necessary when deciding upon how the reconstruction of the post-conflict society is going to take place, especially over the long term. Moreover, in many societies children are charged with significant roles at a local level. They may be home-makers, landowners, breadwinners, and peace brokers. Yet, similarly to other marginalised groups, their specific interests are not represented at the international level. Moving away from the bias of the 'powerful' towards a consideration of the 'knowledgeable' may thus lead to a more rounded consideration of standard security discourses.

Consider the variety of Disarmament, Demobilisation, and Reintegration (DDR) programmes for child soldiers that are in exist-ence in Africa. In Uganda, for example, former members of the Lord's Resistance Army are sent to a reintegration centre for an average of three to six weeks before they are reunited with their families. They may then receive follow-up visits within the community, which monitor their progress. Such efforts are laudable, and necessary, but they need to be carefully examined as to their efficacy. The UN Department of Peacekeeping Operations noted in a 1999 report that what was required for the success of DDR programmes was for chil-dren to be consulted at various stages of the process;[5] the same argu-ments apply for children involved in conflict more generally. They too should be consulted as a source of knowledge – whether cultural or generational – that would be of use in a post-conflict setting. Instead, however, the marginalisation of children in government policy in post-conflict zones around the world results in inadequate care and, in turn, an increased likelihood of social breakdown and, possibly, the resumption of conflict.

Ignoring the specific needs of children when attempting to build peace actually flies in the face of the liberal peacebuilding agenda. The point is not to change the wording of a peace settlement so that 'and children' can be inserted at the relevant points, but rather to under-stand that ignoring children makes it impossible to address crucial elements of conflict resolution. This chapter has already mentioned the centrality of the notion of human rights to the liberal peace discourse; it must be seen, too, that children are central to contemporary conceptions of human rights. The UNCRC – adopted in 1989 and since ratified by almost every country in the world (apart from the United States and Somalia) – is the most widely accepted international rights document in history. This should place children centre stage in the quest for the universal application of human rights, and as such at the heart of the liberal peace project itself. Peace negotiations should not be reserved to those who can speak in the language of the 'liberal club'. They should be open to those who can provide an alternative – and potentially more fruitful – narrative.

The question remains, of course, of what this narrative might potentially include – and for this there are a few immediate answers. First of all, it would have to include an examination of children as complete, as opposed to partial, political actors. Currently there is a temptation to think of children as only being relevant when policies that appear to directly affect them are discussed. Thus they are confined to discussions of issues of education, child health and, when things go wrong, youth crime. Yet to create a stable political regime requires all actors to feel enfranchised by the political environment, and continually allowing children to speak only when they are spoken to does nothing to help in the creation of vibrant democracies – the current problems with youth and political engagement in Western liberal democracies are testament to this. Second, there must be the realisation that the liberal call for an active civil society actually requires liberal policymakers to put their money where their mouths are and give civil society groups real political clout. Only by separating such groups from the political, and allowing them to fully use the knowledge and abilities that they have, will they be able to have the impact that their existence appears to so clearly promise. Third, the dominant policy discourse appears to favour the dominant academic discourse – policymakers thus largely use the expertise of those who tell them what they want to hear. This is in many ways understandable, because to do otherwise entails a sometimes radical shift in the political agenda, and does not offer the short-term solutions that political expediency so clearly requires. Yet continuing to plough in the same furrow means that there is no hope of political change, and within that too no real hope of a long-term and sustainable peace. It also begs the question of whether the current policy regime actually is designed for peace, or whether there is more to gain from the maintenance of uncertainty regarding a return to violence. The ideal for any post-conflict situation should be a return to normality and the withdrawal of peacekeepers and the industry that surrounds them. Yet arguably, in the same way that rebel groups may benefit – economically and otherwise – from the continued threat of violence, the peace industry and those who are connected to it – state and non-state actors, governmental and NGOs, private firms and individuals – may also have a vested interest in the maintenance of a peace that is uncertain, that is requiring of their continued service, and therefore marginalising of those actors and issues that are not directly implicated in its resolution. Only by examining the significance of such vested interests, and exploring how they may be overcome, will there ever really be a notion of a long-term peace – one that is sustainable for our children, and for our children's children.

notes

This chapter draws very heavily on the article: 'Can There Be A "Kindered" Peace?', previously published in *Ethics and International Affairs*, Vol. 22, No. 1, Spring 2008. The author would like to thank Oliver Richmond, Chandra Lekha Sriram, and Zornitsa Stoyanova for their comments at various times during the writing process. All errors remain the author's own.

1. The UN Convention on the Rights of the Child defines as a child everyone under the age of 18.
2. UNHCR, 'What is a Refugee?'
3. H. Urdal, 'The Devil in the Demographics: The Effect of Youth Bulges on Domestic Armed Conflict, 1950–2000', *World Bank Social Development Paper*, No. 14, 2004.
4. Women's Commission for Refugee Women and Children, 'Making the Choice for a Better Life: Promoting the Protection and Capacity of Kosovo's Youth', January 2001.
5. United Nations Department of Peacekeeping Operations, 'Disarmament, Demobilization and Reintegration of Ex-Combatants in a Peacekeeping Environment: Principles and Guidelines', December 1999.

20

art and peacebuilding: how theatre transforms conflict in Sri Lanka

nilanjana premaratna and roland bleiker

Building peace in societies torn apart by violence is a long, frustrating, and extremely difficult process. From the Middle East to Afghanistan, from Somalia to East Timor, years and often decades of conflict have left societies deeply divided and traumatised. New forms of violence constantly emerge, generating yet more hatred. Commentators speak of so-called intractable conflicts: situations where antagonisms have persisted for so long that they have created a vicious cycle of violence.[1]

Sri Lanka is a case in point: for over two decades now the government of Sri Lanka and the Liberation Tigers of Tamil Eelam (LTTE) have been in a tense and often very violent standoff against each other. Deep-seated historical reasons are said to be accountable for the underlying ethnic nature of the conflict. Hatred is meanwhile so widespread and entrenched that even the idea of respectful negotiations among the adversaries seems near-impossible.

Only very few peacebuilding organisations can attract involvement from and support by both conflict parties in Sri Lanka. Jana Karaliya, or *The Theatre of the People*, is such a rare organisation. It is a mobile, multi-ethnic and multi-religious theatre group. Established in 2004, Jana Karaliya has been touring the island with the objective of promoting mutual understanding, tolerance, and trust within and among communities on the island.

The purpose of our chapter is to examine the methods used by Jana Karaliya in its efforts at contributing to peacebuilding in Sri Lanka. How is this organisation able to provide a forum in which both parties to the conflict meet and interact – something that is rarely possible in Sri Lanka? To what extent – and how exactly – can the ensuing interactions contribute to peacebuilding efforts? Drawing on interviews with participants as well as on analyses of performances and documentary evidence, we suggest that theatre can make a modest but symbolically important contribution to peacebuilding by changing conflict attitudes at three related levels: personal, emotional and societal. This is to say that theatre can (1) provide a forum through which individuals can come to terms with their personal experiences of conflict and become more attuned to understanding and appreciating the former enemies; (2) facilitate ways in which individuals and groups can come to terms with the deep emotional wounds inflicted by conflict; and (3) make the surrounding societal discourses more attuned to accommodating parties that were once in conflict, thus creating more inclusive and pluralist historical narratives.

Although we deal with Sri Lanka in particular, we hope that our analysis contributes to a growing scholarly and practical awareness of how the arts can play a crucial role in peacebuilding. All too often peacebuilding efforts focus on processes of institution-building or on holding formal elections. The result is a top-down approach that risks imposing a particular notion of a Western and liberal understanding of peace.[2] But many of the key issues that underlie conflict, such as the existence of deep-seated antagonisms, remain unaddressed. Transforming these attitudes into more peaceful – or at least non-violent – interaction is a long process that requires changing the way people think about themselves and their former enemies. This is why so-called grass-roots activities that promote dialogue and respect for difference are crucial to the long-term success of peacebuilding efforts. Community-based arts projects are part of such activities – and we now proceed to assess the extent to which they can contribute to moving a particular society – Sri Lanka – out of deep-seated patterns of conflict.

background: the conflict in Sri Lanka and the activities of the Jana Karaliya theatre group

Sri Lanka is an island nation with a diverse ethno-religious population going back some 2,500 years. A former colony of the Dutch, Portuguese, and finally the British empires, Sri Lanka is located in a strategically important place in the Indian Ocean. The background of the Sri Lankan conflict provided here is a reduced version that does not encompass the complexities seen on the ground. It is solely meant for the outsider to gain a general understanding of the context for the purposes of relating to theatre as a peacebuilding method, and is not comprehensive by any means.

The key conflict today is between the government and LTTE. The widespread stereotyping of each side to represent the voice of Sinhalese and Tamil ethnicities, respectively, has resulted in the conflict being seen as an ethnic conflict. As in most protracted conflicts, the roots of the conflict in Sri Lanka are disputed. Some focus on the colonial legacy, while others place more emphasis on the political dynamics since independence from Britain in 1948.[3] Others again trace the conflict back through centuries to the periodic invasions of the island kingdom from the Indian subcontinent, especially from Tamil-speaking entities in Southern India.

The violent turn of the conflict started in 1983. The killing of 13 soldiers in Jaffna triggered organised mob actions in the capital against civilian Tamils that lasted several days. The government at the time failed to provide protection and, indeed, was accused of aiding the mobs. These incidents resulted in consolidating the key parties of the conflict as they are seen today, the LTTE and the armed forces of the government. There are other groupings as well, such as militant Muslim groups in the Eastern province of the country, but the key conflict is between the government and the LTTE. The latter demands a separate state for Tamils in the North and the East of the country, which has a strong Tamil-speaking population.

The key points of contention revolve around access to government decision-making pertaining to resource distribution and development, as well as language and religious issues. Sinhala and Tamil languages are largely associated with the respective Sinhalese and Tamil ethnicities. The equal official status of both the languages is not reflected in practice within the country. This results in the marginalisation of minority language speakers on a surface level. In long term, its consequences are seen in the alienation, breakdown of communication, and construction of stereotypes between the two main ethnicities. Recent developments in the conflict witnessed the emergence of a religious tension, mainly spurred on by Sinhala Buddhist groups requesting a united ethno-religious identity associated with the entire island. Hence the centralised government is accused of failing to incorporate the interests and aspirations of the Tamil minority. These grievances and points of contention play a major role in the fight for a separate state for Tamils.

In February 2002, the LTTE and the government signed a ceasefire agreement. But relief was only temporary. A new government, formed

with the support of nationalistic parties, renewed intense military operations in late 2005. These, in turn, triggered a series of suicide bomb-
ings and targeted assassinations. By 2006 the situation had deteriorated
to the point that conflict was in the open again. In January 2008, the
government officially withdrew from the ceasefire agreement.

The Jana Karaliya theatre group we study in this chapter operates in
the context of this deeply entrenched conflict. Meaning 'Theatre of the
People', Jana Karaliya was founded by two veteran artists, Parakrama
Niriella and H.A. Perera. They had two main objectives in mind: to take
high-quality theatre productions to distant areas of the country and
to promote peacebuilding among different ethnicities. Being a mobile
theatre group, Jana Karaliya travels around the country, performing in
a mobile theatre tent that can house 500 people at a time. Apart from
performing within the tent, Jana Karaliya goes into rural schools and
conducts Theatre in Education and Personal Development workshops
with the students and teachers. Activities involved in setting up the
theatre, performing and conducting the workshops are carried out by
the members of the theatre group.

Jana Karaliya is composed of some 20 members from both Sinhala
and Tamil ethnicities. They have Buddhist, Hindu, and Christian
religious backgrounds. Most of the participants had some level of
experience in theatre before joining Jana Karaliya, and they constantly receive more training within the group. When performing,
Jana Karaliya stays in one location for about a month, but the time
could be shorter or longer depending on the situation. The group lives
and travels together except for brief periods when the members visit
their homes. They have a house in Colombo to stay in between performances. Members have their living costs covered and also receive a
monthly allowance.

The productions of Jana Karaliya include Indian and Russian adaptations as well as original scripts. The scripts of the plays are by Parakrama
Niriella, a founder of the group. Often Jana Karaliya plays discuss social
injustice and the marginalised. They problematise the existing system,
revealing that the notions of 'good' and 'bad' have their rationale in
the interest of the dominant social group. Hence the plays invite the
viewers to be critical about their own attitudes and thinking patterns.

Jana Karaliya purposely do not engage with the Sri Lankan conflict
directly in their scripts. Doing so, they believe, would alienate the
audience and only entrench divisive ethnic narratives. The conflict is
addressed indirectly, through scripts about justice and tolerance. They

draw from Sinhala and Tamil traditions and perform the plays in both Tamil and Sinhala languages. Add to this the politically very significant fact that the plays are organised and performed by a multi-ethnic cast who work, travel, and live together.

Jana Karaliya is supported mostly through external funds. Even though they charge a fee for their performances, that income is not sufficient to maintain the group. Various non-governmental organisations have supported the group, such as Hivos and Facilitating Local Initiatives for Conflict Transformation (FLICT) as well as the United States Agency for International Development (USAID). One of the main issues facing the group today is, in fact, the challenge of generating income to ensure the group's sustainability.

transforming individual experiences with conflict through artistic performances

The first component of peacebuilding we stress is a feature that almost all Jana Karaliya members we interviewed identified as essential for their participation: the hope that transforming their own personal experiences with conflict can eventually create a more inclusive and harmonious societal order. This is particularly crucial in Sri Lanka, where communication between the groups in conflict has broken down. Add to this the fact that each of the two major conflict parties has constituted its identity around efforts to demonise the other. Within each ethnic group, the stereotyped other is perceived as undesirable and a threat: Tamils associate the Sinhalese with an oppressive state and a brutal military apparatus. The Sinhalese, by contrast, see the Tamils as a disruptive and dangerous terrorist group.[4]

These antagonistic attitudes become insinuated into the day-to-day ways in which people articulate their views, sense of self, and interactions with others. The resulting stereotypes continuously fuel conflict and dehumanise the enemy.[5] Stereotypes are found in all realms of Sri Lankan society. Even highly educated people often propagate the myth of ancient hatreds, alleging some sort of irremovable natural differences that inevitably breed conflict. Consider a statement by a former Dean of the Faculty of Human and Social Sciences, University of Ruhuna:

I have met with Tamil students and teachers. But I am not in favour of any close association or forming ties with Tamils...I think the differences we see among the races are natural. I think that forming ties with people of another culture is something dishonourable.[6]

Breaking down stereotypes and deep-seated antagonism, as Jana Karaliya have been trying to do in performances across Sri Lanka for several years now, is a long and arduous task. In fact, the very premise of Jana Karaliya is highly controversial: a multi-ethnic cast performing in a country devastated by ethnic conflict. Consider the reaction of Sokkalingam Krishanthan, a Tamil participant from Trincomalee, which has been particularly affected by ethnic violence. He stresses how he was initially afraid of the multi-ethnic cast of Jana Karaliya:

I was seated on a chair in that corner over there and I looked at those around me with great suspicion and mistrust. I was actually quite convinced that one of the guys [Sinhalese] was a member of the CID. [Criminal Investigation Division][7]

Another cast member recollects how theatre resulted in gradually changing similar initial sentiments:

[T]hrough the exercises of drama, singing, music and other activities we were able to forge a strong bond. We were able to overcome many of our preconceived ideas about each other and work together towards a common goal.[8]

And here a similar example from Sumudu Mallawarachchi, another Sinhalese Jana Karaliya member:

Before I joined Jana Karaliya I used to judge people by looking at them but after I joined, I've learned to respect them, their culture and their ideas.[9]

The same kind of initial suspicion – and often hostility – occurred in the communities where Jana Karaliya performed. Consider the case of Padaviya, a predominantly Sinhalese village situated between the fault lines of ethnic conflict. As a result of its location and violent history, the village had a population with very strong anti-Tamil sentiments. Not surprisingly, the multi-ethnic theatre group was not well received initially. But after a few performances and theatre workshops, the situation gradually became less tense. Children who initially reacted to the performance with hostility started to follow R. Kopika, a Tamil member of the cast, wherever she went. Such a change of attitude – and the resulting ability to form relationships where before there was only hostility – is possible after personal experiences with conflict are transformed into narratives that are less vengeful and more accepting of others.

We identify three key elements in this transformation process: encouraging expression, transcending stereotypes, and initiating dialogue.

The first step in this transformation process is the need to express experiences with conflict – whether they be first-hand or learned through others in the community.[10] Jana Karaliya embraces this idea by offering a public forum that gives people the chance to voice their feelings. Doing so allows individuals who experienced conflict a chance to come to terms with past events and perhaps even heal some of the related trauma. In an ideal scenario, sharing testimonies of conflict also gives members of the audience – and perhaps members of the hostile parts of the community – the chance to see how the conflict was experienced from the other side.

The ability of theatre to encourage different forms of communication – including non-verbal ones – is central. The inability to speak each other's language substantially hinders communication between Sinhalese and Tamils in Sri Lanka. This difficulty is surpassed in theatre space, since expression also takes the form of music, dance, and other activities. Not even the different members of Jana Karaliya could talk to each other initially. But their inability to communicate linguistically promoted other, non-verbal forms of communication. Such interactions may actually suit the Sri Lankan context well, since language is one of the divisive issues that heighten the ethnic divisions.[11]

The second component in the individual transformation process relates to how theatre manages to create a distance between a fictional performance and the often brutal reality experienced by the performer or spectator in the real world. Theatre provides the opportunity to take part in conflict narratives outside the risks of real life. The performance is a safe space, so to speak – a space that enables individuals enmeshed in conflict to express themselves in a manner they could not do otherwise. In Sri Lanka, the world outside the theatre is far more volatile and would not necessarily tolerate the types of views that are expressed on stage at Jana Karaliya.

The notion of playing a fictional role, rather than living real life, challenges preconceived perceptions and makes room for multiple voices and views to be heard. Doing so is essential if one is to address the key issues that account for the cycles of violence: hatred, deep-seated antagonisms, and unwillingness to even listen to the arch-enemy. Through forms of theatre such as Jana Karaliya, individuals can take on roles that might often be denied to them in real life, thus giving them the chance to explore new ways of knowing the conflict and expressing its grievances.[12] Neela Selvarajan, a member of Jana Karaliya, notes that many people come to the stage to speak at the end of the performance. They come there to voice their opinions, to share how they felt with others, and often they display vulnerability and an openness that is rarely seen in life outside.[13]

The physical set-up of the Jana Karaliya theatre is designed to take advantage of this opportunity to create a safe space for a multitude of voices. The performance takes place in what is called a 'new arena theatre'. This is to say that the stage is located in the middle of a tent, with the audience completely surrounding the actors' performance. The audience must pass the stage when reaching their seating places, which are in fact simply ascending platforms, built around the stage. The entry into theatrical space thus takes place through a vivid physical experience that clearly separates the theatrical realm from the conflict-bound personal reality that exists outside the tent. This creates a marked enclosure, a separate space for actors and the audience to meet, thus transcending their respective boundaries and roles.

When participating in the performances of Jana Karaliya the actors do not represent particular ethnic, religious, or political groups. They are there as actors. They perform as members of humanity at large. Theatre thus provides individuals with access to – and even ways of acting out – roles that they otherwise would never be able to experience. Consider a youth who attended a performance of Jana Karaliya in Kebithigollewa, another border village that suffered many massacres due to the conflict. He stressed that 'this was one of the most unforgettable moments in my life. I never thought that I would ever speak so freely with a young Tamil woman'.[14]

Jana Karaliya offers participants a chance to slip in and out of different roles, perhaps even to try on the personae of the enemy. Doing so inevitably challenges the stereotypical perceptions that fuel the conflict in Sri Lanka – the idea, for instance, that Tamils are such and such or that Sinhalese behave such and such.[15] These attitudes often change after performances. Numerous Karaliya members we interviewed stress this point. Take Manjula Ramasinghe, a Jana Karaliya member from the strongly Sinhala community in Hambanthota. He used to believe that all the Tamils are terrorists and credited the theatre with helping him overcome the fear of interacting with them. Having engaged through the medium of theatre with other Tamil youths, he is now convinced that he has a lot of things in common with them despite the ethnic, cultural, and religious differences that separate them. These barriers, he stresses, exist mostly in our minds and were established through hostile ways of constructing notions of identity and community.[16]

Jana Karaliya produces the same plays in both Tamil and Sinhala. Each performance features a mixed ethnic cast. When the Tamil actors speak with a Sinhala accent, and vice versa, the performance challenges the stereotypes each group believes in, rendering this very stereotype no longer valid to explain their experiences.

The best example for the potential impact of these role-play reversals can be seen in the way Jana Karaliya was received by both the Sri Lankan Government Army and the LTTE. This is an example very much stressed by Parakrama Niriella, a co-founder of Jana Karaliya. When the group performed in Anuradhapura in a ground close to the Army Hospital, the injured soldiers got so close to the group that they came regularly for performances and often provided food and snacks for the entire group. Similarly, LTTE took responsibility for organising Jana Karaliya performances in Muthur when Jana Karaliya performed in the Eastern Province of the country, which was then under LTTE control. They promised to ensure the safety of the entire group and the LTTE Eastern Commander, inviting the group for tea, voiced that 'this is how we want to live in this country'.[17]

In an ideal scenario, then, role plays and role reversals reach some sort of common humanity in formerly opposed parties. They break down the stereotypes that each side has about the other and open up more inclusive personal narratives and communal relations.

There is a third and directly related element in how theatre transforms personal narratives: it improves communication and understanding between groups in conflict. Performing together is a process that requires communication between performers as well as between performers and the audience.[18] Jana Karaliya promotes dialogue by structural and psychological means. Seating the audience in ascending platforms built surrounding the theatre allows them to watch the performance while seeing the faces of those who are sitting all around them. Manjula, a member of the cast, believes that this is a key feature that encourages community dialogue.[19] The smiles and tears brought onto the faces are able to convey subtle messages that would rarely be satisfactorily captured by words. Hence M. Kalidas, Neela and other commentators do in fact stress that theatre – and the arts in general – are the key instruments through which dialogue can be reintroduced into communities that no longer talk to each other.[20] Needless to say, theatre can only be a starting point. Numerous commentators, such as Parakrama, admit that the next step would require bold initiatives at a more high-profile political level.[21] But the types of lessons learned through community theatre can provide political leaders on both sides of the conflict lines with key insights about how to open up a dialogue that can not only convey grievances but also begin to dismantle the stereotypes that continuously fuel conflict.

theatre and emotional healing after conflict

The second theme under which the role of theatre in peacebuilding can be discussed is its potential in creating more inclusive and less violence-prone communal narratives. Doing so requires engaging the types of collective emotions that fuel the conflict cycle.

Emotions are central in determining how we feel and behave as members of a collective. They are even more central when dealing with the aftermath of conflict – a time when fear and hatred dominate the political landscape. A number of studies have demonstrated that the human mind is more likely to remember incidents with strong emotional associations, for all emotional memories receive preferential processing in registering, storing, and retrieval in comparison to cognitive memories.[22] This privileged position in memory enables emotions to identify specific issues and establish priorities in the general reasoning mechanisms of the mind: hence emotions actively engage in devising strategies to achieve their preferred choices.[23] Through this process of influencing our remembering and decision-making, emotions become critical in deciding where we place ourselves and with whom we form alliances.

In post-conflict societies feelings of anger and revenge are often so strong that they generate whole new and highly dangerous cycles of violence. Consider the stereotypical perceptions that each of the conflict groups in Sri Lanka has of the other. These stereotypes, which continually fuel conflict, are mostly based on anger and fear. They have been formed through the memory of violence and death.

Any peacebuilding effort needs to deal with the role of collective emotions in order to be successful in the long term. The challenge is two-fold: firstly, it consists of recognising how fear and anger create ever more conflict. Secondly, it requires finding a way through which a sense of community can be created around feelings other than hatred: these can be empathy or compassion for the former enemies or a mutual sense of grief. Establishing such an emotional transformation of community attachments and interactions is, of course, a long-term and gargantuan task. This is why it has to start at the local level and gradually work its way through society.

Local theatre groups, such as Jana Karaliya, are ideally placed to initiate and spread such processes of emotional transformation. The capacity to engage with emotions is, indeed, one of the key features of theatre as a peacebuilding method. The role of emotion within theatre can be explored under two main categories.

The first emotional feature of theatre is its ability to provide actors and the audience the opportunity to relive emotions. This allows them to come to terms with their grief and anger. Consider the strong visual impact of theatre, which many commentators associate with the potential of replacing old (conflict-prone) memories with new, different ones.[24] Kalidas[25] astutely picked up on this aspect of theatre in saying that 'people see theatre like pictures. If we do a workshop for theatre, it will end with the day. But because theatre creates pictures it is different. We are remembered'. He further explains his point with an example: 'we stayed in Anuradhapura for about three months, and the people there tell us that when they see the ground, it is always Jana Karaliya they remember. This stays inside people's minds because it is pictures. That is what theatre is.'

The second aspect has to do with how theatre can contribute to the establishment of more inclusive emotional attachments to communities. In the process of reliving emotion, Jana Karaliya might help to attenuate often divisive emotions, such as anger, fear, and hatred. These emotions often become key rallying points after conflict, thus entrenching antagonistic attitudes even more. Grief and loss, by contrast, are often silenced, and so are attempts to show empathy to the opposing side. The resulting culture of fear has to be healed in order to bring reconciliation.

Jana Karaliya brings together communities and enables them to address these issues. In doing so it potentially creates new and less divisive communal narratives. At the end of each performance, the cast introduce themselves, saying their name and home town in the language they are most comfortable with. This is seen as a very emotional moment for the audience. As a group member observes: 'when we talk to them some of them start to cry, there's always a reason behind why they cry and most of the time it's because they feel silly about the grudge they've been holding against the Tamil people'.[26]

Theatre can transform emotions so that anger, fear, and hatred are no longer dominant, but make room for sadness and grief, which, in turn, can be shared and become a source of commonness. Long and Brecke[27] emphasise that reconciliation may come about when certain emotions, such as hatred and anger, are superseded by different ways of engaging with past traumatic events. Focusing on loss and grief, for instance, is much more likely to bring about a shared sense of community. Consider how a member of Jana Karaliya observes interestingly that 'If we've made a change within the people then I feel that this is what we've achieved.'[28] Hence theatre in Jana Karaliya has an emotional aspect and actively engages with emotion, thus facilitating the process of creating inclusive communal narratives of emotion in the place of divisive narratives of hatred and fear.

theatre and the transformation of societal attitudes among parties to the conflict

So far we have examined theatre as a peacebuilding method by focusing on how Jana Karaliya's performances have the potential to transform personal and emotional experiences with conflict. We have suggested that theatre provides a space through which participants and audiences can come together and overcome at least some of the attitudes that have fuelled conflict in Sri Lanka, thus paving the way for the emergence of a culture of reconciliation.

We end this chapter with a few concluding remarks that demonstrate how personal and emotional transformations are part of a larger peacebuilding process that involves transformation of societal attitudes among the parties to the conflict. This is to say that questions of identity, historical memory, and cultural belonging are essential to the process of overcoming conflict. In the Sri Lankan context, each party to the conflict rehearses a different understanding of the past and upholds a different notion of what it means to be a member of society. Very often these forms of identity are highly politicised and involve constituting the other party to the conflict as despicable and inferior.

Jana Karaliya is involved in a process of societal transformation that seeks to change these deeply entrenched societal discourses in a way that makes them more inclusive. For Parakrama Niriella, the very space of theatre is a forum where different cultural and aesthetic traditions can come together and produce a new and more positive attitude.[29]

While there are some similarities between artistic and cultural traditions in the Sinhalese and Tamil communities, there are also some major differences. In producing their plays, Jana Karaliya draws from both traditions. Charandas, one of their productions in both Sinhala and Tamil, is a good example. The Sinhala production of Charandas uses drums and other music instruments along with costumes and steps used in Tamil theatre styles, while the Tamil production does the reverse. Niriella perceives this to be a new turn in Sri Lankan theatre, since this transition of cultural aspects to both ethnicities at the same time has not happened before. In the process of effecting this transition, Jana Karaliya bridges the relationships between Tamil and Sinhala artists.

While theatre exists among both groups as a valued form of art, Tamil theatre is not visible on a national level. It is more or less limited to small areas and small audiences despite the wealth of resource available within it and the artists engaging in it. But Jana Karaliya also plays a critical role in claiming a place for Tamil theatre at the national level through its Tamil language productions. Similarly, as Neela personally testifies, it takes Sinhala plays to communities where Sinhala theatre has not reached before: being a Tamil from a peripheral area, she saw a Sinhala play for the first time after she joined Jana Karaliya.[30]

Take the example of Kalidas,[31] who comes from an estate Tamil community in the upcountry. The impact of Jana Karaliya has been immense upon him and his community. Recipient of the Best Actor Award in the State Drama Festival in 2006, he perceives the momentum of Jana Karaliya and his role in it as a turning point for his entire community. It enables him to open new avenues for his community to belong to the larger society and make themselves heard. For him, it marks the beginning of different, new cultural narratives for a group of people who were marginalised and traditionally limited to a set of given designations that all too often created conflict and violence.

The strategy of Jana Karaliya, to hold repeated performances for an extended period living and working within one area, is the reason for much of their success. It facilitates the time and social engagement required for the gradual formation of new cultural narratives in the place of existing ones. Manjula[32] explains that, after about a month of performances, the villagers start coming every evening to the theatre, not only to see the performances over and over, but also to be in an environment that allows them to associate with various people they would otherwise not interact with, including people from opposing ethnic groups. The gradual breakdown of social hierarchies and divisions within the village that occurs here results in a process of creating more inclusive and collaborative cultural narratives within the community. This goes hand in hand with Jana Karaliya's commitment to live the change they want to see, rather than simply advocating it.

The very strength of this local and extended engagement also demonstrates the limits of the contribution that Jana Keraliya and other theatre groups can make to processes of peacebuilding. Healing the wounds of conflict takes time – often generations. It has to happen at the local level and it inevitably involves compromises and setbacks. We have already stressed that Jana Karaliya shies away from directly engaging with contentious issues related to the ethnic conflict. Doing so could lead to repression from political authorities. More importantly, it could alienate the audience and thus defeat the very idea of promoting peacebuilding processes. Theatre has to tread a fine line between aiming for legitimisation and vocalising its political objective of reconciliation. But recognising these limits, and acknowledging that transformation takes time, does not negate the power of theatre to create spaces that contribute in important ways to peacebuilding processes. These ensuing artistic engagements are crucial both because they create the necessary local preconditions for peace and because they offer hope and insights that political leaders can use to promote reconciliation at the national level.

There are a range of larger lessons we can learn from this – admittedly very brief and limited – study of art and peacebuilding in Sri Lanka. For one, it demonstrates that peacebuilding is far more than the re-establishment of institutions and democratic procedures. Building long-lasting peace requires parties who had been in conflict to deal with – and move beyond – the traumatic past. Doing so is a gargantuan and inevitably long-term task. It requires transforming deep-seated attitudes that people hold of themselves and the enemies they had opposed for years, often decades. It requires coming to terms with death, loss, and grief. Artistic engagements are a good example of community-based activities that can bring people together and give them the chance to step outside the type of role assignments that the conflict has given them. Doing so gives individuals the chance to reassess who they are and how they might relate differently to those who are located behind the – physical and mental – dividing line. Art alone cannot, of course, solve a conflict, but it is part of a larger set of activities that are essential in the process of transforming conflict into peace. Perhaps even more importantly, artistic engagements, as exemplified by the Jana Keraliya theatre group, can serve as a model – a type of experimental spearheading – from which community leaders, politicians, and scholars can draw important lessons about the larger dynamics at play in peacebuilding processes.

notes

1. See R.D. Kaplan, *Balkan Ghosts: A Journey through History*, London: Picador, 2005.
2. See O.P. Richmond, *The Transformation of Peace*, New York: Palgrave, 2005, esp. pp. 149–80.
3. See G. Frerks and B. Klem (eds), *Dealing with Diversity: Sri Lankan Discourses on Peace and Conflict*, The Hague: The Netherlands Institute of International Relations, 2004.
4. These stereotypes are used as a point of analysis here. We need to recognise that the range of attitudes and behaviours of Sri Lankans cannot be reduced to these extreme positions regardless of the context.
5. See C. Cohen, 'Engaging with the Arts to Promote Coexistence', in *Imagine Coexistence*, San Francisco: Jossey-Bass, 2003, pp. 267–79.
6. S. Kariyakarawana, 'Attitude and Responsibilities of the Southern Academics', in *Dealing with Diversity: Sri Lankan Discourses on Peace and Conflict*, The Hague: The Netherlands Institute of International Relations, 2004, pp. 102–3.
7. M. Fernando, 'FLICT Super Stars', Unpublished Document, 2006, p. 1.
8. Ibid, p. 2.
9. Jana Karaliya Group Members, interview by Charlotte Hennessay and Jenny Hughes, 27 September 2005, interview 1, Polonnaruwa, Sri Lanka.
10. See also B. Hosking, 'Playback theatre: A creative resource for reconciliation', Brandeis University, http://www.brandeis.edu/programs/Slifka/vrc/papers/hosking_hutt/index.htm, accessed 24 September 2007.
11. U. Abeyratne, 'The Ethnic Problem and Sri Lankan Political Culture', in *Dealing with Diversity: Sri Lankan Discourses on Peace and Conflict*, The Hague: The Netherlands Institute of International Relations, 2004, p. 93.
12. See A. Boal, *The Aesthetics of the Oppressed*, London: Routledge, 2006; S. Jennings and A. Minde, *Art Therapy and Dramatherapy: Masks of the Soul*, London: Jessica Kingsley publishers, 1993.
13. P. Abeylal, M. Ramasinghe and N. Selvarajan (Jana Karaliya members), interview by Nilanjana Premaratna and Harshadeva Amarathunga, 22 February 2008, interview 2, Thambuththegama, Sri Lanka.
14. M. Fernando, 'FLICT Super Stars', p. 2.
15. For a conceptual discussion see D. Bagshaw and M. Lepp, 'Ethical Considerations in Drama and Conflict Resolution Research in Swedish and Australian Schools', *Conflict Resolution Quarterly*, Vol. 22, No. 3, 2005, pp. 381–96.
16. P. Abeylal, M. Ramasinghe and N. Selvarajan, interview 2.
17. P. Niriella (Jana Karaliya founder), interview by Nilanjana Premaratna and Harshadeva Amarathunga, 22 February 2008, interview 4, Thambuththegama, Sri Lanka.

18. D. Brown, 'Dancing the Darkness Away', *Journal of Undergraduate Research*, 2007, pp. 85–103.
19. P. Abeylal, M. Ramasinghe and N. Selvarajan, interview 2.
20. Ibid., M. Kalidas (Jana Karaliya member), interview by Nilanjana Premaratna and Harshadeva Amarathunga Thambuttegama, Sri Lanka, 22 February 2008, interview 3, Thambuththegama, Sri Lanka.
21. P. Niriella, interview 4.
22. W.J. Long and P. Brecke, *War and Reconciliation: Reason and Emotion in Conflict Resolution*, Massachusetts: the MIT Press, 2003.
23. Ibid. See also E. Hutchison and R. Bleiker, 'Emotional Reconciliation: Reconstituting Identity and Community After Trauma,' *European Journal of Social Theory*, Vol. 11, No. 3, 2008, pp. 385–403.
24. W. Kansteiner, 'Finding Meaning in Memory: A Methodological Critique of Collective Memory Studies', *History and Theory*, Vol. 41, No. 2, 2002, pp. 179–97.
25. M. Kalidas, interview 4.
26. P. Abeylal, M. Ramasinghe and N. Selvarajan, interview 2.
27. W.J. Long and P. Brecke, p. 28.
28. P. Abeylal, M. Ramasinghe and N. Selvarajan, interview 2.
29. P. Niriella, interview 4.
30. P. Abeylal, M. Ramasinghe and N. Selvarajan, interview 2.
31. M. Kalidas, interview 4.
32. P. Abeylal, M. Ramasinghe and N. Selvarajan, interview 2.

interviews

Jana Karaliya Group Members, interview by Charlotte Hennessay and Jenny Hughes, 27 September 2005, interview 1, Polonnaruwa, Sri Lanka.

Palitha Abeylal, Manjula Ramasinghe and Neela Selvarajan (Jana Karaliya members), interview by Nilanjana Premaratna and Harshadeva Amarathunga, 22 February 2008, interview 2, Thambuththegama, SriLanka.

M. Kalidas (Jana Karaliya member), interview by Nilanjana Premaratna and Harshadeva Amarathunga, 22 February 2008, interview 3, Thambuththegama, Sri Lanka.

Parakrama Niriella (Jana Karaliya founder), interview by Nilanjana Premaratna and Harshadeva Amarathunga, 22 February 2008, interview 4, Thambuththegama, Sri Lanka.

21

peacebuilding and environmental challenges

fiona rotberg

introduction

Peacebuilding organisations typically have viewed environmental challenges as second tier to more traditionally recognised pre- and post-conflict issues such as justice sector reforms. There are few examples of where environmental institutions, such as mechanisms to ensure equitable distribution of natural resources, have been fully included in peace accords or post-conflict rebuilding efforts.[1] However, policy and academic research indicates that there is positive movement towards understanding the importance of environmental concerns in peacebuilding. This chapter argues that peacebuilding organisations, in the face of climate change, must raise environmental needs to a first tier priority. Specifically in post-conflict settings, peacebuilding organisations need to work to:

1. Support climate change adaptation activities[2] that provide for livelihood alternatives for local communities;
2. Strengthen or build environmental institutions to provide a governing mechanism to mitigate environmental disagreements.

This chapter uses vignettes from climate change-impacted countries to illustrate the first point and Timor-Leste as a case study to illustrate the second. Through both the case study and the vignettes, this chapter suggests that, if environmental issues that encompass environmental institutions and climate change are not adequately included in global peacebuilding policies, the risk of future violent conflict, and unstable peace, is high.

Poor populations living in war-torn countries often depend on environmental resources such as land for their livelihoods. Thus climate change impacts, such as droughts and floods, make the dependence on natural resources even more unreliable. Weak environmental institutions and complicating factors such as environmental migration of populations in search of livelihood alternatives can lead to increased intrastate and interstate resource and ethnic conflicts.

A brief look at recent events in the Sudan help to substantiate the arguments put forth in this chapter. Climate change impacts such as severe multi-year drought helped lead to environmental conflict (such as disagreements over the scarcity of water and land to graze animals) and contributed to the escalation of violence in the Darfur region of Sudan. The lack of resources from which to derive a living forced many Sudanese to flee the area. Strong environmental institutions were not in place to provide a framework to mitigate conflicts that arose over land and water. Violence inhibited local populations from developing alternative adaptation mechanisms so that they could cope with the drought, instead of migrating from their homes.[3]

Indeed, the causes of the Darfur conflict are numerous and complex, including historical and political grievances, and inequitable distribution and governance of resources. However, as United Nations (UN) Secretary General Ban Ki-moon stated, 'amid the diverse social and political causes, the Darfur conflict began as an ecological crisis, arising at least in part from climate change'.[4] Thus, peace initiatives in countries such as Sudan must include climate change and environmental issues in their policies.

The following research examples suggest that steps are being taken to raise the level of environmental concerns in current peacebuilding initiatives. There is a positive emphasis on understanding the connections between global, national and local environmental governing institutions and adaptation to climate change impacts. Indeed, organisations involved in peacebuilding have much to gain from local experiences: to understand how groups have adapted to climate change vulnerabilities, built local resilience,[5] and avoided environmental conflict in the past.[6] With climate change, there is a new global environmental reality, and thus the peacebuilding establishment needs to raise environmental challenges to the first tier of traditional reforms in post-conflict settings.

Statements by Secretary General Ban Ki-moon indicate this new positive trend. In a United Nations Environment Programme publication, *Global Environmental Outlook* (October 2007), he wrote that: 'natural resources and ecosystems underpin all our hopes for a better world ... climate change can have implications for peace and security'.[7] The publication concluded that: 'environmental cooperation creates an effective path to peace by promoting sustainable resource use and equity within and between countries.'[8] The Action Plan that resulted from the UN Climate Change Conference in Bali in December 2007 outlines that there must be enhanced 'action on adaptation', which includes 'international cooperation to support urgent implementation of adaptation actions' and 'integration of adaptation actions into sectoral and national planning ...'[9]

Another UN document, *Human Development Report 2007/2008*, is entitled *Fighting Climate Change: Human Solidarity in a Divided World*. This report firmly argues for countries to develop adaptation plans to climate change, with the assistance of the international community. The authors also stress that robust governing institutions at the national and local levels are a key component of successful adaptation. The UK Department for International Aid (DFID) developed 'Key Sheets on Climate Change and Poverty' in parallel with its 2007 policy on migration and development, entitled: *Moving out of Poverty: Making Migration Work for Poor People*. DFID also authored *Mapping Climate Vulnerability and Poverty in Africa* (May 2006), which advocates for the international community to address climate change vulnerability at the same time as poverty and peacebuilding. Suggesting that there is a need to further understand the linkages between climate change and peace and security, The German Advisory Council on Global Change (WBGU) (2008) published the most comprehensive work to date on the topic of climate change and security: *World in Transition: Climate Change as a Security Risk*. This volume systematically and thoroughly addresses the multifaceted aspects of climate change and various conflict scenarios. Finally, International Alert, UK (November 2007) published *A Climate of Conflict: The Links between Climate Change, Peace and War*. The main focus of this report is to highlight the consequences of climate change and to understand how they can lead to violent conflict.

Together, these policy publications bolster the argument that the scope of traditional peacebuilding needs to be broadened to include local knowledge, climate change, and adaptation issues. The following section of this chapter argues that peacebuilding efforts should include local climate change adaptation strategies to mitigate the instigation or aggravation of conflicts due to climate change impacts such as resource depletion (direct impact) and migration (indirect impact). This section suggests that peacebuilding initiatives, in addition to including robust environmental institutions, need to address environmental issues that surround climate change impacts and adaptation mechanisms. Vignettes illustrate how the issues of climate impacts, adaptation, and peace building are interlinked. The third section of this chapter uses the United Nations (UN) mission of transitional administration (1999–2002) in Timor-Leste to analyse the UN's role in the rebuilding of Timor-Leste's environmental governing institutions. The fourth section, by way of suggested research questions, provides areas for further research.

climate change adaptation

The International Panel on Climate Change (IPCC) fourth assessment review established firmly not only that climate change is a scientific fact but that it is a result of human action. The IPCC also indicated that adaptation mechanisms can help to further limit the human damage that results from climate change.

Addressing the consequences of climate change, the IPCC writes that, in Africa alone,

> By 2080, it is likely that 1.1 to 3.2 billion people will be experiencing water scarcity; 200 to 600 million, hunger; 2 to 7 million more per year, coastal flooding... Stresses such as increased drought, water shortages and riverine and coastal flooding will affect many local and regional populations. This will lead in some cases to relocation within or between countries, exacerbating conflicts and imposing migration pressures.[10]

Physical consequences of climate change include melting glaciers, sea level rise, droughts, floods, desertification, spread of disease, and less arable land. As a result of these physical consequences, there will be *social and political* consequences of climate change. They include:

- livelihood insecurity,
- food insecurity,
- decreased access to usable water,
- increased social tension,
- increased poverty,
- decreased physical security,
- decline in human health, and
- increased migration.[11]

Each of these consequences of climate change will in turn lead to decreased human security. Decreased human security means a higher potential for unstable peace. Thus the inverse; for sustainable peace, these consequences must be systematically integrated into peacebuilding agendas.

One way of integrating the many consequences of climate change is to include local and national adaptation mechanisms that help enable those who are most exposed to climate impacts. When a group's adaptive capacity is built (or strengthened), social resilience to cope with vulnerabilities will also be bolstered. Groups around the world have already found ways to cope with climate change impacts. In some incidents, they have used their coping strategies not only to sustain their livelihoods but also to sustain peace and avoid violent conflict. Thus, peacebuilding organisations should gain knowledge from current local practice, and adjust policies based on what is working and what is not.

There is evidence of local coping strategies that address the impacts of climate change such as landslides, loss of crops, soil erosion, land degradation, loss of livelihoods, and loss of human settlements. The strategies include alternative cultivation methods, land redistribution, disaster risk management, and livelihood diversification; some with governmental or non-governmental organisation support. For example, to address the impact of sand storms in Niger, women are enlisted by the government to implement a strategy to combat sand storms that destroy crops. The women plant shrub branches and secure them with grass that creates a grid of natural fencing. Thus, the fencing keeps the sand from blowing onto the land that is used for crops and grazing.

Studies from Nigeria, Burkina Faso, and Zimbabwe exemplify how farmers can forecast weather and thus adapt crop rotations accordingly, and adopt to new methods of soil management techniques. Women in these countries traditionally have valuable knowledge about local plants that leads to better food security in times of drought and famine. The use of their 'indigenous knowledge' for climate change policies can prove invaluable to further develop local and sustainable adaptation strategies.[12]

In Mali, 70% of the population live in rural areas and are dependent on sustainable management of natural resources to make a living. Climate change has caused erratic and decreasing levels of rainfall, which in turn has led to a decrease in crop yields – which has led to people migrating to find other sources of income. Alternative growing methods are encouraged by the government so that farmers will use different crop strains that are more resistant to drought. For example, the *jatropha* plant is being grown and used as a biofuel.[13]

In Sri Lanka, rice farmers who have to cope with increased saline levels and reduced water have adapted to new rice varieties to make a living.[14] Flood-prone communities in Nepal have developed early warning systems that allow people to visually see the water rising (from watchtowers) and to employ communication systems so that people are duly informed and can cooperate to stave off the encroaching floods.

Two flood-prone communities in Bangladesh exemplify how social networks play an integral role in coordinating action to cope with floods. In both the Nayanagar Union of Melandaha Thana and the Palbandha Union of Islampur Thana, community flood management committees were established in the aftermath of floods. Based on the voluntary effort of community members, people organised and prepared for a division of labour for flood management. Committee activities include collecting information on the rise and recession of water on a regular basis (mainly using cellular phones to communicate with the nearest water information collection centres), relocating marooned people to shelters, flood shelter management, health care, distribution of potable water, and livestock management. The success of social networks like these helps stave off natural resource-related conflicts, and thus helps build lasting peace.[15]

With increased resilience to cope with climate change impacts, communities will contribute to the reduction of renewed violence or new violence, thus helping to maintain and strengthen peace and peacebuilding initiatives. As the UN suggests, 'Increasing the coping and adaptive capacity of the most vulnerable people and communities requires integration of policies across governance levels and sectors, and over time to address the coping and adaptive capacities of future generations.'[16] As this quote indicates, successful and proper development of adaptation mechanisms to cope with the consequences of climate change will require the UN and other international organisations to work directly with individual states and the local communities where adaptation will be used from day to day.

The next section presents a case study about environmental issues and the rebuilding of the war-torn country of Timor-Leste. This case exemplifies how local inhabitants are directly impacted by governing institutions that do not necessarily take their resource use patterns into account when developing new laws and policies.

Timor-Leste case study

Land and violent conflict are often tightly connected. Populations have fought over land resources for decades. Land tenure and property regimes, and associated environmental institutions, are vital, though often forgotten, components in peacebuilding and reconstruction in post-conflict situations. Analysis of the United Nations' role in the rebuilding of institutions in Timor-Leste demonstrates that the failure to fully include mechanisms to address local land and property issues in peacebuilding, and the failure to establish environmental institutions (that accounted for historical ethnic differences, such as conflicting claims to land), can be linked to the renewed deadly violence of May 2006. The Timor-Leste case shows that sustainable peace operations must target land and property issues that are often central to the cyclical causes and consequences of conflict, and that are often vital to the local (and often poor) resource users who depend on land and property to sustain their livelihoods.

relevant background

On 20 May 2002, three years after the United Nations Transitional Administration in East Timor (UNTAET) arrived in the country, Timor-Leste (formally East Timor) voted to control its own destiny. However, as evidenced by deaths on the streets in 2006, the world's youngest nation was not yet ready to take charge of itself or its destiny. Chaos resumed when more than 30 people were killed in the streets of Dili, the capital. Timor-Leste, or 'Timor of the rising Sun', is located on the eastern part of Timor Island, the easternmost of the Lesser Sunda Islands. Australia is located 500 km across the Timor Sea. The land area of the country is 19,000 km^2, roughly half the size of Belgium. There are between 800,000 and 1,000,000 people living in this small country,[17] yet 41 percent live in poverty, and only 52% are literate.[18] The 2007/2008 UNDP Human Development Report ranks Timor-Leste 150 out of 177 states, indicating that life expectancy is 59 years of age.[19]

Very generally, one can discuss the ethnic population in terms of *firaku* and *kaladi*. Those from the east are *firaku*, while those from the west are referred to as *kaladi*. It is estimated that 30–40% of the population is *firaku*, while 50–70% is *kaladi*.[20] Both the *firaku* and *kaladi* peoples came in the 1940s to Dili to seek access to market spaces and property. Competition was often intense and violent, leading to deaths from clashes between east and west or *firaku* and *kaladi*. It has been said that this historical rivalry became a 'tradition"[21] and was played out again in the 2006 violence in Dili.

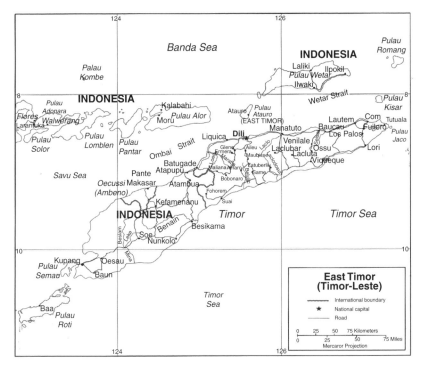

Figure 21.1 **Timor-Leste Map.**
Source: From http://www.lib.utexas.edu/maps/middle_east_and_asia/east_timor_pol_03.jpg, accessed on 10 November 2007.

Timor-Leste has suffered from historical occupation and invasion from outsiders. As such, Timor-Leste's history can be categorised as one of turmoil. The colonial structure that dominated the country's identity can be traced back to 1515, when Portuguese traders settled as soldiers and missionaries. The Portuguese dictatorship finally ended in 1974 when Timor-Leste moved towards independence. Democracy was short-lived, as nine days later, on 7 December 1975, Indonesia invaded the newly established republic. The next three years witnessed fighting and loss of life, with 183,000 Timorese systematically killed.[22] At the same time, food crops, agricultural land, and virtually all land titles and records (a fact that became vital in future land conflict resolution attempts) were destroyed by Indonesian forces. Many East Timorese were forced into refugee camps.[23]

Three distinct political and ideological parties emerged in the mid-1970s: the Timorese Democratic Union (UDT), which favoured continued linkages with Portugal; the Timorese Social Democratic Association (ASDT), which advocated for independence; and the Timorese Popular Democratic Association (APODETI), which advocated for integration with Indonesia. Later in the same year, The Revolutionary Front for the Liberation of East Timor, known as FRETILIN, was born. It is important to mention these different political parties with varying ideologies, as their differences came to the forefront and clashed throughout the next three decades.

Traditionally, Timor-Leste has been a rural, subsistence-based economy, producing coffee as an international export cash crop. In 1998, coffee exports earned \$15 million.[24] Over time, there have been tobacco, cloves, cocoa, vanilla, and nut production as well.[25] Sandalwood and teak are two natural resources that had the potential for long-term economic gain, but are both essentially depleted due to unsustainable logging practices.

Still, today, farming makes up most of the agricultural activity, which includes rice, corn, vegetables, soybeans, and bananas. Forty-two percent (600,000 hectares) is estimated to be viable agricultural land. Of this viable land, half is currently cultivated.[26] There is widespread use of slash and burn shifting agriculture, combined with open grazing and seasonal bush burning that has led to deforestation and soil erosion. In turn, these practices have made it difficult for many people to eke out a living. Timor-Leste's terrain is steep and its soil has little productive use. Approximately 44% of the country has a slope of 40% or greater. This grade makes it extremely difficult to cultivate sustainable crops. The country also has multiple land tenure systems that have contributed to confusion and conflicts.

Timor-Leste's land tenure systems include communally held land and individually held land. Land is generally governed by customary law and is thus unregistered. Today, there are fewer than 47,000 formal titles, 2,709 of which are from the Portuguese colonial era, and 44,091 issued during the Indonesian era.[27] Even though the Timorese have endured resettlement programmes during the Indonesian period of occupation, today customary authorities and local traditional systems still hold the knowledge of land boundaries and purchases and sales. Often unregistered land transactions are verified by the *camat* or subdistrict head.

Land tenure systems in Timor-Leste have been significantly affected by the Indonesian occupation. In the rural areas, many communities were uprooted from their historical territories and placed elsewhere, on others' land. Subsequently, customary systems that prohibited access to certain lands and forests, for example, broke down. This type of land tenure insecurity has over time contributed to bitter disputes.[28] There are often varying levels of '... ownership that relate to different levels of access to and control over resources within family and clan land. Individuals may own, or co-own, many non-contiguous plots of land in different degrees'.[29]

Complexity arises when communities have resettled, or been resettled, onto land that did not come down through their ancestry, and thus claims to land are often deemed ineffective. In turn, this complexity leads to a '... general sense of anxiety among customary communities over "outsiders" getting titles to land'.[30] Meanwhile, because land is often managed in Timor-Leste by a community, it is necessary for the community group to give consent to anyone outside the community who wishes to acquire land use rights. Outsiders may never actually own the land.

1999 was the year of land and property destruction and mass displacement. In August of that year, the Timorese voted (78% in favour) to be freed from Indonesian administration. As a consequence, Indonesian forces 'unleashed militias upon the population' and killed 1,500 people.[31] During these attacks almost 90% of the infrastructure was destroyed, and 500,000 people (75% of the population) were displaced. State buildings and property, including almost all of the official records of land ownership along with the Land and Property Directorate building, were systematically destroyed. The burning of land titles and title deeds helped reawaken the 'endemic cycles of land conflict' which still impact land issues today.[32]

Upon return a year later, in 2000, thousands of people found that 30% of the houses had been completely destroyed. Conflicts immediately arose over who had a legal right to which homes. There was no system in place to account for the number of conflicts that erupted over legal ownership. However, anecdotal evidence suggests that 50% of the housing stock in Dili was illegally occupied. Given that there was already historical confusion about competing claims on titles from the colonial period, and the titles granted during the Indonesian occupation, further fighting ensued. In fact, four categories of people who claimed rights to land, and thus were in competition with each other, were evident:

1. Current occupiers,
2. Traditional communal owners,
3. People with titles from the Portuguese era, and
4. People with titles from the Indonesian era.[33]

Daniel Fitzpatrick explains what he witnessed during this horrific time. When

> ...order was restored a vast mass of people rushed back in...hundreds of thousands over a period of a few months...and there was, of course, a rush to occupy habitable housing...there were terrible machete fights...this was an immediate problem, but it laid the foundations for a longer term problem of land occupation...
>
> In combination with the lack of records...there was almost total lack of awareness in formal terms, in State government terms, of who lived on the land before 1999, who was living on the land after 1999, how to resolve this new jigsaw of land occupation, and this is a problem that plagues East Timor today.[34]

The international community has been criticised for not responding adequately to the hundreds of thousands of persons who were displaced and then subsequently returned after the initial 1999 conflict subsided. For example, no international agency had direct responsibility for the return of the displaced persons. According to a report published in 2000, the UN, through the United Nations High Commissioner for Refugees (UNHCR), initially estimated that some 35,000 houses had been destroyed, and thus distributed emergency shelter kits based on this estimate. As more information was gathered, however, UNHCR revised its estimates of destroyed homes to 85,000.[35] This point brings up a host of issues that surround refugee and migration policy, which deserve separate discussion beyond this chapter.[36]

The direct consequence of not having a clear policy meant that by April 2000, when persons other than the original owners were occupying the standing houses, there was significant overcrowding, and there were conflicts and violence surrounding housing issues.[37] It is impossible to know how many people were evicted from vacant dwellings when the refugees returned. There was no systematic tabulation of the number of evictions. Presumably, conflict over vacant land and dwellings was more acute in Dili than in the countryside, as Dili was the centre of economic activity.[38] As noted previously, given Timor-Leste's customary land system, many consider themselves rightful property owners, even with no formal title in hand.[39] In some cases, one plot of land had 'changed hands' (not legal ownership as no formal records went with the change) many times since 1999.[40] It is against this deadly and complex backdrop that the United Nations Transitional Administration in East Timor (UNTAET) came to Timor-Leste in 1999 and stayed until 2002.

United Nations and land policy

For the most part, the UNTAET period between 1999 and 2002 was about positive change and healing, and the establishment of state institutions. For the first time since 1975, there was an avenue for 'party politics'. UNTAET was given 'overall responsibility for the administration of East Timor' and mandated to 'exercise all legislative and executive authority, including the administration of justice'.[41]

Elections took place in 2001, and FRETILIN won 57 percent of the popular vote. Modern state institutions, such as the National Parliament, the Council of Ministers, local government structures, the police service, and the defence force, were all established in 2000. However, the legitimacy of some institutions was lacking, for example, the defence force and the police service (PNTL). The PNTL even consisted of personnel who had been members of the Indonesian police.[42]

Although this UN mission was originally hailed internationally as a success, some suggest instead that it was an 'assertive peace building' mission that quickly built institutions and, in so doing, highlighted 'the dangers of precipitous and ill prepared liberalisation'.[43] For example, the mission has been criticised for not staying long enough to build needed capacity and institutions in the security and land policy sectors.

Additionally, and tragically, as Harrington explains, the international community misjudged the clashes, battles, and underlying hostilities between different eastern and western Timorese ethnic groups; and thus did not base their policy choices on these historical 'manifestations'.[44] Nor did they account fully for the absence of land title records. As one peacebuilding scholar warns, 'peacebuilding requires carefully calibrated assessments of the needs of a society, and external actors have to tread a fine line between reforming the systems which contributed to instability and vulnerability in the first place and conserving traditional values and structures...'[45]

Naturally, the post-conflict setting being discussed here involves transitional governance, and thus land issues must be dealt within this transitional context. Issues generally arise in these contexts, as they did in Timor-Leste, concerning:

- land law and policy;

- governing and the management of natural resources;
- land administration;
- land titling;
- the need for government land agencies to deal with potential ownership disputes.

In Timor-Leste, the lack of sufficient policy response to deal with land-
related issues left an institutional vacuum and thus helped to fuel
underlying tensions and unresolved issues that resulted in further violence in 2006. As Fitzpatrick explains, 'there was virtually no planned
policy response to the relatively predictable effects on housing of widespread property destruction, mass population return'.[46]

In October 2001, the Constitution of the Democratic Republic of
Timor-Leste was written. In the same year, the UN passed a regulation
which mandated that Indonesian law be adopted, but that decision
immediately raised some complex and confusing questions, for example
what to do with Portuguese land titles that existed on paper from the
past. In the post-conflict transition period, the legal system was being
set up and claims began to come in. But, there was no legal framework
within which to handle these land claims.

Members of the UN and other development and government agencies
had even voiced fears that land and property disputes could become
a serious threat to future security, leading to violence throughout the
country. In fact, the UNTAET Office of the National Security Advisor
and the Land and Property Unit (LPU) authored a report in 2001 which
warned that land-related disputes were 'the major source of conflict and
civil unrest in Timor–Leste'.[47]

Was land the critical prize from the 2006 violence?

> The importance of land issues to post-conflict development is often
> not recognised early enough, and even when it is recognised, it is
> often politically or practically unfeasible to effectively address those
> issues in the immediate post-conflict period.[48]

As this quote suggests, land issues in this small country, as in other
similar countries, are part of the general foundation for development,
especially from the perspective of economic growth, governance, and
the environment. Not only does land serve as the basis of subsistence
farming, but it is a form of security and it is the basis of a social unit.[49]
Land, also viewed as a 'strategic socio-economic asset', especially in

subsistence economies where income and survival are measured by access to land,[50] means that a reliable land administration system is imperative.[51] Land has also been termed the 'critical prize'[52] in the conflicts that have plagued Timor-Leste on and off for decades.

Initially, the causes of the 2006 crisis appeared to be based on lack of trust, old feuds and grudges, and problems with the security sector reform, mostly the restructuring of the army. The Prime Minister and the President were vying for power and had a mutual distrust of each other, leading to a conflict that was sparked after members of the army were sacked. In summary, initially it appeared that the root causes of the 2006 crisis were related to:

- power struggles between the ruling party and opposition party;
- tensions and power struggles between President Xanana Gusmão and Prime Minister Mari Alkatiri;
- unchecked corruption;[53]
- tensions between the police and armed forces;[54]
- lack of strong, functioning institutions, mostly the security forces.[55]

These factors helped to trigger the violence. Land issues and land disputes were also causes of the 2006 unrest.

As mentioned above, at the time of the violence in 2006, the country had:

- no formal land registry;
- no system to record or verify private land transactions;
- no effective regime to govern and legalise foreign interests in land; and
- a weak framework to determine competing and often violent claims to land.[56]

What was UNTAET's role in the causes of violence? Specifically regarding land and housing issues, UNTAET did not adequately provide for the population, and especially the local resource users who depend on land for their livelihoods:

- mechanisms to resolve housing and connected land conflicts;
- an appropriate agency or body to manage and deal with housing conflicts resulting from returnees;
- a system to encourage refugees to return to their original areas.[57]

UNTAET did not establish any land claims commission, or develop any other legal or administrative system to deal with property and title issues, thus leaving 'the whole question of property ownership' to the future government of Timor-Leste.[58] The UNTAET LPU 'was authorised only to file and record property claims' but not to prepare any registration system.[59] UNTAET did establish (in Regulation No.1) that Indonesian law was to be used to resolve questions of land ownership. However, this decision overlooked the historical and divisive fact that most East Timorese people would have difficulty accepting formal law from an oppressive colonial regime.[60] In short, the failure to ensure property rights under good environmental governance laws and practices became a ticking bomb presaging violent conflict later on.

Due to the omission of the establishment of a land claims commission, or any formal method to record land transactions, other regulations were subsequently omitted. Lacking were comprehensive regulations to address:

- formal land administration and a regime for land tax;
- land conflict resolution.[61]
- land use;
- environmental protection.[62]

The lack of these interlinked laws clearly has had an impact on the new nation's ability to address and resolve key land-related issues in the aftermath of the 1999 violence. Fitzpatrick warned in 2002 that '... unless the immediate issues of property destruction and refugee return are handled well, resolution of more long term issues relating to property restitution and land administration in general will be greatly complicated'.[63] Inadequate management of illegal and ad hoc housing occupation and simmering social tensions played a role in the 2006 violence, with further housing destruction and illegal occupations.

renewed violence of 2006

To what extent were there old grievances that stemmed from land disputes involved in the new eruption of violence? Important historical interactions between disputants in the 2006 violence were overlooked. Without proper understanding of conflict with historical roots (sometimes ethnic), resolution is difficult.[64]

Each of the violent episodes that took place in 2006 shares a common social theme where they are 'split along perceived identities', that is, one side is the eastern, or *firaku,* and the other is the western, or *kaladi* Timorese.[65] Harrington writes that:

> The recent breakdown in security and politics was a spark, igniting violence in the security vacuum. During this vacuum, the pre-existing ethnic divide was used by groups and their leaders to achieve political and economic goals. The vacuum gave those from the west the chance to finally reclaim lost or occupied land and properties and to exact vengeance on those who had claimed key properties since 1999.[66]

A clear example of this cultural/ethnic divide can be traced to the rebuilding of the security sector. When the Timor-Leste Defence Force (FDTL) was created in February 2001, 650 of the first 1,500 were ex-combatants. Resentment grew among remaining ex-combatants who were left to roam the streets. In May 2002, when the defence force was renamed FALINTIL-FDTL (F-FDTL), it was split into two battalions that seemed to be divided along the lines of former combatants or new recruits. UNTAET paid great attention to the rebuilding of the security sector and not enough to linked issues. UNTAET 'gave more attention to vetting former Indonesian police and getting them back on the streets than to finding a role for the men in the hills'.[67] As a result, fighters were disgruntled and angry.

It appears that the 2006 violence and destruction of property were orchestrated by socially divided segments of the population who had been organised by armed groups to do so. Harrington's analysis of the 2006 violence, compiled from being in country at the time, buttresses this point well. He asserts that violent actors were mobilised by historical identity and social roles.

> When violence finally erupted on the final day of protests in April, the dividing lines had already been drawn for the east–west rupture within the F-FDTL. The F-FDTL splintered with factions attacking the PNTL while F-FDTL deserters and civilian militias aggravated the situation. Violence can be broken down into three broad categories:
>
> 1. Civilians allying themselves along security force factional lines, meaning by and large east-west lines.

2. Gangs organised, paid (monetary or otherwise), fomented and directed to destroy specifically targeted properties; most of these properties were occupied by easterners.

3. Some political figures and community leaders exploited a perceived east-west divide to improve their relative 'power' position within Timorese society, inciting generic mob violence by gangs; factional east-west violence, looting, and generic property destruction.[68]

Land grievances are likely wrapped up in other grievances that appear more tangible, such as old alliances and wounds that were not mitigated. Fitzpatrick and Monson confirm that:

> To the surprise of many experienced observers, political tensions involving the Prime Minister (Alkatiri) and the President (Gusmão), quickly evolved into violent conflict between 'Easterners' and 'Westerners' in Dili. This conflict largely involved attempts at eviction by Westerners (long-standing Dili residents) of Easterners who occupied houses in Dili in 2000 without license from the pre-2000 owners.[69]

A 2006 assessment similarly concluded that 'these latent tensions, refer back to overlapping land and property claims from Portuguese and Indonesian eras were recognisable through the targeted burning and looting of commercial market stalls, properties and homes'.[70] The authors of this same report warn that the government's current plans are not realistic, and do not include proper mechanisms and tools to resolve historical and outstanding land and property issues. The plans are not 'well designed to avoid causing or exacerbating future conflict'.[71]

The case of Timor-Leste illustrates the importance of including environmental institutions and land policy mechanisms in post-conflict rebuilding efforts. It also suggests that international agencies must account for the complex land and property issues that are often rooted in historical and social factors in war-torn societies. The future inclusion of environmental mechanisms in peacebuilding will hopefully help lead to a reduction in renewed violence in war-torn societies.

International Alert, writing generally about peacebuilding, captures some of the issues evident in Timor-Leste: 'The problem that peace building addresses is that, through the experience of violent conflict, societies lose the capacity to resolve difficult issues peacefully. Variously, they lose the institutions that can mediate and negotiate disputes and differences before they get out of hand, and they lose the cultural habits of compromise and tolerance that are required for serious differences to be settled by agreement. Helping societies regain these attributes is what peace building is about.'[72]

Building on the topics and issues explored in the previous two sections of this chapter, the next section raises some potential research questions, as a way to instigate new thinking and debate. The potential for future research topics that involve peacebuilding and environmental challenges is robust. The questions posed below are but a few ideas.

future research

Generally, research into the many complex linkages between social, economic, cultural, political, and biophysical systems, and how they relate to climate change consequences, adaptation, and peace and development is much needed. There is also a need to recast peacebuilding so that it accommodates the local populations who often depend on natural resources to eke out a living.

Specifically, there is a need for the peacebuilding establishment to better understand:

1. How can environmental institutions be better integrated into traditional security, legal and other institutions in post-conflict settings?
2. How can formal institutions (that is, land and property commissions and judicial mechanisms) and informal institutions (such as non-governmental organisations) be strengthened to help address anticipated impacts of climate change?
3. What actions are being carried out by individuals and groups to address the adverse effects of climate change impacts? What integrated approaches to climate change will help individuals and communities adapt to climate-induced changes? What are the potentials of, and limits to, adaptation as a response to climate change?
4. What are the best mechanisms to understand 'indigenous knowledge systems' about weather and adaptation methods, and how can they be captured and shared as appropriate?

Answers to these questions serve as a conclusion to this chapter. Environmental institutions should no longer be viewed separately from traditional security, justice, and legal reforms: the impacts of climate change necessitate that environmental issues be fully integrated into traditional security threat scenarios and peacebuilding efforts. Land law and land use specialists, for example, need to be included in UN and other teams that are called upon to rebuild obliterated governing institutions in post-conflict settings.

Large institutions typically address peacebuilding from a top-down approach, which in turn runs the risk of further alienating the local resource users who are involved in both the roots and resolution to complex conflicts. Communities that are directly impacted by conflicts are also those that harbour knowledge of important ethnic, cultural, and resource use patterns that is needed to rebuild sustainable environmental institutions in post-conflict settings.

The peacebuilding establishment would benefit from addressing the new environmental reality of today from a bottom-up approach. For example, several of the above questions lend to the recommendation to develop a high-level framework to learn, catalogue, and understand from local communities what they currently are doing to adapt to climate change impacts in their home villages. The development of bottom-up mechanisms would help to make local communities 'stakeholders in peace'[73] and owners of the rebuilding of institutions that serve them. Most importantly, rethinking peacebuilding from the bottom up would help raise environmental issues to a first tier priority.

notes

1. The concept of environmental peacemaking, whereby environmental issues serve as the basis for general and specific cooperation in a conflict-ridden setting, is not new, however. See K. Conca and G. Dabelko (eds) *Environmental Peacemaking*, Baltimore, MD: Johns Hopkins University Press, 2003.
2. Adaptation to climate change refers to adaptation methods in natural or human systems to actual or expected climatic changes. Types of adaptation activities include anticipatory or reactive measures that are collaborative or individual in nature.
3. Migrating is one type of coping mechanism, and thus can be viewed positively. For example, voluntary economic migration can have a positive impact on poverty, through financial remittances. But, in the Sudan case, fleeing was due to the violence that took place after the drought.
4. D. Smith and J. Vivekananda, *A Climate of Conflict: The Links Between Climate Change, Peace and War*, London: International Alert, 2007.
5. Resilience can be described as a 'system's ability to bounce back' after a disaster or disturbance, and of the system (local or national in nature) to

be able to maintain basic equitable functions despite the disturbance. A resilient society is one that is locally or otherwise soundly governed and has mechanisms in place to deal with risks. Social resilience can be viewed as the capacity to cope under stress or unexpected forces, while maintaining basic social and individual structures and mechanisms. See United Nations Development Programme, *Human Development Report, 2007/2008*, 2007.

6. This is not to say that conflicts cannot be traced to environmental causes, because many intrastate and interstate conflicts can indeed be linked to natural resource issues. In fact, the roots of violent conflict can often be traced, at least in part, to natural resource scarcity or land claim issues: for example, the Mexican Revolution of 1912, the Spanish Civil War in 1936–39, the Chinese revolution in 1949, the Cuban revolution of 1959, the El Salvadorian civil war in the 1980s, and more recently in Nepal, Guatemala, Brazil, Sudan, and Zimbabwe.

7. United Nations Environment Programme, *Global Environment Outlook GEO4, Environment for Development*, Foreward, 2007.

8. Ibid., p. 303.

9. United Nations Climate Change Conference Bali Action Plan, 2007, p. 2.

10. Noted in Christian Aid, from Intergovernmental Panel on Climate Change, *Climate Change 2007: Climate Change Impacts, Adaptation and Vulnerability*, Draft of the Technical Summary. Working Group II Contribution to the Fourth Assessment Report, 2007.

11. Smith and Vivekananda, *A Climate of Conflict*, p. 10.

12. M. Boko, I. Niang, A. Nyong, C. Vogel, A. Githeko, M. Medany, B. Osman-Elasha, R. Tabo and P. Yanda, 'Africa', in M.L. Parry, O.F. Canziani, J.P. Palutikof, P.J. van der Linden and C.E. Hanson (eds) *Climate Change 2007: Impacts, Adaptation and Vulnerability. Contribution of Working Group II to the Fourth Assessment Report of the Intergovernmental Panel on Climate Change*, Cambridge, UK: Cambridge University Press, 2007, pp. 433–67, quote on pp. 456–57.

13. Christian Aid, *Climate Change 2007*, pp. 41–3.

14. United Nations Development Programme, *Human Development Report*, p. 171.

15. F. Rotberg, *Humanitarian Challenges to Climate Change Vulnerability*, Project Proposal to Sida. Stockholm, unpublished, 2007.

16. United Nations Environment Programme, *Global Environment Outlook GEO4*, p. 346.

17. Estimates vary. See, for example, CIA, The World Fact Book, https://www.cia.gov/cia/publications/factbook/geos/tt.html, accessed on 13 February 2008.

18. Due to a memorandum of understanding with Australia in July 2001, and a 2006 agreement between the two countries, Timor-Leste will receive 90% of the tax revenues from oil and gas deposits in the Timor Sea. In this way, Timor-Leste is likely to reduce some of its historical economic burden. It has been suggested that these oil and gas revenues will be worth $100 million annually, beginning in 2007–08 and lasting 20 years (Reuters Foundation, 2006, p. 1. Please see alertnet.org).

19. United Nations Development Programme, *Human Development Report*, p. 231.

20. Please refer to A. Harrington, *Ethnicity, Violence, & Land and Property Disputes in Timor-Leste*, Dili: Timor-Leste, 2006 (copy provided to author before publication in *East Timor Law Journal*, 2007), pp. 1–48, for a full discussion on this ethnic distinction.

21. Ibid., pp. 18 and 19.

22. Freedom House, *Countries at the Crossroads 2006, Country Report – East Timor*, Washington, DC: Freedom House, 2006, p. 1.

23. D. Fitzpatrick and R. Monson, *Balancing Rights and Norms: Property Programming in East Timor, the Solomon Islands and Bougainville*, unpublished, Toronto, 2007, p. 4.

24. European Union, 2006, *Country Strategy Paper East Timor 2002–2006*, Brussels: European Union, p. 4.

25. Fitzpatrick and Monson, *Balancing Rights and Norms*, p. 3.

26. Oxfam, *The Customary Use of Natural Resources in Timor-Leste.* Dili: Oxfam, 2003, p. 5.

27. Ibid., p. 6.

28. Ibid., p. 8.

29. Ibid., p. 3.

30. Ibid., p. 4.

31. United Nations, 2006, p. 17.

32. Fitzpatrick and Monson, *Balancing Rights and Norms*, p. 5.

33. D. Fitzpatrick, *Land Policy in Post Conflict Circumstances: Some Lessons from East Timor*, Working Paper (No. 58), New York: UNHCR, 2002, p. 4.

34. The Law Report, 2004, pp. 2–3.

35. COHRE Report, 2000, p. 14.

36. Population displacement is a feature of conflict in the world today. Please see UNHCR, *The State of the World's Refugees*, 2000.

37. D. Fitzpatrick, Land Policy in Post Conflict Circumstances: Some Lessons from East Timor, *The Journal of Humanitarian Assistance*, 24 November 2001, p.11. http://www.jha.ac/articles/a074.htm, accessed 27 January 2008.

38. See http://www.cohre.org/store/attachments/COHRE%20Housing%20 Rights%20East%20Timor%202000.pdf accessed 27 January, 2008 for further discussion on this issue.

39. Harrington, *Ethnicity, Violence, & Land and Property Disputes*, p. 28. See also page 33 for personal correspondence with a UN Judicial Officer about how the UNTAET Land and Property Unit used traditional law and customary mechanism to settle urgent land disputes. See also Fitzpatrick, *Land Policy in Post Conflict Circumstances*.

40. Harrington, *Ethnicity, Violence, & Land and Property Disputes*, p. 33.

41. UN Security Council Resolution 1272, 25 October 1999.

42. See, for example, United Nations, 2006, pp. 17–18.

43. R. Paris, *At War's End. Building Peace After Civil* Conflict Cambridge; New York: Cambridge University Press, 2004, p. 219.

44. Harrington, *Ethnicity, Violence, & Land and Property Disputes*, p. 21.

45. M. Pugh, *Peacebuilding and Spoils of Peace: The Bosnia and Herzegovina Experience*, Plymouth: Plymouth International Studies Centre, 2001, p. 10.

46. Fitzpatrick, *Land Policy in Post Conflict Circumstances*, p. 219. Again, UNHCR and IOM were mandated to manage the return of refugees but neither had complete control.
47. Harrington, *Ethnicity, Violence, & Land and Property Disputes*, p. 40.
48. USAID, 2004, p. 7.
49. Passage of land laws does not necessarily mean there will be security. For example, in many remote areas, wealthy land owners simply push peasants off the land that is rightly theirs. Government corruption and lack of governmental enforcement also fuel this problem. See H. De Soto, *The Mystery of Capital*, New York: Basic Books, 2000 for further discussion on this topic.
50. USAID, 2004, p. 2.
51. Fitzpatrick, *Land Policy in Post Conflict Circumstances*, p. 3.
52. USAID, 2004, p. 1.
53. In Transparency International's annual ranking, Timor-Leste was 111 among 163 countries and earned a 2.6 corruption composite, with a score of 10 being not corrupt and 0 being highly corrupt.
54. Ibid., p. 7.
55. F. Rotberg, 'Why the World Should Care about Timor-Leste', *Asia Media*, June 14, 2006.
56. Fitzpatrick, *Land Policy in Post Conflict Circumstances*, p. 15.
57. Ibid., p. 12.
58. Ibid., p. 15.
59. Fitzpatrick and Monson, *Balancing Rights and Norms*, p. 6.
60. Fitzpatrick, *Land Policy in Post Conflict Circumstances*, p. 15.
61. It has been suggested that part of this omission was due to local politicians wanting to maintain lack of legal clarity so they could gain personally in terms of land claims. See Harrington, *Ethnicity, Violence, & Land and Property Disputes*, p. 30.
62. Fitzpatrick, *Land Policy in Post Conflict Circumstances*, p. 18.
63. Ibid., p. 4.
64. Harrington, *Ethnicity, Violence, & Land and Property Disputes*, p. 13.
65. See Harrington, *Ethnicity, Violence, & Land and Property Disputes*, for an in-depth discussion of how arguments and violence along eastern and western divides can be seen as far back as the 1940s, when market stalls in Dili were relegated along social lines. From Babo Soares, Dionisio da Costa, 'Branching from the Trunk East Timorese Perceptions of Nationalism in Transition', Doctor of Philosophy Thesis, ANU, Department of Anthropology (December 2003), Chapter 8.
66. Harrington, *Ethnicity, Violence, & Land and Property Disputes*, p. 41.
67. International Crisis Group, 'Resolving Timor Leste's Crisis' *Asia Report* No. 120, Dili: International Crisis Group, 10 October 2006, p. 5.
68. Harrington, *Ethnicity, Violence, & Land and Property Disputes*, p. 43. Harrington, in correspondence with the author (2007), indicates that in the wake of the crisis some leaders are now exploiting the situation further for their own gain, acting as peacemakers. See also IISS Strategic Comments,

Turmoil in Timor-Leste: Nation Building Unravels, Vol. 12, Issue 5, International Institute for Strategic Studies, 2006.

69. Fitzpatrick and Monson, *Balancing Rights and Norms*, p. 7.
70. USAID, 2006, p. 21.
71. Ibid.
72. Smith and Vivekananda, *A Climate of Conflict*, p. 30.
73. Pugh, *Peacebuilding and Spoils of Peace*, p. 10.

22

terrorist conflict vs. civil peace in the Basque country

ioannis tellidis

introduction

In an era when the study of terrorism has become fashionable, to the extent that more and more institutions now offer modules on the topic, this chapter employs the Basque case in order to explain the processes under which terrorism is taken up as an option by an ethno-nationalist movement, and the circumstances under which violence substitutes for the means and becomes the end. It is my contention that such processes do not exclusively lead to violence, but instead can be inverted to adopt more civil postures, as is the case in the Basque country, where the civil society seems to have found itself in the middle of two discourses: that of a state that does not recognise calls for independence, even from anti-violent moderates, basing its arguments on the extensive autonomy already granted; and that of a terrorist organisation that has shown no remorse for its selection of targets, including anti-violent moderates. More concretely, this chapter aims to question the power relationships under examination and intends to offer an understanding of their emergence[1] and the reasons behind the specific interpretation of the 'facts',[2] and seeks to determine which elements are universal and which are 'historically contingent'.[3] The implication of the findings is that there are both scope and potential for both civil society and the state to collaborate in the redefinition of the discourse used to manifest concrete political grievances. But, for such a concord to be achieved, the state must first accept its own share of responsibility – that is, it must identify the reasons why its loss of legitimacy was so serious that it pushed groups to contemplate the utilisation of violence as an effective strategy.

Employing Smith's ethno-symbolic paradigm,[4] this chapter intends to question the understandings of reality in the Basque case and critically examine: (a) the defence by the nationalist minority of its historic truth that brings forward its violent demands for self-determination as a protection from the usurpation of the State; (b) the defence by the State that the nationalist grievances have been solved with the Statute of Autonomy, and therefore the only problem in question is that of violence; and (c) the efforts for an end to the problem of violence, which, until recently, have centred only around the two principal actors, that is, the State and ETA, without taking into consideration the role that the Basque civil society can play in the resolution of the conflict and the elimination of violence. It is this last dimension that makes evident the significance of civil societies and the role they can play in peacebuilding, which has traditionally been approached and implemented as a process that focuses exclusively on the 'particular' interests of the conflictive parties, and ignores the 'general' interest, built and based on personal and collective experiences of the conflict. For, even though the potential of the grass-roots level for a 'bottom-up' approach to peace has been highlighted before,[5] peacebuilding often bypasses local needs and remains very much focused on a 'top-down' approach.[6]

This approach is also evident in terrorist conflicts. States often seem incapable of escaping the spiral of violence the terrorists aim to drag them into, thus alienating and radicalising further the movement and the general population. In the Basque case, the formation of the Anti-terrorist Liberation Groups (GAL – Grupos Antiterroristas de Liberación) in the late 1980s, which killed 27 innocent people, is such an example. This non-liberal (or even anti-liberal) stand was coupled with the orthodox discourse that pointed to the use of existing institutionalised channels that every liberal democratic state puts at the disposal of its citizens, particularly minorities, for the voicing and resolving of their grievances and/or concerns.[7] This, as my examination of the Basque case shows, did not take into consideration 'permanent' minorities that were engaged in a futile battle against the wishes and the agendas of a 'permanent' majority. Furthermore, even though there may be numerous rounds of negotiations between the state and the terrorists, they serve to verify that the interests and needs of the civil society are not on the table. In the Basque Country, this led to the catastrophic consequence of the two principal actors, ETA and the State, becoming locked in a war of attrition,[8] which, in turn, over-

looked and ignored the urgent need for peace expressed by the population (local, as well as national). As a result, a movement for peace
began developing towards the mid-1990s, thanks mainly to the aid,
assistance, and initiatives of non-governmental organisations (NGOs)
that were set up precisely for the purpose of educating and informing the extremist minority as well as the centralist majority that the
violence exhibited from both sides of the conflict was detrimental not
only to them as conflictive parties, but also to the very society they
both claimed to represent and/or work for.

The chapter offers a brief historical background of the Basque conflict that will help set the parameters for the analysis of nationalist
terrorism, not least by highlighting the contextual importance of the
nationalist factor in the use of violence, by ETA as well as by the
State's counterterrorist strategies and policies. This is then followed by
a short analysis of the ethno-symbolic[9] paradigm and its contribution
to the explanation of nationalism as an ideology, followed, in turn,
by an analysis of theories of terrorism, and the criticisms they have
received for ways in which research on terrorism has been conducted
so far. My aim is to show the importance, for peacebuilding, of the
continuity links between terrorism and the broader ideological environment by which they are used, and how terrorist end-objectives
are not at all different from those of the social movement of which
they form part. As such, any peacebuilding effort should not focus
solely on the violent manifestation of the discourse, but should rather
attempt to tackle the violence inherent in the discourse itself. In the
final section I show that civil society networks seem to have taken
over the peacebuilding process by positioning themselves against and
between the terrorists and the politicians, thereby manifesting that
nationalisms are neither bad nor good, but, rather, they depend on
the social, political, and economic environment, as well as their historical trajectory, and they can be both at different stages of their
evolution.[10] On the one hand, Basque civil society unequivocally
rejects any manifestation of violence, yet, on the other, it requests
that a political advancement be made on the nationalist demands. In
other words, these networks seem to have substituted for the lack of
political will manifested by statewide as well as local political parties
when it came to establishing a process whereby the conflict would be
resolved, thus breaking away from the bipolar context that peace will
only be achieved once either of the actors in the conflict has admitted defeat and surrendered.

historical background

There are three very important historical moments for Basque nationalism, all of which contributed to the reinforcement of the differentiation
between the Basque and the Spanish identity: (a) the medieval; (b) the end
of the nineteenth and the beginning of the twentieth century, when the
founder of Basque nationalism, Sabino Arana, and his writings appeared;
and (c) from the 1950s onwards, when ETA made its first appearance.
During the first period, the Basque provinces operated under the system
of 'fueros', that is, customary or traditional laws that governed the private
as well as the public sphere,[11] and which the Castilian monarchy had
accepted as a form of agreement granting each province substantial powers of self-government.[12] The most important aspect of the fueros was
that it exempted the local population from state military conscription
and state taxation. The former meant that any military threat would be
dealt with by the Basques themselves, which in turn implied the formation and organisation of some kind of Basque military machine – albeit
for defence purposes. The right, known as hidalguía de sangre (nobility
by blood) or hidalguía colectiva (collective nobility), was granted to the
Basques by the Spanish Crown Kings, who saw in it an alternative to an
efficient border defence system that would limit the intrusions of the
French.[13] On the other hand, the exemption from the state taxation system hinted at a secured economic development for the provinces, especially when compared with the rest of the Spanish regions.

Industrialisation transformed the Basque Country into the motor
of the Spanish economy, and its urban centres expanded suddenly by
attracting many immigrants, from the Basque rural areas as well as from
the rest of Spain. It was at the same time that the first centralising policies began to take place, for example a linguistically unified education[14]
and the abolition of the fueros, as a result of the two Carlist Wars.[15]
These two historical processes, economic immigration and political
centralisation, were taken up by Sabino Arana y Goiri at the end of the
nineteenth century and used as pillars in his nationalist discourse. The
state policies reflected that the Basque was something that belonged to
the past and the way forward was the liberalism that emanated from
Spain, a discourse which the newly formed Basque urban elites found
appealing.[16] According to Arana, the state was aiming to eliminate the
Basque identity, rooted in the community, the language, and the religious devotion. The immigrants, on the other hand, referred to by Arana
as 'maketos' (a racially derogatory term), served as the manifestation

of Spain's degeneration.[17] As Sullivan describes, 'Arana's belief that the maketos constituted a danger to the moral health and social purity of the Basques led him to call for measures which would make life uncomfortable for the maketos.'[18]

Arana's work is of major importance to the comprehension of Basque nationalism, not because of its historicist scope and depth but because of its influence on the establishment and development of Basque claims in more contemporary times. His philosophy, as it is synthesised through his writings, resembles strikingly the ideas of German nationalism and Romanticism, that is, 'an interest in ethnic customs, an attachment to vernaculars, nostalgia for tribal and medieval pageantry and society, [and] religious yearnings'.[19] Arana brought together territory, history, religion, and community – that is, some of the core elements of nationalist ideologies. In the Ikurriña (the Basque flag), for instance, which was designed by Arana, the red background reflects the blood of the historical battles and struggles; the green represents the Basque traditions and spirit of community, and is associated with the Tree of Gernika – the place where historical local representatives met and Spanish monarchs swore allegiance to the Basque 'fueros'; finally, 'both red and green were represented in submission to the purity of the white cross, with religion, of course, forming an integral part of Arana's sacramental nationalism'.[20] He intended to use language as an instrument of political mobilisation,[21] but the fact that it was scarcely spoken not only in the urban sceneries but even in its strongholds, the rural areas, made it a difficult and optimistic undertaking. It is for this reason that race was placed above language when it came to asserting Basque distinctiveness.[22] His discourse attracted the interest of the Basque liberal bourgeoisies, and increasing popular support led him to the formation of the Basque Nationalist Party (PNV). Following its foundation, paradoxically, Arana's understanding of the social changes the Basque country was experiencing was transformed. He realised that, instead of degenerative consequences, the expansion of the economy through the development of the industry could play a major role in the promotion of Basque language and culture.23 Sabino Arana died in 1903 without explaining what had caused that sudden change. The ambivalence, however, between radical and incremental nationalism was to remain with the entire movement until our days.

Some 50 years after his death, and after a brutal submission of the entire population to the Francoist dogma, the nationalist discourse was revived once again, this time by youth organisations of the movement who had

had no experience of the war, other than the narratives of relatives. Motivated by the general apathy and inaction of the party and the population, a group of upper-middle-class young university students founded a magazine, *Ekin* (to do), with the aim of promoting familiarity with the Basque traditions through the writings of Basque intellectuals (mainly Arana's, but also others' whose views on the heroism and the purity of the Basques were very much aligned with the founder of the movement). At the same time, the PNV's youth, EGI, also begun to develop a nationalist action, albeit a more radical one: graffiti and pro-nationalist slogans painted on the walls of the cities and the smaller towns. In 1956, *Ekin* merged with EGI and its representatives asked PNV – which was then in exile in Paris – for recognition and support, a demand that was declined by PNV's cadres. The party's refusal was received by the nationalist youth as an unwillingness or even an inability to confront Franco's authoritarian regime.[24] Their immediate response to PNV's stance was the creation of Euskadi Ta Askatasuna (ETA – Basque Homeland and Freedom). The direct implication was that the PNV would cease to be the only legitimate representative of Basque nationalism.[25]

ETA's emergence brought with it a change in the basic assumptions of Basque nationalism, although it was still very close to Arana's ideological triptych of action–vocation–community. A book titled *Vasconia*, written by Federico Krutwig, one of ETA's most important intellectuals, was to mark the shift from Aranism to modern Basque nationalism. One main difference, espoused by Krutwig, was the subordination of ethnicity to language. As Clark puts it, '[t]he Basques were defined as unique by their ethnicity, which in turn was a product of their language. Were Euskera to disappear, the Basques would disappear as a nation'.[26] A second change concerned the substitution of Arana's racist cronies by the introduction of ideas on revolutionary or guerrilla war, as the only viable way that could lead to the much-desired independence. Finally, in *Vasconia*, Arana's assiduity in Catholicism 'was replaced by the idea of politics as a vocation'.[27] The main reason for this is that the regime espoused the ideals of 'National Catholicism' (nacionalcatolicismo), whereby the Church maintained its silence over the atrocities committed by the regime. In return, the Church was provided with control of secondary education.[28] 'This stiff attitude on the part of the Church was another factor in encouraging many believers to join ETA or support its activists.'[29] The country was occupied by a corrupt and extremely violent (for the Basques at least) regime; and the only way to respond to the violence of such a regime was deemed to be violence.

While ETA counted on the support of a broad sector of the Spanish population during the dictatorship, the use of violence after the transition to democracy became incomprehensible. The continuous splits suffered by the organisation, always between moderates and extremists, and always ending with the reaffirmation of the latter, marked a shift in targets that now included local journalists, politicians, entrepreneurs, and anyone who might oppose ETA's plans. Basque society began to find itself in the middle of a situation where being a nationalist would attract the wrath of the state, and not being nationalist enough could have you targeted by ETA. It is this context that allows us to observe the distancing of the nationalist drive from its traditional violent connotations, replaced by a reaction that has emerged as the principal motor of conflict resolution in the country.

the problem with nationalism

If, as I have claimed, terrorist drives and objectives are very much in line with the broader discourse and/or movement that utilises terrorism, then it makes sense to claim further that one must firstly comprehend the drives and objectives of the movement itself before examining and analysing the terrorist practices and strategies of that movement. Nationalism, as a phenomenon, seems to be just as much an essentially contested concept as terrorism.[30] One of the primary reasons for the theoretical confusion is attributed to the different manifestations of the phenomenon.[31] A normative distinction that has been drawn in order to facilitate understanding is that between civic/political and ethnic/cultural nationalism. The former refers to 'the achievement of a representative national state that will guarantee to its members uniform citizenship rights',[32] whereas the latter operates as 'a movement of moral regeneration', whose aim is to reunite the different aspects of the nation and, thus, reintroduce the national identity.[33]

But, even with that distinction drawn, the explanations and theories offered by students of nationalism are as varied as those centred on terrorism. Early theories focused on the primordial family and religious ties that survived the phases of modernity and industrialisation.[34] The framework of primordiality was utilised for the examination of ethnic ties,[35] whose existence depended on cultural 'givens' (blood, race, language, locality, religion, or tradition),[36] which make an individual feel strongly for his/her compatriots. However, while the effect of those feelings can be observed (for instance, they differentiate between groups[37]), that which makes them emerge remains 'ineffable'. Sociobiological theories[38] that focused on mechanisms of kin selection as a means to maximise inclusive fitness[39] also failed to produce a rigorous explanation, because common descent and the sharing of a common identity need to be, to a certain extent, fictive.[40] Cultural traits, therefore, are necessary for the preservation of identity, even in instances where ethnic groups have undergone an instrumental change of ethnic identity, principally because of circumstances that were affecting their material or socio-political interests.[41]

One common criticism of the aforementioned blocks of theories is that they fail to take into account the historical dimension and how it contributed to the shaping of ethnic identities.[42] This dimension is very much the pillar of modernist explanations of nationalism, labelled as such because they consider nationalism to be an essentially modern phenomenon: either as the product of the German Romanticist movement,[43] a by-product of uneven development that is generated by a speedy and all-encompassing industrialisation,[44] or merely an innovation generated by historically particular circumstances and held together by tradition.[45] However, even though their identification of history as a contributing factor to the emergence of nationalism was correct, modernist scholars failed to explain the mechanisms by which nationalism made use of the past in order to show the degeneration of the present and, thus, project a regenerative future.[46] The postmodernist identification of the necessity to imagine[47] the nation as an extended family – particularly one that has existed since the beginning of time[48] – and the communication of the nationalist ideals through the sphere of imagination were a theoretical step towards a clearer framework. It is in this context that Smith's ethno-symbolic paradigm is of great analytical use, because it identifies a person's primordial feelings for his or her nation as generated not by nationalism but by the power of the symbols the nation carries and projects.[49] The European Union (EU), for instance, is incapable of generating feelings of unity and common descent, precisely because it lacks the symbols and myths that will help it establish a shared past, which, in turn, will project a common future.[50]

These myths and symbols, as I argue in the following section, should not be separated from a contextual analysis of militant nationalist movements. Their regurgitation by the extremist fractions of the Basque nationalist movement cannot be reduced to mere propaganda, for it is they that contribute to the formation and establishment of an ethnic identity, and it is they that determine its strength and its defence by the people that claim it or aspire to share it. The emergence of ETA cannot be solely attributed to the oppression of an authoritarian regime; the symbolisms, myths, and legacies of the nationalist discourse were (and still are) an important motivation for the utilisation of violence. The following section demonstrates that, and highlights the main problems in the analyses of terrorism. More importantly, it explains why a combined investigation of the broader movement that finds refuge in terrorist practices raises the potential for more efficient efforts of the resolution of terrorist conflicts.

the problem with terrorism

Invariably, every study on terrorism begins by highlighting the lack of definitional consensus for the term, and how it hinders the formulation of conventional types of analysis through hypotheses and measurements.[51] Despite the great interdisciplinary wealth of knowledge that has been gathered so far, there seems to be developing a polemic in the field of terrorism studies, according to which research on terrorism lacks a historical perspective and adopts an overtly state-centric approach, which is a consequence of the fact that a number of scholars are funded by the state or are members of institutions that are closely related to State Intelligence and Security agencies. This state-centric approach also explains why most end-products of research on terrorism rush to suggest ways of combating it, without necessarily understanding the phenomenon.[52] Even though these criticisms intend to bypass the fallacies of 'orthodox theories of terrorism',[53] they are not exactly new. Early criticisms on the conduct of research on terrorism concerned the narrow conceptual frameworks and the 'ahistorical linear causal models that ignore the historical and comparative aspects of terrorism',[54] as well as the skewed and biased focus of some studies financed or commissioned by state institutions or agencies linked to these.[55] Studies from other disciplines have claimed that the inability to gather primary material (interviews with terrorists) renders the field inherently inadequate and therefore obsolete.[56]

The states' interpretation and understanding of terrorism has been shaped by the hegemonic practice embedded in the Westphalian traditions of the system of states. States all too often choose to respond to the manifestation of violence with violence, and to superimpose their own core nationalism on peripheral nationalisms. Thus, they choose to ignore academic findings that highlight terrorism's 'agenda-setting function', that is, a broader discourse that surrounds terrorist acts and provides a basis for the terrorist discourse itself, and which cannot be fought against solely punitively by the state.[57] or rational choice theories which suggested that terrorism may be the last decision in a sequence of choices.[58] Furthermore, psychological studies have enhanced our understanding by making clear how group dynamics and group identity evolve,[59] and the implications of this for the severity of violence. More important, however, is the fact that these theories, complemented by peace and conflict theories of human needs[60] and relative deprivation,[61] have implications for the role of the state in its treatment of the violent minority. To put it plainly, while the state is the only actor capable of confronting the violence of terrorists, it is also the only actor that has the capacity to identify (a) the reasons why its legitimacy is in dispute and (b) how to address them in a way that does not lead to further loss of credibility and legitimacy. In nationalist conflicts like the Basque case, the state failed to capitalise on the broad alienation that ETA's radicalisation produced. Instead, and to put it in medical terms, it treated the pain (violence) but ignored the symptoms (anti-centralist feelings). The contextualisation, then, of the utilisation of violence must pass not only through historical analyses of the movement itself, but also through an analysis of the confrontation between the state and the movement: more concretely, the state's understanding of the terrorists and of itself.

During the transition to democracy ETA intensified its campaign: more than 200 attacks took place every year between 1978 and 1982, with 1980 recorded as the bloodiest year in the country's contemporary history.[62] ETA's transformation from the only organisation capable of mounting a serious offensive against the dictatorship into a dictator itself scared away the Spanish public, who quickly became hostile. The Basque public, however, were not so sceptical. As Mees describes, democracy for the Basques equalled self-government, and there is no self-government when there is three-dimensional violence:

> violence used as an instrument of the defenders of the dictatorship – including the anti-ETA terror commandos from the extreme right – against the Basque (nationalist and non-nationalist) opposition, violence as a consequence of the lack of democracy and self-government, and violence as a means of political pressure and intimidation in the hands of the 'armed vanguard' of ETA.63

As many other commentators have noted, the transition was perceived in the Basque country as just another way in which the Spanish state would continue to violate Basque rights and customs.[64] Indeed, the transition was not reflected in the re-formation of state agencies like the security forces and the police stationed in the Basque country. How are things different if the torturers of the dictatorship are now the police officers of the democracy?[65]

Not only has the nationalist dimension always surrounded ETA's terrorist campaign, but, in a sense, it has been the motor behind the perpetuation of violence itself. This chapter regards terrorism in the Basque conflict as *one* method of conducting ethno-nationalist conflicts: a method to incite the kind of violence encountered in war, with all the symbolism that war carries, but lacking the appropriate means to reach the scale. By symbolism of war, I mean that, if war is the ultimate solution and the cause is deemed as significant, men will go on and fight. Indeed, if I may paraphrase Clausewitz, terrorism is politics by other means. It might be war on the cheap,[66] but that does not move away the intention, which in turn is promoted by a greater cause. It is this greater cause, nationalism in this instance, that also contributes to the symbolism of war, with a discourse of past heroes, martyrs, and collective resistance for the common good. The exaltation of ETA's fighting image, which started in the Francoist era, has not been shaken off. On the contrary, as Juan José Echave admitted, 'ETA has never been defined by an ideology (in the strict sense), but by its spirit of struggle'.[67] ETA draws its strength because it is a structure as much as it is a concept, and the constant supremacy of violent fractions is attributed to the nationalist legends that have surrounded ETA itself.[68] The fact that everyone, from academic scholars to people in the street, has referred to and continues to refer to the organisation as ETA, despite its schisms and divisions through the years, verifies its conceptual nature[69] and explains the culture of violence it seems to generate in its immediate social surroundings.[70]

> Political violence became consecrated and the celebration of ETA activists, dead, imprisoned or alive, produced a mystical and emotional aureole around the movement, which penetrated even into the smallest rural area and destroyed familiar and friendship ties between those who joined the movement and those who did not.[71]

Further ethnographic examination of the transfusion of violence into the nationalist discourse makes discernable certain cultural elements that serve as a link between the present and the past, both in terms of identity and in terms of guidance and action. The word *ekintza* means precisely that (action), and it was used during the first moments of ETA and is used until today to describe any violent actions of the organisation. Its verb form, *Ekin* (to do), was the name of ETA's forerunner and its 'founders conceived it as opposed to the static, outdated and passive attitude of the old [...] generation'.[72] The meaning of action in the Basque life has been attributed to the religious doctrine of living a life strictly dictated by religious belief,[73] and it has come to represent Basques virtually as a national definition.[74] As in the Aranist discourse, a true Basque is one who fights for Euskadi's liberation[75] and defends the symbols of the nation's cohesion and differentiation.[76]

It is not the historicism or the symbolism which is important, however, or even the fact that these can be discernible at all in the nationalist–terrorist discourse; it is the fact that they are powerful enough to create belief structures and influence individuals who become agents of violence. 'It is this remembered history, invariably oversimplified, with heroes and villains overdrawn, that mobilises and motivates the next generation.'[77] In a study based on a plethora of interviews with imprisoned former *etarras*, it is highlighted how the mysticism and ritualism that surrounded the organisation, and to a certain extent the entire movement, aided their nationalist sentiment and contributed to their decision to become active members.[78] The issue of independence is not just an occasion for ETA, because, if it is merely a pretext, then from the very moment that the pretext disappears ETA will have no reasons to utilise violence.[79] Reinares' interviewees make particular reference of the fact that independence comes before everything else for ETA's militants, even before the type of regime a future Euskadi would have.[80] In theoretical terms, 'the nationalist triad [of past, present and future] legitimises the use of political violence as it is only the latter that will ultimately restore the nation's original purity'.[81]

These signals, however, were not picked up by the central political authorities in Madrid. In the 1980s, public opinion throughout Spain was shocked by the revelations that 27 innocent people were shot dead by the GAL, formed to target suspected *etarras*. During the 1990s, the general feeling of stupefaction with ETA's practices of targeting virtually anyone and everyone, inside and outside the Basque Country, was picked up by the first government of José Maria Aznar, for whom appeasement was not a viable solution to the problem of violence,[82] when compared with the police efficacy in arresting *etarras* and dismembering the local cells of the organisation. But when a block of all nationalist parties in the Basque Country produced an Agreement in 1998[83] that brought with it the first indefinite and unilateral ceasefire by ETA in its history, Aznar's government saw the opportunity in a clause contained in the document, which recognised the sovereignty of the Basque people, to criminalise the entire nationalist movement.[84] Other commentators have also questioned Aznar's commitment to the ceasefire, considering how in 1999, during a round of negotiations with two of ETA's negotiators in Zurich, the Spanish government leaked the names of the mediators with the arrest of one of the two interlocutors as a result.[85]

In 2000, Aznar was re-elected for a second term, with absolute majority, which offered him the perfect opportunity to promote a set of policies that signalled to the Basque nationalist block that it is not just terrorism the state will not put up with, it is also nationalism. The ban of the political party Batasuna in August 2002, and the closure of *Egunkaria*, the only Basque newspaper, in 2003 and the arrests of its staff were perceived as an attack on freedom of speech and verified to the local population (particularly to the moderate nationalists) their fears that had originated at the beginning of transition: that the State was against the cultural differentiation of the Basque Country. 'The very Francoist roots of [Partido Popular] were now laid bare to see and were rediscovered as an argument of popular polemics.'[86] The direct result of these policies was the radicalisation of the nationalist bloc, extremists as well as moderates. It is this political posture that gives rise to academic calls for the study of the role of the state in the manifestation of terrorism.[87] Undeniably, the Basque conflict highlights instances where the liberal democratic state has not been either very liberal or very democratic, for its own nationalist reasons and perceptions of security. It is precisely this stalemate between the two actors of the conflict that gave rise to the local civil society, and which permitted it to emerge as the primary transformator of the conflict and claim its own right to peace and identity.

peacebuilding and the Basque country

As with terrorism, the state-centricity issue is also the focus of peace and conflict studies. The prominence of the Westphalian system, in an era where most conflicts are intrastate rather than interstate,[88] did not prove very useful in either the management or the resolution of conflicts, particularly terrorist conflicts that contest the hegemony and legitimacy of a state.[89] 'Peace' is yet another contested concept that has attracted multiple interpretations,[90] most of which centre on the Westphalian doctrine of sovereignty, monopoly of violence and inviolability of borders, and the use of force in order to attain peace.[91] While there is a rich account of the evolution of peace and conflict, to which this volume wishes to contribute, this chapter's findings seem to coincide with one of the earliest critical frameworks brought forward, that of human needs and provention. The former explained why some conflicts persisted despite the varying use of power to regulate them,[92] and the latter implied 'the promotion of an environment conducive to harmonious relationships'.[93] Burton's framework, coupled with the findings of the most recent theoretical bloc,[94] which concentrates on an emancipatory dimension of peace that is built on consensus, 'rather than an assumption of consensus tinged with moral superiority',[95] provides a framework for understanding the reaction of the Basque civil society for peace and its emergence as a conflict transformator. If war is seen to derive 'from purposive human conduct situated within deeply embedded institutional frameworks',[96] then peace, too, should be conceptualised as a counter-discourse, seeking 'to understand the structurated legitimation of violence and challenge the militarist order and exclusionist identities which encompass it'.[97] The Basque case makes evident the under-representation, when it comes to peace, of a community that brings forward genuine demands for self-determination with an equally genuine rejection of violence, yet is being targeted by both major actors in the conflict. In the Basque Country, what is evident is an immense need for peace. The general public opinion, which for years remained silent and terrorised, has began a discourse and a movement for peace that wants to continue exploring a nationalist solution, but is determined to do so in the complete absence of violence.

During the 1990s, ETA brought much of its campaign to the Basque Country. Its target selection broadened to include journalists, academics, and moderate nationalists as well as state-party councillors and politicians. In 1997, two of its kidnappings had an important repercussion in the public's perception of and stand against ETA. In the first case, the victim (a prison worker) was held for 532 days and the plan was to starve him to death unless the central authorities agreed to the transfer of Basque prisoners into Basque prisons. The image of a skinny and extremely debilitated young man who emerged from a cellar room brought back memories of Nazi concentration camps and generated great antipathy, even among the organisation's followers.[98] A week after his release, the organisation kidnapped Miguel Ángel Blanco, a young town councillor belonging to the Popular Party (PP – Partido Popular), and gave the authorities 48 hours for all ETA prisoners to be moved to Basque prisons. The small period of time given to the government to complete the task made the victim's execution almost certain. His death provoked massive, multiple, and, most importantly, spontaneous demonstrations with the message directed both towards ETA, to put an end to its attacks, and 'to the policy makers to start working seriously on a solution to the conflict'.[99] The instances of arson and general attacks on the party offices of Herri Batasuna (HB – the political arm of ETA) throughout the Basque Country were the most vivid demonstration of the popular sentiment towards nationalist extremism.[100] Despite the unpopular environment they found themselves in, HB officials blamed the central government's inaction and the moderate nationalists' stand for Blanco's execution. The result, as Mees notes, was the identification of the party by the public as nothing more than ETA itself.[101]

In sum, the majority of the moderate nationalist circles found itself in the middle of the conflict, targeted on the one hand by ETA because of its condemnation of violence, and on the other hand by the state, which opposed non-violent nationalist calls for the right to self-determination. After a ten-year period – branded 'the time of silence'[102] because of the lack of public disagreement with or opposition to ETA – the first non-governmental organisations emerged that allowed citizens to voice their opposition to violence. The first platform that brought together several small pacifist groups was Coordinadora Gesto por la Paz en Euskal Herria (Coordination of a Gesture for Peace in the Basque Country) in 1987. The 'gesture' refers to the silent manifestations following the perpetration of murderous terrorist attacks, and its principal aims were – and still are – to reinforce the social mobilisation and to promote a culture of peace: not simply a culture that is present due to the absence of violence, but a more positive peace, which makes certain that violent phenomena are dealt by the instinctive pacifist social response.[103]

A second organisation whose involvement lies more in the political sphere rather than Gesto's ethical approach, is Elkarri. Unlike Gesto, Elkarri's work goes much further than the simple, yet unambiguous, rejection of violence, because Elkarri recognises that there is a political side to the problem of violence. During ceasefires, as Gorka Espiau, director of Elkarri, explained, nationalist sentiments ran higher, rather than dissipating along with violence, which indicates that there is a cause worthy of investigation that is deeper than a mere fascination with violence.[104] Elkarri is active on three levels: political, social, and international. On the political level, it attempts to facilitate and, in certain instances, initiate a process of dialogue between the political parties. Espiau indicated that the organisation had succeeded in initiating a round table that consisted of all political parties in Euskadi, with the exception of PP and Batasuna (although it was present at the first ever meeting). On the social level, Elkarri's objective is to organise 'dialogue projects' and debates on the local level. At the time this interview was conducted, there were 60 to 100 local dialogue forums that brought together people from all political shades. The topics of these workshops consist of the same issues that are brought by Elkarri to the round tables of the political parties. The conclusions of the workshops are then sent by Elkarri to the political parties in an effort to ensure that the public's view is not ignored by the political parties, as well as providing a map for them to work on a political solution that would reflect the demands and wishes of the popular base. Espiau referred to a petition signed by 122,000 people urging the political parties of the Basque Country and Navarre to initiate a process of dialogue between them for the exploration of possible solutions to the political as well as the violence problem.[105] The international level of Elkarri's work consists mainly of informational actions that aim at making known the dynamics and dimensions of the Basque conflict and, at the same time, attracting support and consultation for conflict resolution projects that can guarantee the institutional stability and development of the Basque country.

Despite the fact that other organisations have been established,[106] Gesto and Elkarri are the biggest and most popular NGOs in the Basque country, not least because they maintain the inherent feeling of a large part of Basque civil society that aspires to a political project of cultural and political differentiation, but does not want to see it materialised with violence. The lack of a serious political actor that would occupy the space between the local nationalist and the state-wide centralist parties made a lot of people support and further organisations like Gesto and Elkarri. This discourse can be translated as a prioritisation of the local civil society's needs:[107] while self-determination and identity are important, peace is more pressing.

conclusion

What this chapter shows is that an end to ethno-terrorist practices is possible if the circumstances of its emergence are interpreted unambiguously, with full awareness of political discourses and biases. On the part of the State, this can be made possible by examining the role and importance of the local discourses as they are expressed, rather than as the State authorities interpret them. The key practice that can allow the isolation of the terrorists from the communities they claim to represent is for the State to provide assurances to those communities, through practical application of liberal pluralist models of government, (a) that it recognises it is the most important actor in the alleviation of their grievances, and (b) that it is working for alleviation in a way that instils confidence in the population that a non-violent, political process is preferable, as a strategy, for the political bargaining entailed in the demands for further concessions to autonomy.

This chapter has clarified the circumstances under which conflict resolution can constitute a tool of intervention in the process by which nationalism gives rise to ethno-terrorism. As the Basque case has shown, the circumstances under which ethno-terrorist practices become tautological with the broader ethno-nationalist discourse can be disrupted if conflict resolution identifies effectively the cultural and symbolic implications that legitimise the use of violence for the sake of the nationalist objective, that is, independence. For that to be achieved, conflict resolution must be directed towards (a) the minority, which perceives both the nationalist as well as the violent dimensions to be legitimate, and (b) the state, which, ultimately, has a vested interest in assuring the minority not only that it possesses the capacity and resources to alleviate possible grievances but also, crucially, that it is willing to adopt or extend any political mechanisms that allow the minority to differentiate itself politically from the central structures without resorting to violence, which is in turn perpetuated by discourses that take advantage of the cultural structures that are the basis for this differentiation. In order for that process to be successful, the state must cooperate with any local actors, such as NGOs, civil society initiative groups, or moderate nationalist platforms that oppose violence. Besides rejection of any temptations to radicalise its anti-terrorist practices that may mistakenly expand to target non-violent nationalist circles, the implementation of the typical tools offered by conflict resolution, such as workshops or informal dialogue, can contribute to the clarification of perceptions and objectives of both sides. Such practices will also be beneficial because they will help persuade the civil society of the state's willingness to attend to their demands and, as a result, will make the utilisation of violence seem a rather 'suicidal' option. I use the term 'suicidal' because, as is evident in the Basque case, where concessions have been made and there exists the political will to further the political cooperation and elaboration of a possible resolution, any violent manifestations may lead the state to back down or reject further concessions – as was the case with the second term in office of Aznar's centre-right government.

By focusing on the critical analyses of the theories of nationalism, terrorism, and conflict resolution, this chapter identifies a section that permits all three to be used conjointly in order to explain the ethno-terrorist nature of a nationalist conflict and the possibilities for its termination. While none of the three fields is new, the critical frameworks that have been brought forward in recent years, and which I have presented briefly, have shown that a correct identification and analysis of the dynamics and practices of all three allow a better contextualisation of ethno-nationalist conflicts and, crucially, bring to the fore the possibilities that such conflicts might be only circumstantially protracted. While I recognise that joining three seemingly different and separate fields of study is a very optimistic undertaking, I argue that it is a more epistemologically, methodologically, and ontologically plausible way of understanding, explaining, and creating frameworks for resolving ethno-terrorist conflicts than current orthodoxies. Perhaps such a framework only seems feasible once the notions of sovereignty, representation, grievance, statehood, and citizenship are redefined and detached from the current exclusionary framework that dominates the international system. On the other hand, and from a macro-level perspective, perhaps these are not even problems or consequences of modern artefacts like the state and the nation; rather, the tendency might be inherent in the human condition to construct 'others' and differentiate from them for social, political, economic or other purposes.

notes

1. R. Bleiker, *Popular Dissent, Human Agent and Global Politics*, Cambridge: Cambridge University Press, 2000, p. 17.
2. R. Cox, *Approaches to World Order*, Cambridge: Cambridge University Press, 1996, p. 88. See also J. Clifford, 'Introduction: Partial Truths', in J. Clifford and G. Marcus (eds) *Writing Cultures: The Poetics and Politics of Ethnography*, Berkeley, CA: University of California Press, 1986.
3. S. Hoffmann, *Janus and Minerva: Essays on the Theory and Practice of International Relations*, Boulder, CO: Westview Press, 1987, p. 237.
4. A.D. Smith, *The Ethnic Origins of Nations*, Oxford: Blackwell, 1986; A.D. Smith, *Nationalism and Modernism*, London; NY: Routledge, 1998; A.D. Smith, *Myths and Memories of the Nation*, Oxford: Oxford University Press, 1999.
5. E. Azar and J. Burton (eds), *International Conflict Resolution: Theory and Practice*, Sussex: Wheatsheaf, 1986; J.P. Lederach, *Building Peace: Sustainable Reconciliation in Divided Societies*, Washington, DC: US Institute of Peace Press, 1997.
6. M. Duffield, *Global Governance and the New Wars*, London: Zed Books, 2001. See also Viktorova Milne's findings in this volume on the relationship between ethnography and conflict resolution.

7. P. Wilkinson, 'Some observations on the relationship between terrorism and freedom', in M. Warner and R. Crisp (eds) *Terrorism, Protest and Power*, Aldershot: Edward Elgar, 1990, pp. 44–53; C. Cruise O'Brien, 'Terrorism under Democratic Conditions: The Case of the IRA', in Martha Crenshaw (ed.) *Terrorism, Legitimacy and Power: The Consequences of Political Violence*, Scranton: Wesleyan University Press, 1983, p. 93.

8. I. S. Cuenca, *ETA Contra el Estado: Las Estrategias del Terrorismo*, Barcelona: Tusquets, 2001.

9. Smith, *Nationalism and Modernism*.

10. P. Alter, *Nationalism*, London: Arnold, 1994, p. 2.

11. D. Conversi, *The Basques, the Catalans and Spain: Alternative Routes to Nationalist Mobilisation*, London: Hurst & Co., 1997, p. 45.

12. R.P. Clark, *The Basque insurgents: ETA 1952–1980*, Madison: University of Wisconsin Press, 1984, p. 12. Author's parenthesis.

13. D. Greenwood, 'Continuity in Change: Spanish Basque Ethnicity as an Historical Process', in Milton Esman (ed.) *Ethnic Conflict in the Western World*, New York: Cornell University Press, 1977, pp. 81–102, quote on p. 92.

14. C. Watson, *Basque Nationalism and Political Violence: The Ideological and Intellectual Origins of ETA*, Reno: Center for Basque Studies, 2008, p. 46.

15. The wars (1833–39 and 1872–76) were named 'Carlist' due to a controversy that broke out in the Spanish crown. King Ferdinand VII wanted to be succeeded by his daughter Isabel, even though succession in Spain could only take place by a male heir to the throne. Don Carlos, Isabel's brother, counted on the support of the traditionalists, whereas his sister had attracted the attention of the liberals as well as that of France and Britain. The Basque country experienced most of the violence, and as a result the wars have been termed by several authors the 'Basque Civil Wars'. See Watson, *Basque Nationalism and Political Violence*, p. 48; M. Heiberg, *The Making of Basque Nation*, Cambridge: Cambridge University Press, 1989, p. 37.

16. At the time, many intellectuals supported this trend. Miguel de Unamuno, for example, considered the Basque language to be an obstacle to human progress. See L. Mees, *Nationalism, Violence and Democracy: The Basque Clash of Identities*, Basingstoke: Palgrave Macmillan, 2003, p. 12.

17. Other intellectuals, like Manuel de Larramendi and Lopez de Isasti, who wrote before Arana, had also focused extensively on the principle of nobility, transfusing racial characteristics in their discourse. In his writings, Larramendi attacked those members of the peasant aristocracy and the urban bourgeoisie because they were rich and powerful, which for him was synonymous with moral tarnishing. As Heiberg notes, Larramendi became 'the ideologue of small landholder and the tenant farmer', while the traditional, rural, Basque life, 'governed by the values of austerity, social harmony and egalitarianism in social relations was, for Larramendi, the original Basque in a state of grace'. See Heiberg, *The Making of Basque Nation*, pp. 33–4.

18. J. Sullivan, *ETA and Basque Nationalism: The Fight for Euskadi 1890–1986*, London; New York: Routledge, 1988, p. 5.

19. A.D. Smith, *Nationalism in the Twentieth Century*, Oxford: Martin Robertson & Co. Ltd, 1979, p. 7.

20. Watson, *Basque Nationalism and Political Violence*, p. 75.
21. Conversi, *The Basques, the Catalans and Spain*, p. 174.
22. J. Corcuera, *Orígenes, Ideología Y Organización del Nacionalismo Vasco*, 1876–1904, Madrid: Siglo XXI, 1979, p. 395.
23. Mees, *Nationalism, Violence and Democracy*, p. 11.
24. Heiberg, *The Making of Basque Nation*, p. 106.
25. Conversi, *The Basques, the Catalans and Spain*, p. 89.
26. Clark, *The Basque Insurgents*, p. 33.
27. Conversi, *The Basques, the Catalans and Spain*, p. 93.
28. R. Carr and J. Pablo Fusi Aizpurua, *Spain: Dictatorship to Democracy*, London: Allen & Unwin, 1979, p. 28.
29. Conversi, *The Basques, the Catalans and Spain*, p. 95.
30. W.B. Gallie, 'Essentially contested concepts', in Max Black (ed.) *The Importance of Language*, Englewood Cliffs: Prentice Hall, 1962, p. 123.
31. P. Alter, *Nationalism*, London: Arnold, 1994, p. 2.
32. J. Hutchinson and A.D. Smith (eds) *Nationalism*, Oxford; NY: Oxford University Press, 1994, p. 124.
33. Ibid., p. 123.
34. Smith, *Nationalism and Modernism*, p. 151.
35. C. Geertz, *The Interpretation of Cultures*, New York: Basic Books, 1973.
36. Ibid., p. 259.
37. The 'primordialist/instrumentalist' debate of the late 1960s and 1970s draws from an earlier socio-anthropological debate that was started off by Edmund Leach's study. Leach argued that 'social units are produced by subjective processes of categorical ascription that have no necessary relationship to observers' perceptions of cultural discontinuities' (C.G. Bentley, 'Ethnicity and practice', *Comparative Studies in Society and History*, Vol. 29, No. 1, 1987, pp. 24–55, quote on p. 24), which departed from the established method of studying the differences projected by the units themselves.
38. Pierre Louis Van den Berghe, 'Race and ethnicity: a sociobiological perspective', *Ethnic and Racial Studies*, Vol. 21, No. 4, 1978, pp. 401–11.
39. 'Inclusive fitness' is a theory according to which 'genes will spread if their carriers act to increase not only their own fitness or reproductive success but also that of other individuals carrying the same genes. A person's inclusive fitness is his or her personal fitness plus the increased fitness of relatives that he or she has in some way caused by his or her actions'. See V. Reynolds, V. Falger and I. Vine (eds) *The Sociobiology of Ethnocentrism: Evolutionary Dimensions of Xenophobia, Discrimination, Racism and Nationalism*, London: Croom Helm, 1987, p. xvii.
40. Pierre Louis van den Berghe, *The Ethnic Phenomenon*, New York; London: Elsevier, 1981.
41. F. Barth (ed.), *Ethnic Groups and Boundaries: The Social Organisation of Culture Difference*, Boston: Little Brown, 1969. See also M. Mazower, *Salonica: City of Ghosts*, London: Harper Perennial, 2005, for an account of the alteration of identity the Jewish populations underwent when they settled in Ottoman Salonica following their expulsion from Spain.
42. C.G. Bentley, 'Ethnicity and Practice', *Comparative Studies in Society and History*, Vol. 29, No.1, 1987, pp. 24–55; R. Jenkins, 'Rethinking Ethnicity:

Identity, Categorization and Power', *Ethnic and Racial Studies*, Vol. 17, No. 2, 1994, pp. 197–223.

43. E. Kedourie, *Nationalism*, 4th edn, Oxford: Blackwell, 2000.
44. E. Gellner, *Thought and Change*, London: Weidenfeld & Nicholson, 1964; and *Nations and Nationalism*, Oxford: Blackwell, 1983.
45. E. Hobsbawm and T. Ranger, *The Invention of Tradition*, Cambridge: Cambridge University Press, 1983.
46. M. Levinger and P.F. Lyttle, 'Myth and Mobilisation: The Triadic Structure of Nationalist Rhetoric', *Nations and Nationalism*, Vol. 7, No. 2, 2001, pp. 175–94. See also D. Muro, 'Nationalism and Nostalgia: The Case of Basque Radical Nationalism', *Nations and Nationalism*, Vol. 11, No. 4, 2005, pp. 571–89.
47. B. Anderson, *Imagined Communities*, London: Verso, 1991.
48. H. Bhabha, 'Dissemination: Time, Narrative, and the Margins of the Modern Nation', in H. Bhabha (ed.) *Nation and Narration*, London; New York: Routledge, 1990.
49. Smith, *Nationalism and Modernism*, 1998, pp. 170–98.
50. Smith, *Myths and Memories of the Nation*, 1999, p. 233.
51. L. Weinberg and W. Eubank, 'Problems with the Critical Studies Approach to the Study of Terrorism', *Critical Studies on Terrorism*, Vol. 1, No. 2, 2008, pp. 185–95, quote on p. 187.
52. R. Jackson, 'The Core Commitments of Critical Terrorism Studies', *European Political Science*, Vol. 6, No. 3, 2007, pp. 244–51, quote on pp. 244–6.
53. Ibid. See also J. Franks, *Rethinking the Roots of Terrorism*, Basingstoke; New York: Palgrave Macmillan, 2006; J. Hocking, 'Orthodox Theories of Terrorism: The Power of Politicised Terminology', *Politics*, Vol. 19, No. 2, 1984, pp. 103–10.
54. R. Crelinsten, 'Terrorism as Political Communication: The Relationship between the Controller and the Controlled', in P. Wilkinson and A. Stewart (eds) *Contemporary Research on Terrorism*, Aberdeen: Aberdeen University Press, 1987, pp. 3–8. See also M. Wieviorka, 'Terrorism in the Context of Academic Research', in M. Crenshaw (ed.) *Terrorism in Context*, University Park: Pennsylvania State University Press, 1995.
55. A. George (ed.), *Western State Terrorism*, London: Polity Press, 1991.
56. D. Brannan, P. Esler and A. Strindberg, 'Talking to "Terrorists": Towards an Independent Analytical Framework for the Study of Violent Substate Activism', *Studies in Conflict and Terrorism*, Vol. 24, No. 1, 1991, pp. 3–24. See also A. Silke (ed.) *Research on Terrorism: Trends, Achievements, Failures*, London: Frank Cass, 2004.
57. M. Crenshaw, "The Logic of Terrorism: Terrorist Behaviour as a Product of Strategic Choice", in W. Reich (ed.), *Origins of Terrorism: Psychologies, Ideologies, Theologies, States of Mind*, Washington DC: Woodrow Wilson International Center for Scholars; Cambridge; New York: Cambridge University Press, 1990, pp. 7–24, quote on p.17.
58. Ibid., p. 11.
59. C. McCauley and S. Moskalenko, 'Mechanisms of Political Radicalization: Pathways Toward Terrorism', *Terrorism and Political Violence*, Vol. 20, No. 3, 2008, pp. 415–33; C. Irvin, *Militant Nationalism: Between Movement and Party*

   in Ireland and the Basque Country, London; Minneapolis, MN: University of
   Minnesota Press, 1999.
60. J. Burton, *Deviance, Terrorism and War*, Oxford: Martin Robertson, 1979, p.
    60; J. Burton (ed.) *Conflict: Human Needs Theory*, Basingstoke: Macmillan,
    1990.
61. T.R. Gurr, *Why Men Rebel*, Princeton, NJ: Princeton University Press, 1970.
62. Colectivo de Víctimas de Terrorismo en el País Vasco, www.covite.org, last
    accessed 24 October 2008.
63. Mees, *Nationalism, Violence and Democracy*, p. 34. Author's brackets.
64. Conversi, *The Basques, the Catalans and Spain*, pp. 148–9. See also R. Clark,
    The Basques: The Franco Years and Beyond, Reno: University of Nevada Press,
    1979.
65. Clark, *The Basques*; P. Preston, *The Triumph of Democracy in Spain*, London:
    Methuen, 1986; Mees, *Nationalism, Violence and Democracy*, p. 35.
66. R. Phillips, 'Terrorism: historical roots and moral justifications', in M.
    Warner and R. Crisp (eds), *Terrorism, Protest and Power*, pp. 68–77.
67. In Conversi, *The Basques, the Catalans and Spain*, p. 226.
68. W. Douglass and J. Zulaika, 'On the Interpretation of Terrorist Violence: ETA
    and the Basque Political Process', *Comparative Studies in Society and History*,
    Vol. 32, No. 2, 1990, p. 254.
69. Ibid., p. 252.
70. D. Conversi, 'Why do peace processes collapse? The Basque conflict and the
    three-spoilers perspective', in E. Newman and O. Richmond (eds) *Challenges
    to Peacebuilding: Managing Spoilers During Conflict Resolution*, New York;
    Tokyo: United Nations University Press, 2006, pp. 173–99, quote on p. 187.
71. Mees, *Nationalism, Violence and Democracy*, p. 57.
72. Conversi, *The Basques, the Catalans and Spain*, p. 204.
73. J. Zulaika, *Basque Violence: Metaphor and Sacrament*, Reno: University of
    Nevada Press, 1988.
74. T. del Valle, 'Basque Ethnic Identity at a Time of Rapid Change', in R. Herr
    and J. Polt (eds) *Iberian Identity: Essays on the Nature and Identity in Portugal
    and Spain*, Berkeley: University of California, 1989, p. 127. See also C. Watson,
    Basque Nationalism and Political Violence, for an analysis of the images of
    saint, prophet, peasant and soldier that Arana infused in the nationalist
    doctrine.
75. Heiberg, *The Making of Basque Nation*, p. 187.
76. Ibid., p. 195.
77. L. Richardson, *What Terrorists Want: Understanding the Terrorist Threat*,
    London: John Murray, 2006, p. 4.
78. F. Reinares, *Patriotas de la Muerte: ¿Quiénes Han Militado en ETA y Por Qué?*,
    Madrid: Taurus, 2001, pp. 112–19. See also interview No. 39, p. 79.
79. Cuenca, *ETA Contra el Estado*, p. 44.
80. Reinares, *Patriotas de la Muerte*, p. 154. Some have even claimed that, as long
    as the decision is made by the Basque nation alone, they would be ready to
    accept whichever type of regime.
81. Muro, 'Nationalism and Nostalgia', quote on p. 586.
82. Aznar, quoted in Mees, *Nationalism, Violence and Democracy*, p. 116.

83. The Pact of Lizarra. The document called for the continuation of negotia-
    tion without the exclusion of any of the implicated parties, even though
    direct mention of ETA was avoided in the document. Furthermore, the
    agreement defined the Basque conflict as a purely political one, it called
    for the continuation of agenda-less negotiations for the resolution of the
    conflict, and, more crucially, it recognised the sovereignty of the citizens
    of the Basque Country. See Mees, *Nationalism, Violence and Democracy*,
    pp. 139–41.
84. Conversi, 'Why do peace processes collapse?', p. 182.
85. Mees, *Nationalism, Violence and Democracy*, p. 139.
86. Conversi, 'Why do peace processes collapse?', p. 185.
87. R. Blakeley, 'Bringing the State Back into Terrorism Studies', *European
    Political Science*, Vol. 6, No. 3, 2007, pp. 228–35.
88. O. Richmond, *Maintaining Order, Making Peace*, Basingstoke: Palgrave, 2002,
    p. 4.
89. O. Richmond, 'Realising Hegemony? Symbolic Terrorism and the Roots of
    Conflict', *Studies in Conflict and Terrorism*, Vol. 26, No. 4, 2003, pp.289–
    309.
90. D. Barash, *Approaches to Peace*, Oxford: Oxford University Press, 2000, p.
    63.
91. O. Richmond, *The Transformation of Peace*, Basingstoke; New York: Palgrave
    Macmillan, 2005, p. 4.
92. Burton, *Deviance, Terrorism and War*.
93. '[W]hereas prevention has negative connotations'. J. Burton, *Conflict:
    Resolution and Provention*, Basingstoke: Macmillan, 1990, pp. 2–3.
94. See indicatively V. Jabri, *Discourses on Violence: Conflict Analysis
    Reconsidered*, Manchester: Manchester University Press, 1996; A. Linklater,
    *The Transformation of Political Community: Ethical Foundations of the Post-
    Westphalian Era*, Oxford: Polity Press, 1997; M. Howard, *The Invention of
    Peace and the Re-Invention of War*, London: Profile, 2002; Richmond, *The
    Transformation of Peace* (note 104).
95. Richmond, *The Transformation of Peace*, p. 185.
96. Jabri, *Discourses on Violence*, p. 75.
97. Ibid., p. 146.
98. B.D. Soto and Antonio José Mencía Gallón, *Diario de un Secuestro: Ortega
    Lara, 532 Días en un zulo*, Madrid: Alianza, 1998.
99. Mees, *Nationalism, Violence and Democracy*, pp. 74–5.
100. Iniciativa Ciudadana ¡Basta Ya!, *Euskadi: Del Sueño a la Vergüenza*, Barcelona:
    Ediciones B, 2004, p. 260.
101. Mees, *Nationalism, Violence and Democracy*, p. 80.
102. Florencio Domínguez Irribarren, *De la Negociación a la Tregua ¿El final
    de ETA?*, 1998, Madrid: Taurus, p. 240 and pp. 253–4. See also Florencio
    Domínguez Irribaren, Florencio, 2000, La Violencia nacionalista de ETA
    in Santos Juliá (ed.), Violencia Política en la España del Siglo XX, Madrid:
    Taurus, pp. 327–364; Mees, *Nationalism, Violence and Democracy*, p. 94.
103. Coordinadora Gesto por la Paz, 2001, *Educándonos para la Paz*, http://www.
    gesto.org/educarparalapaz.htm, last accessed 9 August 2006.

104. Interview with Gorka Espiau, Director of Elkarri, Bilbao, 22 November 2004.
105. See Elkarri, *Propuesta dirigida a los Parlamentos vasco y de Navarra en ejercicio del Derecho de Petición con el apoyo de 122.513 firmas*, 17 June 2004, http://www.elkarri.org/actualidad/object.php?o=1713, last accessed 6 July 2006.
106. From the extremist spectrum, Gestoras Pro Amnistia and Sanideak deal with the issues of prisoners and their relatives respectively. From the state-centric spectrum, Foro de Ermua and ¡Basta Ya! oppose Basque nationalism altogether.
107. Burton, *Deviance, Terrorism and War*.

bibliography

Abu-Lughod L, 'Writing against culture,' in R G Fox (ed.), *Recapturing Anthropology: Working in the present,* Santa Fe: School of American Research Press, 1991.

Addison T and Brück T, 'The Multi-Dimensional Challenge of Mass Violent Conflict' in Addison and Brück, (eds) *Making Peace Work: The Challenges of Social and Economic Reconstruction.* London: Palgrave Macmillan, 2009.

Aggestam K, 'Conflict Prevention: Old Wine in New Bottles?', *International Peacekeeping* Vol. 10, No. 1, 2003.

Ahluwalia P, Bethlehem L and Ginio R (eds), *Violence and Non-Violence in Africa,* London: Routledge, 2007.

Allawi A, *The Occupation of Iraq: Winning the War; Losing the Peace,* New Haven, CT: Yale University Press, 2007.

Ambos K and Othman M (eds), *New Approaches in International Criminal Justice: Kosovo, East Timor, Sierra Leone, and Cambodia,* Freiburg: Max Planck, 2003.

Ambrosetti D, 'Human Security as political resource: A response to David Chandler's 'Human Security: The dog that didn't bark', *Security Dialogue,* Vol. 39, No. 4, 2008.

Anderlini S N, *Women Building Peace: What They Do; Why It Matters,* Boulder, CO: Lynne Rienner, 2007.

Anderson B, *Imagined Communities,* London: Verso, 1991.

Appadurai A, 'The Capacity to Aspire: Culture and the terms of recognition', in V Rao and M Walton (eds) *Culture and Public Action,* Stanford, CA: Stanford University Press, 2004.

Appleby S, Lederach J P, and Philpott D, *Strategic Peacebuilding,* Oxford University Press, forthcoming, 2010.

Arendt H, *Men in Dark Times,* New York; London: Harcourt, Brace and Co, 1968.

Ashdown P, *Swords and Ploughshares: Bringing Peace to the 21st Century,* London: Wiedenfeld and Nicholson, 2007.

Augelli E and Murphy C, *America's Quest for Supremacy and the Third World: A Gramscian Analysis* London: Pinter Publishers, 1988.

Avruch K, *Culture and Conflict Resolution,* Washington, D.C.: United States Institute of Peace Press, 1998.

Avruch K, Black P W and Scimecca J A, *Conflict Resolution: Cross-Cultural Perspectives,* London: Greenwood Press, 1991.

439

Azar E A, 'Protracted International Conflicts: Ten Propositions', *International Interactions*, Vol. 12, No. 1 1985, pp. 59–70.

Azar E A, *The Management of Protracted Social Conflict*, Hampshire, UK: Dartmouth Publishing, 1990.

Azar E and Burton J (eds), *International Conflict Resolution*: Theory and Practice, Sussex: Wheatsheaf, 1986.

Badie B, *The Imported State: the Westernization of the Political Order*, Stanford: Stanford University Press, 2000.

Baker B, 'Post-settlement Governance Programmes: What is being built in Africa?', in O Furley and R May (eds) *Ending Africa's Wars*, Aldershot: Ashgate, 2006.

Bakhtin M, *Problems of Dostoevsky's Poetics*, ed. and trans. C Emerson, introduction by W C Booth, Minneapolis: University of Minnesota Press, 1984.

Bakhtin M, *Speech Genres and Other Late Essays*, trans. V W McGee, ed. C Emerson and M Holquist, Austin: University of Texas Press, 1986.

Bakhtin M, 'Author and Hero in Aesthetic Activity', in M Holquist and V Liapunov (eds), *Art and Answerability: Early Philosophical Essays by M.M. Bakhtin*, trans. V Liapunov, Austin: University of Texas Press, 1990.

Bakhtin M, *Toward a Philosophy of the Act*, trans. with notes by V Liapunov, ed. M Holquist and V Liapunov, Austin: University of Texas Press, 1993[1986].

Balibar E, *Politics and the Other Scene*, London: Verso, 2002.

Ballentine K and Nitzschke H, *Profiting from Peace: Managing the Resource Dimensions of Civil War*, Boulder, CO: Lynne Rienner, 2005.

Barker B, *Jihad vs. McWorld: How Globalism and Tribalism are Reshaping the World*, New York: Ballantine Books, 1996.

Barnett M, 'Building a Republican Peace: Stabilizing States after War', *International Security*, Vol. 30, No. 4, 2006.

Bar-Simon-Tov Y (ed.), *From Conflict Resolution to Reconciliation*, Oxford: Oxford University Press, 2004.

Barth F (ed.), *Ethnic Groups and Boundaries*, Oslo: Norwegian University Press, 1969.

Bartos O J and Wehr P, *Using Conflict Theory*, Cambridge: Cambridge University Press, 2002.

Bastian S and Luckham R (eds), *Can Democracy be Designed?*, London: Zed Press, 2003.

Bauman Z, *Hermeneutics and Social Science: Approaches to Understanding*, London: Hutchinson, 1978.

Bauman Z, *Culture as Praxis*, 2nd edn, London: Sage Publications, 1999.

Bauman Z, *Liquid Modernity*, Cambridge: Polity Press, 2000.

Beck U, 'War is Peace: On Post-National War', *Security Dialogue*, Vol. 36, No. 1, 2005.

Bekthe Elshtain J, *Women and War*. Brighton: Harvester Press, 1987.

Bellamy A and Williams P, 'Peace Operations and Global Order', *International Peacekeeping*, Vol. 10, No. 4, 2004.

Bellamy A, *Responsibility to Protect: The Global Effort to End Mass Atrocities*.Oxford: Polity Press, 2008.

Ben-Porat G (ed.), *The Failure of the Middle East Peace Process?*, London: Palgrave Macmillan, 2008.

Bentham J, 'Panopticon', in Bozovic M (ed.), *The Panopticon Writings*, London: Verso, 1995.

Bentley C G, 'Ethnicity and Practice', *Comparative Studies in Society and History*, Vol. 29, No. 1, 1987.

Bercovitch J, (ed.), *Resolving International Conflicts: The Theory and Practice of Mediation*, London: Boulder, 1996.

Bercovitch J and Rubin J Z, Mediation in IR: Multiple Approaches to Conflict Management, Basingstoke: Macmillan, 1992.

Berdal M and Keen D, 'Violence and Economic Agendas in Civil Wars: Some Policy Implications', *Millennium*, Vol. 26, No. 3, 1997.

Berger M, 'Up From Neo–Liberalism: Free Market Mythologies and the Coming Crisis of Global Capitalism', *Third World Quarterly*, Vol. 20, No. 2, 1999.

Berkowitz L, *Aggression: Its Causes, Consequences and Control*, New York: McGraw-Hill, 1993.

Beschloss M, *The Conquerors: Roosevelt, Truman and the Destruction of Hitler's Germany, 1941–1945*, New York: Simon and Schuster, 2002.

Bhabha H (ed.), *Nation and Narration*, London; New York: Routledge, 1990.

Bhabha H, *The Location of Culture*, London and New York: Routledge, 1994.

Black J, *War in the New Century*, London: Continuum, 2001.

Black P W, 'Surprised by Common Sense: Local understandings and the management of conflict on Tobi, Republic of Belau', in K Avruch, P W Black, and J A Scimecca (eds) *Conflict Resolution: Cross-Cultural Perspectives*, London: Greenwood Press, 1991.

Bleiker R, *Popular Dissent, Human Agency and Global Politics*, Cambridge University Press, 2000.

Bleiker R, 'The Aesthetic Turn in International Political Theory', *Millennium: Journal of International Studies*, Vol. 30, No. 3, 2001.

Bloomfield D, *On Good Terms: Clarifying Reconciliation*, Berlin: Berghof Center for Constructive Conflict Management, 2006.

Boas M and Jennings K M, 'Insecurity and Development: the Rhetoric of the "Failed State"', *The European Journal of Development Research*, Vol. 17, No. 3, 2005.

Boege V, *Bougainville and the Discovery of Slowness: An Unhurried Approach to State-Building in the Pacific*, ACPACS Occasional Paper No. 3, Brisbane: ACPACS, 2006.

Boege V, *A promising liaison: kastom and state in Bougainville*, ACPACS Occasional Paper No. 12, Brisbane: ACPACS, 2008.

Boege V, Brown M A, Clements K and Nolan A, *On Hybrid Political Orders and Emerging States: State Formation in the Context of 'Fragility'*, Berghof Handbook Dialogue No. 8, (Online version), Berlin: Berghof Research Center for Constructive Conflict Management, 2008. Available at: http://www.berghof-handbook.net/uploads/download/boege_etal_handbook.pdf

Boege V, Brown M A, Clements K P and Nolan A, 'States Emerging from Hybrid Political Orders – Pacific Experiences', *The Australian Centre for Peace and Conflict Studies (ACPACS) Occasional Papers Series*, 2008.

Bohman J and Lutz-Bachmann M (eds), *Perpetual Peace: Essays on Kant's Cosmopolitan Ideal*, Cambridge MA: MIT Press, 1997.

Bonta B D, 'Conflict Resolution among Peaceful Societies: The Culture of Peacefulness,' *Journal Of Peace Research*, Vol. 33, No. 4, 1996.

Booth K, 'Security and Emancipation', *Review of International Studies*, Vol. 17, No. 4, 1991.

Bottomore T and Bryan R (eds), *The Capitalist Class: An International Study*, Hemel Hempstead: Harvester Wheatsheaf, 1989.

Bougarel X, Helms E and Duijzings G (eds), *The New Bosnian Mosaic: Identities, Memories and Moral Claims in a Post-War Society*, Aldershot: Ashgate, 2006.

Boulding E, *Cultures of Peace: The Hidden Side of History*, Syracuse, NY: Syracuse University Press, 2004.

Boulding K, 'The Boundaries of Social Policy', *Social Work*, Vol. 12, No. 1, January 1967.

Boulding K, *Beyond Economics: Essays on Society, Religion, and Ethics*, Ann Arbor, MI: University of Michigan Press, 1968.

Bourdieu P, *Outline of a Theory of Practice*, trans. Richard Nice, Cambridge: Cambridge University Press, 1977.

Bourdieu P, *The Logic of Practice*, trans. R. Nice, Cambridge: Polity Press, 1990.

Boutros-Ghali B, *An Agenda for Peace: Preventive Diplomacy, Peacemaking and Peace-keeping*, A/47/277-S/24111, 17 June 1992.

Boutros-Ghali B, 'Beyond Peacekeeping', *New York University Journal of International Law and Politics*, Vol. 25, Fall, 1992.

Boyle M and Sambanis N, *Making War and Building Peace: United Nations Peace Operations*, Princeton, NJ: Princeton University Press, 2006.

Brantzæg B, Pöyry E, Wenping H, Nwoke C, Eriksson A and Agbu O, *Common Causes Different Approaches*, Research Report 2008–014, Oslo: Econ Pöry, 2008.

Brannan D, Esler P and Strindberg A, 'Talking to "Terrorists": Towards an Independent Analytical Framework for the Study of Violent Substate Activism', *Studies in Conflict and Terrorism*, Vol. 24, No. 1, 1991.

Brassett J and Bulley D, 'Ethics in World Politics: Cosmopolitanism and Beyond?', *International Politics*, Vol. 44, 2007, pp. 1–18.

Breau S, 'The Impact of Responsibility to Protect on Peacekeeping', *Journal of Conflict and Security Law*, Vol. 11, No. 3, 2007.

Brigg M, *Asking after Selves: Knowledge and settler-indigenous conflict resolution*, unpublished PhD thesis, University of Queensland, Australia, 2005.

Brigg M and Bleiker R, 'Mediating Across Difference: Indigenous, Oceanic and Asian Approaches to Conflict Resolution', *Dialogue*, forthcoming.

Brown K and Patrick S, *Greater than the Sum of its Parts? Assessing 'Whole of Government' Approaches to Fragile States*. New York: International Peace Academy, 2007.

Brown M, *Theories of War and Peace: An International Security Reader*, Cambridge, MA: MIT Press, 1998.

Brown M A (ed.), *Security and Development in the Pacific Islands. Social Resilience in Emerging States*, Boulder, CO; London: Lynne Rienner, 2007.

Bruemmer Bozeman A, *Politics and Culture in International History*, Princeton, NJ: Princeton University Press, 1960.

Bruemmer Bozeman A, *Conflict in Africa: Concepts and Realities*, Princeton, NJ: Princeton University Press, 1976.

Brumann C, 'Writing for Culture: Why a Successful Concept Should not be Discarded', *Current Anthropology*, Vol. 40, Supplement, 1999.

Brynen R, *A Very Political Economy: Peacebuilding and Aid in West Bank and Gaza*, Washington, DC: United States Institute of Peace Process, 2000.

Buckley-Zistel S, 'In-Between War and Peace: Identities, Boundaries and Change after Violent Conflict,' *Millennium Journal of International Studies*, Vol. 35, No. 1, 2006.

Bukovansky M, 'Liberal States, International Order, and Legitimacy: An Appeal for Persuasion over Prescription', *International Politics*, Vol. 44, Nos. 2–3, 2007.

Burch K and Denemark R (eds), *Constituting International Political Economy*, Boulder, CO: Lynne Rienner, 1997.

Burchell G, Gordon C, and Miller P (eds), *The Foucault Effect: Studies in Governmentality*, Hemel Hempstead: Harvester Wheatsheaf, 1991.

Burton J, *World Society*, Cambridge: Cambridge University Press, 1972.

Burton J and Dukes F, *Conflict: Readings in Conflict Management and Resolution*, Basingstoke: Macmillan, 1990.

Butler J, *Precarious Life, The Powers of Mourning and Violence*. London and New York: Verso, 2004.

Byers M (ed.), *The Role of Law in International Politics: Essays in International Relations and International Law*, Oxford: Oxford University Press, 2001.

Call C T and Cook S E, 'On Democratisation and Peacebuilding', *Global Governance*, Vol. 9, No. 2, 2003.

Cammack P, 'The Governance of Global Capitalism: A New Materialist Perspective', *Historical Materialism*, Vol. 11, No. 2, 2003.

Campbell D, *National Deconstruction: Violence, Identity and Justice in Bosnia*, University of Minnesota Press, 1998.

Caplan P, *Understanding Disputes: The Politics of Argument*, Oxford; Providence, R.I.: Berg, 1995.

Caplan R, *International Governance of War-Torn Territories: Rule and Reconstruction*. Oxford: Oxford University Press, 2005.

Carey H, 'Immigrants, Terrorism, Counter-Terrorism and Social Peace', *Peace Review*, Vol. 14, No. 2, 2002.

Carr R and Aizpurua F, *Spain: Dictatorship to Democracy*, London: Allen & Unwin, 1979.

Chabal P and Daloz J P, *Africa Works: Disorder as a Political Instrument*, Oxford: James Currey, 1999.

Chabal P and Daloz J P, *Culture Troubles: Politics and the Interpretation of Meaning*, London: Hurst & Co., 2006.

Chandler D, 'The Responsibility to Protect? Imposing the Liberal Peace', *International Peacekeeping*, Vol. 11, No. 1, 2004.

Chandler D, *Empire in Denial: The Politics of State-Building*, London: Pluto, 2006.

Chandler D, 'Back to the Future? The Limits of Neo-Wilsonian Ideals of Exporting Democracy', *Review of International Studies*, Vol. 32, No. 3, 2006.

Chandler D, 'EU Statebuilding: Securing the Liberal Peace through EU Enlargement, *Global Society*, Vol. 21, No. 4, 2007.

Chandler D, 'Human Security II: Waiting for the Tail to Wag the Dog – A Rejoinder to Ambrosetti, Owen and Wibben', *Security Dialogue*, Vol. 39, No. 4, 2008a.

Chandler D, 'Human Security: The Dog that Didn't Bark', *Security Dialogue*, Vol. 38, No. 4, 2008b.

Chandrasekaran R, *Imperial Life in the Emerald City: Inside Baghdad's Green Zone*, London: Bloomsbury, 2007.

Chang H J, *Bad Samaritans: The Guilty Secrets of Rich Nations and Their Threat to Global Prosperity*, London: Random House Business Books, 2007.

Chataigner J M and Magro H (eds), *Etats et Sociétés Fragiles*, Paris: Karthala, 2007.

Chomsky N, *Problems of Knowledge and Freedom* London: Barrie and Jenkins, 1972.

Chopra J, 'The Space of Peace Maintenance', *Political Geography*, Vol. 15 No. 3/4, 1996.

Chopra J Chopra (ed.), *The Politics of Peace Maintenance*, Boulder, CO: Lynne Rienner, 1998.

Chopra J, 'The UN's Kingdom of East Timor', *Survival*, Vol. 42, No. 3, 2000.

Chopra J and Hohe T, 'Participatory Intervention', *Global Governance*, Vol. 10, 2004.

Clark R, *The Basque insurgents: ETA 1952–1980*, Madison: University of Wisconsin Press, 1984.

Clifford J, 'Introduction: Partial truths', in J Clifford and George E Marcus (eds), *Writing Culture: The poetics and politics of ethnography*, Berkeley: University of California Press, 1986.

Clifford J, 'On Ethnographic Allegory,' in J Clifford and George E Marcus (eds), *Writing Culture: The poetics and politics of ethnography*, Berkeley: University of California Press, 1986.

Clifford J and Marcus G E (eds), *Writing Culture: The Poetics and Politics of Ethnography*, Berkeley, CA: University of California Press, 1986.

Cochrane F, *Ending Wars*, Cambrige: Polity Press, 2008.

Coker C, 'How Wars End', *Millennium Journal of International Studies*, Vol. 26, No. 3, 1997.

Coker C, *Humane Warfare,* London: Routledge, 2001.

Collier P, *Economic Causes of Civil Conflict and their Implications for Policy*, Washington, DC: The World Bank, 2000.

Collier P, 'Doing Well Out of War: An Economic Perspective', in Berdal M and Malone D (eds), *Greed and Grievance: Economic Agendas in Civil Wars*, Boulder, CO: Lynne Rienner, 2000.

Collier P, *The Conflict Trap*, New York: Oxford University Press for the World Bank, 2003.

Collier P and Hoeffler A, 'On the Economic Causes of Civil War', *Oxford Economic Papers*, Vol. 50, 1998.

Conteh-Morgan E, 'Peacebuilding and Human Security: A Constructivist Perspective', *International Journal of Peace Studies*, Vol. 10, No. 1, 2005.

Conversi D, *The Basques, the Catalans and Spain: Alternative Routes to Nationalist Mobilisation*, London: Hurst & Co., 1997.

Cooke W and Kothari U (eds), *Participation: The New Tyranny?*, London: Zed Books, 2004.

Cooper N, 'On the Crisis in the Liberal Peace', *Conflict, Security & Development*, Vol. 7, No. 4, 2007.

Cooper R, *The Breaking of Nations: Order and Chaos in the Twenty-First Century*, New York: Grove Press, 2003.

Cousens E and Kumar C (eds), *Peacebuilding as Politics*, Boulder, CO: Lynne Rienner, 2001.

Covey J, Dziedzic M J and Hawley L R, *The Quest for Viable Peace. International Intervention and Strategies for Conflict Transformation*, Washington, DC: United States Institute for Peace, 2005.

Cox R, 'Ideologies and the New International Economic Order: Reflections on Some Recent Literature', *International Organization*, Vol. 33, No. 2, 1979.

Cox R, 'Social Forces, States and World Orders: Beyond International Relations Theory', *Millennium: Journal of International Relations*, Vol. 10, No. 2, 1981.

Cox R, *Production, Power and World Order: Social Forces in the Making of History*, New York: Columbia University Press, 1987.

Cox R, *Approaches to World Order*, Cambridge: Cambridge University Press, 1996.

Cramer C, '*Homo Economicus* Goes to War: Methodological Individualism, Rational Choice and the Political Economy of War', *World Development*, Vol. 30, No. 11, 2002.

Cramer C, *Civil War Is Not a Stupid Thing: Accounting for Violence in Developing Countries*. London: Hurst & Co., 2006.

Crapanzano V, 'Hermes' Dilemma: The masking of subversion in ethnographic description', in J Clifford and George E Marcus (eds), *Writing Culture: The poetics and politics of ethnography*, Berkeley: University of California Press, 1986.

Crenshaw M (ed.), *Terrorism, Legitimacy and Power: The Consequences of Political Violence*, Scranton: Wesleyan University Press, 1983.

Crenshaw M (ed.), *Terrorism in Context*, University Park: Pennsylvania State University Press, 1995.

Critchley S, *The Ethics of Deconstruction: Derrida and Levinas*, Oxford: Blackwell, 1992.

Crocker C, Hampson F O and Aall P (eds), *Herding Cats: Multiparty mediation in a complex world*, Washington, DC: United States Institute of Peace Press, 1999.

Cuenca I S, *ETA Contra el Estado: Las Estrategias del Terrorismo*, Barcelona: Tusquets, 2001.

Dahl R, *Polyarchy: Participation and Opposition* New Haven, CT: Yale University Press, 1971.

Darby J (ed.), *Violence and Reconstruction*, Notre Dame, IN: University of Notre Dame Press, 2006.

Darby J and Mac Ginty R, *Contemporary Peacemaking*, London: Palgrave, 2008.

Daya K, '"Honourable Resolutions": Gendered Violence, Ethnicity and the Nation', *Alternatives*, Vol. 27, No. 2, 2002.

De Montclos M A P, 'A Crisis of Humanitarianism', *Forum for Applied Research and Public Policy*, Vol. 16, No. 2, 2001.

Deacon B, *Global Social Policy and Governance*, London: Sage, 2007.

Deacon B, Hulse M and Stubbs P, *Global Social Policy: International Organisations and the Future of Welfare*, London: Sage, 1997.

Deacon B and Stubbs P (eds), *Social Policy and International Interventions in South East Europe*, Edward Elgar: Cheltenham, 2004.

Debrix F and Weber C (eds), *Rituals of Mediation*, Minneapolis, MN: University of Minnesota Press, 2003.

De Certeau M, *The Practice of Everyday Life*, trans. S Rendall, Berkeley: University of California Press, 1984.

Denzin N K and Lincoln Y S (eds), *Handbook of Qualitative Research*, Thousand Oaks, CA: Sage Publications, 2000.

Dey I, *Qualitative Data Analysis: A User-Friendly Guide for Social Scientists*, London: Routledge, 1993.

Diamond L, Linz J and Lipset S, *Democracy in Developing Countries* Boulder, CO: Lynne Rienner, 1988.

Dinnen S, 'The Solomon Islands Intervention and the Instabilities of the Post-Colonial State', *Global Change, Peace & Security*, Vol. 20, No. 3, 2008.

Di Palma G, *To Craft Democracies* Berkeley, CA: University of California Press, 1990.

Dobbins J, Jones S G, Crane K, Rathmell A, Steele B, Teltschik R and Timilsina A, *The UN's Role in Nation-Building: From the Congo to Iraq*, Santa Monica: RAND, 2005.

Dobbins J, Jones S G , Crane K and Cole DeGrasse B, *The Beginner's Guide to Nation – Building*. Santa Monica: Rand Corporation, 2007.

Dodge T, 'Iraq: The Contradictions of Exogenous State-Building in Historical Perspective', *Third World Quarterly*, Vol. 27, No. 1, 2006.

Dollard, D, Miller, M and Sears, *Frustration and Aggression*, New Haven, CT: Yale University Press, 1939.

Dorff R H, 'Failed States after 9/11: What Did We Know and What Have We Learned?', *International Studies Perspectives*, Vol. 6, No. 1, 2005, pp. 20–34.

Douglas M, *Natural Symbols: Explorations in cosmology*, New York: Pantheon Books, 1970.

Douzinas C, *Human Rights and Empire: The Political Philosophy of Cosmopolitanism*, Routledge, 2007.

Duffield M, *Global Governance and the New Wars: The Merging of Development and Security*, London: Zed Books, 2001.

Duffield M, *Development, Security and Unending War: Governing the World of Peoples*, Cambridge: Polity Press, 2007.

Dunn D, *The First Fifty Years of Peace Research*, Aldershot: Ashgate, 2005.

Ekbladh D, 'From Consensus to Crisis: the Postwar Career of Nation-Building in U.S. Foreign Relations', in Fukuyama F (ed.), *Nation–Building: Beyond Afghanistan and Iraq*, Baltimore, MD: Johns Hopkins University Press, 2006.

Eller J D, *From Culture to Ethnicity to Conflict: An Anthropological Perspective on International Ethnic Conflict*, Ann Arbor: University of Michigan Press, 1999.

Ellis S, *The Mask of Anarchy: The Destruction of Liberia and the Religious Dimension of an African Civil War*, London: Hurst & Co., 1999.

Ellis S, 'Interpreting Violence: Reflections on West African wars' in Whitehead N L (ed.), *Violence*, Santa Fe: School of American Research Press, 2004.

Engel U and Erdmann G, 'Neopatrimonialism Reconsidered: Critical Review and Elaboration of an Elusive Concept', *Commonwealth and Comparative Politics*, Vol. 45, No. 1, 2007.

Evans-Pritchard E, *The Nuer*, Oxford: Oxford University Press, 1940.

Fanthorpe R, 'On the Limits of the Liberal Peace: Chiefs and Democratic Centralisation in Post-War Sierra Leone', *African Affairs* Vol. 105, No. 415, 2005.

Farer T (ed.), *Beyond Sovereignty: Collectively Defending Democracy in the Americas*, Baltimore, MD: Johns Hopkins University Press, 1996.

Fatton R, 'Civil Society Revisited: Africa in the New Millennium', *West Africa Review*, Vol. 1, No. 1, 1999.

Faure G O and Rubin J Z (eds), *Culture and Negotiation: The Resolution of Water Disputes*, Newbury Park, CA: 1993.

Ferme M C, *The Underneath of Things: Violence, History and the Everyday in Sierra Leone*, Berkeley, CA: University of California Press, 2001.

Fetherston A B, 'From Conflict Resolution to Transformative Peacebuilding: Reflections from Croatia', Centre for Conflict Resolution, Department of Peace Studies, University of Bradford, working paper no. 4, 2000.

Fetherston A B, 'Peacekeeping, Conflict Resolution and Peacebuilding: A reconsideration of theoretical frameworks', in T Woodhouse and O Ramsbotham (eds), Peacekeeping and Conflict Resolution, London, Portland, OR: Frank Cass, 2000.

Fetherston A and Nordstrom C, 'Overcoming Habitus in Conflict Management: UN Peacekeeping and War Zone Ethnography', *Peace & Change*, Vol. 20, No. 1, 1995.

Fierke K M, 'Meaning, Method and Practice: Assessing the New Security Agenda', in Lawson S (ed.), *The New Agenda for International Relations*, Cambridge: Polity Press, 2002.

Fisher R and Ury W, *Getting to Yes*, 2nd edn, Arrow Books Ltd., 1997.

Foner E, *Reconstruction: America's Unfinished Revolution, 1863–1877*, New York: HarperCollins, 1989.

Foong Khong Y, 'Human Security: A Shotgun Approach to Alleviating Human Misery?', *Global Governance*, Vol. 7, No. 3, 2001.

Foucault M, *Madness and Civilization: A History of Insanity in the Age of Reason*, New York: Random House, 1965.

Foucault M, *The Archaeology of Knowledge & the Discourse on Language*, New York: Pantheon Books, 1972.

Foucault M, *The Birth of the Clinic*, London: Routledge, 1976.

Foucault M, *Discipline and Punish: The Birth of the Prison*, New York: Pantheon 1977.

Foucault M, *Security, Territory, Population*, London: Palgrave, 2007.

Fox R G (ed.), *Recapturing Anthropology: Working in the Present*, Santa Fe: School of American Research Press, 1991.

Franks J, *Rethinking the Roots of Terrorism*, Basingstoke; NY: Palgrave Macmillan, 2006.

Friedman M, *Capitalism and Freedom* Chicago, IL: University of Chicago Press, 1962.

Friedman S, *Building Tomorrow Today: African Workers in Trade Unions, 1970–1984* Johannesburg: Ravan Press, 1987.

Fry D P, *The Human Potential for Peace: An Anthropological Challenge to Assumptions About War and Violence*, New York: Oxford University Press, 2006.

Fukuyama F, *State-Building: Governance and World Order in the Twenty-First Century*, Ithaca, NY: Cornell University Press, 2004.

Galtung J, 'A Structural Theory of Imperialism', *Journal of Peace Research*, Vol. 8, 1971.

Galtung J, *Peace, War and Defense, Essays in Peace Research*, Vol II. Copenhagen: Christian Ejlers' Forlag a-s, 1976.

Galtung J, *Peace by Peaceful Means: Peace and Conflict, Development and Civilization*, London: Sage, 1996.

Gamba V, 'Post-Agreement Demobilization, Disarmament and Reintegration: Towards a New Approach', in Darby J (ed.), *Violence and Reconstruction*. Notre Dame, IN: University of Notre Dame Press, 2006.

Gamble A, *The Free Economy and the Strong State: The Politics of Thatcherism* London: Macmillan, 1988.

Geertz C, *The Interpretation of Cultures*, New York: Basic Books, 1973.

Gellner E, *Thought and Change*, London: Weidenfeld & Nicholson, 1964; and *Nations and Nationalism*, Oxford: Blackwell, 1983.

George J, *Discourses of Global Politics: A Critical reintroduction to International Relations*, Boulder, CO: Lynne Rienner, 1994.

Ghani A and Lockhart C, *Fixing Failed States: A Framework for Rebuilding a Fractured World*. Oxford: Oxford University Press, 2008.

Gibson J, *Overcoming Apartheid: Can Truth Reconcile a Divided Nation?* New York, NY: Russell Sage Foundation, 2004.

Giddens A, *The Nation-State and Violence*. Cambridge: Polity, 1985.

Gill S and Mittelmann J (eds) *Innovation and Transformation in International Studies* Cambridge: Cambridge University Press, 1997.

Gill S and Law D, 'Global Hegemony and the Structural Power of Capital', *International Studies Quarterly*, Vol. 33, 1989.

Gills B, Rocamora J and Wilson R, *Low Intensity Democracy: Political Power in the New World Order* London: Pluto Press, 1993.

Gilpin R, *War and Change in World Politics*, Cambridge: Cambridge University Press, 1981.

Girard R, *Violence and the Sacred*, trans. P. Gregory, London: The Athlone Press, 1988.

Glinavos I, 'Neoliberal Law: Unintended Consequences of Market-Friendly Law Reforms', *Third World Quarterly*, Vol. 29, No. 6, 2008.

Goldstein J, *War and Gender*. Cambridge: Cambridge University Press, 2001.

Good K, 'Development and Democracies: Liberal Versus Popular', *Africa Insight*, Vol. 27, No. 4, 1997.

Gould C, *Rethinking Democracy: Freedom and Social Co-operation in Politics, Economy and Society* Cambridge: Cambridge University Press, 1988.

Gramsci A, *Prison Notebooks*, Vol. 1, ed. by J.A. Buttigieg, trans. by J.A. Buttigieg and A. Callari. New York: Columbia University Press, 1992.

Gramsci A, *Prison Notebooks, Vol. 2*, ed. & trans. J.A. Buttigieg, New York: Columbia University Press, 1996.

Gray C S, *Modern Strategy*, Oxford University Press, 1999.

Greenberg M E and Zuckerman E, 'The Gender Dimensions of Post-Conflict Reconstruction', in Addison and Brück, (eds) *Making Peace Work: The Challenges of Social and Economic Reconstruction*. London: Palgrave Macmillan, 2009.

Groom A J R, 'Paradigms in Conflict: the Strategist, the Conflict Researcher and the Peace Researcher', in Burton J and Dukes F, *Conflict: Readings in Conflict Management and Resolution*, Basingstoke: Macmillan, 1990.

Gulliver P H, *Disputes and Negotiations: A Cross-Cultural Perspective*, New York: Academic Press, 1979.

Gurr T R, *Why Men Rebel*, Princeton, NJ: Princeton University Press, 1970.

Habermas J, *The Theory of Communicative Action, Reason and the Rationalization of Society*, Vol. I. Oxford: Polity Press, 1991.

Habermas J, *Inclusion of the Other*, Cambridge MA: MIT Press, 1998.

Häkli J, 'Discourse in the Production of Political Space: Decolonizing the symbolism of provinces in Finland', *Political Geography*, Vol. 17, No. 3, 1996.

Hall E T, *Beyond Culture*, New York: Anchor Books, 1976.

Hall S, *Thatcherism and the Crisis of the Left: The Hard Road to Renewal*, London: Verso Press, 1988.

Hammarskjold D, *Summary Study UN doc. A/3943*.

Hammer M R, 'The Intercultural Conflict Style Inventory: A Conceptual Framework and Measure of Intercultural Conflict Resolution Approaches,' *International Journal of Intercultural Relations*, Vol. 29, No. 6, 2005.

Hamre J J and Sullivan G R, 'Toward Postconflict Reconstruction', *The Washington Quarterly*, Vol. 25, No. 4, 2002.

Harrison L E and Huntingdon S (eds), *Culture Matters: How Values Shape Human Progress*, New York: Basic Books, 2001.

Harvey D, *The New Imperialism*, Oxford: Oxford University Press, 2002.

Harvey D, *Spaces of Global Capitalism: Towards a Theory of Uneven Geographical Development*, London: Verso, 2006.

Hayner P, *Unspeakable Truths: Confronting State Terror and Atrocity*, London: Routledge, 2001.

Heiberg M, *The Making of Basque Nation*, Cambridge: Cambridge University Press, 1989.

Helander B, 'Who Needs a State? Civilians, security and social services in North-East Somalia', in P Richards (ed.), *No Peace, No War: An anthropology of contemporary armed conflicts*, Athens: Ohio University Press and Oxford: James Currey, 2005.

Herbert C, *Culture and Anomie: Ethnographic Imagination in the Nineteenth Century*, Chicago and London: University of Chicago Press, 1991.

Hesse C and Post R (eds), *Human Rights in Political Transitions: Gettysburg to Bosnia*, Zone Books: New York, 1999.

Hibou B (ed.), *Privatising the State*, London: Hurst & Co., 2004.

Hobsbawm E, *Globalisation, Democracy and Terrorism* London: Little, Brown, 2007.

Hoehne M V, *Traditional Authorities in Northern Somalia: Transformations of Positions and Powers*, Halle/Saale: Max Planck Institute for Social Anthropology Working Paper No. 82, 2006.

Hogan M, *The Marshall Plan: America, Britain and the Reconstruction of Western Europe, 1947–1952*. Cambridge: Cambridge University Press, 1987.

Holman O, 'Transnational Class Strategy and the New Europe', *International Journal of Political Economy*, Vol. 22, No. 1, 1992.

Holquist M, *Dialogism: Bakhtin and His World*, New York: Routledge, 1990.

Hoogvelt A, *Globalization and the Post-Colonial World: The New Political Economy of Development*, Baltimore, MD: Johns Hopkins University Press, 1997.

Howard M, *The Invention of Peace*, New Haven, CT: Yale University Press, 2000.

Hudson V M (ed.), *Culture & Foreign Policy* Boulder, CO: Lynne Rienner, 1997.

Humphrys J, *The Great Food Gamble*, London: Coronet Books, 2002.

Huntingdon S, *The Third Wave: Democratization in the Late Twentieth Century* Norman: University of Oklahoma Press, 1991.

Hurwitz A and Huang R (eds), *Civil War and the Rule of Law: Security, Development, Human Rights*, Boulder, CO: Lynne Rienner, 2008.

Huyse L and Salter M (eds), *Traditional Justice and Reconciliation After Violent Conflict*, Stockholm: International IDEA, 2008.

Hyden G, *Institutions, power and policy outcomes in Africa*, Power and Politics in Africa Discussion Paper No. 2, London: ODI, 2008.

Ignatieff M, *Empire Lite: Nation-building in Bosnia, Kosovo and Afghanistan*, London: Vintage, 2003.

Irvin C, *Militant Nationalism: Between Movement and Party in Ireland and the Basque Country*, London; Minneapolis, MN: University of Minnesota Press, 1999.

Isard W, *Understanding Conflict and the Science of Peace*, Cambridge: Blackwell, 1992.

Jabri V, *Discourses on Violence*, Manchester: Manchester University Press, 1996.

Jabri V, 'Solidarity and Spheres of Culture: The Cosmopolitan and the Postcolonial', *Review of International Studies*, Vol. 33, No. 4, 2007, pp. 715–28.

Jabri V, *War and the Transformation of Global Politics*, London: Palgrave, 2007.

Jackson R, 'The Core Commitments of Critical Terrorism Studies', *European Political Science*, Vol. 6, No. 3, 2007.

Jacoby T, 'Hegemony, Modernisation and Post-war Reconstruction', *Global Society*, Vol. 21, No. 4, 2007.

James A, *Peacekeeping in International Politics*, I.I.S.S., Macmillan, 1994.

Jarstad A K and Sisk T (eds), *From War to Democracy: Dilemmas of Peacebuilding*, Cambridge: Cambridge University Press, 2008.

Jenkins B, 'Rethinking Ethnicity: Identity, Categorization and Power', *Ethnic and Racial Studies*, Vol. 17, No. 2, 1994.

Jenks C, *Culture*, London: Routledge, 1993.

Jeong H W (ed.), *Approaches to Peacebuilding*. Houndsmill, Basingstoke, New York: Palgrave, 2002.

Jeong H W, *Peacebuilding in Post-Conflict Societies: Strategy and Process*, Boulder, CO and London: Lynne Reinner, 2005.

Johnstone I, *Rights and Reconciliation: UN Strategies in El Salvador*, Boulder, CO: Lynne Rienner, 1995.

Jones D, *Cosmopolitan Mediation? Conflict Resolution and the Oslo Accords*, Manchester University Press, 1999.

Just P, 'Conflict Resolution and Moral Community among the Dou Donggo,' in K Avruch, P W Black, and J A Scimecca (eds) *Conflict Resolution: Cross-Cultural Perspectives*, London: Greenwood Press, 1991.

Kahn H, Pfaff W and Stillman E, *War Termination: Issues and Concepts*, Croton-on-Harmon, NY: The Hudson Institute, 1968.

Kaldor M, *New and Old Wars: Organized Violence in a Global Era*, Cambridge: Polity Press, 1999.

Kalyvas S, ' "New" and "Old" Civil Wars – A Valid Distinction?', *World Politics*, Vol. 54, No. 1, 2001.

Kansteiner W, 'Finding Meaning in Memory: A methodological Critique of Collective Memory Studies', *History and Theory*, Vol. 41, No. 2, 2002.

Kant I, *Political Writings*, ed. by Hans Reiss, trans. H B Nisbet, Cambridge: Cambridge University Press, 1970.

Kaplan R D, *The Coming Anarchy: Shattering the Dreams of the Post-Cold War*, New York: Vintage, 2000.

Kaplan R D, *Balkan Ghosts: A Journey through History*, London: Picador, 2005.

Karokhail M and Schmeidl S, 'Integration of Traditional Structures into the State-Building Process: Lessons from the Tribal Liaison Office in Loya Paktia', in Heinrich Boell Foundation (ed.), *Afghanistan*, Berlin: Heinrich Boell Foundation, 2006.

Keane J, *Global Civil Society?*, Cambridge: Cambridge University Press, 2003.

Keck M E and Sikkink K, *Activists Beyond Borders: Advocacy Networks in International Politics*, Ithaca, NY: Cornell University Press, 1998.

Kedourie E, *Nationalism*, Oxford: Blackwell, 2000.

Keen D, *Complex Emergencies*, Cambridge: Polity Press, 2008.

Kelsall T, *Going with the grain in African development?*, Power and Politics in Africa Discussion Paper No. 1, London: ODI, 2008.

Kent R C, 'Security and Local Ownership: Rhetoric and reality', in T Tardy and R Mani (eds), *Pursuing Security in the Post-Conflict Phase: Implications for current and future peace operations*, Report from a workshop of the Geneva Centre for Security Policy (GCSP), 12–13 June 2005, Geneva: GCSP, 2005.

Kerr P, Tow W T and Hanson M, 'The Utility of Human Security Agenda for Policy-Makers', *Asian Journal of Political Sciences*, Vol. 11, No. 2, 2003.

Kiely R, 'Poverty Reduction through Liberalisation? Neoliberalism and the Myth of Global Convergence', *Review of International Studies*, Vol. 33, No. 3, 2007.

Killick J, *The United States and European Reconstruction, 1945–1960*, Edinburgh: Edinburgh University Press, 1997.

King G and Murray C, 'Rethinking Human Security', *Political Science Quarterly*, Vol. 116, No. 4, Winter 2001–2002.

Klein N, *The Shock Doctrine: The Rise of Disaster Capitalism* London: Allen Lane, 2007.

Knight W A, 'Evaluating Recent Trends in Peacebuilding Research', *International Relations of the Asia-Pacific*, Vol. 3, No. 2, 2003.

Koelble T, *The Global Economy and Democracy in South Africa* New Brunswick, NJ: Rutgers University Press, 1999.

Koelble T and LiPuma E, 'Democratizing Democracy: A Postcolonial Critique of Conventional Approaches to Democracy', *Democratization*, Vol. 15, No. 1, 2008.

Kolakowski L, *Positivist Philosophy: From Hume to the Vienna Circle*, trans. N. Guterman, Harmondsworth: Penguin, 1972.

Konca K and Dabelko G (eds), *Environmental Peacemaking*, Baltimore, MD: Johns Hopkins University Press, 2003.

Kotze D, 'Implications of the Democracy-Development Relationship for Conflict Resolution', *African Journal on Conflict Resolution*, Vol. 5, No. 1, 2005.

Kotze D and Solomon H (eds), *The State of Africa: Post-Conflict Reconstruction and Development*, Pretoria: Africa Institute of South Africa, 2008.

Krugman P, 'Dutch Tulips and Emerging Markets', *Foreign Affairs*, July–August, 1994.

Lapid Y and Kratochwil F V (eds), *The Return of Culture and Identity in Ir Theory, Critical Perspectives on World Politics*. Boulder, CO: Lynne Rienner, 1996.

Le Billon P, 'Corrupting Peace? Peacebuilding and Post-Conflict Corruption', *International Peacekeeping*, Vol. 15, No. 3, June 2008.

Le Billon P and Nicholls E, 'Ending 'Resource Wars': Revenue Sharing, Economic Sanction or Military Intervention?', *International Peacekeeping*, Vol. 14, No. 5, 2007.

Lerche C O, 'Truth Commissions and National Reconciliation: Some Reflections on Theory and Practice', *Peace and Conflict Studies*, Vol. 7, No. 1, 2000.

Leal P A, 'Participation: The Ascendancy of a Buzzword in the Neo-Liberal Era', *Development in Practice*, Vol. 17, Nos 4–5, 2007.

Lederach J P, 'Of Nets, Nails and Problems: The Folk Language of Conflict Resolution in a Central American Setting', in K Avruch, P W Black, and J A Scimecca (eds) *Conflict Resolution: Cross-Cultural Perspectives*, London: Greenwood Press, 1991.

Lederach J P, *Preparing for Peace: Conflict Transformation Across Cultures*, Syracuse: Syracuse University Press, 1995.

Lederach J P, *Building Peace: Sustainable Reconciliation in Divided Societies,* Washington DC: United States Institute of Peace, 1997.

Levinger M and Lyttle P F, 'Myth and Mobilisation: the triadic structure of nationalist rhetoric', *Nations and Nationalism*, Vol. 7, No. 2, 2001.

Linklater A and Macmillan J, *Boundaries in Question,* London: Pinters, 1995.

Long W J and Brecke P, *War and Reconciliation: Reason and Emotion in Conflict Resolution*, Massachusetts, the MIT Press, 2003.

Lotman Y, *Universe of the Mind: A Semiotic Theory of Culture*, trans. A. Shukman, London: Tauris & Co., 1990.

Lund M, *Preventing Violent Conflicts,* Washington DC: USIP, 1996.

Luoma-Aho M, 'Body of Europe and Malignant Nationalism: A Pathology of the Balkans in European Security Discourse', *Geopolitics*, Vol. 7, No. 3, 2002.

Mac Ginty R, 'The Role of Symbols in Peacemaking', in J Darby and R Mac Ginty (eds) *Contemporary Peacemaking: Conflict, violence and peace processes*, Basingstoke, New York: Palgrave Macmillan, 2003.

Mac Ginty R, *No War, No Peace: The Rejuvenation of Stalled Peace Processes and Peace Accords*, London: Palgrave, 2006.

Mac Ginty R, 'Reconstructing Post-War Lebanon: A Challenge to the Liberal Peace', *Conflict, Security and Development*, Vol. 7, No. 3, 2007.

Mac Ginty R, 'Indigenous Peace-making versus the Liberal Peace', *Cooperation and Conflict*, Vol. 43, No. 2, 2008.

Macmillan J, *On Liberal Peace. Democracy, War and the International Order,* London: Tauris Academic Studies, 1998.

Maggio J, "'Can the Subaltern Be Heard?': Political Theory, Translation, Representation, and Gyatri Chakravorty Spivak", *Alternatives*, Vol. 32, No. 4, 2007.

Malamud-Goti J, *Game Without End: State Terror and the Politics of Justice*, Norman, OK: University of Oklahoma Press, 1996.

Malinowski B, *Argonauts of the Western Pacific*, London: Routledge, 1922.

Mani R, *Beyond Retribution: Seeking Justice in the Shadows of War,* Cambridge: Polity Press, 2002.

Mann M, *The Sources of Social Power*, Vol. II, Cambridge: Cambridge University Press, 1993.

Marcus G E, 'Contemporary Problems of Ethnography in the Modern World System', in J Clifford and George E Marcus (eds), *Writing Culture: The poetics and politics of ethnography*, Berkeley: University of California Press, 1986.

Marriage Z, *Not Breaking the Rules, Not Playing the Game: International Assistance to Countries at War*, London: Hurst & Co., 2006.

Martin H and Schumann H, *The Global Trap: Globalization and the Assault on Democracy and Prosperity* London: Zed Books, 1997.

Martinez L, *The Algerian Civil War 1990–1998*, (trans. Derrick J) London: Hurst & Co., 1998.

Marx K, *German Ideology* London: Lawrence Wishart, 1970 [1845–46].

Marx K and Engels F, *Manifesto of the Communist Party* Moscow: Foreign Languages Press, 1967 [1850].

Maybury-Lewis D, *Akwe-Shavante Society*, Oxford: Clarendon Press, 1967.

Mayrood C and Katunga J, 'Coltan exploration in Eastern Democratic Republic of the Congo (DRC)', in Lind J and Sturman K (eds), *Scarcity and Surfeit: The Ecology of Africa's Conflicts*, Pretoria: Institute of Security Studies, 2002.

Mazower M, *Salonica: City of Ghosts*, London: Harper Perennial, 2005.

Mccauley C and Moskalenko S, 'Mechanisms of Political Radicalization: Pathways Toward Terrorism', *Terrorism and Political Violence*, Vol. 20, No. 3, 2008.

Mees L, *Nationalism, Violence and Democracy: The Basque Clash of Identities*, Basingstoke: Palgrave Macmillan, 2003.

Mehler A, *Legitime Gewaltoligopole – eine Antwort auf strukturelle Instabilitaet in Westafrika? IAK Diskussionsbeitraege 22*, Hamburg: Institut fuer Afrikakunde, 2003.

Mendelson S, 'The Putin Path: Civil Liberties and Human Rights in Retreat', *Problems of Post-Communism*, Vol.47, No. 5, 2000.

Menkhaus K, 'Governance without Government in Somalia. Spoilers, State Building, and the Politics of Coping', *International Security*, Vol. 31, No. 3, 2006.

Mieksins Wood E, *Empire of Capital*, London: Verso, 2005.

Migdal J, *Strong Societies and Weak States: State-Society Relations and State Capabilities in the Third World*, Princeton, NJ: Princeton University Press, 1988.

Migdal J, *State in Society*, Cambridge: Cambridge University Press, 2001.

Miliband R and Panitch L (eds), *The Socialist Register, 1992* London: Merlin Press, 1992.

Minow M, *Between Vengeance and Forgiveness: Facing History after Genocide and Mass Violence*, Boston: Beacon Press, 1998.

Mittelman J and Pasha M, *Out From Underdevelopment Revisited: Changing Global Structures and the Remaking of World Order* Basingstoke: Macmillan, 1997.

Mooers C (ed.), *The New Imperialists: Ideologies of Empire* Oxford: Oneworld Publications, 2006.

Moore D, 'Reading Americans on Democracy in Africa: From the CIA to "Good Governance'", *European Journal of Development Research*, Vol. 8, No. 1, 1996.

Morvaridi B, *Social Justice and Development*, Basingstoke: Palgrave, 2008.

Mosse D, *Travelling Rationalities: The Anthropology of Expert Knowledge and Professionals in International Development*, Berghahn, 2008.

Mouffe C, *The Return of the Political*, New York: Verso, 1993.

Munckler H, *The New Wars*,Cambridge: Polity Press, 2005.

Murer J, 'Countering the Narratives of Simplification: Embracing complexity as a means of conflict resolution and understanding identity formation,' CPCS paper series in Peace and Conflict Studies, St Andrews, November 2008.

Munro E J, *Multidimensional and Integrated peace operations: Trends and challenges*, GCSP Geneva Papers, Norwegian Ministry of Foreign Affairs, 2008.

Murphy C, *International Organization and Industrial Change* Cambridge: Polity Press, 1994.

Murthy C S R, 'New Phase in UN Reforms: Establishment of the Peacebuilding Commission and Human Rights Council', *International Studies*, Vol. 44, No. 1, 2007.

Nader L and Todd H F (eds), *The Disputing Process: Law in Ten Societies* New York: Columbia University Press, 1978.

Neier A, *War Crimes: Brutality, Genocide, Terror, and the Struggle for Justice*, New York: Times Books, 1998.

Nelson C and Grossberg L (eds), *Marxism and the Interpretation*. Basingstoke: Macmillan, 1988.

Neumann I B, 'European Identity, EU Expansion, and the Integration/ Exclusion Nexus', *Alternatives: Social transformation & humane governance*, Vol. 23, No. 3, 1998.

Nixon R, 'The Crisis of Governance in New Subsistence States', *Journal of Contemporary Asia*, Vol. 36, No. 1, 2006.

Nordstrom C, *Warzones: Cultures of Violence, Militarisation and Peace*, Canberra: Australian National University, Peace Research Centre, 1994.

Nordstrom C, 'Contested Identities/Essentially Contested Powers', in K Rupesinghe (ed.), *Conflict Transformation*, Basingstoke: Macmillan, 1995.

Nordstrom C, *A Different Kind of War Story*, Philadelphia, PA: Pennsylvania University Press, 1997.

Nordstrom C, 'The Tomorrow of Violence', in N L Whitehead (ed.), *Violence*, Santa Fe: School of American Research Press , 2004.

Nordstrom C, *Shadows of War: Violence, Power, and International Profiteering in the Twenty-First Century*, Berkeley, CA: University of California Press, 2004.

Nordstrom C, 'Casting long shadows: War, Peace and Extralegal Economies', in Darby J and Mac Ginty R (eds) *Contemporary Peacemaking: Conflict, Peace Processes and Post-War Reconstruction*, Basingstoke: Palgrave, 2008.

Nordstrom C and Robben A (eds), *Fieldwork under Fire: Contemporary Studies of Violence and Survival*, Berkeley, CA: University of California Press, 1995.

Oakeshott M, *Rationalism in Politics and Other Essays*, London: Methuen & Co., 1962.

OECD-DAC, *Concepts and Dilemmas of State Building in Fragile Situations: From Fragility to Resilience*, OECD-DAC Discussion Paper, Paris: OECD, 2008.

Oren I, *Our Enemies and Us: America's Rivalries and the Making of Political Science* Ithaca, NY: Cornell University Press, 2003.

Osiel M, *Mass Atrocity, Collective Memory, and the Law*, New Brunswick, NJ: Transaction Books, 1997.

Overing J, 'In Praise of the Everyday: Trust and the Art of Social Living in an Amazonian Community,' *s*, Vol. 68, No. 3, 2003.

Owen T, 'Measuring Human Security: Overcoming the Paradox', *Human Security Bulletin*, Vol. 2, No. 3, 2003.

Owen T, 'Human Security – Conflict, Critique and Consensus: Colloquium Remarks and a Proposal for a Threshold-Based Definition', *Security Dialogue*, Vol. 35, No. 3, 2004.

Oyerbeek H (ed.), *Restructuring Hegemony in the Global Political Economy: The Rise of Transnational Neo-Liberalism in the 1980s* London: Routledge, 1993.

Ozerdem A, *Becoming Civilian: Disarmament, Demobilisation and Reintegration*, London: I.B. Tauris, 2008.

Paris R, 'Human Security: Paradigm Shift or Hot Air?', *International Security*, Vol. 26, No. 2, 2001.

Paris R, 'Mission Civilisatrice', *Review of International Studies*, Vol. 28, No. 4, 2002.

Paris R, *At War's End*, Cambridge University Press, 2004.

Parry M L, Canziani O F, Palutikof J P, Van Der Linden P J and Hanson C E (eds), *Climate Change 2007: Impacts, Adaptation and Vulnerability. Contribution of Working Group II to the Fourth Assessment Report of the Intergovernmental Panel on Climate Change*, Cambridge UK: Cambridge University Press, 2007.

Pateman C, *Participation and Democratic Theory* Cambridge: Cambridge University Press, 1970.

Patomaki H, 'The Challenge of Critical Theories', *Journal of Peace Research*, Vol. 38, No. 6, 2001.

Pawlowska K, 'Humanitarian Intervention: Transforming the Discourse', *International Peacekeeping* Vol. 12, No. 4, 2005.

Petras J, 'A Marxist Critique of Post-Marxists', *Links: International Journal of Socialist Renewal*, No. 9, 1997, Links [online], available at http://links.org.au/node/189, accessed 2 November 2009.

Polanyi K, *The Great Transformation: The Political and Economic Origins of Our Time*, Boston: Beacon Press, 1957 [1944].

Pouligny B, *Peace Operations Seen From Below*, London: Hurst & Co., 2006.

Prager C and Govier T (eds), *Dilemmas of Reconciliation: Cases and Concepts*. Waterloo, Ontario: Wilfrid Laurire University Press, 2003.

Pratt M, 'Fieldwork in Common Places', in Clifford J and Marcus G E (eds), *Writing Culture: The Poetics and Politics of Ethnography*, Berkeley, CA: University of California Press, 1986.

Princen T, *Intermediaries in International Conflict*, Princeton University Press, 1992.

Przeworski A, Alvarez M E, Cheibub J A, and Limongi F, *Democracy and Development: Political Institutions and Well-Being in the World, 1950–1990*. Cambridge: Cambridge University Press, 2000.

Pugh M, 'The Political Economy of Peacebuilding: A Critical Theory Perspective', *International Journal of Peace Studies*, Vol. 10, No. 2, 2005.

Pugh M, 'Post-war Economies and the New York Dissensus', *Conflict, Security & Development*, Vol. 6, No. 3, 2006.

Pugh M, Cooper N and Goodhand J, *War Economies in a Regional Context: Challenges of Transformation*, Boulder, CO: Lynne Rienner, 2004.

Pugh M, Cooper N and Turner M (eds), *Whose Peace? Critical Perspectives on the Political Economy of Peacebuilding*, London: Palgrave, 2008.

Pupavac V, 'Human Security and the Rise of Global Therapeutic Governance', *Conflict, Security and Development*, Vol. 5, No. 2, 2005.

Rabar B and Karimi M, *Indigenous Democracy: Traditional Conflict Resolution Mechanisms*, Nairobi: Intermediate Technology Development Group, 2003.

Ranis G, Hu S C and Chu Y P (eds), *The Political Economy of Comparative Development into the 21st Century*, Cheltenham: Edward Elgar, 1999.

Rao V and Walton M, (eds), *Culture and Public Action*, Stanford, CA: Stanford University Press, 2004.

Ramsbotham O, Woodhouse T and Miall H, *Contemporary Conflict Resolution: The Prevention, Management and Transformation of Deadly Conflicts*, Cambridge, UK; Malden, MA: Polity Press, 2005.

Rasmussen M V, *The West, Civil Society and the Construction of Peace*, London: Palgrave, 2003.

Reardon B, *Women and Peace, Feminist Visions of Global Security*. New York: State University of New York Press, 1993.

Reed C and Ryall D (eds), *The Price of Peace. Just War in the Twenty-First Century*, Cambridge: Cambridge University Press, 2007.

Reeves J, *Culture and International Relations: Narratives, Natives and Tourists*, Abingdon; New York: Routledge, 2004.

Reich W (ed.), *Origins of Terrorism: Psychologies, Ideologies, Theologies, States of Mind*, Cambridge: Cambridge University Press, 1990.

Reinares F, *Patriotas de la Muerte: ¿Quiénes Han Militado en ETA y Por Qué?*, Madrid: Taurus, 2001.

Reindorp N, 'Global Humanitarian Assistance', *Humanitarian Exchange*, No. 18, London: ODI, March 2001.

Reinicke W, *Public Policy*, Washington DC: Brookings, 1998.

Reno W, 'Anti-corruption Efforts in Liberia: Are They Aimed at the Right Targets?' *International Peacekeeping*, Vol. 15, No. 3, June 2008.

Richards P, 'New War: An ethnographic approach', P Richards (ed.), *No Peace No War: An anthropology of contemporary armed conflicts*, Athens: Ohio University Press and Oxford: James Currey, 2005.

Richards P (ed.), *No Peace No War: An Anthropology of Contemporary Armed conflicts*, Oxford: James Currey, 2005.

Richardson L, *What Terrorists Want: Understanding the Terrorist Threat*, London: John Murray, 2006.

Riches D (ed.), *The Anthropology of Violence*, Oxford: Basil Blackwell, 1986.

Richmond O P, 'Devious Objectives And The Disputants' View Of International Mediation: A Theoretical Framework', *Journal of Peace Research*, Vol. 35, No. 5, 1998.

Richmond O P, 'Rethinking Conflict Resolution: The Linkage Problematic between "Track I" and "Track II"', *Journal of Conflict Studies*, Vol. 21, No. 2, 2001.

Richmond O P, *Maintaining Order, Making Peace*, London: Palgrave, 2002.

Richmond O P, *The Transformation of Peace*, Basingstoke: Palgrave, 2005.

Richmond O P, 'Critical Research Agendas for Peace: the Missing Link in the Study of International Relations', *Alternatives*, Vol. 32, 2007.

Richmond O P, *Peace in IR*, London: Routledge, 2008.

Richmond O P, 'Eirenism and a Post-Liberal Peace', *Review of International Studies*, Vol. 35, No 3, 2009.

Richmond O P and Carey H (eds), *Subcontracting Peace: the Challenges of NGO Peacebuilding*, Aldershot: Ashgate, 2005.

Richmond O P, and Franks J, *Liberal Peace Transitions: Between Statebuilding and Peacebuilding*, Edinburgh University Press, 2009.

Riles A, *The Network Inside Out*, Ann Arbor: University of Michigan Press, 2000.

Ringmar E, *Identity, Interest and Action. A Cultural Explanation of Sweden's Intervention in the Thirty Years War*. Cambridge: Cambridge University Press, 1996.

Robinson W, *Promoting Polyarchy: Globalisation, U.S. Intervention, and Hegemony* Cambridge: Cambridge University Press, 1996.

Roeder P G and Rothschild D, *Sustainable Peace: Power and Democracy after Civil Wars*, Cornell University Press, 2005.

Roht-Arriaza N (ed.), *Impunity and Human Rights in International Law and Practice*, Oxford: Oxford University Press, 1995.

Ross M H, *The Culture of Conflict: Interpretations and interests in comparative perspective*, New Haven, CT: Yale University Press, 1993.

Rotberg R and Albaugh E, *Preventing Conflict in Africa: Possibilities of Peace Enforcement*, Cambridge, Massachusetts: World Peace Foundation, 1999.

Rotberg R and Thompson D (eds), *Truth v. Justice: The Morality of Truth Commissions*, (Princeton, NJ: Princeton University Press, 2000.

Ruddick S, *Maternal Thinking: Towards a Politics of Peace*. London: The Women's Press. 1989.

Rummel R, *The Common Foreign and Security Policy and Conflict Prevention*, London: International Alert and Saferworld, 1996.

Rumsey A, 'The Articulation of Indigenous and Exogenous Orders in Highland New Guinea and Beyond,' *The Australian Journal of Anthropology*, Vol. 17, No. 1, 2006.

Runciman W, *Relative Deprivation and Social Injustice*, Penguin, 1972.

Rupesinghe K (ed.), *Conflict Transformation*, Basingstoke: Macmillan, 1995.

Said E, *Culture and Imperialism*, London: Vintage, 1993.

Sandole D J, 'John Burton's Contribution To Conflict Resolution Theory And Practice: A Personal View', *International Journal of Peace Studies*, Vol. 6, No. 1, 2001.

Schmeidl S and Karokhail M, *The Failure of "Pret-a-Porter States": How the McDonaldisation of State-building Misses more than just the Story in Afghanistan*, Berghof Handbook Dialogue Series, no 8, Berlin: Berghof Research Center for Constructive Conflict Management, 2009.

Schmid H, 'Peace Research and Politics', *Journal of Peace Research*, Vol. 5, No. 3, 1968.

Schmidt B E and Schröder I W., *Anthropology of Violence and Conflict*, New York: Routledge, 2001.

Schutz A, *Collected Papers, vol. 2*, The Hague: Martinus Nijhoff, 1967.

Schwab K, 'Global Corporate Citizenship: Working With Governments and Civil Society', *Foreign Affairs*, Vol. 87, No. 1, 2008.

Scott D, 'Culture in Political Theory', *Political Theory*, Vol. 31, No. 1, 2003.

Sen A, *Development as Freedom*, Oxford: Oxford University Press, 1999.

Shaw R, *Memories of the Slave Trade: Ritual and the Historical Imagination in Sierra Leone*, Chicago, IL: University of Chicago Press, 2002.

Shilliam R, 'Hegemony and the Unfashionable Problematic of 'Primitive Accumulation', *Millennium, Journal of International Studies*, Vol. 32, No. 1, 2004.

Shostak M, *Nisa: The life and words of a! Kung woman*, Cambridge, MA: Harvard University Press, 1981.

Silke A (ed.), *Research on Terrorism: Trends, Achievements, Failures*. London: Frank Cass, 2004.

Skjelsbaek I and Smith D (eds), *Gender, Peace & Conflict*. London: Sage, 2001.

Sklair L, 'Social Movements and Global Capitalism', *Sociology*, Vol. 29, No. 3, 1995.

Sklair L, 'Social Movements for Global Capitalism: The Transnational Capitalist Class in Action', *Review of International Political Economy*, Vol. 4, No. 3, 1997.

Smith A D, *The Ethnic Origins of Nations*, Oxford: Blackwell, 1986.

Smith A D, *Nationalism and Modernism*, London; NY: Routledge, 1998.

Smith A D, *Myths and Memories of the Nation*, Oxford: Oxford University Press, 1999.

Smith D, *Towards a Strategic Framework for Peacebuilding: Getting the Act Together*, Oslo: Royal Norwegian Ministry of Foreign Affairs, 2004.

Smith D and Vivekananda J, *A Climate of Conflict: The Links Between Climate Change, Peace and War*, London: International Alert, 2007.

Smith K E, *European Union Foreign Policy in a Changing World*, Cambridge: Polity Press, 2003.

Spindler G and Spindler L, 'Cultural Process and Ethnography: An anthropological perspective', *The Handbook of Qualitative Research in Education*, London: Academic Press, 1992.

Sriram C L, *Confronting Past Human Rights Violations: Justice vs. Peace in Times of Transition*, London: Frank Cass, 2004.

Sriram C L, *Globalizing Justice for Mass Atrocities: A Revolution in Accountability*, London: Routledge, 2005.

Sriram C L, *Peace as Governance: Power-Sharing, Armed Groups, and contemporary peace negotiations*, Basingstoke; New York Palgrave, 2008.

Sriram C L and Roth B R, 'Externalization of Justice: What Does it Mean and What is at Stake?' *Finnish Yearbook of International Law*, Vol. 12, 2001, pp. 2–6.

Sriram C L, 'Revolutions in Accountability', *American University International Law Review*, Vol. 19, No. 2, 2003.

Stiglitz J and Bilmes L J, *The Three Trillion Dollar War: The True Cost of the Iraq Conflict*, New York: WW Norton, 2008.

Stubbs R and Underhill G (eds) *Political Economy and the Changing World Order* London: Macmillan, 1994.

Tadjbakhsh S and Chenoy A M, *Human Security: Concepts and Implications*, London: Routledge, 2007.

Talentino A, 'Perceptions of peacebuilding: The dynamic of imposer and imposed upon', *International Studies Perspective*, Vol. 8, No. 2, 2007.

Taylor I, 'China's oil Diplomacy in Africa', *International Affairs*, Vol. 82, No. 5, 2006.

Taylor I, 'What Fit for the Liberal Peace in Africa?', *Global Society*, Vol. 21, No. 4, 2007.

Taylor O, 'The Critique That Doesn't Bite: A Response to David Chandler's '"Human Security: The Dog That didn't bark"', *Security Dialogue*, Vol. 39, No. 4, 2008.

Thorne C, *Border Crossings: Studies in International History*, Oxford: Basil Blackwell, 1988.

Tickner J A, 'Why Women Can't Run the World', *International Studies Review*, Vol. 1, No. 3, 1991.

Tickner J A, 'What Is Your Research Program? Some Feminist Answers to International Relations Methodological Questions', *International Studies Quarterly*, Vol. 49, 2005.

Tiemessen A E, 'After Arusha: Gacaca Justice in Post-Genocide Rwanda', *African Studies Quarterly*, Vol. 8, No. 1, 2004.

Tilly C, *The Formation of National States in Western Europe*. Princeton: Princeton University Press, 1975.

TillY C, 'War making and state making as organized crime' in Evans P et al (eds) *Bringing the State Back In*. Cambridge: Cambridge University Press, 1985.

Tooze R, 'Understanding the Global Political Economy: Applying Gramsci', *Millennium: Journal of International Studies: Journal of International Studies*, Vol. 19, No. 2, 1990.

Toulmin S, *Cosmopolis: The Hidden Agenda of Modernity*, Chicago, IL: University of Chicago Press, 1992.

Toulmin S, *Return to Reason*, Cambridge, MA: Harvard University Press, 2001.

Turner M, 'Taming Mammon: Corporate Social Responsibility and the Global Regulation of Conflict Trade', *Conflict, Security and Development*, Vol. 6, No. 3, 2006.

USAID, *Fragile States Strategy*, PD-ACA-999, Washington, DC: US Agency for International Development, 2005.

Utas M, 'Building a Future? The Reintegration and Re-marginalisation of Youth in Liberia', in Richards P (ed.), *No Peace, No War: An Anthropology of Contemporary Armed Conflicts*, Ohio University Press, 2005.

Uvin P and Mironko C, 'Western and Local Approaches to Justice in Rwanda', *Global Governance*, Vol. 9, No. 2, 2003.

Van Creveld M, *The Rise and Decline of the State*, Cambridge: Cambridge University Press, 1999.

Van Der Pijl K, *Transnational Classes and International Relations,* London: Routledge, 1998.

Van Evera S, *Guide to Methods for Students of Political Science*, Ithaca, NY: Cornell University Press, 1997.

Van Tongeren P, Brenk M, Hellema M and Verhoeven J (eds), *People Building Peace II: Successful Stories of Civil Society,* Boulder, CO: Lynne Rienner, 2005.

Van Tuijl P, 'NGOs and Human Rights: Sources of Justice and Democracy', *Journal of International Affairs*, Vol. 52, No. 2, 1999.

Williams A J, *Liberalism and War: The Victors and the Vanquished*. London: Routledge, 2006.

Väyrynen T, *Culture and International Conflict Resolution*, Manchester: Manchester University Press, 2001.

Väyrynen T, 'A Shared Understanding: Gadamer and International Conflict Resolution', *Journal of Peace Research*, Vol. 42, No. 3, 2005.

Vidich A J and Lyman S M, 'Their History in Sociology and Anthropology,' in N K Denzin and Y S Lincoln (eds), *Handbook of Qualitative Research*, Thousand Oaks, CA: Sage Publications, 2000.

Viktorova J, 'Identity and Alterity: An Apologia for Boundaries', in H van Houtum and E Berg (eds) *Routing Borders between Territories, Discourses and Practices*, Aldershot: Ashgate, 2003.

Von Trotha T, 'Die Zukunft liegt in Afrika. Vom Zerfall des Staates, von der Vorherrschaft der konzentrischen Ordnung und vom Aufstieg der Parastaatlichkeit', *Leviathan*, Vol. 28, 2000.

Wagner R, *The Invention of Culture*, Englewood Cliffs, NJ: Prentice-Hall, 1975.

Walzer M, *Just and Unjust Wars*, 4th edn, New York, Basic Books, 2006.

Warner M and Crisp R (eds), *Terrorism, Protest and Power*, Aldershot: Edward Elgar, 1990.

Watson C, *Basque Nationalism and Political Violence: The Ideological and Intellectual Origins of ETA*, Reno: Center for Basque Studies, 2008.

Weinberg L and Eubank W, ' "Problems with the Critical Studies Approach to the Study of Terrorism', *Critical Studies on Terrorism*, Vol. 1, No. 2, 2008.

Weiss T and Gordenker L (eds), *NGOs, the UN and Global Governance*, Boulder, CO and London: Lynne Rienner, 1996.

Westoby P and Brown M A, 'Peaceful Community Development in Vanuatu: A Reflection on the Vanuatu Kastom Governance Partnership', *Journal of Peacebuilding and Development*, Vol. 3, No. 3, 2007.

Wheeler N, *Saving Strangers: Humanitarian Intervention in International Society*, Oxford: Oxford University Press, 2000.

White G, *Indigenous Governance in Melanesia*, State Society and Governance in Melanesia Discussion Paper, Research School of Pacific and Asian Studies, Canberra: Australian National University, 2006.

Whitehead N L (ed.), *Violence*, Santa Fe: School of American Research Press, 2004.

Wilkinson P and Stewart A (eds), *Contemporary Research on Terrorism*, Aberdeen: Aberdeen University Press, 1987.

Williams A J, *Failed Imagination? The Anglo-American New World Order from Wilson to Bush*, 2nd edn, Manchester: Manchester University Press, 2007.

Williams A J, 'Reconstruction: The Bringing of Peace and Plenty or Occult Imperialism?', *Global Society*, Vol. 21, No. 4, 2007.

Williams A J and Mac Ginty R, *Conflict and Development*, Routledge, 2009.

Williams H, *Britain's Power Elites*, London: Constable, 2006.

Williams P R and Scharf M P, *Peace With Justice? War Crimes and Accountability in the Former Yugoslavia*, Lanham, MD: Rowman and Littlefield, 2002.

Wood E, *Democracy Against Capitalism: Renewing Historical Materialism* Cambridge: Cambridge University Press, 1995.

Woodhouse T and Ramsbotham O (eds), *Peacekeeping and Conflict Resolution*, London: Frank Cass, 2000.

Woods N, 'Whose Aid? Whose Influence? China, Emerging Donors and the Silent Revolution in Development Assistance', *International Affairs*, Vol. 84, No. 6, 2008.

Young T, "A Project to be Realised": Global Liberalism and Contemporary Africa', *Millennium: Journal of International Studies*, Vol. 24, No. 3, 1995.

Yuval-Davis N, *Gender and Nation*, London: Sage, 1997.

Zakaria F, *The Future of Freedom: Illiberal Democracy at Home and Abroad*, New York: W.W. Norton, 2004.

Zartman I W, *The Practical Negotiator*, New Haven, CT: Yale University Press, 1982.

Zartman I W, 'The Timing of Peace Initiatives,' in Darby J and Roger Mac Ginty, *Contemporary Peacemaking*, London: Palgrave, 2003.

Zulaika J, *Basque Violence: Metaphor and Sacrament*, Reno: University of Nevada Press 1988.

index